GREEK:
A COMPREHENSIVE GRAMMAR
OF THE MODERN LANGUAGE

GREEK:
A COMPREHENSIVE
GRAMMAR OF THE
MODERN LANGUAGE

David Holton, Peter Mackridge
and Irene Philippaki-Warburton

London and New York

First published 1997
by Routledge
11 New Fetter Lane, London EC4P 4EE

Simultaneously published in the USA and Canada
by Routledge
29 West 35th Street, New York, NY 10001

Reprinted with corrections 1999

© 1997 David Holton, Peter Mackridge and Irene Philippaki-Warburton

Typeset in Times by The Florence Group, Stoodleigh, Devon
Printed and bound in Great Britain by T.J. International Ltd, Padstow,
Cornwall

British Library Cataloguing in Publication Data
A catalogue record for this book is available from the British Library

Library of Congress Cataloguing in Publication Data
A catalogue record for this book has been requested

ISBN 0–415–10001–1 (hbk)
      0–415–10002-X (pbk)

CONTENTS

PREFACE

Greek is spoken by about 13 to 14 million people. It is the sole official language of the Republic of Greece and (with Turkish) one of the two official languages of the Republic of Cyprus. Since 1981 it has been one of the official languages of the European Community (now European Union). It is spoken as sole mother tongue by 95 per cent of the population of Greece (which totals about 10 million) and by about 600,000 of the inhabitants of Cyprus. It is also spoken by a significant number of people of Greek origin (perhaps 3 or 4 million) who are resident in many parts of the world, chiefly North America, Australia, Germany, the former Soviet Union, and the United Kingdom.

Modern Greek is the sole descendant of Ancient Greek and as such is a member of the Indo-European group of languages. Although until recent times Greek was divided into regional dialects, the vast majority of Greek-speakers now speak a common language with only relatively minor dialectal variations. The only exception to this is the Greek Cypriots, many of whom ordinarily speak a dialect which, although linguistically close to standard Greek, presents some significant differences.

It has long been customary to use the term 'Greek' to refer to the ancient language, while the contemporary language is known as 'Modern Greek'. We believe that, as a living language, contemporary Greek does not need to be qualified by an adjective which implies that it is somehow secondary to the ancient language. For this reason, we use 'Greek' throughout this book to refer to the modern language, adding the adjective 'Ancient' or 'Modern' only when these two chronological stages need to be distinguished.

COMPARISON WITH PREVIOUS GRAMMARS

This is the first comprehensive reference grammar of Modern Greek to have appeared since the pioneering work by Manolis Triandafyllidis and his collaborators, *Νεοελληνική Γραμματική (της Δημοτικής)* [*Modern Greek Grammar (of Demotic)*, Athens 1941]. Nothing to equal the magnitude, scope, accuracy and clarity of Triandafyllidis's grammar has appeared in the meantime, even in Greek. In 1949 Triandafyllidis produced an abridged version of his grammar, called *Μικρή Νεοελληνική Γραμματική*, and a revised edition of this volume is still in official use today in schools; for this reason it is often referred to in Greece as the 'state grammar' or 'official grammar'. In 1967 G. Babiniotis and P. Kontos published their *Συγχρονική γραμματική της κοινής νέας ελληνικής* [*Synchronic Grammar of Common Modern Greek*]. This attempted to describe actual language use in an innovative way, presenting a kind of Greek in which the two language varieties, demotic and *katharevousa*, had merged (for more on demotic and *katharevousa* see below). Nevertheless, some of the material is now outdated; besides, this book was also a teaching manual, and each section presenting a grammatical feature was followed by a set of exercises.

Other grammars of Greek have appeared in English, but they have been either very brief or not widely available. *A Grammar of Modern Greek on a Phonetic Basis*, by J.T. Pring (London 1950), is more of a teaching manual for beginners than a reference grammar, and the author's interest in phonetics led him to provide transcriptions of his material in the International Phonetic Alphabet instead of the Greek alphabet; although reissued many times, it has now been long out of print. The *Reference Grammar of Literary Dhimotiki*, by F.W. Householder, K. Kazazis and A. Koutsoudas (Bloomington 1964) provided a useful presentation of the phonology and morphology, based on what were then up-to-date modern theories and methods, but it devoted a mere thirteen pages to sentential syntax (it is characteristic that at the very end of the book the authors write: 'Greek syntax is enough like English syntax so that the great majority of your problems can be resolved by consulting a good dictionary' [p. 174] – this at a time when 'good dictionaries' of Greek did not exist); moreover, their grammar was reproduced from typescript and was not widely available. Most recently, *Modern Greek: A Contemporary Grammar* by Olga Eleftheriades (Palo Alto 1985) comes nearest to the comprehensiveness of Triandafyllidis, but the theory and method on which it was based was outdated; it too suffers from the lack of a specific and separate treatment of syntax (the author's stated aim was to provide 'a systematic exposition of Greek phonology and morphology'; 'syntax', the author continues, 'is touched upon when the uses of a morphological form are explained' [p. v]); this book too was reproduced from typescript and not readily available.

The difference between the titles of the Triandafyllidis grammar of 1941 and our own book is indicative of the radical shift that the Greek language has undergone in the half-century that separates them. Until 1976, two versions of Greek coexisted: demotic was not only the spoken language but – at least since the turn of the twentieth century – the language of almost all creative literature, while *katharevousa* was reserved for almost all official purposes. *Katharevousa*, a hybrid made up of lexical, morphological and syntactic features from Ancient and Modern Greek thrown together somewhat haphazardly, was never a unified language, but exhibited considerable variation according to the user's education and taste. In reality *katharevousa* was used not only in most official pronouncements but in most of secondary and tertiary education, the law, medicine, the Church, the armed forces, most newspapers, and even to a large extent in broadcasting. Thus the authors of the 1941 grammar had to specify in their title that they were concerned with demotic Greek as opposed to *katharevousa*. Ever since the Greek state decided officially to adopt what it termed 'Modern Greek (Demotic)' as the official language in 1976, such a distinction has no longer been necessary, and the Greek language has come closer to developing a set of universally accepted norms than at any other stage in its history.

One significant difference between our Grammar and the 1941 grammar is, therefore, that the Greek language itself has changed considerably since then. The language described in our grammar is the form spoken and written by educated Greeks from the urban centres of Greece, which, while it is primarily based on demotic vocabulary, phonology, morphology and syntax, displays a significant influence from *katharevousa*.

A second difference is that while Triandafyllidis, in his foreword to the 1941 grammar, claimed that his work was descriptive, he specified that his grammar was 'founded on the basis of the folk songs and of recent literature', and went on to distinguish 'popular' forms, which his grammar chiefly aimed to describe, from 'learned' forms, some of which he felt obliged to include in the morphology because they were used in the common spoken language. Our own grammar concentrates on contemporary spoken and written usage and does not take as its basis the language of literature (let alone the language of folk songs). Yet, despite his claim, Triandafyllidis and his collaborators produced a grammar that was, at least to some extent, prescriptive. Thus, faced with alternative variants of certain morphological forms, the authors of the 1941 grammar tended either to choose just one and omit the rest, or at least to promote one and relegate the rest to footnotes. What is more, some of these choices have proved to be ill-advised, since the form they promoted has not, in some cases, proved to be the dominant one today.

Thirdly, and most importantly, the 1941 grammar almost entirely ignores syntax, devoting well over half its pages to derivational and inflectional morphology. The description of the syntax of Modern Greek was left to Achillefs Tzartzanos, whose *Νεοελληνική Σύνταξις (της Κοινής Δημοτικής)* [*Modern Greek Syntax (of Common Demotic)*, 2nd edn, 2 vols, Athens 1946–53] is a rich treasure-house of syntactical observation, but presents great difficulties in use because it lacks a proper index; in addition, many of its examples (some of them again taken from folk songs and other poetry) are antiquated. A glance at the contents pages of our own Grammar will show that we devote as much space to syntax as to all other features of the grammar put together.

Lastly, while we have attempted to achieve a theoretical neutrality and to reduce modern linguistic terminology to a minimum, we have been able to take advantage of the huge advances that have been made in general linguistics in the past forty years, and in the linguistic study of Greek in the last twenty-five or so. The sections on anaphora, as well as those on variations of word order and the absence or presence of clitics in the expression of topic and focus, are innovations; no previous grammar has covered these phenomena. In general, then, our description of the language is more theoretically sophisticated than those of our predecessors.

In short, we believe that our Grammar is both original and comprehensive. Despite the authority of Triandafyllidis and Tzartzanos, we felt, at all stages of the preparation of the Grammar, that we were unable to use more than a tiny fraction of the material they provided, and that we were having to go back to first principles. We had to reinvent the description of every level of the language: the sound system in the light of generative phonology, the writing system in view of recent orthographic reforms, the morphology in view of radical changes in linguistic attitudes and behaviour brought about by the demise of *katharevousa* as a discrete linguistic code used for official purposes, and the verbal syntax in the light of the substantial amount of trail-blazing work that has been done on it in recent years. Our enterprise was an extremely difficult one, and it proved to be more laborious and time-consuming than we had ever imagined at the outset.

AIMS OF THE GRAMMAR

The Grammar aims to provide a comprehensive explanatory and illustrative description and analysis of contemporary Greek, so as to assist its users in oral and written communication. Our Grammar is not primarily aimed at theoretical linguists, although we hope that they will find it informative. It is intended to be usable by a wide range of people with no formal linguistic training, from adult learners who have only a basic knowledge of Greek to those with a high competence in oral and/or written communication, including native speakers.

By 'description' we mean that it is our aim to inform the reader about which forms are normally used and about how they are used. It is not our aim to instruct the reader as to what is 'correct' and what is 'incorrect'.

The form of the language described is primarily the usage of native Greek-speakers living in the urban centres of Greece who have completed at least their compulsory secondary education. We do not attempt to present all the alternative varieties that are still used today, let alone the plethora of variants to be found in traditional Greek poetry and fiction. Nevertheless, secondary mention is sometimes made of various alternative morphological forms found in literature, as well as of certain alternative *katharevousa* forms still to be found today in newspapers and elsewhere. In view of the wide variety of forms encountered in Greek literature of the nineteenth and twentieth centuries, our Grammar does not aim to cover any but the chief demotic alternatives, and it is beyond its scope to facilitate the comprehension of texts written in *katharevousa*.

We aim to describe both formal and colloquial usage, and we often use these terms when describing a particular feature of the language. In view of the fact that diglossia (the coexistence of two differentiated varieties of the same language used for different purposes) prevailed in Greece until 1976, the sociolinguistic situation is very complex, and we do not attempt to adopt a sociolinguistic approach to the description of Greek. Greek-speakers did not suddenly forget their *katharevousa* when it officially ceased to be used as a variety of Greek that was perceived as being distinct from demotic; they often use *katharevousa* forms when they are trying to speak or write formally, or in jest, or simply because that is the form that comes naturally to them at that particular moment. Nevertheless, it should be borne in mind that when we describe a certain form or usage as 'formal', we generally mean that it has entered the common language from *katharevousa* and is still perceived by speakers as being more appropriate to formal than to informal contexts; but this does not mean that it is not to be found in informal contexts too. Conversely, a form or usage described as 'colloquial' means that it is generally perceived by speakers as being more appropriate to informal speech situations, and it is more likely to be found in such contexts; but this by no means excludes its use in formal contexts.

LAYOUT OF THE GRAMMAR

Greek is a highly inflected language. The nominal system (nouns, adjectives, etc.) displays four grammatical cases, while the verbal system is even more complex. Moreover, the morphology of Greek involves a significant number of alternative forms. For this reason, morphology (the actual forms of the words) has been placed in a separate part of the Grammar, distinct from syntax (which deals with the *use* of the forms). Bearing in mind that this is a work of *reference*, we decided that the reader would be able to find what s/he is looking for more readily if we made a fairly rigid separation between the forms of the words and their syntactic use, rather than dealing with the syntax of each individual morphological class of word along with an account of the forms. We have, of course, included plenty of cross-references to bridge the divisions between phonology, morphology and syntax.

The Grammar is divided into three parts. Part I covers the sound system (phonology, morphophonemics, and suprasegmental features such as stress and intonation) and the writing system (the alphabet, diacritics, and punctuation) in two separate chapters.

Part II covers morphology, dealing with the inflection of each part of speech in turn (articles, nouns, adjectives, adverbs, pronouns, numerals, and verbs), and finally giving an account of the ways of forming derivatives. For ease of reference, the declension and conjugation patterns have been laid out as fully and as explicitly as possible by means of traditional tables, many of which are followed by notes providing details of formation (including alternative forms) that cannot be conveniently fitted into the tables. Obsolete and obsolescent forms that are to be found in older literature have been excluded.

Part III takes a broad view of syntax, detailing the use of the verb and verb phrase (including objects, person and number, mood, voice, aspect, and tense), the noun phrase (including gender, number, case, and the use of the articles, adjectives, numerals, pronouns and determiners), adverbs and adverb phrases, prepositions and prepositional phrases, and finally the clause (including main (independent) and subordinate (embedded) clauses, word order, and other syntactic phenomena). Every syntactic phenomenon described in Part III is illustrated by examples of phrases and sentences that show the phenomenon in action. These examples are not taken from a corpus, but are based, for the most part, on everyday usage.

At the end of the Grammar there are four appendices dealing with features of the language that cannot be readily accommodated in any single part or chapter of the book. These appendices consist of a correspondence table of pronouns, determiners and adverbs; the expression of spatial relations by means of prepositions and adverbs; expressions of time, space and quantity; and agreement of number, gender and case. These appendices are followed by a glossary of select grammatical terms. Finally the reader will find an index of grammatical categories and concepts and of some Greek words of special grammatical interest.

METHODOLOGY AND TERMINOLOGY

Aside from the section on the sound and writing systems, where some phonemic and phonetic transcriptions are used, the Greek in this book is printed in the Greek alphabet, using the simplified 'monotonic' (single-accent) system in use in Greek education and in official and much unofficial communication since 1982. The chapter on the writing system does, however, include an account of the traditional system of diacritics which are still used in a number of publications. All Greek examples are translated into English.

We have attempted to include everything that will be of practical use to the reader. This means that, while full advantage is taken both of modern theoretical approaches and of the most recent work done on Greek from various viewpoints, theoretical statements are for the most part excluded. Our approach does not depend on any one theoretical standpoint. Instead, while it is informed throughout by modern theoretical approaches, the layout of the Grammar is largely traditional, devoting separate parts to the sound and writing systems, the morphology and the syntax. We believe that for this reason this Grammar is easily usable.

It is impossible to describe a language adequately without an arsenal of grammatical terms. We have tried as far as possible to use traditional grammatical terms (terms that have traditionally been used in English, that is, though not necessarily used for Greek) when they are available, and have resorted to terms taken from modern linguistics only when a term for a certain linguistic phenomenon does not exist in the traditional terminology, or where the traditional term has tended to misrepresent the phenomenon it claims to describe. At all events, we do not assume that the reader is familiar with all the grammatical terminology, and every attempt is made to explain it; there is also a glossary of grammatical terms at the end of the Grammar.

We have in fact found ourselves obliged to revaluate the terminology traditionally used for the description of Greek, much of which dates back to descriptions of Ancient Greek by ancient grammarians, and some of which is not suitable for the description of the modern language. Most notable are the terms traditionally applied to the verb forms, particularly 'aorist' and 'subjunctive'. The term 'aorist' (from a Greek word meaning 'indefinite') is not at all appropriate for the description of Modern Greek; besides, it really applied to a verbal aspect rather than to a particular form or tense. We have avoided using this term altogether, and have used the term 'simple past' for the tense traditionally called the 'aorist indicative'; this term brings Greek into line with languages such as English and French. We have redefined the terms 'indicative' and 'subjunctive' not by reference to the verb forms themselves but by reference to the particles with which the verb forms can combine, a subjunctive being a verb introduced by να or ας (and negated by μη[ν]), while an indicative is a verb that is not introduced by να or ας (and is negated by δε[ν]). There is only one present tense in our book, since the old 'present indicative' and 'present subjunctive', as verb forms in themselves, are in fact identical in Modern Greek (unlike in Ancient Greek). As for the traditional 'aorist subjunctive', we have found ourselves forced to invent an entirely new term, namely the 'dependent', since it is the only verb form that cannot normally be used independently of a particle or conjunction.

Parallel with the terms 'present', 'imperfect', 'simple past', and 'dependent', we have also, when the need arises, used other descriptions of the same forms which indicate more transparently the tense and aspect of the forms in question: these terms, not used in grammars of Greek till now but familiar to linguists for several decades, are 'imperfective non-past', 'imperfective past', 'perfective past', and 'perfective non-past'. These terms clearly, faithfully and unambiguously represent the actual status of each verb form, but we have used the other set of terms as far as possible in order to help the non-linguist reader. The three sets of terms are displayed in the table below, which also contains certain other sets of terms where we departed from traditional practice. (The various previous grammars of Greek in English have actually used a variety of terms, not always those classed in our table as 'traditional'.)

Terms used for verb forms
This book does not use the terms classed here exclusively as 'traditional'. 'Technical' terms are those that display tense and aspect; 'non-technical' terms are those used most frequently in this Grammar.

Traditional	Technical	Non-technical
Present indicative	Imperfective non-past	Present
Imperfect	Imperfective past	Imperfect
Aorist indicative	Perfective past	Simple past
Aorist subjunctive	Perfective non-past	Dependent
Simple future	Θα+perfective non-past	Perfective future
Continuous future	Θα+imperfective non-past	Imperfective future
Conditional	Θα+imperfective past	Conditional
Present participle	Gerund (i.e. indeclinable form in -ντας)	Gerund
Infinitive	Non-finite	Non-finite

THE AUTHORS

The three authors of this Grammar come from different and complementary backgrounds. David Holton and Peter Mackridge are British university teachers of Greek language and literature, while Irene Philippaki-Warburton is a Greek linguist who teaches in Britain and has played a leading role in the revolution that has taken place in the linguistic study of Greek in the last decades.

Since two of the authors have produced books on the Greek language before, it is as well to clarify the differences between this Grammar and their previous books. *Modern Greek*, by Brian D. Joseph and Irene Philippaki-Warburton (London 1987), was produced for the Croom Helm Descriptive Language Series. This series was addressed to specialist linguists and had to follow a specific format based on the requirement of the chief editors for grammars that would form the basis for extracting linguistic universals. *Modern Greek* is therefore highly technical in its approach and treatment, and the predetermined format did not permit the authors to decide on the proportionate emphasis to be placed on the various phenomena of the language. *The Modern Greek Language*, by

Peter Mackridge (Oxford 1985), was written to fill the gap left by the absence of a modern comprehensive grammar of Greek. Nevertheless, it was aimed primarily at those who already had a high degree of competence in the language. Rather than providing a comprehensive and systematic description, it concentrated on features of contemporary usage that were not accounted for, or were inadequately covered, in traditional grammars.

Each author of *Greek: A Comprehensive Grammar of the Modern Language* drafted different sections and sent them to the others for scrutiny and comment; all sections were radically revised in the light of comments from the drafter's co-authors. Irene Philippaki-Warburton drafted the sections on the sound system and the verbal and sentential syntax; David Holton drafted the morphology sections; and Peter Mackridge drafted the sections on the writing system, the noun phrase, adverbs and prepositions. Tasos Christidis commented on draft chapters and acted as consultant to the authors at various stages of the preparation of the Grammar. Nevertheless, the Grammar as a whole is the joint responsibility of the three authors.

NOTE ON ORTHOGRAPHY

As mentioned above, this Grammar uses the 'monotonic' accentuation system. It also uses the very slightly simplified orthography that has been taught in Greek schools since 1976. In the case of individual words we have attempted to follow the most recent authoritative concise dictionary of Greek, namely the *Νέο Ελληνικό Λεξικό* by E. Kriaras (Athens 1995). As for the use of the final -ν in certain auxiliary words (the negative particles and the masculine and feminine accusative singular forms of articles and pronouns), we have followed the 'Triandafyllidis rule' in our examples, i.e. we have used the final -ν only when the following word begins with a vowel or a plosive, and have omitted it elsewhere. We recognize that different Greek-speakers adopt different procedures on this and other orthographic matters, and we have adopted our orthography not as an article of faith but in the interests of consistency.

David Holton
Peter Mackridge
Irene Philippaki-Warburton
October 1996

ACKNOWLEDGEMENTS

The authors wish to express their gratitude to Geoffrey Horrocks for having read a draft of the whole Grammar with great care and for alerting them to various inaccuracies and terminological inconsistencies, to Pietro Bortone for having read and commented on some chapters of Part III, to Takashi Tachibana for his discussions of Greek prepositions, and to Tasos Tsangalidis, Marilita Papastathi and Filothei Kolitsi for discussions on morphological matters.

This Grammar has been produced with the help of grants from the European Union LINGUA (now SOCRATES) programme and from the Foundation for Hellenic Culture.

LIST OF CONVENTIONS

*	ungrammatical forms or utterances
?	utterance of doubtful acceptability
bold italics	grammatical terms defined in the Glossary
bold	in examples, indicates the part of the example being discussed
italics	emphasis, or used to highlight terms for easy location by the reader
[]	in Greek examples: indicates material that may be omitted
[]	in English translations: indicates material added to make translation more comprehensible
[]	around letters and symbols indicating sounds: phonetic realization
//	around letters and symbols indicating sounds: phonemic rendering
/	separates alternative forms
†	indicates a verb without a passive perfective form

LIST OF ABBREVIATIONS

acc.	accusative (case)
act.	active (voice)
AG	Ancient Greek
cf.	compare
def. art.	definite article
dep.	dependent (verb form)
e.g.	for example
emph.	emphatic (personal pronoun)
F *or* fem.	feminine
ff.	indicates pages beginning with the specified number
fut.	future (tense)
gen.	genitive (case)
i.e.	that is
imp. *or* imper.	imperative (mood)
imperf.	imperfective (aspect); imperfect (tense)
lit.	literally
M *or* masc.	masculine
N *or* neut.	neuter
nom.	nominative (case)
pass.	passive (voice)
perf.	perfective (aspect)
pl.	plural
pres.	present (tense)
sg.	singular
voc.	vocative (case)

PART I: THE SOUND AND WRITING SYSTEMS

1 THE SOUND SYSTEM

1.1 PHONOLOGICALLY DISTINCT SEGMENTS

The sound system of Greek consists of the following distinct segments or *phonemes*:

(a) *Consonants*
   p, t, k, f, θ, x, v, δ, γ, s, z, l, r, m, n
(b) *Vowels*
   i, e, a, o, u

1.1.1 THE CONSONANTS

1.1.1.1 The pronunciation of each consonant phoneme

Each of the above phonemes may correspond to more than one actual pronunciation, i.e. more than one phonetically different variant or allophone, depending on the sounds adjacent to it, which can affect it in various ways. Below we give each phoneme with its **allophones** and the phonetic environment in which each allophone occurs. The phonemes are placed between slashes //, while the variants or allophones are placed inside square brackets [].

Phoneme	Allophone	Examples
/p/:	[p]	[pódi] πόδι 'foot', [kápu] κάπου 'somewhere'
	[b]	[bóta] μπότα 'boot', [ka(m)bána] καμπάνα 'bell'

The consonant [p] is a voiceless bilabial plosive without aspiration. It occurs in all environments except after a nasal. After a nasal it is pronounced as [b], i.e. as a voiced bilabial plosive, as is clearly shown in [ka(m)bána] 'bell'. However, it may also appear without the nasal in word-initial position as in [bóta] where it contrasts with the voiceless [p]. Nevertheless, even in such circumstances [b] can be analysed as the result of the combination of a nasal + p. This combination gives either a simple [b] in word-initial position [bóta] or a nasal + b in word-medial position. The nasal itself may be reduced even in medial position to a prenasalization feature [ᵐb] ([émboros] 'merchant') or even be omitted completely ([éboros]). The presence or absence of nasal before [b] and the degree of nasality vary in accordance with sociolinguistic factors such as the speaker's place of origin or age, the formality of the context, etc. In some words of foreign origin which have not been assimilated completely to the Greek phonological system, such as [sampánja] σαμπάνια 'champagne', [compjúter] κομπιούτερ 'computer', etc., the sequences nasal + p do not give rise to [(m)b], especially in the speech of educated people.

/t/:   [t]   [télos] τέλος 'end', [potó] ποτό 'drink'
        [d]   [dulápa] ντουλάπα 'wardrobe', [pé(n)de] πέντε 'five'

The consonant [t] is a voiceless dental plosive without aspiration. It occurs in all environments but rarely after a nasal. [d] is a voiced dental plosive and it either occurs after a nasal or as the result of the combination of a nasal + t. As in the case of (m)b, the nasal is absent before [d] in word-initial position ([dáma] ντάμα 'female dancing partner, queen (in cards)'); it is optional in word-medial position and its reduction to a prenasalization feature depends on sociolinguistic factors ([é(n)domo] έντομο 'insect'). The foreign origin of the word may also affect the choice of either omitting the nasal, or retaining the cluster [-nt-] ([anténa] or [a(n)déna] αντένα 'aerial').

/k/:   [k]   [kóri] κόρη 'daughter', [síka] σύκα 'figs'
        [g]   [grína] γκρίνια 'nagging', [a(ŋ)gónas] αγκώνας
               'elbow'
        [k']   [k'ípos] κήπος 'garden', [pak'éto] πακέτο 'package'
        [g']   [g'ónis] γκιόνης 'scops owl', [a(ŋ)g'inára]
               αγκινάρα 'artichoke'

The consonant [k] is a voiceless non-palatalized velar plosive which occurs without a preceding nasal and before a low or a back vowel (see section 1.1.2 for the position of vowels). [g] is a voiced velar plosive which occurs either after a nasal or as the result of the combination of nasal + k. As in the case of [b] and [d], the presence or absence of the nasal and the degree of nasality before [g] in word-medial position depends on sociolinguistic factors, and on the origin of the word.

[k'] is a voiceless palatal plosive. It occurs when there is no preceding nasal and when the following vowel is front. It may also be the result of the combination of k+i when the /i/ is unstressed and a vowel follows: /kiólas/ → [k'ólas] κιόλας 'already'. Its voiced counterpart [g'] occurs after a nasal and before a front vowel. As in the case of [b], [d] and [g], [g'] in initial position represents the combination of nasal + k + front vowel, while in medial position the presence of the nasal and the degree of nasality are optional and are again determined by sociolinguistic factors. [g'] may also be the result of the combination g+i when the /i/ is unstressed and a vowel follows: [giónis] → [g'ónis].

/f/:   [f]   [fóros] φόρος 'tax', [fílos] φίλος 'friend', [néfos]
               νέφος 'cloud, smog', [siɱforá] συμφορά 'disaster'

[f] is the only realization of the phoneme /f/. It is a voiceless labiodental fricative.

/θ/:   [θ]   [θálasa] θάλασσα 'sea', [láθos] λάθος 'mistake', [ánθos] άνθος 'flower'

[θ] is the only realization of the phoneme /θ/. It is a voiceless interdental fricative.

/x/:   [x]   [xará] χαρά 'joy', [víxas] βήχας 'cough', [áŋxos] άγχος 'anxiety'
       [x']   [x'óni] χιόνι 'snow', [vrox'í] βροχή 'rain'

The allophone [x] is a voiceless velar fricative which occurs before a low or a back vowel. The variant [x'] is a palatal voiceless fricative which occurs before a front vowel.

/v/:   [v]   [vulí] βουλή 'parliament', [sovarós] σοβαρός 'serious', [simvulí] συμβουλή 'advice'

The phoneme /v/ has only one realization [v], which is a voiced labiodental fricative.

/δ/:   [δ]   [δóro] δώρο 'gift', [peδí] παιδί 'child', [enδjaféron] or [enδiaféron] ενδιαφέρον 'interesting'

The phoneme /δ/ has only one realization [δ], which is a voiced interdental fricative.

/γ/:   [γ]   [γámos] γάμος 'wedding', [aγápi] αγάπη 'love', [aγóri] αγόρι 'boy'
       [j]   [jíγas] γίγας 'giant', [flojéra] φλογέρα 'flute'

[γ] is a voiced velar fricative which occurs before either a low or a back vowel; [j] is a palatalized voiced velar fricative which occurs before a front vowel. For further discussion of the sound [j] see Section 1.1.3 below.

/s/:   [s]   [sóma] σώμα 'body', [δásos] δάσος 'woods', [vási] βάση 'base'

[s] is the only realization of the phoneme /s/. It is a voiceless dental strident consonant.

/z/:   [z]   [zoí] ζωή 'life', [zíl'a] ζήλια 'jealousy', [xazós] χαζός 'stupid'

[z] is the only realization of the phoneme /z/. It is a voiced dental strident consonant.

/l/:   [l]   [láθos] λάθος 'mistake', [kaló] καλό 'good'
       [l']   [l'ípi] λύπη 'sorrow', [fíl'i] φίλοι 'friends'

The realization [l] of the phoneme /l/ is the only variant for the standard language. It is a voiced apicodental approximant liquid. The variant [l'] is a voiced palatalized apicodental approximant liquid and it occurs before the high front vowel /i/ in some dialects or idiolects.

/r/:   [r]   [rolój] ϱολόι 'clock', [psári] ψάϱι 'fish'

The only realization [r] of the phoneme /r/ is a voiced apicoalveolar flap.

/m/:   [m]   [mónos] μόνος 'alone', [xóma] χώμα 'earth'
       [ɱ]   [siɱfonía] συμφωνία 'agreement'

The realization [m] of the phoneme /m/ occurs in all environments except before a labiodental fricative. It is a voiced bilabial nasal.

The allophone [ɱ] is a voiced labiodental nasal; it occurs before a labiodental fricative.

/n/:   [n]   [nonós] νονός 'godfather', [énas] ένας 'one'
       [ɲ]   [ɲíxta] νύχτα 'night', [áɲiksi] άνοιξη 'springtime',
                [ɲázome] νιάζομαι 'I care'
       [ŋ]   [áŋxos] άγχος 'anxiety', [a(ŋ)gónas] αγκώνας 'elbow'

The phoneme /n/ has three allophones: [n], which is a voiced dental nasal occurring before all vowels; [ɲ], a voiced palatalized nasal which occurs before the high front vowel /i/ or is the result of the combination n+i+vowel when /i/ is unstressed; and [ŋ], a voiced velar nasal which occurs before velar consonants, namely all the allophones of the velar consonant phonemes /k, γ, x/. The palatal allophone [ɲ] is not used by all speakers of standard Greek. It is found in the speech of those whose dialect contains this allophone. Other speakers use [n] in the same context.

1.1.1.2   The sounds [ts] and [dz]

[ts] and [dz] may be analysed as single consonantal segments: [ts] as a voiceless dental affricate, as in [tsépi] τσέπη 'pocket', [papútsi] παπούτσι 'shoe', and [dz] as a voiced dental affricate, as in [dzámi] τζάμι ' window-pane', [pa(n)dzári] παντζάρι 'beetroot'. On the other hand these sounds may be analysed as forming clusters consisting of t + s and d + z respectively.

1.1.2   THE VOWELS

The vowel system of Greek is a very symmetrical one. It consists of five vowels arranged as follows:

	Front	*Back*
High	/i/	/u/
Mid	/e/	/o/
Low	/a/	

All Greek vowels are slightly longer when stressed. There is very little vowel weakening in unstressed syllables but when unstressed and in word-final position the vowels may be slightly shorter and slightly devoiced. For the high vowels /i/ and /u/ there are also non-syllabic allophones as indicated below:

/u/: [u]   [pulí] πουλί 'bird', [fústa] φούστα 'skirt', [kaúra] καούρα 'heartburn'

[w]   [fráwla] φράουλα 'strawberry'

The non-syllabic allophone [w] of the phoneme /u/ is very rare; it occurs only if /u/ is unstressed and is preceded by a vowel.

/i/   [i]   [níki] νίκη 'victory', [peðí] παιδί 'child', [peðía] παιδεία 'education'

[j]   [ðjó] δυο 'two', [karávja] καράβια 'boats', [peðjá] παιδιά 'children', [ajtós] αητός 'eagle'

[x'] [eláfx'a] ελάφια 'deers', [fotx'á] φωτιά 'fire'

The allophones [j] and [x'] of the phoneme /i/ occur in words of demotic origin and those of *katharevousa* origin that have become assimilated to the demotic system, only when /i/ is unstressed and is either preceded or followed by another vowel. The allophone [i] is found in all other environments.

1.1.3 THE PALATALS [j] AND [x']

There are a number of complications associated with the status and distribution of the palatal sounds [j] and [x'].

The sound [j] was described as being derived from two different sources: (a) it represents the palatal allophone of the phoneme /γ/ when it precedes a front vowel; (b) [j] is also derived from the vowel /i/ when it occurs unstressed before a vowel and after a voiced consonant, or in word-initial position, while its voiceless counterpart [x'] derives from unstressed /i/ when it occurs before a vowel and after a voiceless consonant. This rule is not applicable to all Greek words. Thus along with words such as [peðí] παιδί 'child', [peðjá] παιδιά 'children', [vaθís] βαθύς 'deep (masc.)', [vaθx'á] βαθιά 'deep (fem.)', where it is clear that /i/ becomes [j] or [x'] according to the voicing of the preceding consonant when it has no stress and there is a vowel following it, we also find words such as [stádio] στάδιο 'stadium', [áðia] άδεια 'licence', [ánia] άνοια 'dementia', [epétios] επέτειος 'anniversary' etc., where the unstressed /i/ followed by a vowel does not change to the palatal [j]/[x']. So we can find pairs like [áðia] 'licence' and [áðja] 'empty', and many more.

This problem is created by the fact that the Standard Greek vocabulary and with it some morphological and phonological patterns have been derived from two different language sources, the demotic tradition and the *katharevousa* or learned tradition. Vocabulary derived from demotic follows the rule that /i/ becomes [j]/[x'] if unstressed and next to a vowel, while vocabulary from *katharevousa* resists this rule. In view of this historical explanation, we may retain the rule that [j] is not a distinct phoneme but an allophone of either /ɣ/ or /i/ by restricting the application of this rule to the demotic system.

Note that the palatal sound derived from /i/ may become a nasal palatal [ɲ] after the nasal /m/: /miá/ → [mja] → [mɲa] μια 'one'.

The rule which produces a non-syllabic palatal [j]/[x'] from unstressed /i/ next to a vowel does not apply when /i/ is combined with another /i/: [ðiikó] διοικώ 'I govern', [piitís] ποιητής 'poet'. It also fails to apply after a consonant cluster where the second consonant is /r/: [ávrio] αύριο 'tomorrow', [áɣrios] άγριος 'wild', though for some of these words we may also find alternative pronunciations with [j] such as [áɣrjos].

1.2 THE DISTRIBUTION OF DISTINCTIVE SEGMENTS WITHIN THE WORD

1.2.1 CONSONANTS AND CONSONANT CLUSTERS

There are three factors that affect the combinations of consonants into consonant clusters: the position in the word (word-initial, word-medial or word-final), the source of the vocabulary item concerned, and the register or the level of formality of the discourse.

1.2.1.1 Consonants and consonant clusters in word-final position

In the vocabulary of traditional Spoken Greek there are no word-final consonant clusters. In fact, the majority of demotic Greek words end with an open syllable, i.e. a vowel. The only consonants which may appear in word-final position are /n/ and /s/. /n/ is much less frequently used and in any case there is a tendency in speech to avoid final /n/ either by omitting it or by adding the vowel /e/ after the final /n/: [ɣráfune] 'they write' instead of the formal [ɣráfun]. There are some words of *katharevousa* origin restricted only to formal discourse with consonant /r/ in final position, such as ύδωρ 'water', υπέρ 'on behalf of'. We also find final consonants in exclamations: [uf] ουφ, [ax] αχ, etc.

In *katharevousa*, words may also have word-final consonant clusters such as /ks/ /ánθraks/ άνθραξ 'coal' (occurring only in scientific discourse), [vasiléfs] βασιλεύς 'king'.

Foreign loanwords may also contain word-final consonants and consonant clusters: [snob] σνομπ 'snob', [bar] μπαρ 'bar', [boks] μποξ 'boxing'.

1.2.1.2 Consonants and consonant clusters in word-initial position

Word-initial position allows for any consonant and for a rich variety of consonant clusters. All the clusters which occur in initial position may also occur in word-medial position.

The two-consonant clusters which occur in word-initial position can be summarized as follows:

Combinations of a voiceless plosive followed either by /s/ or /r/:

ps	[psomí] ψωμί 'bread', [psiméno] ψημένο 'cooked'
ts	[tsiɣáro] τσιγάρο 'cigarette', [tsépi] τσέπη 'pocket'
ks	[ksílo] ξύλο 'wood', [ksaná] ξανά 'again'
pr	[prépi] πρέπει 'it is necessary', [provlépo] προβλέπω 'I foresee'
tr	[trofí] τροφή 'food', [trávma] τραύμα 'wound'
kr	[krasí] κρασί 'wine', [kremídi] κρεμμύδι 'onion'

Voiceless bilabial plosive /p/ or voiceless velar plosive /k/ followed by /l/ or /n/:

pl	[pliróno] πληρώνω 'I pay', [plíθos] πλήθος 'crowd'
pn	[pnoí] πνοή 'breath', [pníɣome] πνίγομαι 'I am drowning'
kl	[kláma] κλάμα 'crying', [klistó] κλειστό 'closed'
kn	[knizmós] κνησμός 'itching'

Voiceless dental plosive followed by the nasal /m/. This combination is very rare:

tm	[tmíma] τμήμα 'section'

Labial nasal /m/ followed by dental nasal /n/:

mn	[mními] μνήμη 'memory'

Two-consonant clusters in initial position may also be formed by the combination of a voiceless or voiced fricative /f, θ, x, v, δ, γ/ followed by a liquid /l, r/; the combination /δl/ is not attested.

fr	[frík'i] φρίκη 'horror', [frási] φράση 'phrase'
fl	[fláwto] φλάουτο 'flute', [fléva] φλέβα 'vein'
θl	[θliménos] θλιμμένος 'sad'

θr   [θrimatízo] θρυμματίζω 'I shatter'
xl   [xlevázo] χλευάζω 'I jeer'
xr   [xróma] χρώμα 'colour'
vl   [vlávi] βλάβη 'damage'
vr   [vrox'í] βροχή 'rain'
δr   [δraxmí] δραχμή 'drachma'
γl   [γláros] γλάρος 'seagull'
γr   [γráma] γράμμα 'letter'

Another two-consonant combination is formed with the voiceless fricative strident /s/ followed by any other voiceless fricative or plosive:

sp   [spóros] σπόρος 'seed'
st   [stóxos] στόχος 'target'
sk   [skóni] σκόνη 'dust'
sf   [sfirízo] σφυρίζω 'whistle'
sθ   [sθenarós] σθεναρός 'courageous'
sx   [sx'eδón] σχεδόν 'almost'

The combinations /sn/ or /zn/ and /sl/ or /zl/ occur only in foreign words:

sn or zn   [snob] or [znob] σνομπ 'snob'
sl or zl   [slávos] or [zlávos] σλάβος 'Slav'

The combination /zb/ occurs only in the word [zbáros] σμπάρος 'shot'.
    The fricatives /γ, θ, x/ combine with nasal /n/, and voiced /z/ combines with /m/:

γn   [γnómi] γνώμη 'opinion'
θn   [θnitós] θνητός 'mortal'
xn   [xnári] χνάρι 'trace'
zm   [zmínos] σμήνος 'swarm'

The only possible combinations of a voiceless non-strident fricative with a plosive are /ft/, /fk/ and /xt/:

ft   [ftinós] φτηνός 'cheap'
fk   [fk'áno] φκιάνω 'I fix, make' (rather dialectal)
xt   [xtes] χτες 'yesterday'

The only possible combinations of a voiced fricative with another voiced fricative are /vδ, vγ, γδ, zv, zγ/:

vδ   [vδomáda] βδομάδα 'week'
vγ   [vγázo] βγάζω 'I take out'
γδ   [γδérno] γδέρνω 'I skin'
zv   [zvúra] σβούρα 'spinning top'
zγ   [zγurós] σγουρός 'curly'

Combinations of two voiceless fricatives /fθ/, /xθ/ or two voiceless plosives /kt/, /pt/ are also possible:

fθ   [fθáno] φθάνω 'I arrive'
xθ   [xθes] χθες 'yesterday'
kt   [ktíma] κτήμα 'farm'
pt   [ptóma] πτώμα 'corpse'

Combinations of the voiced plosives [b, d, g], which derive from the combination of nasal + voiceless plosive (see above), with a liquid /l , r/, with the exception of [dl], are also found:

bl   [ble] μπλε 'blue'
br   [brávo] μπράβο 'bravo'
dr   [dropí] ντροπή 'shame'
gr   [gremós] γκρεμός 'cliff'
gl   [glítsa] γκλίτσα 'shepherd's crook'

The palatal allophones [j] after voiced consonants and [x'] after voiceless ones, which, as we stated, derive from unstressed /i/ in combination with a vowel, often follow a word-initial consonant, forming various clusters:

δj   [δjóxno] διώχνω 'I send away'
vj   [vjázome] βιάζομαι 'I am in a hurry'
px'   [px'áno] πιάνο 'piano'

The maximum number of consonants which may appear in word-initial position is three; the possible combinations are:

/s/ + voiceless plosive /p, t, k/ + /l/ or /r/

Of the possible combinations of these segments the following are actually attested:

spl   [splína] σπλήνα 'spleen'
spr   [spróxno] σπρώχνω 'I push' (also pronounced as [zbróxno]
         with voiced initial strident)
skl   [sklávos] σκλάβος 'slave'
str   [strofí] στροφή 'bend'
skr   [skríɲo] σκρίνιο 'kind of cupboard'

There is also a three-consonant cluster where the third segment is not a liquid but the nasal /n/:

skn   [sknípa] σκνίπα 'gnat, midge'

In initial position it is also possible to find a three-consonant cluster where /s/ is followed not by a voiceless plosive but by a voiceless fricative. However, this pattern is restricted to /sfr/:

sfr   [sfrajíða] σφραγίδα 'stamp'

1.2.1.3 Consonants and consonant clusters in word-medial position

All of the consonant clusters which occur in word-initial position (see above, Section 1.2.1.2) also occur in word-medial position. In addition to these we also find a number of consonant combinations which occur only in word-medial position. Below are listed the two-consonant clusters which occur only in medial position and the three- and four-consonant clusters which occur only in this position.

Clusters of a plosive or fricative followed by a nasal: /tn, fn, vn, θm, vm/:

tn   [fátni] φάτνη 'manger'
fn   [ksafniká] ξαφνικά 'suddenly'
vn   [evnoikós] ευνοϊκός 'favourable'
θm   [vaθmós] βαθμός 'degree'
vm   [révma] ρεύμα 'draught'

Clusters where the initial segment is a liquid, /l/ or /r/: /rt, rð, rf, rk, rx, rn, rm, rγ/ and /lm, lp, lk, lt, lγ/:

rt   [ártos] άρτος 'bread'
rð   [karðjá] καρδιά 'heart'
rf   [karfí] καρφί 'nail'
rk   [fúrka] φούρκα 'anger'
rx   [árxondas] άρχοντας 'ruler, leader'
rn   [arní] αρνί 'lamb'
rm   [árma] άρμα 'chariot'
rγ   [arγá] αργά 'late'
lm   [álma] άλμα 'jump'
lp   [elpíða] ελπίδα 'hope'
lk   [élkos] έλκος 'ulcer'
lt   [peltés] πελτές 'tomato purée'
lγ   [nostalγós] νοσταλγός 'nostalgic'

Clusters of nasal followed by a fricative: /nθ, nx, mf, ns, nð, mv, nγ, nz/:

nθ   [ánθos] άνθος 'flower'
nx   [áŋxos] άγχος 'anxiety'
mf   [eɱfánisi] εμφάνιση 'appearance'
ns   [ensomatóno] ενσωματώνω 'incorporate'
nð   [enðiazmós] ενδοιασμός 'hesitation'

mv   [emvólio] εμβόλιο 'vaccine'
nγ   [éŋgamos] έγγαμος 'married'
nz   [énzimo] ένζυμο 'enzyme'

Three-consonant clusters found only in word-medial position are /sxr, sxn, sθm, ptr/:

sxr   [esxrós] αισχρός 'horrible'
sxn   [isxnós] ισχνός 'thin'
sθm   [isθmós] ισθμός 'isthmus'
ptr   [kátoptro] κάτοπτρο 'mirror'

Additional three-consonant clusters are created word-medially with the combination of the final consonant of the prefixes /ek/ εκ-, /ef, ev/ ευ-, /en/ εν-, /sin/ συν-, /iper/ υπερ-, /is/ εισ- and /pros/ προσ- in combination with a following consonant or a consonant cluster. Examples of such combinations are:

ktr   [ektropí] εκτροπή 'perversion'
kst   [ékstasi] έκσταση 'ecstasy'
kðr   [ekðromí] εκδρομή 'excursion'
ngl   [siŋglíno] συγκλίνω 'converge'
mbr   [simbráto] συμπράττω 'cooperate'
ftr   [eftrafís] ευτραφής 'well-fed'
fst   [efstáθia] ευστάθεια 'steadiness'
vγl   [évγlotos] εύγλωττος 'eloquent'
rtr   [ipertrofikós] υπερτροφικός 'overgrown'

Examples such as [siŋglíno] and [simbráto] show the effects of two phonological phenomena: (a) the nasal causes the following plosive to become voiced, and (b) the nasal assimilates in point of articulation with the following consonant. Also if we compare [efstáθia] and [évγlotos], both formed with the same prefix spelled ευ-, we see that the final segment of this prefix, a labiodental fricative, is voiceless if the consonant that follows is voiceless and voiced when the following consonant is voiced. In general, clusters in Greek tend to contain either all voiced or all voiceless consonants. This voice assimilation applies only optionally to the last consonant of the prefix εκ-: [ekðúlefsi] and more rarely [egðúlefsi] εκδούλευση 'a favour'.

Due to prefixes with final consonants such as those mentioned above, four-consonant clusters are also created in word-medial position:

kstr   [ekstratía] εκστρατεία 'campaign'
fstr   [efstrofía] ευστροφία 'quickness of mind'

1.2.1.4   Alternations of consonant clusters

It is possible to find the same word with two different consonant clusters and correspondingly different spelling, in either word-initial or word-medial position, as in the following examples:

[fθinós] φθηνός	or	[ftinós] φτηνός 'cheap'
[xθes] χθες	or	[xtes] χτες 'yesterday'
[eptá] επτά	or	[eftá] εφτά 'seven'
[ktíma] κτήμα	or	[xtíma] χτήμα 'farm'
[péktis] παίκτης	or	[péxtis] παίχτης 'player'
[ásx'imos] άσχημος	or	[ásk'imos] άσκημος 'ugly'
[písθik'e] πείσθηκε	or	[pístik'e] πείστηκε 'was persuaded'

The reason for such alternatives is that one of the sources of Standard Greek, namely *katharevousa*, allows for combinations of either two fricatives or two plosives, whereas demotic converts these to a sequence of one fricative and one plosive. This restriction applies only to voiceless consonants. Furthermore, in clusters containing an /s/, it is the non-strident partner that converts to a plosive, while in clusters of voiceless fricatives not containing an /s/, the first of the consonants must be the fricative and the second must be the plosive. The choice between the two alternative forms depends on the degree of formality or the register, in a given discourse, or even individual preference. Thus words with combinations of voiceless fricatives or plosives are more formal than their corresponding forms with one fricative and one plosive.

It is also possible to find words which are morphologically related, in that they are derived from the same root, which have derivatives with clusters of either two plosives or two voiceless fricatives as well as derivatives which contain the corresponding fricative and the corresponding plosive, as in the following examples:

(a)   σχίσμα 'schism', σχισμή 'tear'
(b)   σκίζω 'I tear up', σκισμένος 'torn'

(a)   περίπτερο 'kiosk', άπτερος νίκη 'wingless victory'
(b)   φτερό 'wing', φτερούγα 'wing'

(a)   κλεπταποδόχος 'recipient of stolen goods', κλεπτομανία 'kleptomania'
(b)   κλέφτης 'thief', κλέφτικο '(cooked in the) bandit style'

The words in (a) above belong to more formal, technical or scientific vocabulary, while those in (b) are forms that originate in colloquial speech.

1.2.2   VOWELS AND COMBINATIONS OF VOWELS

All vowels may occur in word-initial, medial and final position. The only restriction concerns unstressed syllabic /i/ in initial and medial position preceded or followed by another vowel. As has already been mentioned, in such contexts the phoneme /i/ is realized as the palatal allophone [j] or [x'] in demotic words and all other words that have assimilated to the demotic pattern.

All syllabic vowels may combine:

eo	[jeoryós]	γεωργός	'farmer'
ii	[ðiik'itís]	διοικητής	'director'
oo	[aθóos]	αθώος	'innocent'
ao	[aóratos]	αόρατος	'invisible'
ua	[ipákua]	υπάκουα	'obediently'

Through compounding, sequences of three vowels may also be produced:

eoe	[neoelinikós]	νεοελληνικός	'neohellenic'
ioa	[vorioanatolikós]	βορειοανατολικός	'north-east'

1.2.3   DIPHTHONGS

Diphthongs are formed by the combination of any vowel adjacent to a non-syllabic allophone [j] or [w] of the phonemes /i/ and /u/ respectively. Diphthongs cannot be formed by combining [i] with [j] or by combining [u] with [w]. Since the reduction of unstressed /i/ and /u/ next to a vowel is optional, diphthongization is also optional:

ej	[kléj]	κλαίει	's/he is crying'
aj	[tsáj]	τσάι	'tea'
oj	[bój]	μπόι	'height'
uj	[akúj]	ακούει	'he listens'
iw	[sk'iwrák'i]	σκιουράκι	'little squirrel'
aw	[fráwla]	φράουλα	'strawberry'

1.3   SUPRASEGMENTAL FEATURES

1.3.1   LENGTH

In Standard Greek length in either consonants or vowels is not distinctive. Vowels, when stressed, may be slightly longer than vowels without stress but this is simply an allophonic (phonetic) and not a distinctive (phonemic) difference. There is also no contrast between long and short consonants. Indeed when two identical consonants come together across the boundaries of two morphemes which are combined in a complex word, the two consonants are simplified to one: from /sin-metoxí/ by assimilation of [n] to [m] we get [sim-metox'í] and by simplification of the two [mm] to a single [m] we get [simetox'í] συμμετοχή 'participation'; similarly [sin-sorévo] → [sis-sorévo] → [sisorévo] συσσωρεύω 'I amass'. In some cases educated people may pronounce each of the two identical consonants separately: [ek-k'endrikós] εκκεντρικός 'eccentric'. There are Greek dialects, such as Cypriot, which have double consonants as a distinctive feature.

1.3.2   STRESS

1.3.2.1   Stress within a single grammatical word

A grammatical word is a unit which is either a simple morpheme or a more complex form derived by processes of inflection and/or derivation.

Stress in Greek is distinctive. Thus words may be differentiated simply by the position of the stress, as in pairs such as [píra] πείρα 'experience', [pirá] πυρά 'fire', [xóros] χώρος 'space', [xorós] χορός 'dance', [ála] άλλα 'others', [alá] αλλά 'but'. In the pronunciation of a word, stress is manifested by extra loudness on the stressed syllable, clearer quality of the vowel and some slight lengthening. The difference in the position of the stress in the pairs listed above shows that the position of the stress in a word is not predictable. However, there are some general rules that constrain the position of the stress. These are as follows:

(a) Every disyllabic or polysyllabic word must, and some monosyllabic ones do, contain one stressed syllable.
(b) *The antepenultimate rule*:
The stress may not fall further from the end than the antepenultimate. It may fall on the last syllable (the ultimate), or the one before the last (penultimate) or the third syllable from the end (antepenultimate).

The effects of these rules will become evident when we discuss changes in the position of the stress in Section 1.5.

1.4   MORPHOPHONEMICS: PHONOLOGICAL PHENOMENA ACROSS MORPHEME AND WORD BOUNDARIES

A number of phonological phenomena which affect the phonological structure of morphemes or words when they are combined together may take place within certain domains. These domains are created either by the combination of morphemes within a grammatical word or by the combination of certain kinds of words into phrasal units, such as the following: (i) the article followed by a noun or an adjective, (ii) a preposition followed by either an adverb or a noun phrase, (iii) the preverbal particles να or θα followed by the verb, (iv) the weak personal pronouns followed by a verb, or (v) a noun, an adjective, a gerund, an imperative verb or an adverb followed by a weak personal pronoun. These phenomena are listed and exemplified in Sections 1.4.1–1.4.3.

1.4.1 ASSIMILATION

Assimilation is a process by which one segment changes its features in such a way as to become more like its adjacent segment. The assimilatory processes applying in Greek are assimilation in point of articulation and assimilation in voice.

(i) Assimilation in point of articulation

This applies to a nasal which assimilates in point of articulation with the consonant that follows it, as in the examples below, where the nasal of the weak pronoun or definite article becomes labial when followed by a labial consonant, labiodental when followed by a labiodental consonant or velar when followed by a velar.

/ton patéra/	→	[to(m)batéra] τον πατέρα 'the father'
/ton fílise/	→	[toɱfílise] τον φίλησε 'she kissed him'
/ton keró/	→	[to(ŋ)g'eró] τον καιρό 'the weather'

This phenomenon is also observed across morpheme boundaries in prefix-ation and compounding, as in the following examples.

/sin-pono/	→	[si(m)bonó] συμπονώ 'I pity'
/sin-filióno/	→	[siɱfiljóno] συμφιλιώνω 'reconcile'
/en-xórios/	→	[eŋxórios] εγχώριος 'local'

(ii) Assimilation in voice

This has two sub-varieties: (i) the voicing of a plosive after a nasal and (ii) the voicing of a segment (other than a nasal or a liquid) if it is followed by any voiced consonant including a nasal or a liquid. These voicing assim-ilations are exemplified below:

(i)	/ðen katálava/	→	[ðe(ŋ)gatálava] δεν κατάλαβα 'I did not understand'
	/ton tímisan/	→	[to(n)dímisan] τον τίμησαν 'they honoured him'
	/ton pólemo/	→	[to(m)bólemo] τον πόλεμο 'the war'
	/tin kálesa/	→	[ti(ŋ)gálesa] την κάλεσα 'I invited her'

and in compounding:

/sin-ponó/	→	[si(m)bonó] συμπονώ 'I pity'

	/én-tomo/	→	[é(n)domo] έντομο 'insect'
	/en-pistévome/	→	[e(m)bistévome] εμπιστεύομαι 'I trust'
	/sin-kátikos/	→	[si(ŋ)gátikos] συγκάτοικος 'flat-mate'
(ii)	/tus γérus/	→	[tuzjérus] τους γέρους 'the old men'
	/as vális/	→	[azvális] ας βάλεις 'you may put'
	/mas δósane/	→	[mazδósane] μας δώσανε 'they gave us'
	/ef-δiáθetos/	→	[evδjáθetos] ευδιάθετος 'in a good mood'
	/is-volí/	→	[izvolí] εισβολή 'attack'
	/ék-δosi/	→	[égδosi] (or [ékδosi]) έκδοση 'edition'

The assimilation rules mentioned above apply across derivational affixes and inflectional affixes and between words forming a phonological word (see below) or phrase. Sometimes, in fast speech, voicing assimilation may be extended across phrases.

1.4.2   DISSIMILATION IN MANNER OF ARTICULATION

As mentioned above, there is a constraint on consonant clusters, both within morphemes and between morphemes, which affects vocabulary derived from the demotic tradition but also words from *katharevousa* that have become assimilated to the demotic system. According to this constraint a consonant cluster with two voiceless fricatives or two plosives is disallowed. This constraint, dealt with in Section 1.2.1.4 above, applies to all clusters both within morphemes and between them but only for vocabulary following the demotic pattern. Its effects are also shown in the inflection of verbs.

There are four rules of dissimilation which bring about the desired combinations.

(a) A fricative (not including nasals or liquids) becomes plosive if it is adjacent to an /s/, irrespective of the order of the two elements. Thus we have the following examples:

/tréx-o/	→	[tréxo] τρέχω 'I run'
/θa tréx-s-o/	→	[θa trékso] θα τρέξω 'I will run'
/klév-o/	→	[klévo] κλέβω 'I steal'
/θa klév-s-o/	→	[θa klépso] θα κλέψω 'I will steal'
/xtíz-o/	→	[xtízo] χτίζω 'I build'
/θa xtiz-θ-ó/	→	[θa xtis-t-ó] θα χτιστώ 'I will be built'

In the above examples a root-final fricative, such as /v/ or /x/, when it comes into contact with the perfective active affix /s/, dissimilates with it in manner of articulation by becoming plosive ([trékso], [klépso]), while the fricative /θ/, the affix of the perfective passive, becomes the corresponding plosive /t/ when preceded by a root-final

/z/ (which devoices to /s/ by the rule of voice assimilation before voiceless /θ/).

(b) If the consonant cluster does not contain an /s/, then it is the order that determines which of the consonants will be the plosive and which one will be the fricative; the first of the two must be the fricative while the second will be the plosive. Thus, if we have two fricatives the second becomes a plosive:

/θa γraf-θ-ó/   →   [θaγraftó] θα γραφτώ 'I will be written'
/plék-θ-ike/   →   [pléxtik'e] πλέχτηκε 'it was knitted'

This rule is also restricted to words of demotic origin. Words of more formal style or of scientific discourse deriving from *katharevousa* do not undergo this rule:

[eléxθi] ελέχθη 'it was said'
[elífθi] ελήφθη 'it was received'

It is also restricted to inflection, while derivation, such as prepositional prefixation, does not seem to be affected, as the following example shows:

/ef-θanasía/   →   [efθanasía] ευθανασία 'euthanasia'

(c) In a combination of two plosives the first becomes a fricative:

/plek-tó/   →   [plextó] πλεχτό 'knitting'

This phenomenon tends to occur in word-medial clusters in words of demotic origin, as in the above example, while vocabulary of *katharevousa* origin generally does not obey it:

[eklektós] εκλεκτός 'excellent'
[andiliptós] αντιληπτός 'noticed'

Clusters with two voiceless plosives may also appear between morphemes after the prepositional prefix εκ-, as in the following examples:

/ektimó/   →   [ektimó] εκτιμώ 'I appreciate',
/ekpémpo/   →   [ekpémbo] εκπέμπω 'I broadcast'

(d) If we have a cluster with a plosive before a fricative the initial plosive will change to a fricative while the following fricative will become a plosive:

/líp-θ-ike/   →   [líf-t-ik'e] λείφτηκε 'was lacking'
/mplék-θ-ike/ →   [bléx-t-ik'e] μπλέχτηκε 'he was implicated'

1.4.3 DELETION

Deletion is a process by which a segment is deleted under certain circumstances. It can be divided into consonant and vowel deletion.

1.4.3.1 Consonant deletion

The following rules describe the conditions under which a consonant may be deleted.

(a) As mentioned above (Section 1.3.1), when a sequence of identical consonants is created within a word or a phrase, one of the two is deleted.

/θa xtíz-s-o/ → [θa xtís-so] → [θa xtíso] θα χτίσω 'I will build'

/mas sósate/ → [masósate] μας σώσατε 'you saved us'

(b) Within words, a nasal is deleted before a liquid /l, r/.

/sin-léɣo/ → [siléɣo] συλλέγω 'I collect'
/sin-roí/ → [siroí] συρροή 'large crowd'

(c) Within words, the final /n/ of the prefix συν- is deleted before a strident /s, z/. But the final /n/ of prefix εν- is not deleted in similar circumstances.

/sin-sítio/ → [sisítio] συσσίτιο 'communal meal', but
/én-simo/ → [énsimo] ένσημο 'official stamp'

(d) The verb root-final /n/ in verbs deletes before /s/ and /θ/ of the perfective active and perfective passive respectively.

/δén-o/ δένω 'I tie'
/θa δén-s-o/ → [θa δéso] θα δέσω 'I will tie'
/θa den-θ-ó/ → [θa deθó] θα δεθώ 'I will be tied'

(e) The final /n/ of the feminine accusative definite article /tin/ is deleted before a fricative including /s/ and /z/ or a liquid /l/ or /r/, but the final /n/ of the masculine definite article /ton/ is only optionally deleted before these sounds. Similarly, the final nasal of the masculine weak pronoun is not deleted before a fricative or a liquid of the following verb.

/tin lípi/ → [tilípi] τη λύπη 'the sorrow'
/tin vási/ → [tivási] τη βάση 'the base'
/tin sinoδévi/ → [tisinoδévi] τη συνοδεύει 'he accompanies her'
/ton fílo/ → [tonfílo] or [tofílo] το(ν) φίλο 'the friend'
/ton sinoδó/ → [tonsinoδó] or [tosinoδó] το(ν) συνοδό 'the escort'

/ton sinoðévi/ → [tonsinoðévi] τον συνοδεύει 'she accompanies him'

/ton lipáme/ → [tonlipáme] τον λυπάμαι 'I feel sorry for him'

(f) The segments /θ/ and /ð/ in root-final position of verbs are deleted before the perfective marker /s/.

/θa pláθ-s-o/ → [θa pláso] θα πλάσω 'I will knead'

1.4.3.2 Vowel deletion

It has been pointed out that within words an unstressed /i/ or /u/, if it is adjacent to another vowel, may reduce to a non-syllabic [j] and [w] respectively. In other combinations of two vowels both vowels remain fully syllabic. Thus hiatus, i.e. the combination of two vowels, is not avoided within a simple word. However, between morphemes within a complex word or between words in a phonological word or phrase, when two vowels come together, it is likely that one of them will be deleted. The factors determining which of the two vowels is to be deleted are fairly complex and involve both phonology and morphology. The most important factor affecting the choice of the vowel to be deleted is the position of that vowel in the *sonority hierarchy*. It has been shown that the five vowels of Greek are arranged on a sonority scale from the most sonorant /a/ to the least sonorant /i/. The scale is a > o > u > e > i, although sometimes /i/ proves stronger than /e/. The more sonorant a segment, the less likely it is to be deleted. Thus, when two vowels come together across morphemes or words within a phrase, the less sonorant will be deleted, leaving the more sonorant behind. Such deletions appear especially across boundaries between a weak pronoun and a following verb with an initial vowel.

/ta ípa/ → [tápa] τα 'πα 'I said it'

/to éfera/ → [tófera] το 'φερα 'I brought it'

/tu éðosan/ → [túðosan] του 'δωσαν 'they gave him'

/mu árese/ → [márese] μ' άρεσε 'I liked it'

In the demotic system we find that both within complex words and within phrases consisting of a weak pronoun followed by a verb (as above), or of one of the preverbal particles να or θα followed by a verb, the deletion of one vowel is optional, with the preference being to keep both vowels intact, especially in more careful and slower speech.

/para-éfaγa/ → [paráfaγa] or [paraéfaγa] παράφαγα or παραέφαγα 'I overate'

/ksana-éðosa/ → [ksanáðosa] or [ksanaéðosa] ξανάδωσα or ξαναέδωσα 'I gave once before'

/θa érθi/   →   [θaérθi] or [θárθi] θα έϱθει or θα 'ϱθει 'he
will come'

Vowel deletion is obligatory in derivational processes of learned origin,
especially in prepositional prefixation. In this case the sonority hierarchy
is not operative; the rule instead is that the last vowel of the prefix is the
one to be deleted.

/para-édosa/   →   [parédosa] παϱέδωσα 'I delivered'
/kata-éxo/   →   [katéxo] κατέχω 'I possess'
/anti-éðrasa/   →   [andéðrasa] αντέδϱασα 'I reacted'
/epi-érxete/   →   [epérx'ete] επέϱχεται 'it is coming'

When the sequence of two vowels is formed by the combination of an
article followed by a noun or adjective, deletion takes place only very
rarely, but when it does, it obeys the sonority hierarchy. Deletion is
avoided when the first vowel is one of the definite articles o (masculine
singular), η (feminine singular) or οι (masculine and feminine plural).

/o alékos/   →   [oalékos] ο Αλέκος 'Alex'
/i alepú/   →   [ialepú] η αλεπού 'the fox'
/i exθrí/   →   [iexθrí] οι εχθϱοί 'the enemy'
/i óres/   →   [ióres] οι ώϱες 'the hours'

In the vowel sequence created by the neuter definite article singular το
or plural τα deletion takes place following the sonority hierarchy. This is
especially common if the article precedes the word άλλος 'other':

/to avγó/   →   [tavγó] τ' αβγό 'the egg'
/to álo/   →   [tálo] τ' άλλο 'the other'

The prepositions σε 'at' (obligatorily) and από 'from' and the adverb μέσα
'inside' (optionally) lose their final vowel when they precede the definite
article:

/se to trapézi/   →   [sto trapézi] στο τϱαπέζι 'at the table'
/apó tin eláda/   →   [aptineláda] or [apotineláda] απ' την
Ελλάδα or από την Ελλάδα 'from
Greece'
/mésa se tin póli/   →   [mesti(m)bóli] or [mesasti(m)bóli] μες
στην πόλη or μέσα στην πόλη 'in the
city'

In the last example there are two vowel deletions, that of /a/ in μέσα and
that of /e/ in σε, and two assimilations: the final nasal /n/ of την assimilates in point of articulation with the bilabial plosive /p/ which follows,
and /p/ in turn assimilates in voice with the preceding nasal. Notice that
the two-plosive cluster /pt/ created by the deletion of the final /o/ of από

does not undergo the dissimilation rule which demands that the first consonant be a fricative.

The final /e/ of a singular imperative verb may be deleted if followed by a weak pronoun with initial /t/:

/δóse to/	→	[δósto] δώσ' το 'give it'
/páre to/	→	[párto] πάρ' το 'take it'
/kópse to/	→	[kópsto] κόψ' το 'cut it'
/γrápse ta/	→	[γrápsta] γράψ' τα 'write them down'

This deletion is normal with imperatives stressed on the penultimate only, but it may also be found in some dialects or idiolects with forms stressed on the antepenultimate:

| /plírose to/ | → | [plírosto] πλήρωσ' το 'pay for it' |

The /e/ of the penultimate syllable of the imperative plural forms is also deleted after /s, r, l/.

| /párete ta/ | → | [párteta] πάρτε τα 'take these' |
| /δióksete ta/ | → | [δjóksteta] διώξτε τα 'send them away' |

The unstressed initial /e/ of the personal pronouns and of the adverbs εδώ 'here' and εκεί 'there' may optionally be deleted if the preceding word ends in a vowel:

/θa páo eγó/	→	[θa paoγó] θα πάω 'γώ 'I will go'
/éla esí/	→	[elasí] έλα 'σύ 'you come (imperative)'
/férta eδó/	→	[fertaδó] φέρ' τα 'δώ 'bring them here'

1.5 PHONOLOGICAL PHENOMENA AFFECTING THE POSITION OF STRESS

The position of the stress in a word remains constant only in a non-inflected word such as a preposition or an adverb; in nouns, adjectives and verbs the position of the stress is affected by phonological and/or morphological factors. We will examine here only the phonologically motivated stress variations.

1.5.1 STRESS PATTERNS IN NOUNS

Nouns may be stressed on the last syllable (η οδός 'the street', η φωλιά 'the nest'), the penultimate (ο φίλος 'the friend', η μοίρα 'the fate') or the antepenultimate (ο δάσκαλος 'the teacher', η θάλασσα 'the sea'). In certain classes of nouns stressed on the penultimate or antepenultimate in the nominative singular this basic stress will move one syllable to the right in the following circumstances:

(a) nouns having their basic stress on the antepenultimate will move the stress to the penultimate if an inflectional ending adds an extra syllable. This change of the position of the stress is motivated by the antepenultimate rule which forbids a word to be stressed further to the left than the antepenultimate.

nom. sg. το **μάθημα**   gen. sg. του **μαθήματος** 'of the lesson'
nom. pl. τα μαθήματα   'the lessons'

This rule also applies to the genitive singular -εως and genitive plural -εων of feminine nouns whose ending in the nominative is either -ις (*katharevousa*) or -η:

nom. sg. η **κυβέρνηση/ις**   gen. sg. της **κυβερνήσεως** 'of the
government'
gen. pl. των **κυβερνήσεων** 'of the
governments'

(b) nouns stressed on the antepenultimate syllable move the stress to the penultimate before the genitive singular ending -ου, the genitive plural -ων, the accusative plural -ους and the nominative and accusative ending -εις, in spite of the fact that no extra syllable is added. There is a historical explanation for this. In Classical Greek these endings contained long vowels or diphthongs which were equivalent to a sequence of two short vowels.

nom. sg. ο **άνθρωπος** 'man'   gen. sg. του ανθρ**ώ**που
gen. pl. των ανθρ**ώ**πων
acc. pl. τους ανθρ**ώ**πους
nom. sg. η **κυβέρνηση/ις**   nom./acc. pl. τις **κυβερνήσεις**

The movement of the stress to the right in the classes of nouns which contain masculines and feminines ending in -ος and neuters in -o does not always take place. There are words which through use have become more acceptable without the change of stress, such as του δάσκαλου 'of the teacher', του τραπεζομάντηλου 'of the table-cloth', etc. Conversely, it is also possible to find stress movement applied to the nominative plural of such nouns: οι ανθρώποι.

(c) For the stress patterns of other classes of nouns see Part II, Sections 2.1–2.4.

1.5.2 ADJECTIVES

Adjectives have what is referred to as *columnar stress*. This means that they keep the stress in its basic position throughout the paradigm. For further discussion and examples see Part II, Section 3.

1.5.3   VERBS

In verbs the stress may move either to the left (in some past tenses, see Part II, Section 7.1.8) or to the right in cases where the inflectional ending has added syllables and the basic stress position violates the antepenultimate rule. The latter case is exemplified by the verb γράφομαι 'I am written':

pass. pres.	**γράφομαι**	pass. imperf.	γρα**φό**μουνα
act. imperf. sg.	έγραφα	act. imperf. pl.	**γρά**φαμε
pass. simple past sg.	**γρά**φτηκα	pass. past pl.	γρα**φτή**καμε

For morphologically conditioned stress variations in the verb system see the tables in Part II, Sections 7.2–7.7.

1.5.4   STRESS WITHIN A PHONOLOGICAL WORD

A *phonological word* is a phrasal unit whose elements are pronounced so closely together as to form a single phonological unit with the result that morphophonemic processes which apply within the word also apply across the word-boundaries of this unit. A phonological word consists of one word from a major grammatical category (noun, verb, adjective, adverb) in combination with monosyllabic or disyllabic unstressed elements which provide grammatical modification for the major constituent. Thus the following combinations form phonological words: a preposition with the phrase that follows it; the definite article + noun or adjective; a noun or adjective with or without definite article + a weak possessive pronoun; one or two weak personal pronouns + a verb; a verb in the imperative + one or two weak personal pronouns; a gerund + weak personal pronouns; an adverbial + a weak personal pronoun. On each occasion the elements forming a phonological word must belong to the same syntactic phrase.

The phonological word is a domain in which, under certain conditions, more than one stress may appear: a basic stress and a derived one. The phenomenon responsible for this situation is referred to as *enclisis of stress*, which can be described as follows:

(a) If a grammatical word (noun, adjective, adverb, verb) is stressed on the antepenultimate and is followed by a weak personal pronoun and this pronoun belongs syntactically to the same phrase as the preceding word, a second stress must be placed on the last syllable of the first word. This rule accounts for the following examples:

[o jítonáz mas] ο γείτονάς μας 'our neighbour'
[fílaksé to] φύλαξέ το 'keep it'
[xárisé mu to] χάρισέ μου το 'give it to me'
[apénandí mas] απέναντί μας 'opposite us'

(b) If a verb in the imperative is stressed on the penultimate and is followed by two weak pronouns, a stress must be placed on the pronoun nearer to the verb. This accounts for examples such as the following:

[δόse tú to] δώσε τού το 'give him it' (alternatively [δóstuto] with deletion of the verb-final -e and no enclisis)
[fére mú ta] φέρε μού τα 'bring them to me'

(c) If a gerund stressed on the antepenultimate is followed by one or two weak pronouns a secondary stress will be placed on the last vowel of the gerund.

[γráfondás mu] γράφοντάς μου 'writing to me'

The phenomenon of enclisis is motivated by the antepenultimate rule. When unstressed elements are phonologically attached to a preceding host word and the result is a sequence of more than three unstressed syllables, we have a violation of the antepenultimate rule which requires that there must be a stress on one of the last three syllables of the word. We saw (in 1.3.2.1) that when this happens within a single grammatical word the basic stress moves to the right; in the case of a phonological word, however, the violation is avoided by the addition of a second stress on the second syllable to the right of the syllable with the basic stress. Of the two stresses the second one, the stress derived by enclisis, is stronger.

1.6   INTONATION

1.6.1   UTTERANCE INTONATIONAL PATTERNS

During the production of an utterance the pitch of the voice may rise or fall, creating what is known as the intonation contour of the utterance. Intonational patterns are not the same in all languages and therefore they have to be learned. Sometimes incorrect intonation may either cause confusion or characterize a speaker as a foreigner.

The results of the very limited studies on Greek intonation show that there is no strict one-to-one correlation between an intonation pattern and the meaning or the force of an utterance, but there are some weak correlations as listed below, the strongest of which is given in (a).

(a) *raised-falling* or *fall to mid-pitch*: This describes the rise of the pitch in utterance-final position and an immediate slight fall. Its presence correlates with a direct yes-no question;

(b) *rising* without subsequent fall: This correlates with incomplete utterances or utterances expressing a rhetorical question, or utterances encouraging continuation on the part of one's interlocutor;

(c) *falling-rising*: correlates with doubt and uncertainty;

(d) *rising-falling*: correlates with contrast or surprise and is equivalent to 'is it so?';

(e) *falling*: correlates with finality, conclusion.

1.6.2 INTONATION PEAK

In a neutral expression the intonation peak of the utterance falls on the last stressed word of the utterance. In the following examples the numbers indicate the degree of stress from the most prominent 1 to the least prominent 3:

$$2 \quad 3 \quad 1 \quad \text{(falling)}$$
(1) Η Μαρία έφυγε νωρίς
'Mary left early'

$$2 \quad 3 \quad 1 \quad \text{(rising + slight fall)}$$
(2) Θα 'ρθει μαζί σου ο Γιάννης
'Will John come with you?'

$$2 \quad 1 \text{ (raised falling)} \qquad 2 \quad 1 \quad 3 \text{ (raised falling)}$$
(3) Η Ελένη δε θα 'ρθει   or Η Ελένη δε θα 'ρθει
'Helen will not come'

The constituent with the intonation peak constitutes the most salient piece of the new information section of the utterance (see also Part III, Section 5.2.4).

1.6.3 EMPHATIC INTONATION

This is achieved by raising the intonation peak above its normal level. It is used to express surprise or emphasis:

$$2 \quad 3 \quad 1+$$
(1) Η Μαρία έφυγε νωρίς
'Mary left (surprisingly) *early*'

1.6.4 CONTRASTIVE STRESS

Contrastive stress may occur on any constituent within the utterance, including unstressed elements, such as articles or even weak pronouns; only one constituent can be contrastive. This constituent not only acquires the intonation peak but also carries extra high stress. Contrastive stress is used to indicate that the stressed element is contrasted with some other alternatives.

       1+   3   2

(1) Η Μαρία έφυγε νωρίς (όχι ο Πέτρος)
    'It is *Mary* who left early (not Peter)'

     2   1+ 3

(2) Η Άννα είναι η φίλη
    'Anna is *the* friend (unique friend, distinct from other friends)'

2 THE WRITING SYSTEM

The writing system of Greek consists of an alphabet of twenty-four letters with the addition of a number of diacritics and a set of punctuation marks.

2.1 THE ALPHABET

Modern Greek uses the same twenty-four letters as Classical Greek. The table below presents each letter in upper and lower case, in alphabetical order, its Greek name and the phoneme(s) to which it corresponds; for details of pronunciation see Sections 1.1–1.1.3.

The Greek alphabet

Form	Name	Phonemic equiv.	Form	Name	Phonemic equiv.
Α α	άλφα	/a/	Ξ ξ	ξι	/ks/
Β β	βήτα	/v/	Ο ο	όμικρον	/o/
Γ γ	γάμα	/γ/	Π π	πι	/p/
Δ δ	δέλτα	/δ/	Ρ ρ	ρο	/r/
Ε ε	έψιλον	/e/	Σ σ (ς at end of word)		
Ζ ζ	ζήτα	/z/		σίγμα	/s/
Η η	ήτα	/i/	Τ τ	ταυ	/t/
Θ θ	θήτα	/θ/	Υ υ	ύψιλον	/i/
Ι ι	γιώτα	/i/	Φ φ	φι	/f/
Κ κ	κάπα	/k/	Χ χ	χι	/x/
Λ λ	λάμδα	/l/	Ψ ψ	ψι	/ps/
Μ μ	μι	/m/	Ω ω	ωμέγα	/o/
Ν ν	νι	/n/			

Each of the following combinations of vowels represents a single sound:

αι	/e/
ει	/i/
οι	/i/
ου	/u/
υι	/i/

The combination αυ represents [af] or [av], according to whether the following sound is voiceless or voiced; similarly, ευ represents [ef] or [ev]. For the purposes of this distinction, the consonants κ, π, τ, χ, φ, θ, σ, ξ, ψ are considered to represent voiceless sounds, while the vowels, together with the consonants β, γ, δ, ζ, λ, μ, ν, ϱ, are considered to represent voiced sounds. Thus: αυτός (demonstrative, masc. nom. sg.) [aftós], αυλή 'yard' [avlí], εύκολος 'easy' [éfkolos], ευεργέτης 'benefactor' [everjétis], ευμενής 'favourable' [evmenís]. At the end of a word they represent [af] and [ef] respectively: άνευ αποδοχών 'without pay' [ánef apoδoxón]. The combination ηυ represents [if] or [iv] according to the circumstances mentioned above: διηύθυνα 'I directed' [δiífθina].

Double consonants (ββ, κκ, λλ, μμ, νν, ππ, ϱϱ, σσ, ττ) normally represent single sounds. An exception is γγ, which may represent [g] or [ŋg], but across morpheme boundaries in words of learned origin may represent [ŋγ] (e.g. εγγονός, 'grandson' [eŋgonós] or [egonós], but εγγράμματος 'literate' [eŋγrámatos]).

The following combinations of letters, when they do not bear an accent and when they are followed by a vowel, may represent [j]: γει, γι, γυ (e.g. γεια σου 'hello; goodbye' [jásu], γιατί 'why' [jatí], γυαλί 'glass' [jalí]).

The following combinations represent voiced plosives (or combinations of nasal + voiced plosive):

γκ   [g] or [ŋg]
μπ   [b] or [mb]
ντ   [d] or [nd]

The combination τζ represents [dz].

2.1.1   VARIATIONS IN SPELLING

Greek uses a *historical orthography*. This means that, as far as possible, Greek words or morphemes that derive from Ancient Greek are spelled as they have been since ancient times. The only aspect of contemporary Greek orthography that contravenes this principle is the diacritics (for which see Section 2.2).

When a word or morpheme does not derive indisputably from Ancient Greek, or when it derives from Ancient Greek but has significantly changed, the current official policy is that the simplest spelling be adopted. The 'simplest spelling' means that the sound [e] is spelled ε, [i] is spelled ι, [o] is spelled ο, [af] and [av] are spelled αφ and αβ, and [ef] and [ev] are spelled εφ and εβ.

This means that [ávγustos] 'August' is spelled Αύγουστος (although the word is ultimately from Latin, it is found, thus spelled, in Greek of the Roman period), while [avγó] 'egg' is spelled αβγό (because, even though the word is ultimately of Ancient Greek origin, the sound [v] is a later addition). The same principle accounts for the spellings of the homophones pronounced [aftí], namely αυτή (fem. sg. of the demonstrative, of Ancient Greek origin) and αφτί 'ear' (of Ancient Greek origin, but the

[f] is a later addition). Many Greeks do not accept these 'simplifications', and continue to use the spellings αυγό and αυτί.

There are many variations in spelling which are due to the differences in educational practice prevailing when the writers concerned were at school; some of the variations in individual words are due to conflicting views on their etymology. Thus while modern practice recommends σβήνω 'I extinguish', many people still write σβύνω, and while κοιτάζω 'I look at' is the normal modern spelling, some writers still spell the word as κυττάζω.

2.1.2 THE TRANSCRIPTION OF UNASSIMILATED FOREIGN WORDS

Foreign words (particularly proper names) that are not assimilated into the Greek morphological system may be either transcribed in Greek characters or written in the Latin alphabet. The transcription system most commonly in use at present entails the simplest transcription of the Greek pronunciation of the word. This means that, for instance, double consonants are avoided, and the sound [e] is rendered by ε, [i] by ι, and [o] by ο (cf. Section 2.1.1): thus Πίτερ 'Peter', Μποντλέρ 'Baudelaire'. Until recently, however, a compromise system between transliterating the orthography of the original and transcribing its sound was in use, involving rather complicated conventions; for instance, English long 'e' was rendered by η, French 'ai' by αι, and French 'au' by ω; thus Πήτερ, Μπωντλαίρ. The non-Greek palato-alveolar sounds found in English ('sh', 'ch', 'j') and French ('ch', 'j') are transcribed with their sibilant equivalents (σ for English 'sh' and French 'ch', ζ for French 'j', τσ for English 'ch', and τζ for English 'j').

2.1.3 THE USE OF LATIN CHARACTERS

The Latin alphabet is used when quoting phrases in Latin and in other languages that use the Latin alphabet (e.g. 'a priori'). In addition, single words and phrases of foreign origin are often printed in the Latin alphabet in the fashionable periodical press. Although prescriptive grammarians advise that such words should be transcribed in Greek characters, both proper names and other items are frequently printed in Latin; this sometimes applies even to Russian or Chinese names. Anglo-American buzz-words such as 'status' or 'glamour' are especially liable to be printed in Latin characters.

The following phrases, printed in capitals, appeared in a single advertisement for a fashionable women's magazine:

(1) EXTRA ΤΕΥΧΟΣ
'special issue [of magazine]'

(2) ΤΑ MUST ΤΟΥ ΧΕΙΜΩΝΑ – 45 ΠΡΟΤΑΣΕΙΣ ΓΙΑ ΤΟ ΠΙΟ
MUST ΣΤΥΛ!
'the musts of winter – 45 suggestions for the mustest style'

(3) 10 WEEK ENDS ΣΤΗΝ ΕΛΛΑΔΑ
'10 weekends in Greece'

In (2), the English word 'must' is used first as an indeclinable plural noun, then as an adjective in the superlative degree; the French word 'style' is transliterated into Greek characters. In (3) the English word 'weekend' is used, in its English plural form, despite the fact that there is a Greek word σαββατοκύριακο 'weekend'; the English word here denotes a weekend trip.

2.1.4   THE USE OF CAPITAL AND LOWER-CASE LETTERS

A capital letter is used at the beginning of a sentence and at the beginning of a proper noun (including the names of the days of the week, the months, and religious festivals). Words derived from proper names, however, normally begin with a lower-case letter. Compare:

(1) ο Έλληνας πρωθυπουργός
'the Greek prime minister'

(2) ο ελληνικός πολιτισμός
'Greek culture'

The word Έλληνας in (1) is a noun, while ελληνικός in (2) is an adjective derived from it.

Titles before personal names usually begin with a lower-case letter:

(3) η κυρία Μπότση
'Mrs Botsi'

In titles of books, only the first word is normally capitalized, except in the case of proper names:

(4) «Ο Χριστός ξανασταυρώνεται»
'Christ Recrucified'

2.2   DIACRITICS (THE MONOTONIC SYSTEM)

In the monotonic system, which has been taught in Greek schools since 1982, there are two diacritics: the **accent** (´) and the *diaeresis* (¨). It is convenient here to add the *apostrophe* (').

According to the monotonic system, the accent appears on every word of more than one syllable when the word is written in lower-case letters; it appears over the vowel which forms the nucleus of the stressed syllable. Thus: φορά 'time, occasion' [forá], but φόρα 'impetus' [fóra]. The accent is written over two vowels within a single word in cases where a word normally stressed on the third syllable from the end receives a stress on its final syllable because of a following weak (clitic) pronoun (φώναξέ τον 'call him': see Section 1.5.4 for this phenomenon).

The accent is written *before* an initial capital representing a stressed vowel: Ἔδεσσα 'Edessa'. However, the accent is not normally used on words written entirely in capitals, though it may, very rarely, be written over a capital in order to emphasize the position of the stress in the word concerned.

Owing to the use of the historical orthography in Greek, there are many instances where a sequence of two written vowels corresponds to a single vowel sound. When a stressed vowel sound is written as two letters, the accent is placed over the second: thus αίμα [éma] 'blood'. Furthermore, the digraphs αυ and ευ correspond to the sounds [af], [av], [ef], and [ev] (see Section 2.1) when the accent is placed over the second letter: θαύμα [θávma] 'miracle', πνεύμα [pnévma] 'spirit'. Conversely, when two written vowels correspond to two separate sounds, the accent is written over the first of the two vowels: thus γάιδαρος [γájðaros] 'donkey', άυλος [áilos] 'immaterial'.

There are certain cases where monosyllabic words take an accent:

(i)   The accent is written on a word that has become a monosyllable as a result of elision or prodelision (i.e. the deletion of the final or initial vowel respectively: see below): thus κόψ' το 'cut it' (reduced from κόψε το), θα 'ρθώ 'I'll come' [θarθó] (reduced from a hypothetical form θα ερθώ); but the accent is not written when, as a result of prodelision, the stress is shifted on to the final vowel of the previous word: thus θα 'ρθω [θárθo] (an alternative reduced form of θα έρθω).

(ii) The following monosyllables take an accent: the disjunctive pronoun ή 'or' (contrast the fem. nom. sg. of the article η) and the interrogative adverbs πού 'where' and πώς 'how' (contrast the complementizers που and πως).

(iii) A weak (clitic) personal pronoun (του, της, τους, etc.), when used before a verb, is written with an accent when it might otherwise be mistaken for a possessive pronoun: thus ο πατέρας **μού** είπε 'the father told **me**' is distinguished from ο πατέρας **μου** είπε '**my** father said'.

(iv) Similarly, a definite article may be written with an accent to distinguish it from a possessive pronoun: thus in ο πατέρας **τού** τότε πρωθυπουργού 'the father of the then prime minister' the τού may be written with an accent to make it clear that the phrase is not to be read ο πατέρας του 'his father'.

(v) A weak (clitic) pronoun which receives a stress because of a weak pronoun that immediately follows it (φέρε **μού** το 'bring me it').

In addition, the accent is used after an Arabic numeral to denote minutes (8.10´ 'ten past eight') and is often used after a letter or group of letters used to represent numbers (e.g. Α´ 'one; first', κδ´ 'twenty-four[th]'). For a table of alphabetic numerals see Part II, Section 6.1.

The *diaeresis* is used to indicate that two adjacent vowels that would otherwise indicate a single sound correspond to two sounds: thus γαϊδάρου [γajδáru] 'donkey (gen.)'; contrast the nominative γάιδαρος, where the position of the accent on the first of the two vowels indicates that they are pronounced as two sounds without the need for the diaeresis. In practice the diaeresis is only written over ι and υ. Where a diaeresis appears over a stressed vowel, the combination is written thus: καΐκι 'caique'.

The *apostrophe* is used to indicate that a vowel has been deleted at the end or the beginning of a word. The deletion of a vowel at the end of a word (e.g. θέλω ν' ανέβω 'I want to go up' for θέλω να ανέβω) is sometimes known as *elision*; the deletion of a vowel at the beginning of a word (e.g. το 'κανα 'I did it' for το έκανα) is sometimes called *prodelision*. Elision and prodelision are never obligatory, but they occur frequently in spoken usage; they may also occur in written usage, especially where the style approximates to speech (see Section 1.4.3.2). Today the normal convention is to write the two words separately, with the apostrophe appearing in the position of the omitted vowel and a space appearing either immediately after the apostrophe (in the case of elision) or before it (in the case of prodelision), as indicated in the above examples.

2.2.1   THE TRADITIONAL DIACRITIC SYSTEM

The traditional diacritic system (polytonic system), which is still used in much writing, though – with few exceptions – not in the mass media and in schoolbooks, was inherited more or less from the Hellenistic period, and consists of an array of diacritical marks written above or below vowels. These marks comprise two *breathings*, three *accents*, the *diaeresis*, and the *iota subscript*. Except in so far as (a) the position (rather than the variety) of the accent and (b) the diaeresis are concerned, these marks have a purely historical significance and are not relevant to pronunciation. (The conventions for the use of the apostrophe in the traditional system are the same as those just outlined in Section 2.2.)

In the traditional system, every initial vowel (and every initial combination of two vowels when their pronunciation consists of or includes a single vowel sound) must carry one of two *breathings*. The two breathings (πνεύματα) are traditionally called 'rough' (δασεία: ʽ) and 'smooth' (ψιλή: ʼ). The rough breathing indicates that in Classical Greek the vowel sound was preceded by an /h/ sound, while the smooth breathing indicates that the vowel was not preceded by /h/. The Greek originals of English derivatives have a rough breathing where English has an 'h': thus ἁρμονία 'harmony', but ἀναλογία 'analogy'. A limited number of words beginning with a vowel or vowels bear the rough breathing over the initial vowel(s): every word beginning with υ has a rough breathing over the initial vowel (or over the second vowel of the digraph υι, as do a number of words beginning with the other vowels, together with their derivatives; all the rest bear the smooth breathing. (For a list of 133 words written with a rough breathing see *Νεοελληνική γραμματική: αναπροσαρμογή της Μικρής νεοελληνικής γραμματικής του Μανόλη Τριανταφυλλίδη* (Athens 1976), pp. 212–13.)

Where a word begins with a single vowel, the breathing is placed above the vowel concerned, or immediately before it in the case of a capital letter ('Αθήνα 'Athens'). Where a word begins with two adjacent vowels pronounced as a single vowel sound, the breathing is written over the second of the two (εἰρήνη 'peace'); similarly the breathing is placed over the second elements of the combinations αυ and ευ when they are pronounced [af], [ef], [av], or [ev] (αὐτός [aftós] (demonstrative), εὐτυχία [eftixía] 'happiness'), but over the first when they are pronounced [ai] and [ei] (ἄυλος [áilos] 'immaterial'). A smooth breathing is placed over a non-initial vowel in the following circumstances: the vowel was the final vowel of a word, and the initial vowel of the following word has been deleted (as in τὄχω 'I have it', from τὸ ἔχω, written το 'χω in the monotonic system), or the vowel sound has come into being in Ancient Greek through the combination of a final and an initial vowel (e.g. τοὐλάχιστον 'at least', deriving from τὸ ἐλάχιστον). The monotonic system has completely dispensed with the breathings.

The three *accents* used in the traditional system are the acute (οξεία: ´), the circumflex (περισπωμένη: ˜), and the grave (βαρεία: `). All words, with a very few exceptions such as the weak (clitic) personal pronouns and the nominative masculine and feminine forms of the definite article, bear an accent. In Modern Greek all of these accents, when they appear in a word of two or more syllables, indicate the same thing, namely that the vowel on which they appear is stressed; in monosyllables the accents are almost always synchronically superfluous.

The choice of accent to be used depends on a complex set of rules which relate partly to the position of the stress and partly to the length of the relevant vowels in Classical Greek, where every vowel was either long or short. In Classical Greek, some written vowels were always long (η, ω, and vowel sounds and diphthongs represented by two letters, e.g. ου, ει, αυ); some were always short (ε and o); while some were sometimes long and sometimes short (α, ι, and υ). At the ends of words, however, -αι and -οι are considered to be short (although -αις and -οις are considered to be long). The basic rules for the position and the kind of accent in the traditional system are as follows (see also the material on stress in Sections 1.3.2.1 and 1.5–1.5.4):

(a) no word can be accented further forward than the third syllable from the end (thus ὄνομα 'name', but gen. sg. ὀνόματος);

(b) words ending in a long syllable cannot be accented further forward than the second syllable from the end (thus gen. pl. ὀνομάτων);

(c) only the acute may be used on words accented on the third syllable from the end (ἀνώριμος);

(d) only the acute or the grave may be used on a final 'short' vowel (καλός or καλὸς 'good');

(e) the circumflex can be placed only over a 'long' vowel, and only when that vowel is the penultimate or final in the word (εὐχαριστῶ 'I thank');

(f) only the circumflex can be placed over a long vowel when that vowel is the penultimate vowel in the word and when the final vowel is 'short' (χῶρος 'space');

(g) only the acute can be placed over the penultimate vowel if the last vowel is 'long' (thus gen. sg. χώρου);

(h) the grave is used only to replace the acute on the final vowel; it replaces it if the word is immediately followed by any word other than a weak (clitic) pronoun (thus ὁ αδελφὸς αὐτός 'this brother', but ὁ ἀδελφός μου 'my brother'), except that the interrogative words τί 'what' and γιατί 'why', as well as the deictic particle νά and the hortatory particle γιά, receive the acute (τί θέλεις; 'what do you want?', νά τὸν Γιάννη! 'there's John!', γιά στάσου! 'just hold on!').

Rules (a) and – almost always – (b) continue to operate in modern Greek: rule (b) is the origin of the shift of stress from nominative to genitive in ἄνθρωπος—ἀνθρώπου 'human being', where the final -o- was short in Classical Greek, whereas the final -ου of the genitive was long. Rules (f) and (g) provide for the accentuation of χῶρος 'place (nom.)', with circumflex, but χώρου (gen.) with acute, because of the same difference in the length of the final vowel as in ἄνθρωπος—ἀνθρώπου. Rule (h) accounts for the different accents used on the last syllable of the noun in the following sentences meaning 'The hunter came':

(1)   ᾟρθε ὁ κυνηγός

(2)   Ὁ κυνηγὸς ἦρθε

In (1) the noun comes at the end of the sentence, and therefore the acute is used; in (2) the grave has to be used because the noun is immediately followed by another word.

As the above examples show, a breathing and an accent can be combined to appear over the same vowel (or before it in the case of a capital letter). When this occurs, the acute or grave is written immediately after the breathing, whereas the circumflex is written above it.

In practice, the grave had been abandoned in favour of the acute in much writing (particularly handwriting and typewriting, but also in some printing) for some decades before the official introduction of the monotonic system in 1982. In addition, the acute was allowed to replace the circumflex in cases where the length of the relevant vowels might not be obvious; previously it was necessary to learn whether the relevant α, ι, or υ was long or short in every individual word. Thus, while in Ancient Greek γλῶσσα was written, in accordance with rule (f) above, with a circumflex because the -ω- was long and the -α happened to be short, in recent times it has tended to be written γλώσσα, with an acute, even in the polytonic system. An exception was made (i) for neuter singular and plural forms in -α and (ii) for first-person singular forms (also in -α) of the past tenses of verbs, in which a 'long' penultimate vowel was always written with a circumflex (θαῦμα, σχολεῖα, and ρωτοῦσα, εἶδα).

The *diaeresis* is used in the traditional system in much the same way as it is in the monotonic system, except that, where the two adjacent written vowels are pronounced as two sounds, the diaeresis appears over the second vowel even when the first is accented: thus γάϊδαρος (contrast γάιδαρος, without diaeresis, in the monotonic system).

The *iota subscript* is hardly used at all today; it appeared under the vowels α, η, ω in certain words, for instance in certain dative singular endings (τῇ χώρᾳ 'to the country', τῷ πολέμῳ 'to the war') and especially in the second- and third-person singular endings of the 'subjunctive' active: thus θέλεις νὰ καθίσῃς 'you want to sit'. These verbal endings have nowadays been replaced by -ει[ς] (as in θέλεις να καθίσεις). In other instances the iota subscript has simply been dropped.

Before 1982 Greek schoolchildren were expected to learn (a) a list of all nouns that were written with the rough breathing, (b) the vowel-length (in Classical Greek) of the crucial syllables in each word, and (c) all the words and endings that included an iota subscript. Since the official introduction of the monotonic system into education, this learning is no longer necessary and is no longer carried out in Greek schools.

2.3 PUNCTUATION

In most respects, Greek punctuation follows normal European practice with respect to the *full stop* (.), *comma* (,), *colon* (:), *exclamation mark* (!), and *parentheses* (( )). Peculiar to Greek is the use of the *raised point* (άνω τελεία: ·), which is used instead of the semicolon. The Greek *question mark* (;) is identical to the Latin semicolon.

The *full stop* (τελεία [.]) is used

(i)   at the end of a sentence;
(ii)   to indicate an abbreviation consisting of a single letter or including a lower-case letter (e.g. ο κ. Α. Παπαδόπουλος 'Mr A. Papadopoulos', and π.Χ. for προ Χριστού 'Before Christ', but οι ΗΠΑ 'the USA');
(iii) to divide large numbers into groups of three figures (thus Greek 1.234.567 corresponds to British and US 1,234,567);
(iv)   to denote clock times (e.g. 10.45).

The *raised point* (άνω τελεία [·]) is used similarly to the semicolon in other European languages, i.e.:

(i)   to divide groups of clauses from each other;
(ii)   before a clause or phrase that clarifies the previous clause.

The *comma* (κόμμα [,]) is used to separate clauses from each other within the same sentence; it most commonly separates two coordinate clauses joined by αλλά 'but' from each other, or a subordinate clause (other than a nominal clause) from a following main clause. It also appears between words and phrases where these serve the same syntactical function within the clause, e.g. in (1), and appears in pairs in order to separate off parenthetical words or phrases from the rest of the clause (2):

(1)   τσιγάρα, σπίρτα, καραμέλες
      'cigarettes, matches, sweets'
(2)   Η κυρία Παπαδοπούλου, η διευθύντρια, μου το είπε
      'Mrs Papadopoulou, the manager, told me so'

It is used to separate off a noun phrase in the vocative from the rest of
the sentence:

(3)   Έλα, Κατερίνα, να φας
      'Come here, Katerina, and eat'

Similarly, an adverbial phrase may be separated off from the rest of the
sentence by commas:

(4)   Για μας, αυτό το ματς ήταν ένας θρίαμβος
      'For us, this match was a triumph'

In practice, a comma tends to appear where one might pause in speech
or reading aloud. Thus a comma is often placed between a topicalized
subject and the immediately following verb (for the topicalization of the
subject see Part III, Section 5.2.2.1). Similarly, the presence or absence
of a comma before and after a relative clause does not always correspond
to the distinction between non-restrictive and restrictive relative clauses,
which are not always distinguished in Greek speech by a pause or absence
of pause (see Part III, Section 5.3.1.1).

A comma is written in the pronoun and determiner ό,τι (also used as
a temporal adverb: ό,τι έφτασε 's/he's just arrived') to distinguish it from
the complementizer ότι; it is written without a space after the comma.

The comma is also used to indicate the decimal point (12,36 in Greek =
12.36 in English). Similarly, the comma is used to separate one unit of measurement, currency, etc., from another: thus 45,50μ. 'forty-five metres fifty'
(45.5m. in English usage), $4,50 'four dollars fifty' ($4.50 in English usage).

The *question mark* (ερωτηματικό [;]) is used at the end of an interrogative sentence. It may also be used in parenthesis after a word or
phrase (;) to indicate the writer's doubt about the truth of what s/he is
writing.

The *exclamation mark* (θαυμαστικό [!]) is used at the end of a sentence
conveying an exclamation or, within a sentence, after an exclamatory
phrase.

The *colon* (δύο τελείες [:]) is used to introduce a piece of direct speech
or a list of items.

Parentheses (παρενθέσεις [()]) are used to isolate a word or phrase,
interpolated into a phrase, clause or sentence, which supplements what is
said but could be omitted without significant loss of meaning.

Two chief conventions are used for the quoting of *direct speech*. These
vary according to the writer or publisher concerned. According to one

commonly observed convention, a piece of direct speech at the beginning of a paragraph is introduced simply by a dash, with no speech-marks indicating the boundary between the speech and the narrative:

(5) — Δυστυχώς, μου είπε, ήρθες αργά
'"Unfortunately", s/he said, "you've come too late"'

According to another convention, direct speech is enclosed within *εισαγωγικά* (« »), which are also used for the quoting or pointing out of individual words or phrases, or for indicating that the word or phrase is being used metaphorically. When the quoted speech begins in mid-paragraph, only εισαγωγικά, not a dash, can be used. For all these purposes the εισαγωγικά may be replaced by double inverted commas (" " or „ „), although inverted commas may also be used to indicate speech quoted within speech that is already enclosed within εισαγωγικά. When the direct speech is interrupted by a brief clause specifying who is speaking and other such details, this clause may or may not be placed outside the εισαγωγικά or inverted commas; if it is, a comma usually does not appear at the break unless it would have appeared had the piece of speech been quoted without a break. Thus:

(6) «Θα προτιμούσα» είπε η Μαρία «να φύγω αμέσως»
'"I would prefer", said Mary, "to leave immediately"'

In one variety of this convention, a comma appears between the closing mark (») and the indication of who is speaking (7), unless the piece of speech itself ends with a punctuation mark (8):

(7) «Δεν ξέρω», απάντησα.
'"I don't know", I replied.'

(8) «Γιατί;» ρώτησε η Μαρία.
'"Why?" asked Maria.'

When the same stretch of direct speech continues into a following paragraph, the paragraph preceding the paragraph break normally ends without εισαγωγικά, while the following paragraph begins with the sign for the end of direct speech (»).

Εισαγωγικά or inverted commas are also used for quoting titles of books, etc.

The *hyphen* (ενωτικό [-]) should be used to join two words, or to indicate a break in a word at the end of a line (see Section 2.3.1), while the *dash* (παύλα [–]) should be used to indicate a break in a sentence (either to show an abrupt change of direction or, in pairs, to isolate a word or phrase from the rest of the sentence). In practice, however, Greek writers and typesetters often fail to observe this distinction.

The *points de suspension* (αποσιωπητικά [...]) may be used to indicate that a sentence is incomplete. Much use is made by comic writers of αποσιωπητικά, usually in order to lead up to the punch-line of a story, or to some word or phrase by which the reader is expected to be surprised.

Some Greek typefaces do not have πλάγια στοιχεία (the equivalent of italics), their place being taken by the spacing out of the letters of the word(s) being emphasized (thus Θέλω δ ύ ο αβγά is the equivalent of Θέλω δύο αβγά 'I want *two* eggs').

2.3.1 HYPHENS AND SYLLABLE DIVISION

The hyphen is used to join two words, e.g. double surnames or Christian names (Πετσάλης-Διομήδης 'Petsalis-Diomidis'), or loose appositional compounds (παιδί-θαύμα 'child wonder'; see also Part III, Section 2.12). The hyphen is not normally used in Greek to indicate a division within a single word, except at a line-break; thus οικονομικοκοινωνικός 'socio-economic', αντιπυρηνικός 'anti-nuclear'.

The hyphen is also used to indicate a word-break at the end of a line. The following are the most common rules governing the division of a word for this purpose:

(a) a word-break may be placed before a consonant that appears between two vowels (έ-χω).

(b) a word-break may be placed between two vowels only if they represent two separate vowel sounds (thus ναός can be broken as να-ός, while ναύτης [náftis] can only be broken as ναύ-της, not να-ύτης).

(c) a word-break may be placed before the first of two consonants which appear between two vowels as long as there is a Greek word beginning with the same pair of consonants (thus λά-σπη [cf. σπίθα], ύπο-πτος [cf. πτώμα]); otherwise, the break must be placed between the two consonants (θάρ-ρος, βαθ-μός).

(d) a word-break may be placed before the first of three or more conso-nants which appear between two vowels as long as there is a Greek word beginning with at least the first two of the three consonants (thus ά-στρο [cf. στρώνω], αι-σχρός [cf. σχέδιο]); otherwise the break must appear after the first consonant (άν-θρωπος, εκ-στρατεία). An older rule specified that the consonant clusters γγ, γκ, μπ, and ντ should either be placed after the word-break or be split by the break according to whether they were pronounced as a single voiced plosive or whether the voiced plosive was preceded by a nasal. In view of the variability in the pronunciation of these clusters, modern practice is normally not to split them.

Rules (c) and (d) presuppose that there is a fixed corpus of Greek words. In practice, the double consonant clusters that are normally considered to be able to appear at the beginning of Greek words are shown below:

βγ, βδ, βλ, βϱ
γδ, γϰ, γλ, γν, γϱ
δϱ
θλ, θν, θϱ
ϰλ, ϰν, ϰϱ, ϰτ
μν, μπ
ντ
πλ, πν, πϱ, πτ
σβ, σγ, σθ, σϰ, σλ, σμ, σν, σπ, στ, σφ, σχ
τζ, τμ, τϱ, τσ
φθ, φϰ, φλ, φϱ, φτ
χλ, χν, χϱ, χτ

PART II: MORPHOLOGY

INTRODUCTION

Greek is a highly inflected language; that is to say, the basic words given in the dictionary are modified in various ways according to their function in a particular context. The system of different but related *forms*, which in Greek is mainly a matter of the different endings attached to the stem of a word, is the language's **morphology**. A thorough familiarity with the full range of forms is an essential part of the proficient use of the language.

In Part II these forms are set out in full by part of speech. Articles (Section 1), adjectives (Section 3), pronouns and determiners (Section 5), and some (but not all) numerals (Section 6) are inflected for gender, number and case. Adverbs (Section 4) may be derived from adjectives according to certain rules and, like adjectives, have degrees of comparison. Nouns (Section 2), which may be of masculine, feminine or neuter gender, are inflected for number and case. Verbs (Section 7) have a complex system of forms which are differentiated by person, number, tense, aspect, voice and (to an extent) mood. Finally, there are various ways of forming new words by means of prefixation, suffixation and compounding; some information on such *derivational morphology* will be given in Section 8.

1 THE ARTICLES

An article is a modifier placed before a noun to limit, individualize or give definiteness or indefiniteness to the noun phrase. Greek has two articles, definite and indefinite. Both are declined for case and gender. The definite article ('the') modifies singular or plural nouns, but the indefinite article ('a[n]') modifies singular nouns only and therefore has only singular forms. The use of the articles as part of a noun phrase is discussed in Part III, Section 2.5. Below we give the tables of forms.

1.1 THE DEFINITE ARTICLE

ο, η, το   'the'

	Sg.			Pl.		
	M	F	N	M	F	N
Nom.	ο	η	το	οι	οι	τα
Acc.	το(ν)	τη(ν)	το	τους	τις	τα
Gen.	του	της	του	των	των	των

1. The masc. and fem. acc. sg. forms *must* have the final -ν when the word immediately following begins with a vowel or with any of the following consonants or consonant clusters: κ π τ γκ μπ ντ ξ ψ. Before other consonants it is possible to omit the -ν, but in the case of the masc. article it is usual to write the full form τον when the noun to which it relates is a proper name, e.g. τον Στέφανο. The neuter sg. article never has a final -ν.

2. The acc. case of the definite article is combined with the preposition σε ('to', 'at', 'in', 'on', etc.) as one word: στο(ν), στη(ν), στο, στους, στις, στα. Σε is also found combined with the gen. case of the definite article in elliptical constructions like στου Γιάννη 'at/to John's [house]', which is shortened from στο σπίτι του Γιάννη. In poetic language, σε can combine with the gen. case of the definite article when separated from its noun by an intervening phrase in the gen. e.g. μες στης αμαρτίας τη μοναξιά 'in the solitude of sin'; the more normal word order would be μες στη μοναξιά της αμαρτίας.

3. There are no vocative forms.

1.2   THE INDEFINITE ARTICLE

ένας, μια, ένα   'a[n]'

	M	F	N
Nom.	ένας	μια	ένα
Acc.	ένα(ν)	μια(ν)	ένα
Gen.	ενός	μιας	ενός

1. The forms of the indefinite article are almost identical to those of the numeral 'one' (Section 6.2). The only differences occur in the feminine forms, and are due to the fact that the numeral can be pronounced emphatically as a two-syllable word, with stress on the first syllable (spelled μία).

2. The final -ν of the acc. forms of the masc. and fem., which is never obligatory, is less often used than is the case with the definite article. It may be used before words beginning with a vowel or a voiceless plosive, e.g. έναν άνθρωπο 'a human being (acc.)', μια φορά κι ένα(ν) καιρό 'once upon a time'.

3. There are no vocative forms.

2 NOUNS

A noun can be defined as a word for a person, a place, a thing, or an abstract quality, an attribute, an action or a condition, e.g. in English, 'girl', 'Mary', 'Greece', 'table', 'beauty', 'loneliness'; in Greek, κορίτσι, Μαρία, Ελλάδα, τραπέζι, ομορφιά, μοναξιά. Greek nouns belong to various *declensions*; by declensions we mean the systems of endings that serve to indicate case and number: nominative, accusative, genitive and vocative cases, and singular and plural number. The complete set of forms for a given noun is referred to as a *paradigm*. The noun paradigms presented below are arranged primarily by *gender*: masculine, feminine, common gender (that is, nouns which can be either masculine or feminine), and neuter.

All nouns in Greek have an inherent gender (for a full discussion see Part III, Sections 2.2 ff.). It is essential to know the gender of a given noun in order to decline it correctly, to prefix it with the correct form of the article, or to modify it with an adjective. The gender can often be deduced from the ending of the word, particularly if one knows its spelling. For example, nouns whose nominative singular ends in -ι are invariably neuter, and those ending in -η are feminine. However, the gender cannot always be inferred so easily: -ος may be the termination of a masculine, feminine or neuter noun, and there are both feminines and neuters that end in -α. In the following lists we therefore divide nouns first by gender, and then by declensional pattern, giving in every instance the appropriate form of the definite article. It is often necessary to classify nouns by the stress of the nominative singular: *oxytone* nouns are stressed on the final syllable, *paroxytone* on the penultimate syllable, and *proparoxytone* on the third syllable from the end. A comparative table of declensional endings is given in Section 2.5.

2.1 MASCULINE NOUNS

2.1.1 NOUNS IN -ας (PARISYLLABIC)

This category consists of nouns in -ας which are *parisyllabic*, i.e. they have the same number of syllables in their plural form as in the singular. (Imparisyllabic nouns in -ας, which add an extra syllable in forming their plural, are dealt with in Section 2.1.5. Masculine nouns in -έας will be found in Section 2.1.4.) There are two types, according to the stress of the genitive plural: (i) those that have a genitive plural with stress on the penultimate (mostly nouns deriving from the Ancient Greek 3rd declension); (ii) those that have a genitive plural with stress on the final syllable (nouns deriving from the Ancient Greek 1st declension, but also including some from the 3rd and some newer formations). With these exceptions, the stress remains on the same syllable as in the nominative singular.

(i)   ο φύλακας 'guard, custodian'

		Sg.		*Pl.*
Nom.	ο	φύλακας	οι	φύλακες
Acc.	το(ν)	φύλακα	τους	φύλακες
Gen.	του	φύλακα	των	φυλάκων
Voc.		φύλακα		φύλακες

Examples:

αγκώνας 'elbow', αγώνας 'struggle', αιώνας 'century', αναπτήρας 'lighter', γείτονας 'neighbour', Έλληνας 'Greek (man)', ενεστώτας 'present tense', ήρωας 'hero', κανόνας 'rule, canon', καύσωνας 'heatwave', κηδεμόνας 'guardian', κόρακας 'crow', λάρυγγας 'throat, larynx', παράγοντας 'factor', πατέρας 'father', πίνακας 'picture, board', πνεύμονας 'lung', πράκτορας 'agent', πρίγκιπας 'prince', πρόσφυγας 'refugee', στρατώνας 'barracks', συνδετήρας 'paper-clip', σωλήνας 'tube', χάλυβας 'steel', χειμώνας 'winter'

(ii)   ο τουρίστας 'tourist'

		Sg.		*Pl.*
Nom.	ο	τουρίστας	οι	τουρίστες
Acc.	τον	τουρίστα	τους	τουρίστες
Gen.	του	τουρίστα	των	τουριστών
Voc.		τουρίστα		τουρίστες

Examples:

άντρας or άνδρας 'man, husband', αριβίστας 'upstart', βήχας 'cough', καρχαρίας 'shark', λοχίας 'sergeant', μήνας 'month', and all other masculine nouns in -ίας and -ίστας

1.   Type (i) includes both paroxytone and proparoxytone nouns; only the latter undergo a *shift* of stress in the gen. pl.; the former have stress on the penultimate throughout.

2.   Alternative forms of the gen. sg., ending in -ος, are sometimes found, e.g. πατρός (learned) instead of πατέρα, αντρός (poetic or dialectal) or ανδρός (learned) instead of άντρα, μηνός (often in dates e.g. στις 10 του μηνός 'on the 10th of the month', deriving from *katharevousa* usage) instead of μήνα.

3. Other learned forms of the nom. sg. are found occasionally in formal contexts. Examples (with the corresponding learned form of the gen. sg. in brackets) are: αγώνς (αγώνος) 'struggle', Έλλην (Έλληνος) 'Greek (man)', κήρυξ (κήρυκος) 'herald', μάρτυς (μάρτυρος) 'witness' instead of the more usual form μάρτυρας, gen. μάρτυρα, γίγας (γίγαντος) 'giant' instead of the more usual γίγαντας, gen. γίγαντα.

4. A few proparoxytone nouns in -ας have a (non-standard) alternative plural in -οι, acc. -ους, with a shift of stress to the penultimate: e.g. ο μάστορας '(skilled) workman', pl. οι μαστόροι or μάστορες, τους μαστόρους or μάστορες.

2.1.2   NOUNS IN -ης (PARISYLLABIC)

These nouns always have stressed -ών in the genitive plural; paroxytone nouns undergo a shift of stress to the final syllable in the genitive plural, but many nouns in this category are oxytone. (For imparisyllabic nouns in -ης see Section 2.1.5, and for nouns with plural in -εις see Section 2.1.4.)

ο κλέφτης   'thief'

		Sg.		Pl.
Nom.	ο	κλέφτης	οι	κλέφτες
Acc.	τον	κλέφτη	τους	κλέφτες
Gen.	του	κλέφτη	των	κλεφτών
Voc.		κλέφτη		κλέφτες

Examples:

Like ο κλέφτης (paroxytone): αναγνώστης 'reader', βιβλιοπώλης 'bookseller', επιβάτης 'passenger', εργάτης 'workman', καθρέφτης 'mirror', ναύτης 'sailor', νεροχύτης 'kitchen sink', πελάτης 'customer, client', στρατιώτης 'soldier', ράφτης 'tailor', φράχτης 'fence'

Oxytone: ανταποκριτής 'correspondent', βουλευτής 'member of parliament, deputy', διευθυντής 'director', εθελοντής 'volunteer', καθηγητής 'professor', μαθητής 'schoolboy, pupil', νικητής 'winner', ποιητής 'poet', σπουδαστής 'student', φοιτητής 'university student'

1. Some oxytone nouns referring to persons have an alternative learned vocative singular in -α, e.g. κύριε καθηγητά 'professor' (only after κύριε).

2. An archaic form of the nom. pl. in -αι is sometimes encountered: οι βουλευταί 'members of parliament', οι φοιτηταί 'students'. Archaic forms of the gen. sing. in -ου and acc. pl. in -ας may also be found: e.g. του καθηγητού, τους καθηγητάς.

3. Surnames in -δης and -της have gen. sg. in either -η or (more formal) -ου, depending on individual preference. The corresponding women's surnames (which are the gen. sg. forms) usually end in -ου, e.g. Παυλίδου, Ανδρεάδου, Πολίτου.

4. Some (mainly paroxytone) nouns of this type have an alternative nom. pl. in -άδες, gen. pl. -άδων, with a shift of stress (cf. the category in Section 2.1.5 below).

Examples include: αφέντης 'master', pl. αφεντάδες or αφέντες, δεσπότης 'bishop, despot', pl. δεσποτάδες 'bishops' (but δεσπότες 'despots'), ψάλτης 'cantor (in church)', pl. ψαλτάδες or ψάλτες. Because the plural ending -άδες is of non-learned, demotic origin, when it is attached to nouns with honorific connotations it has a humorous or depreciative effect, e.g. καθηγητάδες 'professors, "profs"'.

2.1.3 NOUNS IN -ος

Nouns in this very numerous category may be oxytone (ο ουρανός 'sky, heaven'), paroxytone (ο κουμπάρος 'best man (at wedding), godfather (of one's child)', ο φίλος 'friend') or proparoxytone (ο άνθρωπος 'man, human being'). In nouns of the first two kinds, i.e. oxytone and paroxytone, the stress remains on the same syllable throughout the declension:

ο ουρανός   'sky, heaven'

		Sg.		*Pl.*
Nom.	ο	ουρανός	οι	ουρανοί
Acc.	τον	ουρανό	τους	ουρανούς
Gen.	του	ουρανού	των	ουρανών
Voc.		ουρανέ		ουρανοί

Other examples:

αδελφός/αδερφός 'brother', βαθμός 'degree, level', γάμος 'marriage', γιος 'son', δρόμος 'road', εχθρός 'enemy', καιρός 'time', κινηματογράφος 'cinema', κλάδος 'branch (of study)', κόσμος 'world', νόμος 'law', μαραγκός 'carpenter', οδηγός 'driver', όρος 'term', ποταμός 'river', σεισμός 'earthquake', σκοπός 'purpose, tune', σκύλος 'dog', τόπος 'place', ύπνος 'sleep', φόβος 'fear', χώρος 'space, area', ώμος 'shoulder'.

The third kind, that is, proparoxytone nouns, presents two alternative patterns, according to whether the stress moves or remains on the same syllable throughout the declension:

(i)   ο άνθρωπος   'man'

		Sg.		*Pl.*
Nom.	ο	άνθρωπος	οι	άνθρωποι
Acc.	τον	άνθρωπο	τους	ανθρώπους
Gen.	του	ανθρώπου	των	ανθρώπων
Voc.		άνθρωπε		άνθρωποι

(ii)   ο καλόγερος   'monk'

	Sg.			Pl.
Nom.	ο	καλόγερος	οι	καλόγεροι
Acc.	τον	καλόγερο	τους	καλόγερους
Gen.	του	καλόγερου	των	καλόγερων
Voc.		καλόγερε		καλόγεροι

The first type, with shift of stress to the penultimate syllable in the gen. sg. and pl. and the acc. pl., could be called the more conservative: it applies to nouns which are preserved essentially unaltered from Ancient Greek and in general to words likely to occur in more formal contexts. The second type includes more recent formations, especially compounds. We give some examples of the two types:

Like ο άνθρωπος: άνεμος 'wind', αντιπρόσωπος 'representative', διάδρομος 'corridor', δήμαρχος 'mayor', έλεγχος 'check, control', θάνατος 'death', θόρυβος 'noise', Ιανουάριος 'January' (and other names of months), κάτοικος 'inhabitant, tenant', κίνδυνος 'danger', κύριος 'gentleman, Mr', λαβύρινθος 'labyrinth', όροφος 'storey', πόλεμος 'war', πρόεδρος 'president', πρόλογος 'prologue'

Like ο καλόγερος: ανεμόμυλος 'windmill', ανήφορος 'ascent', αντίλαλος 'echo', γάιδαρος 'donkey', δάσκαλος 'teacher', κατήφορος 'descent', λαχανόκηπος 'vegetable garden', παλιάνθρωπος 'rogue', πονοκέφαλος 'headache', χωματόδρομος 'dirt road', ψεύταρος 'big liar'

However, the distinction between the two types is not fixed or absolute: forms without shift of stress like του διάδρομου, or with shift of stress like τους ανεμομύλους or του σιδηροδρόμου may be encountered, possibly serving a particular stylistic purpose ('unshifted' forms belong to a lower stylistic level, those with a shift of stress to a higher stylistic level).

1. Some proparoxytones of this declension have an alternative (non-standard or dialectal) form of the nom. and voc. pl. with the stress on the penultimate: ανθρώποι 'men', δασκάλοι 'teachers', συμπεθέροι 'relations by marriage', συντρόφοι 'comrades'.

2. Proparoxytone surnames in -ος usually preserve the same stress in the gen. sg., e.g. του κυρίου Στεφανόπουλου, and especially when a familiar form of a given name precedes: του Γιάννη Στεφανόπουλου. But, more formally, one might find του κυρίου Ιωάννη Στεφανοπούλου. When such genitive forms are used as women's surnames, there is normally an obligatory shift of the stress to the penultimate: e.g. η κυρία Παπαδοπούλου, η δεσποινίς Πατρικίου. Official street names, named after men, also have the shift of stress: e.g. οδός Αναγνωστοπούλου, οδός Δαιδάλου, πλατεία Αγίου Δημητρίου.

3. In place of the usual -ε termination of the vocative singular, certain nouns have a vocative in -ο (identical to the accusative). They include the following:

(a) Given names and surnames stressed on the penultimate, e.g. ο Νίκος → Νίκο. Thus: Αλέκο, Μάρκο, Πέτρο, Παύλο (but Παύλε is also found), Χρήστο, Βαγιακάκο, Μαρινάτο, Παπασταύρο. Otherwise masculine proper names (including surnames) in -ος have vocative in -ε: Αλέξανδρε, Στέφανε, Χαράλαμπε, Πάγκαλε, Παπαδόπουλε.

(b) Certain common nouns of two syllables: γέρος 'old man', διάκος 'deacon', δράκος 'ogre', λούστρος 'bootblack' (but also λούστρε).

(c) Diminutives in -άκος: φιλαράκος 'little friend'.

4. Nouns of this declension used in certain learned set expressions may have accusative singular in -ον: κατά κόρον 'to satiety', υπό τον όρον 'on condition (that)'.

5. χρόνος 'year' has a genitive plural χρονώ(ν) used for expressions of age (see Appendix 3.2). On the plural forms of this noun see further Section 2.6.

6. For feminine nouns in -ος see Section 2.2.3 and for nouns with the same termination which may be either masculine or feminine (common gender) see Section 2.3.

2.1.4   NOUNS IN -έας

Nouns of this type are declined like those in -ας in the singular, but have plural in -είς, gen. -έων.

ο τομέας   'section, sector'

		Sg.		Pl.
Nom.	ο	τομέας	οι	τομείς
Acc.	τον	τομέα	τους	τομείς
Gen.	του	τομέα	των	τομέων
(Voc.		τομέα		τομείς)

Examples:

αμφορέας 'amphora, urn', βασιλέας 'king', κουρέας 'barber', σκαπανέας 'sapper'.

1. In very formal use, nouns of this type are sometimes declined in the singular according to the Ancient Greek declension from which they derive: nom. -εύς, acc. -έα, gen. -έως, voc. -εύ, e.g. ο Βασιλεύς Παύλος 'King Paul'. (In normal use the form βασιλιάς, pl. βασιλιάδες, corresponding to the type in Section 2.1.5 (i), is the more common.)

2. Many nouns of this type referring to persons are of common gender; for them see Section 2.3.

2.1.5   IMPARISYLLABIC NOUNS IN -άς, -ας, -ής, -ης, -ές, -ούς

Imparisyllabic nouns by definition have a different number of syllables in their singular and plural forms. The plural forms have an extra syllable

and always end in -δες (nom., acc., voc.), -δων (gen.). The nominative
singular of such nouns may be oxytone, as type (i) below, or paroxytone,
as type (ii). Generally speaking, the stress remains on the same syllable
in the plural as in the singular, and the plural ending -δες is added to the
vowel of the singular ending. Exceptions will be discussed with the examples. A third type (iii) are proparoxytone; because of the rule that there
cannot be more than two unstressed syllables at the end of a word (see
Part I, Section 1.5.1), the stress moves one syllable forward in the plural.
Imparisyllabic masculine nouns include many nouns of foreign (especially
Turkish) origin, many words denoting occupations, augmentatives in -άς,
diminutives in -άκης and -ούλης, and proper names in -άς, -ής and -ης.
Examples are given after each type.

(i)   ο παπάς   'priest'

		Sg.		*Pl.*
Nom.	ο	παπάς	οι	παπάδες
Acc.	τον	παπά	τους	παπάδες
Gen.	του	παπά	των	παπάδων
Voc.		παπά		παπάδες

Examples:

Sg. in -άς, pl. -άδες: αρακάς 'pea(s)', βοριάς 'north wind', βραχνάς
'nightmare', γαλατάς 'milkman', καλοφαγάς 'gourmet', κερατάς
'cuckold', κουβάς 'bucket', λεφτάς 'money-bags (= person)', μπαλτάς
'axe', μπελάς 'trouble', μυλωνάς 'miller', παπλωματάς 'quilter',
παράς 'money', σουγιάς 'penknife', σφουγγαράς 'sponge-fisher',
φονιάς 'murderer', χαλβάς 'halva', χαλκιάς 'coppersmith', ψαράς
'fisherman', ψωμάς 'baker', and proper names such as Λουκάς,
Σαμαράς

Sg. in -ής, pl. -ήδες: ατζαμής 'inexperienced person', καταφερτζής
'wheedler, smooth operator', καφετζής 'coffee-house keeper',
μερακλής 'connoisseur', μπεκρής 'drunkard', μπογιατζής 'decorator',
παλιατζής 'second-hand dealer', παπουτσής 'shoe-maker', ταξιτζής
'taxi-driver', and proper names such as Κωστής, Παντελής,
Ραγκαβής, Χατζής

Sg. in -ές, pl. -έδες: γλεντζές 'fun-lover', καναπές 'sofa', καφές
'coffee', κεφτές 'meatball', λεκές 'spot, stain', μεζές 'hors d'oeuvre,
titbit', μενεξές 'violet', μιναρές 'minaret', πανσές 'pansy', πουρές
'purée', τενεκές 'tin', χασές 'calico', χαφιές 'informer'

Sg. in -ούς, pl. -ούδες: παππούς 'grandfather'

(ii)   ο μανάβης 'greengrocer'

	Sg.			Pl.
Nom.	ο	μανάβης	οι	μανάβηδες
Acc.	το(ν)	μανάβη	τους	μανάβηδες
Gen.	του	μανάβη	των	μανάβηδων
Voc.		μανάβη		μανάβηδες

Examples:

Sg. in -ης, pl. -ηδες: αράπης 'Arab, negro' (pl. also αραπάδες), βαρκάρης 'boatman', γκιόνης 'scops owl', δόγης 'doge', καβαλάρης 'horseman', μουσαφίρης 'guest', μπακάλης 'grocer', νοικοκύρης 'landlord, householder' (pl. also νοικοκυραίοι), παππούλης 'little grandad', περιβολάρης 'gardener', τιμονιέρης 'helmsman', χασάπης 'butcher', and many proper names such as Βασίλης, Μανόλης, Παυλάκης, Τρικούπης.

Sg. -ας, pl. -άδες (with shift of stress): κάλφας 'apprentice', μπάρμπας 'uncle, old man'

(iii)   ο φούρναρης 'baker'

	Sg.			Pl.
Nom.	ο	φούρναρης	οι	φουρνάρηδες
Acc.	το(ν)	φούρναρη	τους	φουρνάρηδες
Gen.	του	φούρναρη	των	φουρνάρηδων
Voc.		φούρναρη		φουρνάρηδες

Examples:

(with stress on the antepenultimate in pl.): κοτζάμπασης 'landowner, "squire"';

(with stress on the penultimate in pl.): πρωτόπαπας 'head priest', τσέλιγκας 'shepherd'

Some paroxytone nouns in -άκιας have a plural in -άκηδες, omitting the -ι- in their plural forms. Such are: γυαλάκιας 'bespectacled person, "four-eyes"', κορτάκιας 'womanizer, flirt', τσαντάκιας 'bag-snatcher', τυχεράκιας 'lucky devil'.

2.2 FEMININE NOUNS

2.2.1   NOUNS IN -α (PARISYLLABIC)

These nouns may be oxytone, paroxytone or proparoxytone. As in the case of masculine nouns in -ας, it is necessary to divide this category into two groups according to the stress of the genitive plural. The first group (deriving mainly from Ancient Greek 3rd declension) have the stress on the penultimate in the genitive plural, while the second group (mostly from Ancient Greek 1st declension, but including some new formations and loan-words) have the stress on the final syllable.

(i)   η ελπίδα 'hope'

		Sg.		Pl.
Nom.	η	ελπίδα	οι	ελπίδες
Acc.	την	ελπίδα	τις	ελπίδες
Gen.	της	ελπίδας	των	ελπίδων
Voc.		ελπίδα		ελπίδες

Examples:

ακτίνα 'ray of light; radius', βαρύτητα 'heaviness, gravity', γαρίδα 'shrimp', δυνατότητα 'possibility', εικόνα 'picture, image', εφημερίδα 'newspaper', θυγατέρα 'daughter', ικανότητα 'ability', κλίμακα 'scale', μητέρα 'mother', όρνιθα 'hen', πατρίδα 'fatherland', πέρδικα 'partridge', σάλπιγγα 'trumpet', σειρήνα 'siren', σήραγγα 'tunnel', σταγόνα 'drop', σταφίδα 'raisin', ταυτότητα 'identity, identity card', ταχύτητα 'speed, gear', and proper names like Ελλάδα 'Greece', Σαλαμίνα 'Salamis', Τραπεζούντα 'Trebizond'

1. In addition to the examples given above, this type includes all nouns in -ότητα and -ύτητα, and many nouns in -άδα or -ίδα. Most other feminine nouns in -α follow type (ii), with the exception of the imparisyllabic nouns in Section 2.2.5.

2. All proparoxytone nouns have stress on the penultimate syllable in the gen. pl., e.g. δυνατότητα, gen. pl. δυνατοτήτων. Similarly all other nouns in -ότητα, -ύτητα.

3. Some nouns have a learned alternative gen. sg. in -ος, which may be found in formal contexts, e.g. ικανότητος, κλίμακος, Ελλάδος. Such nouns may also have a learned nom. sg. ending in -ς (or -ξ), e.g. ικανότης, κλίμαξ, Ελλάς. The noun μητέρα has an alternative gen. sg. with movement of stress to the final syllable: μητρός.

(ii)   η θάλασσα 'sea'

		Sg.		Pl.
Nom.	η	θάλασσα	οι	θάλασσες
Acc.	τη	θάλασσα	τις	θάλασσες
Gen.	της	θάλασσας	των	θαλασσών
Voc.		θάλασσα		θάλασσες

Examples:

άγκυρα 'anchor', αίθουσα 'hall', άμαξα 'carriage', άμυνα 'defence', αξία 'value', απεργία 'strike', απόπειρα 'attempt', αχλαδιά 'pear-tree', γέφυρα 'bridge', γλώσσα 'tongue, language', γραβάτα 'necktie', γυναίκα 'woman, wife', δίψα 'thirst', δουλειά 'work', έρευνα 'research', ιδέα 'idea', καρδιά 'heart', κεραία 'antenna, aerial', κυρία 'lady, Mrs', λίρα 'pound sterling', μάζα 'mass', μέλισσα 'bee', (η)μέρα 'day' (gen. pl. always ημερών – other forms with η- are regarded as more formal), μοίρα 'fate; degree (of a circle)', μοτοσικλέτα 'motor-cycle', ντομάτα 'tomato', νύχτα (or νύκτα) 'night', ομορφιά 'beauty', ορχήστρα 'orchestra', πείνα 'hunger', περιφέρεια 'district', πλατεία 'square', ρίζα 'root', σημαία 'flag', τράπεζα 'bank', τρύπα 'hole', φωλιά 'nest', χήνα 'goose', χώρα 'country', ώρα 'hour, time'. Similarly all fem. nouns with the suffixes -τρια (e.g. μαθήτρια 'girl pupil'), -αινα (e.g. λύκαινα 'she-wolf') and -ισσα (e.g. βασίλισσα 'queen'), and abstract nouns in -εια, -ιά, or -οια (e.g. αλήθεια 'truth', έννοια 'meaning'). Proper names, like Θεσσαλία 'Thessaly', Αχαΐα 'Achaea', Μαρία 'Mary', Ουρανία 'Ourania (girl's name)', do not normally have a gen. pl., but note the plural nouns Αντίλλες 'Antilles', Βρυξέλλες 'Brussels', Θερμοπύλες 'Thermopylae', Ινδίες 'India, Indies', Σεϋχέλλες 'Seychelles', all of which have oxytone gen. pl. (e.g. Βρυξελλών).

1. Nouns of type (ii) always have the stress on the final syllable in the gen. pl., irrespective of whether they are oxytone, paroxytone or proparoxytone in the nom. sg.

2. A small number of nouns have an alternative gen. sg. in -ης, with the stress moving to the penultimate if the nom. is proparoxytone. Nouns with stems ending in a vowel or -ρ- retain the ending -ας, but can also have movement of stress to the penultimate. Such forms, which are of learned origin, are sometimes found in formal discourse or official designations: e.g. αμύνης (from άμυνα 'defence'), επικρατείας (from επικράτεια, 'state'), θαλάσσης (from θάλασσα, 'sea'), οικογενείας (from οικογένεια 'family'), τραπέζης (from τράπεζα 'bank'), and place-names such as Αιγίνης (from Αίγινα), Κερκύρας (from Κέρκυρα), Λαρίσσης (from Λάρισσα).

3. The place-name Αθήνα 'Athens' can have the formal gen. pl. Αθηνών in official names, e.g. το Πανεπιστήμιο Αθηνών 'the University of Athens'. Similarly Πάτρα 'Patras' also has a formal gen. pl. Πατρών.

2.2.2 NOUNS IN -η WITH PLURAL -ες

Nouns in this category, like those in -α discussed in Section 2.2.1 (ii), have an obligatory shift of stress to the final syllable in the genitive plural (if they are not stressed on the last syllable throughout). They must be distinguished from other feminine nouns in -η which form their plural in a different way (see Section 2.2.4).

η κόρη   'daughter; pupil of eye'

	Sg.		Pl.	
Nom.	η	κόρη	οι	κόρες
Acc.	την	κόρη	τις	κόρες
Gen.	της	κόρης	των	κορών
Voc.		κόρη		κόρες

Examples:

αγάπη 'love', αλλαγή 'change', αρχή 'beginning, principle', βιβλιοθήκη 'library', γραμμή 'line', διακοπή 'interruption' pl. 'holidays', δίκη 'trial, lawsuit', εκλογή 'choice, election', επιστήμη 'science', μηχανή 'machine', μύτη 'nose', νίκη 'victory', τέχνη 'art, skill', τιμή 'price, honour', φωνή 'voice', ψυχή 'soul', and proper nouns (which do not normally have a plural) like Αφρική 'Africa', Ειρήνη 'Irene', Θράκη 'Thrace', Ιθάκη 'Ithaca', etc. There are also nouns, mostly deriving historically from the category of those in Section 2.2.4, which follow this declension, but lack a gen. pl. They include: βράση 'boiling, heat', δέση 'binding', ζέστη 'heat', κόψη 'cutting-edge', ράχη 'back', χάρη 'favour, charm', and the proparoxytone nouns άνοιξη 'spring', αντάμωση 'meeting', γέμιση 'waxing (of the moon)', δούλεψη 'labour', ζάχαρη 'sugar', θύμηση 'memory', καλοπέραση 'enjoyment', κούραση 'tiredness', κουφόβραση 'sultry weather', λύπηση 'pity', σίκαλη 'rye', τσάκιση 'crease', χώνεψη 'digestion', together with some proper nouns (which do not normally have a plural) such as Άρτεμη 'Artemis', Λυκόβρυση 'Lykovrisi'.

The following form their gen. pl. in -άδων, with the addition of a syllable (like the imparisyllabic nouns in Section 2.2.5): αδελφή/αδερφή 'sister', γιορτή 'celebration, feast, name-day' (but γιορτών also exists), (ε)ξαδέλφη/(ε)ξαδέρφη '(female) cousin', Κυριακή 'Sunday', νύφη 'bride, daughter-in-law'.

2.2.3 NOUNS IN -ος

These feminine nouns, which are of learned origin, have identical endings to masculine nouns in -ος (see Section 2.1.3), but are of course accompanied by the feminine forms of the articles. The stress of those nouns that are proparoxytone moves to the penultimate in the genitive singular and the accusative and genitive plural, as in the example given here in full:

η ήπειρος 'continent'

		Sg.		Pl.
Nom.	η	ήπειρος	οι	ήπειροι
Acc.	την	ήπειρο	τις	ηπείρους
Gen.	της	ηπείρου	των	ηπείρων

Examples:

άβυσσος 'abyss', άμμος 'sand', άνοδος 'ascent', Βίβλος 'Bible', διάλεκτος 'dialect', διάμετρος 'diameter', δοκός 'beam, rafter', εγκύκλιος 'circular, encyclical', είσοδος 'entrance', έξοδος 'exit', επέτειος 'anniversary', θαλαμηγός 'yacht', κάθοδος 'descent', καπνοδόχος 'chimney', κιβωτός 'ark', λεωφόρος 'avenue', μέθοδος 'method', νήσος 'island', οδός 'street', παράγραφος 'paragraph', παρθένος 'virgin', πάροδος 'side-street', περίμετρος 'perimeter', περίοδος 'period', πρόοδος 'progress', σορός 'coffin; corpse', χερσόνησος 'peninsula', ψήφος 'vote' (but often masc. in the pl.).

There are also many names of towns, countries and islands which follow this declension in the singular (they have no plural): e.g. Αίγυπτος 'Egypt', Άνδρος, Ανάβυσσος, Βηρυτός 'Beirut', Επίδαυρος, Κόρινθος, Κύπρος, Νάξος, Οδησσός 'Odessa', Πελοπόννησος, Σκύρος, Χίος and, in fact, almost all names of islands ending in -ος (except monosyllabic names like Κως, gen. Κω, for which see Section 2.2.6). Παξοί 'Paxos' and Αντίπαξοι 'Antipaxos' are, exceptionally, *masculine plural* forms.

1. A plural in -ες is sometimes found, e.g. οι μέθοδες 'methods' (possibly used for humorous effect), but this is rare for other words and would be regarded as non-standard by most people.

2. The vocative case for such nouns is very rare. If used (e.g. in poetic addresses to islands), it is more likely to end in -ο than in the more learned -ε.

2.2.4 NOUNS IN -η WITH PLURAL -εις

Nouns in this category are of learned origin. While in the singular they generally follow the declension of other feminine nouns in -η (see Section 2.2.2), the plural forms are quite different, maintaining the Ancient Greek endings; alternative learned forms are also sometimes found in the singular, particularly in formal contexts (see notes).

η κυβέρνηση 'government'

		Sg.		Pl.
Nom.	η	κυβέρνηση	οι	κυβερνήσεις
Acc.	την	κυβέρνηση	τις	κυβερνήσεις
Gen.	της	κυβέρνησης *or* κυβερνήσεως	των	κυβερνήσεων
Voc.		κυβέρνηση		κυβερνήσεις

Examples:

δύναμη 'force, strength', πίστη 'faith', πόλη 'city', and all feminine nouns ending in -ση, -ξη or -ψη (except those in Section 2.2.2): e.g. αίτηση 'application', απόφαση 'decision', άποψη 'view, opinion', γέννηση 'birth', γνώση 'knowledge', δήλωση 'declaration', εκμετάλλευση 'exploitation', έκφραση 'expression', έλξη 'attraction', ένωση 'union', θέση 'position, place', κίνηση 'movement', μετάφραση 'translation', όρεξη 'appetite', παράδοση 'tradition', παράσταση 'performance', ποίηση 'poetry', σκέψη 'thought', στάση 'stop', σχέση 'relation(ship)', τύψη 'pang of conscience', υπόθεση 'hypothesis; affair', ψύξη 'freezing'. Similarly the toponyms Ακρόπολη 'Acropolis', Κωνσταντινούπολη 'Constantinople, Istanbul', Νεάπολη 'Naples' or 'Neapolis', and the plural toponyms Άνδεις 'Andes', Άλπεις 'Alps'.

1. The stress of two-syllable words remains on the same syllable throughout the declension. The stress of words of more than two syllables moves one syllable forward in the alternative form of the gen. sg. (in -εως) and in all pl. forms.

2. The gen. sg. in -εως tends to be used in more formal contexts, but it is also widely used for certain everyday words, e.g. της πόλεως. A more formal form of the nom. sg., ending in -ις, is also sometimes used, e.g. η κυβέρνησις, η Κωνσταντινούπολις, but it is much less common than the more formal type of gen. sg.

2.2.5   IMPARISYLLABIC NOUNS

Feminine imparisyllabic nouns may be compared to the masculine imparisyllabic nouns discussed in Section 2.1.5. Their plural always ends in -δες (nom., acc., voc.), -δων (gen.), and this ending is added directly to the nominative singular, which always ends in a vowel, either (i) -ά or (ii) -ού. The genitive singular adds -ς to the nominative form. These feminine nouns are always oxytone in their singular forms and the stress remains on the same syllable in the plural.

(i)   η γιαγιά 'grandmother'

		Sg.		Pl.
Nom.	η	γιαγιά	οι	γιαγιάδες
Acc.	τη	γιαγιά	τις	γιαγιάδες
Gen.	της	γιαγιάς	των	γιαγιάδων
Voc.		γιαγιά		γιαγιάδες

Examples:

κυρά 'missus, madam', μαμά 'mummy', νονά 'godmother', νταντά 'nursemaid', οκά 'oka (obsolete measure of weight = 1280 grams)'

(ii)   η αλεπού 'fox'

		Sg.		Pl.
Nom.	η	αλεπού	οι	αλεπούδες
Acc.	την	αλεπού	τις	αλεπούδες
Gen.	της	αλεπούς	των	αλεπούδων
Voc.		αλεπού		αλεπούδες

Examples:

γλωσσού 'gossiping woman', μαϊμού 'monkey (male or female)', παραμυθού 'story-teller', πολυλογού 'chatterbox', υπναρού 'sleepy-head', and many other words referring to females and often corresponding to a masculine noun in -άς or -ής, e.g. φωνακλού 'loud-mouthed woman', φωνακλάς 'loud-mouthed man'.

Such words are mainly confined to non-formal use.

2.2.6 NOUNS IN -ω

The category of feminine nouns ending in -ω consists mainly of proper (given) names, often diminutives, which do not usually have a plural. There are two types, which differ in the formation of their genitive. The stress remains on the same syllable as in the nominative.

(i)   η Φρόσω 'Froso' (diminutive of Ευφροσύνη)

		Sg.
Nom.	η	Φρόσω
Acc.	τη	Φρόσω
Gen.	της	Φρόσως
Voc.		Φρόσω

Examples:

Αργυρώ, Αργώ 'the Argo' (but there is an alternative gen. Αργούς), Δέσπω, Ηρώ, Καλυψώ, Μάρω and most diminutives in -ω from female given names. The names of some Greek islands also follow this pattern in colloquial use, e.g. η Κω (alongside η Κως) 'Kos', gen. της Κως (as an alternative – confusingly – to the standard της Κω).

(ii)   η ηχώ 'echo' (no plural)

		Sg.
Nom.	η	ηχώ
Acc.	την	ηχώ
Gen.	της	ηχούς
Voc.		ηχώ

Examples:

πειθώ 'persuasion', φειδώ 'thrift', and the proper names Ιεριχώ 'Jericho', Λητώ 'Leto' (with an alternative gen. Λητώς)

2.3   NOUNS OF COMMON GENDER

Many nouns denoting persons who carry out certain occupations or other activities are of ***common gender***. In other words, the same forms of the noun are used for both male and female referents, but the article and any other words which modify it (such as adjectives) indicate whether the word denotes a male or female person or persons in the specific context. Thus we have **o** ηθοποιός 'actor', but **η** ηθοποιός 'actress'. First, we give one type of noun which has not yet been mentioned, with singular in -ής and plural in -είς. Strictly speaking, these are adjectives which are used as nouns (corresponding to the adjectives in Section 3.8), but their singular endings are identical with those of the masculine nouns in Section 2.1.2.

o/η συγγενής 'male or female relative'

		Sg.		Pl.
Nom.	o/η	συγγενής	οι	συγγενείς
Acc.	το(ν)/τη(ν)	συγγενή	τους/τις	συγγενείς
Gen.	του/της	συγγενή *or*	των	συγγενών
		συγγενούς		
Voc.		συγγενή		συγγενείς

Other examples:

ασθενής 'sick person, patient', ευγενής 'nobleman or noblewoman'

In these two cases the gen. sg. form in -ούς is the more common (while for συγγενής it is the form in -ή).

Other nouns of common gender follow the declension patterns of masculine nouns, but with masculine or feminine article, etc. as appropriate:

(i)   Like masculine nouns in -ας (Section 2.1.1): o/η επαγγελματίας 'professional person', o/η μάρτυρας 'witness', o/η ταμίας 'cashier'.

(ii) Like masculine nouns in -ης (Section 2.1.2): o/η βουλευτής 'member of parliament', o/η καλλιτέχνης 'artist', o/η ληστής 'robber', o/η πολίτης 'citizen'.

(iii) Like masculine nouns in -ος (Section 2.1.3): o/η γιατρός 'doctor', o/η δικηγόρος 'lawyer', o/η μαθηματικός 'mathematician', o/η νοσοκόμος 'nurse' (fem. νοσοκόμα is more usual), o/η οικονομολόγος 'economist', o/η σύζυγος 'spouse', o/η υπάλληλος 'employee', o/η υπουργός 'minister', o/η ψυχολόγος 'psychologist'.

(iv) Like masculine nouns in -έας (Section 2.1.4): o/η γραμματέας 'secretary', o/η διερμηνέας 'interpreter', o/η εισαγγελέας 'public prosecutor', o/η συγγραφέας 'writer, author'.

Many masculine nouns referring to people form a corresponding feminine noun by adding a suffix, e.g. ο καθηγητής 'male professor', η καθηγήτρια 'female professor', but the list of those that use the same form as the masculine for female referents, as in the above examples, is growing as a result of changes in society (see also Part III, Section 2.2.1).

2.4   NEUTER NOUNS

The accusative forms of neuter nouns are always identical with those of the nominative, for the same number; e.g., sg. το γραφείο 'office' (nom. and acc.), pl. τα γραφεία 'offices' (nom. and acc.).

2.4.1   NOUNS IN -o

Nouns in this category have genitive singular in -ου, but (as in the case of the masculine nouns in -ος in Section 2.1.3) it is necessary to distinguish two types, according to whether proparoxytone nouns undergo a shift of stress in the genitive singular and plural. Type (i) consists of nouns which move the stress to the penultimate in the genitive singular and plural. Type (ii) (and this also includes all oxytone and paroxytone nouns which follow this declension) consists of nouns which normally keep the stress on the same syllable throughout.

(i)   το πρόσωπο   'face, person'

		Sg.		Pl.
Nom.	το	πρόσωπο	τα	πρόσωπα
Acc.	το	πρόσωπο	τα	πρόσωπα
Gen.	του	προσώπου	των	προσώπων
Voc.		πρόσωπο		πρόσωπα

Examples:

άλογο 'horse', αυτοκίνητο 'car', άτομο 'person, individual', διαβατήριο 'passport', δωμάτιο 'room', εισιτήριο 'ticket', εξώφυλλο 'book cover', έπιπλο 'piece of furniture', εστιατόριο 'restaurant', θέατρο 'theatre', κείμενο 'text', μέτωπο 'forehead; front', όργανο 'instrument', πανεπιστήμιο 'university', τηλέφωνο 'telephone', and toponyms such as Μέτσοβο, and those which have plural forms only, e.g. Άγραφα, Ιωάννινα (normally τα Γιάννινα or Γιάννενα, but gen. pl. always Ιωαννίνων), Καλάβρυτα, Τρίκαλα, Φάρσαλα.

(ii)   το αντρόγυνο   'married couple'

		Sg.		Pl.
Nom.	το	αντρόγυνο	τα	αντρόγυνα
Acc.	το	αντρόγυνο	τα	αντρόγυνα
Gen.	του	αντρόγυνου	των	αντρόγυνων
Voc.		αντρόγυνο		αντρόγυνα

Examples (with stress remaining on the same syllable):

αεροπλάνο 'aeroplane', βιβλίο 'book', βουνό 'mountain', δέντρο 'tree', μπάνιο 'bath', νερό 'water', πλοίο 'ship', ποσό(ν) 'amount', φτερό 'feather', χωριό 'village', and the following proparoxytone nouns: δάχτυλο 'finger', κάρβουνο 'coal', κάστανο 'chestnut', κόκκαλο 'bone', κόσκινο 'sieve', λάχανο 'cabbage', μάγουλο 'cheek', μανάβικο 'greengrocer's shop', παράπονο 'complaint', πόμολο 'door knob', ροδάκινο 'peach', σίδερο 'iron', σύννεφο 'cloud', τραπεζομάντηλο 'table-cloth', τριαντάφυλλο 'rose', χαμόγελο 'smile', χασάπικο 'butcher's shop' and all nouns ending in -άδικο, -άρικο, or -όπουλο, as well as many compounds.

1. The division between proparoxytone nouns that have fixed stress and those that move the stress has some flexibility: in formal contexts some nouns may have gen. sg. or pl. with penultimate stress. Nouns that show both types include: αμύγδαλο 'almond', ατμόπλοιο 'steamship', βούτυρο 'butter', γόνατο 'knee', ποδήλατο 'bicycle', πρόβατο 'sheep'.

2. In very formal use, in notices (e.g. names of businesses) and in technical vocabulary, some words have nom. and acc. sg. ending in -ov: e.g. άκρον 'extremity', ποιόν 'character, nature' (found only in nom. and acc. sg.), ποσόν 'amount, quantity', συνεργείον 'repair shop'.

2.4.2   NOUNS IN -ί

Neuter nouns in -ί keep the stress on the final syllable throughout the declension. In all forms except the nominative, accusative and vocative singular the -ι- loses its syllabic value (see Part I, Section 1.1.2).

το παιδί   'child'

		Sg.		*Pl.*
Nom.	το	παιδί	τα	παιδιά
Acc.	το	παιδί	τα	παιδιά
Gen.	του	παιδιού	των	παιδιών
Voc.		παιδί		παιδιά

Examples:

αρνί 'lamb', αφτί 'ear', κλειδί 'key', κρασί 'wine', μαγαζί 'shop', νησί 'island', πουλί 'bird', χαρτί 'paper', ψωμί 'bread'

and all other nouns in -ί stressed on the final syllable.

1. The noun πρωί 'morning' has gen. sg. πρωινού, nom. and acc. pl. πρωινά, gen. pl. πρωινών.

2. The noun ταξί 'taxi' is normally indeclinable; forms such as pl. ταξιά are sometimes heard, but would be regarded as non-standard by some speakers.

2.4.3   NOUNS IN -ι

These nouns are always paroxytone (with one exception, for which see below). In their genitive singular and plural they move the stress to the final syllable, with the -ι- losing its syllabic value (cf. the nouns in Section 2.4.2).

το αγόρι   'boy'

		Sg.		Pl.
Nom.	το	αγόρι	τα	αγόρια
Acc.	το	αγόρι	τα	αγόρια
Gen.	του	αγοριού	των	αγοριών
Voc.		αγόρι		αγόρια

Examples:

αλάτι 'salt', δόντι 'tooth', κορίτσι 'girl', κρεβάτι 'bed', λουλούδι 'flower', παντελόνι 'trousers', παπούτσι 'shoe', σπίτι 'house', τραπέζι 'table', χέρι 'hand'

and all other paroxytone neuter nouns in -ι. The only proparoxytone noun which follows this pattern is φίλντισι 'ivory', gen. φιλντισιού (no pl.).

1. A few nouns are sometimes spelled with -υ (though nowadays they are usually spelled with -ι); they are: βράδυ 'evening', δίχτυ 'net', στάχυ 'ear of corn'. In any case, the pl. forms are normally spelled -ια. An exception is δάκρυ 'tear', spelled with υ in all its forms, which has the following forms: singular δάκρυ (nom./acc.; the gen. is not normally used), plural δάκρυα (nom./acc.), δακρύων (gen.).

2. Neuter nouns in -άι or -όι add a -γ- before the endings in all forms other than the nom., acc. (and voc.) sg., e.g. τσάι 'tea', gen. τσαγιού, κομπολόι 'worry beads', ρολόι 'clock, watch', σόι 'family, lineage'.

3. Diminutives in -άκι and -ούλι, e.g. παιδάκι 'little boy', have no gen. forms, singular or plural.

2.4.4   NOUNS IN -ος

Neuter nouns in -ος may be either paroxytone or proparoxytone. Paroxytone nouns (like κράτος 'state') move the stress to the final syllable in the genitive plural. Proparoxytone nouns (like μέγεθος 'size') also have the stress on the final syllable of the genitive plural, but move the stress to the penultimate in the genitive singular and the nominative and accusative plural (the vocative case is rarely used).

το μέγεθος   'size, magnitude'

		Sg.		Pl.
Nom.	το	μέγεθος	τα	μεγέθη
Acc.	το	μέγεθος	τα	μεγέθη
Gen.	του	μεγέθους	των	μεγεθών
(Voc.		μέγεθος		μεγέθη)

Examples:

βάρος 'weight', δάσος 'forest', έδαφος 'territory', έθνος 'nation', κέρδος 'profit', κόστος 'cost' (no pl. forms), λάθος 'mistake', λίπος 'fat', μέλος 'member', μέρος 'place, part', μήκος 'length', μίσος 'hatred', όρος 'mountain', πέλαγος 'sea', τέλος 'end', ύφος 'style, manner', χάος 'chaos' (no pl. forms), χρέος 'duty, debt'

and all other neuter nouns in -ος.

2.4.5   NOUNS IN -μα

These nouns may be of two syllables, like κύμα 'wave' (with paroxytone stress), or of three or more syllables, like πρόβλημα 'problem' (with proparoxytone stress). The endings of the genitive singular and all plural cases involve an additional syllable, which has implications for the position of the stress. The genitive singular and the nominative and accusative plural of these nouns are always stressed on the antepenultimate; the genitive plural always has the stress on the penultimate.

το πρόβλημα   'problem'

		Sg.		Pl.
Nom.	το	πρόβλημα	τα	προβλήματα
Acc.	το	πρόβλημα	τα	προβλήματα
Gen.	του	προβλήματος	των	προβλημάτων
(Voc.		πρόβλημα		προβλήματα)

Examples:

άγαλμα 'statue', αίμα 'blood', αποτέλεσμα 'result', γράμμα 'letter', διάβασμα 'reading', διάλειμμα 'interval', διάστημα 'space', κλίμα 'climate', μάθημα 'lesson', όνομα 'name', ποίημα 'poem', πράγμα 'thing', σύστημα 'system', σχεδίασμα 'sketch', σώμα 'body', χρώμα 'colour', and all nouns ending in -μα (with two exceptions: κρέμα 'cream' and λάμα 'blade', which are feminine). Some nouns occur only in the plural: e.g., γεράματα 'old age', τρεχάματα 'running around', χαιρετίσματα 'greetings'

2.4.6 NOUNS IN -ιμο

These nouns are all derived from verbs and denote an action. Their nominative singular, which is always proparoxytone, ends in -σιμο, -ξιμο, or
-ψιμο. In the genitive singular and all cases in the plural they have endings
like those of nouns in -μα (Section 2.4.5), with the same pattern of stress.
The genitive plural of these nouns is found infrequently.

το πλύσιμο   '(act of) washing'

		Sg.		Pl.
Nom.	το	πλύσιμο	τα	πλυσίματα
Acc.	το	πλύσιμο	τα	πλυσίματα
Gen.	του	πλυσίματος	(των	πλυσιμάτων)
(Voc.		πλύσιμο		πλυσίματα)

Examples:

γράψιμο 'writing', δέσιμο 'tying', κόψιμο 'cutting', ντύσιμο 'dressing,
dress', σπάσιμο 'breaking, smashing', τρέξιμο 'running', φέρσιμο
'behaviour', φταίξιμο 'fault, blame'.

2.4.7 OTHER NEUTER NOUNS IN -ς

A few neuter nouns end in -ς, but are distinguished from nouns in -ος
(Section 2.4.4) by the different vowel that precedes the final consonant,
or by the position of the stress in the nominative singular. The endings
of the other cases are similar to those of neuter nouns in -μα (Section
2.4.5), without the syllable -μα-. The position of stress varies. In the first
example below, the stress of the genitive singular and the nominative and
accusative plural is on the antepenultimate; in the genitive plural it moves
to the penultimate (cf. neuter nouns in -μα).

το κρέας   'meat'

		Sg.		Pl.
Nom.	το	κρέας	τα	κρέατα
Acc.	το	κρέας	τα	κρέατα
Gen.	του	κρέατος	των	κρεάτων
(Voc.		κρέας		κρέατα)

Examples:

γήρας 'old age' (no pl.), πέρας 'end, conclusion' and τέρας 'monster'

are the only other nouns which follow this pattern.

One other neuter noun ending in -ας constitutes a special case: σέβας 'respect',
pl. σέβη, exists only in these forms, for the nom. and acc. sg. and pl. (it has no
gen. forms).

Other neuter nouns in -ς have the same endings added to the vowel of their stem (-ω- or -ο-). They keep the stress on the same syllable as in the nominative singular, except that the stress must fall on the penultimate in the genitive plural. We give first το φως, which is irregular in that the stress of its genitive singular is on the last syllable:

το φως   'light'

		Sg.		*Pl.*
Nom.	το	φως	τα	φώτα
Acc.	το	φως	τα	φώτα
Gen.	του	φωτός	των	φώτων
(Voc.		φως		φώτα)

Examples (no shift of stress, except that gen. pl. – if it exists – must be stressed on the penultimate):

αεριόφως 'gaslight', γεγονός 'event, fact', ημίφως 'half-light, twilight' (no pl.), καθεστώς 'régime, status quo', λυκόφως 'dusk' (no pl.).

2.4.8   OTHER NEUTER NOUNS ENDING IN VOWELS

Two other nouns which have a genitive singular in -τος present certain peculiarities:

το γάλα   'milk'

		Sg.		*Pl.*
Nom.	το	γάλα	τα	γάλατα
Acc.	το	γάλα	τα	γάλατα
Gen.	του	γάλατος *or*	(των	γαλάκτων)
		γάλακτος		

Similarly:

το μέλι 'honey', gen. του μέλιτος (no plural). Note, however, that
  μέλι more normally follows the pattern of neuter nouns in -ι
  (see Section 2.4.3).

1. The gen. sg. γάλακτος is more formal than γάλατος. The gen. pl. of this noun is very rarely used.

2. For οξύ and ήμισυ see Addenda, p. 520.

2.4.9   OTHER NEUTER NOUNS IN -ν

In this category are a number of nouns which derive from participles, and two other words which have slightly different endings. First we give the nouns originally derived from the neuter forms of participles (cf. the adjective declensions in Section 3.11):

το ενδιαφέρον   'interest'

		Sg.		Pl.
Nom.	το	ενδιαφέρον	τα	ενδιαφέροντα
Acc.	το	ενδιαφέρον	τα	ενδιαφέροντα
Gen.	του	ενδιαφέροντος	των	ενδιαφερόντων

Examples:

ανακοινωθέν 'communiqué', καθήκον 'duty', μέλλον 'future', ον 'being, creature', παρελθόν 'past', παρόν 'present', περιβάλλον 'environment, surroundings', προϊόν 'product', προσόν, 'qualification, advantage', συμβάν 'event', σύμπαν 'universe', συμφέρον 'personal interest, advantage', φωνήεν 'vowel'.

Whether oxytone or paroxytone, these nouns keep the stress on the same syllable as in the nom. sg. throughout, except the gen. pl. that is always stressed on the penultimate.

The noun το παν has a similar declension to the above, except that it is stressed on the final syllable in the genitive singular:

το παν   'everything'

		Sg.		Pl.
Nom.	το	παν	τα	πάντα
Acc.	το	παν	τα	πάντα
Gen.	του	παντός	των	πάντων

Finally in this category, the noun το μηδέν has the following singular forms, but no plural:

το μηδέν   'nil, zero'

		Sg.
Nom.	το	μηδέν
Acc.	το	μηδέν
Gen.	του	μηδενός

2.4.10   NEUTER NOUNS ENDING IN CONSONANTS OTHER THAN -ν or -ς

The vast majority of neuter nouns end in a vowel or -ς. A few end in -ν (Section 2.4.9). Indeclinable neuter nouns may end in various consonants (see Section 2.7), but there are also two declined nouns of Ancient Greek origin which end in -ρ. Their forms are as follows:

το ήπαρ   'liver'

		Sg.		Pl.
Nom.	το	ήπαρ	τα	ήπατα
Acc.	το	ήπαρ	τα	ήπατα
Gen.	του	ήπατος	των	ηπάτων

το πυρ   'fire (usually military)'

		Sg.		Pl.
Nom.	το	πυρ	τα	πυρά
Acc.	το	πυρ	τα	πυρά
Gen.	του	πυρός	των	πυρών

2.5   TABLE OF THE MOST COMMON NOUN ENDINGS

The table below shows the endings of all the common types of noun. (The less common noun types in Sections 2.1.5 (note at the end of section), 2.4.7 and 2.4.8 are omitted.) The endings are grouped by gender, except that most nouns of common gender have identical endings to masculine nouns and have therefore been omitted. The changes in the position of stress cannot easily be represented in a table of this kind. We show the stress only when it falls obligatorily on a syllable of the ending; full information is given in the preceding sections. We show the vocative case only for the singular of nouns of masculine or common gender; in all other instances the vocative form is identical to the nominative.

		Masculine								*Common*
Sg.	Nom.	-ας	-ης	-ος	-έας	-ας	-ης	-ές	-ούς	-ής
	Acc.	-α	-η	-ο	-έα	-α	-η	-έ	-ού	-ή
	Gen.	-α	-η	-ου	-έα	-α	-η	-έ	-ού	-ή/-ούς
	Voc.	-α	-η	-ε	-έα	-α	-η	-έ	-ού	-ή
Pl.	Nom.	-ες	-ες	-οι	-είς	-άδες	-ηδες	-έδες	-ούδες	-είς
	Acc.	-ες	-ες	-ους	-είς	-άδες	-ηδες	-έδες	-ούδες	-είς
	Gen.	-ων	-ών	-ων	-έων	-άδων	-ηδων	-έδων	-ούδων	-ών

		Feminine						
Sg.	Nom.	-α	-η	-ος	-η	-ά	-ού	-ω
	Acc.	-α	-η	-ο	-η	-ά	-ού	-ω
	Gen.	-ας	-ης	-ου	-ης/-εως	-άς	-ούς	-ως
Pl.	Nom.	-ες	-ες	-οι	-εις	-άδες	-ούδες	–
	Acc.	-ες	-ες	-ους	-εις	-άδες	-ούδες	–
	Gen.	-ων	-ών	-ων	-εων	-άδων	-ούδων	–

		Neuter				
Sg. Nom.	-o	-í	-ι	-ος	-μα	-ιμο
Acc.	-o	-í	-ι	-ος	-μα	-ιμο
Gen.	-ου	-ιού	-ιού	-ους	-ματος	-ίματος
Pl. Nom.	-α	-ιά	-ια	-η	-ματα	-ίματα
Acc.	-α	-ιά	-ια	-η	-ματα	-ίματα
Gen.	-ων	-ιών	-ιών	-ών	-μάτων	(-ιμάτων)

2.6 NOUNS WITH A CHANGE OF GENDER IN THE PLURAL

The list below shows nouns which are masculine in the singular, but have a plural of neuter gender, sometimes in addition to the masculine plural form but with a difference of meaning:

ο βράχος 'rock', pl. οι βράχοι or τα βράχια

ο δεσμός 'bond', pl. οι δεσμοί 'bonds' (figuratively), τα δεσμά 'fetters, shackles' (literally)

ο καπνός 'smoke; tobacco', pl. οι καπνοί 'smoke', τα καπνά 'tobacco(es)'

ο λαιμός 'neck, throat', pl. οι λαιμοί 'necks', τα λαιμά 'sore throat'

ο λόγος 'speech; reason; word', pl. οι λόγοι 'speeches; reasons', τα λόγια 'words'

ο πηλός 'clay', pl. οι πηλοί or (non-formal only) τα πηλά

ο πλούτος 'wealth', pl. τα πλούτη 'riches'

ο σανός 'hay', pl. τα σανά

ο σκελετός 'skeleton, framework', pl. οι σκελετοί 'skeletons', τα σκελετά 'shelves or frames for display of merchandise'

ο σταθμός 'station', pl. οι σταθμοί 'stations', τα σταθμά 'weights'

ο χρόνος 'time; year; tense', pl. οι χρόνοι 'times; tenses (of the verb)', τα χρόνια 'years'

2.7 INDECLINABLE NOUNS

Indeclinable nouns have one form only, which serves for all cases, singular and plural. Like all other nouns, however, they are assigned to one of the three genders. There is a large number of nouns of foreign origin which have not been assimilated into the Greek declension system, including place-names and proper names, and we give some common examples below. Also indeclinable are all the names of the letters of the Greek alphabet, which are neuter: το άλφα, το βήτα, etc. See also Part III, Section 2.2.2.

Masculine: μάνατζερ 'manager', ντέτεκτιβ 'detective', ρεπόρτερ
'reporter'
Feminine: πλαζ 'beach', σαιζόν 'season', σπεσιαλιτέ 'speciality', the
toponym Ουάσιγκτον 'Washington', and names of football teams,
e.g. η Λίβερπουλ 'Liverpool'
Common gender: ο/η σταρ 'star'
Neuter: βολάν 'steering-wheel', γκαράζ 'garage', καμουφλάζ 'camouflage', κομπιούτερ 'computer' (also masc.; a pl. κομπιούτερς is
sometimes found), κονιάκ 'cognac', ματς 'match', μετρό 'metro',
νάιλον 'nylon', παρμπρίζ 'windscreen', πάρτι 'party', πουλόβερ
'sweater', ραντεβού 'appointment', ρεπό 'day off', ταμπλό 'picture;
dashboard', τανκς '(military) tank', τρακ 'stage-fright, nerves',
φερμουάρ 'zip'

2.8   LEARNED DATIVE FORMS

The *dative* case of Ancient Greek, although long defunct in the living language,
has left a few remnants in the form of clichés or set phrases. The examples below
are given in the order of the arrangement of declensions in Sections 2.1–2.4. The
dative endings of the nouns are shown in bold:

Masculine nouns in -ος: δόξα τω Θε**ώ** 'thank God', λόγ**ω** 'on account of' (+
gen.), εν λόγ**ω** 'in question', ο υφυπουργός παρά τω πρωθυπουργ**ώ**
'undersecretary to the Premier's office'
Feminine nouns in -α (parisyllabic): απουσί**α** 'in the absence (of)', εν
συνεχεί**α** 'subsequently', πάσ**η** θυσί**α** 'at all costs [lit. by every sacrifice]'
Feminine nouns in -η, pl. -ες: εν ανάγκ**η** 'if need be'
Feminine nouns in -η, pl. -εις: εν γνώσ**ει** 'knowingly', εν δράσ**ει** 'in action',
δυνάμ**ει** 'by virtue (of)', επι λέξ**ει** 'word for word, verbatim', εν πάσ**η**
περιπτώσ**ει** 'in any case', φύσ**ει** 'by nature'. Cf. εντάξ**ει** 'all right'
Neuter nouns in -ο: έργ**ω** 'in practice', μέσ**ω** 'via' (+ gen.).
Neuter nouns in -ος: εν γέν**ει** 'in general', εν τέλ**ει** 'finally, completely'
(usually written as one word: εντέλει).
Neuter nouns in -μα: πράγ**ματι** 'really, in fact'.

For further examples of uses of the dative see Part III, Section 2.4.5.

3 ADJECTIVES

An adjective is a word which denotes a property, quality or characteristic belonging to or associated with a specific noun or noun phrase. An adjective modifies a noun and agrees with it in number, gender and case. (See Part III, Section 2.6 and Appendix 4.) Most (but not all) adjectives have separate forms for masculine, feminine and neuter genders. Some adjectives are indeclinable and have only one form; for them see Section 3.13.

There is a strong tendency for the stress of adjectives to remain on the same syllable throughout the declension ('columnar stress'), unlike what happens with many noun declensions. The principal exceptions to this norm are to be seen in the types examined in Sections 3.8 and 3.11 below.

3.1 ADJECTIVES IN -ος, -η, -ο

This is the commonest type of adjective in Greek. This category includes almost all of the adjectives in -ος which have a stem ending in a consonant or in any unstressed vowel other than /i/ (see Section 3.2 for the exceptions). Adjectives which follow this pattern may be oxytone (e.g. ακριβός 'expensive'), paroxytone (e.g. γεμάτος 'full'), or proparoxytone (e.g. όμορφος 'beautiful'). It will be noticed that the endings of the masculine forms are identical to those of masculine nouns in -ος (see Section 2.1.3), while the endings of the feminine forms are identical to the endings of feminine nouns in -η (Section 2.2.2), and the endings of the neuter forms to those of neuter nouns in -ο (Section 2.4.1).

όμορφος   'beautiful'

	M	Sg. F	N
Nom.	όμορφος	όμορφη	όμορφο
Acc.	όμορφο	όμορφη	όμορφο
Gen.	όμορφου	όμορφης	όμορφου
Voc.	όμορφε	όμορφη	όμορφο

	M	*Pl.* *F*	*N*
Nom.	όμορφοι	όμορφες	όμορφα
Acc.	όμορφους	όμορφες	όμορφα
Gen.	όμορφων	όμορφων	όμορφων
Voc.	όμορφοι	όμορφες	όμορφα

Examples: with stems ending in consonants:

ακριβός 'expensive', άρρωστος 'ill', άσπρος 'white', γαλλικός 'French', γεμάτος 'full', δυνατός 'strong; loud; possible', ελεύθερος 'free', επικίνδυνος 'dangerous', έτοιμος 'ready', εύκολος 'easy', καλός 'good', μαύρος 'black', μεγάλος 'big, great', μικρός 'small', μοναδικός 'unique', νόστιμος 'tasty, nice', ξύλινος 'wooden', πιθανός 'probable', πράσινος 'green', σκοτεινός 'dark', σωστός 'correct', χειμωνιάτικος 'wintry';

with stems ending in vowels:

βέβαιος 'certain, sure', δίκαιος 'just, fair', στέρεος 'solid'

1. Passive present participles in -όμενος, -ώμενος or -ούμενος (see Sections 7.2.2.9, 7.3.2.9 and 7.4.2.9) and passive perfect participles in -μένος (see Sections 7.2.2.10, 7.3.2.10, and 7.4.2.10) follow this adjective declension, as do all comparative adjectives in -τερος, absolute superlatives in -τατος or -ιστος (see Section 3.14), and the ordinal numbers (Section 6.1).

2. The stress normally remains on the same syllable throughout the declension, as in the example above. In the gen. pl. (all genders) proparoxytone adjectives may undergo a shift of stress to the penultimate in certain collocations e.g. διαφόρων εποχών 'of different periods'. This shift of stress, comparable to what happens in many noun declensions, may be occasioned by a more learned register and, perhaps, by considerations of euphony. A similar shift is very occasionally encountered in the masc. acc. pl. and the gen. sg. This shift is normal when such adjectives are used as nouns. (For the substantivization of adjectives see Part III, Section 2.6.1.)

3. The nom. and acc. of the neuter sg. may have the (more learned) ending -ov, especially when a neuter adjective occurs with a complement clause or is used adverbially. (See Part III, Sections 1.9.2 and 5.3.4.2 for examples.) The ending -ov is also sometimes used for the masc. acc. sg., especially when it is used without a noun, e.g. τον ξέρω από μικρόν 'I've known him from a young age'.

4. Adjectives of this type which have stems ending in vowels are sometimes found with fem. sg. in -α, gen. -ας, e.g. βέβαια 'certain' (fem.).

5. Adjectives, including comparatives and superlatives, whose stem ends in -ρ- may sometimes have a feminine in -α, in which case the stress cannot fall earlier than the penultimate syllable. Examples are: η δευτέρα τάξη 'the second class or grade', η Ιερά Οδός 'the Sacred Way', η αριστερά 'the [political] left' (used as a

noun), η Καθαρά (or Καθαρή) Δευτέρα 'Monday of the first week in Lent'. Compare the ending of the noun Δευτέρα 'Monday'.

3.2   ADJECTIVES IN -ος, -α, -ο

The only difference between this type and that in Section 3.1 is that here the feminine singular forms always end in -α (nom. and acc.), -ας (gen.). This category includes all adjectives in -ος which have a stem ending in /i/ (whether or not stressed), or in any other stressed vowel.

μέτριος   'medium, moderate'

| | *Sg.* | | |
	M	*F*	*N*
Nom.	μέτριος	μέτρια	μέτριο
Acc.	μέτριο	μέτρια	μέτριο
Gen.	μέτριου	μέτριας	μέτριου
Voc.	μέτριε	μέτρια	μέτριο

| | *Pl.* | | |
	M	*F*	*N*
Nom.	μέτριοι	μέτριες	μέτρια
Acc.	μέτριους	μέτριες	μέτρια
Gen.	μέτριων	μέτριων	μέτριων
Voc.	μέτριοι	μέτριες	μέτρια

Examples:

άγριος 'wild', άδειος 'empty', αθώος 'innocent', άξιος 'worthy', αρχαίος 'ancient', αστείος 'funny', γαλάζιος 'blue', γελοίος 'ridiculous', δημόσιος 'public', καινούριος 'new', κρύος 'cold', κύριος 'main, principal', μεσαίος 'medium', νέος 'new, young', όρθιος 'upright, standing', πλούσιος 'rich', σιδερένιος 'made of iron', σπάνιος 'rare', σπουδαίος 'important', τέλειος 'perfect', τεράστιος 'huge', τρύπιος 'full of holes', ωραίος 'beautiful'.

Certain other adjectives which do not have stems ending in a vowel also follow this pattern, i.e. they have a fem. sg. in -α. They include:

άκρος 'extreme', γκρίζος 'grey', θρήσκος 'devout, religious', μοντέρνος 'modern', παρθένος 'virgin', σβέλτος 'nimble', σκούρος 'dark', στείρος 'barren, fruitless', στέρφος 'sterile (of animals)', συμφεροντολόγος 'self-interested', and all adjectives with the suffix -ούχος, -φόρος, or -ούργος e.g. προνομιούχος 'privileged', καρποφόρος 'fruitful', πανούργος 'cunning'.

All the adjectives in the above list are paroxytone.

As in the case of the adjectives discussed in Section 3.1, the stress normally remains fixed, but there is sometimes a shift of stress from antepenultimate to penultimate, especially in the gen. pl., mainly in more formal use; e.g. μετρίων διαστάσεων 'of medium dimensions'. This shift also occurs when an adjective is substantivized, e.g. οι υποψήφιοι 'the candidates', gen. των υποψηφίων.

3.2.1 TWO-TERMINATION ADJECTIVES IN -ος

Two-termination adjectives are adjectives which, in certain contexts, do not use separate forms for the feminine gender. They have one set of forms for both masculine and feminine, and the normal neuter forms. Adjectives of this type are of learned origin; in Ancient Greek, adjectives prefixed with privative (negative) α- and most compound adjectives followed this pattern. While some of these adjectives can have feminine forms, exactly as the adjectives in Sections 3.1 or 3.2, in formal or learned contexts they sometimes use the masculine form to modify feminine nouns. (On the other hand, oxytone adjectives like ειδοποιός 'specific' have no separate feminine forms.) This is not to be seen as a fixed category of adjectives: the morphological peculiarity discussed here is conditioned by the context. Essentially this phenomenon is a remnant of *katharevousa* usage. We can tabulate the learned forms of such adjectives as follows:

βόρειος 'northern'

	Sg.		Pl.	
	M/F	N	M/F	N
Nom.	βόρειος	βόρειο	βόρειοι	βόρεια
Acc.	βόρειο(ν)	βόρειο	βορείους/βόρειους	βόρεια
Gen.	βορείου/βόρειου	βορείου/βόρειου	βορείων	βορείων
Voc.	βόρειε	βόρειο	βόρειοι	βόρεια

Examples:

έγγειος 'landed, derived from land' (but fem. pl. may be έγγειες), έγκυος 'pregnant', ειδοποιός 'specific', νότιος 'southern'. Some common phrases exhibiting this type of adjective are: η έγγειος ιδιοκτησία 'landed property', η Βόρειος Ήπειρος 'Northern Epiros' (but also Βόρεια), η Νότιος Αμερική 'South America' (but more usually Νότια), η ειδοποιός διαφορά 'the specific distinction'.

1. The adjective έγκυος 'pregnant' can also (rarely) appear in the fem. sg. form έγκυα. The fem. pl. έγκυες is actually more common than έγγυοι.

2. Some of the feminine nouns in -ος (see Section 2.2.3) are in fact adjectives of this type which have been substantivized with omission of the noun which they originally modified, e.g. η διάμετρος 'diameter', η εγκύκλιος 'encyclical'.

3.3 ADJECTIVES IN -ος, -ια, -ο

Adjectives of this type differ from those in Section 3.1 only in their feminine singular forms, which have the termination -ια rather than -η.

A number of adjectives which end in -κος, -κός, -χός or -θός can optionally follow this type; only a few *must* have -ια for the fem. form. In this
declension the stress remains on the same syllable throughout.

γλυκός   'sweet'

	M	*Sg.* F	N
Nom.	γλυκός	γλυκιά	γλυκό
Acc.	γλυκό	γλυκιά	γλυκό
Gen.	γλυκού	γλυκιάς	γλυκού
Voc.	γλυκέ	γλυκιά	γλυκό

	M	*Pl.* F	N
Nom.	γλυκοί	γλυκές	γλυκά
Acc.	γλυκούς	γλυκές	γλυκά
Gen.	γλυκών	γλυκών	γλυκών
Voc.	γλυκοί	γλυκές	γλυκά

Examples:

(i)   With fem. always in -ια (-ιά): γλυκός 'sweet', φρέσκος 'fresh'.

(ii) With fem. either in -ια (-ιά) or in -η (-ή): βρώμικος 'dirty', γνωστικός
      'sensible', δικός (μου) etc. '(my) own' (see Section 5.3), ελαφρός
      'light, slight', ευγενικός 'polite, kind', θηλυκός 'female, feminine',
      κακός 'bad', μαλακός 'soft', νηστικός 'fasting', ξανθός 'fair-haired',
      παστρικός 'clean', ρηχός 'shallow', ταγκός 'rancid', φτωχός 'poor'.

(iii) Some adjectives denoting local (Greek) origin have a fem. in -ή when
      used adjectivally but in -ιά when used as nouns: η κρητική λογοτεχνία
      'Cretan literature', but μια Κρητικιά 'a Cretan woman or girl'.
      Similarly ζακυ(ν)θινός 'Zakynthian'.

3.4   ADJECTIVES IN -ύς, -ιά, -ύ

This category is a rather small one, but it contains some words in very
frequent use. With the exception of the nominative, accusative and vocative (and alternative genitive) forms of the masculine and neuter singular,
all forms of these adjectives have a non-syllabic -ι- between the stem and
the endings, which are the same endings as those of adjectives discussed
in Section 3.2. The stress is always on the final syllable. The genitive
singular of the masculine and neuter is rarely used.

βαθύς 'deep'

	M	*Sg.* F	N
Nom.	βαθύς	βαθιά	βαθύ
Acc.	βαθύ	βαθιά	βαθύ
Gen.	(βαθιού/βαθύ)	βαθιάς	(βαθιού/βαθύ)
Voc.	βαθύ	βαθιά	βαθύ

	M	*Pl.* F	N
Nom.	βαθιοί	βαθιές	βαθιά
Acc.	βαθιούς	βαθιές	βαθιά
Gen.	βαθιών	βαθιών	βαθιών
Voc.	βαθιοί	βαθιές	βαθιά

Examples:

βαρύς 'heavy', δασύς 'thick, dense', ελαφρύς 'light, slight' (this is an alternative form of ελαφρός, -ή, -ό), μακρύς 'long', παχύς 'fat', πλατύς 'broad', τραχύς 'rough', φαρδύς 'wide'.

Some of these adjectives have alternative forms, when used formally or in set expressions. For these see the following section.

3.5 ADJECTIVES IN -ύς, -εία, -ύ

This declension is the origin of the demotic declension in Section 3.4 (a few adjectives can follow either pattern, depending on the context). The adjectives which follow the paradigm below are used mainly in technical or formal contexts, and in some standard expressions.

ευθύς 'straight, direct'

	M	*Sg.* F	N
Nom.	ευθύς	ευθεία	ευθύ
Acc.	ευθύ	ευθεία	ευθύ
Gen.	ευθέος	ευθείας	ευθέος
Voc.	ευθύ	ευθεία	ευθύ

	M	*Pl.* F	N
Nom.	ευθείς	ευθείς	ευθέα
Acc.	ευθείς	ευθείς	ευθέα
Gen.	ευθέων	ευθέων	ευθέων
Voc.	ευθείς	ευθείς	ευθέα

Examples:

αμβλύς 'blunt, obtuse', βαρύς 'heavy', βραχύς 'short', δριμύς 'pungent, bitter', ευρύς 'broad, wide', θρασύς 'impudent', οξύς 'acute', ταχύς 'fast', τραχύς 'rough'. We give some examples of expressions using these forms: αμβλεία γωνία 'obtuse angle', βαρέα όπλα 'heavy weapons', βραχέα κύματα 'short waves', βραχεία συλλαβή 'short syllable', ευθεία [γραμμή] 'straight line', η ταχεία 'express train'.

3.6 ADJECTIVES IN -ής, -ιά, -ί

The only formal difference between this category and that discussed in Section 3.4 is the spelling of the /i/ vowel in the masculine and neuter singular endings. In the main this category comprises words denoting colour or material, formed in most cases from the relevant noun. All forms are stressed on the final syllable. Unlike the adjectives in Section 3.4, this type is still productive.

μαβής   'dark blue'

	Sg.		
	M	*F*	*N*
Nom.	μαβής	μαβιά	μαβί
Acc.	μαβή	μαβιά	μαβί
Gen.	(μαβιού/μαβή)	μαβιάς	(μαβιού/μαβή)
Voc.	μαβή	μαβιά	μαβί

	Pl.		
	M	*F*	*N*
Nom.	μαβιοί	μαβιές	μαβιά
Acc.	μαβιούς	μαβιές	μαβιά
Gen.	μαβιών	μαβιών	μαβιών
Voc.	μαβιοί	μαβιές	μαβιά

Examples:

βυσσινής 'cherry-coloured', δαμασκηνής 'damson-coloured', θαλασσής 'sea-blue', κανελής 'cinnamon-coloured', καφετής 'brown', κεραμιδής 'tile-coloured', μενεξεδής 'violet', ουρανής 'sky-blue', πορτοκαλής 'orange', σταχτής 'ashen, grey', τριανταφυλλής 'rose-coloured', χρυσαφής 'golden'.

Note also δεξής 'right', an alternative form to δεξιός, -ά, -ό.

Adjectives of this kind are sometimes used uninflected, with the ending -ί for all genders, cases and numbers. This usage is not approved by grammarians.

3.7   THE ADJECTIVE (QUANTIFIER) πολύς

The adjective (or quantifier) πολύς (sg. 'much', pl. 'many') has a unique declension and must be given separately. The majority of its forms have the same endings as adjectives of the type given in Section 3.1; the rest (nom. and acc. of the masc. and neuter sg.) have similar endings to adjectives in -ύς (Section 3.4). Note the important difference of spelling: the first set of forms have double λ, the second a single λ. The genitive singular forms of the masculine and neuter are rarely used, except in very formal registers. On the use of πολύς, see Part III, Section 2.8.3.1.2.

πολύς   'much, many'

	M	*Sg.* *F*	*N*
Nom.	πολύς	πολλή	πολύ
Acc.	πολύ(ν)	πολλή	πολύ
Gen.	(πολλού)	πολλής	(πολλού)

	M	*Pl.* *F*	*N*
Nom.	πολλοί	πολλές	πολλά
Acc.	πολλούς	πολλές	πολλά
Gen.	πολλών	πολλών	πολλών

There are no vocative forms.

3.8   ADJECTIVES IN -ης, -ες

Adjectives of this declension are 'two-termination'; that is, they have a single form for masculine and feminine genders and a separate neuter. Two examples are given below, in order to illustrate the different stress patterns.

(i)   ακριβής   'exact'

	M/F	*Sg.* *N*
Nom.	ακριβής	ακριβές
Acc.	ακριβή	ακριβές
Gen.	ακριβούς	ακριβούς

	M/F	*Pl.* *N*
Nom.	ακριβείς	ακριβή
Acc.	ακριβείς	ακριβή
Gen.	ακριβών	ακριβών

(ii)   συνήθης   'usual'

Sg.		
	M/F	*N*
Nom.	συνήθης	σύνηθες
Acc.	συνήθη	σύνηθες
Gen.	συνήθους	συνήθους

Pl.		
	M/F	*N*
Nom.	συνήθεις	συνήθη
Acc.	συνήθεις	συνήθη
Gen.	συνήθων	συνήθων

Examples:

(i) Like ακριβής, stressed on the final syllable throughout: αβλαβής 'harmless', αληθής 'true', αφελής 'naive', δημοφιλής 'popular', διεθνής 'international', διετής 'two years long', δυστυχής 'unfortunate', εμφανής 'obvious, conspicuous', επικερδής 'profitable', επιμελής 'industrious', ειλικρινής 'sincere', επαρκής 'adequate', ευγενής 'noble', ευλαβής 'pious', ευτυχής 'fortunate', μεγαλοπρεπής 'magnificent', παρεμφερής 'similar, comparable', πολυτελής 'expensive, luxurious', πρωτοετής 'first-year [e.g. student]', σαφής 'clear', συνεπής 'consistent, punctual', συνεχής 'continuous', τριμελής 'three-member', τριμερής 'tripartite', υγιής 'healthy' (fem. sometimes υγιά).

(ii) Like συνήθης, with movement of stress to the antepenultimate in the neuter nom. and acc. sg.: αυθάδης 'impudent', αυτάρκης 'self-sufficient', επιμήκης 'oblong', κακοήθης 'immoral; malignant', κλινήρης 'bedridden'. The adjective πλήρης 'full' keeps the stress on the same syllable in all forms. Adjectives in -ώδης do *not* move the stress in the neuter sg., but the gen. pl. forms are always oxytone: βλακώδης, neuter βλακώδες, gen. pl. βλακωδών 'stupid'; thus θεμελιώδης 'fundamental', θορυβώδης 'noisy', ιδεώδης 'ideal', ονειρώδης 'dreamed of', πυρετώδης 'feverish', στοιχειώδης 'elementary', φρικώδης 'frightful', etc.

1. There is an alternative form of the gen. sg. ακριβή, συνήθη. This form, more common for the masc. than for the fem. or neuter, is certainly less formal and may be regarded as incorrect by some speakers.

2. φρενήρης 'frenzied' keeps the stress on the same syllable throughout: neuter sg. φρενήρες.

3. There are no vocative forms in common use.

3.9   ADJECTIVES IN -ης, -α, -ικο

This is a mixed declensional pattern, shared by a considerable number of adjectives which almost all denote physical appearance, character or mood. The masculine and feminine forms correspond to the noun declensions given in Sections 2.1.5 and 2.2.1 respectively. The neuter takes the suffix -ικο and follows the pattern of many neuter adjectives (cf. those in Sections 3.1, 3.2 and 3.3). The stress is fixed throughout on the last syllable of the stem.

τεμπέλης   'lazy'

| | | *Sg.* | |
	M	*F*	*N*
Nom.	τεμπέλης	τεμπέλα	τεμπέλικο
Acc.	τεμπέλη	τεμπέλα	τεμπέλικο
Gen.	τεμπέλη	τεμπέλας	τεμπέλικου
Voc.	τεμπέλη	τεμπέλα	τεμπέλικο

| | | *Pl.* | |
	M	*F*	*N*
Nom.	τεμπέληδες	τεμπέλες	τεμπέλικα
Acc.	τεμπέληδες	τεμπέλες	τεμπέλικα
Gen.	τεμπέληδων	–	τεμπέλικων
Voc.	τεμπέληδες	τεμπέλες	τεμπέλικα

Examples:

κατεργάρης 'roguish', κατσούφης 'glum, sullen', κουτσομπόλης 'gossipy', μπατίρης 'penniless, broke', τσαχπίνης 'saucy, coquettish', τσιγκούνης 'miserly'.

In addition, this type includes all adjectives ending in -άρης or -ούλης, e.g.

γκρινιάρης 'grumbling', ζηλιάρης 'jealous', κλαψιάρης 'given to crying', παλαβιάρης 'madcap', παραπονιάρης 'complaining', πεισματάρης 'stubborn', φοβητσιάρης 'fearful', ψωριάρης 'scabby', κοντούλης 'short', μικρούλης 'tiny', φτωχούλης 'poor little'.

There are also many compound adjectives with the second element denoting a part of the body, e.g.:

-λαίμης: κοντολαίμης 'short-necked', μακρολαίμης 'long-necked'
-μάλλης: ξανθομάλλης 'fair-haired', μακρομάλλης 'long-haired', σγουρομάλλης 'curly-haired'
-μάτης: ανοιχτομάτης 'open-eyed, wide-awake', γαλανομάτης 'blue-eyed', μαυρομάτης 'black-eyed'
-μύτης: κουτσομύτης 'pug-nosed', ψηλομύτης 'snobbish'
-πόδης: στραβοπόδης 'knock-kneed' or 'bow-legged'

-φρύδης: μαυροφρύδης 'with black eyebrows'
-χέρης: ανοιχτοχέρης 'open-handed'

1. Some of the above compound adjectives also have a fem. form in -ούσα or -ού, e.g. ξανθομαλλούσα or ξανθομαλλού, μαυρομματούσα or μαυρομματού.

2. The adjectives in -ούλης have an alternative neuter in -ι, e.g. μικρούλι.

3.10 ADJECTIVES IN -άς/-ής, -ού, -άδικο/-ούδικο/-ήδικο

This is a small, and rather miscellaneous, category of expressive adjectives which resemble those in Section 3.9, particularly in the addition of a two-syllable suffix to form the neuter. They all have a feminine form in -ού, which may be compared with the imparisyllabic feminine nouns discussed in Section 2.2.5. The majority have a masculine form in -άς (like some of the nouns in Section 2.1.5), as in the following example:

φαγάς   'glutton'

| | *Sg.* | | |
	M	*F*	*N*
Nom.	φαγάς	φαγού	φαγάδικο/φαγούδικο
Acc.	φαγά	φαγού	φαγάδικο/φαγούδικο
Gen.	φαγά	φαγούς	φαγάδικου/φαγούδικου
Voc.	φαγά	φαγού	φαγάδικο/φαγούδικο

| | *Pl.* | | |
	M	*F*	*N*
Nom.	φαγάδες	φαγούδες	φαγάδικα/φαγούδικα
Acc.	φαγάδες	φαγούδες	φαγάδικα/φαγούδικα
Gen.	φαγάδων	φαγούδων	φαγάδικων/φαγούδικων
Voc.	φαγάδες	φαγούδες	φαγάδικα/φαγούδικα

Examples:

With masc. in -άς: κοιλαράς 'big-bellied', λογάς 'talkative', παραμυθάς 'yarn-spinning', πολυλογάς 'chatterbox', υπναράς 'sleepy-head', φωνακλάς 'loud-mouthed'.

With masc. in -τζής, acc., gen. and voc. -τζή, pl. -τζήδες, and neuter forms based on the suffix -τζήδικο: καβγατζής 'quarrelsome', καταφερτζής 'go-getting, slick', τζαμπατζής 'free-loading'.

With masc. in -λής, acc., gen. and voc. -λή, pl. -λήδες, and neuter forms based on the suffix -λήδικο: μερακλής 'choosy, enthusiastic', μπελαλής 'troublesome, mischief-making'.

3.11   ADJECTIVES IN -ων, -ουσα, -ον

These adjectives are in origin the declined active participles of certain Ancient Greek verbs; they can be compared to English adjectives in -ing e.g. 'amusing', 'disappointing'. There are perhaps fewer than a dozen adjectives of this type in common use, although the needs of technical and legal language (particularly when translation is involved) are some-times served by the formation of adjectives of this type. Examples of two types, with different stress patterns, are given in full below. The first type is formed from the stem of the active present of first-conjugation verbs, with the endings -ων, -ουσα, -ον etc. The second type has more varied origins.

(i)   επείγων   'urgent'

Sg.

	M	*F*	*N*
Nom.	επείγων	επείγουσα	επείγον
Acc.	επείγοντα	επείγουσα	επείγον
Gen.	επείγοντος	επείγουσας	επείγοντος

Pl.

	M	*F*	*N*
Nom.	επείγοντες	επείγουσες	επείγοντα
Acc.	επείγοντες	επείγουσες	επείγοντα
Gen.	επειγόντων	επειγουσών	επειγόντων

(ii)   παρών   'present'

Sg.

	M	*F*	*N*
Nom.	παρών	παρούσα	παρόν
Acc.	παρόντα	παρούσα	παρόν
Gen.	παρόντος	παρούσας	παρόντος

Pl.

	M	*F*	*N*
Nom.	παρόντες	παρούσες	παρόντα
Acc.	παρόντες	παρούσες	παρόντα
Gen.	παρόντων	παρουσών	παρόντων

Examples:

Like επείγων: δευτερεύων 'secondary', ενδιαφέρων 'interesting', εποπτεύων 'supervising', ιδιάζων 'peculiar', μέλλων 'future', πρωτεύων 'primary', υπάρχων 'existing', φλέγων 'burning' (usually in the phrase φλέγον ζήτημα 'burning issue').

Like παρών: απών 'absent', αποτυχών 'unsuccessful', επιλαχών 'runner-up', επιτυχών 'successful', τυχών 'chancing to happen'.

1. The gen. pl. of the feminine is sometimes found with what is properly the masc. ending: -όντων (considered incorrect by grammarians).

2. The vocative is rare for such adjectives; when it is used, it is the same as the corresponding nominative.

3. Active present participles from second-conjugation type A verbs (see Section 7.3.1.10) have the endings -ών, -ώσα, -ών, e.g. κυβερνών 'ruling'. The differences between this declension and that of παρών given above are: all the other masc. and neuter endings are spelt with -ώ- instead of -ό-; the fem. endings always have the vowel -ω- (stressed except in the gen. pl., which is stressed on the final syllable). However, many of the forms are rarely found.

4. Active present participles from second-conjugation type B verbs (see Section 7.4.1.10) have nom. sg. endings -ών, -ούσα, -ούν, acc. sg. -ούντα, -ούσα, -ούν, and the vowel -ού- in all other masc. and neuter forms. The fem. forms are as for παρών above. Apart from a few words like επικρατών 'prevailing', διοικών 'managing', these participle forms are rarely used.

5. Some verbs with active perfective stems in -σ-, -ξ- or -ψ- also have active past participles in -ας , -ασα, -αν. For some examples of this marginal part of the Greek verb system see Section 7.12.

3.12 ADJECTIVES IN -ων/-ονας, -ον

There are very few adjectives of this type and some of the forms are extremely rare. Historically there was a single set of forms for masculine and feminine genders, but a distinction is now sometimes made between masculine and feminine forms. For example, there is an alternative masculine nominative singular in -ονας, while feminine forms based on a nominative in -ονη may be found in the language of writers and speakers of extreme demotic. The more established forms are given below (bracketed forms are hardly ever used). In general, it is only the masculine and feminine forms of the nominative (sg. -ων, pl. -ονες) and accusative (sg. -ονα, pl. -ονες) that can be used with confidence. Vocative forms, if used, would be the same as the nominative.

ευγνώμων 'grateful'

| | Sg. | |
	M/F	N
Nom.	ευγνώμων	(ευγνώμον)
Acc.	ευγνώμονα	(ευγνώμον)
Gen.	ευγνώμονος	(ευγνώμονος)

	Pl.	
	M/F	*N*
Nom.	ευγνώμονες	(ευγνώμονα)
Acc.	ευγνώμονες	(ευγνώμονα)
Gen.	ευγνωμόνων	(ευγνωμόνων)

Examples:

γενναιόφρων 'generous', δεισιδαίμων 'superstitious', εθνικόφρων 'nationalist', ειδήμων 'expert', εμπειρογνώμων 'expert, specialist', μετριόφρων 'modest', νοήμων 'intelligent'.

3.13   INDECLINABLE ADJECTIVES

Finally, there are a number of adjectives, principally loanwords from other languages, which are uninflected; a single form is used for all genders and cases, singular and plural.

Examples:

αγκαζέ 'occupied, reserved', γκρι 'grey', καφέ 'brown', κομπλέ 'full, complete', λουξ 'de luxe', μοβ 'mauve', μπεζ 'beige', μπλε 'blue', ριγέ 'striped', ροζ 'pink', σικ 'chic', σόκιν 'shocking', φίσκα 'full up, packed'.

3.14   COMPARISON OF ADJECTIVES

In addition to the basic (or *positive*) forms given above in Sections 3.1 to 3.13, adjectives in Greek have three other degrees of comparison: the *comparative* (Eng. 'smaller'), the ***relative superlative*** ('smallest'), and the ***absolute superlative*** ('most small, extremely small'). For the use of the comparative and superlative forms see Part III, Section 2.6.2. The forms themselves are discussed below.

3.14.1   THE COMPARATIVE

There are two ways of forming the comparative in Greek, although not all adjectives have both possibilities available. (Precisely the same statement could be made about the comparative in English: the comparative of 'clever' is either 'more clever' or 'cleverer'; but the only possible comparative of 'ridiculous' is 'more ridiculous'.) The simpler, and in the spoken language the commoner, form of the comparative uses the word πιο, 'more', in front of the appropriate form of the positive adjective. (As an alternative to πιο, πλέον is sometimes used in formal contexts.) Thus: πιο δύσκολος 'more difficult', πιο γλυκός 'sweeter', πιο βαθύς 'deeper', πιο πολλά βιβλία 'more [lit. 'more many'] books', πιο ζηλιάρα 'more jealous' (fem.), ένα πιο ενδιαφέρον πρόγραμμα 'a more interesting programme', πιο συγκεκριμένες πληροφορίες 'more specific information', κάτι πιο ροζ 'something pinker'. This way of forming the comparative is possible for adjectives of all categories, except for adjectives that cannot logically have a comparative degree.

The second way of forming the comparative is to add the suffix -τερος to the neuter nominative singular form of the adjective. This formation is available for most adjectives of the types discussed in Sections 3.1, 3.2, 3.3, 3.4, 3.5 and 3.8. It does not exist for the types given in Sections 3.6, 3.9, 3.10 and 3.11, or for indeclinable adjectives (3.13), or for present or perfect participles in -όμενος, -ώμενος, -ούμενος or -μένος. In these cases the comparative can only be formed with πιο. Adjectives of the type given in Section 3.12 form a comparative in -ονέστερος, as well as a comparative with πιο. Some adjectives have irregular comparatives; for these see Section 3.14.4. All these one-word comparatives follow the declension of adjectives in -ος, -η, -ο (Section 3.1).

The following table shows the comparative forms for each of the categories presented above in Sections 3.1 to 3.13. A dash (–) indicates that adjectives of this category do not have a one-word comparative form.

όμορφος	πιο όμορφος	ομορφότερος	(3.1)
μέτριος	πιο μέτριος	μετριότερος	(3.2)
γλυκός	πιο γλυκός	γλυκότερος	(3.3)
βαθύς	πιο βαθύς	βαθύτερος	(3.4)
ευθύς	πιο ευθύς	ευθύτερος	(3.5)
μαβής	πιο μαβής	–	(3.6)
πολύς	πιο πολύς	περισσότερος	(3.7; see also 3.14.4)
ακριβής	πιο ακριβής	ακριβέστερος	(3.8)
συνήθης	πιο συνήθης	συνηθέστερος	(3.8)
τεμπέλης	πιο τεμπέλης	–	(3.9)
φαγάς	πιο φαγάς	–	(3.10)
επείγων	πιο επείγων	–	(3.11)
ευγνώμων	πιο ευγνώμων	ευγνωμονέστερος	(3.12)
σόκιν	πιο σόκιν	–	(3.13)

1. Certain comparative forms used to be spelt with -ώτερος rather than -ότερος. This spelling is no longer standard.

2. Sometimes, especially in colloquial speech, the two ways of forming the comparative are combined: πιο μικρότερος, lit. 'more smaller'.

3. For expressions of inferiority (e.g. λιγότερο/πιο λίγο καλός 'less good') see Part III, Section 2.6.2 (end).

3.14.2   THE RELATIVE SUPERLATIVE

The relative superlative is formed in exactly the same way (or ways) as the comparative, except that it is preceded by the definite article.

Adjectives that have a choice of two comparative forms also have two corresponding relative superlatives. One-word relative superlatives follow the declension of adjectives in -ος, -η, -ο (Section 3.1), just like the comparative forms. Thus, ο πιο έξυπνος or ο εξυπνότερος 'the cleverest', η πιο ωραία or η ωραιότερη 'the most beautiful' (fem.), το πιο βαρύ or το βαρύτερο 'the heaviest' (neuter), τα πιο σημαντικά or τα σημαντικότερα 'the most important [things]', το πιο ενδιαφέρον 'the most interesting [point]', οι πιο τσιγκούνηδες 'the meanest [people]'. Irregular relative superlative forms (which are the same as the irregular comparatives, preceded by the definite article) are given in Section 3.14.4. For the use of the relative superlative see Part III, Section 2.6.2.

3.14.3   THE ABSOLUTE SUPERLATIVE

The absolute superlative is used to stress an exceptional property or quality possessed by its referent; compare the English 'What you say is *most interesting*', or 'She is a *most able* teacher', where it is not a matter of making a direct comparison with other things less interesting, or other teachers who are less able, but merely of emphasizing the exceptional degree to which the referent possesses that particular quality. In Greek the absolute superlative is normally formed by adding the suffix -τατος to the neuter nominative singular form of the positive adjective. Examples are: φυσικότατος 'most natural' or 'entirely natural', εξοχότατος 'extremely eminent', βαθύτατος 'very deep indeed, profound', συνηθέστατος 'most usual', κυριότατος 'chief of all'. It will be noticed that English has various ways of expressing the same idea.

The absolute superlative is a rather learned form; it is much less frequently used than the comparative and the relative superlative and cannot be produced for all adjectives. It does *not* exist for those adjectives that cannot have a one-word comparative in -τερος (see Section 3.14.1). Adjectives in -ων, -ον (Section 3.12) can form an absolute superlative in -ονέστατος, e.g. ευγνωμονέστατος 'most grateful'. For irregular forms see the following section. For the use of the absolute superlative see Part III, Section 2.6.2.

3.14.4   IRREGULAR COMPARATIVES AND SUPERLATIVES

The following table lists the principal irregular forms of degrees of comparison. The comparative and relative superlative forms are shown together, the only difference being that the relative superlative is preceded by the definite article.

Positive		Comparative/rel. superlative	Abs. superlative
απλός	'simple'	απλούστερος	απλούστατος
γέρος	'old'	γεροντότερος	–
κακός	'bad'	χειρότερος	κάκιστος ('most wicked')
			χείριστος ('worst')
καλός	'good'	καλύτερος	κάλλιστος ('finest')
			άριστος ('excellent')
κοντός	'short'	κοντότερος ('shorter in height')	κοντότατος
		κοντύτερος ('shorter in length')	κοντύτατος
λίγος	'little'	λιγότερος	ελάχιστος
μεγάλος	'big'	μεγαλύτερος	μέγιστος
μικρός	'small'	μικρότερος	ελάχιστος
πολύς	'much'	περισσότερος	(πλείστος)
πρώτος	'first'	πρωτύτερος ('earlier')	πρώτιστος

The following comparative, relative and absolute superlative forms do not derive from adjectives in the positive degree; some of them derive from other parts of speech, as indicated in the first column (words in brackets are not normally used today):

	Comparative/rel. superlative		Abs. superlative
(άνω 'above')	ανώτερος	'superior'	ανώτατος
κάτω 'below'	κατώτερος	'inferior'	κατώτατος
προτιμώ 'I prefer'	προτιμότερος	'preferable'	–
–	προγενέστερος	'prior'	–
–	μεταγενέστερος	'subsequent'	–
(πλησίον 'near')	πλησιέστερος	'nearer'	πλησιέστατος
(άπω 'far')	απώτερος	'further'	απώτατος
(υπέρ 'over, beyond')	υπέρτερος	'higher'	υπέρτατος

4 ADVERBS

Adverbs are words which modify verbs, adjectives, other adverbs, nouns, numerals or quantifiers, and also whole phrases or clauses, in order to indicate various relationships (time, manner, place, quantity etc.) or to qualify what is being said in some other way. In this section we are concerned with adverbs which stand in a close morphological relationship with adjectives; in other words, we shall be dealing only with adverbs which are formed from the corresponding adjectives according to certain rules or patterns. We shall not, therefore, examine here the many adverbs of place, time, manner, quantity etc. which are not derived directly from declined adjectives. (For types of adverb and their uses see Part III, Sections 3.1 and 3.2.)

There are two main adverbial endings for the forms derived from adjectives: -α and -ως. Some adjectives can use either ending (but with a possible distinction of register or stylistic level and sometimes with a different stress), but for most adjective types there is only one way to form the corresponding adverb. We shall consider in turn the adverbs ending in -α (Section 4.1), those ending in -ως (Section 4.2), and then some irregular forms (Section 4.3). Adverbs are indeclinable, but like adjectives they have degrees of comparison (see Section 4.4).

4.1 ADVERBS IN -α

Adverbs with the ending -α are always identical to the neuter plural (nom. and acc.) form of the corresponding adjective. This type of adverb is found for adjectives in -ος (Sections 3.1, 3.2 and 3.3), including passive perfect participles, for adjectives in -ύς, -ιά, -ύ (Section 3.4), and for adjectives in -ης, -α, -ικο (Section 3.9).

Examples:

> From adjectives in -ος: άγρια 'fiercely', αλύπητα 'mercilessly', αργά 'slowly, late', αριστερά 'on the left', βέβαια 'certainly, of course', γλυκά 'sweetly', δυνατά 'strongly, loudly, aloud', ελληνικά 'in Greek', μάταια 'in vain', ξαφνικά 'suddenly', προφορικά 'orally', σπάνια 'rarely', συγκεκριμένα 'specifically', σωστά 'correctly', τελευταία 'lastly, recently', φτηνά 'cheaply', φτωχά 'poorly', χωριστά 'separately'.

From adjectives in -ύς, -ιά, -ύ: βαθιά 'deep(ly)', βαριά 'heavily; gravely', μακριά 'far away'.

From adjectives in -ης, -α, -ικο: ζηλιάρικα 'jealously', κατσούφικα 'sullenly', τσαχπίνικα 'coquettishly'.

Some adjectives in -ος have an alternative adverb in -ως, for which see the following section.

4.2 ADVERBS IN -ως

Adjectives in -ης, -ες (Section 3.8) form their adverbs with the suffix -ως. The stress remains on the same syllable as the masculine nominative singular of the adjective *except* in the case of adjectives ending in -ώδης: their adverbs have the stress on the final syllable.

Examples:

ακριβώς 'exactly', ασφαλώς 'surely', διαρκώς 'continually', διεθνώς 'internationally', δυστυχώς 'unfortunately', λεπτομερώς 'in detail', μανιωδώς 'furiously', ουσιωδώς 'essentially', πλήρως 'fully', προφανώς 'obviously', σκανδαλωδώς 'scandalously', συνεπώς 'consequently', συνήθως 'usually'.

Two other categories of adjective give rise to adverbs in -ως, though in both cases the adverbs are rather rare: adjectives (from participles) in -ων, -ουσα, -ον or -ών, -ώσα, -όν or -ών, -ούσα, -ούν (see Section 3.11) and those in -ων/-ονας, -ον (Section 3.12). Such adverbs have -ως in place of the -α of the nom. and acc. neuter pl. form, with the stress on the penultimate. (For adverbs formed from adjectives in -ύς, -εία, -ύ see note 3 below.)

Examples:

αρκούντως 'sufficiently' (learned and rare), επειγόντως 'urgently', παρεμπιπτόντως 'incidentally' (the corresponding adjective is very rarely used), ευγνωμόνως 'gratefully'.

Finally, certain adjectives in -ος can also form an alternative adverb in -ως. Adverbs derived from adjectives stressed on the antepenultimate undergo a shift of stress to the penultimate. Adverbs of this kind, which were once more or less limited to *katharevousa*, are in increasing use, facilitating various nuances of register and style. Some common doublets, such as βέβαια/βεβαίως 'certainly', have no difference of meaning and hardly differ in usage. In other cases, however, the -ως form tends to be used in more formal contexts, or for specific stylistic reasons; for example, άδικα and αδίκως 'unjustly', άσχετα and ασχέτως 'irrespectively', σπάνια and σπανίως 'rarely'. Its use in place of the adverb in -α can sometimes avoid an ambiguity when adjacent to a neuter plural adjective. For example, δύο εξαιρετικά πρωτότυπα βιβλία could mean either 'two exceptionally (adverb) original books' or 'two excellent (adjective), original books'. The substitution of the adverbial form εξαιρετικώς would make it clear that the first meaning was intended.

1. Among adverbs from adjectives in -ος which are normally used in the alternative -ως form are: αδιακρίτως 'indiscriminately', αεροπορικώς 'by air[mail]', απολύτως 'absolutely', επανειλημμένως 'repeatedly', επομένως 'consequently', ιδίως 'particularly', κυρίως 'mainly', συνημμένως 'attached'.

2. Sometimes there are differences of meaning or usage between the two forms. We give some important examples:

καλώς 'well, rightly', rather than καλά, is used in certain standardized expressions, such as καλώς ήλθες 'welcome'; καλώς can also mean 'lower second [degree]'
κακώς 'badly, wrongly' is sometimes used in place of the usual κακά
ευχαρίστως means 'with pleasure' while ευχάριστα means 'pleasantly'
τελείως 'completely' is distinguished from τέλεια 'perfectly'
αμέσως means 'immediately', in contrast to άμεσα 'directly'
ίσως 'perhaps' has a quite different meaning from ίσα 'equally'

Many speakers recognize a distinction between the two adverb forms derived from απλός 'simple': απλά means 'simply, in a simple way', while απλώς means 'merely'; this distinction is not always observed in practice.

3. Adjectives in -ύς, -εία, -ύ (Section 3.5) have adverbs ending in -έως, e.g. βαρέως 'heavily, gravely', βραδέως 'slowly', ευθέως 'in a direct manner, straight, honestly' (but note that the adjective itself is also used adverbially of time: ευθύς 'immediately, straightaway'), ευρέως 'widely', ταχέως 'quickly, soon'. These forms are of learned origin and are rarely used in the spoken language.

4.3   OTHER ADVERBS FORMED FROM ADJECTIVES

Some exceptions to the regular formations described in Sections 4.1 and 4.2 must also be noted. In all the following instances the neuter singular form is used adverbially:

άλλος 'other' has an adverbial form άλλο used in the sense 'any more, any longer, any further' (only in questions or in negative statements or commands) and there is also a related adverb αλλιώς 'otherwise'
λίγος 'little' has the adverbial form λίγο '(a) little, to a small extent', e.g. λίγο γνωστός 'little known'
μόνος 'alone, only' has the adverbial form μόνο 'only'
πολύς 'much, many' (for the forms see Section 3.7) has the adverb πολύ 'very, much'

4.4   COMPARISON OF ADVERBS

The comparative degree of adverbs can be formed by prefixing πιο (or sometimes, more formally, πλέον) to the positive form, e.g. πιο ωραία 'more beautifully', πιο ψηλά 'higher', πιο δυνατά 'more loudly, louder', πιο αποτελεσματικά 'more effectively', πιο ευτυχισμένα 'more happily', πιο βαθιά 'more deeply', πιο σαφώς 'more clearly', πιο πολύ 'more, to a greater extent', πιο λίγο 'less, to a lesser extent'. The same forms can also function as relative superlatives in appropriate contexts. (See further Part III, Section 3.1.1.)

Adjectives that have one-word comparative forms also have comparative and absolute superlative forms of their adverb. These adverbs are identical to the neuter plural forms of the corresponding degree of the adjective. We give some examples:

Adverb		Comparative	Abs. superlative
ακριβά	'expensively'	ακριβότερα	ακριβότατα
καλά	'well'	καλύτερα	κάλλιστα/άριστα
φρόνιμα	'prudently'	φρονιμότερα	φρονιμότατα
αργά	'slowly, late'	αργότερα	–
γενικά	'generally'	γενικότερα	γενικότατα
βαθιά	'deeply'	βαθύτερα	βαθύτατα
ακριβώς	'exactly'	ακριβέστερα	ακριβέστατα

The adverbs λίγο '[a] little' and πολύ 'much' have the following degrees of comparison: λίγο – λιγότερο 'less', το λιγότερο or το ελάχιστο 'at the least' (also τουλάχιστο(ν) 'at least'); πολύ – περισσότερο or πιο πολύ 'more', το πιο πολύ 'at the most'.

The following forms of comparative and absolute superlative adverbs are not derived from positive adverbs in the regular way:

Adverb		Comparative	Abs. superlative
ιδίως	'particularly'	ιδιαίτερα	(ιδιαίτατα)
μπροστά	'before; in front'	μπροστύτερα	
νωρίς	'early'	νωρίτερα	νωρίτατα
πρώτα	'first'	πρωτύτερα	–
ύστερα	'later'	υστερότερα	–

5 PRONOUNS AND DETERMINERS

A pronoun is a word which takes the place of a noun phrase and can function as the subject, complement or object of a verb, or as the object of a preposition; it may also be governed by a noun, adverb or other word. For the purposes of this book, determiners are words, other than adjectives and numerals, which modify a noun, e.g. 'every', 'other', 'same'. (Articles are also determiners, but their forms have been given separately in Section 1.) We include here the category of demonstratives ('this (one)', 'that (one)'), which function both as pronouns on their own and as determiners when accompanying a noun. The uses of the full range of pronouns and determiners are discussed in Part III, Section 2.8. Here we are concerned with giving the forms of those pronouns and determiners which are inflected.

The pronouns and determiners which will be discussed in the following sections can be divided into the following categories:

(a) *personal pronouns* ('I', 'you', 'me', 'him', 'we' etc.), which in Greek have emphatic and weak (clitic) forms with different syntactic functions (Sections 5.1 and 5.2 respectively);

(b) *possessive pronouns and determiners*, which in Greek consist of: (i) the weak forms of the personal pronouns (as in Section 5.2) used in the genitive case as possessive pronouns, and (ii) emphatic possessives, which may either directly modify a noun ('my own', 'your own', 'her own' etc.) or take the place of a noun already referred to ('mine', 'yours', 'hers' etc.) (Section 5.3);

(c) *demonstratives* such as 'this', 'that', 'such', and other determiners, e.g. 'all', 'other', 'same' (Section 5.4);

(d) *relative pronouns and determiners* such as 'who', 'which' (Section 5.5);

(e) *interrogative pronouns and determiners* ('who?', 'which?' etc.) (Section 5.6);

(f) *indefinite pronouns and determiners* ('some(one)', 'any(one)' etc.) (Section 5.7);

(g) *reflexive forms* ('myself', 'yourself', 'herself' etc.) (Section 5.8);

(h) the *universal pronoun* ('everyone', 'each one') (Section 5.9).

A complete list of all pronouns and determiners is given in Part III, Section 2.8.4.

5.1   PERSONAL PRONOUNS: EMPHATIC FORMS

The emphatic forms of the personal pronouns function as the subject, complement or object of a verb, when emphasis or distinction is required, or as the object of a preposition, or independently of a clause. The use of these emphatic forms (sometimes called 'strong' forms) is fully discussed in Part III, Sections 2.8.1.1.2 and 5.4.3.4. There are forms for each of the three persons, singular and plural, inflected for case and, for the third person only, gender. (Note that this refers to *grammatical* gender.)

First person

	Sg.	εγώ	*'I'*	Pl.	εμείς	*'we'*
Nom.		εγώ			εμείς	
Acc.		εμένα			εμάς	
Gen.		εμένα			εμάς	

Second person

	Sg.	εσύ	*'you'*	Pl.	εσείς	*'you'*
Nom.		εσύ			εσείς	
Acc.		εσένα			εσάς	
Gen.		εσένα			εσάς	

Third person

Sg.   αυτός, -ή, -ό *'he', 'she', 'it'*   Pl. αυτοί, -ές, -ά *'they'*

	M	F	N	M	F	N
Nom.	αυτός	αυτή	αυτό	αυτοί	αυτές	αυτά
Acc.	αυτό(ν)	αυτή(ν)	αυτό	αυτούς	αυτές	αυτά
Gen.	αυτού	αυτής	αυτού	αυτών	αυτών	αυτών

1. The accusative forms of the first- and second-person pronouns (sg. and pl.) lose their initial vowel when preceded by the prepositions από or για, e.g. για σένα 'for you'. The plural forms then become monosyllabic and are accordingly written without an accent (although, like all strong pronouns, they are in fact stressed in pronunciation), e.g. από σας 'from you', για μας 'for us'. The nominative forms can also lose their initial vowel when they follow a word ending in a vowel in rapid speech. In these cases it is usual to indicate the omission of the vowel with an apostrophe and to retain the written accent (although this is not always done):

(i)   Ξέρω 'γώ;
      'How should *I* know?'
(ii) Ήρθαμε 'μείς
      '*We* have come [and not someone else]'

2. The third-person pronouns are in fact forms of the demonstrative αυτός 'this (one)', which is declined like adjectives in -ος, -η, -ο (Section 3.1), except that the masc. acc. form of the pronoun (as distinct from the corresponding determiner) has a final -ν to distinguish it from the neuter, e.g. απ' αυτόν 'from him', but απ'

αυτό τον κύριο 'from that gentleman'. The fem. acc. form can also, optionally, take a final -ν.

3. There are alternative colloquial forms for the gen. of the third person: masc. and neuter sg. αυτουνού, fem. sg. αυτηνής, pl. αυτωνών (all genders); similarly there is a colloquial masc. acc. pl. αυτουνούς.

4. Other demonstratives can have the same pronominal function as αυτός and are declined in the same way: τούτος, -η, -ο 'this one', 'he', 'she', 'it' etc. and εκείνος, -η, -ο 'that one', 'he', 'she', 'it' etc. They also have alternative genitive forms, which are stressed on the final syllable: masc. and neuter sg. τουτουνού, fem. sg. τουτηνής, pl. (all genders) τουτωνών, similarly εκεινού, εκεινής, εκεινών. Alternative forms are also occasionally used for the masc. acc. pl. τουτουνούς, εκεινούς. For the use of these demonstratives see Part III, Section 2.8.3.2.

5.2 PERSONAL PRONOUNS: WEAK (CLITIC) FORMS

The weak (clitic) forms of the personal pronouns are used only in close connection with verbs, nouns, adverbs and certain other words. They are monosyllabic and unstressed, forming a phonological word with the verb, noun, adverb or other word with which they are syntactically linked (see Part I, Section 1.5.4). The use of these weak forms is fully discussed in Part III, Section 2.8.1.1.1. There are no weak forms for the nominative case of the first and second persons.

First person

	Sg.	Pl.
Acc.	με	μας
Gen.	μου	μας

Second person

	Sg.	Pl.
Acc.	σε	σας
Gen.	σου	σας

Third person

	Sg. M	Sg. F	Sg. N	Pl. M	Pl. F	Pl. N
Nom.	τος	τη	το	τοι	τες	τα
Acc.	τον	τη(ν)	το	τους	τις/τες	τα
Gen.	του	της	του	τους	τους	τους

1. The nom. forms of the weak third-person pronoun have a very restricted range of functions, for which see Part III, Section 2.8.1.1.1.

2. The two fem. acc. pl. forms given above for the third person are not simply alternatives: τις is the obligatory form used before the verb in declarative state-

ments, questions etc., e.g. τις γνωρίζω 'I know them (fem.)', τις είδες; 'did you see them (fem.)?'; τες is used, as an alternative to τις (but one which is preferred by many speakers), only after imperatives and gerunds: φέρε μού τες! 'bring them (fem.) to me!', αφήνοντάς τες 'leaving them'; but after plural imperatives only τις is used: πάρτε τις! 'take them'.

5.3 POSSESSIVE PRONOUNS AND DETERMINERS

The genitive forms of the weak personal pronous are used as possessive pronouns following a noun or as part of a noun phrase, e.g. οι κόρες μου 'my daughters'. The forms are as given in Section 5.2: singular μου, σου, του, της, του, plural μας, σας, τους. For more information about their use see Part III, Section 2.8.1.1.1.

The emphatic possessive δικός μου 'my own, mine' is both a pronoun and a determiner. It is used to give emphasis or to make a distinction ('*my* book', i.e. 'not yours'), or, as the complement of a verb, simply to indicate possession ('this book is *mine*'). These forms are in fact combinations of δικός, which is declined like adjectives in -ος (see Section 3.1) and a weak possessive pronoun μου, σου, του etc. When used attributively it is preceded by the definite article if the noun it qualifies is definite e.g. τα δικά σου παιδιά '*your* children'. For a full discussion of the emphatic possessive see Part III, Section 2.8.3.10. The basic forms, which are declined for case, number and gender, are as follows:

(ο, η, το) δικός, -ή, -ό μου	'my', 'mine'
(ο, η, το) δικός, -ή, -ο σου	'your', 'yours' (referring to a single possessor)
(ο, η, το) δικός, -ή, -ο του	'his'
(ο, η, το) δικός, -ή, -ο της	'her', 'hers'
(ο, η, το) δικός, -ή, -ο μας	'our', 'ours'
(ο, η, το) δικός, -ή, -ο σας	'your', 'yours' (when the possessor is plural, or is addressed in the polite plural form)
(ο, η, το) δικός, -ή, -ο τους	'their', 'theirs'

5.4 DEMONSTRATIVES AND OTHER PRONOUNS AND DETERMINERS

There are three demonstratives: αυτός, τούτος and εκείνος. All are declined like adjectives in -ος. They may function either as emphatic third-person pronouns ('he', 'she', 'it' etc.) or as determiners ('this', 'that') modifying a noun (which must be preceded by the definite article). The forms have been fully described above in Section 5.1 (and notes). For the use of the demonstratives see Part III, Section 2.8.3.2.

The qualitative demonstrative τέτοιος 'such, of such a kind' is fully declined like adjectives in -ος, -α, -ο (Section 3.2). The quantitative demonstrative τόσος 'so much/many' follows the declension of adjectives in -ος, -η, -ο (Section 3.1). The uses of these qualitative and quantitative demonstratives are discussed in Part III, Sections 2.8.3.7 and 2.8.3.8.

The quantifiers όλος 'all' and ολόκληρος 'whole' are also fully declined like adjectives in -ος, -η, -ο. Όλος has an alternative non-formal genitive plural: ολωνών (all genders). On the uses of these and other quantifiers see Part III, Section 2.8.3.1. There is also a quantitative pronoun, which formerly existed in all genders and cases, singular and plural: πας, πάσα, παν 'all, every'. The only forms which occur regularly now are: neuter nom./acc. το παν 'everything' and its pl. τα πάντα (see Section 2.4.9 for the full forms), and the masc. nom. pl. οι πάντες 'all people, everybody'. On the uses of these forms see Part III, Section 2.8.1.2.4.

The intensive pronouns and determiners ίδιος, -α, -ο 'same' and μόνος, -η, -ο 'only' are declined like adjectives. Their uses are described in Part III, Section 2.8.3.11.

Finally, the contrastive pronoun and determiner άλλος 'other, next' is declined like adjectives in -ος, -η, -ο, with the following alternative non-formal forms for the genitive: masc. and neuter sg. αλλουνού, fem. sg. αλληνής, pl. αλλωνών (all genders). For its uses see Part III, Section 2.8.3.12.

5.5   RELATIVE PRONOUNS AND DETERMINERS

Relative pronouns and determiners ('who', 'which', 'that') introduce relative clauses. In Greek there are two ways of expressing the relative pronoun (neither of which is, strictly speaking, a pronoun): (i) the indeclinable *relative complementizer* που, and (ii) the *relative pronoun phrase* ο οποίος, which must agree in gender and number with its antecedent and is declined like adjectives in -ος, -α, -ο (see Section 3.2).

In addition, there are certain other words which introduce free or headless relative clauses. These correlative pronouns and determiners are as follows:

όποιος, -α, -ο	'whoever' (this must be distinguished from the relative pronominal phrase ο οποίος, which always has the definite article and second-syllable stress)
ό,τι	'whatever'
όσος, -η, -ο	'as much as', 'as many as', 'those which'

With the exception of ό,τι, these forms are declined like the respective types of adjective. Όποιος has alternative forms for the gen. sg. οποιανού (masc. and neuter), οποιανής (fem.), gen. pl. οποιανών, and acc. pl. οποιανούς (masc.); these alternative forms are used as pronouns, but not as determiners. The correlative ό,τι is uninflected and may qualify nouns in any gender, number or case. Note that it is written with a comma to distinguish it from the complementizer ότι. For the use of all these relatives and correlatives see Part III, Sections 2.8.3.3, 2.8.3.9 and 5.3.1.

There are also universal correlatives οποιοσδήποτε, οσοσδήποτε and οτιδήποτε; the last of these is indeclinable, but the first two are declined like όποιος and όσος respectively, together with the suffix -δήποτε. (However, οποιοσδήποτε does not have the longer alternative forms which όποιος can have.) For the use of these forms see Part III, Section 2.8.3.9.

5.6 INTERROGATIVE PRONOUNS AND DETERMINERS

There are three interrogative pronouns and determiners: ποιος 'who?', 'which?', τι 'what?' and πόσος 'how much?'. They are determiners when they modify a noun, and pronouns when they stand alone. Of the three, τι is not inflected and may modify nouns of any gender, number or case, while πόσος, -η, -ο is declined like adjectives in -ος (Section 3.1). The forms of ποιος are as follows:

ποιος   'who?', 'which?'

	M	*Sg.* *F*	*N*
Nom.	ποιος	ποια	ποιο
Acc.	ποιον	ποια(ν)	ποιο
Gen.	ποιου/ποιανού	ποιας/ποιανής	ποιου/ποιανού

	M	*Pl.* *F*	*N*
Nom.	ποιοι	ποιες	ποια
Acc.	ποιους/ποιανούς	ποιες	ποια
Gen.	ποιων/ποιανών	ποιων/ποιανών	ποιων/ποιανών

1. In place of the gen. sg. forms of ποιος, τίνος 'whose?' is often used for the masc. and neuter, but never for the fem. There is also a gen. pl. τίνων (all genders).

2. The longer forms of the gen. sg. and pl. and the masc. acc. pl. are used only for humans, and more often as pronouns than as determiners.

3. The uses of these interrogative pronouns and determiners are discussed in Part III, Sections 2.8.3.6 and 5.1.4.4.

5.7 INDEFINITE PRONOUNS AND DETERMINERS

The *indefinite* pronouns and determiners can be divided into two kinds: 'specific', referring to a specific person or thing whose identity is unspecified ('someone', 'something') and 'non-specific', referring to an indefinite person or thing ('anyone', 'anything', or negatively 'no one', 'nothing').

In the first category, Greek has the declinable form κάποιος, -α, -ο 'some[one]' (declined like the adjectives in Section 3.2, with masc. acc. sg. κάποιον and alternative gen. forms: masc. and neuter sg. καποιανού, fem. sg. καποιανής, pl. all genders καποιανών) and indeclinable κάτι 'some[thing]'. The indefinite article ένας is also sometimes used in the sense of 'someone' (for the forms see Section 1.2). We should also mention here ο τάδε and ο δείνα ('such and such', 'so-and-so', 'what's his name'), which consist of the definite article (which is declined for gender, number and case) and the indeclinable words τάδε and δείνα. For the use of these indefinite (specific) words and phrases see Part III, Section 2.8.3.4.

In the second category, the main indefinite non-specific pronouns and determiners are κανείς/κανένας 'any(one), no(one)' (which is declined as below) and the indeclinable τίποτα or τίποτε 'any(thing), no(thing)'. The declension of κανείς/κανένας resembles that of the indefinite article and also has only singular forms:

	M	F	N
Nom.	κανείς/κανένας	καμιά/καμία	κανένα
Acc.	κανένα(ν)	καμιά(ν)/καμία(ν)	κανένα
Gen.	κανενός	καμιάς/καμίας	κανενός

1. There are some important differences in the use of the masc. forms κανείς and κανένας. For these and for all other matters concerning the use of the indefinite (non-specific) forms see Part III, Section 2.8.3.5.

2. The fem. forms with stressed -ι- (καμία, καμίαν and καμίας) are more emphatic than their alternatives.

3. The final -ν may be added to the masc. and fem. acc. sg. forms when they are followed by a word beginning with a vowel or a voiceless plosive (cf. the indefinite article).

4. The neuter κανένα is sometimes shortened in colloquial speech to κάνα, but only when it is used as a determiner, i.e. modifying a noun. There is also an expression κάνα δυο 'a couple (of)', which is used for all genders.

5.8 REFLEXIVE FORMS

Greek has a variety of ways of expressing reflexivity, corresponding to English sentences like 'I wash *myself*', or 'he works for *himself*'. These are discussed in Part III, Section 5.4.3.5ff. The only one which concerns us under the heading of morphology is the reflexive phrase ο εαυτός μου etc. 'myself'. It is a noun phrase consisting of the appropriate masculine forms of the definite article, the declined masculine noun εαυτός, and a weak possessive pronoun. The full range of forms is as follows:

1 sg. 'myself'	Nom.	ο εαυτός μου
	Acc.	τον εαυτό μου
	Gen.	του εαυτού μου
2 sg. 'yourself'	Nom.	ο εαυτός σου
	Acc.	τον εαυτό σου
	Gen.	του εαυτού σου
3 sg. 'himself'	Nom.	ο εαυτός του
	Acc.	τον εαυτό του
	Gen.	του εαυτού του
3 sg. 'herself'	Nom.	ο εαυτός της
	Acc.	τον εαυτό της
	Gen.	του εαυτού της
3 sg. 'itself'	Nom.	ο εαυτός του
	Acc.	τον εαυτό του
	Gen.	του εαυτού του
1 pl. 'ourselves'	Nom.	ο εαυτός μας
	Acc.	τον εαυτό μας or τους εαυτούς μας
	Gen.	του εαυτού μας or των εαυτών μας
2 pl. 'yourselves'	Nom.	ο εαυτός σας
	Acc.	τον εαυτό σας or τους εαυτούς σας
	Gen.	του εαυτού σας or των εαυτών σας
3 pl. 'themselves'	Nom.	ο εαυτός τους
	Acc.	τον εαυτό τους or τους εαυτούς τους
	Gen.	του εαυτού τους or των εαυτών τους

The singular form of εαυτός may be used with both singular and plural possessors (the person or thing to whom or which the weak possessive pronoun refers).
Plural forms of the noun, accusative εαυτούς and genitive εαυτών, are also used
with plural possessors.

5.9   THE UNIVERSAL PRONOUNS καθένας AND καθετί

There are two universal pronouns in Greek: καθένας 'every one, each
one', which may be preceded by the definite article and is inflected, and
the neuter indeclinable (το) καθετί 'each thing'. For the uses of the
universal pronouns see Part III, Section 2.8.1.2.2. The forms of καθένας
are as follows:

	M	F	N
Nom.	καθένας	καθεμιά/καθεμία	καθένα
Acc.	καθένα(ν)	καθεμιά(ν)/καθεμία(ν)	καθένα
Gen.	καθενός	καθεμιάς/καθεμίας	καθενός

1. The above forms are identical to those of the indefinite article (Section 1.2),
prefixed with καθ(ε)-. Compare also the forms of the indefinite pronoun κανείς/
κανένας (Section 5.7). Like both of these, καθένας has no plural forms.

2. The following alternative forms are found: for the masc. nom. καθείς (formal); for the masc. and neuter genitive καθένα (used only when preceded by the definite article); for the fem. genitive the colloquial form καθεμιανής is occasionally heard.

6 NUMERALS

Numerals indicate number, order, size or quantity. They can be classified as *cardinal* ('one, two, three' etc.), *ordinal* ('first', 'second', 'third' etc.), *multiplicative* ('single', 'double', 'treble' or 'triple', etc.), *relative* ('twice as much', 'three times as much', etc.) and *collective* (denoting 'group of two', 'group of three', etc.). The forms of the cardinal and ordinal numerals are fully listed in Section 6.1. Information about the forms of multiplicative, relative and collective numerals is given in notes 10–12 of that section. For the uses of the numerals see Part III, Section 2.7.

6.1 TABLE OF NUMERALS

In the following table the cardinal numerals are given in their nominative masculine forms. Alternative forms are shown separated by an oblique line (/): the form given first is the more common, or the more stylistically neutral, but the choice can be largely a matter of personal preference. Cardinal numerals printed in **bold** are declined, i.e. they have different forms for other genders and cases. For these forms see Section 6.2. The ordinal numerals are all declined like adjectives in -ος, -η, -ο (see Section 3.1). The second column of the table gives the Greek alphabetic system of numerals, which (in either lower-case or upper-case forms) is used for certain purposes (see Part III, end of Section 2.7).

		Cardinal numerals	*Ordinal numerals*
1	α΄	**ένας**	πρώτος
2	β΄	δύο/δυο	δεύτερος
3	γ΄	**τρεις**	τρίτος
4	δ΄	**τέσσερις**	τέταρτος
5	ε΄	πέντε	πέμπτος
6	ς΄/στ΄	έξι	έκτος
7	ζ΄	επτά/εφτά	έβδομος
8	η΄	οκτώ/οχτώ	όγδοος
9	θ΄	εννέα/εννιά	ένατος
10	ι΄	δέκα	δέκατος
11	ια΄	ένδεκα/έντεκα	ενδέκατος
12	ιβ΄	δώδεκα	δωδέκατος
13	ιγ΄	**δεκατρείς**	δέκατος τρίτος
14	ιδ΄	**δεκατέσσερις**	δέκατος τέταρτος

		Cardinal numerals	Ordinal numerals
15	ιε′	δεκαπέντε	δέκατος πέμπτος
16	ις′/ιστ′	δεκαέξι/δεκάξι	δέκατος έκτος
17	ιζ′	δεκαεπτά/δεκαεφτά	δέκατος έβδομος
18	ιη′	δεκαοκτώ/δεκαοχτώ	δέκατος όγδοος
19	ιθ′	δεκαεννέα/δεκαεννιά	δέκατος ένατος
20	κ′	είκοσι	εικοστός
21	κα′	είκοσι **ένας**	εικοστός πρώτος
30	λ′	τριάντα	τριακοστός
40	μ′	σαράντα	τεσσαρακοστός
50	ν′	πενήντα	πεντηκοστός
60	ξ′	εξήντα	εξηκοστός
70	ο′	εβδομήντα	εβδομηκοστός
80	π′	ογδόντα	ογδοηκοστός
90	ϟ′/ϙ′	ενενήντα	ενενηκοστός
100	ρ′	εκατόν/εκατό	εκατοστός
101	ρα′	εκατόν **ένας**	εκατοστός πρώτος
200	σ′	**διακόσιοι**	διακοσιοστός
300	τ′	**τριακόσιοι/τρακόσιοι**	τριακοσιοστός
400	υ′	**τετρακόσιοι**	τετρακοσιοστός
500	φ′	**πεντακόσιοι**	πεντακοσιοστός
600	χ′	**εξακόσιοι**	εξακοσιοστός
700	ψ′	**επτακόσιοι/εφτακόσιοι**	επτακοσιοστός
800	ω′	**οκτακόσιοι/οχτακόσιοι**	οκτακοσιοστός
900	ϡ′	**εννιακόσιοι/εννεακόσιοι**	εννεακοσιοστός
1,000	͵α	**χίλιοι**	χιλιοστός
2,000	͵β	δύο **χιλιάδες**	δισχιλιοστός
3,000	͵γ	τρεις **χιλιάδες**	τρισχιλιοστός
10,000	͵ι	δέκα **χιλιάδες**	δεκακισχιλιοστός
1,000,000		**ένα εκατομμύριο**	εκατομμυριοστός
1,000,000,000		**ένα δισεκατομμύριο**	δισεκατομμυριοστός
1,000,000,000,000		**ένα τρισεκατομμύριο**	τρισεκατομμυριοστός

1. 'Zero' or 'nought' is the neuter noun μηδέν (nom./acc.), which has a genitive μηδενός (see Section 2.4.9).

2. The two-syllable form δύο 'two' is more emphatic than δυο (pronounced as one syllable); the latter form tends to be used in normal speech.

3. The forms of 7, 17 and 700 with the consonant cluster -φτ- and the forms of 8, 18 and 800 with -χτ- are more colloquial and are avoided in more formal, written styles.

4. In counting, all declinable cardinal numerals are used in their neuter forms, e.g. ένα, δύο, τρία, τέσσερα, διακόσια, χίλια.

5. The cardinal numerals up to 20 consist of one word. From 21 onwards, units,

tens, hundreds etc. are written as separate words, e.g. χίλια τριακόσια πενήντα έξι '1,356'.

6. For the hundreds there are also colloquial forms with omission of -ι- in all genders and cases: διακόσοι, τρακόσοι, τετρακόσοι etc.

7. Some other symbols are used as alphabetic numerals in addition to the normal 24 letters of the alphabet: ς or στ (pronounced στίγμα), ϟ or ϙ (κόππα) and ϡ (σαμπί). (These additional symbols have no upper-case forms.) Alphabetic numerals up to 999 are followed by an acute accent, e.g. ρκα' '121'. Alphabetic numerals from 1,000 onwards are also *preceded* by a subscript acute accent (͵), e.g. ͵α ϡ ϙ ζ' '1997'.

8. The ordinal numerals which have their basic stress on the antepenultimate often have a shift of stress to the penultimate (particularly in formal use) in the following cases: fem. sg. (all cases), masc. and neuter gen. sg., masc. acc. pl., and gen. pl. (all genders). Examples: η τετάρτη τάξη 'the fourth class (or grade)', του δεκάτου ενάτου αιώνα 'of the nineteenth century'. There is an alternative fem. form of δεύτερος 'second': δευτέρα, deriving from *katharevousa*. Note also νιοστός 'n[th]'.

9. When the ordinal numerals consist of two words, both words are declined. Ordinal numerals are often written as an Arabic number followed by the relevant adjectival termination (with a written accent if appropriate to the last word replaced), e.g. ο 20ός [= εικοστός] αιώνας 'the 20th century', του 25ου [= εικοστού πέμπτου] κεφαλαίου 'of the 25th chapter'.

10. Multiplicative numerals end in -πλός and are declined like adjectives in -ος, -η, -ο (Section 3.1). They are: απλός 'single' (or 'simple'), διπλός 'double', τριπλός 'treble', τετραπλός 'quadruple', πενταπλός 'quintuple', εξαπλός 'sextuple', etc. Note also πολλαπλός 'multiple'.

11. Relative numerals end in -πλάσιος and are declined like adjectives in -ος, -α, -ο (Section 3.2), e.g. διπλάσιος 'twofold', τριπλάσιος 'threefold', τετραπλάσιος 'fourfold', δεκαπλάσιος 'tenfold', πολλαπλάσιος 'many times as much'.

12. Collective numerals are feminine nouns formed with one of two suffixes: -άδα (*inclusive* collectives, for a definite number) or -αριά (*approximative* collectives, for an approximate number). The latter forms are usually preceded by the indefinite determiner καμιά. Examples: δυάδα 'a group of two', τριάδα 'group of three, Trinity', τετράδα 'group of four', δωδεκάδα 'dozen', καμιά πενταριά 'about five', καμιά εικοσαριά 'twenty or so'. The approximative collective for 'about 100' has a different form: (καμιά) εκατοστή.

6.2 THE DECLINED FORMS OF CARDINAL NUMERALS

The cardinal numerals 1, 3 and 4, when used alone or in any number ending in any of these digits (except for 11 – ένδεκα – which is indeclinable), are declined as follows:

ένας, μία, ένα 'one'

	M	F	N
Nom.	ένας	μία/μια	ένα
Acc.	ένα(ν)	μία(ν)/μια(ν)	ένα
Gen.	ενός	μιας	ενός

1. It will be seen that these forms are identical to the indefinite article (see Section 1.2). The feminine forms μία and μία(ν), pronounced as two syllables, are more emphatic and stress the singularity of the noun referred to. Thus: *μία καρέκλα* '*one* chair [and only one]' can be contrasted with μια καρέκλα 'a chair', '(any) one chair'.

2. An emphatic form μίας is occasionally found for the fem. gen. (Note that this form is not used for the indefinite article, which can never be emphatic.)

τρεις, τρία 'three'

	M	F	N
Nom.	τρεις	τρεις	τρία
Acc.	τρεις	τρεις	τρία
Gen.	τριών	τριών	τριών

The numeral 13 (δεκατρείς) is declined in the same way, as are all numbers ending in 3: είκοσι τρεις, τριάντα τρεις, etc.

τέσσερις, τέσσερα 'four'

	M	F	N
Nom.	τέσσερις	τέσσερις	τέσσερα
Acc.	τέσσερις	τέσσερις	τέσσερα
Gen.	τεσσάρων	τεσσάρων	τεσσάρων

Similarly the numeral 14 (δεκατέσσερις) and all numbers ending in 4.

The other cardinal numerals which decline are the following:

(a) διακόσιοι, διακόσιες, διακόσια 'two hundred' and all the hundreds follow the plural declension of adjectives in -ος (see Section 3.2). The genitive often undergoes an optional shift of stress, e.g. τριακοσίων, as can the masc. acc., e.g. πεντακοσίους (cf. Section 3.1 note 2);

(b) χίλιοι, χίλιες, χίλια 'a thousand' is also an adjective and follows the same declension, with possible shift of stress, as for the hundreds;

(c) the thousands from 2,000 onwards consist of the cardinal numerals 2, 3, 4 etc. with the feminine plural noun χιλιάδες 'thousands', with which they must agree (rather than with any noun to which the number refers), e.g. είκοσι μία χιλιάδες '21,000'. There is a gen. case χιλιάδων, e.g. δεκατεσσάρων χιλιάδων 'of 14,000';

(d) εκατομμύριο 'million', δισεκατομμύριο 'billion' and τρισεκατομμύριο 'trillion' are neuter nouns, declined like the nouns in Section 2.4.1.

Examples: ένα εκατομμύριο 'a/one million'; είκοσι τέσσερα εκατομμύρια '24 million'; ένα ποσό των δεκατριών εκατομμυρίων δραχμών 'a sum of thirteen million drachmas'.

Examples of complex numerals with nouns:

τριακόσιες τριάντα δύο χιλιάδες τετρακόσιοι ενενήντα τρεις
    κάτοικοι: '332,493 inhabitants'
ένα εκατομμύριο πεντακόσιες πενήντα πέντε χιλιάδες τριακόσιες
    δεκατέσσερις δραχμές: '1,555,314 drachmas'
είκοσι μία χιλιάδες εννιακόσια είκοσι ένα βιβλία: '21,921 books'

For the forms of μισός 'half' in combination with cardinal numerals, for the fractions 'one quarter', 'two thirds' etc., and for further details about other uses of numerals, see Part III, Section 2.7.

7 VERBS

7.1 PRELIMINARY NOTES ON THE VERB SYSTEM

A verb expresses an action, a state or a condition, e.g. in Greek γράφω 'I write' or 'I am writing', πήγαν 'they went', θα βρέξει 'it will rain', νιώθαμε 'we felt', έχεις δει 'you have seen', υπάρχουν 'they exist'. It is generally acknowledged that the verb is the most complex part of the Greek morphological system. Whereas English verbs typically have only a small number of different forms to indicate *person*, *tense* etc. (e.g., 'write', 'writes', 'writing', 'wrote', 'written' represent all the different possible word-forms of the verb 'to write'), most Greek verbs have several dozen different forms. The reason for this is that Greek verbs are inflected for person, *number*, tense, *aspect*, *voice* and – to some extent – *mood*. Unlike English, Greek does not have to use subject pronouns. The ending of the verb always makes it clear whether the subject is in the first, second or third person, singular or plural. Thus in the active present tense of γράφω, the six different forms can in themselves indicate the subject of the verb without the need for the subject pronouns 'I', 'you', 'we' etc. which English would have to use. Greek uses the subject pronouns only for emphasis or to make a necessary distinction (see Section 5.1 and Part III, Section 2.8.1.1.2). Tense information is also indicated, to a significant extent, in the endings of the verb, although Greek also employs various other means of expressing tense and mood: these are mainly periphrases, involving a particle or an auxiliary verb. Below we give some general information about the verb system, before proceeding to consider the different types of verb conjugation.

7.1.1 STEMS AND ENDINGS

It is important, first of all, to make a distinction between *stem* and *ending*. For example, γράφω consists of a stem γραφ- and an ending -ω. The stem tells us that the verb is in the *imperfective* aspect, while the ending indicates that the verb is in the first person singular of a non-past *active* tense (i.e. present, if *imperfective*, or *dependent*, if *perfective*). Therefore these two elements taken together tell us that γράφω is the 1st person sg. of the active present tense. Different endings added to the same stem indicate the different persons of the active present tense: γράφ-εις 'you (sg.) write', γράφ-ει 's/he/it writes', γράφ-ουμε 'we write', γράφ-ετε 'you (pl.) write', γράφ-ουν 'they write'. Most verbs have three different stems, and, although some of the stem changes follow certain predictable patterns (see Section 7.9), for each verb it is necessary to learn all three stems. Let us take, as an example, the verb πληρώνω 'I pay', which consists of the imperfective stem πληρων- and the 1st person singular present ending -ω. In the active voice its simple past πλήρωσα 'I paid' is made up of a stem πληρωσ- and personal ending -α, while the simple past of the **passive** voice πληρώθηκα 'I was paid' consists of the stem πληρωθ- plus the appropriate ending -ηκα (actually made up of **affix** -ηκ- and ending -α, the latter indicating 1st person sg. past). It will be seen that different personal endings are used for different tenses.

7.1.2 TENSE

The categories of tense and aspect are inextricably linked in Greek and thus both are indispensable to a full description of the verb system (which must also cover voice and mood). For present purposes we shall make a distinction between *past* and *non-past tenses*. Tense is thus concerned with the time when an action takes place, and the action is viewed as being either in the past or not in the past. (We omit from the present discussion the 'future tense', which in Greek is formed periphrastically using the particle θα followed by a non-past verb form, and also the perfect tenses, for which see Section 7.1.4.) Most verbs in Greek have two sets of past forms, differentiated by aspect, and both existing (in most cases) in active and passive voice forms (see Section 7.1.5). Thus, for πληρώνω 'I pay', there exist the active forms (1st person sg.) πλήρωσα 'I paid' (simple past) and πλήρωνα 'I was paying' or 'I used to pay' (imperfect), with the corresponding passive forms πληρώθηκα 'I was paid' (simple past) and πληρωνόμουν 'I was being paid' or 'I used to be paid'. The non-past forms of the same verb are, in the active voice, πληρώνω 'I pay' or 'I am paying' (present), and πληρώσω (**dependent**, which is not normally found as an independent verb form); in the passive voice the corresponding forms are πληρώνομαι 'I am paid' or 'I am being paid' (present), and πληρωθώ (dependent).

7.1.3 ASPECT

In the examples given in the preceding section, some of the forms are based on a stem πληρων-, others on a stem πληρωσ-, and others again on a stem πληρωθ-. In order to understand the functions of the different stems we need to make a distinction between the two **aspects**, **imperfective** and **perfective**, a distinction which is of fundamental importance in the Greek verb system and interacts with the system of tenses. Most Greek verbs have both imperfective and perfective stems (but for exceptions see

Section 7.1.9). The imperfective stem is used to form one set of forms (imperfective), while the perfective stem is the basis of another set of forms (perfective). (Most verbs in fact have two different perfective stems, for active and passive voices.) These two groups of forms are distinguished formally by the different stem of the verb and semantically by their aspect. Aspect can be defined as the way an action is viewed by the speaker at the time of the utterance (see Part III, Section 1.5). The imperfective aspect is used when an action is seen as in progress, habitual or repeated. The perfective aspect on the other hand is used when the action is seen as a completed whole, or in a neutral way. Thus in Greek the present tense, e.g. γράφω 'I write' or 'I am writing', is imperfective, as is the imperfect έγραφα 'I used to write' or 'I was writing' or 'I wrote [more than once]', and both are formed on the basis of the imperfective stem γραφ-. On the other hand, the simple past έγραψα 'I wrote' is perfective in aspect and it is formed on the basis of the perfective stem γραψ-. In the case of the two past forms, imperfect and simple past, the appropriate stem is prefixed by an **augment**, the syllable ε-. This augment is normally used only when the verb form has a one-syllable stem beginning with a consonant *and* a one-syllable ending; it then carries the stress. (In the active past the stress tends to fall on the third syllable from the end, whereas in the active non-past the stress falls on the same syllable throughout. On the position of stress in the verb see further Section 7.1.8.) The augment is normally found only in forms of the two active pasts: imperfect and simple past. (For a fuller discussion of the augment see Section 7.10, and for verbal aspect see further Part III, Section 1.5.)

In addition to forming the present and imperfect, the imperfective stem is also used to form the imperfective future and the imperfective imperative (which does not indicate tense). The corresponding perfective forms are the perfective future and the perfective imperative. (In some grammars the terms 'continuous' and 'simple' are used for 'imperfective' and 'perfective' respectively.) The two futures are formed periphrastically in Greek, i.e. they consist of a two-word phrase rather than a single word as in some other languages. Both periphrases employ the particle θα. The imperfective future is made up of this particle together with the present: θα γράφω 'I shall write [repeatedly or habitually]' or 'I shall be writing [when something else happens]'. The perfective future consists of the particle θα with the **dependent**: θα γράψω 'I shall write' (viewed as a simple, single action without reference to its duration or frequency). The dependent, which is formed from the perfective stem with the non-past endings, is often referred to in traditional grammars as the 'aorist subjunctive'. An alternative term, favoured by many theorists, is 'perfective non-past'. In this book we call this part of the verb the 'dependent', because it cannot normally exist independently of either a particle (such as θα, μη(ν), να, or ας) or certain conjunctions. (See further Part III,

Section 1.5.2.1.) The two forms of the imperative, imperfective and perfective, do not in fact exist for all verbs and the aspectual distinction between them is somewhat less rigid than is the case with the forms discussed above (present, dependent, imperfect, simple past, and imperfective and perfective futures).

Taking as our example the verb γράφω 'I write', we can now illustrate how tense and aspect combine to produce the various forms we have discussed (the examples are all in the active voice, first person sg., except for the imperatives, which are in the second person singular). The stems are shown separated from the augment (where relevant) and the personal endings by hyphens. The names of the tenses and moods, as used in this grammar, are shown in bold.

Aspect:	*Imperfective*	*Perfective*
Tense/mood:		
Non-past	γράφ-ω 'I write' (present) 'I am writing' **present**	γράψ-ω **dependent**
Past	έ-γραφ-α 'I was writing' 'I used to write' **imperfect**	έ-γραψ-α 'I wrote' **simple past**
Future	θα γράφ-ω 'I shall write' (e.g. 'often') **imperfective future**	θα γράψ-ω 'I shall write' (e.g. 'now') **perfective future**
Imperative	γρά-φε 'write' (e.g. 'often') **imperfective imperative**	γράψ-ε 'write' (e.g 'now') **perfective imperative**

All the forms in the centre column are based on the imperfective stem γραφ-, while those in the right-hand column use the perfective stem γραψ-. It will be seen that, because English does not have the same kind of aspect system as Greek, it is not possible fully to bring out the differences of aspect in the simple English translations given above. Contextual factors are important. It should be noted particularly that the English simple past 'I wrote' can also be used for what in Greek must be expressed by an imperfect, e.g.:

(1) Έγραφα από ένα κεφάλαιο τη μέρα
    'I wrote a chapter a day'

7.1.4   THE PERFECT TENSES AND THE AUXILIARY VERB έχω

Greek also has a set of three perfect tenses which stand outside the aspectual system of imperfective vs. perfective. The perfect tenses, as in many European languages, use the verb 'to have' as an auxiliary. Before examining the perfect tenses themselves, we shall give the relevant forms of the verb έχω 'I have', which also exists as a verb in its own right. There are three sets of tense forms: present, past, and future, set out below. It also has an imperfective imperative, a conditional, and a gerund, which are formed like those of first conjugation verbs (see Section 7.2). There are no perfective forms and no passive forms for this verb.

Present

'I have'

Sg.	1	έχω	Pl.	1	έχουμε
	2	έχεις		2	έχετε
	3	έχει		3	έχουν(ε)

1. All tables of verbs in this book will be set out in the above way.

2. The alternative endings for the third person plural will be discussed in Section 7.2.1.1.

3. An alternative form of the first person plural, έχομε, is sometimes found in formal or regional usage.

Past

'I had'

Sg.	1	είχα	Pl.	1	είχαμε
	2	είχες		2	είχατε
	3	είχε		3	είχαν(ε)

1. There is only one past tense of έχω. It is formed from the stem είχ- with the appropriate past endings: -α, -ες, -ε, -αμε, -ατε, -αν(ε).

2. The stress remains on the same syllable, the stem of the verb, throughout.

Future

'I shall have'

Sg.	1	θα έχω	Pl.	1	θα έχουμε
	2	θα έχεις		2	θα έχετε
	3	θα έχει		3	θα έχουν(ε)

The future of έχω consists of the particle θα plus the present tense.

These three tenses of the verb έχω combine with a particular part of the verb, the **non-finite**, to form the three perfect tenses. (The non-finite is sometimes called the 'infinitive'; however, its sole use in Greek is to form the perfect tenses.) The non-finite is identical with the third person singular of the dependent, and always ends in -ει. The active non-finite of διαβάζω is διαβάσει, giving the following forms for the perfect tenses:

Perfect	έχω διαβάσει 'I have read' etc.
Pluperfect (or past perfect)	είχα διαβάσει 'I had read' etc.
Future perfect	θα έχω διαβάσει 'I shall have read' etc.

In the three perfect tenses it is the auxiliary verb which conjugates to indicate the person of its subject; the non-finite remains unchanged. (For the use of the perfect tenses see Part III, Sections 1.6.5–1.6.7.) Because the non-finite is based on the dependent, it follows that only verbs which have a dependent can form perfect tenses. Those verbs which do not have a perfective stem (see Section 7.1.9) have no dependent form and therefore do not form perfect tenses.

We have now completed our brief description of tense and aspect in the verb system. We have not discussed certain other verb forms which are formed periphrastically: the conditional and the perfect conditional (their forms will be given in the tables of conjugations in Sections 7.2–7.8). Nor have we considered various moods which use particles like να, μη(ν), ας to express non-indicative modalities (imperative, prohibition, obligation, possibility, etc.), since these belong to the area of syntax. For these see Part III, Section 1.3.

7.1.5   VOICE

So far we have been mainly concerned with verbs in the *active voice*. The active voice is used when the subject of the verb is the initiator of the action in question e.g. 'I **am reading** the book'. If the grammatical subject is the person or thing 'acted upon', i.e. the recipient or sufferer of the action, the verb is in the *passive voice*, e.g. 'This book **has been read** by many people'. In Greek most (but not all) verbs have a second set of forms for each tense, which express the passive voice; that is to say, passive voice is a morphological category. However, there are some verbs which are active in meaning but have only passive forms (deponent verbs). Some common examples are δέχομαι 'I receive, accept', αισθάνομαι 'I feel', εργάζομαι 'I work' and έρχομαι 'I come'. It will be seen that the endings of the first person are quite different from those of the other verbs discussed so far, which are active in form as well as active in meaning. In the morphology sections of this grammar we make the distinction active/passive on the basis of the *form* of the verb, i.e. the endings attached to the verb stem, *not* on the basis of meaning. We must further note that the passive in Greek often has a reflexive or reciprocal meaning, e.g. ντύνομαι 'I dress myself', 'I get dressed' (reflexive), αγαπιόμαστε 'we love one another' (reciprocal). (See Part III, Sections 5.4.3.5.1 and 5.4.3.6.1.)

The forms of the passive voice are also based on imperfective and perfective stems, in the same way as the active tenses. For the imperfective forms – present, imperfect, imperfective future – the same stem is used as for the active but with different endings (see the table in Section 7.1.7). The passive perfective forms – simple past and perfective future, and also the passive perfect tenses and the plural of the passive imperative (but not its singular – see Section 7.2.2.8) – are based on a passive perfective stem which can be formed in a number of different ways. (For a full account see Section 7.9.) The passive simple past and dependent use active-type endings (see the table in Section 7.1.7). Below we give a few examples only, in order to illustrate the diversity of stem formation. The stems are shown separated from the augment (where relevant) and from the first-person endings by hyphens:

Present	Meaning	Active past	Passive simple past
διαβάζ-ω	'I read'	διάβασ-α	διαβάστ-ηκα
κοιτάζ-ω	'I look at'	κοίταξ-α	κοιτάχτ-ηκα
ακού-ω	'I hear'	άκουσ-α	ακούστ-ηκα
γράφ-ω	'I write'	έ-γραψ-α	γράφτ-ηκα or γράφ-ηκα
ντύν-ω	'I dress'	έ-ντυσ-α	ντύθ-ηκα
αγαπ-ώ	'I love'	αγάπησ-α	αγαπήθ-ηκα
θεωρ-ώ	'I consider'	θεώρησ-α	θεωρήθ-ηκα
στέλν-ω	'I send'	έ-στειλ-α	στάλθ-ηκα

7.1.6 THE GERUND AND THE PARTICIPLES

Apart from the verb forms already discussed, mention must also be made of the gerund, the active and passive present participles and the passive perfect participle. The **gerund** has an adverbial function and is active in form and meaning: it refers to an action which takes place simultaneously with the action of the main verb of the sentence or clause and which normally has the same subject. It is formed by the addition of the suffix -οντας or -ώντας to the present stem, according to the type of verb.

(1) Φεύγοντας ο Γιάννης άφησε ένα δώρο για την 'Αννα
    'As he left [lit. 'leaving'] John left a present for Anna'

On the use of the gerund see Part III, Section 1.7.

The *active* and *passive present participles* are adjectival in form and both are based on the imperfective stem, but they are available for a rather limited range of verbs. The active present participle ends in -ων and is declined like the adjectives in Section 3.11. The passive present participle ends in -όμενος, -ώμενος or -ούμενος and is declined like adjectives in -ος (see Section 3.1). The *passive perfect participle* is also an adjective and follows the same declension. It always ends in -μένος (with stress on the penultimate syllable), but its formation is a complex matter and will be examined separately in Section 7.11. More information about the use of these participles is given in Part III, Section 1.8.

7.1.7 SUMMARY OF VERB ENDINGS

The system of endings for the various tenses and moods can now be tabulated. Three preliminary remarks are necessary:

(i)   Greek verbs fall into two main categories (or conjugations): *first conjugation* or *paroxytone* (the more numerous) and *second conjugation* or *oxytone*. This distinction is based on the position of the stress in the first person singular of the present active (which is the 'dictionary form' by which verbs are conventionally listed): 'oxytone' means 'stressed on the last syllable', 'paroxytone' means 'stressed on the penultimate syllable'. Verbs of the first conjugation, such as γράφω 'I write', πηγαίνω 'I go', κοιτάζω 'I look at', are stressed on the last syllable of their stem, that is the penultimate syllable of the first person singular of the present tense. Verbs of the second conjugation are stressed on the final syllable of the first person singular, that is on the ending rather than the stem. This stress difference applies throughout the active present tense: we could in fact refer to the two kinds of verb as 'stem-stressed' and 'ending-stressed', as far as their present tense is concerned. The second-conjugation verbs are subdivided into two types according to the system of vowels which characterize their endings. Type A consists of verbs which conjugate like αγαπώ (1st sg.), αγαπάς (2nd sg.), αγαπάει (3rd sg.) etc. The pattern for type B is represented by θεωρώ (1st sg.), θεωρείς (2nd sg.), θεωρεί (3rd sg.) etc. (There is some interchange between the two categories; see Section 7.3.)
(ii) It must be remembered that the endings shown below are added to *either* the imperfective *or* the perfective stem as appropriate.
(iii) There are many alternative forms within the verb system. This variety (known in Greek as πολυτυπία 'multiplicity of forms') sometimes reflects regional or dialectal variation, sometimes differences of register, or simply the idiolect of the speaker or writer. These alternative endings will be set out in the full tables for each type, in Sections 7.2–7.7.

Verb endings

The following contrastive table shows the most commonly used personal endings for the three main kinds of verb, in the active and passive voices (without the full range of variation mentioned above). There are also certain other types of verb whose endings differ slightly from those in the table (see Sections 7.5–7.7).

	1st conjugation		2nd conjugation: type A		2nd conjugation: type B	
Active voice:	Sg.	Pl.	Sg.	Pl.	Sg.	Pl.
Present	΄-ω	΄-ουμε	-ώ	-άμε	-ώ	-ούμε
	΄-εις	΄-ετε	-άς	-άτε	-είς	-είτε
	΄-ει	΄-ουν	-άει	-ούν	-εί	-ούν
Imperfect	΄--α	΄-αμε	-ούσα	-ούσαμε	-ούσα	-ούσαμε
	΄--ες	΄-ατε	-ούσες	-ούσατε	-ούσες	-ούσατε
	΄--ε	΄--αν	-ούσε	-ούσαν	-ούσε	-ούσαν
Dependent	΄-ω	΄-ουμε	΄-ω	΄-ουμε	΄-ω	΄-ουμε
	΄-εις	΄-ετε	΄-εις	΄-ετε	΄-εις	΄-ετε
	΄-ει	΄-ουν	΄-ει	΄-ουν	΄-ει	΄-ουν
Simple past	΄--α	΄-αμε	΄--α	΄-αμε	΄--α	΄-αμε
	΄--ες	΄-ατε	΄--ες	΄-ατε	΄--ες	΄-ατε
	΄--ε	΄--αν	΄--ε	΄--αν	΄--ε	΄--αν
Imperfective imperative	΄--ε/΄-ε	΄-ετε	΄-α	-άτε	(lacking)	-είτε
Perfective imperative	΄--ε/΄-ε	΄-(ε)τε	΄--ε	΄-τε	΄--ε	΄-τε
Gerund	΄-οντας		-ώντας		-ώντας	

Passive voice:	Sg.	Pl.	Sg.	Pl.	Sg.	Pl.
Present	΄-ομαι	-όμαστε	-ιέμαι	-ιόμαστε	-ούμαι	-ούμαστε
	΄-εσαι	΄-εστε	-ιέσαι	-ιέστε	-είσαι	-είστε
	΄-εται	΄-ονται	-ιέται	-ιούνται	-είται	-ούνται
Imperfect	-όμουν	-όμασταν	-ιόμουν	-ιόμασταν	-ούμουν	-ούμασταν
	-όσουν	-όσασταν	-ιόσουν	-ιόσασταν	-ούσουν	-ούσασταν
	-όταν	΄-ονταν	-ιόταν	-ιούνταν	-ούνταν	-ούνταν
Dependent	-ώ	-ούμε	-ώ	-ούμε	-ώ	-ούμε
	-είς	-είτε	-είς	-είτε	-είς	-είτε
	-εί	-ούν	-εί	-ούν	-εί	-ούν
Simple past	΄-ηκα	-ήκαμε	΄-ηκα	-ήκαμε	΄-ηκα	-ήκαμε
	΄-ηκες	-ήκατε	΄-ηκες	-ήκατε	΄-ηκες	-ήκατε
	΄-ηκε	΄-ηκαν	΄-ηκε	΄-ηκαν	΄-ηκε	΄-ηκαν
Imperfective imperative	(lacking)		(lacking)		(lacking)	
Perfective imperative	΄-ου	-είτε	΄-ου	-είτε	΄-ου	-είτε

It can be seen that the two active past tenses and the passive simple past share a common set of endings -α, -ες, -ε, -αμε, -ατε, -αν, except that: (i) in the active imperfect the second-conjugation verbs have an additional syllable -ούσ- before these endings, and (ii) all the passive simple past forms have an affix syllable -ηκ- before the ending. The above table omits one other factor which complicates the picture: the possible presence of an augment in the active imperfect and simple past tenses (this will be discussed, where relevant, in the notes to each paradigm and also in Section 7.10). Finally, the position of stress is indicated in the table with an accent mark over the relevant syllable of the stem or ending (e.g., ΄-α means that the stress is on the antepenultimate, ΄-ω stress on the penultimate). The basic rules of stress in the verb forms are presented in the following section; further information will be given with the complete tables of conjugations.

7.1.8 STRESS

We shall examine separately the stress of past and non-past forms of the verb, since somewhat different rules apply to them. In the *past forms* (imperfect and simple past) the stress follows the antepenultimate rule (see Part I, Section 1.3.2.1), i.e. it retreats to the antepenultimate syllable, or falls on the first syllable in the case of a two-syllable form, e.g. διάβαζες 'you were reading', πληρώσαμε 'we paid', βιάστηκαν 'they hurried', πήραν 'they took', μπήκε 's/he entered'. There are two exceptions: (i) in the active imperfect of second-conjugation verbs the stress always falls on the affix syllable -ούσ-, e.g. μιλούσε 's/he was talking', περπατούσαμε 'we were walking'; (ii) in the passive imperfect the stress falls on the first syllable of the ending, except that in the third person plural of first-conjugation verbs it falls on the antepenultimate, e.g. ερχόταν 's/he was coming', βαριόμασταν 'we were fed up', συναντιούνταν 'they used to meet', but έρχονταν 'they were coming'.

  In the *active non-past forms* (present and dependent) the stress falls on the last syllable of the appropriate stem, except for the present forms of second-conjugation verbs, which are stressed on the first syllable of the ending, e.g. διαβάζουν 'they read/are reading', θα απαντήσουμε 'we shall answer', but φυσάει 'it is windy [lit. it blows]', μιλάτε 'you (pl.) speak/are speaking'. In the *passive present forms* of the first conjugation the stress falls on the antepenultimate, while in second-conjugation verbs the stress falls on the first syllable of the ending, e.g. διαβάζεται 'it is (being) read', εργάζεστε 'you (pl.) work/are working', but βαριέται 's/he is fed up', στερείστε 'you are deprived'. The *passive dependent forms* are always stressed on the first syllable of the ending, e.g. θα δοθεί 'it will be given', θα τηλεφωνηθούμε 'we shall telephone one another'.

Special mention must be made of verbs which have two adjacent vowels in the last syllable(s) of their imperfective stem, of which the first is /i/. It is necessary to know whether the /i/ is pronounced as the vowel [i] or is non-vocalic, because this affects the position of stress in the active imperfect and simple past: non-vocalic /i/ is not counted as a syllable and therefore the stress, if it would normally fall there, retreats to the preceding syllable. This factor also determines whether a verb with a monosyllabic stem takes the augment. For example, αδειάζω [aðjázo] 'I empty' has imperfect άδειαζα [áðjaza] and simple past άδειασα [áðjasa], and διώχνω [ðjóxno] 'I chase away, expel' goes to έδιωχνα [éðjoxna] (imperf.) and έδιωξα [éðjoksa] (simple past), both with augment. In other cases the two vowels retain their syllabic value, e.g. σχεδιάζω [sx'eðiázo] 'I plan', σχεδίαζα [sx'eðíaza] (imperf.), σχεδίασα [sx'eðíasa] (simple past), while a few verbs have imperfect and simple past forms of both types. Some examples follow.

(i)   Verbs with non-syllabic /i/, e.g. νιώθω 'I feel', imperf. ένιωθα, simple past ένιωσα:

αδειάζω 'I empty', αναγαλλιάζω 'I am delighted', αναμαλλιάζω 'I ruffle [someone's hair]', ανατριχιάζω 'I shiver', διώχνω 'I chase away, expel', θεμελιώνω 'I found, establish', θεριεύω 'I grow fast', ισιώνω 'I straighten', κακιώνω 'I sulk', λιώνω 'I melt', μετανιώνω 'I repent', μοιάζω 'I resemble', μονοιάζω 'I reconcile/am reconciled', παλιώνω 'I become old', πιάνω 'I catch', σαλιώνω 'I lick', σιάζω or σιάχνω 'I fix, straighten', στεριώνω 'I make firm', στοιχειώνω 'I become a ghost, haunt', φιλιώνω 'I conciliate, become friends', φτιάχνω 'I make', and most verbs in -ιάζω, except those listed in (ii).

(ii)   Verbs with syllabic /i/, e.g. εντυπωσιάζω 'I impress', imperf. εντυπωσίαζα, simple past εντυπωσίασα:

αγριεύω 'I frighten, rouse', αηδιάζω 'I detest', αιφνιδιάζω 'I surprise', αλλοιώνω 'I alter, spoil', απουσιάζω 'I am absent', βιάζω 'I force, rape', ενθουσιάζω 'I fill with enthusiasm, enthuse', εξουσιάζω 'I dominate, rule', εξυγιαίνω 'I make healthy', επισκιάζω 'I overshadow', θυσιάζω 'I sacrifice', μετριάζω 'I moderate, mitigate', νευριάζω 'I exasperate', παρουσιάζω 'I present', πλησιάζω 'I approach', συνεδριάζω 'I meet in session', σχεδιάζω 'I plan, sketch', σχολιάζω 'I comment on', χλιαίνω 'I make/become lukewarm', ωχριώ 'I become pale'.

(iii) Verbs which can have both types of form, e.g. τελειώνω 'I finish', imperf. τέλειωνα or τελείωνα, simple past τέλειωσα or τελείωσα.

7.1.9   DEFECTIVE, IMPERSONAL AND DEPONENT VERBS

It should be noted that not all verbs have a complete set of forms for all tenses, all persons, or both voices (active and passive). There are three kinds of 'deficiency':

(i) *Defective* verbs have no perfective aspect and exist only in the imperfective forms. Examples:

ανήκω 'I belong', απεχθάνομαι 'I loathe', ασθμαίνω 'I pant/am breathless', βρίθω 'I am full (of)', γειτονεύω 'I am in the neighbourhood (of)', διεγείρω 'I excite', διέπω 'I govern', είμαι 'I am', έρπω 'I crawl', ευθύνομαι 'I am responsible', έχω 'I have', λάμνω 'I row', μάχομαι 'I fight', μέλλω 'I am about to/destined to', ξέρω 'I know', οδύρομαι 'I (be)wail', οφείλω 'I owe/am obliged', περιμένω 'I wait (for)', ρέπω 'I incline', τρέμω 'I tremble', χάσκω 'I gape', χρωστώ 'I owe'

(ii) *Impersonal* verbs have only third-person singular forms (see Part III, Section 1.2.2). Examples:

πρέπει 'it is necessary (that)', πρόκειται 'be about to'

(iii) *Deponent* verbs have only passive *forms* (although they may be active in meaning). Examples (from this very numerous category):

αισθάνομαι 'I feel', απολογούμαι 'I defend myself', αρνούμαι 'I refuse', αφηγούμαι 'I narrate', εργάζομαι 'I work', μιμούμαι 'I imitate', φαίνομαι 'I appear/seem', φοβάμαι 'I fear'.

7.1.10   THE VERB TABLES: PRELIMINARY REMARKS

In Sections 7.2-7.7 we present the full range of forms of all verbs according to their conjugation (first conjugation; second conjugation types A and B; and some deviant patterns that apply to certain verbs only). Notes on the formation of each tense or mood are given after the appropriate paradigm. Alternative forms are discussed and some special factors concerning the usage of different forms are noted. Section 7.8 gives the forms of the copular verb είμαι 'I am'. The formation of the active and passive perfective stems is considered in Section 7.9.

7.2   FIRST CONJUGATION VERBS (PAROXYTONE)

The category of first conjugation (or ***paroxytone***) verbs, which are by far the most numerous in Greek, includes all verbs stressed on the last syllable of their stem in the present tense: that is, active verbs ending in ´-ω and passive or deponent verbs ending in ´-ομαι.

7.2.1   ACTIVE VOICE

7.2.1.1   Present

'I tie'

Sg.	1	δένω	Pl.	1	δένουμε
	2	δένεις		2	δένετε
	3	δένει		3	δένουν(ε)

1. The stress remains on the same syllable throughout.

2. There is an alternative form of the 1st person pl., in -ομε, which is sometimes found in formal use but also in some regional forms of Greek.

3. The form of the 3rd person pl. with the additional syllable -ε is frequent in the spoken language, but less often used in more formal contexts. (Cf. the corresponding forms of the active imperfect, simple past and dependent, and the passive simple past and dependent.)

7.2.1.2   Imperfect

'I was tying/used to tie'

Sg.	1	έδενα	Pl.	1	δέναμε
	2	έδενες		2	δένατε
	3	έδενε		3	έδεναν/δένανε

1. The imperfect is based on the imperfective stem (i.e. the same stem as the present tense), to which the active past endings are attached. When the stem begins with a consonant and the stem and ending together consist of two syllables only, an augment ε- is prefixed to the stem. The stress of the imperfect goes back as far as possible, i.e. to the antepenultimate. Accordingly the augment carries the stress in the singular and in the 3rd person plural form έδεναν. Verbs of more than two syllables like κοιτάζω 'I look at', διαβάζω 'I read', do not normally take an augment.

2. The alternative 3rd person pl. forms are more or less interchangeable (note the difference of stress), though the form with -ε is more colloquial. A form without -ε but with stress on the penultimate is sometimes found in non-formal contexts: δέναν, πηγαίναν.

7.2.1.3   Simple past

'I tied'

Sg.	1	έδεσα	Pl.	1	δέσαμε
	2	έδεσες		2	δέσατε
	3	έδεσε		3	έδεσαν/δέσανε

1. The simple past (the 'aorist' of traditional Greek grammars) is based on the active perfective stem, with the same endings as the imperfect. For the formation of perfective stems see Section 7.9.

2. The rules for augment and position of stress are the same as for the imperfect (see above). Some common verbs have a simple past with a one-syllable stem and no augment, e.g. πήρα 'I took' from παίρνω, ήπια 'I drank' from πίνω (where the η- is a kind of augment), πήγα 'I went' from πηγαίνω, βγήκα 'I went out' from βγαίνω etc. For such irregular forms see the table of irregular verbs in Section 7.13.

3. There is an alternative, non-formal 3rd person pl. in -αν stressed on the penultimate: δέσαν.

7.2.1.4 Dependent

(no equivalent in English)

Sg.	1	δέσω	Pl.	1	δέσουμε
	2	δέσεις		2	δέσετε
	3	δέσει		3	δέσουν(ε)

1. The dependent is based on the active perfective stem (see Section 7.9 for its formation), with the same endings as the present tense. For alternative spellings of the endings see Section 7.12.

2. There is an alternative form of the 1st person pl. in -ομε, which sometimes occurs in formal and regional use.

7.2.1.5 Perfect

'I have tied'

Sg.	1	έχω δέσει	Pl.	1	έχουμε δέσει
	2	έχεις δέσει		2	έχετε δέσει
	3	έχει δέσει		3	έχουν(ε) δέσει

1. The perfect tense is formed periphrastically and consists of the auxiliary verb έχω and the non-finite, which is identical to the 3rd person sg. of the dependent.

2. There is an alternative, but very much rarer, way of forming the perfect tenses when the verb is transitive: έχω is combined with the passive perfect participle, which is an adjective agreeing with the object of the verb: έχω δεμένο 'I have tied'. (The pluperfect and future perfect can also be formed in the same way.) For the distinction between the two constructions see Part III, Section 1.6.9.

7.2.1.6 Pluperfect

'I had tied'

Sg.	1	είχα δέσει	Pl.	1	είχαμε δέσει
	2	είχες δέσει		2	είχατε δέσει
	3	είχε δέσει		3	είχαν(ε) δέσει

The pluperfect consists of the past tense of έχω with the non-finite.

7.2.1.7   Future, conditional, etc. (forms with θα)

The two future forms, together with the future perfect and the conditional and perfect conditional, are all formed with the particle θα, as follows:

Imperfective future	θα δένω etc. (θα + present) 'I shall tie [more than once]'
Perfective future	θα δέσω etc. (θα + dependent) 'I shall tie'
Future perfect	θα έχω δέσει etc. (θα + perfect) 'I shall have tied'
Conditional	θα έδενα etc. (θα + imperfect) 'I would tie'
Perfect conditional	θα είχα δέσει etc. (θα + pluperfect) 'I would have tied'

7.2.1.8   Imperfective imperative

'tie!'

Sg.	δένε	Pl.	δένετε

1. The imperfective imperative has only 2nd-person forms. The singular is formed from the imperfective stem with the ending -ε. The plural is identical to the 2nd person pl. of the present tense. In verbs of more than two syllables the stress of the singular imperative goes back to the antepenultimate: διάβαζε 'read', πλήρωνε 'pay', αντίγραφε 'copy'. For alternative ways of expressing the imperative mood, see Part III, Section 1.3.3.

2. Two common verbs with irregularly formed imperfective imperatives are τρέχω 'I run' (sg. τρέχα, pl. τρεχάτε) and φεύγω 'I leave, go away' (sg. φεύγα, pl. φευγάτε).

7.2.1.9   Perfective imperative

'tie!'

Sg.	δέσε	Pl.	δέστε

1. The perfective imperative, like the imperfective imperative, has only 2nd-person forms. It is formed from the perfective stem, with the endings -ε for the singular and -(ε)τε for the plural. In the plural the ending is normally reduced to -τε when the stem ends in one of the following: λ ρ σ ξ ψ, e.g. στείλτε 'send', πάρτε 'take', καθίστε 'sit down', κοιτάξτε 'look', γράψτε 'write', but μάθετε 'learn', φύγετε 'go away'. The full ending is, however, sometimes used in formal contexts, e.g. περιγράψετε 'describe'. Verbs with a stem ending in -ν- sometimes have the reduced plural ending; the commonest example is κάντε 'do' (pronounced [kánte]). For alternative ways of expressing the imperative mood, see Part III, Section 1.3.3.

2. Singular imperatives which have a stem ending in λ ρ σ ξ or ψ often lose the final -ε when followed by a 3rd-person weak pronoun or a definite article in

the acc. or gen. case. This also occurs in the singular imperative of κάνω 'I do/make'. It is usual to write an apostrophe to indicate the loss of the syllable, e.g. στείλ' τον 'send him', κόψ' το 'cut it', φέρ' τα λεφτά 'bring the money', βούλωσ' το 'shut up!', κάν' το 'do it'. The same thing happens with the singular imperative of δίνω 'I give' when followed by a 1st-person weak pronoun: δώσ' μου 'give me'.

3. Plural imperatives of verbs with a perfective stem ending in ξ or ψ are occasionally found with the consonant changed to χ or φ respectively, e.g. ρίχτε 'throw' alongside ρίξτε, κοιτάχτε 'look' or κοιτάξτε, αλείφτε 'spread, smear' or αλείψτε. A similar sound change may occur in the singular form, when followed by a weak 3rd-person pronoun, e.g. ρίχ' το 'throw it', κόφ' τα 'cut them'.

4. A number of verbs form their perfective imperative in irregular ways. For such verbs see the Table of irregular verbs, Section 7.13.

7.2.1.10 Gerund and participles

Gerund	δένοντας 'tying'
Perfect gerund	έχοντας δέσει 'having tied'
Present participle	(lacking for this verb)

1. The gerund is formed from the imperfective stem with the ending -οντας. The stress falls on the last syllable of the stem. The perfect gerund, which is rather less common, is formed from the gerund of the auxiliary verb έχω and the nonfinite (for which see Section 7.1.4).

2. The active present participle, which is of learned origin, does not exist for all verbs. It is adjectival in form and meaning, consisting of the imperfective stem with the endings -ων, -ουσα, -ον (see Section 3.11 for the declension). Examples: γράφων 'writing', βασιλεύων 'reigning', ισχύων '(being) valid', σημαίνων 'significant'. For the use of the active present participle see Part III, Section 1.8.1.1.

7.2.2 PASSIVE VOICE

7.2.2.1 Present

'I am (being) tied'

Sg.	1	δένομαι	Pl.	1	δενόμαστε
	2	δένεσαι		2	δένεστε/δενόσαστε
	3	δένεται		3	δένονται

1. The passive present tense is formed from the imperfective stem. The stress remains on the stem except in the 1st person pl. and in the alternative 2nd person pl. in -όσαστε.

2. Of the two alternative forms for the 2nd person pl., δένεστε is preferred in formal use, while δενόσαστε is colloquial.

7.2.2.2   Imperfect

'I was being tied/used to be tied'

Sg.	1	δενόμουν(α)	Pl.	1	δενόμασταν/δενόμαστε
	2	δενόσουν(α)		2	δενόσασταν/δενόσαστε
	3	δενόταν(ε)		3	δένονταν/δενόντανε/
					δενόντουσαν

1. The imperfect is based on the imperfective stem, in this case δεν-, with a varied set of endings. For every person at least two options exist. In the 1st and 2nd persons pl. the forms with -αν make a clear distinction between present and imperfect, but the forms in -ε are also very widely used. The sg. forms with a final vowel -α/-ε are colloquial (non-formal). In the 3rd person pl. the form δένονταν is more formal (and tends to be recommended by grammarians), while δενόντουσαν is the more common alternative (at least in Athenian speech).

2. The stress of all these forms falls on the antepenultimate, with the exception of the shorter forms of the singular, which have penultimate stress: -όμουν etc.

7.2.2.3   Simple past

'I was tied'

Sg.	1	δέθηκα	Pl.	1	δεθήκαμε
	2	δέθηκες		2	δεθήκατε
	3	δέθηκε		3	δέθηκαν/δεθήκανε

1. This tense can be seen as consisting of three elements: the passive perfective stem (for the formation see Section 7.9), an affix -ηκ-, and the personal endings – which are identical with those of the active simple past and imperfect. The stress falls on the antepenultimate in all forms.

2. There are also learned forms for the 3rd person sg. and pl., ending in -η and -ησαν respectively, and with augment. They can be found in journalism and other kinds of formal writing, and, to a limited extent, in the spoken language too. These are usually clichés inherited from *katharevousa* and restricted to a rather small range of verbs, e.g. συνελήφθη 's/he was arrested', pl. συνελήφθησαν (from συλλαμβάνω), ελέχθη 'it was said' (from λέγω). For some of these verbs the more demotic forms do not exist. In other cases the two alternatives correspond to more formal and less formal registers: ανεκοινώθη vs. ανακοινώθηκε 'it was announced', προσελήφθησαν vs. προσλήφθηκαν 'they were taken on [as employees]'. For such forms see further Section 7.12.

7.2.2.4   Dependent

(no equivalent in English)

Sg.	1	δεθώ	Pl.	1	δεθούμε
	2	δεθείς		2	δεθείτε
	3	δεθεί		3	δεθούν(ε)

1. The passive dependent uses the same stem as the passive simple past, i.e. the passive perfective stem. The personal endings are identical to those of the active present tense of verbs of the second conjugation, type B. The stress always falls on these endings, never on the stem.

2. The same endings are also used by certain active verbs that have dependents in -ω: βγω from βγαίνω 'I go out', βρω from βρίσκω 'I find', διαβώ from διαβαίνω 'I pass by/through', δω from βλέπω 'I see', μπω from μπαίνω 'I go in', πω from λέω 'I say'; similarly 'ρθώ (only after να or θα) from the irregular deponent verb έρχομαι 'I come'. All these forms are stressed on the endings (but the accent is not written on the monosyllabic forms). See also Section 7.6.

7.2.2.5   Perfect

'I have been tied'

Sg.	1	έχω δεθεί	Pl.	1	έχουμε δεθεί
	2	έχεις δεθεί		2	έχετε δεθεί
	3	έχει δεθεί		3	έχουν(ε) δεθεί

The passive perfect consists of the auxiliary verb έχω and the passive non-finite (identical to the 3rd person singular of the passive dependent).

7.2.2.6   Pluperfect

'I had been tied'

Sg.	1	είχα δεθεί	Pl.	1	είχαμε δεθεί
	2	είχες δεθεί		2	είχατε δεθεί
	3	είχε δεθεί		3	είχαν(ε) δεθεί

The pluperfect is formed like the perfect, but with the past tense of έχω as the auxiliary.

7.2.2.7   Future, conditional, etc. (forms with θα)

These are formed in the same way as their active counterparts, using the corresponding passive forms.

Imperfective future	θα δένομαι etc. (θα + present) 'I shall be tied [more than once]'

Perfective future	θα δεθώ etc. (θα + dependent) 'I shall be tied'
Future perfect	θα έχω δεθεί etc. (θα + perfect) 'I shall have been tied'
Conditional	θα δενόμουν(α) etc. (θα + imperfect) 'I would be tied'
Perfect conditional	θα είχα δεθεί etc. (θα + pluperfect) 'I would have been tied'

7.2.2.8 Perfective imperative

'be tied/tie yourself!'

Sg.   δέσου   Pl.   δεθείτε

1. The singular and plural forms are formed from different stems: the singular adds the ending -ου to the *active* perfective stem (or, in the case of deponent verbs, what the active perfective stem would have been). Examples are: ντύσου 'get dressed', χάσου 'get lost', and from deponent verbs σκέψου 'think' from σκέφτομαι, φαντάσου 'imagine' from φαντάζομαι. The stress is always on the penultimate. The plural form is the same as the 2nd person pl. of the passive dependent, and thus is based on the passive perfective stem.

2. An alternative way of expressing a command is by means of the particle να together with (for the perfective aspect) the 2nd person (sg. or pl.) of the dependent. There is no passive *imperfective* imperative form in existence today. However, an imperfective imperative can also be expressed periphrastically with the particle να and the 2nd person (sg. or pl.) of the passive present, e.g. να ντύνεσαι 'dress yourself'. For such constructions see Part III, Section 1.3.3.

3. The verb σηκώνομαι 'I get up' has an irregular singular imperative σήκω.

7.2.2.9 Present participle

-όμενος, -η, -ο (lacking for this verb)

1. Although δένω lacks a passive present participle, this form is quite often used for some verbs. It is formed from the imperfective stem with the ending -όμενος, and it declines like the adjectives in Section 3.1. Examples:

αναμενόμενος 'expected', διαδραματιζόμενος 'being enacted', διαμαρτυρόμενος 'protesting, protestant', ενδεχόμενος 'possible', επόμενος 'following', εργαζόμενος 'working', ερχόμενος 'coming', προστατευόμενος 'protected, protégé'.

2. It is important to note that the present participle always expresses an action in progress, or a repeated action, or a state or condition; it never refers to a completed action. For the use of this participle see Part III, Section 1.8.2.2.

7.2.2.10 Perfect participle

δεμένος, -η, -ο (declined like adjectives in Section 3.1)

1. The passive perfect participle always ends in -μένος (stressed on the penultimate) and declines like an adjective. The stem is formed in a variety of ways, for which see Section 7.11. For the use of this participle see Part III, Section 1.8.2.1.

2. In a few cases perfect participles show **reduplication**, whereby the initial consonant is repeated with the vowel ε before the stem; or, for verbs beginning with certain consonant clusters, an ε is prefixed to the stem ; or, in the case of stems beginning with ε-, α- or αι-, the vowel becomes η-. This is essentially a learned feature and is non-productive. Some examples:

βεβιασμένος 'forced' (from βιάζω), τετριμμένος 'well-worn, trite' (of e.g. arguments) (contrast the normal perfect participle of τρίβω: τριμμένος 'rubbed'), πεπεισμένος 'convinced' (from πείθω), εσκεμμένος 'deliberate' (from σκέπτομαι), εσφαλμένος 'mistaken' (from σφάλλω), ηνωμένος 'united' (in addition to ενωμένος, from ενώνω).

Further information on reduplication is given in Section 7.11.1.

7.3   SECOND CONJUGATION VERBS (OXYTONE TYPE A)

Second conjugation (or **oxytone**) verbs are defined as those verbs which have an active present 1st person singular stressed on the final syllable. They basically divide into two types: (1) type A, with (usually) an alternative 1st person singular in -άω and characterized by the α vowel in the active present tense endings; (2) type B, with no alternative 1st person singular, and with the vowels ει or ου in the remaining personal endings of the active present tense. There are also differences in the passive imperfective tenses. Some verbs can follow either type. Because dictionaries do not always give this essential information, we list below the most common verbs which follow type A:

αγαπώ 'I love', απαντώ 'I answer', βαστώ 'I bear', βουτώ 'I dive', γελώ 'I laugh', γλεντώ 'I celebrate', διψώ 'I am thirsty', κεντώ 'I embroider', κολλώ 'I stick', κρεμώ 'I hang', κυβερνώ 'I govern', μελετώ 'I study', μετρώ 'I count', μιλώ 'I speak', νικώ 'I conquer', ξενυχτώ 'I stay up at night', ξεχνώ 'I forget', ξυπνώ 'I (a)wake', πατώ 'I step, tread', πεινώ 'I am hungry', περνώ 'I pass', περπατώ 'I walk', πετώ 'I fly, throw', πηδώ 'I jump', πουλώ 'I sell', προτιμώ 'I prefer', ρουφώ 'I suck', ρωτώ 'I ask', σκουντώ 'I shove', σπω 'I break', σταματώ 'I stop', τιμώ 'I honour', τραβώ 'I pull', τρυπώ 'I drill', τσιμπώ 'I prick, sting', φυσώ 'I blow', χαιρετώ 'I greet', χαλώ 'I break, spoil', χτυπώ 'I hit'. (The following do not have the alternative 1st person sg. in -άω, 3rd sg. in -άει, 1st pl. in -άμε, or 3rd pl. in -άνε: αντανακλώ 'I reflect', αντιδρώ 'I react', αποκτώ

'I acquire', αποσπώ 'I detach', διαθλώ 'I refract', διασπώ 'I split, break through', δρω 'I act', επιδρώ 'I influence', προσδοκώ 'I expect', ωχριώ 'I turn pale'.)

The following can follow either type A or type B:

ακολουθώ 'I follow', κατηγορώ 'I accuse', καταφρονώ 'I despise', κινώ 'I set off' (but as type B in the sense 'I move'), κοινωνώ 'I receive communion', κρατώ 'I hold' (but normally as type A), κυκλοφορώ 'I circulate', λαλώ 'I talk, warble' (as type B only in 2nd person sg.), λιποθυμώ 'I faint', μαρτυρώ 'I bear witness', οικονομώ 'I save (money)', παρηγορώ 'I console', προχωρώ 'I go forward', συζητώ 'I discuss', συμπαθώ 'I like, forgive', τηλεφωνώ 'I tele-phone', τυραννώ 'I torture', φιλώ 'I kiss', φυλλομετρώ 'I leaf through', χωρώ 'I fit in, have room' (as type B only in certain phrases). In the case of many of these verbs the use of type B endings is regarded as more formal.

7.3.1   ACTIVE VOICE

7.3.1.1 Present

'I love'

Sg.	1	αγαπώ/αγαπάω	Pl.	1	αγαπάμε/αγαπούμε
	2	αγαπάς		2	αγαπάτε
	3	αγαπάει/αγαπά		3	αγαπούν(ε)/αγαπάνε

The present tense is characterized by the stressed vowel α in its endings although, as will be seen in the table above, the 1st persons sg. and pl. and the 3rd person pl. have alternative endings with a different stressed vowel. The forms in -άω, -άει, -άμε and -άνε are non-formal and are not available for all verbs (see the list in Section 7.3). Otherwise the choice between alternative forms is largely a matter of personal preference, with some regional variation.

7.3.1.2   Imperfect

'I used to love'

Sg.	1	αγαπούσα	Pl.	1	αγαπούσαμε
	2	αγαπούσες		2	αγαπούσατε
	3	αγαπούσε		3	αγαπούσαν(ε)

Alternative forms:

Sg.	1	αγάπαγα	Pl.	1	αγαπάγαμε
	2	αγάπαγες		2	αγαπάγατε
	3	αγάπαγε		3	αγάπαγαν/αγαπάγανε

1. The first of these two sets of forms is available for all second conjugation verbs of both types. The endings attached to the imperfective stem consist of an affix -ούσ-, which always carries the stress, and the same past endings as the paroxytone verbs have.

2. The alternative paradigm is applicable only to second conjugation verbs of type A; while these endings are in frequent use in central and southern Greece, they are much rarer in some parts of northern Greece, particularly Macedonia. These endings have an affix -αγ-, to which the standard past endings are added. The stress retreats to the antepenultimate in all persons. These alternative forms are normally avoided in formal contexts.

3. The augment is not normally used in verbs of this kind.

7.3.1.3 Simple past

'I loved'

Sg.			Pl.		
	1	αγάπησα		1	αγαπήσαμε
	2	αγάπησες		2	αγαπήσατε
	3	αγάπησε		3	αγάπησαν/αγαπήσανε

1. The endings are the same as those of the simple past of first conjugation verbs, added to the active perfective stem, which normally consists of the imperfective stem plus an additional syllable -ησ-. The stress falls on the antepenultimate in all persons.

2. Some verbs of this type form their active perfective stems (from which the dependent and the perfective imperative are formed, as well as the simple past) in other ways. We give some examples below, grouped according to the ending of the simple past:

(i)   in -ασα: αντανακλώ, γελώ, διψώ, κρεμώ, πεινώ, σχολώ, χαλώ.
(ii) in -ασα with omission of the -ν- of the imperfective stem: γερνώ (simple past γέρασα), κερνώ, περνώ, ξερνώ, ξεχνώ.
(iii) in -αξα: βαστώ, πετώ, φυλάω (the present is never *φυλώ).
(iv) in -ηξα: βογκώ, βουτώ, βροντώ (as well as βρόντησα), ζουλώ, πηδώ, ρουφώ, σκουντώ, στραμπουλώ, τραβώ, φυσώ, χυμώ.
(v)   in -εσα: πονώ, χωρώ.

See also Section 7.9.2.

3. There is not normally an augment in the simple past of verbs of this type. However, two verbs do have the augment in the simple past, 1st, 2nd and 3rd persons singular and 3rd person plural: δρω – έδρασα, σπάω – έσπασα (for which there is an alternative present σπάζω).

7.3.1.4   Dependent

(no equivalent in English)

Sg.	1	αγαπήσω	Pl.	1	αγαπήσουμε
	2	αγαπήσεις		2	αγαπήσετε
	3	αγαπήσει		3	αγαπήσουν(ε)

1. The dependent is based on the perfective stem with the same endings and stress as the dependent (and as the present) of first conjugation verbs (see Section 7.2.1.4).

2. There is an alternative form of the 1st person pl. in -ομε, which sometimes occurs in formal and regional use.

7.3.1.5   Perfect

'I have loved'

Sg.	1	έχω αγαπήσει	Pl.	1	έχουμε αγαπήσει
	2	έχεις αγαπήσει		2	έχετε αγαπήσει
	3	έχει αγαπήσει		3	έχουν(ε) αγαπήσει

As for first-conjugation verbs, the perfect consists of the auxiliary verb έχω with the non-finite (which is identical with the 3rd person singular of the dependent).

7.3.1.6   Pluperfect

'I had loved'

Sg.	1	είχα αγαπήσει	Pl.	1	είχαμε αγαπήσει
	2	είχες αγαπήσει		2	είχατε αγαπήσει
	3	είχε αγαπήσει		3	είχαν(ε) αγαπήσει

The pluperfect consists of the past tense of έχω with the non-finite.

7.3.1.7   Future, conditional, etc. (forms with θα)

Imperfective future	θα αγαπώ etc. (θα + present) 'I shall love/ continue to love'
Perfective future	θα αγαπήσω etc. (θα + dependent) 'I shall love'
Future perfect	θα έχω αγαπήσει etc. (θα + perfect) 'I shall have loved'
Conditional	θα αγαπούσα or θα αγάπαγα etc. (θα + imperfect) 'I would love'
Perfect conditional	θα είχα αγαπήσει etc. (θα + pluperfect) 'I would have loved'

7.3.1.8   Imperfective imperative

'love!'

Sg.   αγάπα   Pl.   αγαπάτε

1. The active imperfective imperative consists of the imperfective stem with the endings -α (sg.), -άτε (pl.). The stress falls on the penultimate in both cases.

2. There are also alternative ways of expressing a command, for which see Part III, Section 1.3.3.

7.3.1.9   Perfective imperative

'love!'

Sg.   αγάπησε   Pl.   αγαπήστε

1. The perfective imperative consists of the perfective stem with the endings -ε (sg.) and -τε (pl.). The singular form is stressed on the antepenultimate, while in the plural the stress falls on the penultimate; some further examples (sg. and pl.): κρέμασε, κρεμάστε 'hang', τράβηξε, τραβήξτε 'pull', πέταξε, πετάξτε 'throw'.

2. There is a more formal ending -ετε of the plural, with stress on the antepenultimate, e.g. απαντήσετε 'answer'.

7.3.1.10   Gerund and participles

Gerund   αγαπώντας 'loving'
Perfect gerund   έχοντας αγαπήσει 'having loved'
Present participle   -ών, -ώσα, -ών (lacking for this verb)

1. The gerund of second conjugation verbs has the ending -ώντας, attached to the imperfective stem. The perfect gerund consists of the gerund of έχω with the non-finite.

2. The present participle is declined like an adjective, with nominative singular forms in -ών, -ώσα, ών. (For the full forms see Section 3.11.) Note that the spelling and stress are different from those of the present participles of first-conjugation verbs, and the feminine form has a different vowel. The present participle is rather rare for verbs of this type, being mainly confined to standardized expressions such as το κυβερνών κόμμα 'the ruling party'.

7.3.2 PASSIVE VOICE

7.3.2.1 Present

'I am loved'

Sg.	1	αγαπιέμαι	Pl.	1	αγαπιόμαστε
	2	αγαπιέσαι		2	αγαπιέστε/αγαπιόσαστε
	3	αγαπιέται		3	αγαπιούνται

1. The passive present consists of the imperfective stem with a set of personal endings which resemble those of the passive present of first conjugation verbs (Section 7.2.2.1), but with the following differences: (i) a non-syllabic -ι- is inserted between the stem and ending of all persons; (ii) the first vowel of the 1st person sg. ending is ε (not ο) and of the 3rd person pl. ου (not ο); (iii) in all persons the stress falls on the first syllable of the ending, never on the stem. As in first conjugation verbs, there is an alternative form of the 2nd person pl.

2. Some second conjugation verbs which follow type A in the active present do not use the above endings of the passive present. Their forms are as follows, with the example αποσπώμαι 'I am detached, seconded':

Sg.	1	αποσπώμαι	Pl.	1	αποσπόμαστε/αποσπώμεθα
	2	αποσπάσαι		2	αποσπάστε/αποσπάσθε
	3	αποσπάται		3	αποσπώνται

These endings are similar to those of verbs like φοβάμαι (Section 7.7.1), with the exception of the 1st person sg. and the 3rd person pl. The second forms given for the 1st and 2nd persons pl. are more formal. Other examples: απατώμαι 'I am deceived', αποπειρώμαι 'I attempt', διασπώμαι 'I am split', διερωτώμαι 'I wonder', εγγυώμαι 'I guarantee', εξαρτώμαι 'I depend' (also εξαρτιέμαι), ηττώμαι 'I am defeated', καταχρώμαι 'I misuse', περιπλανώμαι 'I wander' (also περιπλανιέμαι). The present passive of τιμώ 'I honour' may also have 1st person sg. τιμούμαι, 3rd person pl. τιμούνται, but otherwise has the same endings as αποσπώμαι. The passive imperfect of verbs like αποσπώμαι normally has the same forms as the imperfect of φοβάμαι (see Section 7.7.2).

7.3.2.2 Imperfect

'I was being loved/used to be loved'

Sg.	1	αγαπιόμουν(α)	Pl.	1	αγαπιόμασταν/αγαπιόμαστε
	2	αγαπιόσουν(α)		2	αγαπιόσασταν/αγαπιόσαστε
	3	αγαπιόταν(ε)		3	αγαπιόνταν(ε)/αγαπιούνταν(ε)/αγαπιόντουσαν

As in the passive present, a non-syllabic -ι- is inserted between the imperfective stem and the ending in all persons. The endings themselves are the same as those of the passive imperfect of first-conjugation verbs (Section 7.2.2.2), with a similar range of alternative forms, except that in the 3rd person pl. all forms are stressed on the first syllable of the ending and there is also a form in -ιούνταν(ε). The forms with a final vowel -α/-ε (1st, 2nd and 3rd persons sg. and 3rd person pl.) and the 3rd person pl. in -όντουσαν are more colloquial (non-formal).

7.3.2.3 Simple past

'I was loved'

Sg.	1	αγαπήθηκα	Pl.	1	αγαπηθήκαμε
	2	αγαπήθηκες		2	αγαπηθήκατε
	3	αγαπήθηκε		3	αγαπήθηκαν/αγαπηθήκανε

This tense is made up of three elements: the passive perfective stem, in this case formed by adding -ηθ- to the imperfective stem, the affix -ηκ-, and the personal endings, which are the same as the personal endings of the corresponding tense of first conjugation verbs (Section 7.2.2.3). While most verbs of this type have a perfective stem in -ηθ-, those that do not form their active perfective stem in -ησ- (Section 7.3.1.3) also form their passive perfective stem differently. Examples (in the 1st person sg. of the passive simple past): γελάστηκα, ξεχάστηκα, πετάχτηκα, τραβήχτηκα, παραπονέθηκα. For full information on the formation of the passive perfective stem, see Section 7.9.2.

7.3.2.4 Dependent

(no equivalent in English)

Sg.	1	αγαπηθώ	Pl.	1	αγαπηθούμε
	2	αγαπηθείς		2	αγαπηθείτε
	3	αγαπηθεί		3	αγαπηθούν(ε)

The passive dependent of verbs of this type is formed from the passive perfective stem (see Section 7.3.2.3) with the same endings as those of the passive dependent of first conjugation verbs (see Section 7.2.2.4), with the stress on the first (or only) syllable of the endings.

7.3.2.5 Perfect

'I have been loved'

Sg.	1	έχω αγαπηθεί	Pl.	1	έχουμε αγαπηθεί
	2	έχεις αγαπηθεί		2	έχετε αγαπηθεί
	3	έχει αγαπηθεί		3	έχουν(ε) αγαπηθεί

The passive perfect consists of the auxiliary verb έχω and the passive non-finite (identical to the 3rd person sg. of the passive dependent).

7.3.2.6   Pluperfect

'I had been loved'

Sg.	1	είχα αγαπηθεί	Pl.	1	είχαμε αγαπηθεί
	2	είχες αγαπηθεί		2	είχατε αγαπηθεί
	3	είχε αγαπηθεί		3	είχαν(ε) αγαπηθεί

The pluperfect is formed like the perfect, but with the past tense of έχω as the auxiliary.

7.3.2.7   Future, conditional, etc. (forms with θα)

Imperfective future	θα αγαπιέμαι etc. (θα + present) 'I shall be loved'
Perfective future	θα αγαπηθώ etc. (θα + dependent) 'I shall be loved'
Future perfect	θα έχω αγαπηθεί etc. (θα + perfect) 'I shall have been loved'
Conditional	θα αγαπιόμουν(α) etc. (θα + imperfect) 'I would be loved'
Perfect conditional	θα είχα αγαπηθεί etc. (θα + pluperfect) 'I would have been loved'

7.3.2.8   Perfective imperative

'be loved!' (pl. 'love one another!')

Sg.	αγαπήσου	Pl.	αγαπηθείτε

1. The singular is formed from the active perfective stem, with stress on the penultimate. The plural form is identical to the 2nd person pl. of the passive dependent.

2. For alternative ways of expressing a command, see Part III, Section 1.3.3.

7.3.2.9   Present participle

-ώμενος, -η, -ο (lacking for this verb)

1. There is no passive present participle of αγαπώ, but a few other verbs of this type do have it. It is formed from the imperfective stem with the ending -ώμενος, declining like the adjectives in Section 3.1. Examples: εξαρτώμενος 'depending', τιμώμενος 'being honoured'.

2. For the use of such participles, see Part III, Section 1.8.2.2.

7.3.2.10   Perfect participle

'loved'

αγαπημένος, -η, -ο (declined like adjectives in Section 3.1)

1. The passive perfect participle is formed from the stem of the passive simple past, without the -θ-, and with the addition of the ending -μένος (always stressed on the penultimate). Verbs which have passive simple past ending in -χτηκα or -στηκα normally have perfect participles ending in -γμένος or -σμένος respectively, e.g. βουτηγμένος 'dipped' (from βουτώ), περασμένος 'past' (from περνώ). For these and other exceptions see Section 7.11.

2. For the use of this participle see Part III, Section 1.8.2.1.

7.4   SECOND CONJUGATION VERBS (OXYTONE TYPE B)

7.4.1   ACTIVE VOICE

7.4.1.1   Present

'I consider, regard'

Sg.	1	θεωρώ	Pl.	1	θεωρούμε
	2	θεωρείς		2	θεωρείτε
	3	θεωρεί		3	θεωρούν(ε)

The present tense endings are exactly the same as the endings of the passive dependent of both first- and second-conjugation verbs. The stress always falls on the first (or only) syllable of the ending.

7.4.1.2   Imperfect

'I considered/used to consider'

Sg.	1	θεωρούσα	Pl.	1	θεωρούσαμε
	2	θεωρούσες		2	θεωρούσατε
	3	θεωρούσε		3	θεωρούσαν(ε)

The endings added to the imperfective stem, -ούσα etc., are exactly the same as those of second-conjugation verbs of type A (Section 7.3.1.2). The alternative imperfect endings in -αγα etc. do not exist for type B verbs.

7.4.1.3 Simple past

'I considered'

Sg.	1	θεώρησα	Pl.	1	θεωρήσαμε
	2	θεώρησες		2	θεωρήσατε
	3	θεώρησε		3	θεώρησαν/θεωρήσανε

Most second-conjugation verbs of type B add -ησ- to the imperfective stem to form the perfective stem (for exceptions see Section 7.9.2). The endings are the same as those of the simple past of first-conjugation verbs, and the stress falls on the antepenultimate in all persons.

7.4.1.4 Dependent

(no equivalent in English)

Sg.	1	θεωρήσω	Pl.	1	θεωρήσουμε
	2	θεωρήσεις		2	θεωρήσετε
	3	θεωρήσει		3	θεωρήσουν(ε)

The dependent is based on the perfective stem with the same endings and stress as the dependent (and as the present) of first conjugation verbs (see Section 7.2.1.4).

7.4.1.5 Perfect

'I have considered'

Sg.	1	έχω θεωρήσει	Pl.	1	έχουμε θεωρήσει
	2	έχεις θεωρήσει		2	έχετε θεωρήσει
	3	έχει θεωρήσει		3	έχουν(ε) θεωρήσει

As for first conjugation verbs, the perfect consists of the auxiliary verb έχω with the non-finite (which is identical with the 3rd person singular of the dependent).

7.4.1.6 Pluperfect

'I had considered'

Sg.	1	είχα θεωρήσει	Pl.	1	είχαμε θεωρήσει
	2	είχες θεωρήσει		2	είχατε θεωρήσει
	3	είχε θεωρήσει		3	είχαν(ε) θεωρήσει

The pluperfect consists of the past tense of έχω with the non-finite.

7.4.1.7 Future, conditional, etc. (forms with θα)

Imperfective future	θα θεωρώ etc. (θα + present) 'I shall consider'
Perfective future	θα θεωρήσω etc. (θα + dependent) 'I shall consider'
Future perfect	θα έχω θεωρήσει etc. (θα + perfect) 'I shall have considered'
Conditional	θα θεωρούσα etc. (θα + imperfect) 'I would consider'
Perfect conditional	θα είχα θεωρήσει etc. (θα + pluperfect) 'I would have considered'

7.4.1.8 Imperfective imperative

'consider!'

Sg.   (lacking)   Pl.   θεωρείτε

Verbs of this type sometimes form a plural imperfective imperative, which is identical with the 2nd person pl. of the present. A singular form is not found.

7.4.1.9 Perfective imperative

'consider!'

Sg.   θεώρησε   Pl.   θεωρήστε

1. The perfective imperative is formed in the same way as for second-conjugation verbs of type A. It consists of the perfective stem with the endings -ε (sg.) and -τε (pl.). The singular form is stressed on the antepenultimate, while in the plural the stress falls on the penultimate.

2. There is a more formal ending -ετε of the plural, with stress on the antepenultimate, e.g. ευχαριστήσετε 'thank'.

7.4.1.10 Gerund and participles

Gerund	θεωρώντας 'considering'
Perfect gerund	έχοντας θεωρήσει 'having considered'
Present participle	(θεωρών, -ούσα, -ούν) 'considering'

1. The gerund of second conjugation verbs has the ending -ώντας, attached to the imperfective stem. The perfect gerund consists of the gerund of έχω with the non-finite.

2. The present participle is declined like an adjective, with nominative singular forms in -ών, -ούσα, -ούν. (For the complete declension see Section 3.11, note 4.) The forms for θεωρώ above are bracketed because they are not normally used. However, επιθεωρώ 'I oversee' has a present participle, which is often used in

the phrase η επιθεωρούσα επιτροπή 'the overseeing committee'. Another example is επικρατών 'prevailing'. In general the present participle is rather rare and mainly found in standardized formal expressions.

7.4.2 PASSIVE VOICE

7.4.2.1 Present

'I am considered'

Sg.	1	θεωρούμαι	Pl.	1	θεωρούμαστε
	2	θεωρείσαι		2	θεωρείστε
	3	θεωρείται		3	θεωρούνται

1. The passive present consists of the imperfective stem with personal endings which differ from those of first-conjugation verbs. The first vowel of the ending, which always bears the stress, is either ου or ει.

2. For some verbs a more formal alternative ending -ούμεθα is often used for the 1st person pl., e.g. επωφελούμεθα 'we take advantage/profit from'.

7.4.2.2 Imperfect

'I was considered/used to be considered'

Sg.	1	(θεωρούμουν)	Pl.	1	(θεωρούμασταν)
	2	(θεωρούσουν)		2	(θεωρούσασταν)
	3	θεωρούνταν(ε)		3	θεωρούνταν(ε)

Many verbs of this type do not possess a complete set of passive imperfect forms in regular use. The 1st- and 2nd-person forms bracketed above are not normally used for θεωρώ. For the 3rd person of such verbs there are also learned forms, which may have an augment: (ε)θεωρείτο (sg.), (ε)θεωρούντο (pl.). Type B verbs which are, however, often found in the passive imperfect include δικαιολογώ 'I justify', στερώ 'I deprive', and the deponents απολογούμαι 'I defend myself', αρκούμαι 'I confine myself', ασχολούμαι 'I am occupied', διανοούμαι 'I contemplate', μιμούμαι 'I imitate', προσποιούμαι 'I pretend'. Such verbs may also have the additional vowel -α (1st and 2nd persons sg.) and the alternative 1st and 2nd persons pl. in -ούμαστε/-ούσαστε, similar to other passive imperfect types (see Sections 7.2.2.2 and 7.3.2.2).

7.4.2.3 Simple past

'I was considered'

Sg.	1	θεωρήθηκα	Pl.	1	θεωρηθήκαμε
	2	θεωρήθηκες		2	θεωρηθήκατε
	3	θεωρήθηκε		3	θεωρήθηκαν/θεωρηθήκανε

As for second conjugation verbs of type A, this tense is made up of three elements: the passive perfective stem, normally formed by adding -ηθ- to the imperfective stem, the affix -ηκ-, and the personal endings, which are the same as the personal endings of the corresponding tense of first conjugation verbs (Section 7.2.2.3). For full information on the formation of the passive perfective stem, see Section 7.9.2.

7.4.2.4 Dependent

(no equivalent in English)

Sg.	1	θεωρηθώ	Pl.	1	θεωρηθούμε
	2	θεωρηθείς		2	θεωρηθείτε
	3	θεωρηθεί		3	θεωρηθούν(ε)

The passive dependent of verbs of this type is formed from the passive perfective stem (see Section 7.4.2.3) with the same endings as those of the passive dependent of first conjugation verbs (see Section 7.2.2.4), with the stress on the first (or only) syllable of the endings.

7.4.2.5 Perfect

'I have been considered'

Sg.	1	έχω θεωρηθεί	Pl.	1	έχουμε θεωρηθεί
	2	έχεις θεωρηθεί		2	έχετε θεωρηθεί
	3	έχει θεωρηθεί		3	έχουν(ε) θεωρηθεί

The passive perfect consists of the auxiliary verb έχω and the passive non-finite (identical to the 3rd person sg. of the passive dependent).

7.4.2.6 Pluperfect

'I had been considered'

Sg.	1	είχα θεωρηθεί	Pl.	1	είχαμε θεωρηθεί
	2	είχες θεωρηθεί		2	είχατε θεωρηθεί
	3	είχε θεωρηθεί		3	είχαν(ε) θεωρηθεί

The pluperfect is formed like the perfect, but with the past tense of έχω as the auxiliary.

7.4.2.7 Future, conditional, etc. (forms with θα)

Imperfective future   θα θεωρούμαι etc. (θα + present) 'I shall be considered'

Perfective future   θα θεωρηθώ etc. (θα + dependent) 'I shall be considered'

Future perfect	θα έχω θεωρηθεί etc. (θα + perfect) 'I shall have been considered'
Conditional	(θα θεωρούμουν(α) etc.) (θα + imperfect) (see note below)
Perfect conditional	θα είχα θεωρηθεί etc. (θα + pluperfect) 'I would have been considered'

Like the passive imperfect, the passive conditional is not often found for this verb.

7.4.2.8 Perfective imperative

'be considered/consider yourself!'

Sg. θεωρήσου   Pl. θεωρηθείτε

1. The singular is formed from the active perfective stem, with stress on the penultimate. The plural form is identical to the 2nd person pl. of the passive dependent.

2. For alternative ways of expressing a command, see Part III, Section 1.3.3.

7.4.2.9 Present participle

θεωρούμενος, -η, -ο 'being considered, putative'

1. The passive present participle is formed from the imperfective stem with the ending -ούμενος, declining like the adjectives in Section 3.1.

2. For the use of such participles, see Part III, Section 1.8.2.2.

7.4.2.10 Perfect participle

'considered'

θεωρημένος, -η, -ο (declined like adjectives in Section 3.1)

1. The passive perfect participle is formed from the stem of the passive simple past, without the -θ-, and with the addition of the ending -μένος (always stressed on the penultimate). For irregular formations see Section 7.11.

2. For the use of this participle see Part III, Section 1.8.2.1.

7.5 VERBS WITH CONTRACTED ACTIVE PRESENT FORMS

A small group of verbs, the imperfective (present) stem of which ends in a vowel, have 'contracted' forms in the active present tense. The first (or only) vowel of the personal endings of the second person sg., and the 1st, 2nd and 3rd persons pl. is lost. The endings of the present tense are thus: -ω, -ς, -ει, -με, -τε, -ν(ε). We give first the present tense forms of one verb, which provides the model for all such verbs, and then examine some irregularities in the formation of other tenses and moods of individual verbs.

7.5.1 PRESENT

'I say'

Sg.	1	λέω	Pl.	1	λέμε
	2	λες		2	λέτε
	3	λέει		3	λεν/λένε

The other verbs which follow this pattern are: ακούω 'I hear', καίω 'I burn', κλαίω 'I weep', τρώω 'I eat', φταίω 'I am to blame', φυλάω 'I guard, keep' (but also φυλάγω, which is conjugated regularly). Two other verbs follow this pattern: πάω 'I go', which is both an alternative present tense and the dependent of πηγαίνω 'I go'; and φάω, which is the dependent of τρώω.

1. In the case of verbs which have a two-syllable stem, the stress of the 2nd person sg. is on the last syllable: ακούς, φυλάς; so too for the shorter form of the 3rd person pl.: ακούν, φυλάν. In all other forms the stress falls on the penultimate syllable.

2. A more formal alternative to the present of λέω is λέγω, which follows the first conjugation. Its compounds, e.g. διαλέγω 'I choose', always have an imperfective stem ending in -γ-.

7.5.2 OTHER TENSES AND MOODS

The imperfective future of such verbs consists of the present tense (as above), preceded by the particle θα: θα λέω etc. Other parts of these verbs which are based on the imperfective stem insert, in most cases, a -γ- between the stem and the relevant endings:

Active voice
Imperfect	έλεγα, έλεγες, etc. (as the imperfect of first conjugation verbs: Section 7.2.1.2)
Conditional	θα έλεγα, θα έλεγες, etc.
Imperfective imperative	sg. λέγε pl. λέγετε
Gerund	λέγοντας

Passive voice
Present	λέγομαι, λέγεσαι, etc. (as in Section 7.2.2.1)
Imperfect	λεγόμουν(α), λεγόσουν(α), etc. (as in Section 7.2.2.2)
Imperfective future	θα λέγομαι, θα λέγεσαι, etc.
Conditional	θα λεγόμουν(α), θα λεγόσουν(α), etc.
Present participle	λεγόμενος, -η, -ο

However, not all these forms exist for all verbs. It is therefore necessary to give separate notes on each verb.

ακούω: all forms based on the imperfective stem, other than the present, normally have -γ- (the passive present participle is not found), with the exception of the imperfective imperative, which is άκου (sg.), ακούτε (pl.). The simple past is άκουσα.

καίω: all forms except the active present add -γ- to the stem, e.g. active imperfect έκαιγα. There is no passive present participle in normal use. The simple past is έκαψα.

κλαίω: all forms except the active present add -γ- to the stem, e.g. active imperfect έκλαιγα. There is no passive present participle. The simple past is έκλαψα.

πάω: this functions both as the dependent of πηγαίνω and as an alternative present tense with the meaning 'I go/am going'. The other imperfective forms are based on the stem πηγαιν-, e.g. πήγαινα (imperf.), πήγαινε, πηγαίνετε (imperfective imp.), πηγαίνοντας (gerund). The simple past is πήγα. There are no passive forms.

τρώω: except for the active present tense, all other imperfective forms have stem in -γ-. There is no passive present participle. The simple past is έφαγα, dependent φάω (for which see above).

φταίω: except for the active present tense, all other imperfective forms have stem in -γ-. There is no imperative and passive forms do not exist for this verb. The simple past is έφταιξα.

φυλάω: in the active present tense there are also alternative forms with -γ- in the 1st person sg. (φυλάγω) and the 3rd person pl. (φυλάγουν). All other imperfective forms have stem in -γ-. There is no passive present participle. The simple past is φύλαξα.

For the remaining forms of these verbs, see the table of irregular verbs, Section 7.13.

7.6 VERBS WITH OXYTONE ACTIVE DEPENDENT

Certain verbs have active dependent forms which, in the 1st person singular, are monosyllables e.g. βγω, from βγαίνω 'I go out'. These forms conjugate somewhat differently from the normal class of dependents from first-conjugation verbs: since their stem consists of one or more consonants only, it is the endings that have the stress. Their endings are the same as those of the active present of second-conjugation verbs type B (Section 7.4.1.1).

Sg.	1	βγω	Pl.	1	βγούμε
	2	βγεις		2	βγείτε
	3	βγει		3	βγουν/βγούνε

The other dependents which follow this pattern are: βρω (from βρίσκω 'I find'), διαβώ (from διαβαίνω 'I pass (by)'), δω (from βλέπω 'I see'), μπω (from μπαίνω 'I enter'), παραβώ (from παραβαίνω 'I transgress'), πιω (from πίνω 'I drink'), πω (from λέω 'I say'), συμβεί (from συμβαίνει 'it happens'); also, the dependent of έρχομαι 'I come', when its initial vowel is lost by prodelision: (να/θα) 'ρθώ, (να/θα) 'ρθείς, (να/θα) 'ρθεί etc. (Note that these forms are written with an accent because the underlying word is disyllabic. These are alternatives to να 'ρθω etc., in which the stress falls on the particle να or θα.) The perfective imperative forms of βγαίνω are irregular: sg. βγες, pl. βγείτε. This pattern is also followed by βρίσκω, βλέπω, λέω, μπαίνω, πίνω (see the table of irregular verbs for some alternative forms). The perfective imperative forms of διαβαίνω are: sg. διάβα, pl. διαβείτε, and of έρχομαι, sg. έλα, pl. ελάτε. The remaining verbs in the above list do not have perfective imperative forms.

7.7   SECOND CONJUGATION VERBS WITH PASSIVE ONLY

There is a group of four verbs, existing only in passive forms, which are similar to second conjugation verbs in that the imperfective forms are stressed on the endings, although the actual endings differ from those of both types of oxytone verbs. They are: φοβάμαι 'I fear', θυμάμαι 'I remember', κοιμάμαι 'I sleep/go to sleep' and λυπάμαι 'I regret/am sorry'. (The last does in fact have a corresponding active λυπώ 'I distress/make sad', which follows the second conjugation type B, but is rarely found in 1st- or 2nd-person forms.) These four verbs are conjugated as follows:

7.7.1   PRESENT

'I fear/am afraid [of]'

Sg.	1	φοβάμαι/φοβούμαι	Pl.	1	φοβόμαστε
	2	φοβάσαι		2	φοβάστε/φοβόσαστε
	3	φοβάται		3	φοβούνται

The alternative forms given for the 1st person sg. and 2nd person pl. are widely used. Of the two 1st person sg. forms, φοβάμαι is the more normal, while φοβούμαι is regional but is also used sometimes in formal contexts.

7.7.2   IMPERFECT

'I was afraid/used to be afraid [of]'

Sg.	1	φοβόμουν(α)	Pl.	1	φοβόμασταν/φοβόμαστε
	2	φοβόσουν(α)		2	φοβόσασταν/φοβόσαστε
	3	φοβόταν(ε)		3	φοβόνταν(ε)/φοβόντουσαν

The endings, together with the alternatives, are the same as those of the passive imperfect of first conjugation verbs, except that for this type the 3rd person pl. has only the forms stressed on the endings (see Section 7.2.2.2).

7.7.3 SIMPLE PAST

'I became frightened/took fright [at]'

Sg.	1	φοβήθηκα	Pl.	1	φοβηθήκαμε
	2	φοβήθηκες		2	φοβηθήκατε
	3	φοβήθηκε		3	φοβήθηκαν/φοβηθήκανε

The simple past is formed in the same way as the passive simple past of verbs like αγαπώ (see Section 7.3.2.3).

7.7.4 DEPENDENT

(no equivalent in English)

Sg.	1	φοβηθώ	Pl.	1	φοβηθούμε
	2	φοβηθείς		2	φοβηθείτε
	3	φοβηθεί		3	φοβηθούν(ε)

The dependent is formed in the same way as the passive dependent of verbs like αγαπώ (see Section 7.3.2.4).

7.7.5 PERFECT

'I have been afraid [of]'

Sg.	1	έχω φοβηθεί	Pl.	1	έχουμε φοβηθεί
	2	έχεις φοβηθεί		2	έχετε φοβηθεί
	3	έχει φοβηθεί		3	έχουν(ε) φοβηθεί

The perfect consists of the auxiliary verb έχω and the non-finite (identical to the 3rd person sg. of the dependent).

7.7.6 PLUPERFECT

'I had been afraid [of]'

Sg.	1	είχα φοβηθεί	Pl.	1	είχαμε φοβηθεί
	2	είχες φοβηθεί		2	είχατε φοβηθεί
	3	είχε φοβηθεί		3	είχαν(ε) φοβηθεί

The pluperfect is formed like the perfect, but with the past tense of έχω as the auxiliary.

7.7.7 FUTURE, CONDITIONAL, ETC. (FORMS WITH θα)

Imperfective future   θα φοβάμαι/θα φοβούμαι etc. (θα + present)
'I shall fear'

Perfective future   θα φοβηθώ etc. (θα + dependent) 'I shall
become frightened'

Future perfect   θα έχω φοβηθεί etc. (θα + perfect) 'I shall
have become frightened'

Conditional   θα φοβόμουν(α) etc. (θα + imperfect) 'I
would fear/be afraid [of]'

Perfect conditional   θα είχα φοβηθεί etc. (θα + pluperfect) 'I
would have feared/become frightened'

7.7.8 PERFECTIVE IMPERATIVE

'fear/be afraid [of]'

Sg.   φοβήσου   Pl.   φοβηθείτε

The singular is formed from what would be the active perfective stem (if it existed) with the ending -ου; the stress is on the penultimate. The plural is identical to the 2nd person pl. of the dependent. (Compare the passive perfective imperative of second conjugation verbs, Sections 7.3.2.8 and 7.4.2.8.)

7.7.9 PERFECT PARTICIPLE

The four verbs of this type do not follow a single pattern in the formation of their perfect participle, and in fact none exists for θυμάμαι. For the other verbs the forms (all declined like adjectives in Section 3.1) and their meanings are as follows:

φοβισμένος, -η, -ο   'frightened'
κοιμισμένος, -η, -ο   'asleep/having slept'
λυπημένος, -η, -ο   'saddened, sorry'

7.8 THE VERB 'TO BE'

The verb είμαι has only two sets of tense forms: present and past (imperfect). These imperfective forms are combined with the particle θα to form the future and the conditional respectively. There are no perfect tenses. There is a present participle όντας 'being', which is used rather rarely. Other moods (e.g. imperative) are expressed periphrastically (see Part III, Section 1.3.3).

7.8.1   PRESENT

'I am'

Sg.	1	είμαι	Pl.	1	είμαστε
	2	είσαι		2	είστε/είσαστε
	3	είναι		3	είναι

1. The endings of the 1st and 2nd persons singular and plural are similar to those of the passive present of first and second conjugation verbs, but with εί- (always stressed) replacing the first vowel of the endings. The 3rd person singular and plural have the same forms.

2. The first person plural of the present has a learned alternative είμεθα, which is used by some older speakers.

7.8.2   IMPERFECT

'I was/used to be'

Sg.	1	ήμουν(α)	Pl.	1	ήμαστε/ήμασταν
	2	ήσουν(α)		2	ήσαστε/ήσασταν
	3	ήταν(ε)		3	ήταν(ε)

1. Those forms of the singular and of the 3rd person plural with an additional syllable (-α or -ε) are non-formal. Note that the forms ήμαστε and ήσαστε of the 1st and 2nd person plural of the imperfect are distinguished from the corresponding present forms only by their spelling; the alternative imperfect forms in -αν make a clear distinction between the tenses.

2. There is an alternative form ήσαν for the 3rd person plural which is mainly formal, but is also used more generally by some older speakers.

7.8.3   FUTURE AND CONDITIONAL

Future	θα είμαι etc. 'I shall be'
Conditional	θα ήμουν(α) etc. 'I would be'

7.9   FORMATION OF ACTIVE AND PASSIVE PERFECTIVE STEMS

The tables of verbs given in Sections 7.2–7.4 and 7.7 provide detailed information about the endings used in the formation of all tenses. However, in order to produce the perfective forms (active and passive simple past and dependent, and the perfective imperative) and the perfect tenses, it is necessary to know the perfective stems of each verb. Many verbs fit into recognizable patterns in the way they form their perfective stems. In Sections 7.9.1 (first conjugation) and 7.9.2 (second conjugation), verbs are grouped together according to such patterns. For each group we give the last consonant(s) or syllable of (a) the imperfective (present) stem (first conjugation only), (b) the active perfective stem, and (c) the passive perfective stem respectively. (On the phonology of certain passive perfective stems see Section 7.9.3 and Part I, Section 1.4.2.) We then give a number of examples of verbs which follow each pattern, but these lists should not be seen as complete. In particular, we do not show the whole range of compounds formed by prefixing various prepositions to some verbs (only a few examples of common compound verbs are included). In such cases it can normally be assumed that the compound verb follows the simple verb in its stem-formation; e.g. ανελκύω 'I draw up', καθελκύω 'I launch' and προσελκύω 'I attract' form their other stems exactly as ελκύω 'I pull'. Such compound verbs may introduce an internal augment in their past tenses; for the details see Section 7.10.

Many verbs form their perfective stems in ways which do not conform to any of the patterns described here, for example by changing the vowel of the stem (e.g. στέλνω 'I send', έστειλα, στάλθηκα), or using a completely different stem (e.g. βλέπω 'I see', είδα, ιδώθηκα). For these it is necessary to consult the table of irregular verbs in Section 7.13. For verbs with contracted active present forms, see Section 7.5. A dagger (†) indicates verbs which do not have passive perfective forms.

7.9.1 FIRST CONJUGATION VERBS (PAROXYTONE)

In this section first-conjugation verbs are grouped according to their imperfective stem. It should be noted that verbs with similar imperfective stems can diverge into two or more patterns in the formation of their perfective stems. In summary, the kinds of imperfective stem covered in this section are the following:

(i)–(iii)	stems ending in a vowel
(iv)–(vi)	stems ending in a labial consonant (or a consonant cluster which includes a labial)
(vii)	stems ending in a velar consonant (or a consonant cluster which includes a velar)
(viii)	stems ending in a dental consonant (but not -ττ-)
(ix)	stems ending in -σσ- or -ττ-
(x)–(xi)	stems ending in -ζ-
(xii)–(xxi)	stems ending in -ν- (after vowels)
(xxii)	stems ending in -αρ- or -ιρ-

(i)   Imperfective stem ending in a vowel, active perfective -σ-, passive perfective -στ- (or, more formally, -σθ-) (e.g. σείω, έσεισα, σείστηκα):

αχούω 'I hear', αντιχρούω 'I refute', αποκλείω 'I exclude', αποσείω 'I shake off', ελχύω 'I pull', †προσκρούω 'I run into, contravene', σείω 'I shake', †υπακούω 'I obey'.

Similarly the deponent verb:

συγκρούομαι 'I collide'

(ii) Imperfective stem ending in a vowel, active perfective -σ-, passive perfective -θ- (e.g. ιδρύω, ίδρυσα, ιδρύθηκα):

αναλύω 'I analyse', απολύω 'I dismiss', διανύω 'I traverse', διεισδύω 'I infiltrate', †δύω 'I go down, set [of sun]', ενισχύω 'I strengthen', επενδύω 'I invest', ιδρύω 'I establish', †ισχύω 'I am valid', μηνύω 'I bring a charge [against]', †παραλύω 'I paralyse', συνδέω 'I connect'.

Similarly the deponent verbs:

αναδύομαι 'I emerge', υποδύομαι 'I play the part of'.

(iii) Imperfective stem ending in -ε-, active perfective -ευσ-, passive perfective -ευστ- (e.g. εμπνέω, ενέπνευσα, εμπνεύστηκα):

†απορρέω 'I derive from' (simple past απέρρευσα), εμπνέω 'I inspire', †καταρρέω 'I collapse' (simple past κατέρρευσα), †πλέω 'I float, sail', †πνέω 'I breathe', †ρέω 'I flow' (simple past έρρευσα, but rare).

(iv) Imperfective stem ending in -β-/-π-/-πτ-/-φ-/-φτ-, active perfective -ψ-, passive perfective -φτ- (or, more formally, -φθ-) (e.g. βάφω, έβαψα, βάφτηκα):

αλείφω 'I smear', αμείβω 'I recompense', ανάβω 'I light', ανακαλύπτω 'I discover', ανταμείβω 'I remunerate', αποκαλύπτω 'I reveal', απορρίπτω 'I reject', †αστράφτω 'I lighten, flash', βάφω 'I dye', βλάπτω (or βλάφτω) 'I harm', γλείφω 'I lick', †γνέφω 'I nod', γράφω 'I write' (pass. perf. also -φ-), εγκαταλείπω 'I abandon', εξαλείφω 'I obliterate', θάβω 'I bury', θλίβω 'I sadden', καλύπτω 'I cover', κάμπτω 'I bend' (pass. perf. always -φθ-), κλέβω 'I steal' (passive perfective used only in the sense of 'elope'; see also the table of irregular verbs), κρύβω 'I hide', †λάμπω 'I shine', †λείπω 'I am missing', νίβω 'I wash', παραλείπω 'I omit', παραπέμπω 'I refer' (pass. perf. always -φθ-), πασαλείφω (or πασαλείβω) 'I smear', †περιθάλπω 'I nurse', προβλέπω 'I foresee', †προκόβω 'I succeed', ράβω 'I sew', σκάβω 'I dig', †σκοντάφτω 'I stumble', †σκύβω 'I stoop', στέφω 'I crown' (pass. perf. usually -φθ-), στρίβω 'I twist, turn', στύβω 'I squeeze', συνάπτω 'I join, contract', †τέρπω 'I delight', τρίβω 'I rub', υπογράφω 'I sign', †υποκύπτω 'I submit', υποσκάπτω 'I undermine', †χάφτω 'I gobble up'

Similarly the deponent verbs:

επισκέπτομαι 'I visit', σκέφτομαι (or σκέπτομαι) 'I think [about]', υπολείπομαι 'I am left'.

(v) Imperfective stem ending in -αυ-/-ευ-, active perfective -αψ-/-εψ-, passive perfective -αυτ-/-ευτ- (e.g. γιατρεύω, γιάτρεψα, γιατρεύτηκα):

αγγαρεύω 'I force someone to work', αγριεύω 'I make *or* become angry', αναδεύω 'I stir up', ανακατεύω 'I mix', αναπαύω 'I rest' (act. perf. also -αυσ-, though the verb is more common in the passive than the active), †βασιλεύω 'I set [of sun]', βολεύω 'I arrange, fix', γιατρεύω 'I cure', †γνεύω 'I nod', †γυρεύω 'I ask for', δασκαλεύω 'I teach', δουλεύω 'I work', δυσκολεύω 'I make difficult', ζεύω 'I yoke', †ζηλεύω 'I envy', †ζωηρεύω 'I enliven', ημερεύω 'I tame', †θαρρεύω 'I take courage', καβαλικεύω 'I ride', †καλυτερεύω 'I improve', †κινδυνεύω 'I am in danger', κολακεύω 'I flatter', †κοντεύω 'I draw near', μαγειρεύω 'I cook', μαζεύω 'I gather', μπερδεύω 'I confuse', ξοδεύω 'I spend', παζαρεύω 'I haggle', †παλεύω 'I wrestle', παύω 'I cease', †πεζεύω 'I dismount', †περισσεύω 'I am in excess', πιστεύω 'I believe', ρεζιλεύω 'I ridicule', †στενεύω 'I make *or* become narrow', †ταξιδεύω 'I travel', φυτεύω 'I plant', χορεύω 'I dance', and almost all other verbs in -εύω except those listed in (vi). However, some of the verbs listed above can also have an active perfective in -ευσ-, e.g. βασιλεύω (in the sense 'I reign'), κινδυνεύω.

Similarly the deponent verb:

ονειρεύομαι 'I dream'.

(vi) Imperfective stem ending in -αυ-/-ευ-, active perfective -αυσ-/-ευσ- (more rarely -αψ-/-εψ-), passive perfective -αυτ-/-ευτ- (or, more formally, -αυθ-/-ευθ-) (e.g. δεσμεύω, δέσμευσα, δεσμεύτηκα):

†αγορεύω 'I make a speech', †αληθεύω 'I am true', αλιεύω 'I fish', αμνηστεύω 'I pardon', αναγορεύω 'I acclaim', ανιχνεύω 'I detect, trace, track down', αντιπροσωπεύω 'I represent', απαγορεύω 'I forbid' (act. perf. also -εψ-), απλουστεύω 'I simplify', απογοητεύω 'I disappoint', αποθηκεύω 'I store up, save', απομνημονεύω 'I memorize', αποταμιεύω 'I save up', αποχετεύω 'I drain', αρδεύω 'I irrigate', †αριστεύω 'I excel', †αφιππεύω 'I dismount', αχρηστεύω 'I make *or* become useless', βραβεύω 'I award a prize to', γενικεύω 'I generalize', †γνωματεύω 'I give my opinion', δεσμεύω 'I bind', δημεύω 'I confiscate', διακινδυνεύω 'I risk', διακυβεύω 'I gamble', †διανυκτερεύω

'I stay open at night', διαπομπεύω 'I pillory', διοχετεύω
'I channel', †δραπετεύω 'I escape', δυναστεύω 'I oppress',
†εδρεύω 'I am based', ειδικεύω 'I specialize', εκλαϊκεύω
'I popularize', εκπαιδεύω 'I instruct', †εκστρατεύω 'I campaign',
εκτοξεύω 'I shoot, launch', †ελλοχεύω 'I lie in wait', εξιδανικεύω
'I idealize', εξολοθρεύω 'I exterminate', εξωτερικεύω
'I externalize', επιστρατεύω 'I mobilize', εποπτεύω 'I supervise',
ερμηνεύω 'I interpret', θεραπεύω 'I treat, cure', †θριαμβεύω
'I triumph', †ιδιωτεύω 'I retire to private life', ικετεύω 'I entreat',
†ιππεύω 'I ride or mount [horse]', καταπαύω 'I put an end to',
†κατασκοπεύω 'I spy', κηδεμονεύω 'I am guardian [to]',
μεθοδεύω 'I plan carefully', μεταμοσχεύω 'I transplant, graft',
†μεταναστεύω 'I migrate', μεταφυτεύω 'I transplant', μνημονεύω
'I mention', μνηστεύω 'I betroth', †μοιχεύω 'I commit adultery',
†νεύω 'I nod', νοθεύω 'I adulterate', νοσηλεύω 'I nurse, treat',
παγιδεύω 'I trap', παρακινδυνεύω 'I risk', †περιοδεύω 'I tour',
†προεδρεύω 'I preside', προμηθεύω 'I supply', †προοδεύω 'I
progress', προστατεύω 'I protect', †ρητορεύω 'I orate', †σκοπεύω
'I aim', †σταθμεύω 'I park', στηλιτεύω 'I castigate', †στρατοπεδεύω
'I encamp', †συγκατανεύω 'I consent to', συγχωνεύω 'I merge',
συσσωρεύω 'I accumulate', ταριχεύω 'I preserve, embalm',
†τοξεύω 'I shoot', υπαγορεύω 'I dictate', υποθηκεύω 'I mortgage',
υπονομεύω 'I undermine', φυγαδεύω 'I help someone to escape',
χαλκεύω 'I fabricate', ψαύω 'I feel, touch'

Similarly the deponent verbs:

αμφιταλαντεύομαι 'I vacillate', αστιεύομαι 'I joke', γεύομαι 'I
taste', διαπραγματεύομαι 'I negotiate', εκμεταλλεύομαι 'I exploit',
εμπιστεύομαι 'I trust', εμπορεύομαι 'I trade [in]', ερωτεύομαι 'I fall
in love [with]', λογικεύομαι 'I come to my senses', μηχανεύομαι
'I contrive', πορεύομαι 'I march', ταλαντεύομαι 'I swing, oscillate',
υπερηφανεύομαι 'I take pride in', υποπτεύομαι 'I suspect'

(vii) Imperfective stem ending in -γ-/-γγ-/-κ-/-χ-/-χν-, active perfective
-ξ-, passive perfective -χτ- (or, more formally, -χθ-) (e.g. διδάσκω,
δίδαξα, διδάχτηκα):

αδράχνω 'I grasp', αναφλέγω 'I ignite', ανοίγω 'I open', †αντέχω
'I endure', αποδείχνω (present also αποδεικνύω) 'I prove',
αρμέγω 'I milk', †βήχω 'I cough', δείχνω 'I show', διαλέγω
'I choose', †διατρέχω 'I run across', διδάσκω 'I teach', διώκω
'I persecute', διώχνω 'I expel, throw out', εκλέγω 'I elect' (see
also the table of irregular verbs), ελέγχω 'I control', θέλγω
'I charm', θίγω 'I touch' (see also the table of irregular verbs),
†καταλήγω 'I end up', †λήγω 'I expire', †μουλώχνω 'I crouch,

cower', μπήγω 'I drive in', μπλέκω 'I entangle', ξανοίγω 'I open;
catch sight of', ξετυλίγω 'I unwind', περιπλέκω 'I complicate',
πλέκω 'I weave', προσέχω 'I pay attention [to], take care',
προφυλάγω 'I protect', ρίχνω 'I throw', σιάχνω 'I straighten, fix',
σπρώχνω 'I push', †στέργω 'I consent', στριμώχνω 'I crowd
together', σφίγγω 'I squeeze', †τρέχω 'I run', τυλίγω 'I wind,
wrap', †φέγγω 'I shine', φτιάχνω 'I make, fix', φυλάγω 'I guard',
ψάχνω 'I search [for]', ψύχω 'I freeze'

Similarly the deponent verbs:

αποδέχομαι 'I accept', δέχομαι 'I receive', διαδέχομαι 'I succeed
(someone)', ορέγομαι 'I desire strongly', πετάγομαι 'I jump up'

(viii) Imperfective stem ending in -δ-/-θ-, active perfective -σ-, passive
perfective -στ- (e.g. πείθω, έπεισα, πείστηκα):

αλέθω 'I grind', διαψεύδω 'I contradict', επισπεύδω 'I hasten,
bring forward' (passive perfective also -σθ-), †κλώθω 'I spin',
†νιώθω 'I feel', πείθω 'I persuade', πλάθω 'I mould, shape',
†σπεύδω 'I hasten'

(ix) Imperfective stem ending in -σσ-/-ττ-, active perfective -ξ-, passive
perfective -χτ- (or, more formally, -χθ-) (e.g. αναπτύσσω, ανέπτυξα/
ανάπτυξα, αναπτύχθηκα):

αναπτύσσω 'I develop', ανταλλάσσω 'I exchange', αντιτάσσω 'I
oppose', απαλλάσσω 'I exempt', εισπράττω 'I collect [money]',
εναλλάσσω 'I alternate', επιφυλάσσω 'I keep in reserve', κηρύσσω
'I proclaim', πατάσσω 'I punish harshly', πλήττω 'I bore, hit' (see
also table of irregular verbs), συντάσσω 'I draw up, compile',
†φρίττω 'I am horrified'

Similarly the deponent verbs:

ελίσσομαι 'I coil', εξελίσσομαι 'I develop', συναλλάσσομαι 'I do
business', υπαινίσσομαι 'I hint at'

(x) Imperfective stem ending in -ζ-, active perfective -σ-, passive perfective -στ- (and, more formally, -σθ-) (e.g. εξετάζω, εξέτασα,
εξετάστηκα):

†αδειάζω 'I empty', †αηδιάζω 'I disgust or I am disgusted',
†ακμάζω 'I flourish', †αναβλύζω 'I well up', αναγκάζω 'I compel',
αναγνωρίζω 'I recognize', ανεβάζω 'I raise', †αξίζω
'I am worth', αποβιβάζω 'I disembark', αρμόζω 'I befit', †αρχίζω
'I begin', βασίζω 'I base', βιάζω 'I force, rape', βράζω 'I boil',
†γεμίζω 'I fill', †γκρινιάζω 'I complain' (also -ξ-), †δακρύζω
'I weep', δανείζω 'I lend', †δεσπόζω 'I dominate', διαβάζω 'I read',

εξετάζω 'I examine', επηρεάζω 'I influence', εφαρμόζω 'I apply', ζαλίζω 'I make dizzy', κατεβάζω 'I lower, bring down', κουράζω 'I tire', λούζω 'I shampoo', †μπάζω 'I put or take in', πιέζω 'I press', προβιβάζω 'I promote', προσεγγίζω 'I approach', †σκάζω 'I burst', †σπάζω 'I break', συγχύζω 'I upset', σώζω 'I save' (but pass. perf. σωθ-), χωρίζω 'I separate', and the great majority of the numerous verbs in -άζω or -ίζω, other than those listed in (xi)

Similarly the deponent verbs:

αγωνίζομαι 'I struggle', ανακλαδίζομαι 'I squat, stretch myself', αναλογίζομαι 'I contemplate', ανταγωνίζομαι 'I compete', ασπάζομαι 'I embrace', εργάζομαι 'I work', ισχυρίζομαι 'I assert', περιεργάζομαι 'I scrutinize', προοιωνίζομαι 'I augur, portend', προφασίζομαι 'I allege', σπλαχνίζομαι 'I take pity on', στοχάζομαι 'I reflect on', υποψιάζομαι 'I suspect', φαντάζομαι 'I imagine', χρειάζομαι 'I need'

(xi) Imperfective stem ending in -ζ-, active perfective -ξ-, passive perfective -χτ- (and, more formally, -χθ-) (e.g. πειράζω, πείραξα, πειράχτηκα):

αγγίζω 'I touch', †αλαλάζω 'I cheer', αλλάζω 'I change', ανατινάζω 'I blow up', †αράζω 'I moor', αρπάζω 'I seize', βαστάζω 'I bear', †βουίζω 'I buzz', †βουλιάζω 'I sink', διατάζω 'I order', κοιτάζω 'I look at', κράζω 'I call', †κρώζω 'I crow', †λιμάζω 'I am famished', †λουφάζω 'I lie low', †λυσσάζω 'I [en]rage or become enraged', μαλάζω 'I soften', †νυστάζω 'I am sleepy', †ουρλιάζω 'I howl', παίζω 'I play', πειράζω 'I annoy', †πήζω 'I congeal', ρημάζω 'I ruin', σ(ι)άζω 'I straighten, fix', σκιάζω 'I scare', †σκούζω 'I howl', †σπαράζω 'I rend', †στάζω 'I drip', †σταλάζω 'I drip', †στενάζω 'I groan', στηρίζω 'I support', †στίζω 'I dot', στοιβάζω 'I pile up', στραγγίζω 'I strain' (can also follow type (x)), στραμπουλίζω 'I sprain', συνάζω 'I assemble', σφάζω 'I slaughter', †σφυρίζω 'I whistle', τάζω 'I promise', ταράζω 'I agitate', τινάζω 'I shake', τραντάζω 'I rattle', †τρίζω 'I creak', †τρομάζω 'I scare; take fright', †τσιρίζω 'I squeal', †τσούζω 'I sting', †φαντάζω 'I impress', φράζω 'I block', †φρυάζω 'I get mad', †φωνάζω 'I call, shout', χαράζω 'I engrave'

(xii) Imperfective stem ending in -v- (after a vowel), active perfective -σ-, passive perfective -θ- (e.g. ντύνω, έντυσα, ντύθηκα):

ακυρώνω 'I invalidate', ανταμώνω 'I meet', απλώνω 'I spread', αφιερώνω 'I dedicate', βεβαιώνω 'I affirm', γδύνω 'I undress', δένω 'I tie', ισοπεδώνω 'I flatten', λύνω 'I undo', ντύνω 'I dress', ολοκληρώνω 'I complete', προσδένω 'I fasten', σηκώνω 'I lift', στήνω 'I set up', στρώνω 'I spread', σώνω 'I use up, reach', χάνω 'I lose', χύνω 'I pour', χώνω 'I hide, bury', ψήνω 'I roast', and all other verbs in -ώνω (except ζώνω, which follows type (xiii))

Similarly the deponent verbs:

δεξιώνομαι 'I entertain', εναντιώνομαι 'I oppose', καμώνομαι 'I feign'

(xiii) Imperfective stem ending in -ν- (after a vowel), active perfective -σ-, passive perfective -στ- (e.g. κλείνω, έκλεισα, κλείστηκα):

ζώνω 'I belt, encircle', κλείνω 'I shut', ξύνω 'I scratch', πιάνω 'I catch', σβήνω 'I extinguish', †φτάνω 'I arrive, reach', †φτύνω 'I spit'

(xiv) Imperfective stem ending in -ν- (after a vowel), active perfective -ν-, passive perfective -θ- (e.g. κρίνω, έκρινα, κρίθηκα):

ανακρίνω 'I interrogate', διακρίνω 'I distinguish', †κλίνω 'I incline', κρίνω 'I judge'

Similarly the deponent verbs:

ανταποκρίνομαι 'I correspond', υποκλίνομαι 'I bow, curtsey'

(xv) Imperfective stem ending in -ν- (after a vowel), active perfective -ν-, passive perfective -νθ- (e.g. ενθαρρύνω, ενεθάρρυνα, ενθαρρύνθηκα):

αμβλύνω 'I blunt', απευθύνω 'I address', αποθαρρύνω 'I discourage', αποθρασύνω 'I make bold', απομακρύνω 'I remove', †βραδύνω 'I slow down', διευθύνω 'I manage', (δι)ευκολύνω 'I facilitate', (δι)ευρύνω 'I widen', ελαφρύνω 'I lighten', †εμβαθύνω 'I probe into', ενθαρρύνω 'I encourage', εξομαλύνω 'I smooth out', επιβαρύνω 'I aggravate', επιβραδύνω 'I retard, slow down', επιταχύνω 'I accelerate', λαμπρύνω 'I add lustre to', λεπτύνω (also λεπταίνω) 'I make *or* become thin', μεγεθύνω 'I enlarge, magnify', μολύνω 'I pollute', οξύνω 'I sharpen, aggravate', παροτρύνω 'I exhort', σμικρύνω 'I reduce (in size)', †ταχύνω 'I quicken', τραχύνω 'I make *or* become rough'

Similarly the deponent verbs:

αισθάνομαι 'I feel', αμύνομαι 'I defend myself'

(xvi) Imperfective stem ending in -αιν-, active perfective -αν-, passive perfective -ανθ- (e.g. εξυγιαίνω, εξυγίανα, εξυγιάνθηκα):

†ανασαίνω 'I breathe', απολυμαίνω 'I disinfect', διαλευκαίνω 'I clarify', †δυσχεραίνω 'I impede', εξυγιαίνω 'I make healthy',

επισημαίνω 'I point out', ευφραίνω 'I gladden', θερμαίνω
'I warm', κοιλαίνω 'I hollow out', λειαίνω 'I smooth', λευκαίνω
'I whiten', λιπαίνω 'I grease', μιαίνω 'I defile', μοιραίνω 'I appor-
tion', μωραίνω 'I stupefy', †ξεθυμαίνω 'I blow over, let off steam',
ξηραίνω 'I dry', †πεθαίνω 'I die', ραίνω 'I sprinkle' (simple past
έρρανα), ρυπαίνω 'I pollute', †σημαίνω 'I sound, mean',
†συμπεραίνω 'I conclude', υγραίνω 'I moisten', υφαίνω 'I weave',
†φυραίνω 'I shrink', †χλιαίνω 'I make *or* become tepid'

Similarly the deponent verbs:

αποφαίνομαι 'I declare myself', κυμαίνομαι 'I fluctuate',
οσφραίνομαι 'I sniff [at]'

(xvii) Imperfective stem ending in -αιν-, active perfective -αν-, passive
perfective -αθ- (e.g. τρελαίνω, τρέλανα, τρελάθηκα):

απομωραίνω 'I drive mad', βασκαίνω 'I cast the evil eye on',
βουβαίνω 'I strike dumb', †γιαίνω 'I get well' (rarely in the
present), γλυκαίνω 'I sweeten', ζεσταίνω 'I warm', ζουρλαίνω
'I drive mad', κουτσαίνω 'I limp; cripple', κουφαίνω 'I deafen',
λωλαίνω 'I drive mad', μαραίνω 'I wither', μουγγαίνω 'I strike
dumb', μουρλαίνω 'I drive mad', ξεραίνω 'I dry', πικραίνω 'I
make bitter', †σγουραίνω 'I make *or* become curly', τρελαίνω
'I madden', ψυχραίνω 'I chill' (passive perfective also -ανθ- in
certain phrases)

Similarly the deponent verbs:

ξεμωραίνομαι 'I lose my wits', σιχαίνομαι 'I loathe'

(xviii) Imperfective stem ending in αιν-, active perfective -υν-, no passive
perfective forms (e.g. βαραίνω, βάρυνα):

†ακριβαίνω 'I raise the price of', †ανοσταίνω 'I become tasteless',
†απαλαίνω 'I soften', †ασχημαίνω 'I make *or* become ugly',
†βαθαίνω 'I deepen', †βαραίνω 'I weigh down [on]', †ελαφραίνω
'I lighten', †κονταίνω 'I shorten', †λεπταίνω (also λεπτύνω) 'I
make *or* become thin', †μακραίνω 'I lengthen', †μικραίνω 'I make
or become smaller', †ομορφαίνω 'I beautify *or* become beautiful',
†παχαίνω 'I make *or* become fat', †πλαταίνω 'I widen',
†πληθαίνω 'I increase', †σκληραίνω 'I harden', †σκουραίνω 'I
darken', †φαρδαίνω 'I widen', †φτηναίνω 'I cheapen', †φτωχαίνω
'I make *or* become poor', †χοντραίνω 'I get fat'.

Some of these verbs have alternative forms from *katharevousa* with
a stem in -υν-; they then follow type (xv) and may have passive
perfective forms in -υνθ-.

(xix) Imperfective stem ending in -αιν-, active perfective – (syllable dropped), passive perfective irregular or non-existent (e.g. παθαίνω, έπαθα, –):

†απστυχαίνω 'I fail', †λαβαίνω 'I take' (also λαμβάνω), †καταλαβαίνω 'I understand', †λαχαίνω 'I come across, happen', μαθαίνω 'I learn' (passive perfective -ευτ-), †παθαίνω 'I suffer', †πετυχαίνω 'I succeed', †πηγαίνω 'I go' (see table of irregular verbs), †προλαβαίνω 'I have time to do, catch', †τυχαίνω 'I chance' (-τυγχάνω in compounds)

(xx) Imperfective stem ending in -αιν-, active perfective -ασ-, no passive perfective (e.g. χορταίνω, χόρτασα):

†αποσταίνω 'I get tired', †προφταίνω 'I do something in time', †σωπαίνω 'I fall silent', †χορταίνω 'I make or become satisfied'

(xxi) Imperfective stem ending in -αιν-/-αν-, active perfective -ησ-, passive perfective -ηθ- (e.g. αυξαίνω, αύξησα, αυξήθηκα):

†αμαρταίνω or †αμαρτάνω 'I sin', ανασταίνω 'I resurrect', †αρρωσταίνω 'I fall ill', αυξαίνω or αυξάνω 'I increase', †βλασταίνω or βλαστάνω 'I sprout', †ολισθαίνω 'I slide, drift', παρασταίνω 'I depict'

(xxii) Imperfective stem ending in -αρ-/-ιρ-, active perfective -αρισ-/-ιρισ- or -αρ-/-ιρ- (see note below), passive perfective -αριστ-/-ιριστ- (e.g. σοκάρω, σοκάρισα/σόκαρα, σοκαρίστηκα):

αγκαζάρω 'I engage, hire', ακομπανιάρω 'I accompany [musically]', †αμπραγιάρω 'I let in the clutch', γαρνίρω 'I garnish', †γουστάρω 'I have a taste for', †καλμάρω 'I calm (down)', καμουφλάρω 'I camouflage', κουμαντάρω 'I manage', †λασκάρω 'I slacken', λουστράρω 'I shine', μανουβράρω 'I manoeuvre', †μπαρκάρω 'I embark', μπλοκάρω 'I block[ade]', νετάρω 'I finish', πακετάρω 'I pack up', †παρκάρω 'I park', παρκετάρω 'I polish [floor]', †πασάρω 'I pass [on]', πλασάρω 'I sell', †ποζάρω 'I pose', †ποντάρω 'I stake', προβάρω 'I try on/out', ραφινάρω 'I refine', ρεγουλάρω 'I regulate', ρεκλαμάρω 'I advertise', ρετουσάρω 'I retouch', †σαλπάρω 'I weigh anchor', †σαλτάρω 'I jump', σαμποτάρω 'I sabotage', σερβίρω 'I serve', σκιτσάρω 'I sketch', σοκάρω 'I shock', †σουλατσάρω 'I saunter', σταμπάρω 'I stamp', στραπατσάρω 'I damage', τουμπάρω 'I overturn', τρακάρω 'I crash', τσεκάρω 'I check, tick', †φαλίρω 'I become bankrupt, bust', †φλερτάρω 'I flirt [with]', φοδράρω 'I line', †φουμάρω 'I smoke', †φρενάρω 'I brake', φρεσκάρω 'I freshen up', and all other verbs in -άρω and -ίρω (following a consonant)

The active perfective forms with the additional syllable -ισ- are limited to the 1st, 2nd and 3rd person sg. and the 3rd person pl. of the simple past, e.g. παρκάρισα, παρκάρισες, παρκάρισε, παρκάρισαν, with πάρκαρα etc. as alternatives. For all other perfective forms the same stem is used as for the imperfective, e.g. παρκάραμε, θα παρκάρουν, έχω παρκάρει, πάρκαρε (imp.). Some of these verbs have an alternative present in -έρνω, not often used today.

Formation of perfective stems of first-conjugation verbs

The following table summarizes the information given above concerning the various patterns which first-conjugation verbs follow in the formation of their active and passive perfective stems. The more formal alternatives for the passive perfective stems are omitted here, but will be discussed in Section 7.9.3. In the final column of each line the bracketed roman numeral refers to the relevant lists above.

Imperfective stem in	Active perfective stem in	Passive perfective stem in	Type
Vowel	-σ-	-στ-	(i)
	-σ-	-θ-	(ii)
-ε-	-ευσ-	-ευστ-	(iii)
Labial consonant	-ψ-	-φτ-	(iv)
-αυ-/-ευ-	-αψ-/-εψ-	-αυτ-/-ευτ-	(v)
	-αυσ-/-ευσ-	-αυτ-/-ευτ-	(vi)
Velar consonant (or cluster)	-ξ-	-χτ-	(vii)
Dental consonant	-σ-	-στ-	(viii)
-σσ-/-ττ-	-ξ-	-χτ-	(ix)
-ζ-	-σ-	-στ-	(x)
	-ξ-	-χτ-	(xi)
-ν- after vowel	-σ-	-θ-	(xii)
	-σ-	-στ-	(xiii)
	-ν-	-θ-	(xiv)
	-ν-	-νθ-	(xv)
-αιν-	-αν-	-ανθ-	(xvi)
	-αν-	-αθ-	(xvii)
	-υν-	(no passive perf.)	(xviii)
	– (syllable dropped)	(irregular or lacking)	(xix)
	-ασ-	(lacking)	(xx)
-αιν-/-αν-	-ησ-	-ηθ-	(xxi)
-αρ-/-ιρ-	-αρισ-/-ιρισ- or -αρ-/-ιρ- (see note above)	-αριστ-/-ιριστ-	(xxii)

7.9.2 SECOND CONJUGATION VERBS (OXYTONE)

As discussed in Section 7.3, verbs of the second conjugation divide into two types, according to the way they form their active present tense. In the following lists, verbs which follow (or can follow) type A in their present active (see Section 7.3) are identified by (A) or (A/B); verbs not so marked follow type B. However, the vast majority of verbs of both types A and B form their perfective stems in the same, regular, way, i.e. as in (i) below. The exceptions are verbs which have a different vowel (α or ε) before the perfective stem ending, and/or different consonants, i.e. -ξ- (active) -χτ- (passive) at the end of the perfective stem, as in (ii) to (vi), or which have a different vowel and also drop the -ν- of the imperfective (present) stem, as in (vii).

(i)   active perfective -ησ-, passive perfective -ηθ- (e.g. γεννώ, γέννησα, γεννήθηκα):

αγνοώ 'I ignore', †αγρυπνώ 'I stay awake', ακουμπώ (A) 'I lean', απαντώ (A) 'I answer', γεννώ (A) 'I give birth to', †γλεντώ (A) 'I have a good time', †ξυπνώ (A) 'I wake', ομολογώ 'I confess', παρατώ (A) 'I abandon', προτιμώ (A) 'I prefer', φιλώ (A/B) 'I kiss', and the great majority of second conjugation verbs, other than those listed in (ii)–(vii) below.

Similarly the deponent verbs:

αναρωτιέμαι (A) 'I wonder', αρνούμαι 'I refuse, deny', ασχολούμαι 'I am concerned [with]', μιμούμαι 'I imitate'.

(ii)   active perfective -ασ-, passive perfective -αστ- (e.g. κρεμώ, κρέμασα, κρεμάστηκα):

(αντ)ανακλώ (A) 'I reflect', αντιδρώ (A) 'I react', αποσπώ (A) 'I detach, send on secondment', γελώ (A) 'I laugh; deceive', διαθλώ (A) 'I refract', διασπώ (A) 'I split, break through', †διψώ (A) 'I thirst', †δρω (A) 'I act', †επιδρώ (A) 'I influence', κρεμώ (A) 'I hang', ξεγελώ (A) 'I fool', †ξεσπώ (A) 'I break out', †πεινώ (A) 'I am hungry', †σπάω (A) 'I break', †σχολώ (A) 'I stop working', χαλώ (A) 'I spoil', †χαμογελώ (A) 'I smile', †ωχριώ (A) 'I turn pale'.

Similarly the deponent verb:

καταριέμαι (A) 'I curse'.

(iii)   active perfective -εσ-, passive perfective -εστ- (e.g. αποτελώ, αποτέλεσα, αποτελέστηκα):

αποτελώ 'I constitute', αρκώ 'I suffice, limit', †διαρκώ 'I last', †διατελώ 'I remain, am', καλώ 'I call' (but see table of irregular verbs for compounds of -καλώ), †καρτερώ (A/B) 'I wait', †μπορώ 'I can', συντελώ 'I contribute', τελώ 'I perform', †χωρώ (A/B) 'I contain, fit [into]'

(iv) active perfective -εσ-, passive perfective -εθ- (e.g. επαινώ, επαίνεσα, επαινέθηκα):

αναιρώ 'I refute', αφαιρώ 'I remove', †βαρώ (A) 'I beat, sound', διαιρώ 'I divide', εξαιρώ 'I except', επαινώ 'I praise', καταφρονώ 'I despise', †πονώ (A/B) 'I pain, hurt', στενοχωρώ 'I distress' (also -ησ-, -ηθ-), φορώ (A) 'I put on, wear'

Similarly the deponent verbs:

βαριέμαι 'I am bored, fed up', παραπονιέμαι 'I complain'

(v) active perfective -αξ-, passive perfective -αχτ- (e.g. κοιτώ, κοίταξα, κοιτάχτηκα):

βαστώ (A) 'I bear', κοιτώ (A) 'I look at', πετώ (A) 'I throw; fly'

(vi) active perfective -ηξ-, passive perfective -ηχτ- (e.g. τραβώ, τράβηξα, τραβήχτηκα):

βαστώ (A) 'I bear' (but more commonly as type (v)), †βογκώ (A) 'I groan', βουτώ (A) 'I dive', †βροντώ 'I thunder' (active perfective also -ησ-), ζουλώ (A) 'I squeeze', πηδώ (A) 'I jump' (active perfective also -ησ-), ρουφώ (A) 'I suck', σκουντώ (A) 'I prod', τραβώ (A) 'I pull', †φυσώ (A) 'I blow', †χυμώ (A) 'I rush'

(vii) Imperfective stem ending in consonant + -ν-, active perfective -ασ-, passive perfective -αστ- (e.g. ξεχνώ, ξέχασα, ξεχάστηκα):

†γερνώ (A) 'I grow old', κερνώ (A) 'I treat [e.g. to a drink]', ξεπερνώ (A) 'I exceed', ξεχνώ (A) 'I forget', †ξερνώ (A) 'I vomit', περνώ (A) 'I pass'

7.9.3 THE PHONOLOGY OF CERTAIN PASSIVE PERFECTIVE STEMS

In discussing the formation of the perfective stems in Sections 7.9.1–7.9.2 we noted that in certain cases the passive perfective stem has a more formal alternative. We can list the alternatives as follows: -στ- vs. more formal -σθ- (including stems in -ευστ- vs. -ευσθ-), -φτ- vs. more formal -φθ- (including stems in -αυτ- vs. -αυθ- and -ευτ- vs. -ευθ-), and -χτ- vs. more formal -χθ-. The first case consists of a sibilant + a dental plosive (στ), which alternates with sibilant + fricative (σθ); the second and third cases consist of combinations of fricative + dental plosive (φτ, χτ), which alternate with clusters of two fricatives (φθ, χθ). The second, more formal, members of these pairs reflect *katharevousa* phonology, while the less formal have undergone dissimilation according to the normal rules of demotic phonology (see Part I, Section 1.4.2). In the passive perfective forms of the verb, the choice between the two alternatives depends on a number of factors: (i) it may be determined by the verb itself – a colloquial verb will have the less formal consonant cluster, while a word of learned origin will normally attract the more formal stem ending, e.g. colloquial σβήστηκε 'it was put out', but more formal κατασκευάσθηκε 'it was manufactured'; (ii) it may also be determined by the presence of learned morphological elements, e.g. the augment in συνελήφθησαν 'they were arrested', or the learned ending of the 3rd person singular of the passive simple past in ελέχθη 'it was said'; (iii) another possible factor is the presence of other *katharevousa* consonant clusters in the same word, e.g. αναπτύχθηκε 'it was developed' (πτ indicates learned origin, even though the morphology is not in itself learned or formal). In other words, the alternation is connected with **register**, but it is not quite as simple as that. Personal preference and style also play important parts. While some verbs have genuine alternative forms, in many verbs one or the other form has prevailed in actual usage – or is tending to prevail, because the situation is far from being fixed. Consequently, it is important to be aware of the alternative phonologies, but the only true guide is the usage of native-speakers in relation to a particular verb.

7.10   AUGMENT

Augment involves a change to the beginning of the verb stem when the verb is in a past tense. If the verb stem begins with a consonant an additional syllable ε- is prefixed to the stem (*syllabic augment*). If the stem begins with a vowel, the vowel undergoes a change, traditionally described as lengthening (*vocalic augment*). In Ancient Greek all past tenses of verbs had augmentation as a regular morphological feature. In Modern Greek augmentation, when it occurs, can be divided into the following three categories: (i) syllabic augment, which is obligatory when it carries the stress in past tense forms, (ii) vocalic augment in a restricted number of verbs; and (iii) *internal augment*, which can be vocalic or syllabic, in verbs which have a prepositional prefix. These three types of augment are discussed and described in the sections which follow.

7.10.1   SYLLABIC AUGMENT

Syllabic augment is found only in verb forms in a past tense, with a stem beginning with a consonant. It is obligatory when the verb form consists of a one-syllable stem and a one-syllable ending and consequently (because of the antepenultimate rule) the augment carries the stress, e.g. έ-γραψ-α

'I wrote' (simple past), έ-γραφ-ες 'you (sg.) were writing/used to write' (imperfect), έ-πρεπ-ε 'it was necessary'. When the verb stem consists of more than one syllable the augment is not normally used, e.g. φώναξ-α 'I called', φώναζ-ε 's/he was calling/used to call'. Similarly, when a verb with a one-syllable stem has an ending of more than one syllable, the augment is not normally used, e.g. γράψ-αμε 'we wrote', γράφτ-ηκε 'it was written'. Thus, the augment is only obligatory in the active past tense forms (imperfect and simple past) of first conjugation verbs with a one-syllable stem, when they are in the singular or in the 3rd person plural with the ending -αν, e.g. έ-στειλ-αν 'they sent'. There are, however, a small number of verbs which have a simple past with a one-syllable stem but do not have an augment; they are: βγήκα 'I went out' (from βγαίνω, but imperfect έβγαινα, with augment) βρήκα 'I found' (from βρίσκω, but imperfect έβρισκα), μπήκα 'I went in' (from μπαίνω, but imperfect έμπαινα), πήγα 'I went' (from πηγαίνω), πήρα 'I took' (from παίρνω, but imperfect έπαιρνα).

Syllabic augment is also found in certain passive simple past forms of learned origin, where it is unstressed, e.g. ε-λέχθη 'it was said', ε-στάλη 's/he/it was sent'. In addition it occurs in some other past forms of learned origin, e.g. ε-πρόκειτο 'was going to'. In cases of this kind it is largely a matter of cliché expressions which have been taken over from *katharevousa*.

7.10.2   VOCALIC AUGMENT

Vocalic augment, whereby the initial vowel ε-, α- or αι- of a verb stem is changed ('lengthened') to η- in past tense forms, is limited to a small number of verbs. The most common example is ή-λπιζα 'I hoped' (imperfect) from ελπίζω, but the unaugmented form έλπιζα is also used. Vocalic augment does not normally occur when the initial vowel does not carry the stress. Therefore, the 1st and 2nd persons pl. of the imperfect of this verb are always ελπίζαμε, ελπίζατε. Among the few verbs which have vocalic augment, which is hardly ever obligatory, are: ελέγχω 'I check, control' (simple past ήλεγξα), and αίρω 'I lift [e.g. a ban]' (simple past ήρα). Vocalic augment is also found internally, i.e. after a prepositional prefix; see the following section.

Three other verbs have past forms with an augment η- (although this is not strictly vocalic augment): θέλω 'I want', imperfect ήθελα (but without the augment when it would not carry stress, e.g. θέλαμε 'we wanted'); ξέρω 'I know', imperfect ήξερα (but no augment when it would not carry stress); πίνω 'I drink', simple past ήπια (ή- in all persons, but imperfect έπινα etc.).

7.10.3 INTERNAL AUGMENT

Internal augment may be either syllabic or vocalic. It occurs in past tenses of compound verbs, between the prepositional prefix (i.e. prefixes that are derived from Ancient Greek prepositions) and the stem of the verb, and mainly when the stress falls on the augment, e.g. υπ-έβαλα 'I submitted' (from υποβάλλω). The possible prepositional prefixes are the following:

αμφι-
ανα-
αντι-
απο-
δια-
εισ-
εκ- (εξ- before a vowel, e.g. εξαντλώ 'I exhaust')
εν- (εμ- before β, μ, π, φ, ψ, e.g. εμπνέω 'I inspire'; εγ- before γ, κ, ξ, χ, e.g. εγκρίνω 'I approve'; ελ- before λ, e.g. ελλοχεύω 'I lie in wait')
επι-
κατα-
μετα-
παρα-
περι-
προ-
προσ-
συν- (συμ- before β, μ, π, φ, ψ, e.g. συμβαίνει 'it happens', συμπίπτω 'I coincide'; συγ- before γ, κ, ξ, χ, e.g. συγκρούω 'I collide'; συλ- before λ, e.g. συλλαμβάνω 'I arrest'; συρ- before ρ, e.g. συρράπτω 'I stitch together'; συ- before σ, e.g. συστέλλω 'I contract')
υπερ-
υπο-

7.10.3.1 Internal syllabic augment

Those prepositional prefixes which end in a vowel (with certain exceptions) drop the final vowel before an augment, e.g. απο-ρρίπτω 'I reject', simple past απ-έρριψα; επι-βάλλω 'I impose', simple past επ-έβαλα; υπο-δείχνω 'I point out', simple past υπ-έδειξα. The exceptions are περι- and προ-, which always retain the vowel, e.g. περι-πλέκω 'I complicate', simple past περι-έπλεξα. If a prepositional prefix has been assimilated to a following consonant in the present tense, it must be restored to its underlying form when there is a following augment, e.g. συμβαίνει 'it happens', συν-έβη 'it happened'; εγκρίνω 'I approve', εν-έκρινα 'I approved'.

Some verbs have two prepositional prefixes, e.g. επ-ανα-λαμβάνω 'I repeat', παρ-εμ-βάλλω 'I interpose', συμ-περι-λαμβάνω 'I include'. In such cases the augment comes after the second prefix, e.g. επαν-έλαβα 'I repeated'.

Because the syllabic augment is not obligatory except when stressed, a typical past tense paradigm might be as follows:

Simple past of παραδίδω 'I hand over, surrender'

Sg.	1	παρέδωσα	Pl.	1	παραδώσαμε
	2	παρέδωσες		2	παραδώσατε
	3	παρέδωσε		3	παρέδωσαν/παραδώσανε

However, many common verbs with prepositional prefixes never have internal augment, even when it would be stressed. For example, καταλαβαίνω 'I understand' has simple past κατάλαβα (contrast this with κατέλαβα 'I seized, occupied' from καταλαμβάνω); προφτάνω 'I have time to [do something], catch' has simple past πρόφτασα.

Prefixes other than prepositions which can be combined with a verb include: κακο- 'badly', καλο- 'well', ξανα- 'again', παρα- 'too much, over-', πολυ- 'much'. After ξανα- and παρα- the use of the stress-carrying augment is optional, e.g. either ξανάγραψα or ξαναέγραψα 'I rewrote', παράκανα or παραέκανα 'I overdid'. After the rest of these prefixes the augment is not normally found, e.g. κακόμαθε 's/he learned bad habits'.

Internal syllabic augment is also found in forms with learned endings, particularly in the passive simple past, where it is unstressed, e.g. ανεκοινώθη 'it was announced', συνελήφθησαν 'they were arrested'.

7.10.3.2 Internal vocalic augment

Vocalic augment is more common in internal position, i.e. after a prepositional prefix, than it is in initial position (see Section 7.10.2). It is obligatory in the imperfect and simple past of υπάρχω 'I exist' (υπήρχα, υπήρξα). Other commonly encountered examples are: παραγγέλλω 'I order', simple past παρήγγειλα; απεργώ 'I go on strike', simple past απήργησα; απαντώ 'I answer', simple past απήντησα (a formal alternative to απάντησα); εξάπτω 'I inflame', simple past εξήψα.

7.11 THE PASSIVE PERFECT PARTICIPLE

All passive perfect participles end in -μένος and are fully inflected for number, gender and case (see Section 3.1). The stem to which the ending -μένος is attached is usually closely related to the passive perfective stem (see Section 7.9, and for irregular verbs the table in Section 7.13). Some passive perfect participles have a consonant preceding the ending -μένος, while others do not. While intransitive verbs do not normally form passive perfect participles, there are some notable exceptions (see note 4 below). For the use of this and other participle forms see Part III, Section 1.8.

The following list shows the principal regular patterns for the formation of the passive perfect participle from the passive perfective stem – or, in the case of verbs which lack a passive perfective stem, what that stem would be – with some examples of each kind:

-στ-/-σθ-/-νθ-   →   -σμένος
ακουσμένος 'heard' (ακούω), ζαλισμένος 'dizzy' (ζαλίζω), σπασμένος 'broken' (σπάζω/σπάω), γαρνιρισμένος 'garnished' (γαρνίρω), καλεσμένος 'called' (καλώ), κρεμασμένος 'hung' (κρεμώ), περασμένος 'past/passed' (περνώ), θερμασμένος 'heated' (θερμαίνω)

-θ- *(after a vowel, λ or ρ)*   →   *-μένος*
παραλυμένος 'paralysed' (παραλύω), ντυμένος 'dressed' (ντύνω), χαμένος 'lost' (χάνω), πληρωμένος 'paid' (πληρώνω), αγαπημένος 'loved' (αγαπώ), χτυπημένος 'hit' (χτυπώ), αναγγελμένος 'announced' (αναγγέλλω), σπαρμένος 'sown, scattered' (σπέρνω), φερμένος 'brought' (φέρνω), ζεσταμένος 'warmed' (ζεσταίνω), πικραμένος 'embittered' (πικραίνω)

-φτ-/-φθ-   →   -μμένος
αναμμένος 'lit' (ανάβω), καλυμμένος 'covered' (καλύπτω), βλαμμένος 'hurt' (βλάπτω), εγκαταλειμμένος 'abandoned' (εγκαταλείπω)

-χτ-/-χθ-   →   -γμένος
ανοιγμένος 'opened' (ανοίγω), προσεγμένος 'cared for' (προσέχω), βουλιαγμένος 'sunk' (βουλιάζω), εξελιγμένος 'developed' (εξελίσσω), τραβηγμένος 'pulled' (τραβώ)

These basic rules are qualified and supplemented in the following notes concerning exceptions and alternatives:

1. Verbs in -εύω may form their passive perfect participle in either -ευμένος or -εμένος. The former is usual for verbs in more formal use; this group can be roughly equated with verbs that normally have their active perfective stem in -ευσ- (see Section 7.9.1(vi)). The forms in -εμένος are non-formal, e.g. μαγειρεμένος 'cooked', δουλεμένος 'worked, wrought', μαζεμένος 'gathered', ξενιτεμένος 'exiled, living abroad', παντρεμένος 'married'. Some verbs of this kind can take either ending, the choice between them being a matter of register or style.

2. Some verbs with passive perfect participle in -γμένος can optionally drop the velar consonant γ, e.g. πετα(γ)μένος 'thrown' (πετώ), τυλι(γ)μένος 'wrapped' (τυλίγω).

3. Verbs with imperfective stems ending in -αιν- or -υν- present particular problems in the formation of their passive perfect participle. We consider them following the arrangement of perfective stems presented in Section 7.9.1 (xv)–(xxi):

(xv)   mostly -υσμένος, e.g. απομακρυσμένος 'removed, distanced', but αμβλυμμένος 'blunted', αποθαρρημένος 'discouraged', αποθρασυμένος 'emboldened', ενθαρρημένος 'encouraged', επιβαρημένος 'aggravated', οξυμένος 'sharpened, acute'. The remainder do not normally have passive perfect participles.

(xvi)   the following in -ασμένος: απολυμασμένος 'disinfected', εξυγιασμένος 'made healthy', επισημασμένος 'noted', θερμασμένος 'warmed', λιπασμένος 'greased', μιασμένος 'defiled', ρυπασμένος 'polluted', σεσημασμένος 'marked', υφασμένος 'woven'. The remainder have passive perfect participles in -αμένος, e.g. πεθαμένος 'dead', except that verbs with no passive perfective stem do not normally form a perfect participle.

(xvii) all in -αμένος, e.g. βουβαμένος 'struck dumb'.

(xviii) the only verb of this group which has a passive perfect participle is μακραίνω – μακρεμένος 'lengthened'.

(xix)   passive perfect participles, all in -ημένος, are limited to the following: αποτυχημένος 'failed', μαθημένος 'learnt', παθημένος 'suffered', πετυχημένος 'successful'.

(xx)   αποσταμένος 'tired', χορτασμένος 'satiated, "full up"'. The others have no passive perfect participle.

(xxi)   where they exist, the passive perfect participles are in -ημένος, e.g. αυξημένος 'increased'.

4. Some verbs which do not have finite passive forms nonetheless form a passive perfect participle, e.g.

αγαναχτώ 'I am indignant', p.p.p. αγαναχτισμένος 'indignant'
αγρυπνώ 'I stay awake', p.p.p. αγρυπνισμένος 'awake, vigilant'
ακουμπώ 'I lean', p.p.p. ακουμπισμένος 'leaning'
αποσταίνω 'I get tired', p.p.p. αποσταμένος 'tired'
αρρωσταίνω 'I become ill', p.p.p. αρρωστημένος 'ill'
γερνώ 'I grow old', p.p.p. γερασμένος 'aged'
διψώ 'I am thirsty', p.p.p. διψασμένος 'thirsty'
δυστυχώ 'I am unhappy', p.p.p. δυστυχισμένος 'unhappy, unfortunate'
ευτυχώ 'I am happy', p.p.p. ευτυχισμένος 'happy'
θυμώνω 'I get angry', p.p.p. θυμωμένος 'angry'
λιποθυμώ 'I faint', p.p.p. λιποθυμισμένος 'fainted, unconscious'
ναυαγώ 'I become shipwrecked', p.p.p. ναυαγισμένος 'shipwrecked'
πεινώ 'I am hungry', p.p.p. πεινασμένος 'hungry'
ταξιδεύω 'I travel', p.p.p. ταξιδεμένος 'much-travelled'

5. For verbs which form their passive perfect participle in irregular ways, see the Table of irregular verbs (Section 7.13).

6. Some passive perfect participles exhibit **reduplication**; this will be discussed in the following section.

7.11.1 REDUPLICATION

In Section 7.2.2.10 it was noted that reduplication sometimes occurs in the passive perfect participles of certain verbs, and some common examples were given there. It must be stressed that reduplication is not applied to all verbs but is a learned feature, inherited from *katharevousa* and restricted to certain verbs, some of which, however, are in very common use, e.g. συγκεκριμένος 'certain, specific' (from συγκρίνω), having acquired a distinct meaning or function as adjectives. The rules for reduplication are as follows:

1. Verb stems which begin with one of the consonants β, γ, δ, κ, λ, μ, ν, π, σ, or τ are prefixed with an additional syllable consisting of the same consonant + ε, e.g. βεβιασμένος 'forced, hasty' (from βιάζω), δεδηλωμένος 'declared' (from δηλώνω, or rather from the formal δηλώ), δεδομένος 'given' (from δίνω), πεπεισμένος 'convinced' (from πείθω), σεσημασμένος 'marked [a marked man]' (from σημαίνω), τετελεσμένος 'finished, accomplished' (from τελώ), τετριμμένος 'trite'.

2. Verb stems which begin with θ, φ or χ are prefixed with τ, π, or κ respectively + ε, e.g. τεθλιμμένος 'distressed' (from θλίβω), τεθωρακισμένος 'armoured' (from θωρακίζω).

3. Verb stems which begin with ζ, ρ, or ψ, or with σ + one or more other consonants, are prefixed with ε, e.g. εσκεμμένος 'deliberate' (from σκέπτομαι), εσπευσμένος 'hasty' (from σπεύδω), εσφαλμένος 'mistaken' (from σφάλλω).

4. Verbs stems which begin with one of the vowels α, ε, or αι replace the vowel with η, e.g. ηνωμένος 'united' (from ενώνω).

5. When the verb has a prepositional prefix, the reduplication (in accordance with the above rules) comes immediately before the verb stem, e.g. αποδεδειγμένος 'proven' (from αποδεικνύω), αφηρημένος 'abstract' (from αφαιρώ), διακεκριμένος 'distinguished' (from διακρίνω), διατεθειμένος 'disposed' (from διαθέτω), διεστραμμένος 'perverted' (from διαστρέφω), εκτεταμένος 'extended' (from εκτείνω), εξεζητημένος 'recherché' (from εκζητώ), κατεστημένος 'established' (from καθιστώ), κατεψυγμένος 'frozen' (from καταψύχω), προσκεκλημένος 'invited' (from προσκαλώ), συγκεχυμένος 'confused' (from συγχέω), συνδεδεμένος 'connected' (from συνδέω), συνημμένος 'attached' (from συνάπτω), υπογεγραμμένος 'under-signed' (from υπογράφω).

6. Finally, some irregular examples: επανειλημμένος 'repeated' (from επαναλαμβάνω), κατειλημμένος 'occupied' (from καταλαμβάνω).

7.12 LEARNED VERB FORMS

The influence of earlier stages of the language is apparent in the existence of certain learned forms of the verb. In some instances this is merely a matter of different orthography. For example, the 2nd and 3rd person singular endings of the dependent are sometimes spelt with -η instead of -ει, and, in the 1st person pl., -ωμε instead of -ομε (where the more usual ending today is -ουμε). These spellings are sometimes extended to the active present of first-conjugation and second-conjugation type B verbs, when they are combined with a particle (such as να) or follow certain conjunctions (subjunctive use).

Mention has already been made of the learned endings of the passive simple past (Section 7.2.2.3, note 2). The complete set of learned endings of this tense is shown below, using the formal passive simple past of στέλνω, εστάλην 'I was sent' (normally στάλθηκα):

Sg.	1	εστάλην	Pl.	1	εστάλημεν
	2	εστάλης		2	εστάλητε
	3	εστάλη		3	εστάλησαν

Apart from the forms of the 3rd person (sg. and pl.) this learned paradigm is rare. Cliché words in which this morphology may be found include: εξελέγην 'I was elected' (from εκλέγω), εξεπλάγην 'I was surprised' (from εκπλήττω), υπέστην 'I underwent' (from υφίσταμαι, and similarly other compounds of -ίσταμαι, for which see later in this Section). In the table of irregular verbs (Section 7.13), forms of the passive simple past (and certain active simple pasts) which end in -ην follow this pattern, though the forms are not necessarily found for all persons.

The range of participles in common use in Modern Greek is restricted to the active present (Sections 7.2.1.10, 7.3.1.10, 7.4.1.10), the passive present (Sections 7.2.2.9, 7.3.2.9, 7.4.2.9), and the passive perfect (Sections 7.2.2.10, 7.3.2.10, 7.4.2.10, 7.7.9, 7.11). Certain other participles, derived from the complex participle system of Ancient Greek, are sometimes found. They are: an active past (traditionally 'aorist') participle in -ας, -ασα, -αν or -ών, -ούσα, -όν (for the forms see Section 3.11), and a passive past ('aorist') participle in -είς, -είσα, -έν. The active past participle in -ας is formed from the active perfective stem, e.g. ο γράψας 'the writer' [lit. 'the having written']. The only forms which occur are: nom. sg. masc. γράψας, fem. γράψασα, nom. and acc. pl. masc. γράψαντες, acc. sg. masc. γράψαντα, gen. sg. masc. γράψαντος, gen. pl. masc. γραψάντων. Other examples: ο αποβιώσας 'the departed one [i.e. dead]', οι σπουδάσαντες 'those who studied', οι διδάξαντες 'those who taught'. Examples of the other type of active past participle include: ο παθών, η παθούσα, pl. οι παθόντες 'he/she/they who has/have suffered', ο εκλιπών, η εκλιπούσα 'the deceased', ο τυχών, η τυχούσα, το τυχόν 'anyone who comes along/anything that happens', ο επιλαχών, η επιλαχούσα, pl. οι επιλαχόντες 'the runner(s)-up', ο αποτυχών, η αποτυχούσα, pl. οι αποτυχόντες 'he/she/they who has/have failed'.

The passive past participle is based on the passive perfective stem, with the following endings:

	Sg.			Pl.		
	M	F	N	M	F	N
Nom.	-είς	-είσα	-έν	-έντες	-είσες	-έντα
Acc.	-έντα	-είσα(ν)	-έν	-έντες	-είσες	-έντα
Gen.	-έντος	[-είσης]	-έντος	-έντων	[-εισών]	-έντων

Several of these forms are very rare in practice. Examples: ανακοινωθείς 'communicated' (as noun το ανακοινωθέν 'communiqué'), καταργηθείς 'abolished', κατατεθείς 'deposited' (e.g. το σήμα κατατεθέν 'trade-mark'), ληφθείς 'taken' (e.g. τα ληφθέντα μέτρα 'the measures taken'), προταθείς 'proposed', συλληφθείς 'arrested', σχεδιασθείς 'planned'. For the use of these learned participle forms see Part III, Sections 1.8.1.2 and 1.8.2.3.

Two Ancient Greek verbs have given rise to a perplexing array of forms and compounds which need separate consideration. The modern verb θέτω 'I place, pose' derives from Ancient Greek (AG) τίθημι 'I place'. In its active forms it is quite regular: simple past έθεσα, perfect έχω θέσει. Similarly its compounds αναθέτω 'I entrust (something to someone)', διαθέτω 'I have at my disposal', εκθέτω 'I lay out, exhibit', καταθέτω 'I deposit', μεταθέτω 'I transfer', παραθέτω 'I quote', προσθέτω 'I add', συνθέτω 'I compose', υποθέτω 'I suppose' (all have internal augment in past tenses when that syllable carries the stress, e.g. εξέθεσα). The passive of these verbs is quite different. The full forms of the *passive present* are:

Sg.	1	τίθεμαι	Pl.	1	τιθέμεθα
	2	τίθεσαι		2	τίθεσθε
	3	τίθεται		3	τίθενται

(The first- and second-person pl. forms are rarely used.) The passive imperfect is hardly used except in the third person: sg. ετίθετο, pl. ετίθεντο. The remaining passive forms are: simple past τέθηκα, dependent τεθώ, perfect έχω τεθεί. There is a passive present participle τιθέμενος, and a passive perfect participle τεθειμένος.

The second verb, originally from AG ίστημι 'I set up', mainly gives rise to compounds in -ιστώ (all second conjugation, type A), e.g. αντικαθιστώ 'I replace', αποκαθιστώ 'I reinstate', εγκαθιστώ 'I settle (someone)', εφιστώ 'I draw (someone's attention to)', καθιστώ 'I render', συνιστώ 'I recommend'. The θ (instead of τ) and φ (instead of π) in these compounds are due to the fact that the initial vowel of this verb in AG was aspirated. In the simple past, -έστησα, there was no aspiration and the preceding consonants therefore revert to τ and π. Thus, the *simple past* of καθιστώ is:

Sg.	1	κατέστησα	Pl.	1	καταστήσαμε
	2	κατέστησες		2	καταστήσατε
	3	κατέστησε		3	κατέστησαν

Passive present:

Sg.	1	καθίσταμαι	Pl.	1	–
	2	καθίστασαι		2	–
	3	καθίσταται		3	καθίστανται

The passive imperfect is found only in the third-person forms: sg. καθίστατο, pl. καθίσταντο.

Passive simple past:

Sg.	1	κατέστην	Pl.	1	–
	2	κατέστης		2	–
	3	κατέστη		3	κατέστησαν

Passive dependent: καταστώ etc.

The passive present participle is καθιστάμενος and the passive perfect participle κατεστημένος.

Some verbs of this type exist only in the passive, e.g. υφίσταμαι 'I exist' or 'I undergo', συνίσταται 'it consists of/in', pl. συνίστανται (third-person forms only).

The rather formal deponent verb δύναμαι 'I am able' has the same endings as the present passive of καθίσταμαι.

7.13 TABLE OF IRREGULAR VERBS

Irregular verbs are verbs which have active and/or passive perfective stems or passive perfect participles which are not formed according to any of the patterns given in Sections 7.9 and 7.11, or which present irregularities in the formation of some other form(s), e.g. the imperative. In some cases where the forms are not easily predictable, the verbs have been included in order to help the user; for example, we include all second conjugation verbs which form their active perfective stem otherwise than in -ησ-.

In the first column we give the active present tense of the verb, or the passive present tense in the case of *deponent* verbs (see Section 7.1.9). Where a verb stem exists in the given form only in compounds (i.e. with a prepositional prefix), we put a hyphen before the stem, e.g. -άγω. Compound verbs are only listed separately when they present particular irregularities; otherwise they should be sought under the stem of the 'simple' verb. Second-conjugation verbs are marked (A) or (B) to indicate which type the imperfective forms follow. Impersonal verbs are given in the 3rd person singular.

In the second column we give a single basic meaning of the verb (without a personal pronoun); no meaning is given for verbs which exist only in compounds, since these compounds have a variety of meanings.

In the third column the 1st person singular of the active simple past is given; if the dependent (dep.) or perfective imperative (imp.) is irregular, i.e. it cannot be predicted from the simple past, these forms are also given. On occasions we have indicated that the form given for the simple past tense is really an imperfect (imperf.). The simple past of *deponent* verbs is also given in the third column. The fourth column gives the 1st person singular of the passive simple past (and the passive dependent if not regularly formed from the simple past), and the fifth column the passive perfect participle. A dash (−) in the fourth or fifth column indicates that no form exists. An oblique line (/) indicates alternatives, as do the brackets round part of a form. Brackets round a whole word indicate that the form is rarely used.

Present	Meaning	Active simple past	Passive simple past	Passive perfect participle
αγαναχτώ (A)	am indignant	αγανάχτησα	–	αγαναχτισμένος
-αγγέλλω	(–)	-άγγειλα/ -ήγγειλα dep. -αγγείλω	-αγγέλθηκα	-αγγελμένος
-άγω	(–)	-ήγαγα dep. -αγάγω	-άχθηκα/ -ήχθην	-ηγμένος
αίρω	raise	ήρα dep. άρω	άρθηκα	(ηρμένος)
-αιρώ (B)	(–)	-αίρεσα/-ήρεσα dep. -αιρέσω	-αιρέθηκα	-ηρημένος
ακουμπώ (A)	lean	ακούμπησα	–	ακουμπισμένος
ανακλώ (A)	reflect	ανέκλασα	ανακλάστηκα	ανακλασμένος
αναμιγνύω	mix	ανέμιξα	αναμίχθηκα	ανα(με)μιγμένος
ανασταίνω	resurrect	ανάστησα	αναστήθηκα	αναστημένος
ανατέλλω	rise	ανάτειλα/ ανέτειλα	–	–
ανεβαίνω	go up	ανέβηκα dep. ανέβω/ανεβώ imp. ανέβα, ανεβείτε	–	ανεβασμένος
ανέχομαι	tolerate	ανέχτηκα	–	–
αντέχω	endure	άντεξα	–	–
απαλλάσσω	exempt	απάλλαξα	απαλλάχτηκα dep. απαλλαχτώ/ -αγώ	απαλλαγμένος
απελαύνω	deport	απήλασα dep. απελάσω	απελάθηκα	–
απέχω	am far from	(imperf.) απείχα	–	–
απολαμβάνω	enjoy	απήλαυσα dep. απολαύσω	–	–
αποτυχαίνω	fail	απέτυχα dep. αποτύχω	–	αποτυχημένος
αρέσω	please	άρεσα	–	–
αρκώ (B)	suffice	άρκεσα/ήρκεσα	αρκέστηκα	–
αρταίνω	spice	άρτυσα	αρτύθηκα	αρτυ(σ)μένος
αυξάνω/-αίνω	increase	αύξησα	αυξήθηκα	αυξημένος
αφήνω	leave	άφησα imp. άφησε/άσε, αφήστε/άστε	αφέθηκα	αφη(σ)μένος
βάζω	put	έβαλα	βάλθηκα	βαλμένος
-βαίνω	(–)	-έβην dep. -βώ	–	–

Present	Meaning	Active simple past	Passive simple past	Passive perfect participle
-βάλλω	(–)	-έβαλα	-βλήθηκα	-(βε)βλημένος
βαριέμαι	am bored	βαρέθηκα	–	βαριεστισμένος
βαρώ (Α)	strike	βάρεσα	–	βαρεμένος
βαστώ (Α)	bear	βάσταξα/ βάστηξα	βαστάχτηκα/ βαστήχτηκα	βαστα(γ)μένος/ βαστη(γ)μένος
βάφω	paint	έβαψα	βάφ(τ)ηκα	βαμμένος
βγάζω	take out	έβγαλα	βγάλθηκα	βγαλμένος
βγαίνω	go out	βγήκα dep. βγω imp. βγες/έβγα, βγείτε	–	βγαλμένος
βλέπω	see	είδα dep. δω imp. δες, δέστε/δείτε	ειδώθηκα dep. ιδωθώ	ιδωμένος
-βλέπω	(–)	-έβλεψα	–	–
βογκώ (Α)	groan	βόγκηξα	–	–
βόσκω	graze	βόσκησα	(βοσκήθηκα)	βοσκημένος
βούλομαι	wish	βουλήθηκα	–	–
βουτώ (Α)	dive	βούτηξα	βουτήχτηκα	βουτηγμένος
βρέχω	wet	έβρεξα	βράχηκα	βρε(γ)μένος
βρίσκω	find	βρήκα dep. βρω imp. βρες, βρείτε	βρέθηκα	–
βροντώ (Α)	thunder	βρόντηξα/ βρόντησα	–	–
βυζαίνω	suckle	βύζαξα	βυζάχτηκα	βυζαγμένος
γδέρνω	skin	έγδαρα	γδάρθηκα	γδαρμένος
γελώ (Α)	laugh	γέλασα	γελάστηκα	γελασμένος
γέρνω	lean	έγειρα	–	γερμένος
γερνώ (Α)	grow old	γέρασα	–	γερασμένος
γίνομαι	become	έγινα /γίνηκα dep. γίνω/γενώ	–	γινωμένος
γράφω	write	έγραψα	γράφ(τ)ηκα	γραμμένος
-δεικνύω	(–)	-έδειξα	-δείχθηκα	-(δε)δειγμένος
δέομαι	pray	δεήθηκα	–	–
δέρνω	beat	έδειρα	δάρθηκα	δαρμένος
διαβαίνω	pass [by]	διάβηκα dep. διαβώ	–	–
διαθλώ (Α)	refract	διέθλασα	διαθλάστηκα	διαθλασμένος
διαμαρτύρομαι	protest	διαμαρτυρήθηκα	–	διαμαρτυρημένος
-δίδω	(–)	-έδωσα	-(ε)δόθηκα	-δεδομένος

Present	Meaning	Active simple past	Passive simple past	Passive perfect participle
δίνω	give	έδωσα	δόθηκα	δο(σ)μένος/ δεδομένος
διψώ (A)	am thirsty	δίψασα	–	διψασμένος
δρω (A)	act	έδρασα	–	–
εγείρω	erect	ήγειρα	εγέρθηκα	εγερμένος
εκλέγω	elect	εξέλεξα dep. εκλέξω	εκλέχτηκα dep. εκλεγώ	εκλεγμένος
εκπλήσσω	surprise	εξέπληξα	εξεπλάγην dep. εκπλαγώ	–
εκρήγνυμαι	explode	εξερράγην dep. εκραγώ	–	–
επαινώ (B)	praise	επαίνεσα	επαινέθηκα	επαινεμένος
επεμβαίνω	intervene	επενέβηκα/επενέ- βην dep. επέμβω	–	–
έρχομαι	come	ήρθα/ήλθα dep. έρθω/έλθω imp. έλα, ελάτε	–	–
-έρχομαι	(–)	-ήλθα dep. -έλθω	–	–
εύχομαι	wish	ευχήθηκα	–	–
εφευρίσκω	invent	εφεύρα dep. εφεύρω	εφευρέθηκα	εφευρεμένος/ εφευρημένος
εφιστώ (A)	draw [attention to]	επέστησα	επιστήθηκα	–
έχω	have	(imperf.) είχα	–	–
ζουλώ (A)	squeeze	ζούληξα	ζουλήχτηκα	ζουληγμένος
ζω (B)	live	έζησα	–	–
θαρρώ (B)	believe	θάρρεψα	–	–
θέλω	want	θέλησα imperf. ήθελα	–	(η)θελημένος
θέτω	place	έθεσα	τέθηκα	–
-θέτω	(–)	-έθεσα	-τέθηκα	-τεθειμένος
θίγω	touch	έθιξα	θίχτηκα/εθίγην	θιγμένος
θρέφω (cf. τρέφω)	nourish	έθρεψα	θρέφτηκα	θρεμμένος
κάθομαι	sit	κάθισα/έκατσα imp. κάθισε/ κάτσε, καθίστε	–	καθισμένος
καθιστώ (A) pass. καθίσταμαι	render	κατέστησα	κατέστην dep. καταστώ	κατεστημένος

Present	Meaning	Active simple past	Passive simple past	Passive perfect participle
-καθιστώ (Α)	(–)	-κατέστησα	-καταστάθηκα	-κατεστημένος
καίω	burn	έκαψα	κάηκα	καμένος
καλώ (Β)	call	κάλεσα	καλέστηκα	καλεσμένος
-καλώ (Β)	(–)	-κάλεσα	-κλήθηκα	-κεκλημένος
κάνω	make	έκανα/έκαμα	–	καμωμένος
καρτερώ (Α/Β)	wait patiently	καρτέρεσα	–	–
καταναλίσκω	consume	κατανάλωσα	καταναλώθηκα	καταναλωμένος
καταπίνω	swallow	κατάπια	–	–
κατάσχω	confiscate	κατάσχεσα	κατασχέθηκα	(κατασχεμένος)
καταφρονώ (Β)	scorn	καταφρόνεσα	καταφρονέθηκα	καταφρονεμένος
κατεβαίνω	go down	κατέβηκα dep. κατέβω/κατεβώ imp. κατέβα, κατεβείτε	–	κατεβασμένος
κερδίζω	earn	κέρδισα	κερδήθηκα	κερδισμένος
κερνώ (Α)	treat	κέρασα	κεράστηκα	κερασμένος
κλαίω	weep	έκλαψα	κλαύτηκα	κλαμένος
κλέβω	steal	έκλεψα	κλάπηκα (steal)/ κλέφτηκα (elope)	κλεμμένος
κλείνω (-κλείω)	close	έκλεισα	κλείστηκα	κλεισμένος
κόβω (-κόπτω)	cut	έκοψα	κόπηκα	(-κε)κομμένος
κοιτάζω/ κοιτώ (Α)	look	κοίταξα	κοιτάχτηκα	κοιταγμένος
κρεμώ (Α) pass. κρέμομαι	hang	κρέμασα	κρεμάστηκα	κρεμασμένος
κυλώ (Α)	roll	κύλησα	κυλίστηκα	κυλισμένος
λαμβάνω/ λαβαίνω	receive	έλαβα	-λήφθηκα/ -ελήφθην	-ειλημμένος
-λέγω	(–)	-έλεξα	-λέχθηκα/ -λέχτηκα/ -ελέγην	-λεγμένος
λέ(γ)ω	say	είπα dep. πω imp. πες, πέστε/πείτε	λέχθηκα/ ειπώθηκα	ειπωμένος
μαθαίνω	learn	έμαθα	μαθεύτηκα	μαθημένος
μεθώ (Α)	get drunk	μέθυσα	–	μεθυσμένος
μένω	stay	έμεινα	–	–
μηνώ (Β)/ μηνύω	inform/ summons	μήνυσα	μηνύθηκα	μηνυμένος

Present	Meaning	Active simple past	Passive simple past	Passive perfect participle
μπαίνω	enter	μπήκα dep. μπω imp. μπες/έμπα, μπείτε	–	μπασμένος
-νέμω	(–)	-ένειμα	-(ε)νεμήθηκα	-νεμημένος
ντρέπομαι	am ashamed	ντράπηκα	–	ντροπιασμένος
ξαίνω	comb [wool]	έξανα	ξάστηκα	ξασμένος
ξερνώ (A)	vomit	ξέρασα	ξεράστηκα	ξερασμένος
ξέρω	know	(imperf.) ήξερα	–	–
ξεχνώ (A)	forget	ξέχασα	ξεχάστηκα	ξεχασμένος
παθαίνω	suffer	έπαθα	–	παθημένος
παίρνω	take	πήρα dep. πάρω imp. πάρε, πάρτε	πάρθηκα	παρμένος
παρελαύνω	parade	παρέλασα	–	–
παρέχω	provide	(imperf.) παρείχα dep. παράσχω	παρασχέθηκα	–
πάσχω	suffer	έπαθα	–	–
πεινώ (A)	am hungry	πείνασα	–	πεινασμένος
περνώ (A)	pass	πέρασα	περάστηκα	περασμένος
πετώ (A)	throw	πέταξα	πετάχτηκα	πετα(γ)μένος
πέφτω	fall	έπεσα	–	πεσμένος
πηγαίνω/πάω	go	πήγα dep. πάω imp. πήγαινε, πηγαίνετε	–	–
πηδώ (A)	jump	πήδηξα/πήδησα	πηδήχτηκα	πηδηγμένος
πίνω	drink	ήπια dep. πιω imp. πιες, πιέστε/πιείτε	πιώθηκα	πιωμένος
πλάττω/ πλάσσω	mould	έπλασα	πλάστηκα	πλασμένος
πλένω	wash	έπλυνα	πλύθηκα	πλυμένος
πλήττω	am bored	έπληξα	–	–
πνίγω	strangle	έπνιξα	πνίγηκα	πνιγμένος
ποικίλλω	adorn	(ε)ποίκιλα	–	ποικιλμένος
πονώ (A)	hurt	πόνεσα	-πονέθηκα	πονεμένος
πρήζω	swell	έπρηξα	πρήστηκα	πρησμένος
προβαίνω 1.	advance	προέβην dep. προβώ	–	–
2.	appear	πρόβαλα	–	–
προβάλλω 1.	appear	πρόβαλα	–	–

Present	Meaning	Active simple past	Passive simple past	Passive perfect participle
προβάλλω 2.	project	προέβαλα	προβλήθηκα	προ(βε)βλη- μένος
ρεύομαι	belch	ρεύτηκα	–	–
ρουφώ (Α)	suck	ρούφηξα	ρουφήχτηκα	ρουφηγμένος
σέβομαι	respect	σεβάστηκα	–	–
σέρνω (-σύρω)	drag	έσυρα	σύρθηκα	συρμένος
σκουντώ (Α)	prod	σκούντηξα/ σκούντησα	σκουντήχτηκα	σκουντηγμένος
σπέρνω (-σπείρω)	sow	έσπειρα	σπάρθηκα	(-ε)σπαρμένος
στέκομαι/ στέκω	stand	στάθηκα	–	–
-στέλλω	(–)	-έστειλα	-(ε)στάλ(θ)ηκα	-(ε)σταλμένος
στέλνω	send	έστειλα	στάλθηκα	σταλμένος
στενοχωρώ (Α/Β)	distress	στενοχώρεσα/ στενοχώρησα	στενοχωρέθηκα/ στενοχωρήθηκα	στενοχωρημένος
στρέφω	turn	έστρεψα	στράφηκα	στραμμένος
συγχαίρω	congrat- ulate	συγχάρηκα	–	–
συμβαίνει	happens	συνέβη/ συνέβηκε dep. συμβεί	–	–
συμμετέχω	participate	(imperf.) συμμετείχα dep. συμμετάσχω	–	–
συμπίπτω	coincide	συνέπεσα	–	–
σφάλλω	am mistaken	έσφαλα	–	εσφαλμένος
σχολώ (Α)	stop work	σχόλασα	–	σχολασμένος
σώζω	save	έσωσα	σώθηκα	σωσμένος
σωπαίνω	am silent	σώπασα imp. σώπα/σώπασε, σωπάτε/ σωπάστε	–	–
τείνω	tend	έτεινα	-τάθηκα	τεταμένος
τελώ (Β)	perform	τέλεσα	τελέστηκα	(τε)τελεσμένος
τραβώ (Α)	pull	τράβηξα	τραβήχτηκα	τραβηγμένος
τρέπω	turn	έτρεψα	τράπηκα	-(τε)τραμμένος
τρέφω	nourish	έθρεψα	τράφηκα	θρεμμένος

Present	Meaning	Active simple past	Passive simple past	Passive perfect participle
τρώω	eat	έφαγα dep. φάω imp. φά(γ)ε, φάτε	φαγώθηκα	φαγωμένος
-τυγχάνω	(–)	-έτυχα	–	-τυχημένος
υπάρχω	exist	υπήρξα dep. υπάρξω	–	–
υπόσχομαι	promise	υποσχέθηκα	–	(υποσχεμένος)
υφίσταμαι	exist, undergo	υπέστην dep. υποστώ	–	–
φαίνομαι	appear	φάνηκα	–	–
φέρνω (-φέρ(ν)ω)	bring	έφερα	φέρθηκα	φερμένος
φεύγω	leave	έφυγα	-φεύχθηκα	–
φθείρω	corrupt	έφθειρα	φθάρηκα/ εφθάρην	φθαρμένος
φορώ (A/B)	wear	φόρεσα	φορέθηκα	φορεμένος
φταίω	am to blame	έφταιξα	–	–
φυλά(γ)ω	guard	φύλαξα	φυλάχτηκα	φυλαγμένος
φυσώ (A)	blow	φύσηξα	–	–
χαίρομαι/ χαίρω	am glad	χάρηκα	–	–
χαλώ (A)	spoil	χάλασα	–	χαλασμένος
χορταίνω	am satiated	χόρτασα	–	χορτασμένος
χυμώ (A)	swoop	χύμηξα	–	–
χωρώ (A/B)	fit in	χώρεσα	–	–
ψάλλω/ψέλνω	chant	έψαλα	ψάλθηκα	ψαλμένος
ωχριώ (A)	turn pale	ωχρίασα	–	–

8 DERIVATIONAL MORPHOLOGY

In Sections 1–7 we have been concerned with *inflectional morphology*, that is with the changes which words undergo (declension and conjugation) according to their different grammatical functions in a particular context. In this Section we shall deal with *derivational morphology*, which can be defined as the formation of new words by means of various morphological processes. We shall divide the material into **complex** words formed by means of either suffixation (the addition of a **suffix** to the end of the **stem** of a word, so as to create a new word; Section 8.1), or prefixation (the addition of a **prefix** to the beginning of a word; Section 8.2), and the formation of **compounds** (words formed by combining the stems of two or more independent words; Section 8.3). The available material is vast, since all these processes have been widely used to form new words in Greek throughout its long history. We shall limit ourselves to a few examples of each type of formation, with the primary aim of facilitating the reader's recognition of the constituent elements of a complex or compound word. Particular attention will be given to those elements which continue to be productive in the formation of new words.

8.1 SUFFIXATION

Greek possesses a vast range of morphological elements which can be added to the stem of a word in order to modify its meaning or to form *derivatives* (mainly different parts of speech). Our treatment is necessarily selective, concentrating on the most commonly used suffixes and with particular reference to those that are productive of new words.

Diminutives express small size, familiarity, affection or, sometimes, depreciation. The following suffixes are commonly used to form diminutives of nouns:

-άκης (attached to masculine nouns): κόσμος → κοσμάκης 'ordinary person, "the common herd"', and many masculine proper names, e.g. Γιάννης → Γιαννάκης, Δημήτρης → Δημητράκης, Κώστας → Κωστάκης.

-ούλης (attached to masculine nouns): πατέρας → πατερούλης 'dear father, daddy'. This suffix may also be attached to certain adjectives used as nouns, e.g. μικρός → μικρούλης 'youngster', χοντρός → χοντρούλης 'little fat boy/man'. For the declension of adjectives in -ούλης see Section 3.9 and note 2.

-ίτσα (attached to feminine nouns): μπίρα → μπιρίτσα 'little beer', ώρα → ωρίτσα 'just an hour', and feminine proper names, e.g. Αγνή → Αγνίτσα, Ελένη → Ελενίτσα.

-ούλα (attached to feminine nouns): αδελφή → αδελφούλα 'little sister', κάρτα → καρτούλα 'little card', λέξη → λεξούλα 'little word', στιγμή → στιγμούλα 'brief moment', and feminine proper names, e.g. Δήμητρα → Δημητρούλα → Ρούλα, Χρύσα → Χρυσούλα. This suffix is sometimes also attached to adjectives used as nouns, e.g. ξανθός → ξανθούλα 'little fair-haired girl'

-άκι (mainly – but not exclusively – attached to neuter nouns): πρόσωπο → προσωπάκι 'little face', βαπόρι → βαποράκι 'little steamboat', τραπέζι → τραπεζάκι 'little table', λάθος → λαθάκι 'little mistake'. It should be noted that masculine imparisyllabic nouns referring to things (Section 2.1.5) add -δάκι to the singular stem, e.g. καφές → καφεδάκι 'little coffee', and neuter nouns in -μα (Section 2.4.5) add -τάκι, e.g. γράμμα → γραμματάκι 'little letter'. Note also the addition of -γ- to the stem in ρολόι → ρολογάκι 'little clock/watch', τσάι → τσαγάκι 'little [cup of] tea'.

Augmentatives express large size or admiration. A variety of different suffixes are used to form augmentatives (which are always masculine or feminine, never neuter); the following are among the most common:

-α (feminine, but often from neuter nouns), e.g. κεφάλι → κεφάλα 'big head', κουτάλι → κουτάλα 'big spoon', μπουκάλι → μπουκάλα 'big bottle'

-άρα (feminine), e.g. κοιλάρα 'big belly', τρυπάρα 'big hole'

-αράς (masculine, denoting the male possessor of a quality), e.g. κοιλάρα → κοιλαράς 'big-bellied man', δουλευτής → δουλευταράς 'hard-worker'. The corresponding feminine nouns end in -ού; see Section 2.2.5 (ii)

-αρος (masculine), e.g. παιδί → παίδαρος 'big (handsome) lad', πόδι → πόδαρος 'big foot', σκύλος → σκύλαρος 'great big dog'

-άκλα (feminine), e.g. φωνή → φωνάκλα 'loud voice', χέρι → χεράκλα 'big hand'

-ακλάς (masculine, denoting the male possessor of a quality), e.g. φωνάκλα → φωνακλάς 'loud-mouth'. For the corresponding feminine nouns in -ού, see Section 2.2.5 (ii)

-ακλας (masculine), e.g. άντρας → άντρακλας 'great big man'

Other suffixes used to form adjectives or to modify the meaning of existing adjectives include:

-ένιος (adjectives indicating the material from which something is made, but with some other functions), e.g. σίδερο → σιδερένιος 'iron', χώμα → χωματένιος 'earthen', τίποτα 'nothing' → τιποτένιος 'worthless'

-ικός and -ιακός (both extremely common), e.g. διοικητής → διοικητικός 'administrative', μέθοδος → μεθοδικός 'methodical', πλεονεκτώ → πλεονεκτικός 'advantageous', αίσθηση → αισθησιακός 'sensual', ύπαρξη → υπαρξιακός 'existential'

-ειδής ('like', 'resembling', '-oid'), e.g. άνθρωπος → ανθρωποειδής 'humanoid', έμβρυο → εμβρυοειδής 'embryo-like', φασίστας → φασιστοειδής 'fascist-like'

-ιμος ('capable of having something done to it', attached to active perfective verb stems), e.g. διαπραγματεύομαι → διαπραγματεύσιμος 'negotiable', εξάγω → εξαγώγιμος 'exportable', επανορθώνω → επανορθώσιμος 'rectifiable', έφαγα (simple past of τρώω) → φαγώσιμος 'edible, fit to eat'

-ούχος ('possessing'), e.g. προνόμιο → προνομιούχος 'privileged', τάλαντο → ταλαντούχος 'talented' (see Section 3.2 for the declension)

-τέος ('which must be done'), e.g. εξετάζω → εξεταστέος 'which must be examined', παρατηρώ → παρατηρητέος 'which must be observed'

-τός (the usual suffix for forming adjectives with a passive meaning, from verbs), e.g. γράφω → γραπτός 'written', επιθυμώ → επιθυμητός 'desired' or 'desirable', μισώ → μισητός 'hated' or 'detestable', ψήνω → ψητός 'roast(ed)'. Corresponding negative adjectives formed with the prefix α(ν)- have proparoxytone stress, e.g. αδικαιολόγητος 'unjustified' or 'unjustifiable' (see Section 8.2)

-ούτσικος (attached to adjectives and indicating that the quality is present in a moderate amount: '-ish'), e.g. καλός → καλούτσικος 'fairly good', άσχημος → ασχημούτσικος 'rather ugly', κοντός → κοντούτσικος 'shortish'

-ωπός has a similar meaning, e.g. στενός → στενωπός 'narrowish'; it is frequently attached to adjectives denoting colour, e.g. κίτρινος → κιτρινωπός 'yellowish'

A wide variety of suffixes is used to form nouns, including the following:

-μα (neuter, usually denoting the action of a verb or its result), e.g. διαβάζω → διάβασμα 'reading', κατορθώνω → κατόρθωμα 'accomplishment', πειράζω → πείραγμα 'teasing', σκουντώ → σκούντημα 'shoving, jolt'

-ση, -ξη, -ψη (feminine, normally denoting the action of a verb), e.g. εκδικούμαι → εκδίκηση 'revenge', εισπράττω → είσπραξη 'collection [of money]', μετακομίζω → μετακόμιση 'removal', χωνεύω → χώνεψη 'digestion'

-τήρας (masculine nouns, for implements etc.), e.g. ανάβω → αναπτήρας 'lighter', ανεμίζω → ανεμιστήρας 'fan, ventilator', συνδέω → συνδετήρας 'paper-clip'

-τής (masculine nouns for the person, or an appliance, that carries out the action of the verb), e.g. επενδύω → επενδυτής 'investor', μετασχηματίζω → μετασχηματιστής 'transformer', προπονώ → προπονητής 'trainer'

-τητα (feminine nouns, usually denoting abstract qualities, derived from adjectives), e.g. βαρύς → βαρύτητα 'gravity', επίσημος → επισημότητα 'formality', ικανός → ικανότητα 'capability'

For phonological phenomena across morpheme boundaries see Part I, Section 1.4.

8.2 PREFIXATION

The most commonly used prefixes are words which were prepositions in Ancient Greek, although many of them no longer exist as independent prepositions in the modern language. The full list of such prepositional prefixes is as follows:

αμφι-
ανα- (αν- before vowels)
αντι- (αντ- before vowels, ανθ- before vowels which were preceded by /h/ in AG)
απο- (απ- before vowels, αφ- before vowels preceded by /h/ in AG)
δια- (δι- before vowels)
εισ-
εκ- (εξ- before vowels)
εν- (εμ- before β, μ, π, φ, ψ, εγ- before γ, κ, ξ, χ, ελ- before λ, sometimes ερ- before ρ)
επι- (επ- before vowels, εφ- before vowels preceded by /h/ in AG)
κατα- (κατ- before vowels, καθ- before vowels preceded by /h/ in AG)
μετα- (μετ- before vowels, μεθ- before vowels preceded by /h/ in AG)

παρα- (παρ- before vowels)
περι-
προ-
προσ-
συν- (συμ- before β, μ, π, φ, ψ, συγ- before γ, κ, ξ, χ, συλ- before λ,
    συρ- before ρ)
υπερ-
υπο- (υπ- before vowels, υφ- before vowels preceded by /h/ in AG)

Each of these prefixes has a wide range of meanings which cannot be discussed here but will be found in dictionaries. We give examples of verbs which are formed with the above prefixes and the verb -βάλλω:

αμφιβάλλω 'I doubt', αναβάλλω 'I postpone', αποβάλλω 'I expel, miscarry', διαβάλλω 'I slander', εισβάλλω 'I invade', εκβάλλω 'I discharge', επιβάλλω 'I impose', καταβάλλω, 'I overthrow, pay down', μεταβάλλω 'I change, transform', παραβάλλω 'I compare', περιβάλλω 'I surround', προβάλλω 'I project, show', προσβάλλω 'I insult, attack', συμβάλλω 'I contribute', υπερβάλλω 'I exaggerate', υποβάλλω 'I submit'.

(For the possible use of internal augment in the past tenses of such verbs, see Section 7.10.3.) Some verbs combine two, or even three, of these prepositional prefixes, e.g:

αντιδιαστέλλω 'I contradistinguish', εγκαταλείπω 'I abandon', επαναλαμβάνω 'I repeat', συμπεριλαμβάνω 'I include', συγκατανεύω 'I consent to', επανεκδίδω 'I re-issue'.

Prepositional prefixes are not restricted to verbs: other parts of speech are formed from such verbs by means of suffixation and other processes (such as a change of vowel), e.g. nouns: αμφιβολία 'doubt', επανάληψη 'repetition', υπερβολή 'exaggeration'; adjectives: αμφίβολος 'dubious', επιβλητικός 'impressive', υπερβολικός 'excessive'.

The main prepositional prefixes which are still productive in the modern language, with examples of each, are the following:

ανα- ('re-'): αναπαλαιώνω 'I restore' (lit. 'make old again'),
    ανασχηματισμός 'reformation, reshuffle'
αντι- ('in place of', 'vice-', or 'against', 'anti-'): αντιπρόεδρος 'vice-president', αντιφασιστικός 'antifascist', ανθυγιεινός 'insanitary'
απο- ('de-'): αποσύνθεση 'decomposition', απομαγνητισμός 'demagnetization', αφαλατώνω 'I desalinate'
δια- ('inter-'): διαπανεπιστημιακός 'inter-university' (adj.),
    διασύνδεση 'interconnection'

εκ- (denotes a process of change, and often corresponds to English verbs in '-ize' and nouns in '-ization'): εκσυγχρονίζω 'I modernize', εξελληνισμός 'Hellenization', εκλαϊκευτικός 'popularizing' (adj.)

επανα- ('re-'): επανασυνδέω 'I reconnect'

κατα- ('very much'): κατακόκκινος 'bright red', κατάχλωμος 'very pale', καταχαρούμενος 'very glad, delighted', κατενθουσιάζω 'I fill with enthusiasm'

μετα- ('post-', 'meta-'): μεταμοντερνισμός 'postmodernism', μεταπολεμικός 'post-war' (adj.), μεταγλώσσα 'meta-language'

παρα- ('alongside', 'para-' i.e. 'existing unofficially'): παρακράτος 'unofficial state', παραοικονομία 'unofficial ["black"] economy', παραψυχολογία 'parapsychology'

προ- ('before', 'pre-'): προπολεμικά 'before the war' (adv.), προβιομηχανικός 'pre-industrial'

συν- ('joint', 'fellow', 'co-'): συμπαραγωγός 'co-producer', συμφοιτητής 'fellow-student'

υπερ- ('over', 'trans-', 'super-', 'hyper-'): υπεραγορά 'supermarket', υπερατλαντικός 'transatlantic', υπερέντασ

η 'hypertension', υπερηχητικός 'supersonic'

υπο- ('under', 'sub-'): υποανάπτυξη 'under-development', υποδιευθυντής 'sub-director, under-manager', υποκατάστημα 'branch office'

One other prefix, which never occurs as a preposition on its own, is ξε-, which (in addition to other meanings) can have the meaning of 'un-' when combined with verbs and other words formed from verbs, e.g. ξεκουράζω 'I refresh' [lit. 'untire'], ξεσκεπάζω 'I uncover'.

The prefix δυσ- ('difficult to do', 'dys-') is used to form adjectives, e.g. δυσπρόσιτος 'difficult to approach, inaccessible', δύσκαμπτος 'stiff, inflexible', but is also found in nouns and verbs, e.g. δυσλειτουργία 'dysfunction', δυσαναλογία 'disproportion', δυσπιστώ 'I mistrust, dis-believe'.

Finally, the prefix α- (αν- before vowels), the so-called *alpha privative*, is used to express negation, most commonly in the formation of adject-ives. It can be compared with the English prefixes 'un-', 'in-' and 'im-'. When a positive adjective is prefixed with α(ν)-, there is often a shift of stress; compare the following pairs:

δυνατός 'strong', αδύνατος 'weak'; κινητός 'mobile', ακίνητος 'immobile'; αποφευκτός 'avoidable', αναπόφευκτος 'unavoidable'; πιθανός 'probable', απίθανος 'improbable'.

Sometimes there is a difference in the ending of the positive and negative adjectives, e.g.:

συμμετρικός 'symmetrical', ασύμμετρος 'asymmetrical'; τίμιος 'honourable', άτιμος 'dishonourable'; τέλειος 'perfect', ατελής 'imperfect'; χρωματιστός 'coloured', άχρωμος 'colourless'.

However, there are also instances where the prefixation of α(v)- does not affect the basic form of the adjective, e.g. ακριβής 'exact', ανακριβής 'inexact'; επίσημος 'official', ανεπίσημος 'unofficial'; επαρκής 'adequate', ανεπαρκής 'inadequate'. There are also many negative adjectives (usually derived from verbs) for which there is no corresponding positive adjective form, e.g. ακούραστος 'tireless', αμετανόητος 'unrepentant'. In these cases the antonym is the perfect passive participle of the related verb: κουρασμένος 'tired', μετανοημένος 'repentant'. The prefix α(v)- is also found in nouns, e.g. ανισότητα 'inequality', ανοησία 'mindlessness, stupidity', ασυμφωνία 'disagreement', αταραξία 'imperturbability'; and in verbs, e.g. αδυνατίζω 'I become thin', ακινητοποιώ 'I immobilize', ακυρώνω 'I invalidate, cancel'. Such nouns and verbs are usually derived from adjectives with α(v)-.

8.3 FORMATION OF COMPOUNDS

Greek has a large number of *compounds* formed from two or more separate stems. We shall first consider compounds which are verbs, with the first element related to an adverb. Such formations are very productive, particularly in spoken Greek:

κακο- ('badly') and καλο- ('well'): κακοβλέπω 'I dislike, look unfavourably upon', κακομαθαίνω 'I learn bad habits', καλοκάθομαι 'I settle comfortably', καλοπιάνω 'I flatter, coax'

λιγο- ('little'): λιγοψυχώ 'I faint, am faint-hearted'

ξανα- ('again'): ξαναέρχομαι or ξανάρχομαι 'I come again', ξαναδιαβάζω 'I re-read' etc. In the perfect tenses ξανα- can also combine with the auxiliary verb έχω, e.g. δεν τον ξαναείχα δει 'I had not seen him again/before', as an alternative to the more normal δεν τον είχα ξαναδεί.

παρα- ('too much'): παραγεμίζω 'I overfill', παρακάνω 'I do (something) too much', παραμιλώ 'I talk too much, babble, am delirious'; also with the verb 'to be', e.g. παραείναι όμορφη 'she is too beautiful'

πολυ- ('much', 'very'): πολυασχολούμαι 'I am much concerned [with]', πολυενδιαφέρομαι 'I am very interested'. These compounds tend to be more used in negative than in positive sentences.

πρωτο- ('first'): πρωτοβλέπω 'I see for the first time', πρωτομιλώ 'I speak for the first time'

συχνο- ('often'): συχνοκοιτάζω 'I look often', συχνοπηγαίνω 'I go often'

In the following examples the first element gives the verb a reciprocal or reflexive meaning:

αλληλ(ο)- ('one another'): verbs with this prefix, expressing reciprocity, occur only in the plural and in the passive voice, e.g. αλληλοεπηρεάζονται 'they influence one another', αλληλοκοιταχτήκαμε 'we looked at one another'. They also give rise to some nouns, e.g. αλληλεξάρτηση 'interdependence', αλληλεγγύη 'mutual reliance, solidarity', and adjectives, e.g. αλληλοκτόνος 'internecine'.

αυτ(ο)- ('self', in a reflexive sense): αυτοθυσιάζομαι 'I sacrifice myself', αυτοπροβάλλομαι 'I promote myself'. With the same first element we also find nouns, e.g. αυτοδιοίκηση 'self-government', αυτοπεποίθηση 'self-confidence', and adjectives, e.g. αυταπόδεικτος 'self-evident', αυτοδίδακτος 'self-taught'.

Compound adjectives are formed in various ways:

μονο- ('single'), δι- ('double'), τρι- ('triple') etc.: μονομερής 'one-sided', δίγλωσσος 'bilingual', τριήμερος 'lasting three days', τριμερής 'tripartite', τετρασέλιδος 'four-page', πενταμελής 'having five members', εξαγωνικός 'hexagonal', επτάπλευρος 'seven-sided'

νεο- ('new', 'neo-'): νεόπλουτος 'nouveau riche', νεοσύστατος 'newly established', νεοκλασικός 'neo-classical'

ολο- ('entirely'): ολοζώντανος 'full of life', ολοκάθαρος 'spotlessly clean', ολοφάνερος 'totally clear'

παν- ('entirely', 'very'): πανάκριβος 'very expensive', πανέμορφος 'very beautiful', πανευτυχής 'very happy', παγκόσμιος 'worldwide, universal', πάμπλουτος 'immensely rich', πάμφτηνος 'dirt cheap', πανευρωπαϊκός 'pan-European'. Note that παν- becomes παγ- before κ, and παμ- before β, π, φ and ψ.

πρωτο-, δευτερο-, τριτο- etc. ('first', 'second', 'third' etc.): πρωτοετής 'first-year', δευτεροβάθμιος 'secondary' (e.g. education), τριτοκοσμικός 'third-world'

A special type of compound is that in which the two elements belong to the same part of speech and the resultant word combines the meanings of both. Examples include:

compounds of two verbs, e.g. αναβοσβήνω 'I flash on and off', ανεβοκατεβαίνω 'I go up and down', πηγαινοέρχομαι 'I go to and fro'; compounds of two nouns, e.g. αντρόγυνο 'married couple', μαχαιροπίρουνο 'knife and fork', γυναικόπαιδα 'women and children'; compounds of two adjectives, e.g. ασπρόμαυρος 'black and white', μακρόστενος 'long and narrow'.

There are many more types of compound: of two nouns, of noun and verb, of adjective and noun etc. The two components of a compound are characteristically linked with the vowel -o-, as the following examples show:

βίος + γράφω → βιογραφία 'biography', βίος + μηχανή → βιομηχανία 'industry', γράμμα + σειρά → γραμματοσειρά 'character set, font', καπνός + βιομηχανία→ καπνοβιομηχανία 'tobacco industry', κτήνος + τρέφω → κτηνοτροφία 'animal husbandry', κύριος + λέξη → κυριολεξία 'literal meaning', λάρυγγας + λόγος → λαρυγγολόγος 'throat specialist', μυθιστορία + γράφω → μυθιστοριογράφος 'novelist', προίκα + συμφωνία → προικοσύμφωνο 'dowry contract', σκηνή + θέση → σκηνοθεσία 'theatrical direction', τέρμα + φύλακας → τερματοφύλακας 'goalkeeper', φίλος + δόξα → φιλοδοξία 'ambition', φόρος + διαφυγή → φοροδιαφυγή 'tax evasion'

The above notes are far from exhaustive of the range and variety of compound formations that exist in Greek. Compound formation, like other kinds of derivational morphology, continues to be an important means for the creation of new words in the language.

PART III: SYNTAX

1 THE VERB AND THE VERB PHRASE

1.1 THE CONSTITUENTS OF THE VERB PHRASE

The verb is the central element of the clause in that every clause must contain a verb with the exception of some copular clauses where the verb είμαι 'I am' may be omitted (see Section 1.9). Furthermore, the number and the type of constituents that may combine with the verb are determined by the type of the verb. A *verb phrase* is the combination of the verb with its **objects** (direct and indirect, locative, benefactive, etc.) or **predicate complements**, as well as the manner, place and time **adverbials** which modify the verb.

1.1.1 OBJECTS

Objects are those noun phrases which combine with the verb in a very close syntactic–semantic relationship. Depending on the type of the verb, an object may be excluded, as in the case of **intransitive verbs**, or may be required, as in the case of **transitive verbs**. The transitive verbs may require only one object (**monotransitive**) or they may take two such objects (**bitransitive**). These varieties are presented below.

1.1.1.1 Intransitive verbs

Intransitive verbs are those which do not combine with an object noun phrase. They, of course, may combine with adverbs of any type and some may require a subject or clausal **complement**. Intransitive verbs may be subdivided as follows:

(a) Verbs in active voice form expressing action which is not transferred to some other entity, e.g.: ροχαλίζω 'I snore', as in (1):

    (1) Ο Γιάννης ροχαλίζει κάθε βράδυ
        'John snores every night'

Other verbs of this type include: αναπνέω 'I breathe', χαμογελώ 'I smile', δακρύζω 'I have tears in my eyes', μένω 'I stay, reside' etc.

(b) Verbs in active voice expressing state, such as πονώ 'I ache':

    (2) Η Ελένη πονούσε όταν της έβγαλαν το δόντι
        'Helen was in pain when they extracted her tooth'

Other such verbs include: πεινώ 'I feel hungry', πεθαίνω 'I die' φτωχαίνω 'I become poorer', λάμπω 'I shine', ιδρώνω 'I sweat'.

(c) Verbs in passive form expressing an action not transferable to some other entity, such as έρχομαι 'I come':

(3) Ο φίλος του Νίκου έρχεται συχνά στο σπίτι μας
'Nick's friend often comes to our house'

Other such verbs are: εργάζομαι 'I work', ετοιμάζομαι 'I get ready, I prepare myself', ξεκουράζομαι 'I rest', σηκώνομαι 'I get up'.

(d) Verbs in passive form expressing state, such as κοιμάμαι 'I sleep':

(4) Το καλοκαίρι, στην Ελλάδα, κοιμάμαι πάντα το απόγευμα
'In the summer, in Greece, I always sleep in the afternoon'

Other such verbs are: κάθομαι 'I sit', φοβάμαι 'I fear', λιάζομαι 'I sun myself'.

(e) Also intransitive are passive verbs which are typically derived from active transitive ones, such as: αγοράζομαι 'I am bought', derived from active transitive αγοράζω (κάτι) 'I buy (something)':

(5) Το βιβλίο αυτό αγοράστηκε από πολλούς φοιτητές
'This book was bought by many students'

(f) Also intransitive are those verbs in passive form with reflexive meaning which are derived from active transitive ones. E.g. the verb ντύνομαι 'I get dressed', in (6), is derived from ντύνω (κάποιον) 'I dress (someone)':

(6) Η Ελενίτσα τώρα μπορεί και ντύνεται μόνη της
'Little Helen can get dressed by herself now'

(g) There are also verbs which have two different uses, an intransitive and a transitive one with slightly different meaning. Compare intransitive γελώ 'I laugh' and transitive γελώ κάποιον 'I cheat someone', intransitive πονώ 'I ache' and transitive πονώ κάποιον 'I feel sorry for, empathize with someone' or, in a causative sense, 'I cause pain to someone', intransitive γυαλίζω 'I shine' and transitive γυαλίζω κάτι 'I make something shine, I polish something', intransitive δουλεύω 'I work' and transitive δουλεύω κάποιον 'I fool, tease someone', δουλεύω κάτι 'I work on something'. For example:

(7) Η Μαρία δουλεύει στο Πανεπιστήμιο
'Mary works at the University'
(8) Η Μαρία λέει στον Νίκο ότι τον αγαπά αλλά μάλλον
τον δουλεύει
'Mary tells Nick that she loves him but she's probably kidding him'

(9) Η Μαρία δουλεύει τώρα τη διατριβή της
    'Mary is now working on her dissertation'

(h) Also intransitive are the so-called 'linking verbs', such as είμαι 'I am',
    γίνομαι 'I become', etc. These combine not with an object but with
    either a noun phrase or an adjective phrase functioning as a predi-
    cate complement to the subject, e.g.:

(10) Η Σούλα είναι ο πρόεδρός τους
     'Soula is their president'
(11) Η Σούλα είναι πολύ δυναμική
     'Soula is very dynamic'

(See Section 1.9 below.)

(i) There are also intransitive impersonal verbs which require a comple-
    ment clause, e.g.:

(12) Πρέπει να του μιλήσουμε
     'We must speak to him'
(13) Πότε πρόκειται να φύγετε;
     'When are you going to leave?'

(See Section 1.2.2 below.)

1.1.1.2   Monotransitive verbs

Monotransitive verbs combine with a direct object either in the form of
a full noun phrase or in the form of a pronoun. The direct object is marked
by the accusative case.

(1) Πρέπει να καλέσουμε το Γιάννη
    'We must invite John'
(2) Θα καλέσουμε εσάς και την οικογένεια του Μιχάλη
    (εσάς = strong form of the 2nd person pl. pronoun)
    'We will invite **you** and Michalis's family'
(3) Θα σας καλέσουμε στο γάμο
    (σας = weak or clitic pronoun: see Part II, Section 5.2)
    'We will invite you to the wedding'

In more formal discourse we may still find expressions of *katharevousa*
origin containing transitive verbs whose object appears in the genitive case:

(4) Ο καινούριος υπουργός θα επιμεληθεί της καταστάσεως
    'The new minister will take care of the situation'

In Section 1.1.1.2.1 we present further examples of monotransitive verb
phrases with full noun phrase direct object.

1.1.1.2.1 Monotransitives with full noun phrase direct object

Monotransitive verbs either require the obligatory presence of a direct object noun phrase, as in the case of μοιράζω 'I distribute' in (1), or they typically combine with an object, but they may also occur without such an object, as in the case of γράφω 'I write' in (2). Note that verbs such as τρώω 'I eat', πίνω 'I drink' etc., when used without an object, denote simple activities:

(1)a. Ποιος θα μοιράσει τις προσκλήσεις για το χορό;
    'Who will distribute the invitations to the dance?'
  b. *Όλοι μοιράζουν
    'Everybody distributes'

(2)a. Ο Καζαντζάκης έχει γράψει πολλά βιβλία
    'Kazantzakis wrote a lot of books'
  b. Όταν γράφει δε θέλει να τον διακόψει κανείς
    'When he is writing he does not want anybody to interrupt him'
  c. Έγραψε στο Γιάννη χθες
    'She wrote to John yesterday'

Notice that even when a transitive verb like γράφω is used without an explicit object noun phrase an object is still understood. In (2b) we understand an object with general reference (i.e. something) while in (2c) we understand the object to be γράμμα 'letter' because of the linguistic and pragmatic context, i.e. when we write to somebody we are writing a letter to him/her. This omissibility of the direct object, when it is easily understood, is very common in Greek and extends to all transitives. So, in spite of the fact that sentence (*1b) is unacceptable out of context, it is possible to find a context where it is appropriate, such as in the following conversation:

(3)a. Οι αρχηγοί του κόμματος άρχισαν να μοιράζουν
    ρουσφέτια
    'The leaders of the party have begun to distribute favours'
  b. Ε και τι έγινε; Όλοι μοιράζουν
    'So what? They all distribute [i.e. they all do it]'

Monotransitive verbs can either be of active form, as those used in the above examples, or they may have passive form:

(4) Θυμάμαι τον Αλέξανδρο από όταν ήταν μωρό
    'I remember Alexander from when he was a baby'
(5) Ποιος φοβάται τον κακό λύκο;
    'Who's afraid of the bad wolf?'

1.1.1.3   Bitransitive verbs with full noun phrase indirect object

Bitransitives are those verbs which combine with two objects, a direct one, in the accusative case, and an indirect one, which may either be in the genitive case or be expressed by a prepositional phrase.

1.1.1.4   Indirect object in genitive case

The indirect object represents an animate, often human entity which is indirectly affected by the action expressed by the verb. In (1) below, the indirect object is the recipient:

(1)a. Ο Γιάννης έδωσε ένα ωραίο βραχιόλι της Μαίρης *or*
   b. Ο Γιάννης έδωσε της Μαίρης ένα ωραίο βραχιόλι
     'John gave Mary a beautiful bracelet'

In (2) the indirect object expresses the benefactive, i.e. the person who benefits from the result of the action expressed by the verb:

(2) Η Ελένη μαγείρεψε του Νίκου σουτζουκάκια
    'Helen cooked soutzoukakia for Nick'

In (3) the indirect object indicates the source:

(3) Χθες πήραν της Ελένης ένα εκατομμύριο δραχμές
    'Yesterday they took a million drachmas from Helen'

From these examples it is clear that the genitive case does not clearly mark the precise semantic relation of the indirect object to its verb. The precise semantic function of the indirect object is derived by considering the semantics of the verb and of the indirect object as well as the total linguistic and pragmatic context.

As shown in (1a) and (1b) the order of direct and indirect object may vary, since the grammatical function of each noun phrase, as direct or indirect object, is clearly marked by the difference in their case marking: accusative for direct and genitive for indirect object. (On the function of word order changes see Section 5.2.)

We must point out that the use of a simple genitive noun phrase to express the indirect object, as in the examples offered above, is not common. This is because the genitive in these constructions may also be interpreted as a possessive genitive, especially if the direct object is a definite noun phrase. Consider:

(4) Ο Γιάννης έδωσε το ωραίο βραχιόλι της Μαίρης
(5) Η Ελένη μαγείρεψε τα σουτζουκάκια του Νίκου
(6) Χθες πήραν της Ελένης το πορτοφόλι

All three sentences are ambiguous between an indirect object interpretation and one involving a possessive genitive: Mary's bracelet in (4), Nick's soutzoukakia in (5), Helen's purse in (6). This is the reason why the indirect object is more often expressed with a prepositional phrase (see (1–3), Section 1.1.1.5 below) or with the genitive clitic pronoun which more clearly marks the indirect object (see (3) and (6), Section 1.1.1.7 below).

There are some verbs whose direct and indirect objects are both in the accusative case, e.g. μαθαίνω 'I learn, I teach', διδάσκω 'I teach', ρωτώ 'I ask', κερνώ 'I offer a treat':

(7) Φέτος θα διδάξουν τους πρωτοετείς γραμματική
    'This year they will teach the first-year students grammar'

(8) Κεράσανε τους φίλους τους παγωτό
    'They treated their friends to ice-cream'

1.1.1.5   Prepositional phrase indirect object

The functions of recipient, benefactive and source may also be expressed by prepositional phrases introduced by the appropriate preposition.

(1) Έδωσε το βραχιόλι στην Μαίρη
    'He gave the bracelet to Mary'

(2) Η Ελένη μαγείρεψε τα σουτζουκάκια για το Νίκο
    'Helen cooked the soutzoukakia for Nick'

(3) Χθες πήραν από την Ελένη ένα εκατομμύριο δραχμές
    'Yesterday they took one million drachmas from Helen'

1.1.1.6   Transitive verbs with clitic pronouns as objects

Either the direct object or the indirect object of a verb, or both objects at the same time, may be expressed by clitic pronouns instead of either full noun phrases or prepositional phrases. Thus we may have a mono-transitive construction with an accusative clitic pronoun as direct object:

(1) Τον είδα χθες
    'I saw him yesterday'

or a bitransitive construction with both objects expressed by clitics:

(2) Του το είπα πολλές φορές να 'ρθει μαζί μας αλλά ντρέπεται
    'I told him many times to come with us but he is shy'

The use of the object clitic pronouns is very frequent and it often gives rise to idiomatic expressions consisting only of the verb and the clitic:

(3)a. Τα 'μαθες;   'Have you heard (the news)?'
    b. Ναι, τα ξέρω   'Yes, I know (the news)'

c. Τα 'χασα	'I lost (my mind), I got confused'
d. Εμείς τα βρίσκουμε	'We find them [= we get on]'
e. Εμείς τη βρίσκουμε	'We find it [= we have a good time together]'
f. Τα λέμε πάλι	'We will talk again'
g. Τα φτιάξανε	'They fixed them [= they started a relationship]'
h. Τα χαλάσανε	'They spoilt them [= they fell out, they split up]'
i. Τα 'κανες θάλασσα	'You made them a sea [you made a mess of things]'
j. Του την πέσαμε	'To him we threw it down [= we made him a proposition]'

(3j) verges on slang more than the rest.

Whenever clitics are used either on their own or in combination with full noun phrases, and the verb is in either the indicative or the subjunctive mood, the clitics always precede the verb and are attached phonologically to it, forming one phonological word. (See Part I, Section 1.5.) In cases where both direct and indirect object clitics are present, their order is fixed; the indirect object (genitive case) clitic precedes the direct object one (accusative case), as in (2). In those rare cases where both objects are in the accusative it is only possible to use the clitic for the indirect object, and then only in combination with a direct object in the form of a full noun phrase. However, if the indirect object is in the plural it is possible to replace both direct and indirect object by their clitics because plural accusative clitics have the same form as genitive plural clitics and thus the combination is indistinguishable from the accepted pattern of genitive+accusative. Another restriction on the combination of clitic objects is that the direct object must be of the 3rd person while the indirect object clitic may be of the 1st, 2nd or 3rd person. This means that we cannot have the combinations μου σε, σου με, μας σας, μας σε, του με, τους σας etc. Any combination of an item in column A followed by any item in column B is acceptable.

A	B
μου	τον
σου	την
του	το
της	τους
μας	τις
τους	τα
σας	

There is also a use of a personal clitic pronoun in the genitive, accompanying the verb, which is not that of an indirect object. Such a genitive clitic is not restricted to transitive verbs but may accompany any verb including intransitive ones, making a single sentence. This genitive clitic may refer to the speaker, or to the addressee, or even to some third person who is interested or affected by the action expressed by the verb:

(4) Μη μου τη στενοχωρείτε την Κλεία (μου)
     'For my sake [please], do not upset (my) Clea'
(5) Γιατί μας χάλασες την παρέα;
     'Why did you spoil the party for us?'

The genitive clitic in (4) refers to the speaker, who shows, in this way, his emotional involvement in what happens to Clea, who may or may not be his/her daughter, although quite often there is a sense of possession. This genitive clitic is referred to as 'benefactive' or as 'dative of interest' or 'dative of advantage' or 'ethic dative'. (The term 'dative' is used by some grammarians for all indirect objects, because the case which was used to mark the indirect object in Ancient Greek was the dative and this was morphologically different from the genitive.) The genitive clitic μας in (5) indicates again the involvement of the speaker, but here something has happened to the speaker's disadvantage. This use of the genitive clitic is called 'malefactive' or 'dative of disadvantage'.

1.1.1.7 Clitic doubling

The term 'clitic doubling' is used to refer to constructions where we find simultaneously the full noun phrase object (direct and/or indirect) following the verb, and its corresponding clitic pronoun, as shown in (1–3). Clitic left dislocation is a construction where we again find both the object (direct or indirect) noun phrase and its corresponding clitic, but in this construction the object noun phrase is found to the left of the verb, usually at the front of the sentence (4–5).

(1) **Τον** συνάντησα **τον αδελφό της** προχθές
     Lit. 'I met him her brother the day before yesterday'
(2) Πρέπει να **του** μιλήσεις **του Νίκου** εσύ
     Lit. 'It is necessary that you talk to him Nick'
(3) Θα **της το** δώσουνε **της Μαρίας το συμβόλαιο** τελικά;
     Lit. 'Will they give it the contract to her Mary finally?'
(4) **Τα λουλούδια τα** έφερε ο Τάκης
     'Takis brought the flowers' [lit. 'The flowers Takis brought them']
(5) **Της Μαρίας** δεν πρέπει να **της** λες μυστικά
     'You must not tell secrets to Mary'

Unlike the order of the clitics, the order of the noun phrases remains free so that (6a) may also appear as (6b).

(6)a. Θα **της το** δώσουνε **το συμβόλαιο της Μαρίας** τελικά
  b. Θα **της το** δώσουνε **της Μαρίας το συμβόλαιο** τελικά
   'They will give Mary the contract finally'

The function of clitic doubling constructions has to do with making some noun phrase or phrases less prominent in the discourse, in order to allow for some other constituents to be foregrounded, stressed and focal. (For details of this issue see Section 5.2.4.) Clitic doubling or clitic left dislocation constructions where a genitive clitic combines with a genitive noun phrase are much more common than constructions where the indirect object appears as a genitive noun phrase without its clitic. (See (1–3) in Section 1.1.1.4, above.) The reason is that in the presence of the object clitic the role of the genitive noun phrase as object is made clearer and the possibility of confusion with the possessive genitive is avoided.

It must also be pointed out that an indirect object (genitive) clitic cannot co-occur with an indirect object if the latter is expressed with a prepositional phrase. For example, (7) is unacceptable while (8) is correct:

(7)   *Του δώσανε στο Νίκο ένα συμβόλαιο
    'They gave Nick a contract'
(8)a. Του δώσανε του Νίκου ένα συμβόλαιο
  b. Του Νίκου του δώσανε ένα συμβόλαιο
   'They gave Nick a contract'

1.1.1.8   Prepositional phrase complements

In addition to prepositional phrases expressing direction with the preposition σε 'to', benefactive with the preposition για 'for', and source with the preposition από 'from', there are verbs which require, in addition to a direct object, a prepositional phrase which is usually locative. This prepositional phrase is not an indirect object, since its noun is neither human nor animate, nor is it affected by the action of the verb. Because this locative prepositional phrase is required by the specific variety of the verb, it may be viewed, not as a peripheral type of place adverbial, but as a complement to the verb on a par with its objects. Cases of this sort are exemplified in (1–3):

(1) Έβαλαν το φαγητό στο τραπέζι
   'They put the food on the table'
(2) Τους βάλαμε όλους στις θέσεις τους
   'We put everybody in their places'
(3) Έβγαλε τις πατάτες από το φούρνο
   'She took the potatoes out of the oven'

Other prepositional phrases that may be considered complements to the particular verb rather than more peripheral adverbial modifiers are benefactives as in (4), source expressions as in (5), causal expressions as in (6), agentive expressions as in (7), instrumentals as in (8), and comitatives as in (9):

(4) Αυτά τα λουλούδια τα αγόρασε για τη Χρυσούλα
    'He bought these flowers for Chrysoula'   (benefactive)

(5) Να πας να πάρεις τα λεφτά από τη Γιαννούλα
    'You should go to get the money from Giannoula' (source)

(6) Άρχισε να ουρλιάζει από το θυμό της
    'She started screaming out of anger'   (cause)

(7) Ο Τάκης προδόθηκε από τον καλύτερό του φίλο
    'Takis was betrayed by his best friend'   (agent)

(8) Η κονσέρβα αυτή ανοίγει μόνο με ειδικό ανοιχτήρι
    'This can opens only with a special opener'   (instrument)

(9) Δε θα ξαναχορέψει ποτέ με αυτόν τον άνθρωπο
    'She will never dance again with that man'   (comitative)

1.1.2 VERB PHRASE ADVERBIALS

A verb phrase may be modified by an **adverbial**; for the purposes of this treatment an adverbial may be an adverb (1), an adverb phrase (2), a prepositional phrase (3), or an adverbial clause (4):

(1)a. Δούλεψα **χθες**
      'I worked yesterday'

  b. Δούλεψα **καλά**
      'I worked well'

  c. Δούλεψα **πολύ**
      'I worked a lot'

(2)a. Δούλεψα **πολλές φορές**
      'I worked many times'

  b. Δούλεψα **λιγότερο καλά**
      'I worked less well'

(3) Δούλεψα **στην Κρήτη**
    'I worked in Crete'

(4) Δούλεψα **πριν πάω στο θέατρο**
    'I worked before going to the theatre'

A single verb phrase may be modified by a number of adverbials:

(5) **Πολλές φορές** δούλεψα **καλά στην Κρήτη**
    'I've worked well many times in Crete'

(6) **Χθες** δούλεψα **όλη μέρα εδώ πριν πάω στο θέατρο**
    'I worked here all day yesterday before going to the theatre'

The position of adverbials in relation to the verb and in relation to each other is variable, and often depends on matters of **topic** and **focus** (see Section 5.2.2ff.). Nevertheless, a typical position for an adverb of manner is immediately after the verb:

(7)   Να γράψεις **καλά** το όνομά σου
       'Write your name clearly'

For more details about adverbials in general see Sections 3ff. (adverbs and adverb phrases) and 4ff. (prepositional phrases); for adverbs modifying a verb see especially Section 3.2.1. For the following types of adverbial clause see the following Sections: 5.3.5ff. *conditional clauses*, 5.3.6 *concessive clauses*, 5.3.7 *temporal clauses*, 5.3.8 *clauses of manner*, 5.3.9 *clauses of purpose*, 5.3.10 *clauses of result*, 5.3.11 *clauses of cause*.

1.2 PERSON AND NUMBER

Greek verbs have inflectional endings which show three persons and two numbers.

1.2.1 PERSONAL VERBS AND AGREEMENT

Greek verbs inflect for person and number, as shown in the sections on morphology. (See Part II, Sections 7.1–7.1.1.) Thus, we can identify, from the morphological differences in the verb endings, three persons (1st, 2nd and 3rd) and two numbers (singular and plural). In the most common and most typical clauses, the person and the number of the verb agree with the person and the number of the subject noun phrase, as in (1) and (2). (For impersonal verbs see below, Section 1.2.2.)

(1)   Εσείς δε θα του πείτε τίποτα
       'You (2nd pl.) will not tell (2nd pl.) him anything'
(2)   Ο Γιάννης ποτίζει τον κήπο του κάθε πρωί
       'John (3rd sg.) waters (3rd sg.) his garden every morning'

In general, the plural number is used when we wish to refer to more than one item or individual, but, in Greek, as in some other languages, the plural of the second person may also be used when we wish to refer to a single individual in a more polite, respectful manner. This is the so-called 'plural of politeness'. In such cases the verb is also in the 2nd person plural in agreement with the subject. For example, sentence (1) above may refer either to a single individual or to more than one person.

Because the verb itself clearly marks the features of person and number of the subject, when it is a pronoun the subject is generally omitted and this results, very frequently, in sentences without an explicitly stated subject:

(3) Ήρθα να σου πω ότι φεύγω για την Ελλάδα αύριο
    'I came to tell you that I am leaving for Greece tomorrow'
(4) Δεν πρέπει να στενοχωριέσαι τόσο πολύ
    'You must not upset yourself so much'
(5) Κάνει πως δεν καταλαβαίνει
    'He pretends not to understand'
(6) Ελπίζουν πως κάποτε θα φύγουν από δω
    'They are hoping that they will leave here some day'

From the verb endings in the above sentences we know that the subject of the verbs in (3) is the first person singular εγώ (I), in (4) the subject of στενοχωριέσαι is the second person singular εσύ (you), in (5–6) the subject is some 3rd person singular (he or she) and plural (they) respectively. The first- and second-person subject pronouns are more commonly omitted. They are explicitly stated with the pronouns εγώ, εσύ etc. only when we wish to give them some particular emphasis:

(7) **Εγώ** πάντως τον είδα με τα μάτια μου
    '*I,* however, saw him with my own eyes'
(8) **Εσείς** φταίτε για όλα αυτά. Κανείς άλλος
    '*You* are to blame for everything. No one else'

The second person singular is sometimes used with a general indefinite reference instead of the indefinite 3rd-person pronoun κανείς 'one':

(9) Στο εστιατόριο αυτό τρως φτηνά και καλά
    'In that restaurant you can eat cheaply and well'

which could also be expressed as:

(10) Στο εστιατόριο αυτό τρώει κανείς φτηνά και καλά
     'In that restaurant one can eat cheaply and well'

General indefinite reference may also be expressed by the 3rd person plural:

(11) Μπορείτε να μου πείτε πού πουλάνε τσιγάρα εδώ κοντά;
     'Can you tell me where they sell cigarettes around here?'

When we want to speak politely or affectionately to someone we may also address him/her in the 3rd person singular instead of the second. This allows us to include an expression of polite or affectionate address.

(12) Τι θα ήθελε ο κύριος;
     'What would the gentleman want?'
(13) Τι κάνει ο ασθενής μας σήμερα;
     'How is our patient today?'

When we want to give directions or instructions which have a general applicability we often use the first person plural:

(14) Πρώτα σηκώνουμε το ακουστικό και ύστερα ρίχνουμε το
κέρμα
'First we lift the receiver and then we insert the coin'
(15) Καθαρίζουμε το ψάρι και το αλατίζουμε
'We clean the fish and we put salt on it'

The first person plural is also used when the speaker wants to show that
s/he participates emotionally in the meaning of the verb either positively
or negatively:

(16) Πώς αισθανόμαστε σήμερα;
'How are we feeling today?'
(A doctor or nurse talking to a patient and inquiring about
his/her health)
(17) Δε βλέπουμε τα χάλια μας, μόνο κατηγορούμε τους άλλους
'We can't see our own faults but we criticize others'
(Said as a reprimand to someone and implying that the
addressee himself has faults and should not criticize others)

Full noun phrases may appear accompanying plural verbs in the first and
second person. These noun phrases describe or expand the missing and
understood 1st or 2nd person plural subject pronoun.

(18) Σ' αυτό το δωμάτιο μέναμε (1st pl.) τρεις, εγώ και οι δυο
μου αδελφές
'In this room three of us were living, myself and my two
sisters'

1.2.2 IMPERSONAL VERBS

Impersonal verbs are those which appear in the 3rd person singular and
have no noun phrase or pronoun as their subject. A special type of impersonal verbs are the so-called 'weather verbs', such as βρέχει 'it rains',
χιονίζει 'it snows', βροντάει 'it thunders'. There are also impersonal
weather expressions formed with the verb κάνει 'it makes' followed by
an appropriate noun such as κρύο, 'cold', ζέστη 'heat' etc.: κάνει κρύο 'it
is cold', κάνει ζέστη 'it is hot', κάνει ψύχρα 'it is cool' etc.

The 3rd person singular of the verb έχω 'I have' may be used impersonally with the existential meaning of 'there is':

(1) Έχει πολλή φασαρία στην πολυκατοικία μας
'There is a lot of noise in our block of flats'
(2) Έχει ψάρια απόψε;
'Is there fish tonight?'

There are impersonal verbs which are accompanied by a complement
clause, more often in the subjunctive, introduced by να, or in the indicative,

introduced by ότι, depending on the particular impersonal main verb. It can be argued that the clause accompanying the impersonal verb is its syntactic subject.

(3) **Πρόκειται** να πάω στην Ελλάδα σύντομα
'It is likely that I will go to Greece soon'

(4) **Πρέπει** να κόψεις το τσιγάρο
'You must give up smoking'

(5) **Μπορεί** να πάμε αύριο να τον δούμε
'Maybe we will go to see him tomorrow'

(6) **Φαίνεται** ότι οι φίλοι μας προτιμούν την ταβέρνα
'It seems that our friends prefer the taverna'

In (6) the subject of the complement clause, the noun phrase οι φίλοι μας, may occur in a number of positions within its clause, after the verb προτιμούν or after the object την ταβέρνα. In addition, when the main verb is impersonal, the subject of the embedded clause may also be placed before the impersonal. This variation in the order of phrases has stylistic effects (see Section 5.2).

(7) Οι φίλοι μας φαίνεται ότι προτιμούν την ταβέρνα.
'It seems that our friends prefer the taverna'

In such cases, which are very common, the impersonal verb is immediately followed by the embedded verb so that the two verbs form a single verbal expression. Here, it appears that the initial noun phrase is the main clause subject. However, syntactically it is only the subject of the embedded verb, as its agreement clearly shows, while the impersonal verb still has no noun phrase subject of its own (its subject is the whole embedded clause):

(8) Τα παιδιά πρέπει να κοιμούνται νωρίς
'The children must go to bed early'

(9) Οι φίλοι σου πρέπει να κόψουν το τσιγάρο
'Your friends must give up smoking'

1.2.2.1 Impersonal modal verbs

The *modalities* of obligation, possibility, and necessity and their opposites are expressed by the impersonal verbs πρέπει 'it is necessary' and μπορεί 'it is possible' followed by a subjunctive να-clause.

Πρέπει does not have a perfective form. It expresses either obligation or strong probability; to express obligation it may occur in the present πρέπει (obligation in the present), the imperfect έπρεπε (obligation in the past which either has or has not been fulfilled), the future θα πρέπει (obligation in the future), the conditional θα έπρεπε (either a somewhat tentative obligation in the future or an obligation which was not fulfilled in the past). Πρέπει in the sense of obligation is followed by a clause introduced by να with a verb which may be in the imperfective or the perfective non-past, the imperfect or the pluperfect. These combinations are exemplified below:

(1) Οι φίλοι του πρέπει να τον βοηθούν όταν έχει ανάγκη
   'His friends must help him when he is in need'
(2) Οι φίλοι του έπρεπε να τον βοηθούν όταν έχει ανάγκη
   'His friends should help him when he is in need'
(3) Οι φίλοι του πρέπει να τον βοηθήσουν τώρα
   'His friends must help him now'
(4) Οι φίλοι του έπρεπε να τον βοηθήσουν τώρα
   'His friends should help him now'
(5) Οι φίλοι του έπρεπε να τον βοηθούσαν
   'His friends ought to have been helping him'
(6) Οι φίλοι του έπρεπε να τον είχαν βοηθήσει
   'His friends ought to have helped him'

In (1) the impersonal main verb is in the present, indicating an obligation valid for the present or generally valid; the following subjunctive clause is in the imperfective non-past, indicating that the obligation holds for each and every occasion that the need arises. In (2) the impersonal verb is in the imperfect, implying that the speaker thinks that 'his friends' do not or might not really help. In (3) the verb in the subjunctive clause is in the perfective non-past (the dependent), indicating that the obligation to help concerns one specific occasion (now). Accordingly in (4), where the impersonal verb is in the imperfect, the implication is that the friends may help, but they may not (although they should). Similarly in (5) there is an implication that the friends may not have been offering their help as they should. In (6), where the modal is in the imperfect and the verb in the subjunctive clause is in the pluperfect, the implication is that the friends should have offered their help on some occasion in the past but they did not do so.

The negative form of πρέπει expresses disapproval or prohibition.

(7) Η Όλγα δεν έπρεπε να του το είχε πει
   'Olga ought not to have told him'
(8) a. Δεν πρέπει να μιλάς έτσι (with negation in main clause)
   b. Πρέπει να μη μιλάς έτσι (with negation in the complement clause)
   'You should not speak like this'
(9) Δεν έπρεπε να φύγετε τόσο νωρίς
   'You should not have left so early'

Πρέπει may also be used to express strong probability or inference, in which case it may only occur in the present tense followed by a να-clause with a verb in the imperfective non-past (present), the imperfective past (imperfect), the perfective past (simple past), the perfect or the pluper-fect. In this usage it rarely has a negative form.

(10) Από τα λόγια τους καταλάβαινα ότι πρέπει να τον
      αντιπαθούν
      'From their talk I gathered that they must dislike him'

(11) Τα μάτια της είναι κατακόκκινα. Πρέπει να έκλαιγε πολλή
      ώρα
      'Her eyes are very red. She must have been crying for a long
      time'

(12) Πρέπει να τον είδε στη διάλεξη
      'She must have seen him at the lecture'

(13) Πρέπει να την έχει στενοχωρήσει αυτή η κατάσταση
      'This situation must have upset her'

(14) Πρέπει να είχαμε συναντηθεί στο πάρτι του Νίκου
      'We must have met at Nick's party'

(15) Πρέπει να μην κατάλαβες, γι' αυτό θα σου το ξαναπώ
      (negation in the complement clause)
      'You must not [cannot] have understood, so I will repeat
      it'

(16) Δεν πρέπει να κατάλαβες ... (negation in main clause)
      'You probably have not understood ...'

Example (15), with the negative particle in the embedded clause, is equi-valent in meaning to (16), where the negative accompanies the modal.

The impersonal μπορεί followed by a να-clause expresses weak possi-bility. It is generally found in the present tense, rarely in the past, and in this usage it is not negated. All the variations of tense, aspect and nega-tion occur in the embedded να clause:

(17) Μπορεί να συναντήσουμε απόψε το Νίκο
      'It is possible that we will meet Nick tonight [we may meet
      Nick ...]'

(18) Μπορεί όμως και να μην έρθει
      'But he may also not come'

(19) Μπορεί να έφυγαν κιόλας
      'They may have already left'

Ability is expressed by the personal verb μπορώ in all tenses and aspects:

(20) Δεν μπορώ να σε καταλάβω
      'I cannot understand you'

(21) Μπορούσε να φάει δέκα αβγά για πρωινό
      'He could eat ten eggs for breakfast'

Because the 3rd person singular of the personal μπορώ coincides with the impersonal μπορεί there are occasional ambiguities:

(22) Πρόσεχε τι λες γιατί μπορεί να σε καταλάβει
'Be careful of what you say because she can/may understand you'

As in the case of μπορεί – μπορώ, many impersonals have corresponding personal variants with differences in their meaning. For example, in addition to impersonal βρέχει 'it rains' there is personal βρέχω 'I water [something]'.

(23) Όταν κάνει ζέστη πρέπει να βρέχετε συχνά το πρόσωπό σας
'When it is hot you should wet your face frequently'

Weather verbs, which are typically impersonal, may occasionally appear, especially in poetry or songs, with a noun phrase subject:

(24) Βρέχει ο Θεός και βρέχομαι
'God is raining and I am getting wet'

Other such pairs are impersonal φαίνεται 'it seems', personal φαίνομαι 'I appear, I look like', impersonal αξίζει 'it is worth [doing something]', personal αξίζω 'I am worth', etc.

1.2.2.2   Impersonal verbs with a personal clitic pronoun

Some verbs, when used impersonally, may be accompanied by a clitic pronoun in the genitive which represents the so-called 'psychological subject':

(1) Του αρέσει να χορεύει τανγκό
'It pleases him/He likes to dance the tango'
(2) Μου κάνει κέφι να τρώω φρούτο μετά το φαΐ
'It amuses me/I like to eat some fruit after a meal'

The clitic pronoun may also appear in the accusative, as with the verbs πειράζει 'it bothers, it matters', ενοχλεί 'it irritates', στενοχωρεί 'it upsets':

(3) Με πειράζει/με στενοχωρεί/με ενοχλεί να σε βλέπω έτσι
'It upsets me to see you like this'

1.3   MOOD AND MODALITY

The term **mood** is used to refer to a formally differentiated verbal construction associated with a distinct characteristic function. In order to recognize a mood difference between verb forms they have to be distinct either in their morphology (their inflectional endings) or in the choice of particles which precede and modify the verb forms. Mood therefore is viewed as a *grammatically* marked verbal category. The term **modality**, on the other hand, is used to refer to a number of *semantic* uses that the language makes of the basic moods.

Greek has only three formally distinct moods: indicative, subjunctive and imperative. Of these the imperative is differentiated from the other two by specific verbal endings, while the indicative and the subjunctive are distinguished from each other by the choice of verbal particles which accompany the verb and by the choice of the negative particle. Thus (δεν) (θα) + verb represents the forms of the indicative, να/ας (μην) + verb represents the forms of the subjunctive.

1.3.1   INDICATIVE

The basic or characteristic function of the indicative, which we can establish by reference to the most neutral context, namely the main clause, and the most neutral tense, namely the present or past, is to describe objectively an event or a state of affairs. The indicative places the event or state described in the past, present or future and makes a claim which can be judged to be either true or false, e.g. γράφω 'I write' or 'I am writing', έγραφα 'I was writing' or 'I used to write', έγραψα 'I wrote'. In more complex contexts the indicative may be found expressing other modalities which depart sometimes significantly from this characteristic or prototypical use. As a small example of this extension of the use of the indicative consider the future θα γράψω. This form is indicative because it can be negated by the negative particle δεν, which is characteristic of the indicative, and because it can be interpreted as making a claim about the truth. If I make a statement that I will write a letter and then I fail to do so, I can be called a liar. However the future is not something which we can describe objectively, since it has not happened yet. This means that the future of the indicative may also be used to express not what is a fact but what is a possibility or a probability. Therefore the future, which is part of the indicative mood in that it makes a claim about a future state of affairs, also expresses the modalities of possibility and probability.

We classify as indicative all the verb expressions which may be negated with the particle δεν and which cannot be accompanied by the subjunctive particles να or ας. The following clauses are indicative:

> (1)a. (Δε) γράφει συχνά στη μητέρα του
>   'He writes (does not write) often to his mother'
>   b. (Δε) θα γράψω το γράμμα απόψε
>   'I will (not) write the letter tonight'
>   c. (Δεν) το έγραψα για σένα
>   'I wrote (did not write) it for you'
>   d. (Δε) θα το είχε γράψει
>   'He would (not) have written it'

1.3.2   SUBJUNCTIVE

The prototypical, characteristic function of the subjunctive is not to describe situations but to present them as wished for, desired, requested, ordered, conceded, allowed etc., on the part of the speaker in direct speech, or on the part of the main clause subject if the subjunctive occurs in a subordinate clause. The subjunctive is expressed formally by the use of the particles να or ας and by the choice of the negative particle μη(ν). The particle ας occurs only in direct speech; it expresses exhortation, admonition, concession, consent, indifference and the like. When it is combined with the imperfective past ας expresses an unfulfilled wish. Να, on the other hand, in main clauses, expresses a wish, a request, a less forceful command than the imperative etc. The following examples cover some of the uses of the subjunctive and show the differences between να and ας.

(1)a. Να (μη) γράφει στη μητέρα του για τα προβλήματά του
      'He should (not) write to his mother about his problems'
   b. Να μη γράψω το γράμμα απόψε;
      'Shouldn't I write the letter tonight?'
   c. Ας (μην) τον ενοχλήσουμε τώρα
      'Let us (not) bother him now'
   d. Να/ας (μην) του το έλεγες
      'You should (not) have told him that'
   e. Ας (μη) μου δώσεις τα λεφτά
      'Do (not) give me the money. I do not care'

1.3.2.1   Omissibility of the subjunctive particle να

There are some cases where the subjunctive marker να may be omitted while the verb expression remains in the subjunctive, as indicated by the use of the negative particle μη(ν), which is the characteristic negation for the subjunctive mood. Constructions where the particle να may be omitted are the prohibitions discussed below (Section 1.3.2.1.1) and a number of other constructions given in Section 1.5.2.1, where there is a fuller discussion of the *dependent* and the omissibility of either να or θα.

1.3.2.1.1   Prohibitions

In prohibitions we may optionally omit να:

(1)a. (Να) μην του το δώσεις
      'Do not give it to him'
   b. (Να) μην του μιλάς έτσι
      'Do not speak to him like that'
   c. (Να) μην πιστεύεις ό,τι σου λένε
      'Don't believe what they tell you'

1.3.3   POSITIVE IMPERATIVE

The positive imperative has distinct verbal endings (see Part II, Section 7.1.7). Compare the following imperative (1a) to the indicative in (1b) and the subjunctive in (1c):

(1)a. Διάβαζε πιο δυνατά, σε παρακαλώ (imperative)
    'Read louder please'
  b. Διαβάζεις πολύ δυνατά και με ενοχλείς (indicative)
    'You are reading too loud and you are disturbing me'
  c. Να διαβάζεις λίγο πιο δυνατά, σε παρακαλώ (subjunctive)
    'You should read a little louder, please'

The imperative is restricted to the 2nd person singular and plural and only to non-past forms. In addition, the passive voice imperatives are restricted to the perfective aspect. For example, the passive voice of the verb ντύνω 'I dress someone' is ντύνομαι 'I get dressed'. The only possible imperative forms for the passive voice of this verb are in the perfective: ντύσου 'get dressed (sg.)' and ντυθείτε 'get dressed (pl.)'. The only way of giving an order for a repeated or continuous action with passive verbs is by using the subjunctive: να ντύνεσαι 'you (sg.) should dress', να κοιμάστε 'you (pl.) should sleep', etc. The imperative mood cannot be negated. In order to give a negative order and thus to express a prohibition, we must again resort to the subjunctive: να μη γράφεις 'you (sg.) should not write', να μην ντυθείς 'you (sg.) should not dress'.

In addition to its specific endings, which differentiate the imperative from both the indicative and the subjunctive, there is another syntactic feature which characterizes only the imperative and the gerund. The object clitic pronouns follow the imperative and the gerund, whereas they precede the indicative and the subjunctive. This is shown in the following examples:

(2)a. Γράψε τού το (imperative)
    'Write it to him'
  b. Γράφοντάς του το (gerund)
    'While writing it to him'
  c. Του το έγραψα (indicative)
    'I wrote it to/for him'
  d. Να του το γράψεις (subjunctive)
    'You should write it to him'

1.3.4   OTHER MODALITIES

As stated above (Section 1.3) Greek differentiates formally between three moods: indicative, subjunctive and imperative. Each one of these has a characteristic usage: the indicative is normally used for describing facts or states, the subjunctive for talking in general about non-facts, and the imperative for giving orders, making suggestions etc. There are also other, more specific ways of presenting the contents of a sentence. For example, a sentence may express a condition, a clearly marked wish, a possibility, an obligation, a probability etc. These are referred to as **modalities**. These modalities are not marked formally either in the verb ending or by specific particles within the verb group. They are expressed by a variety of means such as through specific combinations of conjunctions and verbal aspect, tense or mood, or by impersonal modal verbs, as we explain below.

1.3.4.1   Conditional

Conditional constructions consist of two clauses: the condition (i.e., the 'if' clause, also known as the **protasis**) and the **apodosis** (the 'then' clause). In Greek the condition is introduced most frequently by the conjunction αν, or less commonly by εάν. The latter occurs in more formal styles. More colloquial alternatives are άμα or έτσι και. Conditional constructions may be divided into *factual* and *counterfactual*. In all cases the verb of the 'if' clause is in the indicative (negative morpheme δεν).

In *factual* conditions the verb may be in the present tense, or the perfective past or the future. The apodosis either uses the same tense as the protasis or is expressed by the subjunctive or imperative.

(1) Αν ξέρεις Αγγλικά είσαι κατάλληλη για τη δουλειά αυτή
    'If you know English you are suitable for this job'   (Present)
(2) Αν (θα) πάω στην Ελλάδα θα προσπαθήσω να τον δω
    'If I go to Greece I will try to see him'   (Future)
(3) Αν θα πας στην Ελλάδα να προσπαθήσεις να τον δεις
    'If you go to Greece you should try to see him'   (Subjunctive)
(4) Αν πας στην Ελλάδα πήγαινε να τον δεις
    'If you go to Greece go and see him'   (Imperative)
(5) Αν βρήκε το γράμμα θα το διάβασε σίγουρα (θα το έχει
    διαβάσει)
    'If he found the letter he must have read it for sure'
                                  (Simple past or perfect)

The same pattern is used to state that some state of affairs obtains as a general rule as a consequence of another state of affairs:

(6) Αν είναι μεσημέρι εδώ, στην Αυστραλία είναι μεσάνυχτα
    'If it is midday here, in Australia it is midnight'

Counterfactual conditions are introduced by αν, εάν, etc., followed again by a verb in the indicative mood but in the imperfective past or the pluperfect. The apodosis is also in the imperfective past or the pluperfect, preceded by the particle θα (conditional or perfect conditional):

(7)   Αν διάβαζες το γράμμα του θα καταλάβαινες
      'If you were to read his letter you would understand'

(8)   Αν είχες διαβάσει το γράμμα του θα καταλάβαινες
      'If you had read his letter you would understand'

(9)   Αν διάβαζες το γράμμα του θα είχες καταλάβει
      'If you had read his letter you would have understood'

(10) Αν είχες διαβάσει το γράμμα του θα είχες καταλάβει
      'If you had read his letter you would have understood'

Sentences (7–10) imply that the subject of the 'if' clause has not read the letter and has not, therefore, understood, but (7) with imperfective past in both clauses allows for the possibility that the wish of reading the letter and understanding may still be realized. In this case the conditional is suppositional rather than counterfactual. On the other hand, the remaining examples, where a pluperfect is used in one or both of the clauses, are more definitely counterfactual.

1.3.4.2   Optative

Optative is the term given to the modality of sentences expressing a wish for something to come about. This is achieved by one of the following means: imperative, subjunctive with either να or ας, or periphrastically with the subjunctive introduced by the exclamatory particle μακάρι or the particle που, or the subjunctive preceded by a main verb expressing a wish.

(1)   Έλα αύριο να τα πούμε
      'Come tomorrow to have a chat'

(2)   Να 'ρθεις αύριο να σε δούμε
      'You should come tomorrow so we can see you'

(3)   Να 'ρχότανε να τον βλέπαμε
      'I wish he would come so we could see him'

The subjunctive used here (3), in both the **protasis** and the **apodosis**, with an imperfective past tense verb, expresses a strong wish for something which is unlikely to happen.

(4)   Ας τον δω κι ας πεθάνω
      'Let me see him and then die'

(5)   Μακάρι/Που να μην τον είχα συναντήσει
      'If only I had never met him'

(6)   Εύχομαι να μην τον ξαναδώ
      'Would that I will never see him again'

1.3.4.3 Obligation

Obligation is expressed by the impersonal main verb πρέπει 'it is neces-sary, must' accompanied by a complement clause in the subjunctive (see also Section 1.2.2.1):

(1) Πρέπει να φύγουμε πριν έρθει ο Γιώργος
    'It is necessary that we leave before George comes'
    'We must leave before George comes'

When there is an explicit subject of the embedded subjunctive clause it is often placed before the main verb πρέπει:

(2) Οι φίλοι σου πρέπει να σε καταλάβουνε
    'Your friends must (should) understand you'

The impersonal verb πρέπει displays neither aspect nor voice distinction. It has, however, four tenses: present πρέπει, past έπρεπε, future θα πρέπει and the future particle θα followed by the past έπρεπε, as in the following examples:

(3)a. Έπρεπε να του το λέγαμε
   b. Έπρεπε να του το πούμε
      'We should have told him'
(4) Έπρεπε να του το είχαμε πει
    'We should have told him' [before some other event in the past]
(5) Θα πρέπει τελικά να πας να του μιλήσεις
    'You will finally have to go and talk to him'
(6)a. Θα έπρεπε να φύγουμε πιο νωρίς
   b. Θα έπρεπε να φεύγαμε πιο νωρίς
   c. Θα έπρεπε να είχαμε φύγει πιο νωρίς
      'We should have left earlier'

The use of θα to introduce sentences (5) and (6) does not alter the basic meaning of the obligation; it is used in order to weaken the impact of the assertion which may sound too strong without it. Thus θα in such contexts makes the assertion less direct and thus more polite.

1.3.4.4 Possibility

Possibility is expressed by the impersonal main verb μπορεί 'it is possible, may' followed by a complement clause in the subjunctive or by the adver-bial ίσως 'perhaps' followed by the subjunctive (see also Section 1.2.2.1):

(1) Μπορεί να βρέξει αύριο αλλά μπορεί και να μη βρέξει
    'Maybe it will rain tomorrow but maybe it will not rain'
(2) Ίσως (να) βρέξει αύριο
    'Perhaps it will rain tomorrow'

In addition to impersonal μπορεί there is also a personal verb μπορώ 'I can' which expresses ability on the part of its subject to do something:

(3) Μπορώ να σηκώσω τη βαλίτσα χωρίς δυσκολία
    'I can lift the suitcase without difficulty'

The personal verb μπορώ is also used to express permission, as in the following examples:

(4) Αν θέλετε μπορείτε να πάτε να τον δείτε
    'If you wish you may go to see him'
(5) Μπορώ να δω τον Νίκο;
    'May I see Nick?'

Because impersonal μπορεί has the ending of the 3rd person singular and this coincides with the personal verb μπορώ when the subject is 3rd singular, we may come across sentences which are ambiguous between a personal (ability or permission) and an impersonal (possibility) reading:

(6) Ο Νίκος μπορεί να ταξιδέψει αύριο
    (i)   'Maybe Nick will travel tomorrow' (impersonal μπορεί
          = possibility)
    (ii) 'Nick is able to travel tomorrow' (personal μπορώ
          = ability)
    (iii) 'Nick is allowed to travel tomorrow' (personal μπορώ
          = permission)

Both personal and impersonal versions have only active voice but, whereas the personal verb occurs in all tenses (except the perfect tense), the impersonal occurs only in the present and the imperfective past.

(7) (Θα) Μπορούσε να είχε καθυστερήσει το τρένο αλλά
     ευτυχώς ήρθε στην ώρα του (impersonal = possibility)
     'The train could (might) have been delayed but fortunately it
     arrived on time'
(8)a. Ο Νίκος μπόρεσε να φύγει χθες (past = personal = ability)
     'Nick was able to leave yesterday [he succeeded in leaving/
     managed to leave]'
   b. Ο Νίκος μπόρεσε και έφυγε χθες
     'Nick managed to leave [lit. 'managed and he left'] yesterday'

The use of θα in (7) contributes again to the indirectness of the assertion. In (8b) the co-ordinating conjunction και is used instead of the subjunctive particle να in order to emphasize the fact that Nick did leave. (Further on the various uses of και see Section 5.4.1.1.)

1.3.4.5   Probability

Probability is a stronger form of possibility. It is expressed with the impersonal main verb πρέπει 'must' followed by a complement clause in the subjunctive. In this case the impersonal verb πρέπει, which as we saw above also expresses obligation, is equivalent to the periphrasis 'It must be the case that'. (See also Section 1.2.2.1).

(1) Πρέπει να έβρεξε τη νύχτα γιατί το έδαφος είναι υγρό
     'It must have rained in the night because the ground is wet'

In most cases the meaning of πρέπει, i.e. whether it expresses obligation or strong probability, is made clear from the whole construction, but we can also find cases of ambiguity. This situation is exactly parallel to the English modal 'must'.

(2) (Θα) Πρέπει να τον αγαπάς πολύ τον αδερφό σου
     (i)   'You should [ought to] love your brother a lot [obligation]'
     (ii) 'I deduce from your behaviour that you must love your
           brother a lot' (strong probability).

The possibility expressed in the above examples is formulated more firmly without the use of θα and more tentatively with it.

An explicit subject of the embedded clause is often placed before an impersonal main verb, while the impersonal verb appears immediately before the embedded subjunctive, creating a complex verbal expression:

(3) Οι φοιτητές **πρέπει να μελετούν** πολύ
     'Students must study a lot' (obligation or probability)
(4) Οι φοιτητές **πρέπει να μη χάσουν** το μάθημα
     'The students must not miss the lecture' (obligation)

1.4   VOICE

Greek verb forms exhibit two different sets of personal endings which correlate with the grammatical category of voice: **active** and **passive** (see Part II, Section 7.1.5). In many cases the same verb can occur in both voices, e.g. γράφω 'I write', γράφομαι 'I am written, I am registered', σπρώχνω 'I push', σπρώχνομαι 'I am pushed'. In such cases the typical or characteristic use of the active voice is to indicate that the subject of the verb acts, i.e. initiates the action conveyed by the verb, causes this action or is the instrument through which the action is implemented. The characteristic use of the corresponding passive is to indicate that the subject undergoes the action conveyed by the verb and/or is affected by it. In such examples it is typically the case that the object (typically the direct object) of the active corresponds to the subject of the passive while the subject of the active corresponds to the **agent**, present or understood, of the passive.

(1) Active: Ο εκδοτικός οίκος Μούτον δημοσίευσε το πρώτο βιβλίο του Τσόμσκι
    'Mouton publishers published Chomsky's first book'
(2) Passive: Το πρώτο βιβλίο του Τσόμσκι δημοσιεύτηκε από τον εκδοτικό οίκο Μούτον
    'Chomsky's first book was published by Mouton publishers'

It is from this type of verb and from such typical uses that the terms active (the subject acts as in (1)) and passive (the subject suffers passively as in (2)) are derived. These terms, active and passive, have subsequently been associated with all the verb paradigms with the endings in -ω, -εις, ει, etc. and -ομαι, -εσαι, -εται, etc., respectively (for morphology see Part II, Section 7.1.5). However, not all verbs belong to this symmetrical pattern. Many verbs appear in only one of the two paradigms and for many the correlation between active or passive voice endings and the meaning of action or suffering does not hold. We must, therefore, restrict the terms active and passive voice to the formal distinction between the two sets of verbal endings and then proceed to give the various uses that we can find associated with each.

1.4.1 ACTIVE

As we explained above, a typical use of the active voice is to express action initiated or caused by the subject. If this action is transferred to another entity, then we have a transitive construction. In many cases, this type of active transitive construction gives rise to a corresponding passive, as described above (Section 1.4). Below we give one more such example:

(1) Active transitive: Ο Εφιάλτης πρόδωσε τους Σπαρτιάτες
                          'Ephialtes betrayed the Spartans'
(2) Passive: Οι Σπαρτιάτες προδόθηκαν από τον Εφιάλτη
                          'The Spartans were betrayed by Ephialtes'

We will now describe a number of types of verb which depart to a greater or lesser degree from this pattern. Some active transitive verbs may express action but have no corresponding passive, such as φέρνω 'bring', μαλώνω 'scold', φωνάζω 'call, shout'.

(3) Ο θυρωρός μάς φέρνει τα γράμματα κάθε πρωί
    'The porter brings us the letters every morning'
(4) Αφού είσαι άρρωστος πρέπει να φωνάξουμε το γιατρό
    'Since you are unwell we must call the doctor'

There are active transitive verbs which express not action but state, such as πιστεύω (κάτι) 'I believe [something]', μοιάζω (κάποιου) 'I look like [someone]'.

(5) Ο Νίκος πάντα πιστεύει την Ελένη
    'Nick always believes Helen'
(6) Λένε πως ο Στέφανος μοιάζει του πατέρα του
    'They say that Stefanos looks like his father'

There are also active verbs which do not express action and appear only in intransitive constructions, such as μένω 'I stay, reside', τρέμω 'I tremble', etc.

(7) Ο Αλέκος μένει στην Αθήνα
    'Alekos lives in Athens'
(8) Τρέμει από το φόβο του
    'He trembles with fear'

Some verbs with active voice endings do not express action but a certain feeling or perception, such as, πονάω 'I ache', νιώθω 'I feel', ακούω 'I hear', βλέπω 'I see', ξέρω 'I know'. Some of these, such as ακούω, βλέπω and ξέρω, may be transitive, while others, such as ακούω, may even occur in the passive.

(9) Ο Γιάννης ένιωσε μια παράξενη επιθυμία
    'John felt a strange desire'
(10) Active: Η Μαρία άκουσε το Γιάννη να μιλάει στο
               διπλανό δωμάτιο
               'Maria heard John talking in the next room'
(11) Passive: Ο Γιάννης ακούστηκε να μιλάει στο διπλανό
               δωμάτιο
               'John was heard speaking in the next room'

There are also active voice verbs which occur in both transitive and intransitive constructions, such as περπατώ, intransitive 'I walk', transitive 'I take somebody for a walk', τρέχω, intransitive 'I run', transitive 'I take somebody for a run', γελώ, intransitive 'I laugh', transitive 'I fool somebody, I make him laughable', πεθαίνω, intransitive 'I die', transitive 'I make someone die', ζωντανεύω, intransitive 'I revive', transitive 'I revive someone'. In many such cases the transitive version has a causative meaning, as shown in the following examples:

(12) Ο Νίκος περπατάει μια ώρα την ημέρα
    'Nick walks for an hour every day'
(13) Ο Νίκος περπατάει το σκύλο του μια ώρα την ημέρα
    'Nick walks his dog for an hour every day'

1.4.2   PASSIVE

As stated above (Section 1.4), the 'true' passive is found with verbs which occur in both active transitive and passive constructions. In such cases the passive indicates that its subject undergoes or is affected by the action expressed by the verb. The initiator of the action, i.e. the agent, is either omitted in the passive or is expressed by a prepositional phrase typically introduced by the preposition από (see examples in Section 1.4.1 above). Whereas the active is used to focus on the *action* of the verb, the passive is used to emphasize the *result* of this action, e.g.:

(1) Active: Η ανάπτυξη του τουρισμού κατάστρεψε το χωριό
                 'The development of tourism destroyed the village'

(2) Passive: Το χωριό καταστράφηκε (από την ανάπτυξη του
                 τουρισμού)
                 'The village has been destroyed (due to the develop-
                 ment of tourism)'

The passive is used more in formal, scientific or journalistic discourse influenced by *katharevousa*, especially when the agent of the action is either not relevant or easily understood from the context and need not be mentioned.

(3) Θεωρείται απαραίτητο να διεξαχθούν συζητήσεις . . .
     'It is considered essential that discussions be conducted . . .'

(4) Στο τέλος θα οδηγηθούμε σε κάποια διεθνή κυβέρνηση
     'In the end we will be led to some sort of international government'

Another function of the passive is to present the element which corresponds to the object of the active verb as the topic of the sentence, i.e. the entity that the sentence is about. Compare (5) and (6) (on topicalization see Section 5.2.2):

(5) Ο κόσμος δε θεωρεί τους πολιτικούς έντιμους
     'People do not consider politicians honest'

(6) Οι πολιτικοί δε θεωρούνται έντιμοι (από τον κόσμο)
     'Politicians are not considered honest (by people)'

In example (6) the entity which is more topical, more central to the sentence, is 'οι πολιτικοί', while the phrase 'από τον κόσμο' is so general that it can be easily understood and can, therefore, be omitted. However, in Greek there is another way to make the object of the corresponding active into the topic of the sentence without resorting to the passive. This can be achieved by adding the object clitic pronoun to the construction and optionally bringing the object phrase to the beginning of the sentence, as below:

(7) Το Νίκο τον απολύσανε χθες ενώ το Γιάννη δε θα τον
     απολύσουν
     'As for Nick, they fired him yesterday, whereas they will not fire
     John'

(8) Τα βιβλία του Ελύτη τα πούλησαν όλα
    'As for Elytis's books, they sold them all'

Notice that in English the above sentences are more likely to be expressed with the passive:

(7)a. 'Nick was fired yesterday, whereas John will not be fired'
(8)a. 'Elytis's books were all sold'

In the rather rare cases where an animate, often human, agent is explicitly present in the sentence it is expressed with the preposition από. This preposition can also express the cause rather than the true agent, as in the following example:

(9) Πολλά σπίτια καταστράφηκαν από τις βροχές
     'Many houses were destroyed by the rain'

With verbs expressing emotion the cause of this emotion may either be expressed as agency with the use of the preposition από, or as instrument, in which case the preposition με 'with' may be used instead.

(10) Απογοητεύτηκε από/με τη συμπεριφορά του
      'She was disappointed by/with his behaviour'

Passives in the present tense often have the meaning of 'be able to' or 'allow oneself to':

(11) Είναι άνθρωπος που συμπαθιέται πολύ εύκολα
      'S/he is the sort of person who is liked very easily'
(12) Το φαΐ αυτό δεν τρώγεται
      'This food is not edible'

1.4.2.1 The reflexive use of the passive

The most typical reflexive construction involves an active transitive verb with the reflexive phrase τον εαυτό μου, τον εαυτό σου, τον εαυτό του, etc., in direct object position (see Section 5.4.3.5.3) as in the examples below:

(1) Κοίταξε τον εαυτό της στον καθρέφτη
     'She looked at herself in the mirror'
(2) Σκοτώνεις τον εαυτό σου με τη δουλειά αυτή
     'You are killing yourself with this work'

However, another way of expressing reflexivity with a number of verbs, mostly of bodily care, is through the use of passive morphology and without an object. Such verbs are πλένομαι 'I wash myself', χτενίζομαι 'I comb my hair', κουρεύομαι 'I have my hair cut', ξυρίζομαι 'I shave myself', ντύνομαι 'I get dressed; I have my clothes made', ετοιμάζομαι 'I get myself ready'.

(3) Κοιτάχτηκε στον καθρέφτη
    'She looked at herself in the mirror'
(4) Σκοτώνεσαι στη δουλειά
    'You are killing yourself with work'

These passives may also have a factitive meaning, 'I have somebody do something for me', such as in the examples below:

(5) Ντύνεται στον καλύτερο ράφτη
    'He gets his clothes made [lit. is dressed] at the best tailor'
(6) Χτενίζεται στο κομμωτήριο της γειτονιάς της
    'She gets her hair done [lit. is combed] at the hairdresser's of her neighbourhood'

With this kind of verb it is often the wider context that leads to the reflexive or factitive interpretation. However, the reflexive can be made clear by the use of μόνος μου, μόνος σου, μόνος του 'on my own, by myself', etc.

(7) Λούζομαι πάντα μόνη μου αλλά δεν μπορώ να χτενιστώ μόνη μου
    'I always wash my hair myself but I cannot set my hair on my own'

With other verbs, not indicating bodily care, the prefix αυτο- 'self-' may be added to the passive verb form to indicate reflexivity, e.g. καταστρέφω 'I destroy', passive καταστρέφομαι 'I am destroyed', periphrastic reflexive καταστρέφω τον εαυτό μου 'I destroy myself', monolectic reflexive αυτοκαταστρέφομαι 'I am destroying myself'.

1.4.2.2   The reciprocal use of the passive

To express reciprocity (see Section 5.4.3.6) we usually use the expression ο ένας τον άλλο 'each other' or add the prefix αλληλο- 'each other' to the passive verb:

(1) Ο Τάκης και η Όλγα αγαπούν πολύ ο ένας τον άλλο
    'Takis and Olga love each other very much'
(2) Αλληλοκοιτάχτηκαν άγρια
    'They looked at each other angrily'

In addition, reciprocity may also be expressed with passive morphology alone:

(3) Ο Τάκης και η Όλγα αγαπιούνται πολύ
    'Takis and Olga love each other [lit. are loved] very much'
(4) Δεν πρέπει να φιλιέστε έτσι μπροστά στον κόσμο
    'You should not kiss (each other) like this in front of people'

1.4.3   DEPONENT VERBS

The term *deponent* verb refers to a verb which appears with passive morphology but is active in its meaning. Such verbs may be transitive, such as θυμάμαι κάποιον 'I remember someone', δέχομαι κάποιον 'I receive, accept someone', λυπάμαι κάποιον 'I pity, feel sorry for someone', φοβάμαι κάποιον 'I fear someone', περιποιούμαι κάποιον 'I take care of someone', etc.

(1) Δέχτηκε την πρότασή μας αμέσως
    'He accepted our proposal immediately'
(2) Η Ελένη φοβάται το σκοτάδι
    'Helen is afraid of the dark'

Deponent verbs may also be intransitive, such as έρχομαι 'I come', κοιμάμαι 'I sleep', κουράζομαι 'I get tired', ξεκουράζομαι 'I rest', γίνομαι 'I become':

(3) Όταν έρχομαι στην Αθήνα κουράζομαι πολύ
    'Whenever I come to Athens I get very tired'

Some of the transitive deponent verbs may also appear as intransitives, λυπάμαι 'I am sad', φοβάμαι 'I am scared', etc.:

(4) Φοβάται και λυπάται χωρίς να ξέρει γιατί
    'He is fearful and sad without knowing why'

1.5   ASPECT

Aspect is a grammatical category which indicates a certain difference in the way the action expressed by the verb is viewed by the speaker and presented to the hearer. An action may be presented in its totality, as a single and complete event, as repeated habitually, as being in progress, or as completed in the past where its completion is relevant to the present state of things. Greek verbs differentiate morphologically, i.e. within the verb form itself, between two aspects, namely perfective and imperfective. In addition, verbs may display a third aspect, namely the perfect; they do this periphrastically, by means of auxiliary verbs.

1.5.1   IMPERFECTIVE

The imperfective aspect in Greek presents the action or state expressed by the verb either as a single but continuous event (progressively) or as a habitually repeated one. In the most regular case the imperfective aspect is expressed by the plain verbal root without any morphophonological modification:

(1) Δε γράφει στη μητέρα του πολύ συχνά
    'He does not write to his mother very frequently'
(2) Τα πρώτα χρόνια μάς έγραφε κάθε βδομάδα
    'During the first years she used to write to us every week'

In the above examples the unmodified root γραφ- corresponds to the imperfective aspect, while the adverbs συχνά in (1) and κάθε βδομάδα in (2), which indicate repetition of the action, lead us to interpret the action as *habitual*. In examples (3) and (4) below, the same imperfective aspect is interpreted as describing a *progressive* or *continuous* action because of the other elements in the sentence:

(3) Μην τον διακόπτεις τώρα γιατί γράφει
    'Do not interrupt him now because he is writing'
(4) Έγραφα ένα γράμμα στο Νίκο την ώρα που τηλεφώνησες
    'I was writing a letter to Nick when you telephoned'

In (3) the adverb τώρα in combination with the other verb in the sentence μην τον διακόπτεις points to the interpretation of γράφει as continuous. In (4) we have two clauses; the first of which, in the imperfective past, acts as a background, a setting, within which the action expressed by the perfective past (single complete action) τηλεφώνησες took place.

It has been stated that adverbials expressing frequency (συχνά 'often', κάθε βδομάδα 'every week', etc.) point to the habitual interpretation of the imperfective, while adverbials indicating a specific point of time (τώρα 'now', αυτή τη στιγμή 'at this moment') or some other expression which indicates a single point in time, as in (4), point to a continuous-progressive interpretation of the imperfective. However, there are cases where such adverbials may not be present and others where, even if they are present, they do not always correlate with one interpretation or the other. In the majority of cases it is the wider linguistic and pragmatic context that allows us to give the correct interpretation of the imperfective aspect either as habitual or as continuous progressive. For example, the same question in (5) can receive different answers. In these answers it is the semantics of the individual verbs in combination with the semantics of the rest of the words that determine the meaning of the imperfective aspect.

(5)a. Τι κάνει ο Νίκος;   'What is Nick doing?'
   b. Τρώει   'He is eating'
   c. Διδάσκει   'He teaches, *or* he is teaching'
   d. Διδάσκει γλωσσολογία   'He teaches linguistics'

Answer (b) can only mean that he is eating now; it, therefore, corresponds to the progressive-continuous interpretation of the question. This is because the verb τρώει cannot normally be an appropriate answer to what someone does habitually, say as a job. In (c) we have a case of ambiguity because the response can mean either 'he is teaching right now' (in the pragmatic context of a school environment) or that his profession is to teach; that is what he does habitually to earn his living. The answer in (d) is not ambiguous. It indicates the habitual-repetitive interpretation. This is so because of the presence of the other phrases, which are more likely to be used when we talk about teaching as a profession.

The imperfective can also be used to indicate capability, or more frequently the lack of it, in negative sentences:

(6)a. Κόβει αυτό το ψαλίδι;
     'Do these scissors cut [Are they sharp]?'
  b. Αυτό το μολύβι δε γράφει
     'This pencil does not write [It is not possible to write with it]'

There are some temporal/aspectual verbs which may be followed by an embedded subjunctive clause whose verb is always in the imperfective. Such verbs are αρχίζω 'I begin', εξακολουθώ, συνεχίζω 'I continue', σταματώ and παύω 'I stop'.

(7)a. Και ξαφνικά άρχισε να κλαίει
     'And suddenly she started crying'
  b. Εμείς φύγαμε αλλά αυτός συνέχισε να τραγουδάει
     'We left but he carried on singing'

In embedded subjunctive clauses after verbs of perception, such as ακούω 'hear', βλέπω 'see', αισθάνομαι 'feel', αντιλαμβάνομαι 'become aware', φαντάζομαι 'imagine', etc., we more frequently find the imperfective, although the perfective is sometimes also possible.

(8)a. Δεν τον ακούσαμε ποτέ να παραπονιέται (imperfective)
     'We never heard him complain'
  b. Δεν τον ακούσαμε ποτέ να παραπονεθεί (perfective)
     'We never heard him complain (once)'
(9)a. Τον είδα να τη φιλάει (imperfective)
     'I saw him kissing her'
  b. Δεν είδα να τη φίλησε (perfective)
     'I did not see whether he kissed her'

In (8b) and (9b) the main verbs followed by the perfective aspect indicate that the speaker is informed or has realized that something is the case, rather than that the speaker has direct perception, as is the case with (8a) and (9a) where the main verb is followed by the imperfective aspect. Notice that the difference in the meaning between the imperfective in (8a) and the perfective in (8b) can be best captured in English by the use of the adverb 'once' for the latter.

There are some other main verbs which may only take the imperfective in their embedded subjunctive clause such as μαθαίνω 'learn [how to]', ξέρω 'I know [how to]'.

(10) Έμαθες επιτέλους να κολυμπάς;
'Have you finally learned how to swim?'

A sentence with μαθαίνω as main verb followed by a να-clause in the perfective is ungrammatical:

(11) *Έμαθα να κολυμπήσω

1.5.2   PERFECTIVE

The perfective aspect in Greek expresses an action (less so a state) which is viewed in its totality as a single and complete event. It is normally marked by a morphophonological modification of the stem itself. (See Part II, Section 7.1.3.)

The perfective and imperfective aspects combine with the category of time reference to give us two past tenses: simple past (which combines the properties of perfective aspect and past) έγραψα (see Section 1.6.3) and imperfect (which combines the properties of imperfective aspect and past) έγραφα (see Section 1.6.2). The present tense, as we already mentioned, can only appear with the imperfective aspect, γράφω (see Section 1.6.1). This means that the verb form which combines the categories perfective aspect and non-past, γράψω, cannot function as a tense on its own, which is why we refer to it as the **_dependent_** (see below).

1.5.2.1   The dependent

The dependent is the verb form which combines the properties perfective (as indicated by its perfective stem) and non-past (as indicated by its inflectional endings). Examples of the dependent are γράψω, διαβάσω, αγαπήσω (see Part II, Section 7.1.3). This form does not constitute an independent tense or an independent mood but appears normally in constructions where it is preceded by one of the particles θα, να or ας. With the future particle θα it forms the perfective future θα γράψω 'I will write' (a complete act of writing); with the particles να or ας it forms the perfective subjunctive, referring again to a complete action. These possibilities are illustrated in the following examples:

(1) **Θα μιλήσω** στον Τάσο γι' αυτό
'I will speak to Tasos about it'
(2) Θέλει **να μιλήσει** στον Τάσο γι' αυτό
'S/he wants to speak to Tasos about it'
(3) **Ας του μιλήσει** για το θέμα αυτό η ίδια
'Let her speak to him (on this occasion) about this topic herself'

Notice that after θα we may have the present (i.e. imperfective non-past), thus forming the imperfective future. If instead of the present we have the dependent the result is the simple future, since the only difference between θα γράφω 'I will be writing' and θα γράψω 'I will write [once]' is the difference in the aspect of the two verb forms. Similarly after να or ας we may find the present tense (imperfective non-past), thus forming a subjunctive expressing a continuous or repetitive action; if we find the dependent instead we obtain a subjunctive referring to a complete action. Again the only difference between the present tense verb form and the dependent verb form is that of aspect. The following examples illustrate this:

(4)   Αύριο **θα γράφω** όλη μέρα
      'Tomorrow I will be writing all day'
(5)   Το βράδι θέλει **να βλέπει** τηλεόραση
      'In the evening she [always] wants to watch television'
(6)   **Ας μιλάει** όσο θέλει
      'Let him speak as much as he wants'

Thus the basic difference between the dependent and the other verb forms is the fact that the dependent normally requires one of the particles θα, να or ας, while the other verb forms may occur either after the same three particles or independently of them.

There are some constructions where the dependent may be found without the particles. Such constructions are the following:

(i)   After the conditional or temporal conjunctions αν, εάν, έτσι και, όταν, άμα, μόλις, αφού. In these constructions the dependent may either appear without a particle or it may optionally be preceded by the future particle θα:

(7)a.   Αν (θα) τον δεις να μην του μιλήσεις
        'If you see him do not talk to him'
   b.   Θα του το δώσω όταν (θα) τον δω
        'I will give it to him when I see him'

It is possible, therefore, to interpret the dependent in (7) as a reduced form derived from the omission of θα. Notice that other verb forms may also appear in this construction with or without θα and with the negative particle δεν:

(8)   Αν (θα) τον έβλεπες θα στενοχωριόσουνα
      'If you were to see him you would be upset'

(ii) After the conjunctions πριν 'before' and ίσως 'perhaps'. In these cases we may optionally use the subjunctive marker να, as shown by the following examples:

(9)a.   Πρέπει να το κοιτάξεις καλά πριν το αγοράσεις
        or πριν να το αγοράσεις
        'You must look at it carefully before you buy it'

b. Ίσως έρθει να μας δει
Ίσως να έρθει να μας δει
'He may come to see us'

We may therefore interpret these clauses as being reduced forms of the subjunctive.

(iii) After the correlative pronouns and adverbs όποιος 'whoever', όποτε 'whenever', όπου 'wherever', όπως 'however'. In these cases too we may find either the more reduced expressions with the correlative followed directly by any verb form including the dependent, or the more expanded constructions which contain either και αν or και να. Thus these forms without και αν or και να may also be interpreted as reductions of the longer forms which include them. This context is again one where either the indicative or the subjunctive is possible.

(10)a. Όποιος μιλήσει βρίσκει τον μπελά του
Όποιος και αν μιλήσει . . .
Όποιος και να μιλήσει . . .
'Whoever speaks gets into trouble'
  b. Όπου ρωτήσεις θα σου πουν το ίδιο πράγμα
Όπου και αν (θα) ρωτήσεις . . .
Όπου και να ρωτήσεις . . .
'Wherever you ask they will tell you the same thing'

(iv) The bare dependent may also occur in idiomatic 'either . . . or' constructions like the following:

(11) Μιλήσεις δε μιλήσεις δε σε ακούει κανείς
'Whether you speak or not no one listens to you'

The above expressions are also reductions from the fuller versions such as that given below, which contains the particle αν and optionally also the future particle θα:

(12) Κι αν (θα) μιλήσεις κι αν δε (θα) μιλήσεις
'Whether you speak or not'

(v) The only context where we can find the dependent (as well as all other verb forms) without an optional particle, either θα or να, is the more learned expression είτε...είτε 'whether . . . or':

(13) Είτε τη μαλώσεις είτε όχι μου είναι αδιάφορο
'Whether you scold her or not it is of no interest to me'

1.5.3   PERFECT

The term perfect covers a combination of both the categories of aspect and tense and it will be discussed below in Section 1.6.5.

1.6   TENSE

In general we may say that tense, in the most unmarked indicative mood, and most clearly in main clauses, is the verbal category which places the action or state of the verb at a point in time: past έγραφα 'I was writing', έγραψα 'I wrote', present γράφω 'I write, I am writing', future θα γράφω, 'I will be writing', θα γράψω 'I shall write', perfect έχω γράψει 'I have written', pluperfect είχα γράψει 'I had written'. The point in time in main clauses is defined in relation to the time of the utterance. Because aspect, whether imperfective or perfective, is marked in every verb form, tense is always the result of a combination of time reference and aspect. Some of the tenses are formed **monolectically**, i.e. by modification within the verb form itself (present, simple past, imperfect), while others are formed **periphrastically** (perfective future and imperfective future, conditional, perfect conditional and future perfect) with the use of the preverbal particle θα. The more complex perfect and pluperfect use the auxiliary έχω (see Part II, Section 7.1.4).

1.6.1   PRESENT

The present tense always has imperfective aspect and is interpreted as describing either a continuous-progressive action or state, or a repetitive-habitual one:

(1) Αυτόν τον καιρό γράφω πολλά γράμματα
    'Nowadays I write many letters'
(2) Μη μου μιλάς γιατί τώρα γράφω
    'Do not talk to me because I am writing now'

In the examples above, the adverbials αυτόν τον καιρό and τώρα refer to the present time in relation to the time when the speaker uttered the sentences. In these examples the speaker of the utterance is the same as the subject of the verb. Notice, however, that if we have a more complex structure, such as indirect or reported speech, the present tense of the embedded clause is interpreted as including the point of time when the whole complex sentence was uttered, i.e. 'today', as in (3):

(3) Ο Γιάννης μάς έλεγε χθες ότι γράφει πολλά γράμματα
    'John was telling us yesterday that he writes many letters'

In (3), in spite of the fact that John's utterance took place yesterday, the time reference of the ότι-clause includes the day when the speaker is reporting on this. In fact (3) also describes a habitual, timeless activity.

In addition to this basic function of the present to describe an action or state in the present either as continuous or habitual, it can also be used to describe an action which took place in the past. This usage of the present is known as 'the historic present' and it occurs within narrative in order to give vividness to the description.

(4) Εκεί που τρώγαμε σηκώνεται ο Νίκος ξαφνικά, ανοίγει την πόρτα και φεύγει
'As we were eating, suddenly Nick gets up, opens the door and leaves (the room)'

The present is also used in sports commentaries:

(5) Ο Γκίκας τρέχει βρίσκει τη μπάλα και σουτάρει
'Gikas runs, finds the ball and shoots'

The present tense is also used in places where English would use the continuous perfect:

(6) Μένω σ' αυτό το σπίτι τρία χρόνια τώρα
'I have been living in this house for three years now'

(7) Διαβάζω αυτή την εφημερίδα από το 1984
'I have been reading this newspaper since 1984'

The present tense may also be used to refer to an action which will take place in the immediate future:

(8) Εγώ αύριο εξαφανίζομαι
'Tomorrow I [will] disappear'

1.6.2 IMPERFECT

This tense is the result of the combination of the categories imperfective and past. It describes an action or state which was either taking place repeatedly or habitually in the past, as in sentence (1) below, or was taking place continuously, i.e. was in progress, at some past time, as in (2):

(1) Όταν ήμουν στην Αθήνα έβλεπα συχνά την Ελένη
'When I was in Athens I used to see Helen frequently'

(2) Έβλεπε το παιδί που έκλαιγε αλλά δεν του μιλούσε
'He was watching the child crying but was not speaking to him'

As mentioned above (Section 1.5), the imperfect is often used to provide a background against which an action expressed in the perfective past took place:

(3) Μιλούσε στο Νίκο όταν άκουσε το κουδούνι να χτυπάει
'He was speaking to Nick when he heard the door bell ring'

1.6.3   SIMPLE PAST

This tense is formed by the combination of the categories perfective and past. It describes an action or state which took place and was completed at a particular point of time in the past.

(1) Είδα το Γιώργο και του μίλησα για σένα
    'I saw George and I spoke to him about you'
(2) Έγραψα πέντε γράμματα χθες
    'I wrote five letters yesterday'

For many verbs which express a change of state, known as inchoative verbs, the simple past tense often conveys a change which started at a point of time in the past but whose consequences are relevant to the present. In similar circumstances English uses either the simple past or the perfect. Some examples are: αρρωσταίνω 'I become ill', κουράζομαι 'I become tired', καταλαβαίνω 'I understand', θυμώνω 'I get angry' and others:

(3) Θύμωσα, γι' αυτό δεν πρόκειται να πάω στο πάρτι
    'I got angry (and I am still angry) and for this reason I will not
    go to the party'
(4) Βαρέθηκε και θέλει να φύγει
    'S/he is bored and wants to leave'

The meaning of the verb in the simple past, θύμωσα of (3), is that the anger started at some point in the past but it carries on to the time of the utterance and it is this current anger that makes the speaker decide not to go to the party. The same thing is true of (4), which means that s/he became bored and is still bored to the extent that s/he wants to go somewhere else.

Even with verbs which are not inherently inchoative we can detect the semantic nuance of a past action with consequences relevant to the present when the verb is in simple past.

(5) Φόρεσες βλέπω κι εσύ το μίνι
    'I see that you have put on a mini-skirt too'
(6) Βλέπεις αγοράσαμε κι εμείς αυτοκίνητο
    'You see we also (have) bought a car'

English would be more likely to render sentences (5) and (6) with the perfect. It is probably safe to say that in Greek the two tenses simple past and perfect overlap in meaning to a large extent. Their difference is that in the simple past what is stated is that the event was established (took place) in the past and what is implied, either because of the semantics of the verb or because of the semantics and pragmatics of the whole discourse, is the current relevance of the consequences of this event. In the perfect, on the other hand, what is stated and focused on is the current relevance of the result and what is implied is that these results came about through some action that started in the past.

The simple past without the conditional conjunction αν, but with an interrogative intonation contour, may also be used to express the hypothesis (the **protasis**) in a conditional construction:

(7) Αρρώστησες στο χωριό; Αλίμονό σου
    'Did you get ill in the village? Bad luck' [i.e. were you to get ill . . .]

The simple past has another interesting function. It can be used to refer to urgent and imminent or very certain future action. For example, when in a restaurant the customer gets impatient and calls the waiter, the most likely reply from the waiter is έφτασα ('I arrived'), meaning 'I will be there so soon that it is as good as if I have already done so':

(8) Αν σε πιάσει ο Αλέκος χάθηκες
    'If Alekos catches you, you are lost [are finished]'

In (8) the simple past χάθηκες indicates that your future demise is so certain given the fulfilment of the condition that it is as if it has already taken place. This usage is found most frequently with threats or promises.

1.6.4   FUTURE AND CONDITIONAL

The future tense is formed periphrastically with the particle θα followed by either the perfective non-past or the imperfective non-past. When θα combines with the imperfective non-past we have the future continuous or future progressive, e.g. θα γράφω ('I will be writing'). When it combines with the perfective non-past we have the simple future θα γράψω ('I will write'). Notice that the clitic object pronouns are placed between the particle θα and the verb form:

(1) Θα του το στείλω
    'I will send it to him'

1.6.4.1   Imperfective future

This is formed with the particle θα followed by the imperfective non-past verb form. It describes an action or state which will be taking place in the future either as a repeated, habitual event or as a continuous, progressive one:

(1) Είπε ότι θα μας μαζεύει στο σπίτι της πότε πότε για κανένα
    ουζάκι
    'She said that she will bring us together at her house now and
    then for an ouzo'

(2) Αύριο τέτοια ώρα θα μαζεύουμε τις ελιές
     'This time tomorrow we will be gathering the olives'

The future continuous can also be used in a modal sense to express a strong possibility, almost a certainty, that something is the case:

(3) Θα τον φροντίζει, φαντάζομαι, ο ανιψιός του
     'His nephew will be taking care of him, I imagine'

In (3) the particle θα does not have the force of the true future but is equivalent to 'it is most probably the case that ...' Notice the use of μάλλον ('rather') in (4):

(4) Θα τον φοβάται μάλλον, γι' αυτό δεν του φέρνει αντίρρηση
     'She must be afraid of him, that is why she does not confront him'

1.6.4.2   Perfective future

This tense is formed with the particle θα and the perfective non-past verb form (the dependent). It expresses an action or state which will take place and be completed at a future point in time:

(1) Θα σου τηλεφωνήσω αύριο το πρωί
     'I will telephone you tomorrow morning'

The simple future is also used to describe a habitual timeless action:

(2) Κάθε πρωί θα σηκωθεί, θα πιει το καφεδάκι του, θα διαβάσει
     την εφημερίδα του και κατά τις 8.30 θα φύγει για το γραφείο
     του
     'Every morning he will get up, drink his coffee, read his news-
     paper and at approximately 8.30 he will leave for the office'

In such cases we can replace the simple future with a present tense. However, the use of the future indicates that the action or state is not only happening now but will go on happening exactly like this in the future.

The simple future is also used in a modal sense indicating either probability or obligation:

(3) Έλα μη στενοχωριέσαι, θα σε πληρώσουν αύριο
     'Come on, do not be upset, they are sure to pay you tomorrow'
(4) Όχι, θα μου το επιστρέψεις αυτό το γράμμα αμέσως
     'No, you will give this letter back to me immediately [You must
     return this letter ...]'

Another use of the simple future is to give polite instructions:

(5) Θα περπατήσετε περίπου 50 μέτρα, ύστερα θα στρίψετε δεξιά
και θα βρείτε το σπίτι στα αριστερά σας
'You will walk about 50 metres, you will then turn right and you
will find the house on your left'

It is also found in questions used to express polite requests:

(6) Θα μου δώσετε λίγο νερό παρακαλώ;
'Would you give me some water please?'

Another less common use of the simple future is found in descriptions of
someone's past actions and achievements:

(7) Ο Κ γεννήθηκε και μεγάλωσε στο Ηράκλειο. Εκεί θα τελειώσει
και το δημοτικό και το γυμνάσιο αλλά μετά το στρατιωτικό
του θα μεταφερθεί οριστικά στην Αθήνα
'K was born and grew up in Iraklion. It was there that he would
finish his primary and secondary education, but after his
military service he would move permanently to Athens'

The use of the future in such descriptions of past actions adds the implication that these actions or events were willed or intended either by the
person him/herself or perhaps by some higher power.

1.6.4.3   *Θα* with imperfective past (conditional)

This construction is a combination of the particle θα with the imperfect
verb form. Semantically it is not so much a tense as a modality, hence
the term **conditional**. It is used to express suppositions or counterfactual
conditions, as in the **protasis** of (1) or in the **apodosis** of (2). According
to the context it may have a present, past or future reading:

(1) Θα πήγαινα κι εγώ στο Παρίσι αλλά δεν είχα λεφτά
'I would have gone to Paris too but I did not have the money'
(2) Αν τον άκουγες πόσο ωραία μιλούσε δε θα το πίστευες
'If you heard how beautifully he spoke you would not believe it'
(3) Αν διάβαζες το γράμμα του θα με καταλάβαινες
'If you were to read his letter you would understand me
[yesterday, today or tomorrow]'

In indirect speech, after a past tense main verb of reporting, we usually find
the same tense as the corresponding direct speech, but the conditional may
also be used without a suppositional/counterfactual interpretation. There it
often expresses a future whose time reference must be determined in terms
of the time it was uttered in a direct speech.

(4) Μου έλεγε/είπε ότι   θα 'ρθει να μας δει
θα 'ρχότανε να μας δει
'He said that he would come to see us'

(5) Original report:
Θα 'ρθω να σας δω
'I will come to see you'

1.6.4.4   *Θα* with perfective past

This construction is a combination of the particle θα with the perfective past verb form. Its functions are also modal. It expresses inference, possibility and probability that something took place. The future particle θα in this case corresponds to 'It is likely that':

(1) Θα πήγε να δει το Νίκο
'He must have gone to see Nick [It is likely that he went . . .]'

1.6.5   PERFECT

The perfect is a verb form which is both a tense and an aspect. It is an aspect because it describes an action or state as completed, and it is a tense because it places the action in time. More precisely, the perfect describes an action that is anterior to the time of the utterance but whose consequences are relevant to the present.

The perfect tense is formed by the use of the auxiliary verb έχω in the present tense followed by the ***non-finite*** verb form, e.g. έχω γράψει 'I have written', έχω πάει 'I have gone', έχω κουραστεί 'I have got tired'. The object clitic pronouns are placed before the auxiliary έχω: του το έχω δώσει 'I have given it to him'. The perfect tense is, in most cases, interchangeable with the simple past tense, especially in those cases where the simple past is likely to be interpreted as a completed action with current relevance.

(1)a. Κουράστηκα πολύ σήμερα
'I got very tired today'
   b. Έχω κουραστεί πολύ σήμερα
'I have got very tired today'

The perfect can be replaced by the simple past even in cases where an action has been repeated a number of times from the past till today and in cases where we have adverbials such as μέχρι τώρα 'up to now', μέχρι σήμερα 'till today', κιόλας 'already', where English will use the perfect.

(2)a. Έχω γράψει δέκα σελίδες μέχρι τώρα
'I have written ten pages up to now'
   b. Έγραψα δέκα σελίδες μέχρι τώρα
'I have written ten pages so far'
(3)a. Έχω φάει κιόλας δυο παγωτά
'I have already eaten two ice-creams'

    b. Έφαγα κιόλας δυο παγωτά
      'I already ate two ice-creams'

However, there is a semantic difference between the simple past and the perfect. The perfect focuses more on the current relevance, while the simple past focuses on the completion of this action in the past. As a consequence of this difference we can find situations where only one of these tenses is appropriate. This is clearly seen if we compare (4) and (5) below:

   (4) Κουράστηκα πολύ σήμερα αλλά έκανα ένα μπάνιο και τώρα
       νιώθω καλά
      'I got very tired today but I had a bath and I now feel well'
   (5) ?Έχω κουραστεί πολύ σήμερα αλλά έκανα ένα μπάνιο και
       τώρα νιώθω καλά
      'I have got very tired today but I had a bath and now I am
      feeling well'

In (4) it is quite natural to continue with the second clause, while the same second clause in (5) creates some sort of contradiction because the perfect implies that the subject is still tired at the time of the utterance and therefore s/he cannot simultaneously also feel well.

This semantic difference between the two tenses is also seen in the following examples:

   (6) Έχεις πάει στο Λονδίνο;
      'Have you been to London?'
   (7) Πήγες στο Λονδίνο;
      'Did you go to London?'

The first sentence, where the perfect tense is used, must be given an interpretation which includes current relevance. It is, therefore, understood to mean: 'Have you ever been to London?' Sentence (7), on the other hand, has no such implication necessarily, and thus it could be interpreted as being placed at a number of points in the past: 'Did you go to London last week?' 'Did you go to London as you were planning to do?', etc.

The fact that the perfect is more appropriate when the consequences of the verb have current relevance is also seen in the following examples:

  (8)a. Ο Ταχτσής έχει γράψει μόνο ένα μυθιστόρημα
      'Tachtsis has written only one novel'
    b. Ο Ταχτσής έγραψε μόνο ένα μυθιστόρημα
      'Tachtsis wrote only one novel'
  (9)a. Ο Ταχτσής γεννήθηκε το 1927.
      'Tachtsis was born in 1927'
    b. ?Ο Ταχτσής έχει γεννηθεί το 1927
      'Tachtsis has been born in 1927'

In (8a) we can use the perfect because the number of novels that Tachtsis has written is still relevant in spite of the fact that he is dead. In (9) however we cannot use the perfect because the consequences of Tachtsis's birth, namely his being alive, are no longer valid.

1.6.6 PLUPERFECT

The *pluperfect* is the past perfect. It is formed by using the past tense of the auxiliary έχω and the *non-finite* verb form: είχα γράψει 'I had written', είχα πάει 'I had gone', είχα κουραστεί 'I had got tired'. It describes an action or state as having been completed in the past with consequences relevant to another, subsequent point in time, also in the past, which is either explicitly specified or implied.

(1) Είχα δει τον αδερφό σου πολλές φορές στο Λονδίνο
    'I had seen your brother many times in London [by the time I left London]'

(2) Την περασμένη Δευτέρα δεν είχα ακόμη στείλει το γράμμα
    'Last Monday I had not yet sent the letter'

The pluperfect may be replaced by a simple past, but only very rarely. This is possible in (1) where an action took place several times over a period of time. Thus in (1) we can replace είχα δει 'I had seen' with the simple past είδα 'I saw'. In (2) the pluperfect cannot be replaced by the simple past. The adverbials ήδη 'already', κιόλας 'already', δεν ... ακόμη 'not ... yet' and similar expressions, if they refer to a completed action with relevance to some point in the past, can only combine with the pluperfect.

(3) Είχε ήδη/κιόλας μιλήσει μαζί του όταν τη συνάντησα
    'She had already spoken to him when I met her'

The pluperfect is also used in the protasis, i.e. the conditional clause, of a counterfactual conditional construction, as in (4), where the implication is that the subject has not seen George and therefore has not told him:

(4) Αν είχα δει το Γιώργο θα του το έλεγα/θα του το είχα πει
    'If I had seen George I would have told him about this'

The pluperfect is used in Greek in cases where it would not be used in English, especially in subordinate clauses:

(5) Όταν την είχα γνωρίσει για πρώτη φορά σπούδαζε ακόμα στο Πανεπιστήμιο
    'When I met her [lit. had met her] for the first time she was still studying at the University'

The pluperfect is also used instead of the simple past in sentences containing adverbs referring to a point of time in the past:

(6)a. Πέρσι το καλοκαίρι είχα πάει στην Κρήτη
   'Last summer I went to Crete'
   b. Είχαμε πάει στην ταβέρνα χθες το βράδι
   'We went to the taverna last night'

1.6.7   FUTURE PERFECT

The future perfect is formed with the future particle θα followed by the perfect: θα έχω γράψει ('I shall have written'), θα έχω πάει ('I shall have gone'), θα έχω κουραστεί ('I shall have got tired'). It describes an action or state which will have been completed at some future time which is either explicitly stated or implied. Furthermore the consequences of this action or state will be relevant to that point in time:

(1) Μέχρι την άλλη Δευτέρα θα έχω γράψει το πρώτο κεφάλαιο
   'By next Monday I shall have written the first chapter'
(2) Το θέμα θα έχει κιόλας τακτοποιηθεί πριν έρθεις εσύ
   'The matter will have been taken care of before you come'

As in the case of other verb constructions using the particle θα, the perfect can also be used in a modal sense:

(3) Θα έχει θυμώσει μαζί σου, γι' αυτό δε σου μιλάει
   'He must have got angry with you and that is why he is not
      speaking to you'
(4) Πιστεύω ότι θα έχει κουραστεί πολύ
   'I believe that she must have got very tired'

In (3) the particle θα does not refer to a future time but is used with the epistemic modal sense of 'It must be the case that ...', while the consequences of the completed action or state of the verb are relevant to the present.

1.6.8   Θα WITH PLUPERFECT (PERFECT CONDITIONAL)

The future pluperfect is formed with the future particle θα followed by the pluperfect tense: θα είχα γράψει 'I would have written', θα είχα πάει 'I would have gone', θα είχα κουραστεί 'I would have got tired'. It describes an action or state which would have been completed at some point in the past but failed to do so. The particle θα indicates that at some point in time there was a possibility that the action of the verb might have taken place, but because the verb is in the past this possibility no longer exists. It is, therefore, the irrealis expression and for this reason it is used in the **apodosis** of a counterfactual conditional construction:

(1) Αν με είχες ϱωτήσει θα σου το είχα πει/θα σου το έλεγα
   'If you had asked me I would have told you'
(2) Αν είχαμε λεφτά θα είχαμε πάει/θα πηγαίναμε κι εμείς στο Παρίσι
   'If we had had money we would have gone to Paris too'

As indicated in (1–2), the perfect conditional, in the apodosis of counter-factual conditions, may be replaced by the conditional. The difference between these alternatives is that the pluperfect focuses more on the result, the consequences, rather than the action itself.

As with all other constructions using θα, the perfect conditional too may be interpreted in a modal sense.

(3) Θα τον είχαν ειδοποιήσει, γι' αυτό έφυγε αμέσως
   'They must have warned him; that is why he left right away'
(4) Θα είχε εξετάσει το ζήτημα μόνος του
   'He must have examined the issue himself'

In such cases the counterfactuality of this construction is removed. What is expressed instead is a strong likelihood that something must have been the case. The choice between the counterfactual and the modal (i.e. prob-ability) interpretation is determined by the context. In the apodosis of a conditional construction the perfect conditional is always counterfactual. In constructions such as (3), where the second clause indicates the evidence for the speaker's conclusion that someone must have warned the subject, it is clear that we have the modal sense. In (4) however we have no clue as to which of the two senses is intended. (4) could mean either that the subject has not examined the issue on his own but would have done, but for some obstacle, or that he must have examined the issue on his own. In fact the second – strong possibility – is more likely here.

1.6.9   ALTERNATIVE PERFECT CONSTRUCTIONS

Another, much less common, way of forming perfect tenses is with the use of the auxiliary έχω followed by the passive perfect participle. This construction is restricted to those active transitive verbs which can also occur in the passive. The passive participle takes its gender and number from the object of the verb which is present in the construction: το έχω γϱαμμένο 'I have written it'.

(1) Στις δώδεκα είχε και το φαΐ μαγειϱεμένο και τα ϱούχα πλυμένα και σιδεϱωμένα
   'At twelve o'clock she had cooked the food and washed and ironed the clothes'

This construction with έχω and the passive perfect participle focuses even more on the result of the action of the verb to the extent that it is now presented as a property of the object itself. Thus we may say that we have a progression from the action to the result, as shown by the use of the participle. However, we are still operating in an active construction due to the auxiliary έχω, which allows the agent of the actions to remain the subject of the construction. Compare:

(2)a. Έγραψα το γράμμα   'I wrote the letter'
   b. Έχω γράψει το γράμμα   'I have written the letter'
   c. Έχω γραμμένο το γράμμα   'I have written the letter'
   d. Το γράμμα είναι γραμμένο   'The letter is written'

We can interpret the progression from (2a) to (2d) as follows: (2a) I performed the action of writing the letter, (2b) I wrote the letter and this past action carries on being relevant now, (2c) I performed the action of writing and as a result the letter is now written, and (2d) the letter is written and it does not matter who did the writing.

The perfect formed with έχω and passive perfect participle may occur more frequently in some dialects such as those of rural Crete. It is rare in Standard Greek but is found in idioms:

(3) Έχει δεμένο το γάιδαρό του
     'He has tied up his donkey = He has nothing to worry about'
(4) Σ' έχω γραμμένο στα παλιά μου τα παπούτσια
     'I have written you on my old shoes = I ignore you, I don't give
       a damn about you'
(5) Τα έχει χαμένα (τα μυαλά του)
     'He has lost his mind = he is crazy'

Needless to say, this construction can also occur in the pluperfect (το είχα γραμμένο 'I had written it'), future perfect (θα το έχω γραμμένο 'I will have written it'), and perfect conditional (θα το είχα γραμμένο 'I would have written it').

1.7 THE GERUND

The **gerund** is formed by adding the suffix -οντας to the imperfective stem of first conjugation verbs: γράφ-οντας ('writing'), τρέχ-οντας ('running'), or -ώντας to the stem of second-conjugation verbs: μιλώντας ('speaking'). The gerund is used adverbially. It describes an action which takes place in parallel with the action of the verb it modifies, and it expresses either the manner in which something is done or the means or the time during which something is done or is taking place.

(1) Ο Γιάννης ήρθε τρέχοντας όταν άκουσε τα νέα
     'John came running when he heard the news' (manner)

(2) Τόσο στενοχωρέθηκε που έφυγε κλαίγοντας
'She was so upset that she left crying' (accompanying action)
(3) Περπατώντας προς το γραφείο του ο Νίκος συνάντησε ένα
παλιό του φίλο
'While walking towards his office Nikos met an old friend of his'
(time)
(4) Μόνο μιλώντας λογικά θα καταφέρεις να τους πείσεις
'Only by speaking logically will you manage to persuade them'
(manner leading to result)

In general only active-voice verbs have the gerund, which is traditionally referred to as the 'active present participle'. However, there are some marginal cases of gerunds of passive verbs, such as όντας 'being' from the verb είμαι, and possibly others:

(5) Δούλευε στην επιχείρηση του πατέρα του όντας ακόμη φοιτητής
'He was working in his father's business while he was still a university student'

The gerund is almost always *subject-controlled*, i.e. it has the same subject as that of the verb it modifies, as in the examples given above (see Section 5.4.3.1). On some rare occasions the gerund is used with a different subject, in which case the subject of the gerund is also in the nominative:

(6) Δύοντας ο ήλιος άρχισε να πέφτει υγρασία
'As the sun set, dampness started falling'
(7) Φεύγοντας ο δάσκαλος διέλυσε η τάξη
'Upon the teacher's departure the class dispersed'

1.8   PARTICIPLES

A characteristic of participles is that they inflect for gender, case and number in the same way as adjectives.

1.8.1   ACTIVE VOICE PARTICIPLES

The only active voice participles are those introduced into Standard Greek from *katharevousa*. They are found in *katharevousa* writings and even today in journalistic writings or in discourse which uses *katharevousa* features to achieve high style, formality or irony. These forms are (a) the active present participle and (b) the active past participle.

1.8.1.1   Active present participle

This participle is formed with the endings -ων, -ουσα, -ον, or -ών, -ώσα, -ών, or -ών, -ούσα, -ούν, depending on the class of the verb (see Part II,

Sections 7.2.1.10, 7.3.1.10 and 7.4.1.10) added to the imperfective stem of the verb; it is used as an adjective:

(1) Υπάρχουν τρελοί που την τρέλα τους την εκμεταλλεύονται οι καιροφυλακτούντες γνωστικοί
'There are crazy people whose madness is taken advantage of by sane opportunists'

(2) Δε θέλει να ανατρέψει το τρέχον γούστο
'He does not wish to overturn current taste'

1.8.1.2   Active past participle

This participle is formed with the endings -ας, -ασα, -αν added to the perfective stem. It is even more rare than the present active participle and it occurs in journalistic discourse.

(1) Οι επιζήσαντες προσκυνητές ενίσχυσαν αυτήν την υποψία
'The surviving pilgrims strengthened this suspicion'

1.8.2   PASSIVE VOICE PARTICIPLES

There are three passive voice participles, as described below.

1.8.2.1   Passive perfect participle

The most common passive participle is that formed with the endings -μένος, -μένη, -μένο added to a stem (see Part II, Section 7.11). In general these participles are formed from transitive verbs which have both an active and a passive voice. The construction with the verb είμαι and the passive perfect participle, e.g. το γράμμα είναι γραμμένο 'the letter is written', is considered to be equivalent to the perfect passive το γράμμα έχει γραφτεί 'the letter has been written'.

(1)a. Το βιβλίο αυτό δε θα είναι γραμμένο πριν από το Μάρτη
'This book will not have been written before March'
  b. Το βιβλίο αυτό δε θα έχει γραφτεί πριν από το Μάρτη
'This book will not have been written before March'
(2)a. Η ανακοίνωση ήταν διατυπωμένη σε αυστηρή γλώσσα
'The announcement was expressed in strict language'
  b. Η ανακοίνωση είχε διατυπωθεί σε αυστηρή γλώσσα
'The announcement was expressed in strict language'

There are, however, some fine semantic differences between these two constructions, which are discussed in Section 1.6.9.

This passive participle is also used as an adjective, e.g. πεταμένα λεφτά 'money that has been thrown away (wasted)', οι κληρωμένοι λαχνοί 'the lottery tickets that have been selected', etc.

In addition to this perfect passive participle, we also find a construction with the verb μιλώ 'I speak', where the subject corresponds to the indirect object of the corresponding active, as in (3), and with the verb περπατώ 'I walk', where the passive participle is formed even though the verb is not transitive, as in (4):

(3) Ο πολιτικός αυτός είναι μιλημένος
     'This politician has been spoken to [and has been persuaded to follow a certain course of action]'
(4) Ο άνθρωπος αυτός ξέρει πολλά γιατί είναι περπατημένος
     'This man knows a lot because he has travelled [lit. is walked]'

1.8.2.2 Passive present participle

The passive present participle has entered the language through *katharevousa* and is formed with the endings -όμενος, -όμενη, -όμενο or for second-conjugation verbs -ούμενος, -ούμενη, -ούμενο, or -ώμενος -ώμενη, -ώμενο, depending on the class of verb, added to the imperfective stem, e.g. αυξανόμενος 'increasing', προβλεπόμενος 'predicted', απειλούμενος 'threatened', ερωτώμενος 'questioned'. This participle is also restricted in usage in the same way as other participle forms of *katharevousa* origin:

(1) Κατά τα λεγόμενα θα έχουμε εκλογές σύντομα
     'According to what is being said we will have elections soon'
(2) Ποιο είναι το ζητούμενο στην υπόθεση αυτή;
     'What is the objective in this affair?'
(3) Τα κρατούμενα εδάφη
     'The occupied lands'

1.8.2.3 Passive past participle

This participle is also a *katharevousa* form restricted in usage in the same way as the other participles of *katharevousa* origin mentioned above. It is formed with the ending -είς, -είσα, -έν added to the passive perfective stem (see Part II, Section 7.12), e.g. απολυθείς, απολυθείσα, απολυθέν 'dismissed, fired'. These participles are sometimes used in newspapers and in more formal discourse, as in the following:

(1) Για να εξασφαλίσει την απόδοση των εξαγγελθέντων μέτρων . . .
     'In order to secure the results of the measures announced . . .'
(2) Τα μη εισπραχθέντα χρέη του δημοσίου
     'The non-collected debts of the state'

1.9   THE SYNTAX OF LINKING (COPULAR) VERBS

Linking or *copular* verbs, the most typical of which is the verb είμαι 'I am', are those which link the subject of the sentence with a nominal (1) or adjectival predicate (2) or with an adverbial complement in the form of an adverb or a prepositional phrase (3). The predicate describes the subject as having a property or a characteristic, or as being in a certain state:

(1) Η Χριστίνα είναι η πιο καλή μου φίλη
    'Christina is my best friend'
(2) Ο Νίκος είναι συμπαθητικός
    'Nick is likeable'
(3) Η Μαρία δεν είναι ποτέ καλά
    'Maria is never well'

1.9.1   THE VERB είμαι WITH ADJECTIVAL AND NOMINAL PREDICATES

The verb είμαι is the most typical and the most frequently used verb in copular sentences. It has only three tenses: present είμαι, είσαι, είναι, etc., past ήμουν(α), ήσουν(α), ήταν(ε), etc., and future θα είμαι, θα είσαι, θα είναι, etc. (see Part II, Section 7.8). When there is a nominal or adjectival predicate it must be in the nominative case to agree with the nominative case of the subject of the sentence. Adjectival predicates must also agree in number and in gender with the subject (see also Appendix 4 on Agreement), as in the following examples:

(1)a. **Ο Γιάννης** (masc. sg.) είναι **έξυπνος** (masc. sg.)
      'John is intelligent'
   b. **Η Μαρία** (fem. sg.) είναι **έξυπνη** (fem. sg.)
      'Mary is intelligent'
   c. Εμείς **οι Έλληνες** (masc. pl.) είμαστε πάντα **ανυπόμονοι** (masc. pl.)
      'We Greeks are always impatient'

When the subject is not present in the sentence or is a personal pronoun in the singular, not accompanied by a noun phrase (2a–2c), the adjectival or nominal predicate agrees with the natural sex of the person understood to be the subject:

(2)a. Είμαι πολύ **κουρασμένη** (fem. sg.)
      'I am very tired'
   b. Εσύ, είσαι **κουρασμένος** (masc. sg.);
      'And you, are you tired?'
   c. Είμαι **μια φίλη** (fem. sg.) της Ελένης
      'I am a friend of Helen's'

From the feminine singular ending of the adjective predicate in (2a) and (2c) we understand that the first-person subject of the clause is female. Similarly, from the masculine singular ending in the adjective predicate in (2b), we understand that the second-person subject here is male.

When the subject of the verb είμαι is in the plural and this plural represents a set of people comprising both feminine and/or neuter and masculine members, or even feminine and neuter members alone, the adjectival or nominal predicate is in the masculine gender (3a–c). When the subject represents a set of inanimate objects of different genders, then the predicate is either in the neuter plural or in the gender of the noun phrase nearest to the verb (3d–e):

(3)a. Άνδρες (masc.) και γυναίκες (fem.) πρέπει να είναι
αγαπημένοι (masc.)
'Men and women must be loving'

b. Οι γυναίκες (fem.) και τα παιδιά (neut.) να είναι έτοιμοι
(masc.)
'The women and children should be ready'

c. Αυτοί οι άνδρες (masc.) και τα παιδιά (neut.) είναι όλοι φίλοι
(masc.) μας
'These men and children are all our friends'

d. Οι πόρτες (fem.) και τα παράθυρα (neut.) είναι βαμμένα (neut.)
μπλε
'The doors and the windows are painted blue'

e. Οι δρόμοι (masc.) και οι πλατείες (fem.) ήταν γεμάτα (neut.)
or γεμάτες (fem.) κόσμο
'The roads and the squares were full of people'

When the subject of the sentence is in the 2nd person plural but this plural is used to refer politely to a single individual, the adjectival or nominal predicate appears in the singular in spite of the fact that the subject pronoun, if present, and the verb είμαι appear in the plural. The addressee in the following examples is a single individual:

(4)a. Εσείς (pl.) να είστε (pl.) πολύ προσεκτικός (masc. sg.)
'You should be very careful'

b. Εσείς (pl.) είστε (pl.) η καθηγήτριά (fem. sg.) του;
'Are you his teacher?'

With nominal predicates the noun phrase used as predicate may appear in three different ways with differences in meaning: without any determiner (5a), or with an indefinite determiner such as the indefinite article (5b), or with the definite article (5c) (see Section 2.5):

(5)a. Ο Γιώργος είναι φίλος μας
'George is a friend of ours'

b. Ο Γιώργος είναι **ένας** φίλος μας
   'George is a certain friend of ours [one of our friends]'
c. Ο Γιώργος είναι **ο** φίλος μας
   'George is our friend [the one and only friend of ours or the friend we were telling you about]'

Where the predicate is a noun phrase and the verb είμαι equates the subject with the predicate noun phrase, the restrictions on gender and number agreement do not apply. The meaning of such constructions is 'X is equal/equivalent to Y', where X and Y are two different noun phrases and thus may be of different gender and number:

(6)a. **Ο Νίκος** (masc. sg.) θα είναι πάντα **το μωρό** (neut. sg.) της
      'Nick will always be her baby'
   b. **Αυτός ο γιατρός** ήταν **η σωτηρία** μας
      'That doctor was our salvation'
   c. **Τα παιδιά** του είναι **η μεγαλύτερή** του αδυναμία
      'His children are his greatest weakness'

The most common and most neutral order of the elements in copular sentences is subject – verb – predicate. Different orders are usually associated with more marked intonation and more contrastive meaning. (On focus see Section 5.2.4.)

(7)a. Η Μαρία είναι **πολύ καλή δασκάλα**
   b. Είναι **πολύ καλή δασκάλα** η Μαρία
      'Mary is a very good teacher'
   c. **Πολύ καλή δασκάλα** είναι η Μαρία
      'Mary is really a very good teacher'

Other orders are less natural. On rather rare occasions the verb είμαι may be omitted, but only if the sentence describes something which is true at the time of the utterance:

(8) Τελικά αποφασίστηκε. Πρόεδρος η Μαρία και αντιπρόεδρος η Σούλα
    'Finally it was decided. The president [is] Mary and the vice-president [is] Soula'
(9) Άσχημα τα νέα σήμερα
    'The news today [is] bad'

1.9.2   THE VERB είμαι WITH ADVERBIALS AND PREPOSITIONAL PHRASES

The most typical adverbials combining with the copula είμαι are the adverbs καλά, καλύτερα, πολύ καλά, όχι πολύ καλά, μέτρια, έτσι κι έτσι and similar ones pertaining to health and to mood.

(1)a. Είσαι καλά σήμερα;
   'Are you well today?'
   b. Όχι, δεν είμαι καθόλου καλά. Είμαι χάλια
   'No, I am not at all well. I am in an awful state'
   c. Ο Γιάννης είναι έτσι κι έτσι και η Μαρία πότε έτσι πότε αλλιώς
   'John is so-so and Mary [is] sometimes this way sometimes another way'

Instead of the adverbial complement the verb είμαι may be followed by a prepositional phrase:

(2)a. Είναι πάντα με το χαμόγελο στα χείλια
   'She is always with a smile on her lips [i.e. she is always smiling]'
   b. Δυστυχώς ο Γιάννης είναι και χωρίς λεφτά και χωρίς δουλειά
   'Unfortunately John is both without money and without a job'

The verb είμαι in its impersonal third-person form may be omitted with adverbs in the comparative or with neuter adjectives used adverbially, such as καλύτερα or πιο καλά 'better', προτιμότερο 'preferable', δυνατό(ν) 'possible', αδύνατο(ν) 'impossible', πιθανό(ν) 'probable', απίθανο(ν) 'improbable':

(3)a. (Είναι) καλύτερα να μην του το πείτε ακόμη
   '[It is] better not to tell him yet'
   b. (Είναι) προτιμότερο να μείνω εγώ
   '[It is] better that I stay'
   c. (Είναι/ήταν) αδύνατον να τον πείσω
   '[It is/it was] impossible to persuade him'

1.9.3   OTHER LINKING VERBS TAKING NOMINAL AND ADJECTIVAL PREDICATES

As mentioned above, the verb είμαι is the most typical linking verb and the one combining with all types of predicates, nominal and adjectival, with adverbials and with prepositional phrases in copular constructions proper as well as in equational ones. Other linking verbs are the following: γίνομαι 'I become', φαίνομαι 'I seem', εμφανίζομαι 'I appear', παρουσιάζομαι 'I present myself as', αποδεικνύομαι 'I prove to be', λέγομαι 'I am called', καταντώ 'I am reduced to', πάω για 'I am going for', εκλέγομαι 'I am elected', διορίζομαι 'I am appointed', etc.:

(1)a. Ο Γιάννης έγινε πιο σοβαρός
    'John became more serious'
  b. Η Καίτη θα γίνει γιατρός
    'Katie will become a doctor'
  c. Έγινε ένας καλός γιατρός
    'He became a good doctor'
  d. Έγινε διευθυντής του νοσοκομείου
    'He became director of the hospital'
  e. Η Ελένη θα γίνει η τιμωρία της
    'Helen will become her punishment'
  f. Πώς έγινες έτσι χωρίς καρδιά;
    'How did you become so heartless?'
(2)a. Η Ελένη μού φάνηκε συμπαθητική
    'Helen seemed to me likeable'
  b. Η Ελένη μού φαίνεται ευαίσθητη κοπέλα
    'Helen seems to me to be a sensitive girl'
  c. Η μητέρα σου φαίνεται καλά
    'Your mother looks well'
  d. Ο αρραβωνιαστικός της φαίνεται με πολλά λεφτά
    'Her fiancé seems to have [lit. with] a lot of money'
(3) Τώρα πάει για υπουργός
    'Now he is going for the office of minister'

The order possibilities in these constructions are the same as those with the verb είμαι (see Section 1.9.1).

2 THE NOUN AND THE NOUN PHRASE

2.1 THE CONSTITUENTS OF THE NOUN PHRASE

The chief functions of the noun phrase are:

(i)   to act as the **subject** *of a verb* (in the nominative)
(ii)   to act as a **subject predicate** (in the nominative)
(iii)   to act as the **direct object** *of a verb* (in the accusative)
(iv)   to act as an **object predicate** (in the accusative)
(v)   to act as the **indirect object** *of a verb* (in the genitive; this construction is less common, however, than σε followed by a noun phrase in the accusative)
(vi)   to *be governed by a* **preposition** (normally in the accusative)
(vii)   to *depend on* another noun (in the genitive).

(1) **Ο πατέρας του Γιώργου** χτύπησε **τη μύτη του** στον τοίχο
'George's father banged his nose on the wall'

Example (1) contains four noun phrases:

ο πατέρας (in the nominative) is the **subject** of the verb χτύπησε
τη μύτη (in the accusative) is the **direct object** of the verb χτύπησε
τον τοίχο (in the accusative) is governed by the **preposition** σ[ε]
του Γιώργου (in the genitive) depends on the **head** *of the* **noun phrase** ο πατέρας

In addition, the noun phrase τη μύτη του contains the weak personal pronoun του (in the genitive).

(2) **Ο Γιώργος** είναι **φοιτητής**
'George is a student'

In example (2) the noun φοιτητής is a **subject predicate** that attributes a property to the subject (i.e. George).

(3) Ο Γιώργος έδωσε **της Ελένης** ένα βιβλίο
'George gave **Helen** a book'

In example (3) the noun phrase της Ελένης is the **indirect object** of the verb έδωσε (see also Section 1.1.1.4).

(4) το αυτοκίνητο **της Ελένης**
'Helen's car'

In example (4) the noun phrase της Ελένης depends on the noun αυτοκίνητο and is in the genitive to indicate that Helen is the possessor of the car.

A noun phrase must contain one of the following:

(a) noun
(b) a pronoun other than a weak (clitic) personal pronoun
(c) any other part of speech or phrase acting as a noun

In addition, a noun phrase may contain one or more of the following:

(d) adjectival phrase (see also Section 2.6)
(e) cardinal or ordinal numeral (see also Section 2.7)
(f) article (see also Section 2.5)
(g) determiner not otherwise listed here (see also Section 2.8.2ff.)
(h) weak (clitic) personal pronoun (see also Section 2.8.1.1.1)
(i) adverbial (see also Section 2.9)
(j) clause connective (see also Section 2.10)

A noun phrase can also be further extended through the addition of a complement (see Section 5.3.4.3) or a relative clause (see Sections 5.3.1–5.3.1.3).

The **head** or nucleus of a noun phrase is a noun (πατέρας, Γιώργου, μύτη, τοίχο in example (1)), and a noun may form a noun phrase by itself. Nevertheless, any word in categories (b) to (e) above may stand for a noun, and may even constitute a phrase on its own, e.g.:

(a) noun (κρέας 'meat'): Τρώω κρέας 'I eat meat'
(b) pronoun (εγώ 'I'): Εγώ θα πάω '*I*'ll go'
    (τι 'what'): Τι θέλεις; 'What do you want?'
    (κάποιος 'someone'): Κάποιος σε ζητάει
        'Someone's looking for you'
(c) other part of speech or phrase acting as noun (ευχαριστώ 'thank you'): Χίλια ευχαριστώ! 'A thousand thanks!'
(d) adjective (μαύρα 'black'): Φοράει μαύρα 'S/he wears black'
(e) numeral (δέκα 'ten'): Ήρθαν δέκα 'Ten came'

In addition, a nominal clause functions as a noun phrase (e.g. as the subject or object of a verb, as in the following example):

(5) **Όσα μου είπαν** ήταν ψέματα
    '**What they told me** was lies'

For nominal and nominalized clauses see Sections 5.3.1.4 and 5.3.4.4.

2.2   GENDER

Every Greek *noun* belongs to one of three gender classes: *masculine, feminine,* or *neuter* (for the small number of nouns that change their gender in the plural see Part II, Section 2.6). These three categories are largely conventional, and they do not necessarily correspond to the division between male, female and inanimate (for the correlation between natural and grammatical gender see Section 2.2.1). Nevertheless, the following general tendencies can be observed.

Nouns denoting *human beings* are usually (but not always) masculine if the person is male, and feminine if the person is female. Thus άντρας 'man (male); husband' and Πέτρος 'Peter' are masculine, γυναίκα 'woman; wife' and Μαρία 'Mary' are feminine. However, κορίτσι 'girl' and αγόρι 'boy' are both neuter.

Many nouns – most of them denoting people who practise particular professions – are of *common* gender. Although their endings follow the masculine declension patterns, they may be either masculine or feminine, depending on the sex of the person denoted. (See Section 2.2.1 for the relationship between natural and grammatical gender and Part II, Section 2.3 for the declension of nouns of common gender.)

For the gender of nouns denoting *animals* see Section 2.2.1.

Nouns denoting *inanimate objects, substances,* and *natural phenomena* may be masculine, feminine, or neuter. Thus αέρας 'air; wind' is masculine, καρέκλα 'chair' is feminine, and αλεύρι 'flour' is neuter.

Most *abstract* nouns are feminine, but some are neuter or masculine. Thus γνώση 'knowledge' is feminine, but κέφι 'high spirits' is neuter and περιορισμός 'limitation' is masculine.

The gender class to which a noun belongs is generally reflected in its *endings*, and always in the form of any modifier (article, adjective, determiner, etc.) that accompanies it. The form of a noun given in dictionaries (the *dictionary form*) is the nominative singular (see below).

Masculine nouns (as well as nouns of *common* gender) have dictionary forms ending in -ς (e.g. όροφος 'storey', πατέρας 'father', μαθητής '(male) pupil or school student', καφές 'coffee', παππούς 'grandfather') and decline according to the patterns given in Part II, Sections 2.1ff.

The dictionary form of most *feminine* nouns ends in a vowel (usually -α or -η: e.g. μαθήτρια '(female) pupil or school student', δραχμή 'drachma'); they decline according to the patterns in Part II, Sections 2.2ff. However, some feminine nouns have a dictionary form ending in -ος and decline like masculines (see Part II, Section 2.2.3).

Most *neuter* nouns have a dictionary form ending in -ο, -ι, or -μα, although some end in -ς (e.g. δωμάτιο 'room', δόντι 'tooth', πράγμα 'thing', έθνος 'nation': see Part II, Sections 2.4ff. for their declension patterns).

Most members of the other word-classes that make up the ***nominal system*** (adjectives, articles, some numerals, and determiners) inflect so as to agree with the gender of the noun they modify (or, in the absence of a noun, the sex of the real person or item they denote). Thus if the noun is masculine, the words that modify it (i.e. articles, adjectives, and other determiners) must also be masculine:

(1) αυτός (masc.)   **ο** (masc.)   καλός (masc.)   άντρας (masc.)
    determiner   *article*   *adjective*   *noun*
    'this   good   man/husband'

If the noun is feminine, so must the words that modify it:

(2) αυτή (fem.) **η** (fem.) καλή (fem.) γυναίκα (fem.)
    'this good woman/wife'

If it is neuter, then the words that modify it have to be neuter too:

(3) αυτό (neut.) **το** (neut.) καλό (neut.) παιδί (neut.)
    'this good child'

Where a noun is of common gender (i.e. a noun that may be either masculine or feminine), it may be necessary or desirable to indicate the sex of the person which it denotes. Compare the two ways of saying 'a good writer'; the masculine forms of modifiers are used if he is a man (4a), while the feminine forms of the modifiers are used if she is a woman (4b):

(4)a. **ένας** (masc.) καλός (masc.) συγγραφέας
   b. **μια** (fem.) καλή (fem.) συγγραφέας

When the sex of the person is not known or not specified, the masculine may be used:

(5) **ο** (masc.) συγγραφέας αυτού του βιβλίου
    'the author of this book'

The author referred to in (5) may be a woman, but the speaker either does not know it or is not concerned to specify it. If the speaker wishes to make it clear that s/he is referring to a female writer or writers only, s/he can say (6a) or (6b); if s/he wishes to refer only to a male writer or writers, it is possible to say (6c) or (6d):

(6)a. μια γυναίκα συγγραφέας
     'a woman/female writer'
   b. οι γυναίκες συγγραφείς
     'women/female writers'
   c. ένας άντρας συγγραφέας
     'a man/male writer'
   d. οι άντρες συγγραφείς
     'men/male writers'

In the constructions illustrated in (6) above, the word συγγραφέας or συγγραφείς is, grammatically speaking, a noun phrase in apposition to the noun phrase that precedes it, and both noun phrases appear in the same case. Such appositional constructions involving γυναίκα may be used even when the other noun is feminine:

(7) μια γυναίκα διευθύντρια
'a woman director'

Here, although the feminine noun διευθύντρια (the feminine counterpart of the masculine διευθυντής) is available and is being used, the speaker is stressing the fact that the director is a woman; on its own, μια διευθύντρια implies 'a director who happens to be a woman'.

Most *adjectives* and some *determiners* have separate sets of forms for each gender. The dictionary form of adjectives and determiners is the nominative singular of the masculine.

When no noun is mentioned, male humans are normally denoted by the masculine forms of adjectives, pronouns, etc., female humans by the feminine forms of adjectives, pronouns, etc., and other items (objects, concepts, etc.), by neuter adjectives, pronouns, etc. (although babies too are usually referred to by neuter adjectives):

(8)a. Είναι ωραίος
'**He**'s handsome'
b. Είναι ωραία
'**She**'s beautiful'
c. Είναι ωραίο
'**It**'s lovely'

When humans are referred to without a noun being mentioned and when the gender of the referent is immaterial, the masculine is used. Thus 'Who came?' can be rendered in either of the following ways if the speaker does not wish (or is unable) to specify the sex of the person(s) concerned:

(9)a. Ποιος (masc. sg.) ήρθε; (when referring only to one person)
b. Ποιοι (masc. pl.) ήρθαν; (when referring to more than one)

In (9a) the speaker may mean 'Which person came?' or 'Which man came?', while in (9b) the speaker may mean 'Which people came?' or 'Which men came?' If the speaker is talking exclusively about women, s/he will say one of the following two sentences:

(10)a. Ποια (fem. sg.) ήρθε;
b. Ποιες (fem. pl.) ήρθαν;

Example (10a) means 'Which woman came?', while example (10b) means 'Which women came?'

The masculine is the appropriate case for an adjective used as a generic noun (see also Section 2.5.1):

(11) Συχνά **ο** πλούσιος περιφρονεί **το** φτωχό
'A rich [person] often despises a poor [one]'

Similarly, the masculine is used when a mixed group of men and women is referred to:

(12) Όλ**οι** σας τον ξέρετε
'All of you know him'

Here the speaker may be talking to a group of males or to a mixed group of men and women, whereas if a group of women is being addressed the feminine form is used:

(13) Όλ**ες** σας τον ξέρετε

When counting, the neuter form of declinable cardinal numerals is used:

(14) η σελίδα τέσσερ**α**
'page four'

Contrast:

(15) τέσσερ**ις** σελίδες
'four pages'

where the numeral is in the feminine form to agree with the feminine noun σελίδες which it modifies.

2.2.1   NATURAL AND GRAMMATICAL GENDER

The table below gives examples of the various correlations between natural and grammatical gender with reference to *humans*:

Natural and grammatical gender with reference to humans

		Gender	
		natural	*grammatical*
ο άνθρωπος	'person'	either	masc.
ο άντρας	'man'	male	masc.
η προσωπικότητα	'personality'	either	fem.
ο/η πρόεδρος	'president'	either	common
ο ποιητής	'poet'	either	masc.
η ποιήτρια	'poet'	female	fem.
το παιδί	'child'	either	neut.
το αγόρι	'boy'	male	neut.
το κορίτσι	'girl'	female	neut.
τα αδέρφια	'siblings'	both	neut.

All words that modify the noun (article, adjective, determiner, etc.) appear in the same gender as the noun, irrespective of the sex of the person whom it denotes:

(1) Ο Γιάννης (masc.) έγινε μεγάλη (fem.) προσωπικότητα (fem.)
    'John has become a great personality'
(2) Η Μαρία (fem.) είναι το (neut.) μεγαλύτερο (neut.) παιδί (neut.)
    'Mary is the oldest/biggest child'

Only with nouns of common gender do the words that modify them appear in either the masculine or the feminine according to the sex of the person denoted (see Section 2.2).

Noun phrases in apposition to each other do not have to agree with each other in gender:

(3) η γυναίκα (fem.)-φάντασμα (neut.)
    'the phantom woman'
(4) ο άντρας (masc.) μοντέλο (neut.)
    'the male model'

The gender of nouns denoting *animals* does not usually correlate with the sex of the animal concerned. Some familiar animals have three terms, one generic (non-sex-specific), one for the female, and one for the male, e.g.:

(5)a. το πρόβατο (neut.)
      'sheep'
   b. η προβατίνα (fem.)
      'ewe'
   c. το κριάρι (neut.)
      'ram'

In addition to these items there is also το αρνί (neut.) 'lamb'.

Some other domesticated animals have two terms, one serving both as the generic term and to denote one sex, the other term denoting the other sex, e.g.:

(6)a. η γάτα (fem.)
      'cat; she-cat'
   b. ο γάτος (masc.)
      'tom-cat'
(7)a. ο σκύλος (masc.)
      'dog; he-dog'
   b. η σκύλα (fem.)
      'bitch'

In addition to the items listed in (6) and (7) above there are the neuter forms το γατί and το σκυλί, which do not specify the sex of the animal; το γατί is a *diminutive* (denoting a kitten), while το σκυλί may either be used simply as an alternative for ο σκύλος or η σκύλα, or it may have a diminutive meaning (although there is also an additional item το κουτάβι 'puppy').

Most wild animals have only one term, e.g.:

(8) η αλεπού (fem.)
'fox'

(9) ο ελέφαντας (masc.)
'elephant'

In these cases, if the sex of the animal is to be specified, the word has to be accompanied by the adjective for 'female' or 'male', the adjective and other modifiers agreeing with the gender of the noun rather than with the sex of the animal:

(10) η (fem.) αρσενική (fem.) αλεπού (fem.)
'the male fox'

(11) ο (masc.) θηλυκός (masc.) ελέφαντας (masc.)
'the female elephant'

2.2.2 THE GENDER OF INDECLINABLE NOUNS

While the vast majority of loanwords taken from foreign languages inflect according to Greek patterns, an increasing number of nouns that have entered the language in recent times have not been adapted to the Greek declension system; the same applies to most names of foreign people and places. Nevertheless, every foreign noun, when used in Greek, must be assigned to one of the three genders. (See also Part II, Section 2.7.)

In general, if there is no compelling reason to do otherwise, an indeclinable noun is assigned to the masculine or feminine if it denotes a human, otherwise to the neuter:

(1) ο/η μάνατζερ (common: masc. or fem.)
'manager [e.g. of a sports team or rock group]' (from English)

(2) το ασανσέρ (neut.)
'lift, elevator' (French *ascenseur* [masc.])

However, the allocation of an originally non-Greek noun to a particular gender category may be influenced by one or more of the following factors: (i) its gender in the donor language; (ii) its ending; (iii) its meaning; and (iv) the gender of some Greek noun that is understood.

(i) While French masculines tend to become neuters in Greek, French feminines often remain feminine:

(3) η πλαζ (fem.)
'beach' (French *plage* [fem.])

Many feminine nouns which in French end in mute '-e' are declined in Greek like feminines in -α:

(4) η πρεμιέρα (gen. της πρεμιέρας)
     'première [= first performance]'

(ii) Italian feminines in '-a' and masculines in '-o' tend to be treated as feminine and neuter respectively in Greek. Many of these are inflected like Greek feminines in -α and Greek neuters in -o respectively:

(5) η πίτσα (gen. της πίτσας)
     'pizza'
(6) το πιάνο (gen. του πιάνου)
     'piano'

Conversely, many comparatively recent toponyms in -a are assigned to the feminine gender without being declinable:

(7) η Αγκόλα (gen. της Αγκόλα)
     'Angola'

(iii) Some foreign nouns are assigned to the gender of the equivalent word in Greek, e.g.:

(8) οι Τάιμς (masc. pl.)
     'the Times' [by analogy with the masculines χρόνος and καιρός 'time']

(iv) The names of many non-Greek football teams are feminine, the feminine noun ομάδα 'team' being understood:

(9) η Σέφιλντ
     'Sheffield [Wednesday]'

Contrast the use of the neuter to denote the town itself:

(10) το Σέφιλντ
     'Sheffield'

The brand-names of many products are likewise feminine or masculine according to the gender of the generic noun denoting the product:

(11) μια Ολιβέτι (fem.)
     'an Olivetti' [sc. γραφομηχανή (fem.) 'typewriter']
(12) ένας Μάκιντος (masc.)
     'a Macintosh' [sc. υπολογιστής (masc.) 'computer']

Some brand-names of cars (especially large ones) are feminine (13), while most are neuter (14):

(13) μια Ρολς-Ρόις
    'a Rolls-Royce'
(14) ένα Πεζό
    'a Peugeot'

Names of ships and of companies, including Greek ones, are normally not declined. Names of ships are normally neuter, a word such as πλοίο (neut.) 'ship' being understood, e.g.:

(15) ο καπετάνιος του Λήμνος
    'the captain of the Limnos' [cf. the name of the island η Λήμνος (fem.)]

Names of companies are normally feminine, εταιρεία (fem.) 'company' being understood, e.g.:

(16) ο πρόεδρος της Παπαστράτος
    'the chairman of Papastratos'

2.3 NUMBER

Every declinable word (noun, pronoun, adjective, article, numeral, or determiner) indicates in its inflection whether it denotes a single item (singular) or more than one item (plural). Almost every noun has a separate set of inflections for each of the two numbers, singular and plural, though a few have only singular or plural forms. There is however no single way for a noun to distinguish between singular and plural; the endings employed depend on which declension class the noun belongs to (see morphological tables in Part II, Sections 2ff.). The number of the subject is also indicated in the verb: see Section 1.2.1.

Many abstract nouns exist only in the singular, e.g.

ειρήνη 'peace'
γαλήνη 'calm; serenity'
πίστη 'belief, faith'
κύρος 'authority, validity'

Conversely, a number of nouns are used either exclusively in the plural or more commonly in the plural than in the singular. These tend to be nouns denoting entities that naturally occur in sets, and the vast majority are neuter. Examples include the following (gender specified if not neuter):

various sets: άμφια 'vestments', άρματα 'arms, weapons', γένια
    'beard', κάλαντα 'carols', κιάλια 'binoculars'
times of life: νιάτα 'youth', γεράματα 'old age'
relatives: αδέρφια 'siblings', γονείς (masc.) 'parents', ξαδέρφια
    'cousins', πεθερικά 'in-laws'

certain categories of foodstuffs: πουλερικά 'poultry'
certain compound nouns: γυναικόπαιδα 'women and children',
    μαχαιροπίρουνα 'cutlery', μικροπράγματα 'trifles'
charges made for services: δίδακτρα 'tuition fees', ναύλα 'fare'
languages (originally neuter plurals of adjectives): ελληνικά 'Greek',
    etc.
certain festivals: Χριστούγεννα 'Christmas', Επιφάνια 'Epiphany'
certain toponyms: Παξοί (masc.) 'Paxos', Σπέτσες (fem.) 'Spetses',
    Χανιά 'Chania' (neut.)
areas: περίχωρα 'outskirts'

There are some *collective nouns*, i.e. singular nouns that denote a collection
of items. Examples include ομάδα 'team', δωδεκάδα 'group of twelve',
η αστυνομία 'the police', and ο κόσμος 'the world', which is frequently
used to mean 'people' (as in όλος ο κόσμος 'everybody').

A countable noun may be used in the singular with the definite article
to denote a genus or species or a commodity:

(1) Το άλογο είναι χρησιμότατο ζώο
     'The horse is a most useful animal'
(2) Η ντομάτα έχει 150 δραχμές το κιλό
     'Tomatoes are 150 drachmas a kilo'

A few nouns have different meanings in the singular and plural:

μαλλί (sg.) 'wool'; μαλλιά (pl.) 'hair [on human head]'
φυλακή 'prison [as an abstraction]' (είναι στη φυλακή 's/he's in
    prison'); φυλακές 'prison [an actual building]' (είναι στις φυλακές
    Λαμίας 's/he's in/at Lamia prison')

Some nouns have two different plural forms, sometimes with different
meanings: see Part II, Section 2.6.

Some nouns denoting substances (e.g. το αίμα – τα αίματα 'blood', το
νερό – τα νερά 'water', το χιόνι – τα χιόνια 'snow') may be used in the
singular with the definite article to indicate the substance in general (3a)
or a specified amount of it (3b), whereas the plural may indicate an unspecified quantity of the substance (3c):

(3)a. Το αίμα (sg.) κυκλοφορεί στις φλέβες
       'Blood circulates in the veins'
   b. μια σταγόνα αίμα (sg.)
       'a drop of blood'
   c. Τα ποτάμια γέμισαν αίματα (pl.)
       'The rivers filled with blood'

In addition, the plural of such words may mean 'varieties':

(4) Το νοσοκομείο διαθέτει διάφορα αίματα (pl.)
   'The hospital has various kinds of blood'

Alternatively, the plural may denote two or more items (τρία νερά 'three
waters' [i.e. bottles or glasses of water]). Some other nouns have plurals
that denote large amounts (e.g. οι ζέστες 'the spell of hot weather').

Proper nouns may be used in the plural to indicate two or more indi-
viduals of the same name (e.g. πολλοί Γιάννηδες 'many Johns'). The plural
may also be used metonymically to denote works of art by a particular
artist (e.g. τρεις Βολωνάκηδες 'three Volonakises' [i.e. three paintings by
Volonakis]). The plural of proper nouns may also be used jocularly in
phrases such as:

(5) Άσε με με τα Λονδίνα σου!
   [lit. 'leave me with your Londons!']

in which the speaker is expressing irritation at what s/he takes to be the
addressee's obsession with London.

As with gender, all words modifying the head of the noun phrase agree
with the head and with each other in number. Thus:

(6) πολλές (fem. pl.) καλές (fem. pl.) γυναίκες (fem. pl.)
   'many good women/wives'

A subject in the singular (7a–b), including a collective noun, requires a
verb in the singular, while a subject in the plural (7c), or a combination
of more than one subject (7d), requires a verb in the plural:

(7)a. Ήρθε ο αδελφός μου
     'My brother came'
   b. Το 90% (sg.) των κατοίκων ασχολείται (sg.) με την
      κτηνοτροφία
      '90% of the inhabitants are engaged in stock-breeding'
   c. Ήρθαν οι αδελφοί μου
      'My brothers came'
   d. Ήρθαν ο αδελφός και η αδελφή μου
      'My brother and sister came'

Unlike in English, the expression 'more than one' requires the head noun,
together with its other modifiers and (when it is the subject) its verb to
be in the plural:

(8) Σκοτώθηκαν (pl.) περισσότερα (pl.) από ένα πουλιά (pl.)
   'More than one bird was killed'

When someone is being addressed in the *polite plural*, the plural forms
of the personal pronoun and the verb are used even when the addressee
is a single person:

(9) Εσείς είστε ο κύριος Λαμπρόπουλος;
    'Are you Mr. Lambropoulos?'

For further details on number agreement see Appendix 4.

2.4   CASE

The cases in Greek are:

nominative (see Section 2.4.1)
accusative (see Section 2.4.2)
genitive (see Section 2.4.3)
vocative (see Section 2.4.4)

In addition Greek contains traces of the ancient dative case (see Section 2.4.5).

Every declinable word, whether it be a noun, pronoun, adjective, article, numeral, or determiner, inflects for case, although in practice a word may not always indicate unambiguously which case it is in. Only one class of nouns has a separate form for each of the four cases, and then only in the singular, namely most masculines in -ος. All declinable nouns and adjectives (that is, all nouns and adjectives except some recent loanwords) possess separate forms for the nominative and genitive singular and the nominative and genitive plural. The accusative singular of nouns other than those in -ος is generally either the same as the nominative (as in all neuters and most feminines) or as the genitive (as in most masculines); the definite article however distinguishes between all these three cases (nominative, accusative and genitive) in the masculine and the feminine, though in the neuter the nominative and accusative are again identical. For the various forms corresponding to the cases see Part II, Sections 1–3 and 5–6.

As with gender and number, all declinable words modifying the head of the noun phrase must be in the same case:

(1)a. ο (nom.) άλλος (nom.) τραγουδιστής (nom.)
   b. τον (acc.) άλλο (acc.) τραγουδιστή (acc.)
   c. του (gen.) άλλου (gen.) τραγουδιστή (gen.)
      'the other singer'

In addition, all other words that denote the same item and are used in the same clause must be in the same case:

(2)a. Ο Γιάννης (nom.) θεωρείται καλός τραγουδιστής (nom.)
      'John is considered a good singer'
   b. Δε θεωρώ το Γιάννη (acc.) καλό τραγουδιστή (acc.)
      'I don't consider John a good singer'

For case agreement see Appendix 4.

2.4.1   NOMINATIVE

The nominative is considered to be the basic case; dictionaries normally give declinable words in the nominative singular form. A title or a place-name used to specify another noun phrase also appears in the nominative:

(1) ο συγγραφέας του μυθιστορήματος (gen.) *Το τρίτο στεφάνι* (nom.)
    'the author of the novel *The Third Wedding*'
(2) ο διευθυντής του ξενοδοχείου (gen.) Η Ωραία Ελένη (nom.)
    'the manager of the Hotel Belle Hélène'
(3) στο χωριό (acc.) Άσσος (nom.)
    'in the village [of] Assos'

The nominative is used to indicate the **subject** of a verb (i.e. the person, thing, etc. that is said to do something or have something done to him/her/it):

(4) Ήρθε **η Μαρία**
    '**Mary** came'
(5) Φυλακίστηκε **ο κλέφτης**
    '**The thief** was imprisoned'

In addition, the nominative is used to indicate a **subject predicate** (i.e. a word or phrase denoting the same person, thing, etc., as the subject):

(6) Ο Γιάννης είναι **γιατρός**
    'John is **a doctor**'
(7) Ο Γιάννης σπουδάζει **γιατρός**
    'John is studying [to be a] **doctor**'
(8) Τον ξέρω από **μικρός**
    'I've known him since [I was] **a child**'
(9) Αυτό το βιβλίο χρησιμεύει για **οδηγός** [*or* σαν **οδηγός**]
    'This book serves as a **guide**'
(10) Περνάει για **ωραίος**
    'He is reputed to be **handsome**' [lit. 'He passes for handsome']

The nominative is also used in certain more-or-less fixed expressions, e.g.:

(11) στις τρεις **η ώρα**
    'at three **o'clock**'

Finally, the nominative of the weak personal pronoun can be used only after πούν' 'where is/are' and να 'there':

(12) Πούν' **τος**;
    'Where is he?'
(13) Να **τος**!
    'There he is!'

2.4.2 ACCUSATIVE

The accusative has two chief uses. The first is to indicate the **direct object** of a verb (i.e. the person, thing, etc. that is acted upon by the subject; see also Sections 1.1.1ff.):

(1) a. Η αστυνομία έπιασε **τον κλέφτη**
      'The police caught **the thief**'
    b. Η αστυνομία **τον** έπιασε
      'The police caught **him**'

Similarly, the accusative is used to express an **object predicate**:

(2) Τον θεωρώ **φίλο μου**
    'I consider him **my friend**'
(3) Τον ξέρω από **μικρόν**
    'I've known him since [he was] **a child**' (contrast example (8) in Section 2.4.1)
(4) Δεν είδα τον αδελφό μου **γυμνό**
    'I didn't see my brother **naked**'
(5) Βρήκα τον πατέρα μου **καθισμένο** στην πολυθρόνα
    'I found my father **seated** in the armchair'

Secondly, the accusative is used for the object of most prepositions (for more on prepositions see Section 4):

(6) Η Μαρία είναι από **την Αθήνα**
    'Mary is from **Athens**'
(7) Χάρισα το βιβλίο **στον Πέτρο**
    'I gave the book to **Peter**'

The accusative has a variety of other uses. It is used after certain types of words other than verbs and prepositions, such as γεμάτος 'full [of]', όλος 'all', and certain past participles meaning 'loaded with' and 'dressed [in]':

(8) Η πόλη είναι γεμάτη **σκύλους**
     'The town's full of **dogs**'
(9) Ήταν όλος **καλοσύνη** και **τρόπους**
     'He was all **kindness** and [good] **manners**
(10) Κυκλοφορούσε πάντα φορτωμένος **έναν μπόγο** με ρούχα
     'He always went around loaded [with] **a bundle** of clothes'
(11) ντυμένος **την καινούρια του στολή**
     'dressed in **his new uniform**'

and after certain exclamatory words such as μα 'by' (in oaths), καλώς 'welcome', πανάθεμα 'a curse on', and κρίμα '[it's a] pity [about]':

(12) Μα **το Θεό**!
     'By **God**!'

(13) Καλώς **το Γιάννη**!
'Welcome, **John**!'
(14) Έλα δω, **πανάθεμά σε**!
'Come here, damn **you**!'
(15) Κρίμα **τη λεκάνη**!
'Pity about **the basin** [which got broken]'

In addition, the accusative is used in a particular kind of exclamatory expression of pity or indignation, which may be either addressed to someone or uttered about him/her:

(16) **Τον καημένο τον Γιάννη**! 'Poor John!'
(17) **Τον ηλίθιο**! 'The idiot!'

2.4.2.1 The accusative in adverbial use

Noun phrases in the accusative may also have an adverbial function, especially in expressions of measurement in time or space.

(i) Duration (time)

(1) Δούλεψα **όλο το χρόνο**
'I worked **all year**'

(ii) Distance (space or time)

(2) Έτρεξα **δυο χιλιόμετρα**
'I ran **two kilometres**'
(3) Κράτησε **ένα μήνα**
'It lasted **a month**'

(iii) Point in time

(4) νύχτα
'at night'
(5) τη νύχτα
'during the night'
(6) την Τρίτη το πρωί
'on Tuesday morning'
(7) το Μάρτιο
'in March'
(8) την πρώτη Οκτωβρίου
'on the first of October' (contrast the days of the month after the first, which are expressed by στις and the feminine of the cardinal numeral, e.g. στις είκοσι μία Οκτωβρίου 'on the twenty-first of October')

(9)   την άλλη μέρα
      'the next day'
(10) το χειμώνα
      'in winter'
(11) τα Χριστούγεννα
      'at Christmas'
(12) τρεις φορές
      'three times'

Note however that the time of day is expressed by a prepositional phrase introduced by σε (στις τρεις 'at three o'clock').

(iv)   Rate (time or weight)

(13) τριάντα χιλιόμετρα **την ώρα**
      'thirty kilometres **per hour**'
(14) χίλια δολάρια **τον τόνο**
      'a thousand dollars **a ton**'

(v)   Measurement (space)

(15)a. ένα ξύλο **δέκα πόντους** μακρύ
       'a stick **ten centimetres** long' or
    b. ένα ξύλο **δέκα πόντους μήκος**
       'a stick **ten centimetres [in] length**'
(16)   Αυτό το σπίτι έχει ύψος **δέκα μέτρα**
       'This house has [a] height [of] **ten metres**'
(17)a. ένα σπίτι **δέκα μέτρα** ψηλό
       'a house **ten metres** high'
    b. ένα σπίτι **δέκα μέτρα** ύψος
       'a house **ten metres [in] height**'
(18)   Το σπίτι μου είναι **δυο χιλιόμετρα** μακριά
       'My house is **two kilometres** away'

Examples (15a) and (15b) are two alternative ways of saying the same thing, as are (17a) and (17b).

(vi)   Degree of separation (space or time)
Expressions of relation may include a noun phrase in the accusative denoting the degree of separation between two terms:

(19) Μένω **δυο δρόμους** παρακάτω
      'I live **two streets** further down'
(20) Η αδελφή μου είναι **ένα χρόνο** μεγαλύτερη από μένα
      'My sister is **one year** older than me'

(vii)   Goal or aim

(21)   Πήγα **περίπατο** *or* **βόλτα**
       'I went **for a walk**'
(22)   Θα πάμε **εκδρομή**
       'We'll go on an excursion'
(23)   Πήγα **επίσκεψη** στο μουσείο
       'I visited the museum' [lit. 'I went **visit** to the museum]'

(viii)   Other expressions
Apart from the expressions of time and place that have been listed above,
there are many idiomatic expressions in which the accusative of a noun
is used as an adverb (usually as an adverb of manner):

(24)   Τα φέρνω **βόλτα**
       'I manage, get by'
(25)   Πήγα **παρέα** με την Άννα
       'I went **together** with [**in the company** of] Anna'
(26)   Έφυγε **τρεχάλα**
       'S/he left **at a run**'
(27)   Λείπει **ταξίδι**
       'S/he's away **on a journey**'
(28)   Στέκομαι **προσοχή**
       'I stand **at attention**'
(29)   Με πήραν τα αίματα **ποτάμι**
       'I bled profusely' [lit. 'the blood took me **river**']
(30)   Το έσκισα **κομμάτια**
       'I tore it **to pieces**'
(31)   Το έκοψα **φέτες**
       'I cut it **in slices**'
(32)   ένα μαντήλι δεμένο **κόμπο**
       'a handkerchief tied **in a knot**'
(33)   Σε πήρα **τηλέφωνο**
       'I phoned you' [lit. 'I took you **telephone**']
(34)   Η Μαρία πήρε το μωρό **αγκαλιά**
       'Mary took the baby **in her arms**'

In colloquial use, the accusative of nouns denoting locations, particularly
institutions such as σπίτι 'house', σχολείο 'school', and φυλακή 'prison',
but also places of entertainment and even place-names, is used to convey
'motion to' or 'location at':

(35)a. Πάω σπίτι
       'I'm going home'
    b. Πάω σχολείο
       'I'm going to school'

    c. Πάω φυλακή
      'I'm going to prison'
    d. Πάω σινεμά
      'I'm going to the cinema'
    e. Πάω Αμπελοκήπους
      'I'm going to Ambelokipi'
(36) Είμαι σπίτι
     'I'm at home'

There are other idiomatic adverbial uses of the accusative in which the noun is repeated, e.g.:

(37)a. άκρη άκρη
     'at/along the very edge'
    b. βράχο βράχο
      'from rock to rock'
    c. γιαλό γιαλό
      'along the shore'
    d. τοίχο τοίχο
      'along the wall'
    e. χέρι χέρι
      'hand-in-hand'
    f. στάλα στάλα
      'drop by drop'

In some of these constructions the definite article is inserted between the two instances of the noun:

(38) **Χρόνο το χρόνο** γερνάμε
     'We get older **year by year**'
(39) Τρώει ήσυχα, **μπουκιά την μπουκιά**
     'S/he eats gently, **mouthful by mouthful**'

In others a preposition is used before the article:

(40) Βελτιώνεται **μέρα με τη μέρα**
     'S/he/it's improving **day by day**'

Lastly, a small number of nouns are used adverbially in the *accusative of reference*; in this construction the noun is always preceded by the definite article:

(41) Είναι γιατρός **το επάγγελμα**
     'S/he's a doctor **by profession**'
(42) Ήρθε ένας χωριανός, Νίκος **το όνομα**
     'A villager came, Nikos **by name**'
(43) Είμαι Ελληνίδα **την καταγωγή**
     'I'm Greek **by descent**'

2.4.3   GENITIVE

The genitive has two quite separate sets of syntactical functions, according to whether it is governed by a verb or dependent on a noun. When governed by a verb it most commonly indicates the indirect object (see Section 2.4.3.1). When it depends on a noun the genitive may indicate various relations of dependency: most commonly it indicates the possessor of the noun on which it depends, but it may indicate various other, more abstract, relations instead (see Section 2.4.3.2).

2.4.3.1   The genitive governed by a verb

When it is governed by a verb, the genitive form of a personal pronoun or a noun phrase normally indicates that the pronoun or noun phrase is the ***indirect object*** of a verb. (For the indirect object from the point of view of the verb phrase see Section 1.1.1.4.) In examples (1–3) the indirect object denotes the person, thing, etc., *to* which something is given or said:

    (1) **Μου** έδωσε ένα κολιέ
         'S/he gave **me** a necklace'
    (2) Το έδωσε **της Κατερίνας**
         'S/he gave it **to Catherine**'
    (3) **Της** είπα τα νέα
         'I told **her** the news'

With regard to example (2) it is, however, more usual for the noun phrase acting as indirect object to appear in a prepositional phrase introduced by σε (Το έδωσε **στην Κατερίνα**).

In example (4) the indirect object denotes the person *for* whom the action is done:

    (4) Πιάσε **μου** το αλάτι
         'Get **me** the salt'

In (5) the indirect object may be interpreted as the person *from* whom something is removed:

    (5) **Του** πήραν τα γυαλιά
         'They took the glasses **from him**'

The possessive pronoun may optionally be added to the direct object in such circumstances:

    (6) Του πήραν τα γυαλιά του
         'They took [away] his glasses'

Alternatively, the indirect object in (5) may be interpreted, as in (4), as the person *for* whom the action took place ('They bought the glasses **for him**'). The appropriate interpretation depends on the context.

In the following examples the indirect object indicates the person *affected* by the action of the verb:

(7) **Του** κόψανε το χέρι
'They cut **his** hand/arm off'

(8) **Μου** κλέψανε το αυτοκίνητο
'They've stolen the car **from me**'

In both (7) and (8) the possessive pronoun may optionally be added to the noun. In the latter case, the possessive pronoun may be added to the direct object to make it clear that it was *my* car that was stolen (9a); otherwise some other possessive genitive expression may be used to indicate whose car it was (9b):

(9)a. Μου κλέψανε το αυτοκίνητό μου
'They've stolen my car from me' (i.e. 'My car's been stolen')

   b. Μου κλέψανε το αυτοκίνητο της αδελφής μου
'They've stolen my sister's car from me'

In (10) the optional presence of the genitive form of the first-person weak (clitic) pronoun indicates the *interested party*:

(10) Τι **μου** κάνεις;
'How are you?' [lit. 'What to-me do-you-do']

In (10) the presence of the genitive pronoun implies the speaker's affectionate interest in the addressee's well-being.

The genitive is also used to indicate the indirect object (usually a weak pronoun) of certain verbs that do not take direct objects, such as αρέσω 'please', πάω 'suit', and φαίνομαι 'seem':

(11) Δε **μου** αρέσει αυτό το κρασί
'I don't like this wine'

(12) **Σου** πάει αυτή η φούστα
'This skirt suits **you**'

(13) Δύσκολο **μου** φαίνεται
'It seems difficult **to me**'

There are some verbs originating in *katharevousa* which in formal styles may take only the genitive even when this does not indicate the indirect object. With such verbs, the genitive cannot be replaced by σε+accusative; with all of them except διαφεύγω the object must normally be a noun phrase, not a weak personal pronoun. These verbs include διαφεύγω 'escape', επιζώ 'survive', επωφελούμαι 'take advantage of', προηγούμαι 'precede', προεδρεύω 'preside over', προπορεύομαι 'march ahead of', προϋπάρχω 'pre-exist', υπερισχύω 'prevail', and sometimes επιμελούμαι 'be in charge of, take care of' and στερούμαι 'be deprived of':

(14) **Μου** διαφεύγει το όνομά του
'His name escapes **me**'

(15) **Του γεύματος** προηγήθηκε συνέντευξη τύπου
       '**The luncheon** was preceded by a press conference'

In (15) συνέντευξη τύπου is the subject, του γεύματος the object. With some verbs the genitive may sometimes be replaced by από+accusative (Από το γεύμα . . .). Others, such as επιμελούμαι and στερούμαι, take the accusative instead of the genitive in less formal contexts. (See also Section 1.1.1.2.)

2.4.3.2   The genitive dependent on a noun

The genitive is the only case that displays a hierarchical relationship between two noun phrases. The genitive of a noun phrase dependent on a noun covers a much wider variety of functions in Standard Greek than it did in traditional demotic. In older colloquial usage the genitive of a noun phrase dependent on a noun was for the most part confined to the possessive genitive, and then only if the possessor was animate. A further complication, traces of which still survive today, is that some nouns lack a normal genitive plural form. Thus, for instance, whereas 'the legs of the hen' is τα πόδια **της κότας**, 'the legs of the **hens**' is normally expressed by using a prepositional phrase introduced by από instead of the genitive plural: τα πόδια **από τις κότες** (instead of τα πόδια **των κοτών**).

In the types of construction outlined below the item in the genitive can always be a noun phrase; by contrast, a weak pronoun in the genitive may normally depend on a noun only in the possessive genitive and in the subjective and objective genitive (items (i) and (ii) below).

When the item in the genitive is a noun phrase (and especially when the head is definite), this noun phrase in the genitive may precede the head, generally for purposes of contrastive emphasis. This normally applies only to the *possessive genitive* and the *genitive of quality*, but not to the other genitive constructions (see examples (1c–d) and (22–24)). Noun phrases in the above-mentioned genitive constructions, and also in the *genitive of measurement*, may also be used ***predicatively*** (see examples (1e), (25–27) and (34–36)).

(i)   Possessive genitive

When a noun phrase or pronoun is in the genitive it may indicate that the person, thing, etc., which it denotes is the possessor of the person, thing, etc., which is denoted by the noun on which it depends:

(1)a. το σπίτι **της Λουκίας**
       '**Lucy's** house'
   b. το σπίτι **της**
       '**her** house'
   c. **της Λουκίας** το σπίτι
       '*Lucy's* house [rather than anyone else's]'

d. **αυτηνής** το σπίτι
'*her* house [rather than anyone else's]'
e. Αυτό το σπίτι είναι **της Λουκίας**
'This house is **Lucy's**'

A sub-category of the possessive genitive is one where the phrase in the genitive expresses the whole of which the other phrase represents a part:

(2)a. τα κλαριά **των δέντρων**
'the branches **of the trees**'
b. τα κλαριά **τους**
'**their** branches'

(ii) Subjective and objective genitive

A noun phrase or weak pronoun in the genitive dependent on an abstract noun may indicate a more abstract relationship:

(3)a. Ο υπουργός ευθύνεται για τη δημιουργία **αυτής της**
κατάστασης
'The minister is responsible for the creation **of this situation**'
b. Ο υπουργός ευθύνεται για τη δημιουργία **της**
'The minister is responsible for **its** creation'

In (3a) the relationship between the two noun phrases τη δημιουργία and αυτής της κατάστασης may be seen by translating the sentence as '... for creating this situation'; here the noun phrase in the genitive corresponds to the direct object of a verb (*objective genitive*). In some circumstances, however, the genitive may correspond to the subject (*subjective genitive*), or it may not be clear whether it corresponds to the subject or the object:

(4)a. η υποστήριξη **της οικογένειάς του**
'the support **of his family**'
b. η υποστήριξή της
'its support'

Example (4a) may refer to the fact that he is supporting **his family** (υποστηρίζει **την οικογένειά του**) or that his family is supporting **him** (**τον** υποστηρίζει **η** οικογένειά του).

It is possible, though rare, for a subjective genitive expressed by a weak pronoun to co-occur with an objective genitive expressed by a noun phrase:

(5) η υποστήριξή του **αυτής της οικογένειας**
'his support **of this family**'

A noun phrase in the subjective genitive does not normally co-occur with a noun phrase in the objective genitive; the co-occurrence of two weak pronouns after the same head is in any case excluded.

(iii)   Genitive of place, time or cause

A noun phrase in the genitive may specify the place (6) or time (7) at which something takes place, or the cause of something (8):

(6) η Μάχη **της Κρήτης**
'the Battle **of Crete**'

(7) οι Έλληνες **του δέκατου ένατου αιώνα**
'the Greeks **of the nineteenth century**'

(8) η πίκρα **του χωρισμού**
'the sorrow **of parting**'

(iv)   Genitive of purpose

A definite noun phrase in the genitive may indicate the purpose for which something is used, usually the contents for which a receptacle is intended:

(9) ένα ποτήρι **του κρασιού**
'a **wine**-glass'

(10) το κουτί **των τσιγάρων**
'the **cigarette** box'

(v)   Specific genitive

A noun phrase in the genitive may make the meaning of the other noun more specific:

(11) ένας καθηγητής **της φιλολογίας**
'a **literature** teacher/professor'

(12) γυμνάσιο **θηλέων**
'girls' high school' [lit. 'gymnasium **of-females**']

(13) στυλό **μιας χρήσεως**
'non-refillable pen' [lit. 'pen **of one use**']

This kind of genitive construction is of learned origin, and the noun phrase in the genitive is often characterized by the lack of an article and by the use of learned forms, as in examples (12–13).

(vi)   The genitive in street names

The genitive is used in almost all street names:

(14) οδός **Μαυρομιχάλη**
'**Mavromichalis** Street'

Again, the noun phrase in the genitive appears without an article and normally uses learned forms.

(vii)   Genitive of quality

With the genitive of quality the person, thing, etc., denoted by the other noun could be said to possess the quality denoted by the noun phrase in the genitive. Many of these phrases are stereotyped, having been translated from other European languages, and often contain genitive forms of learned origin:

(15) η σοκολάτα **πολυτελείας**
      '**luxury** chocolate' (French *de luxe*)
(16) άνθρωποι **τέτοιου είδους**
      'people **of such a kind**'
(17) αεροπλάνο **άλλου τύπου**
      '[an] aeroplane **of another type**'
(18) διευκολύνσεις **πάσης φύσεως** *or* **κάθε μορφής**
      'facilities **of every nature**' *or* '**of every form**'
(19) οι πολίτες **δεύτερης κατηγορίας**
      '**second-class** citizens'
(20) συζητήσεις **υψηλού επιπέδου**
      '**high-level** discussions'
(21) άνθρωπος **καλού χαρακτήρος**
      '[a] man **of good character**'

A noun phrase in the genitive of quality (though not, it seems, if it consists of a single noun) may be placed immediately before the head of the principal noun phrase:

(22) **τέτοιου είδους** άνθρωποι (=16)
(23) Έχουμε **δυο ειδών** ποτήρια
      'We've got two kinds of glasses [lit. '**of two kinds** glasses']
(24) οι **αποφασιστικής σημασίας** συζητήσεις
      'discussions **of decisive importance**'

A noun phrase in the genitive of quality may act as a predicate:

(25) Αυτή η σοκολάτα είναι **πολυτελείας** (cf. 15)
      'This chocolate is **de luxe**'
(26) Αυτό το ξενοδοχείο είναι **τρίτης κατηγορίας**
      'This hotel is [a] **third class** [one]'
(27) Τα ποιήματά της είναι **δυο ειδών**
      'Her poems are **of two kinds**'

(viii) Genitive of measurement
Measurement of time and space may be expressed with the use of a noun phrase in the genitive:

(28) ένα παιδί **τριών χρονών**
      'a **three-year-old** child'
(29) μια αναβολή **δύο χρόνων**
      'a **two-year** delay'

(30) κατά τη μακρά περίοδο **τριάντα ετών**
    'during the long period **of thirty years**'
(31) μια τηλεόραση **είκοσι τεσσάρων ιντσών**
    'a **24-inch** television'
(32) σε απόσταση **εκατό μέτρων**
    'at a distance **of 100 metres**'

In expressions of spatial measurement there may be two noun phrases in the genitive, one indicating the dimension ('height', 'length', etc.), the other the number of units of measurement:

(33) Έπεσα σ' ένα λάκκο **βάθους σαράντα εκατοστών**
    'I drove [lit. 'fell'] into a forty-centimetre-deep pothole [lit. 'a
    pothole **of-depth of-forty centimetres**']'

The genitive of measurement may also be used predicatively:

(34) Το παιδί μου είναι **τριών χρονών**
    'My child is **three years old**' (cf. 28)
(35) Η τηλεόρασή μου είναι **είκοσι τεσσάρων ιντσών**
    'My television is **twenty-four inch**' (cf. 31)
(36) Ο προϋπολογισμός είναι **του ύψους των 150.000 λιρών**
    'The budget is £150,000 [lit. '**of-the height of-the £150,000**']'

Apart from the expression of age (example 28), the genitive of measurement belongs to rather formal styles. For more colloquial expressions of measurement involving the accusative, see Section 2.4.2.1(v).

(ix) Genitive of content
With the genitive of content the noun phrase in the genitive indicates what the item denoted by the other noun consists of (contrast the use of με in Section 4.2.2.10(iv), which indicates what the first noun contains):

(37) μια σειρά **δέκα διαλέξεων**
    'a series **of ten lectures**' (cf. the simpler appositional
    construction in Section 2.12, example 21)
(38) μια παρέα **εννέα γυναικών**
    'a group **of nine women**'

For more colloquial versions of such expressions see Sections 2.12 (appositional constructions) and 4.2.2.2(ii)(g) (prepositional phrases with από).

A related use of the genitive is in expressions of time such as the following:

(39) στιγμές **ευτυχίας**
    'moments **of happiness**'
(40) ύστερα από τόσα χρόνια **φιλίας**
    'after so many years **of friendship**'

(x) Partitive genitive

With the partitive genitive the head noun denotes a portion of the item denoted by the noun phrase in the genitive:

(41) μια μεγάλη μερίδα **του λαού**
      'a large portion **of the people**'
(42) ούτε ένα ίχνος **ανησυχίας**
      'not a single trace **of unease**'
(43) μια γενναία ποσότητα **αφρού**
      'a goodly quantity **of foam**'

Related to these last two functions are constructions with εκατοντάδες 'hundreds', χιλιάδες 'thousands', μυριάδες 'myriads', and εκατομμύριο 'million':

(44) οι μυριάδες **των ξένων**
      'the myriads **of foreigners**'
(45) τα δέκα εκατομμύρια **των Ελλήνων**
      'the ten million **Greeks**'

Again, such constructions with the genitive tend to belong to formal styles. For more colloquial alternatives see Section 2.12 (appositional constructions).

(xi) The genitive in surnames

The genitive is also used in the masculine and feminine forms of certain surnames derived from Christian names, and in the feminine form of other surnames. Surnames originating in the genitive of Christian names may be used for both men and women, and they are not declinable (e.g. Αγγέλου from Άγγελος, Ιωάννου from Ιωάννης, and various surnames beginning with Παπα- and Χατζη- such as Παπανδρέου [from Ανδρέας] and Χατζηπαύλου). Similarly, feminine surnames derived from masculine surnames are not declinable (such as the feminine Μητσάκη from the masculine Μητσάκης, and the feminine Μητσάκου from the masculine Μητσάκος).

Surnames derived from genitives usually appear in their *katharevousa* form. The examples Αγγέλου, Ιωάννου and Παπανδρέου have been given above. The following examples illustrate the types of feminine surname that usually appear in their *katharevousa* form (names with masculine forms in -άδης, -ίδης, -της, -όπουλος):

masc.	*fem.*
Αναστασιάδης	Αναστασιάδου
Πετρίδης	Πετρίδου
Πολίτης	Πολίτου
Παπαδόπουλος	Παπαδοπούλου

With the feminine form Παπαδοπούλου (with shift of accent) compare the normal genitive of the masculine form, Παπαδόπουλου. With regard to the other types of surname illustrated above, some women prefer to use the demotic genitive version of their surname Αναστασιάδη, Πετρίδη, and Πολίτη. See also Part II, Section 2.1.2, note 2, and Section 2.1.3, note 2.

2.4.3.3   The genitive dependent on an adjective, numeral, pronoun, or determiner

A noun phrase or pronoun in the genitive may depend on an adjective, numeral, pronoun, or determiner. Such constructions may be divided into three groups according to whether the genitive expression (i) is necessarily a noun phrase in itself, (ii) is necessarily a weak personal pronoun, or (iii) may be either a noun phrase or a weak personal pronoun.

(i)   Noun phrase in the genitive
In formal styles a small number of adjectives may be followed by a noun phrase in the genitive:

(1) Είναι **ένοχη/αθώα του εγκλήματος**
    'She is **guilty/innocent of the crime**'
(2) Θα σας κρατήσω **ενήμερο των εξελίξεων**
    'I shall keep you **informed of developments**'
(3) Είναι ποιητής **άξιος του ονόματος**
    'He is a poet **worthy of the name**'
(4) ένα ωράριο **διπλάσιο του κανονικού**
    'a working day **twice the normal** [in length]'

Where the adjective is derived from a verb, such a construction may correspond to a phrase consisting of verb+object (objective genitive: cf. Section 2.4.3.2(ii)):

(5) Τέτοιες ενέργειες είναι **αντιπροσωπευτικές της νοοτροπίας** της αντιπολίτευσης
    'Such actions are **representative of the mentality** of the opposition'

This corresponds to:

(6) Τέτοιες ενέργειες **αντιπροσωπεύουν τη νοοτροπία** της αντιπολίτευσης
    'Such actions **represent the mentality** of the opposition'

The genitive may depend on an adjective denoting colour:

(7) μια φούστα **κόκκινη της φωτιάς**
    'a **fire-red skirt**'

A noun phrase in the genitive may depend on a noun modified by an adjective in the superlative:

(8) ο πλουσιότερος εφοπλιστής **του κόσμου**
'the richest shipowner **in the world**'

(ii)   Weak personal pronoun in the genitive
Numerals and certain adjectives and pronouns may be followed by a weak personal pronoun in the genitive which specifies more narrowly the scope of the word on which it depends (*clarificatory genitive*). (If the item that depends on any of these words is a noun phrase, this noun phrase has to be in the accusative preceded by από.) Examples:

(9)   οι τρεις σας
      'the three of you'
(10) κανένας τους
      'none/any of them'
(11) καθένας σας
      'each of you'
(12) κάποιος τους
      'a certain one among them'
(13) ο πρώτος μας
      'the first of us'
(14) άλλοι τους
      'others of them'
(15) όλοι μας
      'all of us'

The intensive pronoun μόνος 'alone' may be followed by a weak personal pronoun in the genitive, the whole phrase meaning 'by oneself', in the sense of either 'without company' or 'without help' (see also Section 2.8.3.11):

(16) Καθόταν **μόνη της**
      'She was sitting **all alone**'
(17) **Μόνοι μας** το κάναμε
      'We did it **all by ourselves**'

The use of the genitive of the weak personal pronoun is compulsory with the emphatic possessive pronoun and determiner δικός [μου] '[my] own' (see also Section 2.8.3.10):

(18) Έχει **δικό της** σπίτι
      'She has **her own** house'
(19) Αυτή η καρέκλα είναι **δική σου**
      'This chair is **yours**'

The genitive of the weak personal pronoun may be used after the comparative or superlative of an adjective:

(20) Η Μαρία είναι δυο χρόνια **μεγαλύτερή του**
'Mary is two years **older than him**'

(21) Ο Παύλος είναι **ο καλύτερός μας**
'Paul is **the best of us**'

In practice, however, the comparative and superlative are more usually followed by από+accusative (see Section 5.4.2.).

(iii)   Noun phrase or weak personal pronoun in genitive
Adjectives expressing comparison or similarity (αντίστοιχος 'equivalent, corresponding', όμοιος 'similar', ισοδύναμος 'of equal force', συνομήλικος 'contemporary [=of the same age]', σύγχρονος 'contemporary [=of the same time]', συνώνυμος 'synonymous') or opposition or dissimilarity (ανόμοιος 'dissimilar', αντίθετος 'opposite') may be followed by a noun phrase or a weak personal pronoun in the genitive:

(22) Δε βρήκαμε **τον όμοιό του**
'We haven't found **his like**'

(23) οι σύγχρονοί μας
'our contemporaries'

(24) οι σύγχρονοί του ποιητές
'the poets of his time' [lit. 'his contemporary poets']

(25) Ο Σωκράτης ήταν σύγχρονος του Αριστοφάνη
'Socrates was [a] contemporary of Aristophanes'

Alternatively these adjectives may be followed by με+accusative (see Section 4.2.2.10). For the genitive of the weak pronoun dependent on adverbs see Section 3.2.7.

2.4.3.4   The genitive in exclamations

The weak pronoun in the genitive may depend on certain exclamatory words in greetings, wishes, and other exclamations. The pronoun here has a clarificatory function, i.e. it specifies the person to or for whom the wish, etc., is made:

(1) Καλημέρα σας!
'Good day to you!'

(2) Μπράβο της!
'Good for her!'

(3) Περαστικά του!
'I hope he gets well soon!' [lit. '[may it be] passing to him']

(4) Γεια σου
'Hello/Goodbye!'

(5) Ντροπή τους!
'Shame on them!'

(6) Αλίμονό τους!
   'Woe betide them!'

The exclamatory words να and ορίστε may be followed by a weak pronoun in the genitive, indicating the person who the speaker implies should be interested in the situation:

(7) Να σου τον!
   'There he is, you see!'
(8) Να τα μας! *or* Ορίστε μας!
   'What a [shameful] situation [for us]!'

2.4.3.5 Idiomatic noun phrases in the genitive

In colloquial usage there are certain fixed expressions consisting of noun phrases in the genitive, which have a metaphorical adverbial or adjectival use. Here are a few examples:

(1) Δε βρήκα φόρεμα **της προκοπής**
   'I didn't find a dress [that was] **any good**'
(2) Έγινε **της κακομοίρας** *or* **της τρελής**
   'There was **a terrible commotion**'
(3) Η ορχήστρα έπαιζε **του κουφαμού**
   'The orchestra was playing **deafeningly loud**'
(4) Έπεσε **του θανατά**
   'S/he was at death's door'
(5) Η κοντή φούστα είναι **της μόδας**
   'Short skirts are **in fashion**'
(6) Έφαγα **του σκασμού**
   'I've eaten **a bellyfull**'
(7) Κάνει **του κεφαλιού του**
   'He does **just as he pleases**'
(8) Κοιμόταν **του καλού καιρού**
   'S/he was sleeping **like a log**'

The most common expression of this sort, however, is the adverbial expression του χρόνου 'next year', which is not confined to colloquial usage.

2.4.3.6 The genitive governed by a preposition

Certain prepositions whose use is chiefly confined to formal contexts govern the genitive; see Sections 4.2.2ff. and 4.2.3.

2.4.3.7   The genitive of noun phrases in elliptical constructions

A noun phrase in the genitive may sometimes be considered as being dependent on a noun which has been omitted:

(1) Πήγα **στου Γιάννη**
    'I went to **John's**' ('house' omitted)
(2) Αυτό το παλτό μοιάζει με **του Γιάννη**
    'This coat is like **John's** [coat]'
(3) **Του Γιάννη** είναι μεγαλύτερο
    '**John's** is bigger' (some neuter singular noun omitted)
(4) Ο στρατός τους είναι μεγαλύτερος από **των Γερμανών**
    'Their army is bigger than **the Germans**'' (το στρατό 'the army' is understood)
(5) Θα πάρω **των δώδεκα**
    'I'll take **the twelve o'clock**' ('bus', 'train', etc., omitted)
(6) του Αγίου Γεωργίου
    '[on] St. George's [day]' ('festival' omitted)

2.4.3.8   The genitive absolute

The genitive absolute construction has been inherited from Ancient Greek. It consists of a parenthetical noun phrase in the genitive containing a participle and a head (usually a noun). Some of these phrases are stereotyped (1), while others may include the use of the appropriate form of συμπεριλαμβανόμενος 'being included' (2) or δεδομένος 'given' (3):

(1) τηρουμένων των αναλογιών
    'mutatis mutandis' [lit. 'the proportions being-preserved']
(2) Όλα τα κράτη-μέλη της Ευρωπαϊκής Ένωσης, **συμπεριλαμβανομένης και της Ελλάδας**, συνεισφέρουν σ' αυτό το ταμείο
    'All the member-states of the European Union, **including Greece**, contribute to this fund'
(3) **δεδομένης της άρνησής του** να απαντήσει, . . .
    '**given his refusal** to answer, . . .'

Two single forms deriving from archaic passive participles are used in genitive absolute expressions, namely δεδομένου (ότι) and προκειμένου (για/να). The former means 'given that'. The latter, which derives from the impersonal verb πρόκειται, is used with για to mean 'as far as [. . .] is concerned', while its meaning with να is easier to illustrate than to define; it may mean 'when it comes to' (6), or it may express purpose, 'with a view to' (7):

(4) Δεδομένου ότι ο Νίκος δε θα έρθει, ας ξεκινήσουμε
    'Given that Nick won't come, let's set off'
(5) Προκειμένου για ζώα που ζουν στα δάση . . .
    'As far as animals that live in forests are concerned . . .'
(6) Προκειμένου να τα χάσει όλα, προτίμησε να συμβιβαστεί
    'Faced with the prospect of losing everything, s/he preferred to compromise'

(7) Προθυμοποιήθηκαν να με διορίσουν, προκειμένου να με ξεχρεώσουν
   'They showed themselves eager to appoint me [i.e. give me a job], with
   a view to getting me out of debt'

2.4.4 VOCATIVE

The vocative indicates that the person, thing, etc., denoted by the noun
is being addressed:

(1) Έλα, Πέτρο!
   'Come on, Peter!'
(2) Δολοφόνε!
   'Murderer!'

A word in the vocative may, in familiar usage, be preceded by the exclamatory words μωρέ, ρε, or βρε, which are uninflected for case, number, and
gender. Any of these exclamatory words may also be used on its own.
While these forms of address may show affection if the addressee is an
intimate of the speaker, they are considered impolite when used to
strangers.

(3) Σώπα, ρε Γιάννη!
   'Be quiet, John!'
(4) Βρε ηλίθιε!
   'You imbecile!'
(5) Έλα, μωρέ!
   'Oh, come on!' (either literally encouraging the addressee to
      come, or expressing disbelief, protest, etc.)

2.4.5 DATIVE

The ancient dative has survived in a number of fixed adverbial expressions such
as the following (for the forms of the dative see Part II, Section 2.8):

(1) βάσει (+gen.) 'on the basis [of]'
(2) δυνάμει 'potentially'
(3) ελλείψει (+gen.) 'in the absence [of]'
(4) τοις εκατόν 'per cent'
(5) καλή τη πίστει 'in good faith'
(6) τοις μετρητοίς 'in cash; at face value'
(7) παρουσία (+gen.) 'in the presence [of]'
(8) ποιητική αδεία 'by poetic licence'
(9) λόγω (+gen.) 'by reason of'

Many of these dative constructions are found in prepositional phrases introduced
by ancient prepositions such as εν 'in' (see also Section 4.2.3):

(10) εν ανάγκη 'if need be'

(11) εν μέρει 'in part'
(12) εν πάση περιπτώσει 'in any case'

Some of these phrases are now written – and thought of – as a single word:

(13) εντάξει 'OK'
(14) εντούτοις 'nevertheless'

Outside fixed expressions, the dative is not used productively in Greek, except very occasionally for jocular purposes.

2.5   THE ARTICLES

Greek possesses a distinct ***definite article***, which inflects for gender, number, and case. The numeral ένας/μια/ένα 'one' also acts as the ***indefinite article***; this inflects for gender and case, but only exists in the singular.

The definite and indefinite articles always precede the head of the noun phrase and agree with it in number, gender, and case:

(1) αυτός **ο** σκύλος (masc. nom. sg.)
    'this dog'
(2) **ένας** σκύλος (masc. nom. sg.)
    'a dog'
(3) **οι** σκύλοι (masc. nom. pl.) **της** γυναίκας (fem. gen. sg.)
    'the woman's dogs'
(4) **τα** παιδιά (neut. nom./acc. pl.) **του** γείτονα (masc. gen. sg.)
    'the neighbour's children'

The uses of the articles in Greek are broadly similar to those in English: where English has 'the', Greek normally has the definite article, and where Greek has the indefinite article English has 'a[n]'. Nevertheless, the Greek definite article is also used in contexts where English does not use 'the'; conversely, there are many contexts in which English uses 'a[n]' but Greek does not use an article at all. The uses of the articles are covered in Sections 2.5.1 and 2.5.2, while contexts where an article is not used are treated in Section 2.5.3.

2.5.1   THE DEFINITE ARTICLE

A noun phrase that includes the definite article denotes a specific item that has already been mentioned, or is present before the speaker and/or hearer, or is assumed by the speaker or writer to be in some other way identifiable by the hearer or reader. Thus the definite article is used when the existence of the item denoted by the noun phrase in question is presupposed by the speaker or writer. Compare the following groups of sentences, in which the first of each group (a) contains a noun phrase with the definite article, and each of the others contains a noun phrase without the definite article (on the presence or absence of the definite article see Section 2.5.3):

(1)a. Ἦϱθε **ο** φίλος της Κατεϱίνας
'Katerina's friend came'

  b. Ἦϱθε ένας φίλος της Κατεϱίνας
'A friend of Katerina's came'

  c. Ἦϱθε κάποιος φίλος της Κατεϱίνας
'Some friend of Katerina's came'

(2)a. Ἦϱθε **ο** φίλος της
'Her friend came'

  b. Ἦϱθε ένας φίλος της
'A friend of hers came'

  c. Ἦϱθε κανένας φίλος της;
'Did any friend of hers come?'

  d. Είναι φίλος της
'He's a friend of hers'

(3)a. Θέλω **την** κόκκινη φούστα
'I want the red skirt'

  b. Θέλω μια κόκκινη φούστα
'I want a red skirt'

  c. Φοϱούσε κόκκινη φούστα
'She was wearing a red skirt'

(4)a. Ἦϱθε **η** κοπέλα που είδαμε χθες
'The girl we saw yesterday came'

  b. Ἦϱθε μια κοπέλα
'A girl came'

(5)a. Βλέπεις **την** καϱέκλα στη γωνία;
'Can you see the chair in the corner?'

  b. Βλέπεις καθόλου καϱέκλα;
'Can you see a chair at all?'

(6)a. **τα** καλύτεϱα αποτελέσματα
'the best results'

  b. καλύτεϱα αποτελέσματα
'better results'

Example (1a) clearly refers to a particular friend, and the speaker assumes that the hearer knows about this friend's existence. Example (2a) similarly refers to a specific friend. When compared with (2b–d), (2a) shows that in Greek the possessive pronoun (της in these examples) can be used with or without a definite article according to whether or not the noun phrase is definite. Examples (3a–c) show how a noun phrase may be definite or indefinite when it is modified by an adjective. Examples (4a–b) and (5a–b) show that a noun phrase may be definite when it is modified by a restrictive relative clause (4a) or an adverbial or prepositional phrase (5a).

Examples (6a–b) illustrate the way in which the presence or absence of
the definite article results in a comparative form of an adjective or adverb
being given either a relative superlative or a comparative meaning respectively (for more on the comparison of adjectives and adverbs see Sections
2.6.2 and 3.1.1).

The definite article is also used with names of people (7), places (8: but
cf. the end of Section 2.5.3), heavenly bodies (9), parts of the day (10),
days of the week (11), months (12), seasons (13), and festivals (14), where
the name denotes a specific person or item; it is also used when specifying years (15), and dates and times (16):

(7)   Ξέρεις **τον** Πέτρο;
       'Do you know Peter?'

(8)   Πήγαμε **στο** Λονδίνο
       'We went to London'

(9)   **Ο** Δίας είναι πλανήτης
       'Jupiter is a planet'

(10)   Θα σε δω **το** μεσημέρι
       'I'll see you at midday (in the middle of the day)'

(11)   Θα σε δω **την** Κυριακή
       'I'll see you on Sunday'

(12)   **Ο** Δεκέμβριος είναι ο πιο βροχερός μήνας
       'December is the rainiest month'

(13)   Δε μ' αρέσει **ο** χειμώνας
       'I don't like winter'

(14)   **Το** Πάσχα είναι η πιο σημαντική γιορτή του χρόνου
       'Easter is the most important festival of the year'

(15)   **Το** 1995 ήταν καλύτερο
       '1995 was better'

(16)   **στις** τρεις (fem. pl.)
       'on the third [of the month]; at three [o'clock]'

Some of the above kinds of noun may be used without the definite article
when the item denoted is not definite:

(17)a. Δεν ξέρω κανένα Πέτρο
       'I don't know any Peter'

    b. Με λένε Πέτρο
       'My name is Peter'

(18)   Την είδα μια Κυριακή
       'I saw her one Sunday'

(19)   Την είδα ένα μεσημέρι
       'I saw her once in the middle of the day [lit. 'one midday']'

(20)   Είχαμε πολύ βαρύ χειμώνα
       'We had a very harsh winter'

The definite article is also omitted when a name is used in the vocative:

(21) Έλα, Γιάννη! 'Come on, John!'

When proper names are preceded by titles, the definite article precedes the title (ο κύριος Παυλόπουλος 'Mr Pavlopoulos', ο βασιλιάς Γεώργιος 'King George').

The definite article is obligatory in a noun phrase containing a demonstrative (αυτός, τούτος, εκείνος):

(22) **αυτός ο** σκύλος
     'this dog'

It is also used in expressions of rate (in the accusative):

(23) εκατό χιλιόμετρα **την** ώρα
     'a hundred kilometres an hour'

The definite article is used when referring to an institution whose existence is presupposed:

(24) Το είδα σ**την** τηλεόραση
     'I saw it on television'
(25) Ήρθα με **το** τρένο
     'I came by train'

Similarly it is used with nouns denoting abstract concepts:

(26) Δε φοβάμαι **το** θάνατο
     'I'm not afraid of death'
(27) Ζει με **την** ελπίδα
     'S/he lives in hope'

Generic specification in the singular or the plural is expressed with the definite article (28–29, which have the same meaning):

(28) **Το** άλογο είναι ωραίο ζώο
     'The horse is a lovely animal'
(29) **Τα** άλογα είναι ωραία ζώα
     'Horses are lovely animals'

Sentences such as (28–29) are ambiguous as to whether they denote specific or generic items. Thus example (28) may denote the horse as a genus or the particular horse in question; example (29) may in addition mean 'The horses [in question] are lovely animals'. Words denoting substances are used with the definite article when these substances are talked about generally:

(30) **Το** μελάνι είναι μαύρο
     'Ink is black'

(31) Προτιμώ **το** κρασί από **την** μπίρα
'I prefer wine to beer'

Sentences such as (30) and (31) can also have a specific meaning. Thus example (29) may mean 'The ink [in question] is black', while example (31) may mean 'I prefer this particular wine to this particular beer'.

Some nouns denoting either substances or individual items (such as πέτρα 'stone') may be used in three different ways, namely in generic, specific, and individual use, according to whether they are used with one of the articles or without, and according to the context:

(32) η πέτρα
'stone' (generic); 'the stone' (individual item); 'the kind of stone' (specific, e.g. marble or granite)
(33) μια πέτρα
'a stone' (individual item); 'a kind of stone'
(34) [οι] πέτρες
'stones' (generic); '[the] stones' (individual examples); '[the] kinds of stone' (specific)
(35) Αυτή η πέτρα είναι σκληρή
'This stone is hard' (*either* this kind of stone *or* this particular item)

The definite article is used in expressing fractions (36) and percentages (37):

(36) **τα** τρία τέταρτα των Ελλήνων
'three quarters of the Greeks'
(37) **το** εβδομήντα τοις εκατό των Ελλήνων
'seventy per cent of the Greeks'

The definite article may be used with an adjective, numeral, or other modifier in the absence of a noun (see Section 2.6.1 for substantivized adjectives in elliptical uses). This may occur when we are talking about a particular person or persons, or about a certain class of people (e.g. ο πλούσιος 'the rich man', η πλούσια 'the rich woman', οι πλούσιοι 'the rich'), or when we are referring to an object or objects which are either present to the speaker and hearer or have already been mentioned, e.g.:

(38) – Ποιο μολύβι θέλεις, **το** μαύρο ή **το** κόκκινο; – Και **το** ένα και **το** άλλο
'"Which pencil do you want, the black one or the red one?" "Both of them [lit. 'and the one and the other']"'
(39) Από τα πέντε μολύβια που αγόρασα, λείπουν **τα** τρία
'Of the five pencils I bought, three are missing'

The neuter forms of the definite article may be used to substantivize any part of speech (and even whole phrases and clauses) in a variety of ways.

(a)   The neuter singular forms are used:

(i)   To substantivize another part of speech

> (40) στην Ελλάδα **του σήμερα** (adverb of time)
> 'in the Greece of today'
> (41) Μη ρωτάς **το γιατί** (interrogative adverb)
> 'Don't ask why'
> (42) Αυτός σκέφτεται μόνο **το εγώ του** (personal pronoun)
> 'He thinks only of himself [lit. 'his ego']'

(ii) To introduce a nominalized clause beginning with a question word
(especially when the clause is not the direct object of a verb)

> (43) Το μόνο που τον ενδιαφέρει είναι **το** πόσο θα κερδίσει
> 'The only thing that interests him is how much he will earn'
> (44) **Το** τι τράβηξα δε λέγεται
> 'I can't tell you how much I've suffered' [lit. 'the what I-
> pulled not is-said']
> (45) Διαφωνούν για **το** πώς έγινε το ατύχημα
> 'They disagree about how the accident happened'

(iii) When talking about a particular word or phrase

> (46) Πώς γράφεται **το** "λεωφόρος";
> 'How is "λεωφόρος" spelled?'
> (47) Πώς είναι ο παρατατικός **του** "επιμένω";
> 'What's the imperfect of "επιμένω"?'

(iv) When quoting the title of a text, song, etc.

> (48) **το** Πάτερ ημών
> 'the Lord's prayer' [lit. 'the Our Father']

(b)   The neuter plural forms are used:

(i)   In front of certain adverbs of place (especially εδώ, εκεί, κάτω, πάνω,
μπρος and πίσω when preceded by προς)

> (49) Έλα λίγο προς **τα** εδώ
> 'Come this way a little'
> (50) Πήγαμε προς **τα** κάτω
> 'We went downwards'

(ii) In idiomatic collocations, in front of neuter plural forms of adjectives
(which may be interpreted as adverbs)

> (51) Φύγανε σ**τα** γρήγορα
> 'They left in a bit of a hurry'

With the last example contrast Φύγανε γρήγορα 'They left quickly'.

Finally, as a relic of earlier formal usage, the article is used substantively in phrases such as και ο μεν και ο δε 'both the one and the other'; in such constructions the article is inflected for gender, number and case.

2.5.2   THE INDEFINITE ARTICLE

The indefinite article is used when referring to a singular person, thing, concept, etc., when this is not already known to the hearer/reader (for noun phrases without an article see Section 2.5.3):

(1) Ήρθε **ένας** φίλος σου
     'A friend of yours came'
(2) Είναι **μια** αφόρητη κατάσταση
     'It's an intolerable situation'
(3) Είδα **ένα** αυτοκίνητο
     'I saw a car'

The indefinite article is often used to emphasize the particularly intense quality of the item denoted:

(4) Έχω **μια** πείνα
     'I've got a [great] hunger'
(5) Έριχνε **μια** βροχή
     'It was pouring down' [lit. 'it-was-throwing a rain']
(6) **Μια** ολόκληρη Αγγλία δεν μπόρεσε να τους νικήσει
     'Even England itself [lit. 'a whole England'] wasn't able to
     defeat them'

For the uses of ένας as a numeral see Section 2.7. For its uses as a pronoun and determiner see Section 2.8.3.4.

2.5.3   NOUN PHRASES WITHOUT AN ARTICLE

Subject and object predicates normally appear without an article:

(1) Είναι καθηγητής
     'He's a professor'
(2) Έγινε καθηγητής
     'He became a professor'
(3) Τον διόρισαν καθηγητή
     'He was appointed professor' [lit. 'they appointed him
     professor']
(4) Με λένε Μάρκο
     'My name is Mark' [lit. 'They call me Mark']

However, the indefinite article may optionally accompany the predicate if the noun is made more specific in some way, e.g. by an adjective:

   (5) Είναι ένας καλός καθηγητής
       'He's a good professor'

The article can be omitted from noun phrases following σαν 'like' unless the noun phrase denotes a specific person or thing:

   (6) σκληρό σαν πέτρα
       'hard as stone'
   (7) Έτρεμε σαν πουλί [also σαν το πουλί]
       'S/he was trembling like a bird'

When a noun is used in a *partitive* sense (whether it is plural or denotes a substance or abstract concept), it is used without an article. In such cases the noun denotes neither a specific instance of the item concerned, nor all of this item in general:

   (8) ένα ποτήρι **νερό**
       'a glass of water'
   (9) ένα άγαλμα από **πέτρα**
       'a statue [made] of stone'

Further examples of partitive uses are the following; here the noun phrases act as direct objects of verbs:

   (10) Μ' αρέσει να τρώω **ψάρι**
        'I like eating fish' (neither a particular fish, nor all fish, but simply
          the fish I eat)
   (11) Γράφει **βιβλία**
        'S/he writes books' (cf. Αγαπάει **τα βιβλία** 'S/he loves books *or*
          the books': in the first case, books as a whole are referred to)
   (12) Θέλω **ψωμί**
        'I want some bread' (neither particular bread, nor all bread in
          general)
   (13) Έχω **λεφτά**
        'I have money *or* some money'
   (14) Μυρίζεις **κολόνια**
        'You smell of cologne'

The article is also omitted in partitive expressions where the noun phrase concerned is the subject of a verb:

   (15) Υπάρχει ψωμί
        'There's bread'
   (16) Χύθηκε νερό στο τραπέζι
        '[Some] water has spilt on the table'

Apart from such partitive expressions, subjects do not normally appear as bare indefinites (i.e. without an article or determiner). However, it is possible to have an indefinite subject with a postmodifier when it does not denote a specific item:

(17)   **Γυναίκα που δεν αγαπάει τα παιδία της** είναι λύκαινα
'**[A] woman who doesn't love her children** is a she-wolf'

In journalistic styles (and not only in headlines) an indefinite subject often appears with specific reference:

(18)   **Πατέρας** σκότωσε το γιο του
'**[A] father** killed his son'

The article may be absent from a noun phrase acting as the direct object of a verb, where the speaker does not feel the need to stress the specificity of the object but only its kind:

(19)   Γράφω βιβλίο
'I'm writing **[a] book**'
(20)   Δίνω διαταγή
'I give **[an] order**'
(21)   Φορούσε κόκκινο πουκάμισο
'He was wearing **[a] red shirt**'

The presence or absence of the indefinite article distinguishes between non-specific and specific meanings of a noun:

(22)a. Αυτό το έργο θυμίζει **ένα ντοκιμαντέρ** που είδα πέρσι
'This film is reminiscent of a documentary I saw last year' (i.e. a particular documentary)
  b. Αυτό το έργο θυμίζει **ντοκιμαντέρ**
'This film is reminiscent of a documentary' (not a particular documentary, but documentaries as a class)
(23)a. Βρήκα **ένα ρολόι**
'I found [*or* I've found] a watch' (e.g. one that someone has left in my house)
  b. Επιτέλους βρήκα **ρολόι**
'At last I found [*or* I've found] a watch' (i.e. I didn't have one before)

The presence of an article is not necessary in a direct object noun phrase in clauses that are not positive and assertive (e.g. negative (24–25), interrogative (26) or conditional (27)):

(24)   Δεν έχω **γάτα**
'I haven't got **[a] cat**'
(25)   Δεν οδηγώ **αυτοκίνητο**
'I don't drive **[a] car**'

(26) Έχεις **μολύβι**;
'Have you got **[a] pencil**?'
(27) Αν είχα **ρολόι** θα ήξερα τι ώρα είναι
'If I had **[a] watch** I would know what time it is'

In many more or less fixed collocations consisting of verb+noun object the noun is *not* accompanied by an article. The verbs that appear most frequently in such expressions are έχω 'I have' and κάνω 'I do/make'. Such expressions include: έχω διάθεση (να) 'I'm in the mood (to)', έχω δίκιο 'I'm right', δεν έχω ιδέα 'I've no idea', έχω καιρό (να) 'I have time (to); I haven't [done something] for some time', έχω πεποίθηση (σε) 'I have confidence (in)', έχω πονοκέφαλο 'I've got a headache', έχει σημασία 'it's important', έχω σκοπό (να) 'I intend (to)', έχω χρέος (να) 'I have a duty (to)', κάνω εμετό 'I vomit', κάνω εντύπωση 'I make an impression', κάνει ζέστη 'it's hot [of weather]', κάνω μάθημα 'I'm having/giving a lesson', κάνω μπάνιο 'I have a bath/swim', κάνω νόημα 'I signal', κάνω φασαρία 'I make a fuss/row'. Other such expressions without the article include δηλώνω συμμετοχή 'I register my entry [for a competition, etc.]', σπουδάζω μουσική 'I study music', παίζω πιάνο 'I play the piano'.

In addition, the article is absent from a large number of other collocations consisting of preposition+noun phrase, usually in cases where the preposition is being used in a non-concrete sense (e.g. σε τελευταία ανάλυση 'in the last analysis', από επιστημονική άποψη 'from a scientific viewpoint', σε κοινωνικό επίπεδο 'on a social level', με προθυμία 'willingly' [lit. 'with willingness'], κατά προσέγγιση 'approximately' [lit. 'according-to approximation']); in addition, the preposition μέσω 'via' normally takes a noun phrase without an article (μέσω Αθηνών 'via Athens'). The article is also absent from the second noun phrase in many fixed collocations consisting of noun phrase+noun phrase, in which the second noun is abstract and in the genitive (e.g. λόγος υπάρξεως '*raison d'être*', άδεια οδηγήσεως 'driving licence', δελτίο ταυτότητος 'identity card'). The article is also absent from the genitive noun phrase in street names and titles of institutions (e.g. η οδός Κοραή 'Korais Street', το Πανεπιστήμιο Αιγαίου 'the University of the Aegean', ο Δήμος Αίγινας 'Aegina Council'). In such cases, where a noun phrase in the genitive without an article depends on another noun, the second noun often appears in its *katharevousa* form (as illustrated by υπάρξεως, οδηγήσεως and ταυτότητος above).

2.6   THE ADJECTIVE

The adjective normally inflects for gender, number, and case. (There are a few exceptions, namely indeclinable adjectives such as μπλε 'blue'.) The prime function of an adjective is to modify a noun, to which it attributes a certain quality (for elliptical uses of the adjective see Section 2.6.1). An adjective normally modifies a noun in one of two ways: *attributively* or *predicatively*.

In *attributive* use an adjective modifies a noun within the same noun phrase:

(1) μια **κόκκινη** καρέκλα
    'a red chair'
(2) ο **ωραίος** άντρας
    'the handsome man'

In attributive use the adjective must agree with its noun in gender, number, and case.

The normal position of an adjective in attributive use is before the noun; where an article is present, the adjective appears between the article and the noun, as in examples (1–2). The adjective may however appear after the noun for special emphasis; in such cases, if the noun is preceded by the definite article, the definite article must be repeated before the adjective:

(3) μια καρέκλα **κόκκινη**
    'a *red* chair'
(4) ο άντρας **ο ωραίος**
    'the *handsome* man'

In *predicative* use an adjective appears as a subject predicate, in which case it modifies and agrees with the subject (5–8), or an object predicate, in which case it modifies and agrees with the direct object (9–10):

(5) Αυτή η καρέκλα είναι **κόκκινη**
     'This chair is red'
(6) Εκείνος ο άντρας είναι **ωραίος**
     'That man is handsome'
(7) Ο Γιώργος παντρεύτηκε **μικρός**
     'George got married young'
(8) Το τσάι πίνεται **ζεστό** ή **κρύο**
     'Tea is drunk hot or cold'
(9) Έβαψαν την καρέκλα **κόκκινη**
     'They painted the chair red'
(10) Ο Θεός τον έπλασε **ωραίο**
     'God created him handsome'

In predicative use an adjective must agree in gender, number, and case with the noun or 3rd-person pronoun that it modifies. In the absence of a noun or a 3rd-person pronoun, as in examples (11–12), the predicative adjective normally agrees with the gender and number of the subject or object:

(11) Είναι **ωραίος** (masc.) *or* **ωραία** (fem.) (subject predicate)
     'S/he's handsome'
(12) Σε βλέπω **χλωμό** (masc.) *or* **χλωμή** (fem.) (object predicate)
     'You look pale to me' [lit. 'I see you pale']

A whole clause may be modified by an adjective in predicative use, whether the clause is the subject (13) or the direct object (14) of the verb; clauses are neuter singular:

(13) Είναι **άγνωστο** πότε θα έρθει
     'It is not known when s/he/it will come'
(14) Θεωρώ **βέβαιο** ότι θα κερδίσουμε τις εκλογές
     'I consider it certain that we will win the elections'

Certain adjectives may be used in the neuter singular in exclamatory single-word sentences:

(15) Περίεργο! Δεν το πρόσεξα.
     '[It's] strange! I never noticed.'

Here it is the fact that I never noticed that is strange.

The adjective can also be used in apposition to a noun phrase, which it may either precede or follow:

(16)a. Σοβαρός, ο καθηγητής συνέχισε το μάθημα
    b. Ο καθηγητής, σοβαρός, συνέχισε το μάθημα
       'Serious [i.e. 'still serious' or 'once again serious'], the
        professor continued the lesson'

Examples (16a–b) have the same meaning.

The *passive perfect participle* functions in the same way as an adjective:

(17) η **βαμμένη** καρέκλα (attributive)
     'The painted chair'
(18) Είναι **καμωμένος** έτσι (predicative: subject predicate)
     'He's made that way'
(19) Το άσπρο κρασί πίνεται **παγωμένο** (predicative: subject
        predicate)
     'White wine is [best] drunk chilled'
(20) Τον βρήκαμε **πεσμένο** στο πάτωμα (predicative: object
        predicate)
     'We found him lying [lit. 'fallen'] on the floor'

For further details on the use of the passive perfect participle see Section 1.8.2.1.

Adjectives may be modified by adverbs (21), prepositional phrases (22), noun phrases in the genitive (23), and weak personal pronouns in the genitive (24):

(21) Το πρόβλημα είναι **καθαρά** οικονομικό
     'The problem is purely economic'
(22) Είναι δυνατή **στα μαθηματικά**
     'She's good [lit. 'strong'] at maths'
(23) ένας ποιητής άξιος **του ονόματος** (objective genitive)
     'a poet worthy of the name' (cf. Αξίζει το όνομα 'He deserves
     the name')
(24) ένας γνωστός **μου** γιατρός
     'a doctor who is an acquaintance of mine' [lit. 'a known-to-me
     doctor']

An adjective may have a clause as a complement (25–26: see also Section
5.3.4.3):

(25) Είναι ικανός **να κάνει τη δουλειά;**
     'Is he capable **of doing the job?**'
(26) Είμαι σίγουρη **ότι δε θα έρθουν**
     'I'm sure **they won't come**'

As in English, most adjectives may be used both attributively and predicatively, yet some may have different meanings in attributive and
predicative use. Some adjectives that commonly modify certain nouns in
attributive use can hardly do so at all in predicative use (27–28); others
cannot do so with the same meaning (29–32), and some of these can
modify the same nouns predicatively only in unusual contexts (33–36):

(27)a. ο κύριος λόγος
       'the chief reason'
   b. *αυτός ο λόγος είναι κύριος, but
   c. αυτός ο λόγος είναι **ο** κύριος
       'this reason is the chief [one]'
(28)a. ο αστικός κώδικας
       'the civil code'
   b. *αυτός ο κώδικας είναι αστικός
(29)a. νομικός σύμβουλος
       'legal adviser'
   b. αυτός ο σύμβουλος είναι νομικός
       'this adviser is a jurist' (here νομικός acts as a noun)
(30)a. μεγάλος ψεύτης
       'a big liar'
   b. αυτός ο ψεύτης είναι μεγάλος
       'this liar is big [in size *or* grown-up *or* old]'
(31)a. ο μόνος φίλος
       'the only friend'
   b. αυτός ο φίλος είναι μόνος
       'this friend is lonely', but

c. αυτός ο φίλος είναι **ο** μόνος
'this friend is the only [one]'

(32)a. έτοιμα ρούχα
'ready-made (off-the-peg) clothes'

b. αυτά τα ρούχα είναι έτοιμα
'these clothes are ready'

(33)a. στενός φίλος μου
'a close friend of mine'

b. ?ο φίλος μου είναι στενός
'my friend is narrow'

(34)a. παλιός φίλος μου
'an old friend'

b. ?ο φίλος μου είναι παλιός
'my friend is an old habitué, etc.'

(35)a. αληθινός ήρωας
'a real hero'

b. ?αυτός ο ήρωας είναι αληθινός
'this hero is for real'

(36)a. καθαρό μίσος
'pure hatred'

b. ?αυτό το μίσος είναι καθαρό
'this hatred is pure'

For agreement of gender, number, and case between an adjective and more than one noun see Section 1.9.1 and Appendix 4.

A noun may be modified by more than one adjective. In attributive use these may simply be placed together before the noun, possibly separated from each other by commas or by comma intonation:

(37) ένα **μικρό, ωραίο, χαριτωμένο** παιδί
'a little, beautiful, charming child'

(For the order of adjectives modifying a single noun see Section 2.11.)
In both attributive and predicative use two adjectives may be linked by και or αλλά:

(38) ένα **καθαρό και γρήγορο** τραίνο
'a clean, fast train'

(39) Το τραίνο είναι **καθαρό και γρήγορο**
'The train is clean and fast'

(40) ένα **καλογραμμένο αλλά ανιαρό** βιβλίο
'a well-written but boring book'

(41) Αυτό το βιβλίο είναι **καλογραμμένο αλλά ανιαρό**
'This book is well-written but boring'

Alternatively, when two adjectives are used attributively to modify the same noun, one of them may appear before the noun and one after it:

(42) ένα **γρήγορο** τραίνο **καθαρό**
      (almost same meaning as example (38), but with (possibly
      contrastive) emphasis on καθαρό)

An adjective in attributive use normally follows the noun that it modifies
if the adjective is itself modified by a phrase or clause:

(43) τρία βιβλία **παρόμοια με το προηγούμενο**
      'three books similar to the previous one'

In formal styles, however, an adjectival phrase consisting of an adjective
or past participle passive modified by a phrase may be placed before the
noun that it modifies:

(44) **αποκλεισμένα από το χιόνι** χωριά
      'villages cut off by the snow'

Although Greek frequently uses substantivized adjectives (see Section
2.6.1), the adjective and the noun constitute distinct categories, as is shown
by the fact that the adjective, unlike the noun, has sets of forms for each of
the three genders. One area in which the distinction between noun and
adjective is not the same as in English is the one which concerns nouns
and adjectives denoting nationalities. In Greek a noun, not an adjective,
denoting nationality is used to modify another noun denoting a person.
Examples (45a–b) show the masculine and feminine form of the *noun* being
used for a male and female respectively, while (45c–e) show the *adjective*
being used in all three genders to modify nouns denoting non-humans:

(45)a. ο Γάλλος (masc.) πρωθυπουργός
     b. η Γαλλίδα (fem.) πρωθυπουργός
         'the French Prime Minister'
     c. ο γαλλικός προϋπολογισμός
         'the French budget'
     d. η γαλλική κουζίνα
         'French cuisine'
     e. το γαλλικό χιούμορ
         'French humour'

2.6.1 THE SUBSTANTIVIZATION OF ADJECTIVES

An adjective may act as the head of a noun phrase, that is, without a
noun being present. Examples of this phenomenon, which occurs particularly with an adjective in the masculine or feminine denoting a person
or persons (ένας πλούσιος 'a rich man', μια πλούσια 'a rich woman', οι
πλούσιοι 'the rich'), have already been given in Section 2.5.1, as have
elliptical uses of an adjective denoting an item that has already been
mentioned (το μαύρο 'the black one').

Greek also uses a large number of substantivized adjectives (i.e. adjectives used as nouns) that have taken on specific meanings in this elliptical use. In such cases the adjective acts as the head of the noun phrase, while the noun itself, which is omitted, is 'understood'. The adjective appears in the gender and number appropriate to the noun that has been omitted. This way of substantivizing an adjective is productive, in the sense that new examples of substantivized adjectives can readily be created. In each of the following examples the substantivized adjective is followed by the omitted noun in square brackets:

(1) το δημοτικό [σχολείο]
     'primary school'
(2) η δημοτική [γλώσσα]
     'the demotic language'
(3) οι δημοτικές [εκλογές]
     'municipal elections'
(4) ο περσικός [κόλπος]
     'the Persian Gulf'
(5) καθηγητής της αγγλικής [γλώσσας]
     'teacher of English'
(6) Λείπει με δίωρη [άδεια]
     'S/he's away on two-hour leave'
(7) ο κωδικός [αριθμός]
     'code' (esp. area code in telephone numbers, or postcode)
(8) η Φιλοσοφική [Σχολή]
     'the Arts Faculty'
(9) ο τελικός [αγώνας]
     'the final (in sport)'
(10) το τετραγωνικό [μέτρο]
     'the square metre'
(11) Προτιμώ το πράσινο παρά το κόκκινο [χρώμα]
     'I prefer green to red'

Different meanings of the same adjective may be distinguished by gender, as in examples (1–3). In some cases, however, the same adjective in the same gender may have more than one meaning, according to the context:

(12) η λαϊκή
     [αγορά] 'street-market'
     [γλώσσα] 'slang'
(13) η πρώτη
     [παράσταση] 'première'
     [ταχύτητα] 'first gear'

The neuter singular of an adjective is often used to denote a national or international political problem (14: with ζήτημα 'question' or πρόβλημα 'problem' understood), whereas the neuter plural of an adjective (often a derivative of a noun denoting a month) is used to denote a series of incidents that took place at a particular time (15):

(14) το κυπριακό
'the Cyprus question'
(15) τα Δεκεμβριανά
'the December events [in Athens in 1944]'

An adjective may be considered to have become so thoroughly substantivized that it may itself be modified by an adjective:

(16) ο ισπανικός εμφύλιος [πόλεμος]
'the Spanish Civil War'

Some neuter adjectives have become substantivized without the omission of a noun, e.g. το ενδιαφέρον '[the] interest', το γλυκό '[the] sweet'.
The neuter form of an adjective may be used as an abstract noun:

(17) Το καλό/κακό με το Γιάννη είναι ότι . . .
'The good/bad thing about John is that . . .'

The abstract use of a neuter adjective is often found in theoretical discourse, perhaps through the omission of στοιχείο 'element':

(18) το φανταστικό και το ονειρώδες στην τέχνη
'the imaginary and the dreamy [element] in art'

In formal styles, the neuter singular of an adjective (often in its *katharevousa* form with final -v) may be used as an abstract noun when there is no separate abstract noun derived from it. Such a substantivized adjective is typically followed by a noun phrase in the genitive:

(19) **Το νεαρόν της ηλικίας τους** δεν τους επέτρεπε να έχουν απόλυτη συναίσθηση ευθύνης
'Their young age [lit. '**the young[ness] of their age**'] did not permit them to have a full sense of responsibility'
(20) Η ύπαρξη της συμφωνίας αυτής αποτελεί προϋπόθεση **του παραδεκτού της αίτησης** (παραδεκτός 'acceptable')
'The existence of this agreement constitutes a precondition **for the acceptability of the application**'

2.6.2   THE COMPARATIVE AND SUPERLATIVE OF ADJECTIVES

The *comparative* of the adjective indicates that the item denoted by the noun possesses a higher degree of the attribute denoted by the adjective as compared with something else. The comparative is normally formed in one of two ways: (i) morphologically, through the use of the inflection

-τερος, and (ii) syntactically, through the use of πιο. Thus: φυσικός 'natural', φυσικότερος or πιο φυσικός 'more natural'. The comparative of adverbs is formed in a similar way (φυσικά 'naturally', φυσικότερα or πιο φυσικά 'more naturally'); see Part II, Section 3.14 for further details on the formation of the comparative of adjectives, and Part III, Section 5.4.2.1 for the syntax of comparison. In more abstract styles πιο is sometimes replaced by περισσότερο, although this is never necessary: περισσότερο φυσικός 'more natural'. There is no difference of usage or meaning between the two types of comparative. The use of both the syntactical and the morphological constructions at the same time (e.g. πιο καλύτερος, lit. 'more better'), although frequently found in speech and writing, is disapproved of by some grammarians.

There is no morphological form of the comparative of passive perfect participles. Instead, the construction with πιο or περισσότερο is used: thus πιο [or περισσότερο] κουρασμένος 'more tired', πιο [or περισσότερο] φορτισμένος 'more highly charged'.

The comparative forms of the adjective are also used in certain comparative constructions involving the phrases όσο μπορώ (in the appropriate form), όσο γίνεται, όσο το δυνατόν (all these three phrases have the same meaning) or the correlative pronoun ό,τι:

(1) Πάρε όσο μπορείς/όσο γίνεται/όσο το δυνατόν πιο μεγάλα/
    μεγαλύτερα αβγά
    'Get as large eggs as you can [as possible]'
(2) Πάρε ό,τι καλύτερο
    'Get the best thing there is'

Greek adjectives have two types of *superlative* forms, each with a different meaning.

The *relative superlative*, which indicates that the item denoted by the noun phrase possesses comparatively the highest degree of the attribute denoted by the adjective, is formed in exactly the same way as the comparative, but with the addition of the definite article in front of it. Thus:

(3) Οι γιατροί διαφωνούν για το ποιος είναι **ο φυσικότερος** [*or* **ο
    πιο φυσικός**] τρόπος γέννησης
    'Doctors disagree as to which is the most natural method of
    childbirth'

The relative superlative is sometimes used instead of the comparative in constructions such as the following:

(4) ο καλύτερος από όλους τους άλλους
    'the best of all' [lit. 'the best from all the others']

Such a construction is an alternative for (5a) and (5b):

(5)a. ο καλύτερος από όλους
'the best of all'
  b. καλύτερος από όλους τους άλλους
'better than all the rest'

The *absolute superlative*, which indicates that the item denoted by the noun phrase possesses absolutely the highest degree of the attribute denoted by the adjective, is formed through the ending -τατος, e.g. φυσικότατος. There is no exact equivalent of the absolute superlative in English; it might be rendered in some such way as 'very natural', 'absolutely natural', 'totally natural', etc.:

(6) Τέτοια συμπεριφορά είναι φυσικότατη
'Such behaviour is completely natural'

The converse of the comparative and the relative superlative (i.e. 'less' and 'least') is expressed by [o] λιγότερο + adjective:

(7) ένας λιγότερο φυσικός τρόπος γέννησης
'a less natural method of childbirth'
(8) ο λιγότερο φυσικός τρόπος γέννησης
'the least natural method of childbirth'

2.7 NUMERALS

A numeral is a word that expresses a number. Numerals are divided into *cardinals* ('one', 'two' 'three', etc.) and *ordinals* ('first', 'second', 'third', etc.).

From the morphological point of view Greek *cardinal numerals* may be divided into three categories: (a) *indeclinable cardinals*, (b) *declinable cardinals*, and (c) *cardinals behaving like nouns*. (For further information on forms see Part II, Section 6.)

(a) Indeclinable cardinals
All cardinal numerals are indeclinable except 'one', 'three', and 'four'; the hundreds from 'two hundred' to 'nine hundred' inclusive; 'thousand'; and 'million' (and 'billion', etc.). Thus, as in examples (1–3), πέντε 'five' does not inflect for gender and case:

(1) οι πέντε άντρες (masc. nom.)
'the five men'
(2) τις πέντε γυναίκες (fem. acc.)
'the five women'
(3) των πέντε παιδιών (neut. gen.)
'of the five children'

(b) Declinable cardinals

The following cardinal numerals behave like adjectives, in that they are declinable and they agree in gender, number, and case with the noun or other item that they modify (see Part II, Section 6.2 for details on their inflection):

ένας, μια, ένα 'one'
τρεις, τρία 'three'
τέσσερις, τέσσερα 'four'
διακόσιοι, διακόσιες, διακόσια 'two hundred', τριακόσιοι,
   τριακόσιες, τριακόσια 'three hundred', etc.
χίλιοι, χίλιες, χίλια 'one thousand' (for 'two thousand' and above see
   (c) below)

(4) ένας άντρας
     'one man'
(5) μια γυναίκα
     'one woman'
(6) ενός παιδιού
     'of one child'
(7) στους πεντακόσιους επιβάτες
     'to the five hundred passengers'
(8) πεντακόσιες εργάτριες
     'five hundred women workers'
(9) πεντακόσια αγόρια
     'five hundred boys'
(10) χίλιοι άντρες
     'a thousand men'
(11) χίλιες γυναίκες
     'a thousand women'
(12) των χίλιων παιδιών
     'of the thousand children'

When counting, the neuter form of the numerals is used (ένα, δύο, τρία, τέσσερα, etc.).

(c) Cardinals behaving like nouns

The following cardinal numerals behave like nouns:

[δυο, τρεις, etc.] χιλιάδες (fem. pl.) '[two, three, etc.] thousand' (for 'one thousand' see (b) above; χιλιάδες is also an *inclusive*: see below)
ένα εκατομμύριο (neut. sg.) 'one million'; plural [δυο, τρία, etc.] εκατομμύρια '[two, three, etc.] million'
ένα δισεκατομμύριο (neut. sg.) 'one billion'; plural [δυο, τρία, etc.] δισεκατομμύρια '[two, three, etc.] billion'

The numerals in (c) normally appear in the same case as the nouns which they modify:

(13) Το δάσος περιέχει **τρεις χιλιάδες δέντρα** (acc. pl.)
'The forest contains three thousand trees'
(14) ένα ποσόν **τεσσάρων εκατομμυρίων δραχμών** (gen. pl.)
'a sum of four million drachmas'

For more details on these constructions (including the alternative construction in which the noun phrase after the numeral appears in the genitive) see Section 2.12. For cardinal numerals followed by weak personal pronouns see also Section 2.4.3.3(ii).

'Zero' is expressed by the noun μηδέν (neut. sg.). It may be used with or without the definite article:

(15) τρεις βαθμοί κάτω από το μηδέν
'three degrees below zero'
(16) Του έβαλα μηδέν
'I gave him nought' (i.e. when marking his school-work)

When 'zero' or 'nought' denotes the symbol '0', it is called μηδενικό:

(17) τρία μηδενικά
'three noughts'

'Halves' are expressed in the following way. 'Half of a/the' (followed by a word denoting a thing, substance, etc.) is expressed by μισός, which is an *adjective* that agrees with the noun or other item that it modifies:

(18) Δώσ' μου μισό πορτοκάλι
'Give me half an orange'
(19) Δώσ' μου το μισό πορτοκάλι
'Give me half of the orange'
(20) Δώσ' μου τα μισά πορτοκάλια
'Give me half of the oranges'

When 'a/the half' does not modify a noun phrase, it is expressed by the neuter *noun* μισό (21); when 'a/the half' is accompanied by an abstract noun, the noun μισό may again be used (22):

(21) Θα φας το άλλο μισό;
'Will you eat the other half?'
(22) το μισό του πληθυσμού
'half of the population'

Greek has a special way of expressing a whole number followed by a half ('one and a half' to 'nineteen and a half' inclusive) by means of compound words.

When 'one and a half' is used to modify a noun, it is fully inflected. Not only are the gender and case of the noun reflected in the ending, but its gender is also reflected in the first part of the compound word: ενάμισης (masc. nom.), ενάμιση (masc. acc. and gen.), μιάμιση (fem. nom. and acc.), μιάμισης (fem. gen.), ενάμισι (neut. all cases). Note that these forms are singular and modify a singular noun:

(23) ενάμισης τόνος (masc. nom.)
       'one and a half tons'
(24) ένα φορτίο ενάμιση τόνου (masc. gen.)
       'a load of one and a half tons'
(25) στη μιάμιση (fem. acc.)
       'at half past one'
(26) ένα μάθημα μιάμισης ώρας (fem. gen.)
       'a one-and-a-half-hour lesson'
(27) ενάμισι κιλό (neut. nom./acc.)
       'one and a half kilos'
(28) ένα μπουκάλι ενάμισι λίτρου (neut. gen.)
       'a one-and-a-half-litre bottle'

Δυόμισι 'two and a half' is indeclinable, while τρεισήμισι (masc. and fem.), τριάμισι (neut.) 'three and a half', and τεσσερισήμισι (masc. and fem.), τεσσεράμισι (neut.) 'four and a half' have two separate gender forms each but do not distinguish case. The following forms are indeclinable: πεντέμισι 'five and a half', εξήμισι 'six and a half', εφτάμισι 'seven and a half', οχτώμισι 'eight and a half', εννιάμισι 'nine and a half', δεκάμισι 'ten and a half', εντεκάμισι 'eleven and a half', and δωδεκάμισι 'twelve and a half'. The forms from μιάμιση to δωδεκάμισι are frequently used in telling the time (as in example 25 above); the feminine forms are used where they exist. Δεκατρεισήμισι, δεκατριάμισι 'thirteen and a half', and δεκατεσσερισήμισι, δεκατεσσεράμισι 'fourteen and a half' distinguish between masc./fem. and neuter, while the rest of these forms, from δεκαπεντέμισι 'fifteen and a half' to δεκαεννιάμισι 'nineteen and a half', are indeclinable. All these compounds may be used when expressing young people's ages. All except ενάμισης modify plural nouns. (Note on spelling: the rule laid down in Greek school grammars is that masculine or feminine forms meaning 'one and a half' end in -η[ς], while the neuter, together with all other forms meaning 'n and a half', end in -ι.)

Alternatively, 'one and a half', etc., may be expressed by using the numeral for the whole number followed either by και μισό when there is no noun present or understood, or by a noun and και μισός in the appropriate form to agree with the noun:

(29) ένας τόνος και μισός
       'one and a half tons' (=23)

(30) μία ώρα και μισή
'one and half hours'

(31) στη μία και μισή
'at half past one' (=25)

This construction (numeral+και μισός) may be used with all numerals.
Other *fractions* are expressed with *ordinal* numerals (see below).

Similar to the cardinal numerals included in (c) above are two types of
collective noun indicating groups (see also Part II, Section 6.1, note 12):

(i)   *inclusive collective* nouns indicating 'a group of [a certain number]'
      (μονάδα 'unit', δυάδα 'set of two; dyad', τριάδα 'group of three;
      Trinity', τετράδα 'group of four', πεντάδα 'group of five', etc.). In the
      singular these are normally followed by the genitive plural (μια
      πεντάδα εκπροσώπων 'a group of five representatives'). Inclusives
      denoting larger round numbers (δεκάδες 'tens', εκατοντάδες
      'hundreds', χιλιάδες 'thousands', μυριάδες 'tens of thousands;
      myriads') are frequently used, typically in the plural, where they may
      modify a noun in the same case (χιλιάδες πουλιά 'thousands of birds').
      They may also be used in the plural, without modifying a noun, in
      phrases such as the following:

      (32) Οι χιτλερικοί στρατιώτες εξόντωναν **με τις εκατοντάδες** τους
            "συμμορίτες"
            'Hitler's troops used to exterminate the "bandits" by the
            hundred [*or* in their hundreds]'

(ii) *approximative collective* nouns, which indicate an approximate number
      from 'ten' upwards (usually a multiple of ten, but also 'twelve' and
      'fifteen'). Approximatives are normally preceded by καμιά. When an
      approximative is followed by a noun, this noun appears in the same
      case as the approximative:

      (33) Ήρθαν καμιά δεκαριά φίλοι μας
            'About ten friends of ours came'
      (34) Είδαμε καμιά δωδεκαριά φίλους μας
            'We saw about a dozen friends of ours'
      (35) καμιά εκατοστή άτομα
            'about a hundred people'

The noun ντουζίνα 'dozen' is not necessarily accompanied by καμιά:

      (36) μια ντουζίνα μπουκάλια
            'a dozen bottles'

Ordinal numerals indicate the order in which the relevant item occurs in
a series (e.g. πρώτος 'first', δεύτερος 'second', τρίτος 'third', τελευταίος
'last'). They are declinable adjectives that agree with the noun or other

item that they modify. For a list of the ordinal numerals see Part II, Section 6.1. Among their other uses, ordinals can denote the number of a king, patriarch, pope, etc. (e.g. ο Γεώργιος ο Δεύτερος 'George the Second'); in addition, they are often used in Greek where English uses cardinals (e.g. Κεφάλαιο Τέταρτο 'Chapter Four', Σκηνή Τρίτη 'Scene Three').

The neuter form of ordinals is also used to express *fractions* apart from 'half' (for which see above). The expression of a fraction normally consists of def. art.+cardinal+ordinal (all in the neuter), optionally followed by a noun phrase in the genitive:

(37) το ένα τέταρτο του κιλού
      'a quarter of a kilo'
(38) τα τρία πέμπτα του πληθυσμού
      'three fifths of the population'

Two other types of adjectives are related to numerals:

(a) *multiplicatives*, meaning 'single', 'double', 'triple', etc. 'Single' is usually απλός (also 'simple'), but μονός when talking about beds or hotel rooms (for the other forms see Part II, Section 6.1, note 10):

(39) ένα απλό εισιτήριο
      'a single ticket' (i.e. not a return ticket)
(40) ένα μονό δωμάτιο
      'a single room'
(41) ένα διπλό κρεβάτι
      'a double bed'
(42) μια τριπλή νίκη
      'a triple victory'

(b) *relatives*, expressing multiples, i.e. διπλάσιος 'twice as big/much', τριπλάσιος 'three times as big/much' (for forms see Part II, Section 6.1, note 11); these may be used as adjectives or neuter nouns:

(43) ένα κρεβάτι διπλάσιο
      'a bed twice the size' (contrast 41)
(44) Ο μισθός σου είναι διπλάσιος από το δικό μου
      'Your salary is twice as big as mine'
(45) Πλήρωσα τα τριπλάσια
      'I paid three times as much'

Word order

Most types of numeral normally immediately precede the noun which they modify (or the adjective if there is one):

(46) δυο τραπέζια
      'two tables'

(47) τα δυο τραπέζια
      'the two tables'
(48) και τα δυο κόκκινα τραπέζια
      'both of the red tables'

When a cardinal and an ordinal both modify the same noun, the cardinal normally precedes the ordinal, although the reverse order is also possible:

(49) τα δυο πρώτα τραπέζια *or* τα πρώτα δυο τραπέζια
      'the first two tables'
(50) τα δυο τελευταία τραπέζια *or* τα τελευταία δυο τραπέζια
      'the last two tables'

Ordinals, multiplicatives and relatives, which are really adjectives, may appear before or after the noun they modify. The ordinal appears after the noun in titles of kings, patriarchs, popes, chapters, scenes, etc. (as in the examples Ο Γεώργιος ο Δεύτερος, Κεφάλαιο Τέταρτο, Σκηνή Τρίτη, given earlier in this Section). See example (43) above for an example of a relative numeral used after a noun.

Pairs of cardinal numerals may be used in two different ways. The *same* numeral when repeated means 'one by one', etc.:

(51) Τα ζώα μπήκαν δύο δύο
      'The animals came in two by two'

When two *different* cardinal numerals appear together they express approximation. Although in such expressions the declinable numerals agree in gender, number and case with the noun they modify, the neuter expression ένα δυο (alternatively κάνα δυο) may be used colloquially with a plural noun in any gender or case:

(52) Ήρθαν μία δύο *or* ένα δυο *or* κάνα δυο φίλες μου
      'One or two (a couple) of my [female] friends came'
(53) Έμεινα τρεις τέσσερις μήνες στην Ελλάδα
      'I stayed in Greece for three or four months'
(54) σε είκοσι τριάντα χρόνια
      'in twenty or thirty years'

When expressing *hours and dates* the feminine forms of the cardinal numerals are used (55–56), except for the first of a month, when the feminine singular of the ordinal πρώτη is used (57):

(55) Είναι τρεις η ώρα
      'It's three o'clock'
(56) στις τέσσερις
      'at four [o'clock]; on the fourth [of the month]'
(57) την πρώτη Απριλίου *or* την πρώτη του Απρίλη
      'on the first of April'

Years are expressed by cardinal numerals, usually with the neuter singular form of the definite article:

(58) Γεννήθηκα το [χίλια εννιακόσια] σαράντα έξι
      'I was born in [nineteen] forty-six'

Arithmetical operations are expressed in a variety of ways. There are two alternative ways of expressing 'plus' (59) and two alternative words for 'minus' (60). There is yet another, more colloquial, way of expressing 'minus' (see alternative in brackets in 60). In multiplication the feminine forms of the multiplied numerals are used, optionally with the feminine article between them (61), or alternatively the neuter forms with or without επί while in all operations the word for 'equals' (ίσον) may be omitted:

(59) 2 + 3 = 5   δύο και/συν τρία [ίσον] πέντε
(60) 6 − 5 = 1   έξι πλην/μείον πέντε (*or* πέντε από έξι) [ίσον]
                     ένα
(61) 3 × 4 = 12   τρεις οι τέσσερις (*or* τρία [επί] τεσσερα) δώδεκα
(62) 20 ÷ 4 = 5   είκοσι διά τέσσερα *or* το τέσσερα στο είκοσι
                     [ίσον] πέντε

When specifying the measurements of areas, επί is used:

(63) ένα κελί τρία επί τέσσερα
      'a three by four [metre] cell'

Percentages are expressed by the phrase τοις εκατό (πέντε τοις εκατό 'five per cent'), or more colloquially by στα εκατό (πέντε στα εκατό).

Decimals are expressed in a variety of ways. For example, Anglo-American 2.25 'two point two five' is expressed as follows:

(64) 2,25: δύο και είκοσι πέντε, *or* δύο είκοσι πέντε, *or* δύο κόμμα
      είκοσι πέντε

The first of these alternatives is used to express two different decimal units of currency (e.g. pounds and pence, dollars and cents).

Numbers containing many digits (such as telephone numbers) are normally expressed in speech by being divided into pairs, each pair being expressed in terms of tens and units; where there are three digits left at the end, the first is expressed either as a unit or as a hundred:

(65) 39-41-657: τριάντα εννέα σαράντα ένα έξι (*or* εξακόσια)
      πενήντα επτά
      [lit. 'thirty-nine forty-one six (*or* six hundred) fifty-seven']

The *numerical* expression of *cardinal* numbers is normally the same as elsewhere in Europe (outside Britain), i.e. Arabic numerals are used, with the point being used to divide numbers consisting of more than three digits, and the comma used to separate an integer from decimals. Thus in Greek

1.000.000 is 'one million', while 2,25 (as in 64 above) is 'two point two five'. *Ordinal* numbers may be expressed *numerically* by the number (in figures) followed by the inflexional ending (which is accented if it is stressed):

    (66) 19ος (=δέκατος ένατος) '19th'
    (67) 20ός (=εικοστός) '20th'

Numbers can be expressed *alphabetically* by means of Greek letters supplemented by a small number of special signs that are not found in the Greek alphabet (for a complete list see Part II, Section 6.1). Each combination of these symbols, used in lower-case or capital form, is followed by the acute accent. (For the numerical expression of thousands, the relevant letter is preceded by a subscript symbol that resembles an acute accent: ͺα = 1000.) The lower-case forms are often used (like small roman numerals in English) in the pagination of introductory sections of books and in the numbers of items in a list:

    (68) στη σελίδα ια´
           'on page xi'

The capital forms are used (like capital roman numerals in English) after the names of kings, patriarchs, popes, etc., but also to express the number of a chapter, scene, etc.:

    (69) ο Γεώργιος Β´ (=ο Γεώργιος ο Δεύτερος)
           'George II'
    (70) Κεφάλαιο Δ´ (=Κεφάλαιο Τέταρτο)
           'Chapter 4'

Both capital and lower-case forms may be used to express centuries:

    (71) τον ΙΘ´ (*or* ιθ´) αιώνα
           'in the 19th century'

2.8 PRONOUNS AND MISCELLANEOUS DETERMINERS

The following sections deal with the pronouns and with the various determiners that have not yet been covered, i.e. all those except the articles and the adjective.

A ***pronoun*** is a word that has the function and, in general, the distribution, of a noun phrase. It is neither a noun nor an adjective, but it functions as the subject, complement, or object of a verb, or the object of a preposition; it may (in the case of weak personal pronouns) appear in the genitive and depend on a noun, adverb, etc. Pronouns include *personal pronouns* ('I', 'you', 'he', 'she', 'it'), and *other pronouns* (e.g. 'something', 'someone', 'everyone', 'everything', 'nobody', 'nothing', 'who?').

A ***determiner*** is a word that is not an adjective or a numeral but which accompanies a noun (e.g. 'every', 'other', 'same'); although articles belong to the category of determiner, they are treated separately in this book (Sections 2.5ff.). As far as word order is concerned, a determiner normally precedes the noun it accompanies and may be separated from it only by an adjective or another determiner. Exceptions are the qualitative τέτοιος 'such a' and the contrastive άλλος 'other', which may appear either before or after a noun. The quantifiers όλος 'all' and ολόκληρος 'whole' and the demonstratives αυτός, τούτος 'this', and εκείνος 'that' are different from other determiners in that they stand outside the definite article+noun complex.

Since in Greek some of these words may be used either as pronouns or as determiners, while others may be used only as one or the other, it will be convenient to deal first with those that are pronouns alone (Section 2.8.1), then with those that are only determiners (2.8.2), and lastly with those that may perform either function (2.8.3–2.8.3.12). For a correspondence table of pronouns, determiners, and adverbs, see Appendix 1.

2.8.1   PRONOUNS

Pronouns may be divided into *personal pronouns* and *other pronouns*.

2.8.1.1   Personal pronouns

Personal pronouns (εγώ 'I', εσύ 'you', etc.), so called because they indicate whether they refer to the first, second or third person, are inflected for number and case; the third-person pronouns are in addition inflected for gender. For the forms see Part II, Sections 5.1 and 5.2.

Personal pronouns are divided into ***weak (clitic) pronouns*** and ***emphatic pronouns***.

2.8.1.1.1   Weak (clitic) personal pronouns
Weak (clitic) personal pronouns are monosyllabic and unstressed. They are used when the speaker or writer does not wish to emphasize the pronoun.

A weak personal pronoun may

(i)   act as the *direct object* (in the accusative) or the *indirect object* (in the genitive) *of a verb*;

(ii) in the genitive, *depend on a noun*, where the pronoun indicates that the item it denotes *possesses* the item denoted by the noun (possessive pronoun), or where the pronoun indicates the agent or patient of the action indicated by the noun (subjective or objective genitive);

(iii) in the genitive, *follow an adjective, numeral, pronoun, quantifier, or determiner*;

(iv) in the genitive, *depend on an adverb*.

There are also what appear to be nominative forms of the weak pronouns: for their forms see Part II, Section 5.2. Nevertheless, the weak pronoun is not normally used as the subject of a verb: where there is no overt subject present, the personal ending of the verb unambiguously indicates person and number without the need for a pronoun (μπαίνω 'I go in', μπαίνεις 'you (sg.) go in', μπαίνουν 'they go in'). Thus the use of the nominative forms of the weak pronoun is restricted to exclamatory and interrogative constructions involving the words να 'there' and πούν' 'where is/are' (να τος! 'there he is!', πουν' τος; 'where is he?': see Section 2.4.1).

(i)   Weak pronoun as object of verb
(See also Sections 2.4.2 and 2.4.3.1.)

The weak pronoun may act as the object of a verb. When it is the direct object, it appears in the accusative; when it acts as the indirect object, it appears in the genitive. When it is used as the object of a verb, the weak pronoun immediately precedes the verb, except where the imperative or the gerund is used, in which case it immediately follows the verb form. Nothing may separate the weak pronoun from the verb form.

Two weak pronoun objects may co-occur only when (a) the first of them denotes a person *and* (b) the second of them is a third-person form. When two weak pronouns are used, the indirect object (μου in examples 1–4) precedes the direct object (το in examples 1–4); nevertheless, after imperatives and gerunds, the direct object is sometimes found after the indirect object (3–4):

(1) Μου το έδωσες
     'You gave it to me'
(2) Δε θα μου το δώσεις
     'You will not give it to me'
(3) Δώσ' μου το *or* Δώσ' το μου (imperative)
     'Give (sg.) it to me'
(4) δίνοντάς μου το *or* δίνοντάς το μου (gerund)
     'giving it to me'

For the stress phenomenon exemplified in (4) see the end of this section.

In colloquial usage, when the genitive (indirect object) form of the second person singular precedes a third-person singular pronoun before the verb, the σου may be reduced to σ':

(5) Σ' το έδωσα (=Σου το έδωσα, sometimes written Στο έδωσα)
     'I gave it to you'

The neuter singular of the weak pronoun may refer to a whole clause:

(6) – Δεν είμαι καλά σήμερα. – Το ξέρω.
'"I'm not well today." "I know it [i.e. that you're not well today]."'
(7) Γέλασα χωρίς να το θέλω
'I laughed without wanting to [lit. 'wanting it', i.e. 'wanting to laugh']'

The neuter plural of the weak pronoun is used to introduce the announcement of some news:

(8) Τα 'μαθες; Η Μαρία παντρεύτηκε.
'Have you heard? [lit. 'Did you learn it?'] Mary's got married.'

The weak pronoun is used in various forms in colloquial idiomatic phrases where there is no explicit referent. This kind of construction is highly productive, and new expressions are constantly being coined, especially by younger speakers. Here are a few examples out of very many such expressions (see Section 1.1.1.6 for further examples):

(9) την κοπανάω
'I make off'
(10) το παίρνω απόφαση
'I accept the inevitable'
(11) τα βγάζω πέρα
'I get by' (esp. financially)
(12) τη βγάζω [με]
'I get by [with]' (i.e. I survive)
(13) τη βρίσκω [με]
'I get a kick [out of]'
(14) [μου] τη σπάει
'S/he gets on [my] nerves'

The weak pronoun is not normally used as the object of a participle.

(ii)   Weak pronoun dependent on noun
(Pronoun in genitive; see also Section 2.4.3.2.)

The genitive of the weak personal pronoun is used as a *possessive* pronoun:

(15) ο πατέρας **μου**
'**my** father'
(16) τα σπίτια **τους**
'**their** houses'

It is also used to indicate the agent or patient of an action. Example (17) illustrates the *subjective genitive*, where the weak pronoun indicates the person carrying out the action, while example (18) illustrates the *objective genitive*, where the weak pronoun indicates the thing to which something has been done:

(17) η βοήθειά **σου**
    '**your** help' (i.e. the help offered by you)
(18) η κατάργησή **του**
    '**its** abolition' (i.e. the action of abolishing it)

In these uses the weak personal pronoun always follows the noun (except in cases covered in (iii) below).

(iii) Weak pronoun after an adjective, numeral, pronoun, or quantifier (Pronoun in genitive; see also Section 2.4.3.3(ii))

The genitive of the weak personal pronoun may serve a possessive function after an adjective, numeral, or quantifier that precedes a noun. This is usually a stylistic alternative to placing the possessive pronoun after the noun, and it is still the noun that denotes the item possessed:

(19) το παλιό **μου** αυτοκίνητο
    '**my** old car'
(20) οι πέντε **της** κόρες
    '**her** five daughters'
(21) με όλη **μου** την καρδιά
    'with all **my** heart'

In addition, the weak personal pronoun may be used after these classes of word with meanings other than possession.

It may be used after the comparative form of an adjective to express the second term of a comparison (22), or after the relative superlative form of an adjective to indicate the group of items among which the item denoted by the adjective possesses the relevant attribute to the highest degree (23):

(22) Ο Γιάννης είναι μεγαλύτερός **μας**
    'John is bigger/older **than us**'
(23) Ο Γιάννης είναι ο μεγαλύτερός **μας**
    'John is the biggest/oldest **of us**'

The weak pronoun in the genitive plural may be used after a numeral (24), pronoun (25–28), or quantifier (29) in order to specify the person (1st, 2nd, or 3rd) which that term denotes:

(24) οι τρεις **μας**
    'the three **of us**'
(25) κανένας **σας**
    'none **of you**'
(26) μόνος **του**
    'by himself, on **his** own'

(27) ο καθένας **μας**
'each **of us**'

(28) άλλοι **τους**
'others **of them**'

(29) όλοι **τους**
'all **of them**'

(iv) Weak pronoun dependent on an adverb

A weak pronoun in the genitive may also depend on a number of adverbs (mostly adverbs of place; for a list of these adverbs see Section 3.2.7):

(30) ανάμεσά τους
'between them'

(31) μπροστά μου
'in front of me'

As far as stress and intonation are concerned, the weak pronoun is phono-logically attached to the word (verb, noun, adjective, or adverb) on which it depends, forming a single unit with that word. When a weak pronoun follows the word on which it depends and the combination would other-wise result in a series of more than two unstressed syllables after the last stress, the next-but-one syllable after the original stressed syllable also receives a stress. This is illustrated in examples (17), (18), (22), (23), and (30) above, and in (32) below. This phenomenon may also occur when two weak pronouns follow the word on which they depend, as is shown in example (4) above, and in (33) below:

(32) γράφοντάς του
'[while] writing to him'

(33) Δώστε μού το
'Give (pl.) it to me'

For further details on this phenomenon see Part I, Section 1.5.4. For clitic doubling see Part III, Section 5.4.3.3.

2.8.1.1.2 Emphatic personal pronouns
The basic forms of the emphatic personal pronouns consist of more than one syllable (but see below) and are stressed. Separate forms of the emphatic pronouns exist for the first and second persons; these only distin-guish between nominative and oblique cases (i.e. the accusative and genitive are identical). For the third person the demonstratives (αυτός, εκείνος, τούτος) are used (for more details, see Section 2.8.3.2); these decline like adjectives, except that when used as pronouns the masculine accusative singular forms normally have final -ν (αυτόν, εκείνον, τούτον); there are separate emphatic genitive forms (e.g. masc. and neuter gen. sg.

αυτουνού, fem. gen. sg. αυτηνής, all genders gen. pl. αυτωνών) which may be used in colloquial styles instead of the more regular adjectival formations. (For the declension of emphatic personal pronouns see Part II, Section 5.1.)

Emphatic pronouns are used when the speaker or writer wishes to emphasize the pronoun. An emphatic pronoun may stand as the chief or only word in a verbless sentence:

(1) – Ποιος το έκανε; – Εγώ.
    '"Who did it?" "I [did]."'
(2) – Ποιος θέλει κρασί; – Όχι εγώ.
    '"Who wants [some] wine?" "Not me."'
(3) – Εμένα το έδωσαν! – Όχι, εμένα!
    '"They gave it to *me*!" "No, *me*!"'

An emphatic pronoun may also act:

(i)   as the *subject* or the *direct or indirect object of a verb*;
(ii) as the *object of a preposition*;
(iii) in tandem with a weak pronoun, as *a direct or indirect object*, or as *a possessive*;
(iv) *in apposition* to a noun.

(i)   Emphatic pronoun as subject or object of verb
An emphatic pronoun may stand as the subject of a verb when the person of the verb is emphasized for contrastive purposes (4–6) or when the subject is ***topicalized*** (7–10: for topicalization see Sections 5.2.2ff.):

(4) **Εγώ** το έκανα
    '*I* [and no one else] did it'
(5) **Εσύ** το έκανες
    '*You* [and no one else] did it'
(6) **Αυτός/αυτή** το έκανε
    '*He/she* [and no one else] did it'
(7) **Εγώ** δεν έχω καμιά γνώμη
    '**As for me**, I have no opinion'
(8) **Εσύ** δεν έχεις καμιά γνώμη
    '**As for you**, you have no opinion'
(9) **Αυτός/αυτή** δεν έχει καμιά γνώμη
    '**As for him/her**, s/he has no opinion'
(10) **Εγώ** που δεν είχα ξαναπάει στην Αθήνα, εντυπωσιάστηκα
     από το Αρχαιολογικό Μουσείο
     '**I**, who had never been to Athens before, was impressed by the Archaeological Museum'

Similarly an emphatic pronoun may function as the direct or indirect object of a verb when the object is emphasized for contrastive purposes (11–12):

(11) Όχι, **εσένα** είδα!
'No, it was *you* [and no one else] I saw!'
(12) **Εσένα** μιλάω!
'It's *you* [and no one else] I'm talking to!'

When preceded by the focalizer και, an emphatic pronoun may be highlighted to mean 'I too', etc.:

(13) Κι εγώ σε είδα
'I saw you too' (i.e. 'I too saw you', 'I wasn't the only one who saw you')
(14) Κι εσένα είδα
'I saw you too' (i.e. 'You weren't the only one I saw')

(ii) Emphatic pronoun as the object of a preposition
(Pronoun in the accusative: see also Sections 4.2.2ff.)

An emphatic pronoun in the accusative may act as the object of certain prepositions. When preceded by the prepositions από and για, the pronouns εμένα, εσένα, εμάς, εσάς lose their initial vowel; when they are preceded by the prepositions με and σε, the preposition loses its final vowel, and an apostrophe is written in its place. Emphatic pronouns are regularly used in a neutral way after χωρίς and σαν, but after από, για, με and σε they are normally used only where contrastive emphasis is required:

(15) Πήγαν χωρίς εμένα
'They went without me'
(16) Δεν ξέρω κανέναν άλλον σαν εσένα
'I don't know anyone else like you'
(17) Το έμαθα από σένα
'I learned it from *you*'
(18) Το έκαναν για μας
'They did it for *us*'
(19) Θα πάω μ' εσάς
'I'll go with *you* [rather than someone else]' (cf. neutral Θα πάω μαζί σας 'I'll go with you')
(20) Το έδωσαν σ' εμένα
'They gave it to *me* [rather than to someone else]' (cf. neutral Μου το έδωσαν 'They gave it to me')

Similarly the emphatic pronouns (preceded by από, σε, etc.) are used instead of the weak pronouns to indicate contrastive stress after a number of adverbs (see Section 3.2.7):

(21) πάνω από μας
'above *us* [rather than above anyone else]' (μας here is an
emphatic pronoun, despite being written identically to the
corresponding weak pronoun: see Part II, Section 5.1)

(22) ανάμεσα σ' εμάς και σ' εσάς
'between *us* and *you* [rather than between anybody else]'

(iii) Emphatic pronoun in tandem with weak pronoun as direct or
indirect object of verb or as possessive
(See also Section 5.2.2.3.)

A topicalized emphatic pronoun may function in tandem with a weak
pronoun (for topicalization see Sections 5.2.2ff.), either as a direct object
(23) or an indirect object (24–5) of a verb, or as a possessive (26):

(23) **Εσένα** σε είδα κιόλας
'**As for you**, I've already seen you'

(24) **Εσένα** σου μίλησα κιόλας
'**As for you**, I've already spoken to you'

(25) **Εσένα** που έκανες τόσο πολλά για μένα, δε θα σου μιλούσα
έτσι
'You who have done so much for me, I wouldn't talk to you
like that'

(26) – Ο πατέρας μου είναι ναυτικός. – Ε και; Εμένα ο πατέρας
μου είναι δικηγόρος
'"My father's a sailor." "So what? My father's a *lawyer*"'

As in the reply in example (26), this doubling may serve to indicate that
the noun on which the weak pronoun depends is already given (the conversation is already about fathers); at the same time it may indicate a contrast
between the person of the pronoun ('my') and some other pronoun used
earlier in the conversation and to place the focus on the subject predicate (δικηγόρος).

(iv) Emphatic pronoun accompanied by a noun phrase in apposition
An emphatic pronoun may be accompanied by a noun phrase in apposition
to it; both items may appear in the nominative (27), accusative (28), or
genitive (29):

(27) εμείς οι Έλληνες
'we Greeks'

(28) σ' εμάς τους Έλληνες
'to us Greeks'

(29) Βλέπω τη ζωή **εσάς των νέων** και με πιάνει τρόμος
'I see the lives **of you youngsters** [i.e. 'that you youngsters
lead'] and I get scared'

2.8.1.2   Other pronouns

A small number of items function solely as pronouns. These are the following:

2.8.1.2.1   The indefinite (assertive) pronoun κατιτί
Κατιτί 'something' is a less commonly used stylistic alternative to κάτι, from which it differs solely in that κατιτί is used only as a pronoun, while κάτι may be used either as a pronoun or as a determiner (see Section 2.8.3.4):

(1) Έχει μέσα κατιτί
    'There's something inside it'

2.8.1.2.2   The universal pronouns καθένας and καθετί
Καθένας 'every one, each one' may optionally be preceded by the definite article as ο καθένας. It is fully inflected for gender and case, but has no plural (see Part II, Section 5.9).

(1) Το ξέρει ο καθένας
    'Everyone knows it'
(2) Αυτά τα κουνουπίδια έχουν 200 δραχμές το καθένα
    'These cauliflowers are 200 drachmas each'

When καθένας indicates each one of a specific group, it may be followed either by από+noun or emphatic pronoun ([ο] καθένας από τους στρατιώτες 'each one of the soldiers', ο καθένας απ' αυτούς 'each of them') or by a genitive plural form of the weak pronoun to specify the person (first, second, or third) that it denotes (ο καθένας τους 'each one of them'). Otherwise it often means 'everyone' in general (as in example (1) above).

Καθετί 'each thing' is itself indeclinable, but it is usually preceded by the neuter singular of the article, whose form indicates whether it is being used in the nominative/accusative or the genitive:

(3) Παραπονιέται για το καθετί
    'S/he complains about every single thing'
(4) θαυμαστής του καθετί που είναι ωραίο
    'admirer of everything that is beautiful'

2.8.1.2.3   The reflexive pronoun phrase ο εαυτός μου
The reflexive phrase ο εαυτός μου is actually a noun phrase consisting of the masculine definite article, the masculine noun εαυτός (which inflects for case and number but not for gender), and the genitive of the weak pronoun in the gender and number appropriate to the possessor[s] of the self:

(1) Μιλούσε στον εαυτό της
    'She was talking to herself'

When talking about more than one person, the singular of εαυτός is commonly used, though the plural may be used as an alternative, especially where εαυτός is modified by some other word:

(2) Πρέπει να φροντίσουμε τον εαυτό μας
    'We must look after ourselves'
(3) Είχαν αρχίσει να μην αισθάνονται **τον εαυτό τους** (sg.) πολύ
    ξένο (sg.)
    'They had begun to stop feeling [lit. 'to not feel'] themselves so
    foreign'
(4) Θεωρούν **τους εαυτούς τους** (pl.) πολύ σημαντικούς (pl.) στην
    κοινωνία
    'They consider themselves very important in society'

Since ο εαυτός μου is just one of several ways of expressing reflexivity in Greek, this topic is covered in separate sections (Section 5.4.3.5–5.4.3.5.3).

2.8.1.2.4   The quantifiers το *παν, οι πάντες, τα πάντα*
In addition to όλος 'all' (for which see below, Section 2.8.3.1.1), various forms of the ancient adjective πας 'each; all' are used. The neuter singular noun το παν means 'everything' in the sense of 'the most important thing', or else in the fixed phrase κάνω το παν 'I do everything possible':

(1) Είσαι το παν για μένα
    'You are everything to me'
(2) Έκανε το παν για να μ' ευχαριστήσει
    'S/he did everything [s/he could] to please me'

The masculine and neuter plural forms are used with the article to mean 'everybody' or 'everything':

(3) Ήρθαν οι πάντες στη δεξίωση
    '[Absolutely] everybody came to the reception'
(4) Αυτός ξέρει τα πάντα
    'He knows [absolutely] everything'

While οι πάντες and τα πάντα are generally stronger in meaning than όλοι and όλα, example (4) can be distinguished from example (5) by the fact that (4) means 'everything there is to know' in general, while (5) denotes everything there is to know about a specific topic.

(5) Αυτός τα ξέρει όλα
    'He knows everything'

2.8.2   THE DISTRIBUTIVE DETERMINER κάθε

The only word that may act solely as a determiner and not as a pronoun is the *distributive determiner* κάθε 'each, every'. Like almost all determiners, κάθε precedes the noun it determines. It is uninflected, but it may accompany a noun in any case. When it determines a noun in the singular, it may optionally be preceded by the definite article:

(1) [Η] κάθε μητέρα θυσιάζεται για τα παιδιά της
    'Every mother sacrifices herself for her children'

Κάθε may also accompany a noun in the plural, either when a numeral is present (2) or when the noun has no singular (3) or is used in a different meaning in the singular (4):

(2) κάθε τρεις μήνες
    'every three months'
(3) κάθε Χριστούγεννα
    'every Christmas'
(4) Το συντηρητικό κόμμα κέρδισε σε κάθε εκλογές από το 1979
    'The conservative party had won in each election since 1979'
    [εκλογές in the sense of 'election[s]' is always plural]

It may also accompany a quantitative pronoun or determiner (e.g. κάθε τόσο 'every so often', κάθε πόσα χρόνια; 'every how many years?') and may even introduce a που-clause, where κάθε που is equivalent to κάθε φορά που 'each time that':

(5) Κάθε που έρχεται στο σπίτι μου, στρογγυλοκάθεται και ανάβει
    ένα τσιγάρο
    'Each time s/he comes to my house, s/he makes him/herself
      comfortable and lights a cigarette'

2.8.3   TERMS FUNCTIONING AS BOTH PRONOUNS AND DETERMINERS

A large variety of words may be used either on their own as pronouns, or as determiners accompanying nouns. They may be divided into the following categories:

quantifiers (2.8.3.1)
demonstratives (2.8.3.2)
the relative pronoun phrase ο οποίος (2.8.3.3)
indefinite (specific): κάποιος, ένας, κάτι, ο τάδε, ο δείνα (2.8.3.4)
indefinite (non-specific): κανείς, κανένας, τίποτα (2.8.3.5)
interrogative: ποιος, τι, πόσος (2.8.3.6)
qualitative demonstrative: τέτοιος (2.8.3.7)

quantitative demonstrative: τόσος (2.8.3.8)
correlative: όποιος, ό,τι, όσος, οποιοσδήποτε, οτιδήποτε, οσοσδήποτε
   (2.8.3.9)
emphatic possessive: δικός μου (2.8.3.10)
intensive: ίδιος, μόνος (2.8.3.11)
contrastive: άλλος (2.8.3.12)

2.8.3.1 Quantifiers

For the purposes of this book a quantifier is defined as a word that
expresses quantity without specifying number (e.g. 'all', 'many', 'few');
numerals are treated separately in Section 2.7. Quantifiers can be divided
into two categories according to the way they function within the noun
phrase. The first category consists of όλος 'all' and ολόκληρος 'whole'
(2.8.3.1.1), while the second contains the rest (2.8.3.1.2). For the quantifiers το παν, οι πάντες, τα πάντα, which are used exclusively as pronouns,
see Section 2.8.1.2.4.

2.8.3.1.1 *Όλος* and *ολόκληρος*

The quantifiers όλος 'whole; all' (in singular or plural) and ολόκληρος
'whole' (especially in the singular) regularly perform syntactically in the
same way as demonstratives (see Section 2.8.3.2), in that they stand outside
the article+noun complex:

   (1) όλος ο κόσμος
       'all the world; everybody' (cf. αυτός ο κόσμος 'this world')
   (2) όλες οι γυναίκες
       'all [the] women' (cf. αυτές οι γυναίκες 'these women')
   (3) ολόκληρο το σπίτι
       'the whole house' (cf. αυτό το σπίτι 'this house')

Like demonstratives, these quantifiers may follow the article+noun complex:

   (4) ο κόσμος όλος (=1; cf. ο κόσμος αυτός)
   (5) οι γυναίκες όλες (=2; cf. οι γυναίκες αυτές)
   (6) το σπίτι ολόκληρο (=3; cf. το σπίτι αυτό)

These quantifiers may also be used, in either attributive or predicative
use, without an article. The plural of ολόκληρος may function attributively,
as in (7a) and (7b):

   (7)a. **ολόκληρες** ώρες
      b. ώρες **ολόκληρες**
         '[for] hours on end'

Both όλος and ολόκληρος may be used predicatively, either as subject
predicates, as in (8) and (9), or as object predicates, as in (10) and (11):

(8) Είμαι **όλος** αφτιά
     'I'm **all** ears'
(9) Τινάχτηκε **ολόκληρος**
     'He shook **all over**'
(10) Την πίτα την έφαγα **όλη**
     'I ate **all** the pie'
(11) Την πίτα την έφαγα **ολόκληρη**
     'I ate the pie **whole**'

The plural of όλος also functions as a pronoun, either indicating something already mentioned, as in (12), or used absolutely to mean 'everyone'
(in the masculine) or 'everything' (in the neuter), as in (13) and (14):

(12) Τα βλέπεις τα ραδιόφωνα; **Όλα** είναι σκάρτα
     'Do you see the radios? They're **all** useless'
(13) **Όλοι** το ξέρουν
     '**Everyone** knows it'
(14) Αλλάξανε **όλα**
     '**Everything** has changed'

When όλος is used pronominally as the object of a verb, the verb is
normally accompanied by a doubling clitic:

(15) Τους είδα όλους
     'I saw them [masc.] all; I saw all of them [masc.]'
(16) Αυτός τα ξέρει όλα
     'He knows everything'

For clitic doubling see Section 5.4.3.3.
   The neuter singular όλο also functions as an adverb ('all [wholly]; all
the time').

In formal usage the singular of the quantifier όλος, meaning 'whole' and accompanying an abstract noun, may behave like a normal adjective with respect to
word order:

(17) η όλη κατάσταση
     'the whole situation'
(18) η όλη αυτή κατάσταση
     'this whole situation'

2.8.3.1.2 Other quantifiers
Other quantifiers include the following:

πολύς 'much, a lot [of]; too much' (pl. 'many; too many');
   comparative περισσότερος 'more' (note that Greek does not
   normally distinguish between 'much/many' and 'too much/many')
αρκετός 'quite a lot [of]'

κάμποσος/καμπόσος 'quite a lot [of]'
μπόλικος 'plenty [of]'
λίγος '[a] little' (pl. 'few'); comparative λιγότερος 'less' (plural 'fewer')
λιγοστός 'little' (pl. 'few')
ελάχιστος 'very little' (pl. 'very few')
τόσος 'so much' (pl. 'so many')
όσος 'as much as' (pl. 'as many as') (for τόσος and όσος see also below, Sections 2.8.3.8 and 2.8.3.9)
ο υπόλοιπος 'the rest [of]' (always with definite article)

These quantifiers, which may be used with or without a noun, inflect like adjectives, and agree in gender, number and case with the relevant noun or with the item which they denote:

(1) Ήρθε πολύς κόσμος
    'Many people came'
(2) Ήρθαν πολλές [φοιτήτριες]
    'Many women [students] came'
(3) Ήρθε αρκετός κόσμος
    'Quite a lot of people came'
(4) Ήρθαν αρκετές [φοιτήτριες]
    'Quite a lot of women [students] came'
(5) Ήρθε ελάχιστος κόσμος
    'Very few people came'
(6) Ήρθαν ελάχιστες [φοιτήτριες]
    'Very few women [students] came'
(7) Τι θα κάνουμε το υπόλοιπο κρέας;
    'What shall we do with the rest of the meat?'
(8) Οι περισσότεροι είχαν κρυολόγημα, οι υπόλοιποι όμως είχαν γρίππη
    'Most had colds, but the rest had flu'

The neuter singular forms of some of these quantifiers may also function as adverbs: πολύ 'very; much' (comparative περισσότερο 'more'); λίγο 'a little' (comparative λιγότερο 'less'); τόσο 'so'; όσο 'as much as'. The adverb corresponding to αρκετός is αρκετά.

The quantifier μερικοί 'some' is always used in the plural, while ορισμένοι 'certain' and διάφοροι 'various' are normally used in the plural:

(9) μερικές φοιτήτριες
     'some [female] students'
(10) ορισμένες φοιτήτριες
     'certain [female] students'
(11) διάφορες φοιτήτριες
     'various [female] students'

Apart from these, there are other words or phrases that may be considered to be quantifiers, such as πλήθος 'a crowd [of], a large number [of]', and the indeclinable ένα σωρό 'a whole lot [of]', which is used with a noun in the case appropriate to its function in the clause. Both are used only with a plural noun:

(12) Ήρθαν πλήθος φοιτήτριες
      'A large number of [female] students came'
(13) Ήρθαν ένα σωρό φοιτήτριες
      'A whole lot of [female] students came'

For the determiners τίποτα 'any[thing]; no[thing]' and καθόλου 'any at all; no . . . at all', see Section 2.8.3.5.

In formal usage the archaic quantifier αμφότεροι 'both' is occasionally used:

(14) αμφότερα τα κόμματα
      'both the parties'

Αμφότεροι cannot be used predicatively.

2.8.3.2 The demonstratives *αυτός, τούτος, εκείνος*

Any of the **demonstratives** αυτός, τούτος, and εκείνος may function as a determiner (with a noun accompanied by the definite article: 'this; that') or as an emphatic third-person pronoun ('he, she, it', etc.). When used as a determiner, the demonstrative stands outside the article+noun complex, as shown in examples (1–4) and (7–8) below. For the forms of the demonstratives see Part II, Section 5.1; for more on word order involving demonstratives see Part III, Section 2.11.

Traditionally the three demonstratives were semantically distinguished from each other as follows. Αυτός was normally used for items situated close to the hearer, τούτος for items close to the speaker, and εκείνος for items distant from both. In modern usage, however, τούτος tends to be used only when emphasizing the closeness of the item to the speaker (in free alternation with αυτός, except that it is not considered particularly polite to talk about a human as τούτος), while αυτός may be used either to indicate proximity or as an all-purpose demonstrative without distinguishing between proximity and distance, εκείνος continuing to be used for items distant from hearer and speaker. In order to emphasize the proximity or distance of the item indicated, the adverbs εδώ 'here' and εκεί 'there' are sometimes used with the demonstratives in the collocations αυτός εδώ, τούτος εδώ, εκείνος εκεί (cf. colloquial English 'this here', 'that there'). Examples (1–4) show the demonstratives functioning as determiners, while (5–6) show them functioning as pronouns:

(1) **Αυτό** το δέντρο είναι λεύκα
'This tree is a poplar'

(2) **Τούτο** εδώ το δέντρο είναι πλάτανος
'This tree here is a plane'

(3) **Εκείνη** η φούστα είναι κόκκινη
'That skirt is red'

(4) **Εκείνος** εκεί ο σωλήνας έχει τρυπήσει
'That pipe there has burst'

(5) **Εκείνη** το έκανε
'*She* did it' (contrastive emphasis on the subject)

(6) Δώσ' το σ' **αυτόν**
'Give it to *him*' (contrastive emphasis on the indirect object)

Note that, when it functions as a pronoun, the masculine accusative singular form of the demonstrative normally ends in -ν: αυτόν, τούτον, εκείνον.

Αυτός and εκείνος may also be used to distinguish between proximity and distance in time rather than place:

(7) Αυτή η παράσταση είναι καλύτερη από την προηγούμενη
'This performance is better than the previous one'

(8) Εκείνη την εποχή ζούσαμε πιο καλά
'We lived better in those days [lit. 'in that period']'

When the demonstratives are used to indicate an item that is present in the discourse rather than in reality, αυτός may stand in opposition to εκείνος, αυτός indicating 'the latter' and εκείνος 'the former':

(9) Ο Γιάννης και ο Γιώργος ήρθαν μαζί. **Αυτός** όμως έφυγε νωρίς, ενώ **εκείνος** έμεινε μέχρι τα ξημερώματα
'John and George came together, but the latter left early while the former stayed till dawn'

The demonstratives may also be used to substitute for a word that has already appeared in the sentence:

(10) Η πρεσβεία της Μόσχας δεχόταν περισσότερες πληροφορίες από **εκείνη** του Λονδίνου
'The Moscow embassy used to receive more information than **that** of London'

Αυτός and εκείνος may be used to indicate a change of grammatical subject:

(11) Παρακάλεσε την κόρη της να γυρίσει πίσω, αλλά **εκείνη** δεν την άκουσε
'She begged her daughter to come back, but she [i.e. the daughter] did not listen'

Without εκείνη, the above example could be misunderstood as meaning that the mother did not listen to the daughter, i.e. that the subject of the second verb was the same as the subject of the first.

Both αυτός and εκείνος may be modified by a relative clause to indicate an indefinite subject:

(12) **Αυτοί/Εκείνοι** που λένε τέτοια πράγματα θα έπρεπε να τιμωρηθούν
      'Those who say such things ought to be punished'

The neuter αυτό may be used to denote the content of a whole clause:

(13) Ποιος τον σκότωσε; **Αυτό** να μου πεις
      'Who killed him? Tell me that'

In colloquial speech, αυτός preceded by the definite article may be used pronominally as a substitute for a noun that the speaker cannot think of or does not wish to utter: thus ο αυτός is equivalent to 'whatsisname', η αυτή to 'whatsername', and το αυτό to 'the thingy'; similarly the vocative αυτέ or αυτή can be used vulgarly to address someone whose name the speaker has forgotten. This colloquial use of ο αυτός should not be confused with the archaic use of the same collocation, still sometimes found in the sense of 'the same' (see Section 2.8.3.11).

For the pronouns and determiners τέτοιος 'such a; this/that kind of' and τόσος 'so much', which are also demonstratives, see Sections 2.8.3.7 and 2.8.3.8 respectively.

2.8.3.3   The relative pronoun phrase *ο οποίος*

The relative pronoun phrase ο οποίος 'who, that, which' is fully inflected, consisting of the definite article followed by οποίος, which declines like adjectives such as ωραίος (see Part II, Section 3.2). It agrees in gender and number with its antecedent (i.e. the noun which it modifies), while it appears in the case appropriate to its syntactical function within the relative clause. For discussion and examples see Section 5.3.1.2. Ο οποίος is a stylistic alternative for the far more commonly used που, which is not inflected and is not strictly a pronoun, although it does the work of the English relative pronouns 'who, that, which' (for its uses in relative clauses see Section 5.3.1.3).

In non-restrictive relative clauses (see Section 5.3.1.1), ο οποίος is occasionally used as a determiner, especially where the relative expression is separated from its antecedent by other words or by a pause, or by both:

(1) Είδα το Γιάννη χθες – ο οποίος Γιάννης μου διηγήθηκε το εξής ανέκδοτο
     'I saw John yesterday – who (John) told me the following story'

2.8.3.4   Indefinite (specific): *κάποιος, ένας, κάτι, ο τάδε, ο δείνα*

Κάποιος 'someone' and κάτι 'something' are used as *pronouns* to denote a specific person or thing whose identity is nevertheless not specified. When used as pronouns κάποιος can be applied only to a person or persons, and κάτι only to a thing. Κάποιος is fully inflected for gender, number, and case, although it is normally used in the masculine singular unless it is obvious that it indicates two or more people who have already been mentioned, or that it indicates a woman; κάτι is uninflected and, when used as a pronoun, is singular. They may be used in any kind of sentence (assertive positive or negative, interrogative, subjunctive, etc.):

(1) **Κάποιος** ήρθε και σε ζητούσε
     'Someone came asking for you'
(2) Είδες **κάποιον** στο γραφείο μου;
     'Did you see someone in your office?'
(3) **Κάτι** μπλέχτηκε στα γρανάζια
     'Something's got caught up in the cog-wheels'
(4) **Κάτι** δεν πάει καλά
     'Something's wrong' [lit. 'something's not going well']

As a *determiner* κάποιος may be used in the singular or plural to mean 'some . . . or other, [a] certain':

(5) **Κάποιος** φίλος σου ήρθε και σε ζητούσε
     'Some friend of yours came asking for you'
(6) Οι διαρρήκτες μπήκαν στο γραφείο **κάποιου** φίλου μου
     'The burglars entered the office of a friend of mine'
(7) **Κάποιοι** φίλοι σου ήρθαν και σε ζητούσαν
     'Some friends of yours came asking for you'
(8) Έχω **κάποια** επιφύλαξη γι' αυτή την απόφαση
     'I have a certain reservation about this decision'

In the singular the determiner κάποιος is equivalent in meaning to the indefinite article ένας, which may also be used as a pronoun instead of the pronoun κάποιος in positive declarative sentences:

(9)   **Ένας** φίλος σου ήρθε και σε ζητούσε (=5)
      'A friend of yours came asking for you'
(10) **Ένας** ήρθε και σε ζητούσε (=1)
      'Someone came looking for you'

The plural κάποιοι (as in example 7 above) can act as the plural of ένας (example 9).

Κάτι may be used as a determiner before plural nouns of any gender and in any grammatical case to mean 'some' (i.e. a quantity of); in such uses it is equivalent to the plural of κάποιος or ένας:

(11) Κατι φίλοι σου ήρθαν και σε ζητούσαν (=7)
(12) Βρήκα κάτι παλιά χαρτιά στο συρτάρι
      'I found some old papers in the drawer'
(13) Άκουσα τα ονόματα κάτι παιδιών
      'I heard the names of some children'

Κάτι may be used with plural nouns in exclamations expressing admiration or amazement:

(14) Έχει κάτι μάτια!
      'S/he's got *some* eyes!' (i.e. beautiful or in some other way
        remarkable)

Κάτι may be modified by a following adjective, with or without the definite article:

(15) κάτι το ωραίο
      'something lovely'
(16) κάτι συνηθισμένο
      'something usual'

Ο τάδε 'such and such' consists of the definite article and the indeclinable τάδε. It is only used in the singular, but the article inflects according to gender and case. It is used as a pronoun or determiner to denote someone or something that is definite but not specified. When two persons are talked about in this way, ο τάδε may alternate with ο δείνα:

(17) Έδωσαν ραντεβού με τον τάδε και το δείνα για την τάδε ώρα
        στο τάδε μέρος
      'They made a date with so and so and such and such for such
        and such a time at such and such a place'

The adverbial counterparts of κάποιος and κάτι are κάποτε 'at some time, once', κάπου 'somewhere', and κάπως 'somewhat'.

2.8.3.5 Indefinite (non-specific): κανείς, κανένας, τίποτα

Κανείς or κανένας 'any[one]; no [one]' and τίποτα 'any[thing]; no[thing]' are normally used in negative or interrogative clauses, or in other clauses which do not make a statement. When used as *pronouns* they are singular. Κανένας is inflected for case, while τίποτα is uninflected. (For the declension of κανείς/κανένας see Part II, Section 5.7. Κανείς is normally a less colloquial stylistic alternative of κανένας, but see below.)
  Examples of interrogative use:

(1) Ήρθε κανένας στο γραφείο μου;
     'Did anyone come to my office?'

(2) Είδες κανέναν να περνάει από δω;
'Did you see anyone pass by here?'
(3) Θέλεις τίποτα;
'Do you want anything?'

Examples of negative use (see also Section 5.1.5.2.4(i)):

(4) Δεν ήρθε κανένας στο γραφείο μου
'No one came to my office'
(5) Δεν είδα κανέναν να περνάει από δω
'I didn't see anyone pass by here'
(6) Δε θέλω τίποτα
'I don't want anything'

Κανείς/κανένας and τίποτα may be used as the sole or chief word of a verbless sentence, in which case they always have a negative meaning:

(7) – Ποιος ήρθε σήμερα; – Κανένας.
'"Who came today?" "No one."'
(8) – Τι θέλεις; – Τίποτα.
'"What do you want?" "Nothing"'

These indefinite (non-specific) pronouns are also typically used in sentences or clauses that do not make *statements* about the past or present. That is, in practice, they are used in subjunctive, conditional, or imperative clauses, or sentences referring to future time:

(9) Άς ρωτήσουμε κανέναν
'Let's ask someone'
(10) Αν βρεις κανέναν, ρώτησέ τον
'If you find someone, ask him'
(11) Για φέρε μου τίποτα να φάω
'Do bring me something to eat'

Although κάποιος and κάτι may be used instead of κανένας and τίποτα in the above sentences, the speaker in (9–11) has in mind no particular person or thing, but rather 'anyone/anything that happens to be about'.

Κανείς/κανένας and τίποτα may also be used as *determiners*. In such uses κανείς/κανένας may accompany only a singular noun, while τίποτα may accompany only a plural form (τίποτα is not normally used as a determiner in negative clauses). In the following examples, these words are used interrogatively (12–13), both interrogatively and negatively (14), negatively (15), and positively (16–18):

(12) Ήρθε κανένας πελάτης στο μαγαζί;
'Did any customer come to the shop?'
(13) Θέλεις τίποτα φρούτα;
'Do you want any fruit?' (φρούτα is plural)

(14)   Δεν ήρθε κανένας πελάτης στο μαγαζί;
       'Didn't any customer come to the shop?'
(15)   Όλη μέρα το μαγαζί ήταν άδειο: κανένας πελάτης, κανένας
       περαστικός
       'The shop was empty all day: no customer, no passer-by'
(16)   Ας ρωτήσουμε κανέναν αστυφύλακα (cf. 9)
       'Let's ask a policeman'
(17)   Αν βρεις κανένα ποτήρι, φέρ' το (cf. 10)
       'If you find a glass, bring it'
(18)   Για φέρε μου τίποτα φασολάκια (cf. 11)
       'Do bring me some beans'

In interrogative sentences such as (13) above, τίποτα may be replaced by
καθόλου '[not] any at all', which is also more usual than τίποτα as a determiner of a plural noun in negative sentences such as (19):

(19)   Δε θέλω καθόλου φρούτα
       'I don't want any fruit at all'

Even though it may only be used in the singular, as a determiner in positive sentences κανείς/κανένας may imply more than one of the persons,
objects, etc., denoted by the noun. Thus in example (17) above it is not
clear whether the speaker is asking for one or more glasses; this can only
be inferred from the context.

Κανένας may also be used in positive assertive clauses which make
statements; in such cases the use of κανένας rather than κάποιος implies
that the speaker is referring to more than one person or object:

(20)   Από τα κοντινά χτήματα ερχόταν λαχανιασμένος κανένας
       μικρός να μάθει ποιος πέθανε
       'From the nearby farms a young lad would come [every so
       often], puffing and panting, to find out who had died'

In the English rendering of (20), the phrase 'every so often' has been added
to show that the speaker is referring to a number of different young lads;
this is made clear by the use of the imperfective form of the verb ερχόταν.
Κανένας tends to have a vague meaning when used in positive assertive
clauses. Thus the common phrase καμιά φορά means 'occasionally' (not
'never', except when it constitutes a whole sentence, and then only given
the appropriate intonation), and καμιά is typically found with approxi-
matives (καμιά δεκαριά 'about ten': see Section 2.7). Also the common
compound κάνα δυο (short for κανένα δυο: uninflected but used with
plural nouns of any gender or case) means 'one or two; a couple of'. Other
examples:

(21)   Θα έρθω σε καμιά ώρα
       'I'll come in about an hour'

(22) Πέρασα κανένα μήνα εκεί
    'I spent about a month there'

Τίποτα, like κάτι (see Section 2.8.3.4 above) may be modified by a
following adjective, with or without the definite article:

(23) Δεν ήταν τίποτα το σπουδαίο
    'It wasn't anything important'
(24) Δεν ήταν τίποτα ασυνήθιστο
    'It wasn't anything unusual'

A small number of other words act in a rather similar way to indefinite
non-specific pronouns, being used chiefly in negative clauses or as the only
word in a verbless sentence. An example is κουβέντα, which is in other
respects a noun meaning 'word, remark, talk'; another is τσιμουδιά, which
is not used outside such contexts:

(25) Δεν είπε κουβέντα
    'S/he didn't say a word'
(26) Μη λες κουβέντα! (or Μη βγάζεις τσιμουδιά!)
    'Don't say a word!'
(27) Κουβέντα! or Τσιμουδιά!
    'Not a word!'

Example (27) could be uttered either as a reply to a question whether
someone said anything, or as a command to the hearer not to speak.
    The adverbial counterparts of κανείς/κανένας and τίποτα are ποτέ
'[n]ever', πουθενά 'anywhere; nowhere', and καθόλου '[not] at all'.

2.8.3.6   Interrogative: ποιος, τι, πόσος

The interrogative pronouns and determiners are ποιος 'who; which', τι
'what', and πόσος 'how much'. Ποιος and πόσος are fully inflected, while
τι is uninflected (for the inflection of ποιος see Part II, Section 5.6; for
more on the syntax of interrogative pronouns and other question-words
in direct and indirect questions see Sections 5.1.4.4ff. and 5.3.2.2).

    As a *pronoun*, ποιος may be either singular or plural and normally indi-
cates a person or persons ('who'), in which case it normally appears in
the masculine; it may, however, indicate either a person or persons or a
thing or things ('which one[s]') that has/have already been mentioned, in
which case it appears in the appropriate gender:

(1) Ποιος (masc. nom. sg.) ήρθε;
    'Who came?'
(2) Ποιον (masc. acc. sg.) είδες;
    'Who did you see?'

(3) Ποιανού (masc. gen. sg.) το έδωσες;
    'Who did you give it to?'
(4) – Δώσ' μου τα βιβλία. – Ποια; (neut. acc. pl.)
    '"Give me the books." "Which ones?"'
(5) Ποιες έφερες; (fem. acc. pl.)
    'Which ones did you bring?'

In example (5) ποιες indicates some feminine plural item that has already been mentioned (e.g. women or τσάντες 'handbags').

When used as a pronoun, τι, which is singular, may not refer to a person:

(6) Τι θέλεις;
    'What do you want?'

As a *pronoun* πόσος may indicate, in the singular, the amount of a substance or, in the plural (all genders), a quantity of persons or things:

(7) Πόσο (neut. acc. sg.) έχει αυτό;
    'How much does this cost?'
(8) – Παίρνω ζάχαρη. – Πόση (fem. acc. sg.) παίρνεις;
    '"I take sugar." "How much do you take?"'
(9) Πόσοι (masc. nom. pl.) ήρθαν;
    'How many people came?'

As a *determiner*, ποιος may modify, in the singular or plural, a noun denoting a person or persons or an inanimate or inanimates (10–11); τι may accompany a noun in the singular or plural denoting a person or persons or an inanimate or inanimates (12–14); πόσος may be used in the singular to indicate an inanimate and in the plural to indicate persons or inanimates (15–16):

(10) Ποιος καθηγητής σού το 'πε αυτό;
     'Which teacher/professor told you that?'
(11) – Δώσ' μου τα βιβλία. – Ποια βιβλία; (cf. 4)
     '"Give me the books." "Which books?"'
(12) Τι άντρας είσαι;
     'What [sort of] man are you?'
(13) Τι δουλειά κάνεις;
     'What job do you do?'
(14) Τι βιβλία θέλεις;
     'What books do you want?'
(15) Πόση ζάχαρη παίρνεις; (cf. 8)
     'How much sugar do you take?'
(16) Πόσες γυναίκες ήρθαν στη συγκέντρωση; (cf. 9)
     'How many women came to the meeting?'

The difference in meaning between ποια βιβλία ('which books': 11) and τι βιβλία ('what books': 14) is that the former normally implies that there is a set of books already known to both speaker and hearer, and the speaker is asking the hearer to specify which books out of this set s/he is referring to; while in the latter the speaker implies 'which books out of all the books that exist'.

'What sort of' may also be expressed by τι είδος (τι είδους (gen.) in more formal usage) followed by a noun in the case appropriate to its function in the clause; there is also a more colloquial, but now rather old-fashioned, alternative, τι λογής:

(17) Τι είδος [*or* είδους *or* λογής] άνθρωπος είναι;
    'What sort of person is s/he?'

Note that ποιος has three alternative sets of genitive forms:

(a) ποιου/ποιας/ποιων, used especially in attributive use, normally where the noun it accompanies is abstract:

(18) Ποιας κατηγορίας είναι αυτό το ξενοδοχείο;
    'What class of hotel is this?' [lit. 'Of which category is this hotel?']

(b) ποιανού/ποιανής/ποιανών, used especially (but not exclusively) for humans:

(19) Ποιανού είναι αυτή η ομπρέλα; *or* Ποιανού ομπρέλα είναι αυτή;
    'Whose is this umbrella?'
(20) Ποιανού η κόρη διορίστηκε στην τράπεζα;
    'Whose daughter was appointed at the bank?'
(21) Σε ποιανού στρατού τις νίκες θα προσδοκούσαμε;
    'In the victories of which army would we place our expectations?'
(22) Ποιανής φοιτήτριας είναι αυτό το βιβλίο;
    'Which [female] student does this book belong to?' [lit. 'which student (fem. gen.) is this book']

(c) τίνος (plural τίνων rare), which is interchangeable with ποιανού (or ποιανών) only, i.e. only in masculine and neuter:

(23)a. Τίνος είναι αυτή η ομπρέλα;
   b. Τίνος ομπρέλα είναι αυτή;
    'Whose umbrella is this?'
(24) Τίνος παιδιού είναι αυτό το βιβλίο;
    'Which child does this book belong to?' [lit. 'Of which child is this book']

Note that when the pronoun τίνος is immediately followed by the noun on which it depends (as in 23b), the noun is more often used without the article. As a determiner τίνος (as in 24) is not as common as ποιανού.

Τι and πόσος are used in exclamations:

(25) Τι όνειρα έκανα!
      'What dreams I had!'
(26) Πόσα πράγματα είχα να κάνω!
      'How many things I had to do!'

In colloquial usage τι may be used adverbially instead of γιατί 'why' in simple sentences (cf. English 'what for'):

(27) Τι με κοιτάς έτσι;
      'What are you looking at me like that for?'

Τι, like κάτι and τίποτα, may be modified by an adjective, which is normally preceded by the definite article:

(28) Τι το καινούριο είχε συμβεί;
      'What new thing [lit. 'what the new'] had happened?'

Τι is also used adverbially to accompany an adjective or adverb in an exclamation:

(29) Τι ωραίος που είναι!
      'How handsome he is'
(30) Τι ωραία που το περιέγραψε!
      'How beautifully s/he described it!' or 'How nice [it is] that s/he described it!'

The adverbial counterparts of ποιος, πόσος, and τι are πόσο 'how much', πότε 'when', πού 'where', and πώς 'how', which may likewise be used in direct and indirect questions and in exclamations (e.g., τι πολλά! 'what a large quantity!' [lit. 'what many']).

2.8.3.7 Qualitative demonstrative: τέτοιος

Τέτοιος 'such [a]; of such a kind; this/that sort of', which is fully inflected, functions as a pronoun and as a determiner. As a *pronoun* it may be used in the singular to indicate an unspecified thing, and in the plural to indicate persons or things:

(1) Θέλω ένα τέτοιο (perhaps accompanied by a pointing gesture)
     'I want one of those [lit. 'a/one such (neut.)']'
(2) Έχουμε πολλούς τέτοιους (masc. acc. pl.) στη χώρα μας
     'We have a lot of such people in our country'
(3) Δε θέλουμε τέτοια
     'We don't want such things'

As a *determiner* τέτοιος may be used in the singular or plural to indicate a person or persons or an inanimate or inanimates:

(4) Δε θέλω ένα τέτοιο πουκάμισο
   'I don't want a shirt like that [lit. 'a such shirt']'
(5) Έχουμε πολλούς τέτοιους ανθρώπους στη χώρα μας (=2)
(6) Δε θέλουμε τέτοια πράγματα (=3)
(7) Έχτισαν το σπίτι με τέτοιο τρόπο που γκρεμίστηκε μέσα σε
   τρεις μήνες
   'They built the house in such a way that it fell down within
      three months'

Τέτοιος behaves so much like an adjective that it can also be used predicatively:

(8) Η δύναμη της έκρηξης ήταν τέτοια που έσπασαν όλα τα τζάμια
   σε ακτίνα ενός χιλιομέτρου
   'The force of the explosion was such that all the window-panes
      broke within a radius of one kilometre'

When τέτοιο co-occurs with κάτι it appears second: κάτι τέτοιο 'something like that'.

2.8.3.8 Quantitative demonstrative: *τόσος*

Τόσος 'so much/many; that much/many' is fully declinable. It may be used
as a pronoun or a determiner in any gender, number, or case:

(1) – Ήρθαν χίλιοι; – Ναι, τόσοι περίπου ήτανε
   '"Did a thousand [of them] come?" "Yes, there were about that
      many"'
(2) Μη βάζεις τόση ζάχαρη
   'Don't put in so much sugar'

Other quantitatives are the interrogative πόσος 'how much' and the correlative όσος 'as much as' (see Sections 2.8.3.6 and 2.8.3.9 respectively).
Frequently τόσος co-occurs with these:

(3) – Πόση ζάχαρη θέλεις; – Τόση.
   '"How much sugar do you want?" "That much."'
(4) Σήμερα ήρθαν **τόσοι όσοι** ήρθαν και χθες
   'As many came today as came yesterday'

For more details on constructions with τόσος and όσος (correlative
comparison) see Section 5.4.2.2.
   Like πόσος, τόσος is used in exclamations:

(5) Είχα τόσα πράγματα να κάνω!
   'I had so many things to do!'

The adverbial counterpart of τόσος is τόσο; nevertheless, the plural of the
determiner is often used, instead of the adverb, with the plural of πολύς:

(6) τόσο [or τόσα] πολλά βιβλία
    'so many books'
(7) τόσο [or τόσες] πολλές γυναίκες
    'so many women'

2.8.3.9 Correlative: *όποιος, ό,τι, όσος, οποιοσδήποτε, οτιδήποτε, οσοσδήποτε*

(See also Section 5.3.1.4.)

The correlative pronouns and determiners όποιος, ό,τι, and όσος belong semantically to both the main clause and the nominal or adverbial clause which they introduce. Ὁποιος and όσος are fully declinable. Although ό,τι is uninflected, as a determiner it may accompany a noun in any gender, number, or case. (Note that the correlative ό,τι is distinguished from the complementizer ότι 'that' by the comma between the first and second letters.)

The correlatives have two slightly different sets of meanings; these uses are termed *definite* and *indefinite*. In definite use they typically introduce clauses containing verbs in a past tense, or in the present tense with present reference; in indefinite use the clause they introduce typically contains a verb in the dependent.

In *definite* use όποιος means 's/he who, any who/which' (examples 1–2 below), ό,τι means 'what (that which)' (3–4), and όσος 'the amount or number which' (7); in addition, the plural of όσος may function as an alternative to the plural of όποιος (i.e. 'those who/which': 5–6). Thus, in definite use, όποιος is the equivalent of αυτός που or εκείνος που, ό,τι is the equivalent of αυτό που or εκείνο που, while the plural όσοι is the equivalent of αυτοί που or εκείνοι που.

In definite use (i.e. with a verb in the past or present) όποιος, ό,τι, and όσος indicate a specific item or items; examples (1), (3), (5), and (8–9) show these words being used as pronouns, while examples (2), (4), (6), and (7) show them used as determiners; (8) and (9) show the pronoun ό,τι being modified by an adjective:

(1) Ο Μιχάλης έδερνε όποιον έκλεβε τα μήλα του
    'Michael used to beat up anyone who stole his apples'
(2) Ο Μιχάλης έδερνε όποιο παιδί έκλεβε τα μήλα του
    'Michael used to beat up any boy who stole his apples'
(3) Θα επιστρέψω ό,τι μου δάνεισες
    'I'll return what you lent me'
(4) Θα επιστρέψω ό,τι λεφτά μου δάνεισες
    'I'll return what money you lent me'
(5) Όσοι διέπραξαν αυτά τα εγκλήματα θα τιμωρηθούν
    'Those who committed these crimes will be punished'

(6) Όσοι κακούργοι διέπραξαν αυτά τα εγκλήματα θα τιμωρηθούν
    'Those malefactors who committed these crimes will be punished'
(7) Όση ζάχαρη περίσσεψε θα τη βάλουμε στο κέικ
    'We'll put what sugar is left over into the cake'
(8) Θα σου δώσω ό,τι καλό έχω
    'I'll give you whatever I have that's good [lit. 'what good I have']'
(9) Θα σου δώσω ό,τι καλύτερο έχω
    'I'll give you the best thing[s] I have [lit. 'what better I have']'

Ό,τι is also used in comparative constructions in which the two terms being compared are not noun phrases in the same relationship with the verb:

(10) Ήρθες αργότερα **απ'** ό,τι περίμενα
     'You came later than I expected'

For further details on comparative constructions see Sections 5.4.2ff.
Όσοι, rather than που, is normally used after όλοι:

(11) Όλοι όσοι δεν έχουν εισιτήρια να προσέλθουν στο λογιστήριο
     'All those who haven't got tickets should present themselves at the purser's office'
(12) Δεν μπορώ να σου διηγηθώ όλα όσα έγιναν από τότε
     'I can't tell you all the things that have happened since then'

When the neuter plural όσα is used as a pronoun, it is often preceded by the definite article:

(13) Τα όσα τράβηξα δεν περιγράφονται
     'What I've suffered can't be described'

Όσος is used in comparative constructions involving the expression of amounts:

(14) Του αφιερώνει περισσότερες σελίδες της ανθολογίας της **απ'**
     όσες στον Γκάτσο
     'She devotes more pages of her anthology to him than to Gatsos'

Here όσες implies 'the number of pages which [she devotes]'. For more details see Sections 5.4.2ff.

In *indefinite* use, with the verb typically in the dependent, the correlatives indicate not specific items but anyone or anything (e.g., in (15), it is possible that no one may come at all). In indefinite use they correspond to English 'whoever', 'whichever', 'whatever', and 'however much/many'. In (15), (17), and (19) the correlative functions as a pronoun, while in (16), (18), and (20) it functions as a determiner of a noun:

(15) Όποιος έρθει, πες του να καθίσει
     'Whoever comes, tell him to sit down'

(16) Όποιος πελάτης έρθει, πες του να καθίσει
      'Whichever customer/client comes, tell him to sit down'
(17) Θα φάω ό,τι μου δώσεις
      'I'll eat what[ever] you give me'
(18) Θα φάω ό,τι κρέας μου δώσεις
      'I'll eat what[ever] meat you give me'
(19) Όσοι έρθουν, πες τους να καθίσουν
      'Whoever comes, tell them to sit down'
(20) Όσοι πελάτες έρθουν, πες τους να καθίσουν
      'Whichever [or however many] customers/clients come, tell
      them to sit down'

In addition, όποιος is characteristically found in proverbial statements such as the following, where no one in particular is referred to:

(21) Όποιος πονάει γαϊδουρινά φωνάζει
      'He who is in pain shouts like a donkey'

The indefiniteness of the correlative may be intensified through the use of κι αν or και να before the verb in the clause introduced by the correlative. In such cases a concessive sense is often introduced. For examples see Sections 5.3.1.4(9) and 5.3.6.

Όποιος may also be used with the definite article and a noun to mean 'whatever it/they may be, if any':

(22) Τα όποια λάθη τους μπορούν να αποδοθούν στην έλλειψη
      πείρας
      'Whatever mistakes, if any, they may have made [or may be
      making or may make] may be attributed to lack of
      experience'

Όσος often co-occurs with τόσος 'so much': see Section 5.4.2.2. The adverb corresponding to όσος is όσο 'as much as; however much'.

The *universal correlative* pronouns and determiners οποιοσδήποτε 'whoever', οτιδήποτε 'whatever', and οσοσδήποτε 'however much' are used in much the same way as the correlatives presented above, both with and without κι αν or και να. Their indefiniteness is even greater than that of the corresponding correlatives.

In addition to introducing nominal or adverbial clauses, the universal correlatives may be used as simple pronouns, with the following meanings: οποιοσδήποτε 'anyone whatever', οτιδήποτε 'anything whatever', οσοσδήποτε 'any quantity whatever [of]':

(23) Δε θα το έδινα σε οποιονδήποτε
      'I wouldn't give it to just anyone'
(24) – Ποιο βιβλίο να πάρω; – Οποιοδήποτε.
      '"Which book should I take?" "Whichever [you like]."'

(25) – Τι να σου δώσω; – Οτιδήποτε.
    '"What should I give you?" "Whatever [you like]."'
(26) – Πόσοι χωράνε στο σπίτι; – Οσοιδήποτε.
    '"How many can fit into the house?" "As many [as need to]."'

The corresponding adverbial forms are οσοδήποτε 'however much' and οπωσδήποτε 'in whatever way'.

2.8.3.10 Emphatic possessive: δικός μου

The emphatic possessive pronoun and determiner δικός μου 'my own; mine' consists of two elements, the adjective δικός, which inflects to show the gender, number, and case of the word it accompanies, and the genitive of the weak personal pronoun, which inflects to indicate the person, number, and (in the third person singular only) gender of the possessor.

Like an adjective, δικός μου may be used attributively (1–2, in which case it is equivalent to 'my own'), predicatively (3), as the object of a preposition (4), or as a predicate complement (5, in which cases it is equivalent to 'mine'). Δικός μου is preceded by the definite article if the noun it modifies is definite, as in (1) and (4), but not otherwise:

(1) Το δικό της αυτοκίνητο είναι μαύρο
    'Her own car is black'
(2) Θέλει δικό της αυτοκίνητο
    'She wants a car of her own'
(3) Το μαύρο αυτοκίνητο είναι δικό της
    'The black car is hers'
(4) Πάμε στο σπίτι μου ή στο δικό σου;
    'Shall we go to my house or yours?'
(5) Όλα τα θέλει δικά του
    'He wants everything [or them all] for himself'

Without a noun, δικός μου is often used to mean 'one of my people', i.e. one of my relatives or compatriots:

(6) Φοβόμουνα μήπως ήταν εχθρός, αλλά ήταν δικός μας
    'I was afraid it might have been one of the enemy, but it was one of our chaps'
(7) Τι κάνουν οι δικοί σου;
    'How are your folks?'

The phrase και στα δικά σου *or* σας, especially when addressed at a wedding to someone other than the bride and bridegroom, expresses a wish for the future marriage of the person addressed.

2.8.3.11   Intensive: *ίδιος, μόνος*

The intensive pronoun and determiner ίδιος has two chief uses, in both of which it is normally preceded by the definite article. ('Ίδιος inflects like an adjective, as in Part II, Section 3.2. For further details on its use see Part III, Section 5.4.3.7.)

As a *pronoun*, ο ίδιος means either 'the same' (1–3) or 'myself' (4) according to the context:

(1) – Άλλος είναι. – Όχι, ο ίδιος είναι.
     '"It's someone else." "No, it's the same one/man."'
(2) Πάλι τα ίδια!
     'It's the same thing all over again!'
(3) Είτε φύγεις είτε όχι, το ίδιο μου κάνει
     'Whether you leave or not, it's the same to me'
(4) Ήρθε η ίδια
     'She herself came' (i.e. she came in person)

As a *determiner*, when it immediately precedes the noun it accompanies, ίδιος means 'same':

(5) Όλοι μας γεννηθήκαμε στην ίδια πόλη
     'All of us were born in the same town'

When the definite article is repeated before the noun it accompanies, or when it follows an emphatic pronoun, ο ίδιος is used to emphasize the identity of the item denoted by the noun or pronoun; in this use it is the equivalent of 'myself', etc. In this construction, ο ίδιος may either precede or follow the article+noun complex:

(6) Ήρθε η ίδια η Μαρία *or* η Μαρία η ίδια
     'Mary herself came'
(7) Εγώ ο ίδιος το έκανα
     'I myself did it'

'Ίδιος may also be used to mean 'my own', especially with words for parts of the body and with the reflexive pronoun phrase ο εαυτός μου 'myself', when a contrast is not being made with anyone else's:

(8) Το είδα με τα ίδια μου τα μάτια
     'I saw it with my own eyes'
(9) Δεν το ομολόγησε ούτε στον ίδιο τον εαυτό της
     'She didn't admit it even to her own self'

'Ίδιος can also be used adjectivally, either attributively or predicatively, to mean 'the same' in the sense of 'identical'; here it is used without the definite article:

(10) Αυτά τα παιδιά μοιάζουν μεταξύ τους – ίδιες φάτσες, ίδια
      ρούχα
      'These kids look alike – the same faces, the same clothes'
(11) Όλες αυτές οι καραμέλες είναι ίδιες
      'All these sweets are the same'
(12) Είναι ίδιος ο πατέρας του
      'He's just like his father'

The adverbial counterpart is το ίδιο 'equally': see Section 3.1(9).

In addition, in formal usage, the archaic construction ο αυτός is occasionally used in the sense of 'the same'. Both the article and αυτός inflect to agree with the noun which they accompany:

(13) Ενέργησε με **την αυτήν** απροσεξία που έδειξε την προηγούμενη φορά
      'S/he acted with **the same** lack of care as s/he showed the previous time'

This construction should not be confused with the normal demonstrative use of αυτός, in which αυτός stands outside the article+noun complex (με αυτή την απροσεξία 'with this lack of care'), for which see Section 2.8.3.2.

As an adjective used attributively, μόνος means 'only':

(14) Είσαι η μόνη γυναίκα που αγάπησα
      'You're the only woman I've loved'

Used as a predicate and followed by the genitive of the weak personal pronoun, μόνος [μου] can mean 'alone' (i.e. without company):

(15) Μένει μόνη της
      'She lives alone'

Alternatively, μόνος [μου] can mean 'by myself' (i.e. without assistance from anyone else):

(16) Μόνη της το έκανε
      'She did it by herself'

The adverbial equivalent is μόνο 'only'; for its use see Section 3.1(10).

2.8.3.12 Contrastive: *άλλος*

The contrastive pronoun and determiner άλλος 'other; next' distinguishes one person or thing from another person[s] or thing[s]. (It inflects like an adjective, except that it has a set of alternative colloquial forms for the genitive, especially when it is used as a pronoun proper; see Part II, Section 5.4.)

(1) Όχι, αυτός που ήρθε ήταν άλλος
'No, the one who came was someone else'
(2) Πηγαίνετε στην άλλη κυρία
'Go to the other lady'
(3) Άλλο παιδί έχεις;
'Have you got another child?'
(4) Θα σε δω τον άλλο μήνα
'I'll see you next month'

Άλλος may follow the pronouns and determiners κάποιος, κανένας, ποιος, and όποιος. In such cases it is the equivalent of 'else':

(5) Κάποιος άλλος ήθελε να με δει
'Someone else wanted to see me'
(6) Κανένας άλλος δεν ήθελε να με δει
'No one else wanted to see me'
(7) Ποιος άλλος ήθελε να με δει;
'Who else wanted to see me?'
(8) Όποιος άλλος έρθει να με δει, διώξτε τον
'Whoever else comes to see me, send him away'

When used with a numeral and a noun, άλλος may either precede or follow the numeral, but with different meanings. If it precedes, the phrase indicates a number of identical items (i.e. more of the same), while if it follows, the phrase indicates a number of different items:

(9) Φέρε άλλα δύο ποτήρια
'Bring [us] two more glasses' (i.e. in addition to that or those we already have)
(10) Φέρε δύο άλλα ποτήρια
'Bring [us] two different glasses' (i.e. to replace the ones we have, which we don't want, e.g. because they are dirty or cracked)

When used with τόσος, άλλος may also have different meanings according to the order of the words: τόσος άλλος means 'so much other', while άλλος τόσος means 'as much again' (i.e. 'twice as much'):

(11) Υπάρχουν **τόσοι άλλοι** που μπορούν να κάνουν αυτή τη δουλειά
'There are so many others who can do this job'
(12) Χρειάζονται **άλλοι τόσοι** για να γίνει αυτή η δουλειά
'As many people again are needed for this job to be done'

Άλλος is used in a pair (άλλος . . . άλλος) when making a contrast between two items or two sets of items:

(13) Άλλος πλουτίζει, άλλος πεθαίνει της πείνας
'One person gets rich, another dies of hunger'

(14) Άλλοι πλουτίζουν, άλλοι πεθαίνουν της πείνας
'Some get rich, others die of hunger'

(15) Στα αγγλικά, άλλα λέμε κι άλλα γράφουμε
'In English we speak differently from the way we write [lit. 'we say other-things and we write other-things']'

(16) Άλλο (neut. sg.) η πίστη κι άλλο (neut. sg.) ο φανατισμός
'Faith is one thing and fanaticism is another'

Ο άλλος is often contrasted with ο ένας. This may be simply to distinguish between two members of a pair:

(17) Έχω δυο γιους. Ο ένας είναι πολιτικός μηχανικός κι ο άλλος είναι γιατρός.
'I've got two sons. One is a civil engineer and the other is a doctor.'

In addition, in reciprocal use ο ένας (in the nominative) is used with ο άλλος (in the accusative or genitive according to its function in the clause) to mean 'one another, each other'. For details of this and other reciprocal constructions see Section 5.4.3.6.3.

There are two adverbs of manner corresponding to άλλος, namely άλλο and αλλιώς. For an illustration of the use of άλλο see Section 3.1(11). Αλλιώς means 'otherwise, in a different way' and is often contrasted with έτσι 'thus'. Also corresponding to άλλος are the adverb of place αλλού and the adverb of time άλλοτε.

2.8.4 ALPHABETICAL LIST OF PRONOUNS AND DETERMINERS

The following list indicates the section where the uses of each pronoun and determiner are treated.

άλλος 'other' (2.8.3.12)

αυτός/-ή/-ό: third-person emphatic personal pronoun (2.8.1.1.2); demonstrative (2.8.3.2)

[ο] δείνα 'so-and-so; such-and-such' (2.8.3.4)

δικός μου 'own' (emphatic possessive) (2.8.3.10)

[ο] εαυτός μου 'myself' (reflexive) (2.8.1.2.3)

εγώ, εμένα, εμείς, εμάς: first-person emphatic personal pronoun (2.8.1.1.2)

εκείνος/-η/-ο: third-person emphatic personal pronoun (2.8.1.1.2); demonstrative (2.8.3.2)

ένας/μια/ένα 'a[n]' (indefinite article) (2.5.2); 'one' (numeral) (2.7); 'a certain' (2.8.3.4)

εσύ, εσένα, εσείς, εσάς: second-person emphatic personal pronoun (2.8.1.1.2)

ίδιος 'same; self; identical' (2.8.3.11)

κάθε 'each, every' (2.8.2)
καθένας 'each one' (2.8.1.2.2)
καθετί 'each thing' (2.8.1.2.2)
καθόλου 'any/none at all' (2.8.3.5)
κανείς, κανένας 'any[one]; no [one]; one' (2.8.3.5)
κάποιος 'someone' (2.8.3.4)
κάτι 'some[thing]' (2.8.3.4)
κατιτί 'something' (2.8.1.2.1)
με, μου, μας: first-person weak personal pronoun (2.8.1.1.1)
μόνος 'by [my]self, on [my] own' (2.8.3.11)
ο/η/το 'the' (definite article) (2.5.1)
όλος: 'all' (2.8.3.1.1)
ολόκληρος 'whole' (2.8.3.1.1)
όποιος 'whoever, whichever' (2.8.3.9)
[ο] οποίος 'who, that, which' (relative) (2.8.3.3)
οποιοσδήποτε 'anyone whatever' (2.8.3.9)
όσος 'however much/many; as much/many as; those who' (2.8.3.9)
οσοσδήποτε 'any quantity whatever of' (2.8.3.9)
ό,τι 'that which, what' (2.8.3.9)
οτιδήποτε 'anything whatever' (2.8.3.9)
[το] παν 'everything', οι πάντες 'everyone', τα πάντα 'everything'
    (2.8.1.2.4)
ποιος 'who; which' (interrogative) (2.8.3.6)
πόσος 'how much/many' (2.8.3.6)
σε, σου, σας: second-person weak personal pronoun (2.8.1.1.1)
[ο] τάδε 'so-and-so; such-and-such' (2.8.3.4)
τέτοιος 'such [a]' (2.8.3.7)
τι 'what' (interrogative) (2.8.3.6)
τίποτα 'no[thing]; any[thing]' (2.8.3.5)
τος/τη/το: third-person weak personal pronoun (2.8.1.1.1)
τόσος 'so much/many' (2.8.3.8)
τούτος/-η/-ο: third-person emphatic personal pronoun (2.8.1.1.2);
    demonstrative (2.8.3.2)

2.9   ADVERBIALS WITHIN THE NOUN PHRASE

The chief function of adverbials (i.e. adverbs, adverb phrases and preposititonal phrases) is to modify verbs (see Section 3.2.1) and whole sentences (see Section 3.2.5). However, they may also modify nouns, adjectives, quantifiers, and numerals.

A *noun* may be modified by a following adverb phrase (1: see Section 3.2.7) or prepositional phrase (2–3: see Sections 4.1–4.2):

(1) το δέντρο **δίπλα στο σπίτι μας**
'the tree **next to our house**'
(2) Το παιδί **στη γωνία** είναι ο γιος του Γιάννη
'The boy **in the corner** is John's son'
(3) ένας άνθρωπος **σαν το Γιάννη**
'a man **like John**'

Brief adverbials of place and time modifying a noun may appear between the article and the noun, where they act semantically as adjectives:

(4) η **κάτω** πόρτα
'the **lower/downstairs** door'
(5) η **παραπάνω** παράγραφος
'the **above** paragraph'
(6) η **πρώην** σύζυγός του
'his **former** wife'
(7) η **μέχρι τώρα** έρευνα
'the research **hitherto**'
(8) ο **τότε** πρόεδρος
'the **then** president'
(9) οι **μετέπειτα** εξελίξεις
'the **subsequent** developments'
(10) οι **περαιτέρω** αυξήσεις των μισθών
'the **further** increases in salaries'

In addition, the stereotyped clause καθώς πρέπει 'comme il faut' may be placed either between article and noun or after the noun:

(11)a. μια **καθώς πρέπει** κυρία
b. μια κυρία **καθώς πρέπει**
'a **prim and proper** lady'

In both attributive and predicative uses, *adjectives* may be modified by adverbs and adverb phrases (see also Section 3.2.2).

The adverbial normally precedes the adjective when the latter is predicative:

(12) Οι λόγοι μου ήταν **καθαρά** πρακτικοί
'My reasons were **purely** practical'
(13) Κόψ' τα **όσο γίνεται** πιο μικρά
'Cut them as small **as possible**'

The adverbial may precede or follow an *adjective* in attributive use, or a *numeral*, or a *quantifier*.

Most types of adverbial, including adverbs of manner, normally precede the adjective they modify:

(14) για **καθαρά** πρακτικούς λόγους (cf. 12)
      'for **purely** practical reasons'

(15) ένα **καλά** οργανωμένο συνέδριο
      'a **well**-organized conference'

(16) μια **πολιτικά** σκόπιμη ενέργεια
      'a **politically** expedient action'

(17) ένα **πολύ** καλό κομμάτι
      'a **very** good piece'

(18) **τόσο** ωραία λουλούδια
      '**such** beautiful flowers'

(19) ένα **πιο** περιορισμένο θέμα
      'a **more** restricted topic'

(20) **τρεις φορές** περισσότερα χρήματα
      '**three times** more money'

(21) η **αμέσως** επόμενη λέξη
      'the **immediately** following word'

(22) τα πρώτα **κάπως** πειστικά συμπεράσματα
      'the first **somewhat** convincing conclusions'

Adverbials expressing qualification (doubt, approximation, etc.: 23–26) or clarification (27–28) normally follow the adjective, quantifier, or numeral:

(23) αντικειμενικοί **τάχα** επιστήμονες
      '**supposedly** objective scientists/scholars'

(24) τα πιο ενδιαφέροντα **ίσως** βιβλία
      '**perhaps** the most interesting books'

(25) όλα **σχεδόν** τα παιδιά
      '**almost** all the children'

(26) δέκα **περίπου** φοιτητές
      '**about** ten students'

(27) ο τριαντάχρονος **σήμερα** Γιαννόπουλος
      'Yannopoulos, [who is] **now** 30 years old'

(28) Δεν έχουν καμιά **απολύτως** παράδοση
      'They have **absolutely** no tradition'

Such a clarificatory adverbial after an adjective may be a parenthetical phrase consisting of several words:

(29) το τρίτο, **ύστερα από δύο συλλογές διηγημάτων**, βιβλίο της
      'her third book, **after two collections of stories**'

The following example shows a noun modified by two adjectives, the second of which is in turn modified by two adverbials, one before and a second one (a prepositional phrase) after:

(30) η δύσκολη αλλά **καθόλου** άχαρη **γι' αυτές** ζωή τους
      'their life, [which is] difficult but **not completely** unpleasant **for them**'

In contrast to the above examples, an adverbial or prepositional phrase (31) or a clause (32) may act as a *complement* to an adjective. In such cases the adverbial follows the adjective:

(31) τα αποκλεισμένα **από τα χιόνια** χωριά
'cut off **by the snow** villages' (i.e. 'villages cut off by the snow')

(32) ο ανίκανος **να ενεργήσει** πρόεδρος
'the incapable **of acting** president' (i.e. 'the president, who was incapable of acting')

The more complex of these constructions, such as those in examples (29–32), are confined to formal and literary usage.

A parenthetical clause may be used adverbially to express something tentatively:

(33) κατά τον ίδιο **θα έλεγα** τρόπο
'in the same way, **I would say**'

Here the parenthetical clause θα έλεγα modifies the intensive determiner ίδιο, in the same way as the adverb περίπου in (34):

(34) κατά τον ίδιο **περίπου** τρόπο
'in **more or less** the same way'

2.10   CLAUSE CONNECTIVES WITHIN THE NOUN PHRASE

Certain clause connectives may appear within a noun phrase in formal and literary contexts, although they are not semantically integral to the noun phrases that contain them. These include μεν and δε, which cannot appear as the first word of a phrase, and όμως and λοιπόν, which regularly appear after the first word of a clause.

The ancient connectives μεν 'on the one hand' and δε 'on the other' often co-occur in formal styles (see example (1)), though each may appear on its own. They tend to be placed immediately after the article.

(1) Ο **μεν** κύριος Παπαδόπουλος θα έρθει· για την **δε** κυρία Παπαδοπούλου δεν ξέρω
'Mr Papadopoulos will come, but I don't know about Mrs Papadopoulos'

Λοιπόν 'so, then, thus' and όμως 'however' may appear at the beginning of a clause, but their normal position is after the first phrase of a clause. They may, however, appear within the noun phrase, though not between the definite article and the noun:

(2) Ένα **λοιπόν** πλέγμα απ᾽ αυτούς τους παράγοντες . . .
'**Thus** an aggregate of these factors . . .'

(3) Ένα **όμως** πράγμα που δεν πρέπει να ξεχνάμε είναι το εξής ...
'One thing **however** that we must not forget is the following ...'
(4) Η πράξη της **όμως** αυτή ...
'This action of hers, **however**, ...'

2.11 COMBINATIONS AND ORDER OF ELEMENTS IN THE NOUN PHRASE

The parts of speech listed in Section 2.1 can be combined in the following ways. When two or more of these constituents with the same referent are used together in the same noun phrase, all of them have to agree with each other in gender, number and case.

Within a noun phrase a *noun* may be modified by any one of the following alone: (a) an article, (b) an adjective, (c) a cardinal or ordinal numeral, (d) a quantifier, (e) a determiner ((1) interrogative, (2) indefinite, or (3) distributive); and it may accompany (f) a weak personal pronoun in the genitive or (g) a noun phrase in the genitive that depends on it:

(a) το άλογο 'the horse'
(b) μεγάλα δέντρα 'big trees'
(c) πέντε σπίτια 'five houses'
(d) μερικοί πελάτες 'some customers'
(e1) ποιος ηλίθιος 'which idiot'
(e2) κάποια ηθοποιός 'some actress'
(e3) κάθε σπίτι 'each house'
(f) στρατιώτες μας 'soldiers of ours'
(g) το σπίτι του Γιάννη 'John's house'

Articles always precede the noun. Numerals and determiners normally precede the noun too. The weak personal pronoun always follows. The neutral position of the adjective is before the noun, but it may follow when it is heavily emphasized:

(1) δέντρα μεγάλα
'*big* trees'

When an adjective is placed after the noun it modifies, and the noun is accompanied by the definite article, the adjective too must be preceded by the definite article:

(2) τα δέντρα τα μεγάλα
'the *big* trees'

The following can modify a noun only when the latter is preceded by a definite article: (h) the quantifier όλος 'all' and (j) a demonstrative. The quantifier and/or demonstrative cannot appear immediately after the article; its normal position is before the article, as in examples (3a) and

(4a), although for stylistic reasons or for reasons of emphasis the demonstrative may be placed after the noun, as in examples (3b) and (4b):

    (3)a. όλες οι καρέκλες
       b. οι καρέκλες όλες (emphasis on όλες)
         'all the chairs'
    (4)a. αυτές οι καρέκλες
       b. οι καρέκλες αυτές
         'these chairs'

When an adjective modifies a noun accompanied by a demonstrative, the most normal order is for the demonstrative to precede the article + adjective complex, which in turn precedes the noun (5a). For stylistic reasons, however, different orders are possible (5b–d), though the order art.+adj.+noun+demonstrative (5e) is normally excluded:

    (5)a. εκείνες οι ωραίες καρέκλες
       b. οι ωραίες εκείνες καρέκλες
       c. οι καρέκλες εκείνες οι ωραίες
       d. οι καρέκλες οι ωραίες εκείνες
       e. ?οι ωραίες καρέκλες εκείνες
         'those lovely chairs'

When both όλος and a demonstrative modify a noun, όλος normally precedes the demonstrative:

    (6)a. όλες αυτές οι καρέκλες
       b. όλες οι καρέκλες αυτές
       c. οι καρέκλες αυτές όλες
         'all these chairs'

When a larger number of these elements is used together, the normal order is:

quantifier	demonstrative	article	numeral	adjective	noun	poss. pron.
(7) όλοι	εκείνοι	οι	πέντε	μεγάλοι	ζωγράφοι	μας
'all	those		five	great	painters	of ours'

Interrogative, indefinite and distributive determiners, which come first in the phrase, do not co-occur with each other, nor do they co-occur with an article, with the quantifiers όλος and ολόκληρος, or with demonstratives; in addition, indefinite correlative determiners do not co-occur with numerals:

    (8) ποιοι πέντε μεγάλοι ζωγράφοι μας;
        'which five great painters of ours?'
    (9) κάποιοι μεγάλοι ζωγράφοι μας
        'certain great painters of ours'

(10) μερικοί μεγάλοι ζωγράφοι μας
      'several great painters of ours'

The order of the various other determiners is a complex question. Other quantifiers, such as πολύς 'much' (pl. 'many'), λίγος 'little' (pl. 'few'), and τόσος 'so much' tend to come first (after the quantifier όλος or ολόκληρος and the demonstrative and the article, if these are present); so do the indefinite determiners κάποιος 'a certain' and κανένας 'no/any', which cannot be accompanied by a demonstrative or the definite article. Then comes άλλος 'other', which precedes τέτοιος 'such'; these and ίδιος 'same' precede δικός [μου] '[my] own'; and all these precede numerals and regular adjectives:

(11)a. πολλά άλλα τέτοια παιχνίδια
     b. άλλα πολλά τέτοια παιχνίδια
     c. τέτοια άλλα πολλά παιχνίδια
         'many other such toys'
(12) αυτά τα ίδια τρία παιδιά
      'these same three children'
(13) κανένας άλλος μεγάλος ήρωας
      'no other great hero'

Ίδιος can however be placed between the article and demonstrative:

(14) την ίδια αυτή εποχή
      'at this same period'

A phrase such as the following, while unlikely to be used in practice, contains a large variety of elements placed together in the grammatically correct order:

(15) όλες εκείνες [or εκείνες όλες] οι πολλές άλλες τέτοιες δικές
      μου πράσινες χάντρες
      'all those numerous other such green beads of mine' [lit. 'all
      those many other such my own green beads']

When two adjectives modify the same noun attributively, they may both be placed before it. As in English, an adjective denoting an inherent quality or fundamental attribute tends to be placed nearest to the noun:

(16) ωραία ξύλινα τραπέζια
      'lovely wooden tables'

Here the adjective ξύλινα denotes an inherent quality of the tables, while the adjective ωραία expresses an opinion about them. Nevertheless, unlike English, this tendency regarding the relative order of adjectives is not a fixed rule, and the opposite order is possible, as is illustrated in (17) and (18b):

(17) ξύλινα ωραία τραπέζια (=16)

(18)a. Φορούσε τριμμένο μαύρο παλτό

  b. Φορούσε μαύρο τριμμένο παλτό
   'S/he wore a worn black coat'

One adjective may precede the noun while the other follows; the following examples are equivalent to (16–17):

(19)a. ξύλινα τραπέζια ωραία
   [lit. 'wooden tables – lovely']

  b. ωραία τραπέζια ξύλινα
   [lit. 'lovely tables – wooden']

Alternatively, both adjectives may follow the noun:

(20)a. τραπέζια ξύλινα ωραία

  b. τραπέζια ωραία ξύλινα

Here again, particular emphasis is placed on these following adjectives. If the noun is preceded by the definite article and one or more adjectives follow the noun, the article has to be repeated before each of the adjectives that follow:

(21)a. τα ξύλινα τραπέζια τα ωραία (cf. 19a)

  b. τα ωραία τραπέζια τα ξύλινα (cf. 19b)

  c. τα τραπέζια τα ξύλινα τα ωραία (cf. 20a)

  d. τα τραπέζια τα ωραία τα ξύλινα (cf. 20b)
   'the lovely wooden tables'

2.12 APPOSITIONAL CONSTRUCTIONS

Two or more noun phrases in the same case placed side-by-side may serve the same syntactic function within the sentence. Thus in

(1) **Εσείς οι άλλοι** είδατε **τη φίλη** μου **την Καίτη**;
   'Have **you others** seen **my friend Katy**?'

the two noun phrases εσείς and οι άλλοι, placed in apposition to each other and both in the nominative, jointly function as the subject of the sentence, while the two phrases τη φίλη μου and την Καίτη, placed in apposition to each other and both in the accusative, jointly function as the direct object.

A noun may modify the head noun after which it is placed. There is a small repertoire of fixed combinations in traditional Greek, which are normally used only with the appropriate form of the verb είμαι 'I am', but may also serve an exclamatory function when used on their own. Among these expressions are the following:

(2) θάλασσα λάδι
   'smooth sea' [lit. 'sea oil']
(3) παιδί μάλαμα
   'marvellous lad' [lit. 'boy gold'; cf. English 'as good as gold']
(4) σκοτάδι πίσσα
   'pitch dark'
(5) **γέννημα θρέμμα** της Θεσσαλονίκης
   '**born and bred** in Thessaloniki'
(6) κίνδυνος θάνατος
   'mortal danger'

Example (6) is found on warning signs at electrical installations, but may also be used as a subject or object predicate.

In more recent usage there is an increasing number of loose appositional compounds, some of which began as loan translations from other European languages. Whereas the traditional expressions are normally written as two separate words, the more recent combinations are written with a hyphen:

(7) θέση-κλειδί
    'key position'
(8) παιδί-θαύμα
    'child prodigy'
(9) ταξίδι-αστραπή
    'lightning trip'
(10) πρόγραμμα-πιλότος
    'pilot programme'
(11) κράτος-μέλος
    'member state'

The semantic relationship between the two nouns is not always the same: while in (7–10) the second term is metaphorical, in (11) both terms denote the same thing in a quite literal manner. While both terms in (11) inflect together (gen. sg. κράτους-μέλους, nom./acc. pl. κράτη-μέλη, etc.), the second (metaphorical) term in the other examples may remain uninflected when the first term inflects, although there is a considerable wavering in actual usage. The second term can in some cases become attached to a wide variety of heads: e.g. -κλειδί, with its sense of 'crucial', may become attached to various nouns, while -αστραπή may give the sense of 'performed very speedily' to a range of head-nouns.

A number of other types of appositional construction are concerned with the expression of *quantity* (and are typically introduced by a cardinal numeral or quantifier), but may be distinguished into the following groups according to the semantic relationship between the two noun phrases. In more formal usage the genitive is often preferred to these appositional constructions (see Section 2.4.3.2). For the sake of convenience, all of the following examples show the noun phrases in the nominative.

(a)   Quantity+substance or objects quantified

    (12)   δυο κιλά πατάτες
          'two kilos of potatoes'

    (13)   μια ώρα δρόμος
          'an hour's journey' [lit. 'one hour road']

    (14)   δέκα τόνοι τσιμέντο
          'ten tons of cement'

When it acts as the subject, a construction such as (14), where the noun phrase denoting the quantity is plural and the noun phrase denoting the item quantified is singular, normally takes a plural verb.

(b)   Container+substance or objects contained

    (15)   μερικά κουτιά σπίρτα
          'several boxes of matches'

    (16)   ένα ποτήρι νερό
          'a glass of water'

    (17)   δυο σακούλια πατάτες
          'two bags of potatoes'

Neither noun phrase in such a construction is emphasized more than the other; with (17) contrast δυο σακούλια **με** πατάτες 'two sacks **containing** potatoes' (see Section 4.2.2.10(iv)), where the focus is on 'potatoes'.

(c)   Group+objects grouped
(Compare the genitive of content, Section 2.4.3.2(ix).)

    (18)   πλήθος γυναίκες
          'a crowd of women'

    (19)   ένα κοπάδι πρόβατα
          'a flock of sheep'

    (20)   ένα ζευγάρι παπούτσια
          'a pair of shoes'

    (21)   μια σειρά πηδήματα
          'a series of leaps'

    (22)   ένα μάτσο γλαδιόλες
          'a bunch of gladioli'

As with the constructions in (b) above, neither noun phrase is emphasized more than the other; with (22) compare ένα μάτσο **από** γλαδιόλες (see also Section 4.2.2.2(i)(c)), where the meaning is almost identical, except that the focus is on 'gladioli'.

(d)   Number+objects enumerated

Here the number is expressed by an *approximative* (see Section 2.7), or by εκατοντάδες 'hundreds', χιλιάδες 'thousands', μυριάδες 'myriads', or εκατομμύριο 'million':

(23) καμιά δεκαπενταριά άνθρωποι
      'about fifteen people'
(24) εκατοντάδες πρόβατα
      'hundreds of sheep'
(25) τρεις χιλιάδες φώτα
      'three thousand lights'
(26) δέκα εκατομμύρια Έλληνες
      'ten million Greeks'

(e)   Division+substance divided

(Compare the partitive genitive, Section 2.4.3.2(x).)

(27) ένα κομμάτι ψωμί
      'a piece of bread'
(28) μια στάλα νερό
      'a drop of water'

Appositional constructions of the kinds exemplified in (12–28) are readily usable when they consist simply of [numeral or quantifier+]noun+noun. If the first noun is modified by some other term, the construction may become problematic and an alternative construction may be used; nevertheless, it has to be said that even these alternatives are sometimes problematic and may be avoided. When the first noun is preceded by the definite article, it is sometimes possible to retain the appositional construction as long as the second noun too is accompanied by the definite article:

(29) **τα** δυο κιλά **οι** πατάτες
      '**the** two kilos of potatoes' (contrast 12)
(30) **το** ποτήρι **το** νερό
      '**the** glass of water' (contrast 16)
(31) **το** ζευγάρι **τα** παπούτσια
      '**the** pair of shoes' (contrast 20)
(32) **το** κομμάτι **το** ψωμί
      '**the** piece of bread' (contrast 27)

In many other cases, however, and especially where the first noun phrase is in the plural and the second in the singular (33–34), or if the first is modified by some term other than the definite article (35–36), or if no numeral or quantifier is present, the appositional construction is often replaced by a construction with the genitive:

(33) τόνοι **τσιμέντου** (contrast 14)
      'tons **of cement**'
(34) χιλιάδες **λαού**
      'thousands **of people**'
(35) μια **ωραία** σειρά **μαθημάτων** (contrast 21)
      'a lovely series **of lessons**'
(36) ένα **μεγάλο** πλήθος **γυναικών**
      'a **large** crowd **of women**' (contrast 18)

Constructions similar in meaning to type (b) above but with the first noun phrase introduced by the definite article may be replaced by constructions involving a prepositional phrase introduced by με:

(37) **το** κουτί **με τα σπίρτα** (contrast 15)
      '**the** box **of matches**'
(38) **τα** δυο σακούλια **με τις πατάτες** (contrast 17)
      '**the** two bags **of potatoes**'

Constructions of type (c), but containing modifiers for the second noun, may be replaced by constructions involving a prepositional phrase introduced by από:

(39) μια σειρά από τεράστια πηδήματα
      'a series of huge leaps'

Otherwise the second noun phrase is normally in the genitive, as in Section 2.4.3.2 (37–38):

(40) **τα** δυο κιλά **του καφέ**
      '**the** two kilos **of coffee**'
(41) **οι** δυο χιλιάδες **των επιβατών**
      'the two thousand **passengers**'
(42) **τα** δέκα εκατομμύρια **των Ελλήνων**
      '**the** ten million **Greeks**' (contrast 26)
(43) **τα** κομμάτια **του ψωμιού**
      '**the** pieces **of bread**' (contrast 27)

On the other hand, the following type of construction is very commonly used with δεκάδες, εκατοντάδες and χιλιάδες:

(44) τα εκατοντάδες πρόβατα (cf. 24)
      'the hundreds of sheep'
(45) τα τρεις χιλιάδες φώτα (cf. 25)
      'the three thousand lights'

In (44) the phrase εκατοντάδες modifies the noun phrase τα πρόβατα as if the former were an adjective; similarly, in (45), τρεις χιλιάδες modifies τα φώτα.

Other, more stereotyped, appositional constructions include the following:

(46) Τι **είδος** άνθρωπος είναι;
      'What **sort of** person is s/he?'

The genitive είδους may be used here in more formal styles.

3 THE ADVERB AND THE ADVERB PHRASE

An adverb or an adverb phrase may function in any of the following ways:

(a) to modify a verb (see Section 3.2.1);
(b) to modify an adjective or another adverb (3.2.2);
(c) to modify a noun (3.2.3);
(d) to modify a numeral or quantifier (3.2.4);
(e) to modify a whole clause or sentence (3.2.5).

An adverb phrase is a phrase whose head is an adverb:

> (1) Το βιβλίο είναι **πάνω στο τραπέζι**
>   'The book is **on the table**'
> (2) Τρέχει **πολύ γρήγορα**
>   'S/he runs/is running **very fast**'

In example (1) the adverb πάνω is the head of the adverb phrase πάνω στο τραπέζι. In (2) the adverb γρήγορα is the head of the adverb phrase πολύ γρήγορα, in which it is modified by πολύ.

Although these sections will concentrate on adverbs and adverb phrases, they will sometimes mention other adverbials. An adverbial is any word, phrase or clause that functions adverbially, and may consist of (3) a single adverb, a phrase – for instance (1–2) an adverb phrase or (4) a noun phrase in the accusative – or (5) a clause:

> (3) Θα έρθω **αύριο**
>   'I'll come **tomorrow**'
> (4) Θα έρθω **την άλλη μέρα**
>   'I'll come **the next day**'
> (5) Θα έρθω **όταν είμαι έτοιμος**
>   'I'll come **when I'm ready**'

Prepositional phrases (i.e. phrases introduced by prepositions), including those in adverbial functions, are covered in Sections 4ff.

From a semantic point of view, most adverbials specify the *manner* in which an action takes place (or the manner in which a situation exists), or the *place* or *time* at which the action takes place (or the place or time at which the situation exists), or qualify what is being said in some other way. The adverbials in examples (3–5) above all indicate *time*.

Sections 3.1–3.2.5 will concentrate on the meaning and form of adverbials (almost exclusively single-word adverbs) and their relationship to the items listed in (a–e) above (though the relationship between verb phrase adverbials and the verb is covered in greater detail in Section 1.1.2). Sections 3.2.6–3.2.7 cover the construction of adverb phrases. For the syntax of adverbial clauses see Sections 5.3.5–5.3.5.2 (conditional clauses), 5.3.6 (concessive clauses), 5.3.7 (temporal clauses, as in example (5) above), 5.3.8 (clauses of manner), 5.3.9 (clauses of purpose), 5.3.10 (clauses of result), and 5.3.11 (clauses of cause).

3.1   TYPES OF ADVERB: MANNER, PLACE, TIME, QUANTITY, ETC.

Adverbs are most commonly used to specify *manner, place, time, or quantity.*

Adverbs of manner (e.g. καλά 'well', εύκολα 'easily') are regularly formed from adjectives and many passive perfect participles according to the rules laid down in Part II, Sections 4.1–4.3. Most adverbs from adjectives in -ος end in -α, but some end in -ως, as do adverbs from most adjectives in -ης. A few adjectives form two different adverbs with two different uses. Thus απλός 'simple' forms απλά and απλώς 'simply', the first meaning 'in a simple manner', and the other meaning 'just, only'; similarly, ευχάριστος forms ευχάριστα 'pleasantly' and ευχαρίστως 'with pleasure':

(1)a. Το έκανε απλά
      'S/he did it simply'
   b. Απλώς κοιτάζω
      'I'm just looking'
(2)a. Πέρασα ευχάριστα τις διακοπές μου
      'I spent my holidays pleasantly'
   b. Θα το κάνω ευχαρίστως
      'I'll do it with pleasure'

The most common *adverbs of manner,* apart from those formed from adjectives, include:

πώς	how (interrogative)
όπως	however (correlative)
έτσι	thus; in this/that way
αλλιώς	otherwise; differently, in another way
κάπως	in some way
καθόλου	[not] at all
οπωσδήποτε	in some way or another; by all means; certainly
μόνο	only
μαζί	together

Κάπως and καθόλου are also adverbs of quantity. None of the adverbs listed above has a comparative or superlative form. Έτσι and αλλιώς are often contrasted with each other:

(3) Εμείς το κάνουμε έτσι, εσείς το κάνετε αλλιώς
'We do it like this, you do it differently'

The most common *adverbs of place* are the following:

πού	where (interrog.)		
όπου	where[ever] (relative and correlative)		
εδώ	here	κοντά	near
εκεί	there	μακριά	far
κάπου	somewhere	ανάμεσα	between
αλλού	somewhere else	απέναντι	opposite
παντού	everywhere	δίπλα, πλάι	nearby
πουθενά	nowhere	γύρω	around
οπουδήποτε	anywhere	χάμω	on the ground
πάνω	up; above	πέρα	beyond
κάτω	down; below	ψηλά	high up
μέσα	inside	χαμηλά	low down
έξω	outside	δεξιά	to/on the right
εμπρός, μπροστά	in front	αριστερά	to/on the left
πίσω	behind		

Μπροστά can also mean 'present', as in

(4) Δεν ήσουν μπροστά
'You weren't present'

Few of the adverbs of place listed above have a comparative or super-lative form, although some may be preceded by πιο to form the equivalent of a comparative (see below, Section 3.1.1). A number of adverbs of place may be followed by a weak personal pronoun or by a prepositional phrase (see Section 3.2.7).

The majority of the most common *adverbs of time* can be divided seman-tically into (a) those indicating *point in time*, (b) those indicating *frequency*, and (c) others:

(a)   Adverbs indicating point in time

πότε	when (interrogative)		
όποτε	whenever (correlative)		
οπότε	at which point, whereupon (conjunctive)		
τώρα	now	πρώτα	first
τότε	then [at that point]	πριν	before; ago
		μετά	afterwards, later

άλλοτε	at another time; formerly	μεθάυριο	the day after tomorrow
κάποτε	at some time; once	απόψε	tonight
νωρίς	early	ύστερα, έπειτα	then; next
αργά	late	ήδη, κιόλας	already
οποτεδήποτε	at any time	αμέσως	immediately
προχθές	the day before yesterday	επιτέλους	at last
χθες	yesterday	μόλις	just
σήμερα	today	πρόπερσι	two years ago
αύριο	tomorrow	πέρ[υ]σι	last year
		φέτος	this year
		του χρόνου	next year

Πριν and μετά are used adverbially to mean 'before, earlier' and 'afterwards, later':

(5) Θα 'πρεπε να το 'χες κάνει πριν
'You ought to have done it before'
(6) Θα το κάνω μετά
'I'll do it later'

When temporal distance is expressed with μετά and πριν, it may be done by means of a following από-phrase (7a and 8a), or by a noun phrase in the adverbial accusative (see Section 2.4.2.1(vi)) either before (7b and 8b) or after (7c and 8c) the temporal adverb. In these expressions, πριν means 'ago' or 'previously', while μετά means 'later' or even (with a future verb) 'in . . . time' (8d):

(7)a. Έγινε πριν από ένα χρόνο
   b. Έγινε ένα χρόνο πριν
   c. Έγινε πριν ένα χρόνο
   'It happened a year ago/before'
(8)a. Έγινε μετά από ένα χρόνο
   b. Έγινε ένα χρόνο μετά
   c. Έγινε μετά ένα χρόνο
   'It happened a year later'
   d. Θα γίνει μετά ένα χρόνο
   'It will happen in a year's time'

Πριν and μετά also function as prepositions (see Sections 4.2.2.15 and 4.2.2.11), and πριν (with or without να) as a temporal conjunction (Section 5.3.7).

(b) Adverbs indicating frequency

(τρεις) φορές	(three) times	καμιά φορά	from time to time
συχνά	often, frequently	σπάνια	rarely
κάπου κάπου	from time to time	τακτικά	regularly
πότε πότε	occasionally	συνήθως	usually

Also phrases introduced by κάθε 'every', e.g.:

κάθε πόσο	how often	κάθε φορά	every time
κάθε τόσο	every so often	κάθε Σάββατο	every Saturday

(c)   Other adverbs of time

πάλι, ξανά	again	όλο	all the time
πια, πλέον	[any/no] more	ποτέ	[n]ever
ακόμα	still; yet	ουδέποτε	never
πάντα	always		

Ακόμα is also an adverb of quantity ('more'). Ουδέποτε, whose use is normally confined to formal contexts, differs from ποτέ in its use, in that it can only have negative force and may be used with a positive verb.

Some adverbs denoting point in time and frequency have comparative forms (see Section 3.1.1 below).

The chief *adverbs of quantity* are the following:

πόσο	how much (interrogative)
όσο	as much as (correlative)
οσοδήποτε	however much (universal correlative)
τόσο	so much; this/that much
κάμποσο/καμπόσο	quite a lot
κάπως	somewhat
πολύ	very; much, a lot; too [much]
περισσότερο	more (comparative)
λίγο	a little
λιγότερο	less (comparative)
ελάχιστα	very little (absolute superlative)
τελείως	completely
αρκετά	quite [a lot]
σχεδόν	almost
τουλάχιστον	at least
πάνω κάτω	approximately
περίπου	approximately; more or less
καθόλου	[not] at all
μάλλον	rather
εξίσου	equally

| πάρα | (intensifying adverb used regularly before πολύ: πάρα πολύ 'very much; too much') |
| πιο | more (used in front of adjective or adverb to form a comparative) |

Some of the above are comparative or superlative forms; these are the only comparative forms of adverbs of quantity (see Section 3.1.1 below).

A small number of adverbs do not fit into any of the above categories. These include *sentential adverbs* (adverbs that modify a whole sentence: see Section 3.2.5) as well as the intensive adverbs μόνο 'only, just' (adverbial equivalent of the intensive pronoun and determiner μόνος) and το ίδιο 'in the same way, equally' (equivalent of the pronoun and determiner ο ίδιος), and the contrastive adverb άλλο 'more, any further' (equivalent of the contrastive pronoun and determiner άλλος):

(9) Η Άννα είναι το ίδιο ανόητη με τον Πέτρο
     'Ann is just as stupid as Peter'

(10) Δεν είδα άντρες εκεί, μόνο γυναίκες
     'I didn't see [any] men there, only women'

(11) Μην προχωράς άλλο!
     'Don't go any further forward!'

Conjunctive adverbs are those that join clauses or sentences together semantically without being strictly conjunctions. These include:

όμως	however
ωστόσο	nevertheless
παρ' όλα αυτά	nevertheless
διαφορετικά	otherwise
πάντως	still, at any rate
λοιπόν	well then
άρα	therefore
επομένως	consequently
άλλωστε, εξάλλου	besides
τότε	then
τώρα	now
έτσι	thus
λες και	it's as though

Τώρα is often used to express the beginning of a new stage in an argument, while τότε is often used to introduce a clause expressing a conclusion ('then' in the apodosis of a conditional sentence (12), or 'in that case' (13)):

(12) **Τώρα** αν νομίζεις ότι είδες το δολοφόνο, **τότε** πρέπει να ειδοποιήσεις την αστυνομία
     '**Now** if you think you saw the murderer, **then** you must inform the police'

(13) – Δε θέλω να βγω. – Ε, **τότε**, γιατί είπες ότι θα βγούμε μαζί;
      '"I don't want to go out." "In that case, why did you say we
      would go out together?"'

The noun αλήθεια is used adverbially to mean 'by the way', or 'now you
come to mention it':

(14) Αλήθεια, τι κάνει η Μαρία;
      'By the way, how is Mary?'

Various kinds of *noun phrase* are used adverbially. These are normally in
the accusative and may be used as adverbs of place (15–16), time (17–18),
or quantity (19):

(15) πάμε **σπίτι/σχολείο/περίπατο/εκδρομή/παρέα**
      'We're going **home/to school/for a walk/on a trip/together**'
(16) γιαλό γιαλό
      'along the seashore'
(17) συνέχεια
      'constantly'
(18) τη νύχτα
      'during the night'
(19) **δέκα μέτρα** βαθύ
      '**ten metres** deep'

For more details of the accusative of noun phrases in adverbial use see
Section 2.4.2.1.

3.1.1   THE COMPARATIVE AND SUPERLATIVE OF ADVERBS
(See also Part II, Section 4.4.)

Most adverbs of manner that are derived from adjectives form single-
word comparatives and absolute superlatives in the same way as adjectives
(see Section 2.6.2), but with the -α ending; alternatively, the comparative
may be expressed by the basic form preceded by πιο:

εύκολα 'easily'
ευκολότερα *or* πιο εύκολα 'more easily' (comparative)
ευκολότατα 'very easily' (absolute superlative)

Adverbs do not normally form a relative superlative; the comparative
form is used instead:

(1) Αυτό που μου άρεσε καλύτερα ήταν η μουσική
     'What I liked better/best was the music'

Nevertheless, a phrase consisting of το+neuter singular of the comparative
form of the adjective is used to express 'as . . . as possible':

(2) Σας παρακαλώ στείλτε τη συνδρομή σας το συντομότερο [*or* το
συντομότερο δυνατόν]
'Please send your subscription as soon as possible'

Some adverbs of place may be preceded by πιο to form the equivalent
of a comparative (εδώ, εκεί, πάνω, κάτω, μέσα, έξω, μπροστά, πίσω,
κοντά, μακριά, χάμω, πέρα), e.g.:

(3) πιο εδώ
'more this way, more in this direction'
(4) πιο πάνω
'higher up'
(5) πιο μέσα
'further in'
(6) πιο μπροστά
'further forward'
(7) πιο κοντά
'nearer'
(8) πιο πέρα
'further along, further down'

Some adverbs of time form single-word comparatives and absolute
superlatives (cf. Part II, Section 4.4):

νωρίς 'early' – νωρίτερα 'earlier'
αργά 'late' – αργότερα 'later'
πρώτα 'first' – πρωτύτερα 'earlier'
συχνά 'often' – συχνότερα 'more often' – συχνότατα 'very often'
σπάνια 'rarely' – σπανιότερα 'more rarely' – σπανιότατα 'very
rarely'
συνήθως 'usually' – συνηθέστερα 'more usually' – συνηθέστατα 'very
frequently'
τακτικά 'regularly' – τακτικότερα 'more regularly' – τακτικότατα
'very regularly'

All the above (except συνήθως) may alternatively form comparatives by
adding πιο to the basic form, as can πριν and ύστερα:

πιο πριν 'previously, earlier'
πιο ύστερα 'later'

The single-word comparative forms of the quantitative adverbs πολύ and
λίγο are περισσότερο and λιγότερο respectively. These are the only
adverbs of quantity that can be used in the comparative degree.

3.2   THE SYNTACTICAL USES OF THE ADVERB

Many adverbs may be used on their own as single-word responses. These include not only those listed in Section 3.1 above, but a number of adverbs of manner used as exclamations to express a view about what has just been said, e.g.:

ακριβώς!	exactly, precisely!
βέβαια! *or* βεβαίως!	certainly, of course!
έκτακτα!	excellent!
καλά!	good!
λαμπρά!	splendid!
σαφώς!	obviously!
ωραία!	fine, lovely!

Other adverbs too are used as response utterances, e.g.:

ναι	yes
όχι	no
μάλιστα	certainly
ίσως	perhaps
πράγματι	indeed

The chief syntactic function of the adverb, however, is to modify a verb (3.2.1), an adjective or adverb (3.2.2), a noun (3.2.3), a numeral or quantifier (3.2.4), or a clause or sentence (3.2.5).

3.2.1   ADVERB MODIFYING A VERB
(See also Section 1.1.2.)

Adverbs of manner (1), place (2), time (3), or quantity (4) may modify a verb:

(1) Δούλεψα **καλά**
    'I worked **well**'
(2) Δούλεψα **εδώ**
    'I worked **here**'
(3) Δούλεψα **χθες**
    'I worked **yesterday**'
(4) Δούλεψα **πολύ**
    'I worked **a lot**'

Often, particularly in more literary usage, an adverb of manner is replaced by a prepositional phrase consisting of με . . . τρόπο (5) or με+abstract noun (6):

(5) Εξήγησε το κείμενο **με απλό τρόπο**
    'S/he explained the text **simply**'

(6) Μίλησε **με απλότητα**
   'S/he spoke **simply** [lit. 'with simplicity']'

3.2.2   ADVERB MODIFYING AN ADJECTIVE OR ADVERB

An adverb of manner may modify an *adjective*:

(1) **καλά** οργανωμένος
   '**well** organized'

A few adverbs of time may modify an adjective:

(2) το **αμέσως** επόμενο βήμα
   'the **immediately** following step'

An adverb of quantity modifying an adjective conveys the degree of the quality denoted by the adjective:

(3)a. **πολύ** καλός
     '**very** good; **too** good'
   b. **πιο** καλός
     'better'
   c. **πολύ** καλύτερος
     '**much** better'
   d. **κάπως** καλύτερος
     '**somewhat** better'
   e. **λίγο** καλύτερος
     '**a bit** better'
   f. **τρεις φορές** καλύτερος
     '**three times** better'
   g. **λιγότερο** καλός
     '**less** good'
   h. **τόσο** καλός
     '**so** good'
   i. **πόσο** καλός
     '**how** good' (question)
   j. **όσο** καλός
     '**however** good'
   k. **αρκετά** καλός
     '**quite** good'
   l. **τι** καλός!
     '**how** good!' (exclamation; cf. Section 5.1.6.1)
   m.**φοβερά** καλός
     '**terribly** good'
   n. **ελάχιστα** κατανοητό
     '**hardly** comprehensible'

    ο. **καθόλου** ευχάριστο
    'not at all pleasant'

In some cases the relationship is not so simple:

  (4)a. **καθαρά** οικονομικό
     'purely economic'
    b. **πολιτικά** ανώριμος
     'politically immature'

It would perhaps be sensible to treat καθαρά as an adverb of quantity. The last phrase is an example of a 'viewpoint adverb', i.e. one that denotes the point of view from which the adjective is applied ('from a political point of view'). In some idiolects or styles the adverb may sometimes appear in its *katharevousa* form in these more complex combinations:

  (5)a. **καθαρώς** οικονομικό
    b. **πολιτικώς** ανώριμος

For further details about adverbs within the noun phrase see Section 2.9.
    An adverb may modify an *adverb* (especially an adverb of manner) in much the same way as it may modify an adjective:

  (6)a. **πολύ** καλά
     'very well'
    b. **πάρα** πολύ καλά
     'very well' (stronger than 6a)
    c. **πιο** καλά
     'better'
    d. **πολύ** καλύτερα
     'much better'
    e. **κάπως** καλύτερα
     'somewhat better'
    f. **λίγο** καλύτερα
     'a bit better'
    g. **τρεις φορές** καλύτερα
     'three times better'
    h. **λιγότερο** καλά
     'less well'
    i. **τόσο** καλά
     'so well'
    j. **πόσο** καλά
     'how well' (question)
    k. **αρκετά** καλά
     'quite well'
    l. **τι** καλά!
     'how well!' (exclamation)

m. **φοβερά** καλά
   '**terribly** well'

More complex combinations of adverb + adverb tend to be replaced with a phrase made up of με . . . τρόπο:

(7) με καθόλου ευχάριστο τρόπο
     'not at all pleasantly' [lit. 'in [a] not-at-all pleasant way']

An adverb may also modify an adverb of place or time. Such modification is of two kinds. In the first, the modifying adverb precedes the one modified, while in the second the modifying adverb follows. In both cases, the range of combinations of adverbs is limited.

Adverbs that precede the adverb which they modify include πιο, πολύ, αρκετά, τόσο, αμέσως. Πιο may be used with an adverb indicating location and almost any adverb of place indicating relative direction (e.g. πάνω/κάτω, μπροστά/πίσω, μέσα/έξω, κοντά/μακριά, πέρα) as well as with some adverbs denoting relative time. Examples:

(8)a. πιο εδώ/εκεί
       'on this/that side [of a certain point]'
   b. πιο πάνω/κάτω
       'further up/down'
   c. πιο ψηλά/χαμηλά
       'higher/lower'
   d. πιο αριστερά/δεξιά
       'more to the left/right'
   e. πιο ανατολικά/δυτικά
       'further east/west'
   f. πιο νωρίς/αργά
       'earlier/later'
   g. πιο πριν/ύστερα
       'previously/subsequently'

Πολύ and αρκετά may be used with adverbs of place and time which have a relative sense:

(9)a. πολύ/αρκετά πάνω/κάτω
       'very/quite far up/down'
   b. πολύ/αρκετά ψηλά/χαμηλά
       'very/quite high/low'
   c. πολύ/αρκετά αριστερά/δεξιά
       'very much to the left/right'
   d. πολύ/αρκετά ανατολικά/δυτικά
       'very much to the east/west'
   e. πολύ/αρκετά νωρίς/αργά
       'very/quite early/late'

f. πολύ/αρκετά πριν/ύστερα
'very much previously/subsequently'

They may also be used to modify comparative adjectives and adverbs:

(10)a. πολύ/αρκετά πιο καλός/καλά
'very much better'
b. πολύ/αρκετά πιο πάνω/κάτω
'considerably further up/down'

Τόσο can be used with some of the adverbs of place and time that have a relative sense:

(11)a. τόσο πάνω/κάτω
'so far up/down'
b. τόσο ψηλά/χαμηλά
'so high/low'
c. τόσο νωρίς/αργά
'so early/late'

Αμέσως may be used with πριν/ύστερα and πιο:

(12)a. αμέσως πριν/ύστερα
'immediately before/after'
b. αμέσως πιο πάνω/κάτω
'immediately further up/down'

The other kind of combination of adverbs is the one in which the modified adverb of place or time comes after the modifying adverb. The most common type of combination involves εδώ or εκεί followed by an adverb indicating relative position or direction, e.g.:

(13)a. εδώ/εκεί πάνω/κάτω
'up/down here/there'
b. εδώ/εκεί κοντά
'near here/there'
c. εδώ/εκεί πέρα
'over here/there'
d. εδώ/εκεί ψηλά/χαμηλά
'up/down here/there'

Περίπου is used before or (more commonly) after some adverbs of place and time to indicate approximation:

(14)a. εδώ περίπου
'more or less here'
b. τότε περίπου
'more or less at that time'
c. στις δέκα περίπου
'at about ten; on about the tenth'

3.2.3   ADVERB OR ADVERB PHRASE MODIFYING A NOUN

An adverb or adverb phrase may modify a following (1–2) or preceding (3) noun:

(1) η **πίσω** πόρτα
     'the **back** door'
(2) ο **τότε** υπουργός
     'the **then** minister'
(3) τα δέντρα **εκεί πέρα**
     'the trees **over there**'

For further details see Section 2.9.

3.2.4   ADVERB MODIFYING A NUMERAL OR QUANTIFIER

An adverb may modify a numeral or quantifier:

(1)a. **σχεδόν** όλα *or* όλα **σχεδόν**
      '**almost** all'
   b. **τουλάχιστον** τρεις φορές
      '**at least** three times'
   c. για ένα μήνα **περίπου**
      'for **about** one month'
   d. **τι** πολλά δέντρα!
      '**what** a lot of trees!' [lit. 'what many trees']
   e. **τόσο** πολλά δέντρα
      '**so** many trees'

3.2.5   ADVERB MODIFYING A CLAUSE OR SENTENCE

An adverb modifying a whole clause or sentence (sometimes known as a *sentential adverb*) expresses the speaker's evaluation of the meaning of the whole clause or sentence:

(1) **Ευτυχώς** το βρήκαμε
     '**Luckily** we found it'
(2) **Δυστυχώς** δεν το βρήκαμε
     '**Unfortunately** we didn't find it'
(3) **Ειλικρινά** δεν ξέρω
     '**Frankly** I don't know'

Other sentential adverbs include απλώς 'simply', βέβαια 'of course', ίσως 'perhaps', περιέργως 'curiously enough', πραγματικά 'in fact', σίγουρα 'for sure', τελικά 'finally', and φυσικά 'naturally'.

Word order, combined with context, may distinguish between two uses of the same adverb, whether modifying a verb (4a) or a sentence (4b):

(4)a. Θα μιλήσω **φυσικά**
  'I'll speak naturally [=in a natural manner]'
   b. **Φυσικά** θα μιλήσω
  'Naturally [=of course] I'll speak'

3.2.6   COMPLEMENTS OF ADVERBS

Many adverbs may be followed by prepositions, e.g.:

ανάλογα με	'according to'
ανεξάρτητα από	'independently of'
αριστερά/δεξιά από	'to the left/right of'
ενάντια σε	'against'
όσο για	'as for'
πριν από	'before'
σύμφωνα με	'according to'
σχετικά με	'in relation to'
ύστερα από	'after'

For certain adverbs of place followed by prepositional phrases see Section 3.2.7.
A few evaluative adverbs of manner such as καλά and ωραία may be followed by a που-clause:

(1) Καλά που το θυμήθηκες
  'It's a good thing you remembered it'

Some adverbs of place and time may be modified by a που-clause (εδώ που, εκεί που, πάνω που, τώρα που, τότε που, μετά που); see Section 5.3.1.3.
The quantitative adverb όσο may introduce either a που-clause or a να-clause (όσο που, όσο να, which are equivalent to ώσπου and ώσπου να respectively):

(2) Όσο που πέρασε [*or* Όσο να περάσει] το λεωφορείο, είχαμε
    γίνει μούσκεμα
  'By the time the bus came by, we'd got soaking wet'

Μετά and πριν also function as prepositions (see Sections 4.2.2.11 and 4.2.2.15).
Εκτός, which may also function as a preposition (see Section 4.2.3) generally functions as an adverb, in which case it may be followed by από, αν or που:

(3) Όλοι πήγαν, εκτός από το Γιάννη
  'Everyone went except John'
(4) Εκτός από πολυέξοδο, είναι και κουραστικό
  'Apart from being expensive, it's tiring'

(5) Θα είμαστε τρεις, εκτός αν θέλει κι η Μαρία να έρθει μαζί μας
'There'll be three of us, unless Mary wants to come with us too'

(6) Ο Γιώργος, εκτός που όλο τρώει τα νύχια του, είναι και
αντιπαθητικός τύπος
'George, quite apart [from the fact] that he continually bites his
nails, is an unpleasant character'

3.2.7   ADVERBS OF PLACE USED WITH WEAK PERSONAL PRONOUN OR PREPOSITIONAL PHRASE

A number of adverbs, chiefly indicating relative location or direction, may
be followed by a weak personal pronoun in the genitive. Examples:

ανάμεσά τους	'between/among them'
απέναντί μας	'opposite us'
γύρω της	'around her'
δίπλα σου	'next to you'
κοντά σου	'near you'
μαζί σου	'with you'
μακριά του	'far away from him'
μέσα μας	'inside us'
μπροστά μου	'in front of me'
πάνω του	'on him/it' (απάνω and επάνω are alternative forms of πάνω)
πίσω σας	'behind you'
πλάι του	'beside him'

Such constructions may be preceded by από 'from':

από μπροστά τους	'from in front of them', etc.

Έξω and κάτω are not normally used with a weak pronoun without themselves being introduced by από:

απ' έξω του	'outside him/it' *or* 'from outside him/it'
από κάτω μας	'under/below them' *or* 'from under/below them'

In addition, πάνω+weak pronoun is preceded by από when it means 'over'
or 'above' (e.g., *either* location at a point above but not in contact, *or*
passage over) rather than 'on' (e.g. location on the surface of):

(1) Στεκόμουν από πάνω του
'I stood over/above him/it'
(2) Πήδηξα από πάνω του
'I jumped over him/it'

When μέσα+weak pronoun means 'through' (passage) rather then 'inside' (motion into or location inside), it too is preceded by από:

    (3) Η σφαίρα πέρασε από μέσα του
        'The bullet passed through him/it'

In addition, the adverb of *time* ποτέ '[n]ever' may be followed by a weak pronoun in the genitive referring to the subject in order to intensify its meaning:

    (4) Ποτέ μου δε θα έκανα τέτοιο πράγμα
        'I would never ever do such a thing'

If, however, these adverbs (to which can be added έξω and κάτω) are used with a noun or an emphatic pronoun, this noun or emphatic pronoun must be contained within a prepositional phrase introduced by one of the prepositions σε or από (the relevant preposition is placed in brackets after the adverb in the list below; for further details about the semantic differences indicated by the alternative use of σε and από with adverbs of place see Section 4.2.1):

ανάμεσα (σε)	'between, among'
απέναντι (από/σε)	'opposite'
γύρω (από/σε)	'around'
δίπλα (σε)	'next to'
έξω (από)	'outside'
κάτω (από)	'under, below'
κοντά (σε)	'near'
μαζί (με)	'[together] with'
μακριά (από)	'far from, away from'
μέσα	(σε) 'inside'; (από) 'through; from inside'
μπροστά (από/σε)	'in front of'
πάνω	(σε) 'on [top of]'; (από) 'above'
πίσω (από)	'behind'
πλάι (σε)	'beside'

The use of an emphatic pronoun in such cases (as in 9, 13, 15, 20 below) often indicates contrast. Examples:

    (5) ανάμεσα στα βιβλία
        'between/among the books'
    (6) απέναντι στο σπίτι της
        'opposite her house'
    (7) γύρω από τη φωτιά
        'round the fire'
    (8) δίπλα στο Γιάννη
        'next to John'

(9)   δίπλα σ' **εσένα**
      'next to *you* [rather than next to anyone else]'
(10) έξω από το σπίτι
      'outside the house'
(11) κάτω από το τραπέζι
      'under the table'
(12) κοντά στην Αθήνα
      'near Athens'
(13) κοντά σ' **εμάς**
      'near *us* [rather than near anyone else]'
(14) μαζί με τους άλλους
      'together with the others'
(15) μαζί μ' **αυτούς**
      'with *them* [rather than with anyone else]'
(16) μακριά από την πόλη
      'away/far from the town'
(17) μέσα στην εκκλησία
      'inside the church'
(18) μέσα από το δωμάτιο
      'through the room; from inside the room'
(19) μπροστά στο σπίτι
      'in front of the house'
(20) μπροστά σ' **αυτούς**
      'in front of *them* [rather than in front of anyone else]'
(21) πάνω στο τραπέζι
      'on the table'
(22) πάνω από το τραπέζι
      'above the table'
(23) πίσω από το δέντρο
      'behind the tree'
(24) πλάι στο δέντρο
      'beside the tree'

Although the adverb is more frequently placed before the prepositional phrase, it may optionally follow it. If the adverb would have been used with a σε-phrase had the adverb come first, the order can simply be reversed:

(25) στην εκκλησία μέσα (=17)
(26) στο σπίτι μπροστά (=19)
(27) στο τραπέζι πάνω (=21)

On the other hand, if the adverb would have been used with an από-phrase had the adverb come first, the prepositional phrase is commonly introduced by σε and the adverb by από:

(28) στο σπίτι απ' έξω (=10)
(29) στο τραπέζι από κάτω (=11)
(30) στο τραπέζι από πάνω (=22)
(31) στο δέντρο από πίσω (=23)

For other adverbs commonly used in combination with a prepositional phrase, but not in combination with a weak personal pronoun see Section 3.2.6.

In addition to the *spatial* relations indicated by these adverbs, they are also used *metaphorically* to indicate non-spatial (usually abstract) relations. Some examples:

(32) η θέση μου **απέναντι** σ' αυτό το ζήτημα
      'my position **vis-à-vis** this question'
(33) ένα βιβλίο **γύρω** στο Σολωμό
      'a book **about** Solomos'
(34) Την παράσταση την είδαν **γύρω** στους διακόσιους θεατές
      'The performance was seen by **about** two hundred spectators'
(35) Δεν μπορώ να ζήσω **κάτω** από τέτοιες συνθήκες
      'I can't live **under** such conditions'
(36) Τελειώσαμε τη δουλειά **μέσα** σε τρεις μήνες
      'We finished the job **within** three months'
(37) Αυτό δεν είναι τίποτα **μπροστά** στη ζημιά που πάθαμε
      'That's nothing **compared with** the damage we've suffered'
(38) Δεν έχω λεφτά **πάνω** μου
      'I've got no money **on** me'
(39) Γράφει διατριβή **πάνω** στο ρόλο των Άγγλων στην Κατοχή
      'S/he's writing a thesis **on** the role of the English [i.e. British]
          in the Occupation'
(40) Ήρθαν **πάνω** από τριακόσιοι φοιτητές
      '**Over** three hundred students came'

In (40) the noun phrase τριακόσιοι φοιτητές is nominative because the whole phrase introduced by πάνω από functions as the subject of the verb.

In addition to all that has been said above, all these adverbs may be accompanied by a σε-phrase in a looser relationship, in which the prepositional phrase does not depend on the adverb but is in apposition to it. The interpretation of such constructions usually depends on pragmatic factors, as is shown in (41–43). An adverb that is typically found with από may be accompanied by a σε-phrase in apposition to it, as in (44–46). Unlike the kind of construction treated so far, in these looser constructions there may optionally be a pause between the adverb and the prepositional phrase:

(41) Ο Νίκος είναι **πάνω** στη σοφίτα
      'Nick's **up in** the attic' (not *on* the attic)

(42) Ο Νίκος είναι απέναντι στο μαγαζί
   'Nick's **opposite in** the shop' (otherwise '*opposite* the shop')

(43) Ο Νίκος είναι δίπλα στο μαγαζί
   'Nick's **next door at** the shop' (otherwise '*next to* the shop')

(44) Ο Νίκος είναι κάτω στο υπόγειο
   'Nick's **down in** the cellar' (cf. κάτω από το υπόγειο '*under* the cellar')

(45) Ο Νίκος είναι έξω στον κήπο
   'Nick's **out in** the garden' (cf. έξω από τον κήπο '*outside* the garden')

(46) Ο Νίκος γύρισε πίσω στο σπίτι
   'Nick's gone **back to** the house' (cf. πίσω από το σπίτι '*behind* the house')

4 THE PREPOSITION AND THE PREPOSITIONAL PHRASE

A **preposition** is typically placed immediately before a noun phrase in order to indicate the relation of this phrase to some other phrase. A phrase introduced by a preposition is known as a **prepositional phrase**.

Prepositions will be dealt with in terms first of their syntactic characteristics (Section 4.1), then of their semantics (4.2).

Constructions such as πάνω στο τραπέζι 'on the table', consisting of an adverb of place followed by a prepositional phrase, are dealt with in Section 3.2.7. Even though collocations such as πάνω σε are sometimes called 'complex prepositions', they actually consist of adverb+preposition; they are therefore treated in this book under adverbs.

4.1 GENERAL SYNTACTIC CHARACTERISTICS OF PREPOSITIONS AND PREPOSITIONAL PHRASES

Except in their purely grammatical functions (e.g. to express the *indirect object* or the *agent*), prepositional phrases function like adverbs. Compare the prepositional phrase in (1) and (3) with the adverb in (2) and (4):

   (1) Πήγα **στη γωνία**
      'I went to the corner'
   (2) Πήγα **εκεί**
      'I went there'
   (3) Ο κύριος **στη γωνία**
      'The gentleman in the corner'
   (4) Ο κύριος **εκεί**
      'The gentleman there'

A prepositional phrase may modify or complement a verb (5: see also Sections 1.1.1.8 and 1.1.2), a noun (6), a pronoun (7), an adjective (8), or an adverb (9):

   (5) Πήγα **στο σινεμά**
      'I went **to the cinema**'
   (6) Το δέντρο **στην αυλή μας** είναι λεύκα
      'The tree **in our yard** is a poplar'
   (7) Κανένας **στην τάξη μας** δεν ήξερε ν' απαντήσει
      'No one **in our class** knew the answer [lit. 'knew to reply']'

(8) Είναι δυνατή **στα μαθηματικά**
    'She's good **at maths**'
(9) Το βιβλίο είναι πάνω **στο τραπέζι**
    'The book is on top **of the table**'

From the viewpoint of the internal construction of prepositional phrases, the chief Greek prepositions may be grouped into three categories:

(i) The two *basic prepositions*, with their most frequent meanings, are:

  από (optionally reduced to απ' before definite article or before a word beginning with a vowel): 'from'; 'since' (time); 'by' (agent), '[made] of'; 'than'; also sometimes used instead of genitive
  σε (σ before definite article; optionally σ' before a word beginning with a vowel): location: 'at', 'in', 'on'; motion: 'to', 'into', 'on to'

These are the most frequently used prepositions. Although the 'meanings' of the prepositions are often dictated by the linguistic or situational context, the primary relations expressed by the basic prepositions are relations of space.

  The basic prepositions may be used with noun phrases (including emphatic personal pronouns) in the accusative, but not with a weak pronoun:

(10)a. από την Αθήνα
       'from Athens'
    b. από μας [reduced from από εμάς]
       'from/than/by us'
    c. στη Θεσσαλονίκη
       'to/in Thessaloniki'
    d. σ' εμένα
       'to *me*' (with contrastive emphasis; otherwise μου)

The basic prepositions are also frequently found after a range of adverbs of place (see Section 3.2.7).

(ii) The next group consists of the remaining prepositions that govern the accusative:

αντί   'instead of'
για   (optionally γι' before a word beginning with
                           α) 'for', 'because of', 'about' (concerning)
κατά   'according to'; time: 'about; during; at the
                           time of' (but cf. Section 4.2.2.9)
με   (optionally μ' before a word beginning with a
                           vowel): 'with' (accompaniment or instrument)
μετά   'after'
μέχρι/ως/έως/ίσαμε: time: 'until'; place: 'as far as'

παρά	(optionally παρ' before όλο, όλη, etc.) 'despite; contrary to'
πριν	'before'
προς	'towards'
σαν	'like'
χωρίς/δίχως	'without'

Για, κατά, με, μέχρι/ως/έως/ίσαμε, σαν and χωρίς/δίχως may, like από and σε, be used with noun phrases (including emphatic pronouns) in the accusative:

(11) a. για το Γιάννη
        'for John'
     b. για μένα
        'for me'
     c. κατά τη γνώμη μου
        'in my opinion'
     d. με τη Μαρία
        'with Mary'
     e. μ' αυτό
        'with it' [where 'it' denotes an instrument]
     f. μέχρι τις τρεις
        'until three [o'clock]; until the third [of the month]'
     g. μέχρι εμένα
        'as far as me'
     h. σαν τη μητέρα της
        'like her mother'
     i. σαν εσένα [or σαν κι εσένα]
        'like you'
     j. χωρίς τη Μαρία
        'without Mary'
     k. χωρίς εμάς
        'without us'

A number of prepositions (αντί, για, μέχρι, παρά, πριν, σαν, χωρίς/δίχως) may introduce a να-clause:

(12) a. Το βράδι η κυκλοφορία, **αντί να** ελαττωθεί, αυξήθηκε
        'In the evening the traffic, **instead of** diminishing, increased'
     b. Πήρα αυτή τη θέση **για να** μην πεινάσουν τα παιδιά μου
        'I took this job **so that** my children wouldn't starve'
     c. Θα περιμένω **μέχρι να** τελειώσει το έργο
        'I'll wait **till** the film finishes'
     d. Προτιμούσα να πάω με τα πόδια **παρά να** πάρω το
        λεωφορείο
        'I preferred to walk **than to** take the bus'

e. **Πριν να** κοιμηθώ, ήπια ένα τσάι
   '**Before** I went to sleep, I drank a [cup of] tea'
f. Φέρεται **σαν να** πήρε ήδη τη θέση
   'S/he's behaving **as though** s/he's already got the job'
g. Έφυγαν **χωρίς να** πάρουν τη Μαρία
   'They left **without** taking Mary'

When παρά introduces a να-clause (as in example (12d) above), it may be considered a conjunction (see also Section 5.4.2.1).

Μέχρι, μετά and ως may introduce a που-clause. Μέχρι may be followed by a που-clause in an expression of an event that has already taken place. In addition, μετά may be followed by a που-clause as an alternative to the conjunction αφού:

(13)a. Περίμενα **μέχρι που** τελείωσε το έργο
       'I waited **till** the film finished'
   b. **Μετά που** έφυγες, κοιμήθηκα αμέσως [= Αφού έφυγες . . .]
       '**After** you left, I went to sleep immediately'

Ως is also regularly followed by a που-clause, but in such cases the combination is written as one word (ώσπου 'until; by the time that': see Section 5.3.7).

The prepositions από, για, με, σε and a number of other prepositions may be followed by numerals and by most types of non-personal pronoun:

(14)a. για τρεις
       'for three'
   b. με τι
       'with what, what with'

A number of prepositions (από, για, μέχρι/ως) may be followed by an adverb of time or place:

(15)a. από παλιά
       'from of old'
   b. μέχρι/ως εδώ
       'up to here'

(iii) A few prepositions (or other words used as prepositions) may govern noun phrases (including emphatic personal pronouns) or weak personal pronouns in the genitive, notably εναντίον 'against', εξαιτίας 'because of', μεταξύ 'among, between (of place, of time, or metaphorically)'. For their uses see the section on each of them (Sections 4.2.2ff.). For prepositions of *katharevousa* origin used in formal discourse (including λόγω 'by reason of', which is mentioned below) see Section 4.2.3.

When a noun phrase after a preposition is a subject complement, the noun phrase appears in the nominative:

(16)a. Παραιτήθηκε από καθηγητής (nom.)
    'He resigned as [lit. 'from'] professor'
  b. Οι άνεμοι (nom.) θα είναι από μέτριοι (nom.) έως ισχυροί (nom.)
    'The winds will be moderate to strong [lit. 'from moderate until strong']'
  c. Ο Παύλος (nom.) πάει για βουλευτής (nom.)
    'Paul's standing for parliament' [lit. 'Paul is-going for member-of-parliament']

Prepositions may not normally be separated from the noun phrase that they govern. The terms εξαιτίας and λόγω are originally noun forms that take a genitive, although they can be treated as prepositions for most purposes. However, unlike most true prepositions, they may be separated from the noun phrase that depends on them:

(17)a. εξαιτίας **και** του κρύου **και** της βροχής
    'because of both the cold and rain'
  b. λόγω **κυρίως** της βροχής
    'chiefly because of the rain'

The particles μεν and δε may nevertheless separate a true preposition from its noun phrase:

(18) Για **μεν** τους Έλληνες είναι σωστό, για **δε** τους ξένους όχι
    'For the Greeks, on the one hand, it is right, but for the foreigners [it is] not'

4.2 THE USES OF INDIVIDUAL PREPOSITIONS

The semantic characteristics of individual prepositions will be dealt with in the following sections. For an alphabetical list of all prepositions see Section 4.3. For a summary of spatial relations expressed by Greek prepositions and adverbs see Appendix 2.

In view of the basic semantic opposition between από and σε in spatial expressions, these oppositions will be discussed first, in Section 4.2.1. Sections 4.2.2ff. deal alphabetically with each of the prepositions belonging to the common language (namely αντί, από, για, δίχως, εναντίον, εξαιτίας, έως, ίσαμε, κατά, με, μετά, μεταξύ, μέχρι, παρά, πριν, προς, σαν, σε, χωρίς, and ως), while Section 4.2.3 lists prepositions of *katharevousa* origin whose use is normally confined to formal discourse or to fixed expressions.

4.2.1 SEMANTIC OPPOSITIONS BETWEEN σε AND από IN SPATIAL AND TEMPORAL EXPRESSIONS

With verbs implying *motion*, σε and από are often semantically opposed. In such cases, σε is used to express *goal* ('to'), while από is used to express *source, origin, or starting-point* ('from'), as in (1). Included in these senses are 'into' and 'out of' respectively, as in (2); Greek prepositions do not distinguish between (a) motion to or from a point and (b) motion into or out of a container (e.g. a building, box, etc.):

(1) Πήγα **από** την Αθήνα **στη** Θεσσαλονίκη
    'I went **from** Athens **to** Thessaloniki'
(2) Βγήκα **από** το σπίτι και μπήκα **στον** κήπο
    'I came **out of** the house and went **into** the garden'

The other chief basic spatial use of σε is to indicate *location*: 'in; at'. Unlike English, Greek distinguishes between 'motion to' and 'location' by means of the verb alone, not the preposition. In the expression of location, σε typically co-occurs with verbs denoting existence in a location (for examples see Section 4.2.2.18(2a–b)). Just as Greek does not distinguish, by single prepositions alone, between (a) motion to or from and (b) motion into or out of, so it does not distinguish between (c) location at a point and (d) location inside a container (including a building).

Σε does not necessarily imply motion to or location at a precise point (i.e. contact with that point); instead, it may simply imply proximity (see Section 4.2.2.18(2c). Thus σε may mean 'location on or near the surface of' (see Section 4.2.2.18(2d); it can also mean 'motion on to the surface of', while από means 'motion from the surface of' (3):

(3) Η γάτα πήδηξε από το γραφείο στο τραπέζι
    'The cat jumped off the desk on to the table'

With an adverb of place or time, motion or location away from is expressed by placing από before the adverb (4a), while motion to or location at a point is regularly expressed by the bare adverb (4b–c):

(4)a. Από πού ήρθες;
       'Where did you come from?' (motion away from)
   b. Πού πας;
       'Where are you going?' (motion to)
   c. Πού είσαι;
       'Where are you?' (location at)

We have seen that σε and από do not in themselves specify the precise spatial relationship between the relevant item and the location denoted by the prepositional phrase. Instead they imply proximity (σε) and distance (από). The most convenient way to specify the precise spatial relation between the relevant item and the location denoted in the prepositional phrase is to put an adverb of place next to the prepositional phrase (for further details on adverbs of place used with prepositional phrases see Section 3.2.7). Most of these adverbs of place are followed by either σε or από. In some cases there is a syntactic as well as a semantic contrast between a pair of adverbs, one of which is typically used with a σε-phrase, while the other typically co-occurs with an από-phrase. Thus whereas (5a) vaguely states the location of the subject (John) in relation to the place (the house), without specifying whether he is inside or outside it, (5b) makes it clear that he is inside the house, while (5c) makes it clear that he is outside the house (although he may possibly be right outside and therefore still be 'at home'):

(5)a. Ο Γιάννης είναι στο σπίτι
'John's at home'
b. Ο Γιάννης είναι μέσα στο σπίτι
'John's in[side] the house'
c. Ο Γιάννης είναι έξω από το σπίτι
'John's outside the house'

As well as μέσα and έξω, there are three other contrastive pairs of such adverbs of place, namely πάνω 'above' and κάτω 'below', μπροστά 'in front' and πίσω 'behind', and κοντά 'near' and μακριά 'far'. Just as μέσα typically collocates with σε and έξω with από, so πάνω, μπροστά and κοντά typically collocate with σε, while κάτω, πίσω and μακριά are accompanied by από:

(6)a. πάνω στο τραπέζι
'on the table'
b. κάτω από το τραπέζι
'under the table'
(7)a. μπροστά στο σπίτι
'in front of the house'
b. πίσω από το σπίτι
'behind the house'
(8)a. κοντά στο σπίτι
'near the house'
b. μακριά από το σπίτι
'[at some distance] away from the house'

Some adverbs of place may be followed by a prepositional phrase introduced by either σε or από. The following pairs of phrases, each of which contains an adverb used with σε and από, may have the following meanings (for the sake of simplicity, these phrases exemplify only the binary opposition location/passage: for από in the expression of passage see Section 4.2.2.2(ib)):

(9)a. Μένουν κάπου **γύρω στο** Ρέθυμνο
'They live somewhere round Rethymno' (location)

b. Έτρεξαν **γύρω από** το σπίτι
'They ran round the house' (passage)

(10)a. Μένουν **δίπλα στο** σπίτι μου
'They live near my house' (location)

b. Πέρασαν **δίπλα από** το σπίτι μου
'They went right by my house' (passage)

(11)a. Μένουν **κοντά στο** σπίτι μου
'They live close to my house' (location)

b. Πέρασαν **κοντά από** το σπίτι μου
'They passed close by my house' (passage)

(12)a. Σταμάτησαν **μπροστά στο** σπίτι μου
'They stopped in front of my house' (location)

b. Πέρασαν **μπροστά από** το σπίτι μου
'They passed in front of [i.e. went past] my house' (passage)

The situation with μέσα is more complex. While μέσα σε expresses motion into (13a) or location inside (13b), μέσα από expresses not only motion from inside (13c) and passage through (i.e. from outside to inside and then out again at a different point: 13d), but also situations in which, for example, someone situated *inside* a container is looking at something outside (13e), or someone inside is looking *through* something at something outside (13f), or vice versa (13g); in these last two cases the subject's gaze is considered as passing from inside to outside or vice versa:

(13)a. Μπήκαν μέσα στο σπίτι
'They went inside the house' (motion from outside to inside)

b. Έμειναν μέσα στο σπίτι
'They stayed inside the house' (location inside)

c. Βγήκαν μέσα από την κουφάλα
'They came out from [inside] the hollow' (motion from inside to outside)

d. Η σφαίρα πέρασε μέσα από το χέρι του
'The bullet passed through his hand' (passage from outside to inside to outside)

e. Προτιμούσε να βλέπει τον έξω κόσμο μέσα από το σπίτι του
'He preferred to see the outside world from inside his house' (vision from inside to outside)

f. Ο φυλακισμένος έβλεπε τον έξω κόσμο μέσα από μια τρύπα στον τοίχο του κελιού του
'The prisoner could see the outside world through a hole in the wall of his cell' (vision from inside to outside by way of)

g. Έβλεπα το εσωτερικό της σπηλιάς μέσα από μια τρύπα
'I could see the interior of the cave through a hole' (vision from outside to inside by way of)

Where μέσα από is used, it is frequently, though optionally, preceded by από, e.g.:

(14)a. Βγήκαν από μέσα από την κουφάλα (=13c)
   b. Προτιμούσε να βλέπει τον έξω κόσμο από μέσα από το σπίτι του (=13e)

In addition, μέσα σε is used in the temporal sense of 'within':

(15) Το έκανα μέσα σε τρεις ώρες
   'I did it within three hours'

Μπροστά, as we have seen, may be used with σε or από:

(16)a. Ένα δέντρο φύτρωσε μπροστά στο σπίτι μου
   'A tree has grown in front of my house' (location)
   b. Έβγαλαν το δέντρο μπροστά από το σπίτι μου
   'They removed the tree from in front of my house' (motion away from)
   c. Πέρασαν μπροστά από το σπίτι μου
   'They went by my house' (passage)

Nevertheless, even in expressions of location, μπροστά may be used with either σε or από, with two slightly different implications. Given the appropriate context, μπροστά σε may be used simply to express position, while μπροστά από may imply relative position in contrast to another:

(17)a. Ποιος είναι αυτός που στέκεται μπροστά στο Γιάννη;
   b. Ποιος είναι αυτός που στέκεται μπροστά από το Γιάννη;
   'Who's that standing in front of John?'

Example (17a) implies that John is facing the unknown person, while (17b) perhaps implies that the unknown person is ahead of John in a queue. Again, in non-spatial expressions μπροστά is only used with σε:

(18) Βρισκόμαστε μπροστά σ' ένα δίλημμα
   'We are faced by a dilemma' [lit. 'we-are-found in-front-of a dilemma']

Ανάμεσα and απέναντι, which may be used with σε or από to express location (19) and only with από to express motion (20), may be used only with σε in abstract senses (21: απέναντι σε is used in the sense of behaviour or attitude towards):

(19)a. Μένουμε ανάμεσα στην Πατησίων και στην Αχαρνών
'We live between Patision and Acharnon [Streets]'
   b. Μένουμε απέναντι στο φούρνο *or* από το φούρνο
'We live opposite the bakery'
(20)a. Βγήκαν ανάμεσα από τις γρίλιες
'They came out from between the grilles'
   b. Περάσαμε απέναντι από το φούρνο
'We passed by opposite the bakery'
(21)a. Πρέπει να διαλέξεις ανάμεσα στο γάλα και στον καφέ
'You must choose between milk or coffee'
   b. Δε μ' αρέσει η συμπεριφορά του απέναντι στη Μαρία
'I don't like his behaviour towards Mary'

4.2.2 PREPOSITIONS USED IN THE COMMON LANGUAGE

4.2.2.1 Αντί

Αντί 'instead' may govern noun phrases (including emphatic personal pronouns) in the accusative. It is used to express a contrast whereby something occurs rather than something else:

(1) Αντί το Φίλιππα, ήρθε ο Στέφανος
'Instead of Philip, Stephen came'
(2) Αντί εμένα, στείλανε το Στέφανο
'Instead of me, they sent Stephen'

Alternatively, αντί may be used with a για-phrase:

(3) Αντί για το Φίλιππα, ήρθε ο Στέφανος (=1)
(4) Αντί για μένα, στείλανε το Στέφανο (=2)

Clearly, when followed by για, αντί is not really a preposition, as is also shown by the fact that it can be followed by other prepositions than για when contrasting two phrases introduced by the same preposition:

(5) Το πήρα από το σαλόνι αντί από την κουζίνα
'I took it from the lounge instead of the kitchen'
(6) Πήγα με ταξί αντί με το λεωφορείο
'I went by taxi instead of by bus'
(7) Το έδωσα στο Φίλιππα αντί στο Στέφανο
'I gave it to Philip instead of to Stephen'

The more formal construction in which αντί governs a noun phrase in the genitive is also occasionally used:

(8) Αντί του Φίλιππα, ήρθε ο Στέφανος (=1)

In addition, αντί may be followed by a να-clause:

(9) Αντί να στείλουν το Φίλιππα, στείλανε το Στέφανο
     'Instead of sending Philip, they sent Stephen'

4.2.2.2 Από

Από is normally constructed with noun phrases (including emphatic personal pronouns) in the accusative. Its varied semantic uses can be classified under the following categories:

(i) concrete (spatial and temporal) relations
(ii) abstract (including grammatical) relations

For semantic oppositions between από and σε in the expression of spatial and temporal relations see Section 4.2.1.

(i) Concrete (spatial and temporal) relations

(a) Space: motion away from (1a–b), origin from (1c), location at a distance from (1d)

   (1)a. Έφυγαν από την Κρήτη
          'They left Crete' (i.e. they went away from Crete)
      b. Έβγαλε τα πόδια του από το τραπέζι
          'He took his feet off the table'
      c. Είμαι από την Κρήτη
          'I'm from Crete' (i.e. I was born and/or bred there *or* I live there permanently now)
      d. Μένω τριάντα χιλιόμετρα από το Ρέθυμνο
          'I live thirty kilometres from Rethymno'

(b) Space: passage
     Από is frequently used in expressions of passage ('through, along, across, past, by way of', etc.), typically, but not exclusively, with περνώ 'I pass':

   (2)a. Πέρασα από το τούνελ
          'I went **through** the tunnel'
      b. Πέρασα από την οδό Κοραή
          'I went **along** Korais Street'
      c. Τον πέρασα από τη γέφυρα
          'I transported/escorted him **across** the bridge'
      d. Πέρασα από το Λευκό Πύργο
          'I went **past/by way of** the White Tower'
      e. Πέρασα από το γραφείο σου αλλά δε σε βρήκα
          'I went **by** [*or* dropped in at] your office, but I didn't find you'

(3) Ελάτε από δω
   'Come this way'
(4) – Από ποιο δρόμο ήρθες; – Από τη Λαμία.
   '"Which way did you come?" "Via Lamia."' [lit. '"From which
   road you-came?" "From Lamia."']

In such expressions of passage as those in (2), the precise nature of
the subject's movement (walking, running, driving, swimming, flying,
etc.) and its spatial relation to the place denoted by the prepositional
phrase (above, below, etc.) are not specified, but are left to the hearer
to infer pragmatically.

(c) Group+items grouped
   Από is often used to express the components of which a set is
   made up; like the appositional construction (Section 2.12), this
   construction is a colloquial alternative for the more formal genitive
   of content (Section 2.4.3.2(ix)):

(5) μια σειρά από δέκα διαλέξεις
   'a series [made up] of ten lectures'

(d) Time: starting-point of a situation ('from or since')

(6)a. Τον περίμενα από τις έξι μέχρι τις επτά
      'I waited for him from six till seven (or from the sixth till
      the seventh)'
   b. Τον περιμένω από τις έξι και δε φάνηκε ακόμα
      'I've been waiting for him since six (or the sixth) and he
      hasn't appeared yet'

(ii)   Abstract (including grammatical) relations

(a) Ablative ('from')
   The ablative sense of από in the expression of 'taking from' is clearly
   related to spatial uses:

(7) Το πήραν από τον Πέτρο και το έδωσαν στον Παύλο
   'They took it from Peter and gave it to Paul'

(b) Agent, cause, or reason ('by')
   Από may introduce a phrase specifying the *agent* of an action, i.e. the
   person or thing that performed the action when this person or thing
   is not the grammatical subject of the verb. This construction is regularly used with verbs in the passive voice (8a–b), but example (8c)
   shows that the agent may be expressed by means of από even when
   the verb is morphologically active; example (8d) shows από expressing
   the agent after a deverbal adjective:

(8)a. Σκοτώθηκαν από άτακτους στρατιώτες
'They were killed by irregular troops'

b. Τα δέντρα ξεριζώθηκαν από τον άνεμο
'The trees were uprooted by the wind'

c. Η παράσταση έγινε από ερασιτέχνες
'The performance was carried out [lit. 'became'] by amateurs'

d. Η φρεγάτα "Έλλη" είναι απλησίαστη από εχθρικές επιθέσεις
'The frigate "Elli" is unapproachable by enemy attacks'

Από may also be used to introduce a phrase expressing *cause*:

(9)a. Γελούσε από τη χαρά της
'She was laughing for joy [lit. 'from her joy']'

b. Πέθανε από δηλητηρίαση
'S/he died of food poisoning'

c. Από το πολύ φως έβλεπα τον κόσμο μαύρο
'The light was so bright that the world looked black to me'
[lit. 'From the much light I saw the world black']

d. ο ενθουσιασμός από την ανακάλυψη
'the enthusiasm [caused] by the discovery'

Από may also express *reason* when the phrase it introduces expresses some emotion:

(10) Το πέταξα από φόβο μήπως δε σου αρέσει
'I threw it away for fear that you might not like it'

(c) *Material* out of which something is made

(11)a. ένα φόρεμα από φτηνό ύφασμα
'a dress [made out] of cheap material'

b. ένα κολιέ από μαργαριτάρια
'a pearl necklace' (lit. 'a necklace from pearls')

(d) In *partitive* constructions
Από is used to express the total of which a portion is singled out; the phrase introduced by από normally depends on something other than a noun (contrast Section 2.4.3.2(x)):

(12)a. δύο από τους φίλους μου
'two of my friends'

b. οι περισσότεροι από τους φίλους μου
'most of my friends'

c. Ο Καβάφης είναι από τους ποιητές που θέλεις να τους
ξαναδιαβάζεις
'Cavafy is [one] of those poets you want to keep re-reading'

d. Κανένας άλλος από την οικογένειά μου δεν είχε πάει στο
πανεπιστήμιο

'No one else from my family had gone to university'
e. Ήπια απ' αυτό το κρασί
   'I've drunk [some] of that wine' [i.e. 'I've tasted it']

(e) In *comparative* constructions

Από is used after comparative and superlative forms of adjectives and adverbs ('than' or 'of'), and after words expressing contrast such as άλλος 'other' ('than') and διαφορετικός or αλλιώτικος 'different' ['from']:

(13)a. Η Μαρία είναι πιο ψηλή από τον Δημήτρη
       'Mary is taller than Dimitris'
   b. Η Μαρία είναι η πιο ψηλή απ' όλους
      'Mary is the tallest of all'
   c. Η Μαρία γράφει καλύτερα από το Δημήτρη
      'Mary writes better than Dimitris'
   d. Η γυναίκα που γνωρίσαμε χθες δεν είναι άλλη από την
      κόρη εκείνου του ζωγράφου
      'The woman we met yesterday is none other than that
      painter's daughter'
   e. Η Μαρία είναι διαφορετική (*or* αλλιώτικη) από τους άλλους
      'Mary is different from the rest'

For more details of comparative constructions see Section 5.4.2.1.

(f) *Distributive* use

In distributive use από+numeral is the equivalent of 'numeral+each':

(14) Φάγαμε από δυο αβγά
      'We ate two eggs each'

The noun phrase introduced by από appears in the case appropriate to its function in the clause; for instance, από is followed by the nominative when the noun phrase functions as the subject of the clause:

(15) Δεξιά κι αριστερά υπάρχει από ένας τοίχος (nom.)
      'There is a wall on each side' [lit. 'right and left there-is from
      one wall']

(g) *Colloquial alternative to genitive*

Από+accusative is often used as a colloquial alternative to the genitive, particularly the possessive genitive, the genitive of type, the genitive of content, or the partitive genitive (cf. Section 2.4.3.2(x)). In such constructions the από-phrase modifies a noun phrase.

In colloquial styles από+accusative plural may be used as an alternative to the genitive plural in a possessive sense; this normally occurs only with feminine nouns in -α denoting an everyday object, whose genitive plural would entail a shift of stress to the last syllable:

(16) τα πόδια απ' τις καρέκλες (*or* τα πόδια των καρεκλών)
'the legs of the chairs'

Από may be used in a restricted range of expressions expressing type:

(17) μολύβια απ' όλα τα χρώματα
'pencils of all colours'

(h) *Various other uses*

Από is used after a huge range of verbs, nouns, adjectives, and other parts of speech in a variety of senses other than those covered above.
   Από may be used to express a sense of being rid of something:

(18) Το 1821 οι Έλληνες απελευθερώθηκαν από την Οθωμανική
      Αυτοκρατορία
      'In 1821 the Greeks liberated themselves from the Ottoman
      Empire'

It is used to specify the part of something by which the subject holds it:

(19) Τον άρπαξε από το χέρι
      'S/he grabbed him by the hand/arm'

It expresses subtraction in arithmetic:

(20) Δυο από πέντε τρία
      'Two from five [makes] three'

It is used in spatial expressions of location (21a) and in abstract expressions (21b) with μέρος or μεριά 'side':

(21)a. από την άλλη μεριά του δρόμου
       'on the other side of the street'
     b. από τη μια μεριά ... από την άλλη ...
        'on the one hand ... on the other...'

It expresses a change of state:

(22) Από φτωχός (nom.) που ήταν, έγινε πλούσιος εφοπλιστής
      'From being poor [lit. 'From poor that he was'], he became a
      rich shipowner'

In expressions of this sort the phrase after από appears in the case appropriate to its function in the clause (φτωχός is a subject predicate in the above example).
   In many of these senses, however, από after verbs, nouns, and adjectives can simply be interpreted as 'with respect to':

(23)a. Είναι ορφανή από μητέρα
       'She's lost her mother' [lit. 'She's orphan from mother']

   b. Το τοπίο ήταν έρημο από ανθρώπους
      'The landscape was deserted' [lit. 'deserted from people']
   c. Το δωμάτιο είναι γεμάτο από διάφορες αντίκες
      'The room is full of various antiques'
   d. Μείναμε από βενζίνη
      'We ran out of petrol' [lit. 'we remained from petrol']
        (perhaps cause)
   e. Δεν ξέρω από μουσική
      'I don't know anything about music'
   f. Από φαΐ τι έχεις;
      'What have you got in the way of food?' [lit. 'From food
       what have you?']
   g. ένα κουτί από μπισκότα
      'a biscuit tin' (i.e. one that used to have biscuits in)

Finally, από is used in a variety of purely abstract expressions originating
in formal styles, e.g.:

   (24) από οικονομική άποψη
        'from an economic point of view'

In a small number of fixed archaic expressions από governs the genitive:

   (25)a. από καθέδρας
       'ex cathedra'
     b. από αρχαιοτάτων χρόνων
       'from the most ancient times'

In certain fixed expressions of *katharevousa* origin, από is reduced to αφ' when
followed by a vowel which in the traditional diacritic system carried a rough
breathing:

   (26) αφ' ενός . . ., αφ' ετέρου . . . (each of these is usually written today as
        one word: αφενός, αφετέρου)
      'on the one hand . . ., on the other . . .'

4.2.2.3 Για

Για is normally constructed with noun phrases (including emphatic
personal pronouns) in the accusative.

(i) Benefit

   (1) Το 'κανα για σένα
      'I did it for you'

(ii) Purpose or aim

(2)a. Πήγε στη βρύση για νερό
'S/he went to the tap/spring for water'
b. Το 'κανα για πλάκα
'I did it for fun'

(iii) Reason

(3) Ήταν γνωστός για τις απόψεις του
'He was well known for his views'

(iv) Destination

(4)a. Αύριο φεύγω για την Ισπανία
'Tomorrow I'm leaving for Spain'
b. Ποιο είναι το τραίνο για τη Θεσσαλονίκη;
'Which is the train for Thessaloniki?'

(v) Price

(5) Το αγόρασα για δέκα χιλιάδες
'I bought it for ten thousand'

(vi) Topic of discussion ('concerning')

(6)a. ένα βιβλίο για τη Ρωσία
'a book about Russia'
b. Μιλούσαμε για το Χρήστο
'We were talking about Christos'

(vii) In expressions of emotion

(7)a. Συγνώμη για την καθυστέρηση
'I'm sorry about [i.e. I apologize for] the delay'
b. Σε συγχαίρω για το διορισμό σου
'I congratulate you on your appointment'

(viii) Time: duration
In some expressions of duration (e.g. 8a), a noun phrase is more frequently used in the bare accusative, without για, while in others (e.g. 8b) the preposition cannot be omitted:

(8)a. Η μάχη κράτησε (για) πολλές μέρες
'The battle lasted for many days'
b. Ήρθα για τρεις μέρες
'I've come for three days'

(ix) Time: occasion (with φορά)

(9) Πήγα για πρώτη φορά
'I went for the first time'

(x) 'Instead of'

(10) Σε πήρα για την Άννα
'I [mis]took you for Anna'

(xi) To introduce a subject or object predicate
In such constructions the noun phrase following για appears in the case appropriate to its function in the clause:

(11)a. Περνάει για ωραίος (nom.)
'He passes for [being] handsome'
  b. Δεν κάνει για δάσκαλος (nom.)
'He won't do as a teacher' [lit. 'he doesn't do for teacher']
  c. Χρησιμεύει για οδηγός
'It serves as a guide'
  d. Πάει για βουλευτής (nom.)
'He's standing for parliament' [lit. 'he goes for member-of-parliament']
(12)a. Σε είχα για πιο πεισματάρη (acc.)
'I thought you were more stubborn' [lit. 'I had you for more stubborn']
  b. Πρότεινε τον εαυτό του για υποψήφιο δήμαρχο (acc.)
'He proposed himself as prospective mayor'

In examples (11a–d) the noun phrase after για is a subject predicate, i.e. it modifies the subject; in examples (12a–b) the noun phrase after για is an object predicate, i.e it modifies the direct object (σε and τον εαυτό του).

(xii) In idiomatic constructions with repeated noun

(13) Δεν έμεινε **τραπέζι για τραπέζι**
'There wasn't a single table left' [lit. 'there didn't remain **table for table**']

The preposition για should not be confused with the hortatory particle για which may be placed before positive imperative forms of the verb to indicate encouragement.

4.2.2.4   Δίχως

Δίχως 'without' is semantically and syntactically identical to χωρίς, except that δίχως tends to be confined to non-standard use. For its uses see Section 4.2.2.19.

4.2.2.5   Εναντίον

Εναντίον is used with noun phrases (including emphatic personal pronouns) and with weak personal pronouns; it is always followed by the genitive. It expresses opposition ('against'):

(1)a. Πολέμησαν γενναία εναντίον των εχθρών
   'They fought bravely against the enemy'
   b. Δεν έχω τίποτα εναντίον σας
   'I haven't got anything against you'

4.2.2.6   Εξαιτίας

Εξαιτίας is used with noun phrases (including emphatic personal pronouns) and with weak personal pronouns; it is always followed by the genitive. It is used to express reason or cause:

(1) Δεν έφυγα εξαιτίας του καιρού
   'I didn't leave, because of the weather'

4.2.2.7   Έως

Έως 'until' is in most respects semantically and syntactically identical to μέχρι. For uses see Section 4.2.2.13.

4.2.2.8   Ίσαμε

Ίσαμε 'until' is in most respects semantically and syntactically identical to μέχρι, except that it is largely confined to non-standard use. For its uses see Section 4.2.2.13.

4.2.2.9   Κατά

Κατά is used in two different kinds of construction. Although it is always written in the same way, it is pronounced without stress when followed by the accusative, but it is stressed on the last syllable when followed by the genitive.

With the *accusative* it is used to express the following:

(i) Time or place: 'about'

(1)a. κατά τις έξι
      'about six [o'clock]'
   b. Μένουν κατά τα Πατήσια
      'They live somewhere around Patisia'

(ii) Time: 'during' or 'at the time of'

(2)a. κατά το Δεύτερο Παγκόσμιο Πόλεμο
      'during the Second World War'
   b. Σημειώθηκαν ορισμένα ασήμαντα επεισόδια κατά την άφιξή
      του στο αεροδρόμιο
      'Some trivial incidents took place at the time of his arrival at
      the airport'

It is also used in the fixed expression κατά τη διάρκεια + gen. 'during,
throughout', which has a more emphatic alternative καθ' όλη τη διάρκεια
+ gen. 'throughout'.

(iii) Space: 'towards'

(3) Τράβηξε κατά το χωριό
    'S/he went off towards the village'

This use of κατά is no longer common and has largely been superseded
by προς or για.

(iv) In accordance with

(4)a. κατά τους ειδικούς
      'according to the experts'
   b. κατά τις πληροφορίες που διαθέτουμε
      'according to the information we have at our disposal'
   c. κατά τη γνώμη μου
      'in my opinion'

(v) Manner (with τρόπο)

(5)a. κατά κάποιον τρόπο
      'in some way'
   b. κατά περίεργο τρόπο
      'in a curious way'

(vi)   Measure of difference or extent

(6)a. αύξηση κατά 40%
     'a 40% increase'
   b. κατά πόσο[ν]
     'to what extent'

(vii)   Distributive

(7)a. Πέρασαν κατά τετράδες
     'They went by in fours'
   b. Ψηφίζουμε κατά περιφέρεια
     'We vote according to [our] constituency'

Κατά is also used in fixed expressions such as κατ' αρχήν 'first of all', κατ' εξοχήν '*par excellence*', κατ' ευθείαν 'directly' (these three expressions are often written as one word), κατά βάθος 'at bottom, basically', κατά κανόνα 'as a rule', κατά λάθος 'by mistake', κατά τύχη 'by chance', κατά μήκος 'lengthways; (+gen.) along', κατά συνέπεια 'as a result', and κατά τα άλλα 'in other respects'.

It is also used with the *genitive* in expressions of opposition ('against'):

(8)a. Πολέμησαν κατά των Ιταλών
     'They fought against the Italians'
   b. Ψήφισα κατά της πρότασης
     'I voted against the proposal'

In this sense κατά may also be used as an adverb or a noun:

(9)a. Ψήφισα κατά
     'I voted against'
   b. τα υπέρ και τα κατά
     'the pros and cons'

As is shown in some of the above expressions, κατά may be reduced to κατ' before a vowel, especially in fixed expressions. In fixed expressions of *katharevousa* origin, κατά is reduced to καθ' when it is followed by a vowel which in the old diacritic system carried a rough breathing. The only commonly used expression of this sort is κατά followed by a form of όλος, as in:

(10)   καθ' όλη τη διάρκεια της Κατοχής
      'throughout the whole duration of the Occupation'

4.2.2.10   Με

Με 'with' may be followed by noun phrases (including emphatic personal pronouns) in the accusative.

(i)   Accompaniment

(1) Πήγαμε με τον πατέρα μου
   'We went with my father' [alternatively, 'I went with my father']

In expressions of accompaniment, με may co-occur with μαζί for greater emphasis ('together with, along with'):

(2)a. Κατάπια το ψάρι μαζί με τα κόκκαλα
   'I swallowed the fish together with [*or* along with] the bones'
   b. – Πόσοι είσαστε; – Τέσσερις μαζί με τον οδηγό
   '"How many are you?" "Four including the driver."'

Μαζί με can only be used in expressions of *spatial* accompaniment.
Με can also be used in expressions of *temporal* accompaniment:

(3)a. Γυρίσαμε σπίτι με το σούρουπο
   'We returned home at dusk [lit. 'with the dusk']'
   b. Το πανηγύρι έκλεισε με τραγούδια και χορούς
   'The festival ended with singing and dancing' [lit. 'songs and dances']

(ii)   Instrument ('by means of', 'with the help of') or material ('with')

(4)a. Τον χτύπησε με το τηγάνι
   'S/he hit him with the frying-pan'
   b. Το 'γραψα με μελάνι
   'I wrote it in ink'
   c. Διάβαζα με το φως του φεγγαριού
   'I was reading by the light of the moon'
   d. Πήγα με τα πόδια
   'I went on foot'
   e. Πήγα με αυτοκίνητο
   'I went by car'
   f. Το σκέπασα μ' ένα χαλί
   'I covered it with a carpet'

(iii)   Manner, in the construction με το να+verb
Με το να+verb is used to mean 'by doing':

(5) Με το να κάθεσαι με σταυρωμένα τα χέρια, δε λύνεις το
   πρόβλημα
   'By sitting with your arms folded you're not solving the problem'
   (i.e. 'You won't solve the problem by doing nothing')

This construction is an alternative to the gerund (see Section 1.7).

(iv)   Content

The phrase introduced by με denotes what the first noun contains (contrast the genitive of content (Section 2.4.3.2(ix)), which denotes what the first noun consists of):

(6)a. ένα φάκελο με χρήματα
    'an envelope containing money'
  b. ένα δάσος με βελανιδιές
    'a forest of oak-trees'

For appositional constructions expressing content see Section 2.12(b); with με the focus is on the content rather than the container.

(v)   Basis of calculation

(7)a. Τα πορτοκάλια πουλιούνται με το κιλό κι όχι με το κομμάτι
    'The oranges are sold by the kilo, not by the piece'
  b. Πληρώνομαι με το μήνα
    'I'm paid by the month'
  c. Πίνει ούζο με το μπουκάλι
    'S/he drinks ouzo by the bottle'
  d. Κάθεται με τις ώρες
    'S/he sits for hours on end'

(vi)   Identity or similarity

Με is regularly used with words expressing identity or similarity, such as αντιστοιχώ 'correspond', μοιάζω 'resemble', [ο] ίδιος 'the same', αντίστοιχος 'corresponding', ισοδύναμος 'of equal force', πανομοιότυπος 'identical', παρόμοιος 'similar', σύγχρονος 'contemporary [of the same time]', συνομήλικος 'of the same age', συνώνυμος 'synonymous' and ταυτόχρονος 'simultaneous':

(8)a. Αυτά τα παπούτσια μοιάζουν με τα δικά μου
    'These shoes are like mine'
  b. Αυτά τα παπούτσια είναι ίδια με τα δικά μου
    'These shoes are the same as mine'
  c. Αυτά τα παπούτσια είναι παρόμοια με τα δικά μου
    'These shoes are similar to mine'
  d. Ο Παύλος είναι συνομήλικος με τη Δήμητρα
    'Paul is the same age as Demetra'

(vii)   Accordance or relation

Με is used after various verbs, nouns, adjectives, and adverbs expressing accordance with or relation to, such as ανάλογα 'accordingly', σχέση 'relation', σχετίζομαι 'be related', σχετικά 'relatively', σύγκριση 'comparison', and σύμφωνα 'according':

(9)a. Παίρνω περισσότερα ή λιγότερα λεφτά ανάλογα με τις
    περιστάσεις
    'I earn more or less money according to the circumstances'
  b. Σχετικά με το θέμα αυτό θα ήθελα να πω το εξής
    'In relation to this subject, I would like to say the following'
  c. Σε σύγκριση με τον Παύλο, δεν πίνω πολύ
    'I don't drink much in comparison with Paul'
  d. Σύμφωνα με τις επίσημες στατιστικές, η εγκληματικότητα
    αυξάνεται συνεχώς
    'According to the official statistics, the crime rate is constantly
    increasing'

(viii)   Opposition or contrast ('against')

(10)a. Πολέμησα με τους Ιταλούς
    'I fought with the Italians' (in the appropriate context this
      could also mean 'I fought on the side of the Italians')
  b. Μαλώνει με τα παιδιά του
    'He quarrels with his children'
  c. Σε αντίθεση με τους Έλληνες, οι Ρώσοι δεν πίνουν πολύ κρασί
    'In contrast to the Greeks, the Russians don't drink much wine'

**(ix)   Various other expressions describing the expression or stance of
animates**

(11)a. Στεκόταν με χαμένο ύφος
    'S/he stood with a lost expression [on his/her face]'
  b. Στεκόταν με το καπέλο στο χέρι
    'S/he stood with hat in hand'
  c. Στεκόταν με άδεια τα χέρια
    'S/he stood empty-handed [lit. 'with empty the hands']'

This construction may be used in conjunction with a να-clause:

(12) Στεκόταν με τα χέρια του να τρέμουν
    'He stood with his hands trembling'

(x)   *με*+noun phrase+noun phrase or *να*-clause

Με may be used to introduce a noun phrase followed by either a second
noun phrase in the accusative (13) or a να-clause (14: 12 is an additional
instance):

(13)a. με βάση τα επίσημα στοιχεία
      'on the basis of the official figures'
   b. Όλοι οι κάτοικοι έφυγαν από την πόλη, με εξαίρεση μερικές
      εκατοντάδες
      'All the inhabitants left the town, with the exception of a few
      hundreds'
(14)a. Έκανε τις αποκαλύψεις με σκοπό να δυσφημήσει τους
      αντιπάλους του
      'He made the revelations with the aim of discrediting his
      opponents'
   b. Το πανηγύρι έκλεισε με τους νέους να τραγουδάνε και να
      χορεύουνε (cf. (3b) above)
      'The festival closed with the young people singing and
      dancing'

(xi)   Various other uses

Με has a wide variety of other uses, some of which are related to the
uses covered above: wearing (clothes: 15); physical characteristics (16);
weather conditions (17); cause (after verbs expressing emotion: 18); contra-
riety ('despite'), always with the appropriate form of όλος (19); division
(20); manner (followed by abstract noun: 21); time of termination when
time of beginning is also specified ('till': 22); dimensions ('by': 23); approximation when two numbers are mentioned ('to': 24); 'in relation to' (25);
exchange (26); and, in expressions with repeated nouns, gradual progress
over time (27):

(15)a. Παρουσιάστηκε με φανέλα και σώβρακο
      'He appeared in a vest and underpants'
   b. το κορίτσι με τα μαύρα
      'the girl in black'
(16)   η δασκάλα με τα χρυσά μάτια
      'the schoolmistress with the golden eyes'
(17)   Δεν ταξιδεύω με τέτοια βροχή
      'I'm not travelling in rain like this'
(18)a. Γέλασαν με την αμηχανία του
      'They laughed at his embarrassment'
   b. Θύμωσα με τα λόγια της
      'I got angry at her words'
   c. Απορούσα με τη σιωπή του
      'I was puzzled by his silence'

(19) Με όλα τα ελαττώματά του, είναι το καλύτερο λεξικό που
      έχουμε
      'For all its faults, it's the best dictionary we have'
(20) Το 32 δε διαιρείται με το 3
      '32 isn't divisible by 3'
(21) Με βοήθησε με προθυμία [=πρόθυμα]
      'S/he helped me with willingness' (=willingly)
(22) Έχουμε μάθημα δέκα με έντεκα [also written '10-11']
      'We've got a lesson from ten till eleven'
(23) ένα σίδερο πέντε μέτρα μήκος με δέκα εκατοστά φάρδος
      'a piece of iron five metres long by ten centimetres thick'
(24) Ήρθαν δυόμισι με τρεις χιλιάδες
      'About two and a half to three thousand came'
(25) Έχει μανία με το κυνήγι
      'S/he's crazy about hunting'
(26) Άλλαξαν τις χάντρες με χρυσό
      'They exchanged the beads for gold'
(27) Κάνει περισσότερη ζέστη μέρα με τη μέρα
      'It's getting hotter day by day'

4.2.2.11 Μετά

Μετά 'after' is used as a preposition with a definite noun phrase in the
accusative (1a). When it is followed by an indefinite noun phrase (including
an emphatic personal pronoun), it is usually linked to the noun phrase by
από (2a and 3). Nevertheless, there is some variation in use, and the
converse of the above tendency is found with noun phrases other than
emphatic pronouns (1b and 2b):

(1)a. **μετά** τον πόλεμο
   b. μετά από τον πόλεμο
      'after the war'
(2)a. **μετά από** έναν πόλεμο
   b. μετά έναν πόλεμο
      '**after** a war'
(3) **μετά από** μένα
      '**after** me'

When used with από, μετά functions as an adverb. Μετά is used as an
adverb meaning 'afterwards, later': see Section 3.1(6 and 8).

Μετά is also used with the genitive in a number of fixed expressions originating
in *katharevousa*. Here it has its ancient meaning 'with', e.g. μετά τιμής [lit. 'with
honour', a formal expression for ending a letter], μετά χαράς 'with pleasure' [lit.
'with joy'].

4.2.2.12 Μεταξύ

Μεταξύ 'between (of place or time); among' is followed by noun phrases (including emphatic personal pronouns) or weak personal pronouns in the genitive:

(1)a. μεταξύ Λονδίνου και Αθήνας
'between London and Athens'

   b. μεταξύ Δευτέρας και Τετάρτης
'between Monday and Wednesday'

(2)   μεταξύ ζωής και θανάτου
'between life and death' [i.e. half-alive]

(3)   μεταξύ μας
'between/among us; between ourselves' [i.e. confidentially]

Except in fixed expressions such as (2) and the metaphorical meaning of μεταξύ μας ('confidentially'), μεταξύ may normally be replaced by ανάμεσα (σε).

4.2.2.13 Μέχρι

Μέχρι is used with noun phrases (including emphatic pronouns) in the accusative to express 'as far as, up to' (of place: 1) and 'until, up to' (of time: 2), or figuratively (3):

(1) Θα σε πάω μέχρι το Σύνταγμα
'I'll take you as far as Constitution Square'

(2) Θε σε περιμένω μέχρι τις οχτώ
'I'll wait for you till eight'

(3) Είναι χρεωμένος μέχρι το λαιμό
'He's up to his neck in debts'

It is also used, of time, to express time at or before which ('by'):

(4) Το κοστούμι σας θα είναι έτοιμο μέχρι το Σάββατο
'Your suit will be ready by Saturday'

What has been said here about μέχρι applies also to έως, ίσαμε, and ως.
   Μέχρι is also used to introduce (a) που-clauses and (b) που να-clauses or να-clauses. In the first case (5) the clause expresses something that has happened, while in the second (6) it expresses something that may happen:

(5) Σε περίμενα μέχρι που νύχτωσε
'I waited for you till it got dark'

(6) Θα σε περιμένω μέχρι [που] να νυχτώσει
'I'll wait for you till it gets dark'

Ίσαμε and ως may introduce clauses in the forms ίσαμε να and ώσπου [να].

In certain fixed expressions originating in formal styles, μέχρι is followed by the genitive, and appears in the form μέχρις before a vowel (μέχρις ενός σημείου *or* μέχρι ένα σημείο 'up to a point', μέχρι στιγμής 'up to now', μέχρι τέλους 'right up to the end', μέχρις αηδίας 'ad nauseam'). In formal use μέχρι που or μέχρι να is occasionally replaced by μέχρις ότου (also έως ότου).

4.2.2.14 Παρά

Παρά may govern a noun phrase, though not normally an emphatic personal pronoun. It exists in two forms, one pronounced without stress and the other pronounced with stress on the last syllable, although they are written in the same way. These forms should be distinguished from the intensifying adverb πάρα, with stress on the first syllable (as in **πάρα** πολύ 'very much').

Both forms of παρά are followed by the accusative. The *unstressed* form expresses the following:

(i)   Amount lacking

(1)a. τρεις παρά τέταρτο
    'a quarter to three' ['three lacking quarter']
   b. Έχασε την εκλογή παρά μία ψήφο
    'S/he lost the election by [a margin of] one vote'
   c. Παρά τρίχα [*or* παρά λίγο] να σκοτωθούμε στο ατύχημα
    'We were nearly killed in the accident' ['by a hair's breadth' or 'by a small margin']

(ii)   Temporal alternation

(2) μέρα παρά μέρα
    'every other day'

The *stressed* form means 'against, despite, contrary to':

(3)a. Έφυγαν παρά τη θέλησή του
    'They went away against his will/wishes'
   b. παρά την υπόσχεσή του
    'contrary to his promise'

In the sense of 'despite' it is used in a number of fixed phrases (e.g. παρ' ελπίδα 'against all hope'). It is frequently followed by the appropriate form of όλος:

(4) Απέτυχε, παρ' όλες τις προσπάθειές του
    'He failed, despite all his efforts'

Especially common are the fixed expressions παρ' όλα αυτά 'despite this' and παρ' όλο που 'despite the fact that'; the latter is used as a conjunction.

Παρά may introduce a να-clause expressing what something is preferred to:

(5) Προτιμώ να φύγω παρά να κάτσω εδώ
    'I prefer to leave than to stay here'

It may also be followed by an ότι-clause optionally introduced by το ('despite the fact that'):

(6) Παρά το ότι (or παρ' ότι) μου μίλησε ειλικρινά, δεν τον συμπαθώ
    'Despite the fact that he spoke to me frankly, I don't like him'

In addition, παρά is used as a conjunction (see Section 5.4.2.1).

4.2.2.15   Πριν

Πριν 'before' tends to function more as an adverb than as a preposition. Nevertheless it may be used as a preposition followed by a definite noun phrase (but not an emphatic personal pronoun) in the accusative (1a). This is an alternative construction to πριν από, which may be used before a definite or indefinite noun phrase (including an emphatic pronoun):

(1)a. πριν τον πόλεμο
   b. πριν από τον πόλεμο
      'before the war'
(2) πριν από ένα πόλεμο
    'before a war'
(3) πριν από μένα
    'before me'

Πριν also functions as an adverb (see Section 3.1(5) and (7)), and (with or without να) it may introduce a temporal clause (see Section 5.3.7).

Πριν is used with the genitive in a small number of fixed expressions originating in formal usage (e.g. πριν της ώρας 'before [my, etc.] time').

4.2.2.16   Προς

(i) Space: 'towards'
In the spatial sense of 'towards', προς may be followed by a noun phrase (including an emphatic personal pronoun) in the accusative, or by το μέρος and the genitive of the weak personal pronoun:

(1)a. Οδηγούσα προς τη θάλασσα
      'I was driving towards the sea'
   b. Κοίταξε προς την άλλη κατεύθυνση
      'S/he looked in the other direction'

   c. Γύρισε προς το μέρος μου
    'S/he turned towards me'

It can also be followed by a small number of adverbs of place when they are substantivized with the neuter plural form of the article:

  (2)a. προς τα δω
     'in this direction' [lit. 'towards the here']
    b. προς τα κει
     'in that direction' [lit. 'towards the there']
    c. προς τα πάνω
     'upwards' [lit. 'towards the up']
    d. προς τα πού
     'in what direction' [lit. 'towards the where'] (interrogative)

(ii)   Time: 'towards'

   (3) Φτάσαμε προς το βράδι
     'We arrived towards evening'

(iii)   Abstract: 'towards', 'in respect of'

   (4)a. η υποστήριξη του ΟΗΕ προς τους Κούρδους
     'the UN support for the Kurds'
    b. η αντίθεσή του προς κάθε ξένο στοιχείο
     'his opposition towards any foreign element'

(iv)   Abstract: purpose

   (5) Έγινε αυτοψία προς εντοπισμό στοιχείων για τους δράστες
     'An on-the-spot investigation took place with the aim of locating
     the culprits'

This use is confined to formal contexts.

(v)   Abstract: 'by' between two identical nouns

   (6) βήμα προς βήμα
     'step by step'

(vi)   Abstract: 'at' a specified price

   (7) Τα πουλήσαμε προς χίλιες δραχμές το καθένα
     'We sold them for a thousand drachmas each'

(vii)   Abstract: 'to' in ratios

    (8) μια αναλογία ένα προς δέκα
       'a ratio of one to ten'

(viii)   Abstract: 'to' in expression of emotions
A phrase introduced by προς may be used to express the emotion caused
by what is mentioned in the rest of the sentence:

    (9) Προς μεγάλη μου έκπληξη, έφερε και τις δυο φιλενάδες του
       'To my great surprise, he brought both of his girl-friends'

(ix)   In various fixed phrases
In addition, προς appears in various fixed phrases, mostly originating from
formal usage (e.g. προς το παρόν 'for the present', προς στιγμήν 'for the
moment', προς τιμήν του 'in his honour'). In certain fixed phrases προς
is followed by the genitive, e.g. προς Θεού 'for God's sake!'

Ως προς is used to mean 'with respect to; as far as . . . is concerned'.

4.2.2.17   Σαν

Σαν 'like' is used in comparative constructions with a noun phrase in the
nominative or accusative, or an emphatic personal pronoun in the
accusative. When the noun phrase that follows it is in the nominative (1),
the noun phrase essentially denotes the *same* person or thing as the subject
(i.e. it is a subject predicate), while a noun phrase in the accusative (2)
denotes someone or something that *resembles* the subject:

    (1) Τρώει σαν βασιλιάς (nom.)
       'He eats like a king'
    (2) Τρώει σαν το βασιλιά (acc.)
       'He eats like the king'

Example (1) means that he eats as if he himself were a king, while in the
appropriate context (2) may imply that he eats in the way that a particular king eats.
    When σαν governs an emphatic pronoun it may optionally be followed
by και:

    (3) σαν εμένα *or* σαν κι εμένα
       'like me'

Σαν also has the meaning 'as' ('in one's capacity as'), with no sense of
comparison:

    (4) Υπηρετεί σαν δάσκαλος
       'He's serving as a teacher'

Some grammarians advise that the conjunction ως should be used instead of σαν in such cases:

(5) Υπηρετεί ως δάσκαλος (=4)

If σαν is used in such constructions as example (4), it is not clear whether the subject is actually serving as a teacher or doing the job of a teacher without really being one; in the former sense the use of ως is often preferred. Nevertheless, in the construction σαν ... που είμαι, etc., σαν definitely means 'in my capacity as':

(6) Κάθεται καλά σαν το καλό παιδί που είναι
     'He's sitting nicely like the good boy he is'

Σαν may introduce a να-clause in comparative constructions:

(7) Τρώει σαν να είναι ο βασιλιάς της Αγγλίας
     'He eats as though he's the king of England'

For more on the use of σαν see Section 5.4.2.3.

In old-fashioned literary and non-standard usage σαν is also used as a temporal conjunction ('when'):

(8) Σαν τέλειωσε ο πόλεμος, γυρίσαμε στα σπίτια μας
     'When the war ended, we returned to our homes'

4.2.2.18 Σε

Σε may be followed by noun phrases (including emphatic personal pronouns) in the accusative. Σε is the most commonly used preposition; indeed, it is probably used more frequently than all the other prepositions put together.

The prime uses of σε are to introduce the indirect object, and to express location at or motion to a point in space or time, but it has a variety of additional functions. (For semantic oppositions between σε and από see Section 4.2.1.)

(i)   Indirect object
Σε is used with noun phrases (including emphatic personal pronouns) to express the indirect object:

(1)a. Το έδωσα στον Αντώνη
      'I gave it **to** Antony'
   b. Το έδωσε σ' εμένα
      'S/he gave it **to** *me*' (contrastive emphasis)

(ii)   Space: location at or motion to

(2)a. Μένω στην Πάτρα
    'I live **in** Patras'
  b. Είμαι στο κρεβάτι
    'I'm **in** bed'
  c. Μένω στη λίμνη
    'I live **at/by** the lake'
  d. Το βιβλίο είναι στο τραπέζι
    'The book is **on** the table'
  e. Πήγα στην Πάτρα
    'I went **to** Patras'
  f. Πέρασα στο άλλο δωμάτιο
    'I went **into** the other room'
  g. Πήδηξε στο τραπέζι
    'S/he jumped **on to** the table'

'At' followed by expression of someone's house, shop, etc., may be expressed by σε with the accusative (3a), or with the genitive (3b); in the latter case a phrase such as το σπίτι 'the house' is understood:

(3)a. Μένω στο Δημήτρη
    'I'm staying **with** Dimitris'
  b. Μένω στου Δημήτρη
    'I'm staying **at** Dimitris's'

(iii)   Time: location at a point in time or length of time
Σε is used to specify location at a point in time (4a), or the length of time during or after which something happens (4b–c):

(4)a. Θα σε δω στις έξι η ώρα
    'I'll see you at six o'clock'
  b. Θα σε δω σε έξι ώρες
    'I'll see you in six hours'
  c. Κάναμε τη δουλειά σε έξι ώρες
    'We did the job in six hours'

For the bare accusative to express point in time or duration see Section 2.4.2.1(i–iii).

(iv)   Figurative uses
Σε is used in a huge variety of figurative uses, which include many idioms. In many cases the phrase introduced by σε acts as a clarificatory complement of a verb, including a passive perfect participle (5: see also Section 1.1.1.8), noun (6) or adjective (7):

(5)a. Υπάκουσαν στις διαταγές της
'They obeyed her orders'

b. Θα αντισταθούμε στη βία
'We shall resist force/violence'

c. Επιτέθηκαν στην πρωτεύουσα
'They attacked the capital'

d. Δεν έφταιγες σε τίποτα
'You weren't to blame in any way [lit. 'in anything']'

e. Τον μαύρισαν στο ξύλο
'They beat him black and blue' [lit. 'They blackened him to the wood']

f. Το έσχισαν στα δύο
'They tore it in two'

g. Με πέθανε στη φλυαρία
'S/he killed me with [his/her] chatter'

h. Ήταν ντυμένη στα μαύρα
'She was dressed in black'

i. Η Αθήνα είναι πνιγμένη στο τσιμέντο
'Athens is drowning in cement'

(6)a. Δεν υπάρχει φάρμακο σ' αυτή την αρρώστια
'There is no cure [lit. 'medicine'] for this illness'

b. η όξυνση στις σχέσεις με την Τουρκία
'the exacerbation of relations with Turkey'

c. η περιεκτικότητα των τροφίμων σε λίπος
'the fat content of foodstuffs' [lit. 'the content of foodstuffs in fat']

d. Είμαι πτώμα στην κούραση
'I'm dead tired' [lit. 'I'm corpse to the tiredness']

(7)a. Σε τι είναι καλύτερη;
'In what respect is she better?'

b. Είναι δυνατή στα μαθηματικά
'She's good at maths'

c. Είναι μεγαλύτερος στα χρόνια
'He's older' [lit. 'bigger in the years', i.e. as opposed to bigger in size]

The verbs in examples (5a–c), namely υπακούω 'I obey', αντιστέκομαι 'I resist' and επιτίθεμαι 'I attack', are intransitive, unlike their equivalents in English.

In expressions of transformation σε may express what something turns into:

(8) Θέλω ν' αλλάξω λίρες σε δραχμές
'I want to change pounds into drachmas'

In expressions of rate, σε may mean 'in every' or 'out of every':

(9) Ο ένας στους τρεις κερδίζει
'One [person] in three wins [e.g. a lottery]'

In many cases, especially in idioms, the semantic function served by σε is difficult to specify:

(10)a. Ήρθαν στα χέρια
'They came to blows [lit. 'to the hands']'
 b. Ήπιαμε στην υγεία σου
'We drank to your health'

There is a large number of fixed abstract phrases introduced by σε, most of them originating from formal usage, e.g. σε τελευταία ανάλυση 'in the last analysis', σε μηνιαία βάση 'on a monthly basis', σε σημαντικό βαθμό 'to a significant degree'. Likewise, there is a range of expressions consisting of σε+abstract noun+preposition and expressing various relationships, e.g. σε αντίθεση με/προς 'in contrast *or* opposition to', σε σχέση με 'in relation to', σε συνδυασμό με 'in combination with', σε συνεργασία με 'in collaboration with', σε σύγκριση με 'in comparison with'.

4.2.2.19 Χωρίς

Χωρίς 'without' may be followed by noun phrases (including emphatic personal pronouns) in the accusative:

(1)a. χωρίς τη βοήθειά σου
'without your help'
 b. Δε θα το 'κανα χωρίς εσένα
'I wouldn't/couldn't have done it without you'

Χωρίς often co-occurs with the indefinite (non-specific) pronouns and determiners κανένας 'any[one]', τίποτα 'anything' and καθόλου 'any at all':

(2) Έκανα τη δουλειά χωρίς καμιά βοήθεια [*or* χωρίς καθόλου βοήθεια]
'I did the job without any help'

It can also introduce a να-clause:

(3) Χωρίς να το καταλάβω, βρέθηκα μπροστά στο Δημαρχείο
'Without realizing it, I found myself in front of the Town Hall'

What is said here applies equally to δίχως.

4.2.2.20   Ως

Ως 'until; up to' is in most respects semantically and syntactically identical to μέχρι. For uses see Section 4.2.2.13. The preposition ως should not be confused with the conjunction ως 'as' (see Section 5.4.2.3).

Ως may introduce a temporal clause in the form ώσπου [να] 'until' (see Section 5.3.7).

Ως και, followed by a noun phrase in the case appropriate to its function in the clause, has an intensive use ('even'):

(1)   Ως κι η Ελένη ήρθε στο πάρτι
      'Even Helen came to the party'

4.2.3   Prepositions of katharevousa origin used in formal discourse

There are some *prepositions of katharevousa origin*, which govern a noun phrase in the accusative, genitive, or dative. Their use tends to be confined to formal usage or (in colloquial usage) to fixed phrases. Some of them originate in mathematical discourse.

ανά	+ acc.	various: ανά δύο μέρες 'every two days', ανά πάσαν στιγμήν 'at any moment', ανά χείρας 'at hand'
	+ case appropriate to function of phrase in clause: 'in groups of': ανά διακόσιοι 'in groups of two hundred'	
άνευ	+ gen.	'without': άνευ αποδοχών 'without remuneration', άνευ όρων 'unconditional[ly]' [lit. 'without conditions'], άνευ προηγουμένου 'unprecedented' [lit. 'without precedent'], άνευ σημασίας 'without importance, trivial'
διά	+ nom.	'divided by': τριάντα διά τρία ίσον δέκα 'thirty divided by three equals ten'
	+ gen.	'through; by means of': διά της βίας 'by force'
εις	+ acc.	'in, at, etc.': εις βάρος [+ gen.] 'at the expense [of]', εις είδος 'in kind', εις αναζήτησιν τροφής 'in search of food', εις υγείαν! 'cheers!' (toast)
εκ	+ gen.	'from' (εξ before vowel): εκ γενετής 'from birth', εκ μέρους [μου] 'on my behalf', εκ του μηδενός 'from nothing', εκ περιτροπής 'alternately', εκ των προτέρων 'in advance', εκ πρώτης όψεως 'at first sight', εξ ακοής 'by repute', εξ όψεως 'by sight'
εκτός	+ gen.	'outside': εκτός Αθηνών 'outside Athens', εκτός εαυτού 'beside himself' (e.g. with rage), εκτός κινδύνου 'out of danger'
		'apart from; except': εκτός τούτου 'apart from this'; see also Section 3.2.6(3–6)
εν	+ dat.	'in': εν ανάγκη 'if need be' [lit. 'in need'], εν μέρει 'in part', εν πάση περιπτώσει 'in any case', εν λόγω 'in question', εν όψει 'in view', εν γνώσει 'in [full]

		knowledge', εν πρώτοις 'in the first place', εν τέλει 'in the end, finally', εν τούτοις 'nevertheless', εν ψυχρώ 'in cold blood'
εντός	+ gen.	'within': εντός ολίγου 'within a short time'
επί	+ acc.	'for the duration of': επί τρεις μήνες 'for three months' 'by (dimensions)': ένα κελί τρία επί τέσσερα 'a cell three by four [metres]'
	+ gen.	'on': επί τόπου 'in situ, in the spot' 'over, at the expense of': μια νίκη επί της ΑΕΚ 'a victory over AEK [football team]' 'in the time of; under the rule of': επί Τουρκοκρατίας 'under Turkish rule'
	+ dat.	'on': επί πιστώσει 'on credit', επ' αυτοφώρω 'red-handed', επί ίσοις όροις 'on equal terms'
	+ dat.	various: επί τη ευκαιρία 'by the way' [lit. 'on the occasion'], επί θύραις 'in the offing' [lit. 'at the gates']
κατόπιν	+ gen.	'after': κατόπιν εντολής 'by order [of]', κατόπιν εορτής 'after the event', κατόπιν συνεννοήσεως 'after consultation'
λόγω	+ gen.	'by reason of, because of': το ματς ματαιώθηκε λόγω κακοκαιρίας 'the match was cancelled because of bad weather'
μείον	+ nom.	'minus': τέσσερα μείον δύο ίσον δύο 'four minus two equals two' (also πλην)
μέσω	+ gen.	'via': μέσω Θεσσαλονίκης 'via Thessaloniki'
περί	+ acc.	'about (approximately)': περί τα δύο εκατομμύρια 'about two million'
	+ gen.	'about (concerning)': περί τίνος πρόκειται; 'what's it all about?'
πλην	+ gen.	'less, minus; except': όλοι χάθηκαν πλην ενός 'all were lost, except one'
προ	+ gen.	'before (of time or place); ago': προ Χριστού 'before Christ', προ δέκα ετών 'ten years ago', προ ημερών 'some days ago', προ καιρού 'some time ago'
συν	+ nom./acc.	'plus': δύο συν τρία ίσον πέντε 'two plus three equals five'
	+ dat.	'with': συν τοις άλλοις 'among other things', συν τω χρόνω 'in time'
υπέρ	+ acc.	'over and above': υπέρ το εκατομμύριο 'over a million', υπέρ το δέον 'excessively, inordinately'
	+ gen.	'for, in favour of, on behalf of': είμαι υπέρ της δημοκρατίας 'I'm in favour of democracy'
υπό	+ acc.	'below, under': τρεις βαθμοί υπό το μηδέν 'three degrees below zero', η υπό εξέταση περίοδος 'the period under investigation', υπό την αιγίδα 'under the aegis/auspices' [+ gen.], υπό την προστασία

'under the protection' [+ gen.], υπό τον όρο ότι 'on
condition that'

In addition, there are the relics of two *postpositions* from Ancient Greek, namely
ένεκεν 'on account of' and χάριν 'for the sake of'. They are equivalent in use to
prepositions, except that they follow the noun phrase that they govern. They both
take the genitive and are used exclusively in fixed expressions:

(1) τιμής **ένεκεν**
     'as a token of respect' [lit. 'for the sake of honour']
(2) παραδείγματος **χάριν**
     'for example'

4.3   CHECKLIST OF PREPOSITIONS

ανά	various meanings (4.2.3)
άνευ	'without' (4.2.3)
αντί	'instead of' (4.2.2.1)
από	'from' (3.2.7, 4.2.1, 4.2.2.2)
για	'for' (4.2.2.3)
διά	'divided by; through; by means of' (4.2.3)
δίχως	'without' (4.2.2.4)
εις	'in, at, etc.' (4.2.3)
εκ	'from' (4.2.3)
εκτός	'outside; apart from' (4.2.3)
εν	'in' (4.2.3)
εναντίον	'against' (4.2.2.5)
εντός	'within' (4.2.3)
εξαιτίας	'because of' (4.2.2.6)
επί	'for the duration of; (multiplied) by; on; in the time of; under the rule of; over, at the expense of' (4.2.3)
έως	'until, up to' (4.2.2.7)
ίσαμε	'until, up to' (4.2.2.8)
κατά	'about', 'towards', 'during', 'in accordance with', etc. (4.2.2.9)
κατόπιν	'after' (4.2.3)
λόγω	'by reason of' (4.2.3)
με	'with' (4.2.2.10)
μείον	'minus' (4.2.3)
μέσω	'via' (4.2.3)
μετά	'after' (4.2.2.11)
μεταξύ	'between, among' (4.2.2.12)
μέχρι	'until, up to' (4.2.2.13)
παρά	'by', 'despite' (4.2.2.14)
περί	'about (approximately); about (concerning)' (4.2.3)
πλην	'less, minus; except' (4.2.3)

πριν	'before' (4.2.2.15)
προ	'before' (4.2.3)
προς	'towards' (4.2.2.16)
σαν	'like' (4.2.2.17)
σε	'in, to, at, etc.' (3.2.7, 4.2.1, 4.2.2.18)
συν	'with; plus' (4.2.3)
υπέρ	'over and above; for, in favour of' (4.2.3)
υπό	'below, under' (4.2.3)
χωρίς	'without' (4.2.2.19)
ως	'until, up to' (4.2.2.20)

5 THE CLAUSE

The *clause* is the smallest syntactic unit which contains (explicitly or implicitly) a subject and a verb phrase. The term **sentence** is sometimes used to refer either to a single independent clause or to a more complex structure consisting of more than one clause, one of which is the main clause while the others are structurally dependent either on the main clause or on one of the other dependent ones.

5.1   MAIN (INDEPENDENT) CLAUSES/SENTENCES

We will present first independent sentences consisting of only one clause. Depending on their structural characteristics and their most common use or function these sentences are divided into: *indicative* (Section 5.1.1), *non-indicative* (5.1.2), *imperative* (5.1.3), and *exclamatory* (5.1.6). Indicative and non-indicative clauses may appear in positive, interrogative (5.1.4ff), negative (5.1.5), or negative interrogative forms (5.1.5.2.2).

5.1.1   INDICATIVE SENTENCES (STATEMENTS)

There are no special structural or intonational features to characterize an indicative sentence. There is no introductory particle for these sentences and the intonational contour is at its most neutral, unless one wants to stress one of the constituents in order to give it emphasis (see Section 5.2.4 below). An indicative sentence or statement contains a verb in the indicative mood (see Section 1.3) and its characteristic use is to express a proposition which may be either true or false.

(1)a. Ο καιρός σήμερα είναι καλός
       'The weather today is fine'
   b. Οι φίλοι μας πήγαν στην Κρήτη πέρσι το καλοκαίρι
       'Our friends went to Crete last summer'
   c. Το μετρό της Αθήνας θα τελειώσει σε δυο χρόνια
       'The Athens metro will be completed in two years'

The above sentences are statements in the indicative mood expressing something which may be true or false at the time of the utterance (1a), in the past (1b) or in the future (1c).

5.1.2   NON-INDICATIVE SENTENCES (SUGGESTIONS, WISHES, PROMISES)

These independent sentences are differentiated by the use of the subjunctive mood indicated by the particles να or ας. Their characteristic function is to make a wish, a suggestion or a promise, or to express something as a possibility or as a hypothesis etc.:

(1)a. *Suggestion*
   Να πάτε να τον δείτε
   'You should go to see him'
   b. *Wish*
   (Μακάρι) **να** τον είχαμε δάσκαλο. Τί ωραία που θα ήταν!
   'If only we had him as our teacher. How wonderful it would
      be!'
   c. *Request*
   Να μου γράφεις συχνά.
   'Please write to me often'
   d. *Hypothesis*
   Και να με καλούσες δε θα ερχόμουνα
   'Even if you invited me I wouldn't come'
   e. *Suggestion*
   Ας πάμε να τον δούμε
   'Let's go and see him'
   f. *Concession*
   Ας μη μου μιλάει. Δε με νοιάζει
   'I don't care if he doesn't speak to me' [lit. 'Let him not speak
      to me. I do not care']
   g. *Strong wish*
   Ας τον έβλεπα έστω και για λίγο
   'If only I could see him even for a little while'

Main clauses with a verb in the bare subjunctive introduced by the particle να are not very frequent. It is more common to find subjunctives introduced by a modal (see Section 1.2.2.1) or some other main verb which makes the meaning of the sentence more precise, as shown below:

(2)a. **Πρέπει να** πάτε να τον δείτε
   'You must go to see him'
   b. **Θα ήθελα να** τον είχαμε δάσκαλο
   'I wish we had him as a teacher'
   c. **Θέλω/Θα ήθελα να** μου γράφεις συχνά
   'I would like you to write to me often'

5.1.3 POSITIVE IMPERATIVE SENTENCES

Positive imperative sentences are characterized by the use of a verb in the imperative mood, which has four morphologically distinct forms: second person singular and second person plural, imperfective and perfective (see Section 1.3.3; for negative imperative sentences see Section 5.1.5.2.3).

(1)a. **Μίλα** (2nd sg. imperf.) πιο αργά γιατί δε σε καταλαβαίνω
   'Speak more slowly because I cannot understand you'
   b. **Μίλα** βρε παιδί μου, βουβάθηκες;
   'Come on, speak my child. Have you lost your voice?'
   c. **Μίλησε** (2nd sg. perf.) με το Γιάννη γι' αυτό
   'Speak to John about this'

In (1a) the imperfective expresses a continuous action and it is equivalent to 'continue speaking'. However, imperfective imperatives may also be used to ask for immediate action, as in (1b), i.e. 'start speaking'. In (1c), where the verb is in the perfective, the action is viewed as one which will be completed, and the meaning of the sentence is equivalent to 'have a chat with John'.

With verbs in the passive form the perfective alone is used:

(2)a. **Ντύσου** πιο καλά γιατί κάνει κρύο
   'Put on more clothes [lit. 'dress better'] because it is cold'
   b. **Φαντάσου** την έκπληξή του όταν μας είδε
   'Imagine his surprise when he saw us'
   c. **Κοιμήσου** ακόμη λίγο. Είναι νωρίς
   'Sleep a little longer. It is early'

To express an order or an instruction in the imperfective of passive verbs or in persons other than the second, we may resort to the use of the subjunctive (with the particles να or ας):

(3)a. Ας μην ντύνεται κομψά
   'I don't care if he is not elegantly dressed [lit. 'Let him not be elegantly dressed']'
   b. **Να ντύνεσαι** πιο ζεστά τώρα το χειμώνα
   'You should wear warmer clothes [lit. 'dress warmer'] now in the winter'

Another characteristic of imperative verb forms is that the object clitic pronouns follow the verb, while in both indicative and subjunctive they precede (see also Section 2.8.1.1.1):

(4) **Δώσε τού το** αμέσως το βιβλίο του
   'Give his book to him right away' [lit. 'Give him it immediately his book']

To weaken the impact of a direct order and to make it sound more like a suggestion, the imperative sentence is sometimes introduced by the particle για:

(5)a. **Για έλα** εδώ μια στιγμή
'Just come here a minute'

b. **Για πες** μου, βρε παιδί μου, γιατί γκρινιάζεις;
'Just tell me, my child, why are you grumbling?'

The use of the plural of politeness, i.e. the second person plural imperative verb form, to refer to a single individual, makes the order less abrupt and less offensive. The order becomes milder and more polite if we accompany it with παρακαλώ 'please', which may occur at the beginning of the sentence or at the end.

(6)a. (Σας) παρακαλώ, ελάτε μέσα κύριε Μαρκόπουλε
'Please come in, Mr Markopoulos'

b. Ελάτε μέσα, κύριε Μαρκόπουλε, παρακαλώ
'Come in, Mr Markopoulos, please'

5.1.4   DIRECT QUESTIONS

Interrogative sentences, that is sentences that express questions, are most typically used to seek information. The information sought may relate to the whole sentence, namely whether or not it is the case that . . ., in which case they are called *yes/no questions*. Alternatively, they may question one element of the sentence; these are referred to as *constituent questions*.

5.1.4.1   Yes/no questions

These seek either a 'yes' or a 'no' answer. Yes/no questions are available for both indicative and subjunctive clauses introduced by the particle να, but are less frequent with subjunctives introduced by ας. Questions are not available for imperatives.

To form a yes/no question from an indicative or a subjunctive main clause it is necessary to use a special intonation which is characterized by a rise of the voice pitch followed immediately by a slight fall of the voice pitch at the end of the sentence. In interrogatives, the verb is often placed first. However, since this order with the verb at the beginning of the sentence is not unique to interrogatives but may also occur in statements, the clearest marker of interrogation is the characteristic intonation contour of rise and fall at the end of the construction. Intonation is, of course, restricted to the spoken language, while in the written language an interrogative sentence is indicated by the use of the question mark. In some circumstances the interrogative sentence may be introduced by a special particle: μη(ν), μήπως, άραγε.

(1)a. Ο Γιάννης θα δει την Ελένη;
   'Will John see Helen?'
   b. Θα δει την Ελένη ο Γιάννης;
   'Will John see Helen?'
   c. Να φέρει ο Γιάννης την Ελένη στο πάρτι;
   'Should John bring Helen to the party?'
   d. **Μήπως** θα δεις την Ελένη σήμερα;
   'Will you see Helen today, by any chance?'
   e. **Άραγε** θα είναι κλειστά αύριο τα καταστήματα;
   'Will the shops be closed tomorrow, I wonder?'

To answer a positive yes/no question either the particle ναι 'yes' (for agreement) or the particle όχι 'no' (for disagreement) is used:

(2)a. Θα πάτε διακοπές φέτος;
   'Will you be going on holiday this year?'

Answer:

   b. Ναι = Ναι, θα πάμε   'Yes (we will go)'
   c. Όχι = Όχι, δε θα πάμε   'No (we will not go)'

5.1.4.2   Alternative (either/or) yes/no questions

These are formed by combining a positive interrogative sentence with either a full negative interrogative one or with the particle όχι. The two parts are joined with the conjunction ή 'or':

(1)a. Το καταλαβαίνεις αυτό ή δεν το καταλαβαίνεις;
   'Do you understand this or don't you understand it?'
   b. Το καταλαβαίνεις αυτό ή όχι;
   'Do you understand this or not?'

5.1.4.3   Leading yes/no questions

A speaker who makes a statement in the indicative, whether positive or negative, may decide to seek confirmation about the truth of his or her proposition by adding, after the end of the statement, the tag έτσι δεν είναι; or δεν είναι έτσι; 'isn't it so?' which is accompanied by the characteristic question intonation:

(1)a. Ο Γιάννης το πήρε το δάνειο. Δεν είναι έτσι/έτσι δεν είναι;
   'John got the loan, didn't he?'

   b. *Answer with agreement*:
     Ναι, το πήρε
     'Yes, he got it/Yes, he did'
   c. *Answer with disagreement/contradiction*:
     Όχι, δεν το πήρε
     'No, he didn't [get it]'
(2)a. Ο Γιάννης δεν το πήρε το δάνειο. Δεν είναι έτσι;
     'John didn't get the loan, did he?'
   b. *Answer with agreement*:
     Ναι, δεν το πήρε
     'No, he didn't [get it]'
   c. *Answer with disagreement/contradiction*:
     Όχι, το πήρε
     'Yes, he did [get it]'

The answers in examples (2b–c) indicate that Greek and English use opposite particles in responses. But if we simply have a negative question without the tag, as in (3), the agreeing answer can be introduced either by ναι or by όχι:

(3)a. Δεν πήρε ο Γιάννης το δάνειο;
     'Didn't John get the loan?'
   b. *Answer with agreement*:
     Όχι, δεν το πήρε
     'No, he didn't [get it]'
   c. Ναι, δεν το πήρε
   d. *Answer with disagreement*:
     Πώς, το πήρε/Ναι, το πήρε/Όχι, το πήρε

5.1.4.4 Constituent questions

These interrogative sentences ask information about one constituent of the sentence which is expressed by an appropriate question word, such as ποιος 'who', πού 'where', πότε 'when', γιατί 'why', πώς 'how', τι 'what':

(1)a. **Ποιος** θα αναλάβει την υπόθεση αυτή;
     'Who will undertake this affair?'
   b. **Τι** να κάνει τώρα ο πρωθυπουργός;
     'What should the Prime Minister do now?'
   c. **Πού** να βάλω αυτό το τραπεζάκι;
     'Where should I put this table?'
   d. **Γιατί** δεν κάλεσαν τον Αλέκο;
     'Why didn't they invite Alekos?'

5.1.4.5   What constituents may be questioned

In principle it is possible to question any constituent of a sentence except the verb. Thus we can question subject noun phrases, object noun phrases, prepositional phrases and adverbials of all kinds. The question words commonly used for noun phrases are inflected for gender, case and number, e.g. ποιος, ποια, ποιοι, ποιανού, ποιον, etc. (see Section 2.8.3.6). They are used either as pronouns to replace the questioned noun phrase completely or as determiners accompanied by a head noun and agreeing with it in gender, number, and case:

(i)   Questioning the subject

(1)a. **Ποιος** θα αναλάβει την υπόθεση αυτή;
      'Who will undertake this affair?'
   b. **Ποιος δικηγόρος** θα αναλάβει την υπόθεση αυτή;
      'Which lawyer will undertake this affair?'

(ii)   Questioning the direct object

(2)a. **Ποιον** είδες χθες στην ταβέρνα;
      'Whom did you see at the taverna yesterday?'
   b. **Ποιον φίλο μας** είδες χθες στην ταβέρνα;
      'Which friend of ours did you see at the taverna yesterday?'

(iii)   Questioning the indirect object in the genitive

(3)a. **Ποιανού** έδωσες το γράμμα;
      'Who did you give the letter to?'
   b. **Ποιανού ηλίθιου** έδωσες το γράμμα;
      'Which idiot did you give the letter to?'

(iv)   Questioning the indirect object in a prepositional phrase

(4)a. **Σε ποιον** να το πω αυτό;
      'Who should I say this to?'
   b. **Σε ποιον άνθρωπο** να το πω αυτό;
      'Which person should I say this to?'

There is also the word τι 'what', which may be used pronominally or in combination with a head noun as a neuter subject (5a) or as a neuter object (5b). It can also be used in the genitive τίνος for the indirect object (5c), for either the masculine or the neuter, but not for the feminine. It may also be used as an indeclinable determiner followed by a noun of any gender and number, but only in nominative predicate constructions (5d–e):

(5)a. Τι (φαγητό) σε πείραξε;
       'What (food) has upset you?'
   b. Τι (έργο) είδατε χθές;
       'What (film) did you see yesterday?'
   c. Τίνος (φίλου σου) το είπες;
       'Who (which friend of yours) did you tell it to?'
   d. Τι άνθρωπος είναι αυτός βρε παιδί μου;
       'What kind of a man is he?'
   e. Τι (είδους) γυναίκα είναι αυτή;
       'What kind of a woman is she?'

The word τίνος in (5c) may be replaced by ποιανού without any difference in meaning.

(v)   Questioning prepositional phrases
A prepositional phrase is questioned by using the appropriate question word for the noun phrase object of the preposition and moving the whole prepositional phrase to the beginning of the sentence:

(6)a. Με ποιον πήγες στο σινεμά χθες;
       'Who did you go to the cinema with yesterday?'
   b. Από ποιον φίλο μου να δανειστώ τα λεφτά;
       'Which friend of mine should I borrow the money from?'
   c. Για ποιον μιλούσατε στο τηλέφωνο;
       'Who were you talking about over the phone?'
   d. Για τι μιλούσατε χθες τόση ώρα;
       'What were you talking about for such a long time yesterday?'

The sequence για τι in (6d) consists of the preposition για 'about' and the neuter question pronominal τι 'what'. It is thus different from the single lexical item γιατί 'why'. Instead of για τι 'what about' longer expressions may be used, such as για τι πράγμα or για ποιο πράγμα 'about what thing'.

(vi)   Questioning adverbials
The most typical question word for time in general is πότε 'when'; it is also possible to have more specific expressions questioning the day, the week or the month, etc. and these are formed by the question word appropriate to the questioned noun followed by that noun.

(7)a. Πότε θα γίνουν οι εκλογές;
       'When will the elections take place?'
   b. Ποια μέρα γίνονται οι εκλογές;
       'On what day do elections take place?'
   c. Ποιο μήνα αρχίζουν τα μαθήματα στο πανεπιστήμιο;
       'What month do classes start at the university?'

The question word used for place is πού 'where', the one for manner is πώς 'how' and for reason or cause γιατί 'why'. Note that the question words πού and πώς, though monosyllabic, must be assigned a stress mark in order to differentiate them from the complementizers που and πως 'that'. Again it is possible to use longer expressions with questioned noun phrases.

(8)a. Πού να φυτέψουμε το γιασεμί;
      'Where should we plant the jasmine?'
   b. Σε ποιο μέρος να φυτέψουμε το γιασεμί;
      'In which place should we plant the jasmine?'
(9)a. Πώς να τον παρηγορήσουμε;
      'How should we console him?'
   b. Με ποιον τρόπο να τον παρηγορήσουμε;
      'In what way should we console him?'
(10)a. Γιατί δεν είσαι πιο προσεκτικός;
      'Why aren't you more careful?'
    b. Για ποιο λόγο δεν είσαι πιο προσεκτικός;
      'For what reason are you not more careful?'

The question word πού may also be used as a complement to a preposition: από πού 'where from', για πού 'for where' (i.e. where to), προς τα πού 'towards where'. Πού is also used in the idiomatic expression από πού (κι) ως πού to mean 'why on earth' or 'on what grounds'.

(11)a. Από πού αγόρασες το καινούριο σου ταγέρ;
      'Where did you buy your new suit from?'
    b. Για πού το βάλατε πρωί πρωί;
      'Where are you off to so early in the morning?'
    c. Προς τα πού περπατούσε όταν τον συναντήσατε;
      'Which direction was he walking in when you met him?'
    d. Από πού (κι) ως πού μας ζητάει αυτός δανεικά;
      'Why on earth is he asking to borrow money from us?'

(vii)   Multiple questions
It is possible to question more than one constituent within the same sentence, but in this case only one of the question words will be placed at the beginning of the sentence while the other will remain in the position it occupies in the corresponding statement. The questions in (12) with the characteristic question intonation and with both question words stressed are asking information about both of these items.

(12)a. Τι έδωσες σε ποιον;
      'What did you give to whom?'
    b. Σε ποιον έδωσες τι;
      'Who did you give what to?'

Two question words can be placed together at the beginning of a sentence, but only if they are conjoined by και 'and':

(13) Με ποιον και γιατί μαλώνεις;
      'Who are you quarrelling with and why?'

5.1.5   NEGATION

Negation may be subdivided into denial or disagreement (Section 5.1.5.1) and true negation (5.1.5.2).

5.1.5.1   Denial or disagreement

Denial presupposes that something has been stated or suggested immediately before in the discourse with which the speaker disagrees. The particle όχι 'no' is the appropriate negative marker to introduce the denial in such circumstances; it is used either on its own or accompanied by a whole sentence. Thus όχι is the opposite of ναι 'yes', which expresses agreement with a previous statement or suggestion.

(1)a. Νομίζω ότι ο Νίκος αγόρασε καινούριο αυτοκίνητο
      'I think that Nick has bought a new car'
   b. *Denial*:
      Όχι, δεν αγόρασε
      'No, he didn't'

(2)a. Να φορέσεις το κόκκινο πουλόβερ
      'You should wear the red pullover'
   b. *Denial*:
      Όχι, δε θα το φορέσω
      'No, I will not wear it'

5.1.5.2   True negation

Negation, like interrogation, may affect the whole sentence (sentence negation) or a constituent within the sentence (constituent negation). We will present each one of these types separately.

5.1.5.2.1   Sentence negation

Sentence negation in Greek is formed differently for sentences in the indicative and the subjunctive. To form a negative statement, i.e. a negative indicative, the negative morpheme δε(v) is added before the verb (1a) if there are no other verbal particles, i.e. θα or clitic pronouns, accompanying the verb; otherwise δε(v) is added before the first particle (1b):

(1)a. Η μουσική **δεν ακουγόταν** πολύ καλά
   'The music could not be heard very well'
  b. Οι συγγενείς του **δε θα του δώσουν** καμιά βοήθεια
   'His relatives are not going to give him any help'

Sentences in the subjunctive mood are negated by a different negative morpheme from the one used for indicatives. The subjunctive negative marker is μη(ν); it is placed immediately after the subjunctive marker να or ας:

(2)a. **Να μην** του δώσεις άλλα λεφτά
   'You should not give him any more money'
  b. **Ας μην** το συζητήσουμε άλλο
   'Let us not discuss this any more'

The subjunctive particle να may optionally be omitted in negative subjunctive sentences:

(3) **Μην** του δώσεις άλλα λεφτά
   'Do not give him any more money'

5.1.5.2.2 Negative interrogative sentences

Negative interrogative sentences (see also 5.1.4.3) are formed by a combination of an interrogative intonational contour and the negative particle appropriate to the mood of the sentence.

(1)a. Δε θα δει ο Γιάννης την Ελένη;
   'Won't John see Helen?'
  b. *Answer with agreement*:
   (i) Όχι, δε θα τη δει
   (ii) Ναι, δε θα τη δει
   'No, he won't [see her]'
  c. *Answer with disagreement*:
   (i) Όχι, θα τη δει
   (ii) Πώς/Ναι, θα τη δει
   'Yes, he will [see her]'

In the first answer (1b(i)) the negative element όχι is used to strengthen the negation of the sentence, while in (1c(i)) the negation indicates the disagreement of the second speaker, who wants to deny the suggestion that John will not see Helen. The introductory ναι in (1b(ii)), on the other hand, indicates that the second speaker confirms that John will not see Helen.

A negative question in the subjunctive is either asking for some sort of permission or is more of a rhetorical question expecting a positive answer:

(2)a. Να μη δεχτεί ο Γιάννης την πρόταση;
   'Shouldn't John accept the offer?'

b. *Answer*:
   (i) Όχι, να μην τη δεχτεί
   (ii) Ναι, να μην τη δεχτεί
   'No, he shouldn't [accept it]'
   (iii) Όχι, να τη δεχτεί
   (iv) Ναι, να τη δεχτεί
   'Yes, he should [accept it]'

(3)a. Να μη σου δώσω ένα φιλάκι τώρα;
   'Shouldn't I give you a kiss now?'

b. *Answer*:
   (i) Όχι, να μη μου δώσεις
   (ii) Ναι, να μη μου δώσεις
   'No, you shouldn't'
   (iii) Όχι, να μου δώσεις
   (iv) Ναι, να μου δώσεις
   'Yes, you should'

The particle ναι may be replaced by the stronger affirmative word μάλιστα 'certainly, of course' or πώς 'sure'.

5.1.5.2.3 Negative commands

As mentioned in Section 1.3.3, sentences with a verb in the imperative form cannot be negated. To express a negative command or a prohibition the negative subjunctive with either the particle ας or να is used. The particle να may also be omitted, in which case the prohibition becomes more direct. Μη can also be used on its own to forbid or advise against something expressed before.

(1)a. Να μην του το πεις
   'You should not tell him'

b. Μην του το πεις
   'Do not tell him'

c. Ας μην του το 'λεγες
   'You shouldn't have told him'

d. Μη
   'Don't'

5.1.5.2.4 Constituent negation

Sentence negation (see above) is expressed by negating the verb of the sentence. It is also possible to negate only a single constituent of the sentence. For constituent negation a variety of means are used, such as the following:

(i) Negation with indefinite pronouns, determiners and adverbials

Indefinite pronouns such as κανείς/κανένας 'anyone, no one' (see Section 2.8.3.5), which may be used either pronominally to replace a whole noun phrase, as in (1a), or as determiners followed by a noun, such as κανένα βιβλίο 'any book, no book' as in (1c), acquire their negative meaning when they are within negative sentences. The same is true of τίποτα 'anything, nothing', which is only used pronominally in negative sentences (1d) and in questions. Indefinite adverbials are either expressed with a single adverb, such as ποτέ 'ever, never', πουθενά 'anywhere, nowhere' or in more complex expressions such as με κανένα τρόπο, κατά κανένα τρόπο, 'in any way/in no way', σε κανένα μέρος 'in any place/in no place', με κανένα λόγο 'on any account/on no account', καθόλου 'at all, not at all', and επουδενί 'on no account' which is used only within a negative sentence. Negative sentences which contain one of these words or expressions must also contain the negative particle δεν or μην according to the mood of the verb.

(1)a. **Δεν** ήρθε **κανείς** να με δει όταν ήμουνα άρρωστη
   'No one came to see me when I was unwell'

   b. **Κανείς** να **μην** πάει να τον βοηθήσει
   'No one should go to help him'

   c. **Κανένα** του βιβλίο **δεν** άξιζε
   'No book of his was worth anything'

   d. **Δεν** πήρε **τίποτα** μαζί του
   'He left without taking anything with him'

   e. Να **μην** αφήσετε **πουθενά** τα ίχνη σας
   'You should not leave your traces anywhere'

   f. **Ποτέ δεν** είδαμε τόσο πολύ κόσμο σε συγκέντρωση
   'We have never seen so many people at a meeting'

Note that the words κανείς, τίποτα, καθόλου, ποτέ, πουθενά have a negative meaning also in sentences without a negative particle if these sentences contain the negative word χωρίς 'without':

(2)a. Μπήκε μέσα χωρίς να τον δει κανείς
   'He entered without anyone seeing him'

   b. Έφυγε χωρίς να πάρει τίποτα
   'He left without taking anything'

They also have a negative meaning when used alone as single-word utterances:

(3)a. Ποιος θα τολμήσει να του πει την αλήθεια;
   'Who will dare tell him the truth?'
   Answer:
   Κανείς
   'No one'

b. Πότε θα πάμε κι εμείς διακοπές;
   'When will we ever go away on holiday?'
   Answer:
   Ποτέ
   'Never'

However, it is important to note that in the context of a positive, an interrogative or even a negative interrogative sentence these words function
as indefinites, as shown in the translations of the following examples (see
also Section 2.8.3.5):

(4)a. Ήρθε **κανείς** να με ζητάει;
      'Did anybody come looking for me?'
   b. Δεν ήρθε **κανείς** να με ζητάει;
      'Didn't anyone come asking for me?'
   c. Μήπως δώσατε **κανενός** άλλου μαθητή την εργασία μου;
      'Did you, by any chance, give some other student my essay?'
   d. Λέει **κανείς** να αλλάξει αλλά δεν μπορεί
      'One means to change but one can't'
   e. Να προσέχεις όταν πηγαίνεις **πουθενά** χωρίς εμένα
      'You should be careful when you go anywhere without me'
   f. Έλα σε **καμιά** ωρίτσα και θα είμαι έτοιμη
      'Come in about an hour or so and I will be ready'

Notice that if a negative word or phrase is the subject of a yes/no interrogative sentence this subject cannot occur in sentence-initial position.

(ii)   Constituent negation with the particle *όχι*
Όχι is used to negate a constituent in constructions with contrastive
negation.

(5)a. Να ψηφίσουμε το Δημητρακόπουλο και **όχι** τον Καλογεράκη
      'We should vote for Dimitrakopoulos and not for Kalogerakis'
   b. Να περάσουνε μέσα οι γυναίκες αλλά **όχι** οι άνδρες
      'Let the women come in but not the men'
   c. Φέρε μου τα κλειδιά σε καμιά ώρα, **όχι** τώρα
      'Bring me the keys in an hour or so, not now'
   d. **Όχι** μόνο δε χιόνισε αλλά ούτε έβρεξε καλά καλά
      'Not only did it not snow, but it hardly rained'
   e. **Όχι** πως θα το παινευτώ αλλά η κόρη μου είναι ένα
      καταπληκτικό κορίτσι
      'Not that I want to brag about it, but my daughter is a
      wonderful girl'

(iii) Constituent negation with *ούτε ... ούτε*

The negative expression ούτε ... ούτε 'neither ... nor' is also used within negative sentences. It may accompany any kind of constituent, as in the following examples:

(6)a. Δεν τόλμησε να μιλήσει **ούτε** η γυναίκα του **ούτε** η αδελφή
     του
     'Neither his wife nor his sister dared speak'
   b. Απόψε δεν πρέπει **ούτε** να φας **ούτε** να πιεις
     'Tonight you should neither eat nor drink'

(iv) Constituent negation with the negative particle *μη(ν)*

The negative particle μη is used to negate gerunds, participles and sometimes adjectives and nouns. This pattern is of learned origin and it is restricted in use. Notice that this negative particle does not appear with final -ν even if the word that follows begins with a vowel or a voiceless plosive. The only exception is when the negated word is a gerund, in which case the final -ν may appear if the gerund begins with a vowel (7a) or a plosive (7b).

(7)a. Ο ομιλητής, μη(ν) έχοντας άλλα επιχειρήματα, σταμάτησε
     'The speaker, not having any more arguments, stopped'
   b. Μη(ν) ξέροντας τι να πει, άνοιξε την πόρτα κι έφυγε
     'Not knowing what to say, he opened the door and left'
   c. Θα υπογράψεις το χαρτί αυτό θέλοντας και μη
     'You will sign this paper whether you want to or not [willy
       nilly]'
   d. Η κυβέρνηση θα δώσει κάποιο επίδομα στους μη
     εργαζομένους
     'The government will give a bonus to those who are not in
       work'
   e. Οι μη αξιόλογοι άνθρωποι είναι συχνά φθονεροί
     'People of no importance are often envious'
   f. Υπάρχουν εστιατόρια που είναι μόνο για μη καπνιστές
     'There are restaurants which are only for non-smokers'

Μη is also used on its own after the conjunction και 'and' to express the opposite of what was expressed by some adjective, adverb or noun in the first part of the phrase (8):

(8) Οι λογαριασμοί, εξοφλημένοι και μη (ή όχι), πρέπει να
     φυλάγονται
     'The bills, whether paid or not, must be kept'

Notice that if the conjunction is ή 'or', rather than και 'and', the negative particle following is όχι.

Μη is also used in some idiomatic expressions:

(9) Και μη χειρότερα!
'May it not get any worse!' [= 'God forbid!']

5.1.6 EXCLAMATIONS

Exclamations are used to express delight, admiration or their opposite, and they are associated with a specific intonation contour. The whole exclamation is pronounced at a higher pitch level than either a statement or a question; this pitch level stays constant all the way to the end of the utterance, unlike questions, where the pitch falls at the end. This exclamation contour is represented in the written language by the exclamation mark (!).

5.1.6.1 Typical exclamations

Exclamations may be optionally introduced by a repetition (twice or three times) of the exclamatory particle πω πω πω 'wow'. In the most typical cases, the exclamatory structure itself consists of a question word, generally τι 'what' followed by the element of the sentence that gives rise to the exclamation, i.e. the focus of the exclamation, followed by the relative clause complementizer που and the verb.

(1)a. (Πω πω πω!) Τι χαριτωμένη που είναι η κορούλα σας!
'How charming your daughter is!'
   b. Τι ωραία που μιλάει αυτός ο άνθρωπος!
'How beautifully that man talks!'
   c. Τι φριχτά που μας ξεγέλασε!
'How terribly he betrayed us!'
   d. Πω πω. Τι χάλια!
'What a mess!'

The section που + verb may be omitted, leaving only τι followed by the focus of the exclamation and the subject:

(2)a. Τι συμπαθητικός ο αρραβωνιαστικός της!
'How charming her fiancé (is)!'
   b. Τι θαύμα! Τι φρίκη! Τι συμφορά!
'How wonderful!' 'How appalling!' 'What a disaster!'

Exclamations may also be formed by using the corresponding constituent question, accompanying it with the exclamation intonation:

(3)a. Πόσο μας κόστισε όλη αυτή η ιστορία!
'How costly this business was for us!'
   b. Ποιος θα το πίστευε!
'Who would have believed it?!'

5.1.6.2   Echo-questions as exclamations

Exclamations expressing wonderment or disbelief at something mentioned before may be formed by combining the structure of a question with the intonation of an exclamation.

(1)a. *Statement:*
   Η Ελένη θα παντρευτεί το Δημήτρη
   'Helen will marry Dimitris'
(2)a. *Echo question:*
   Η Μαρία **θα παντρευτεί το Δημήτρη**!
   (exclamatory intonation)
   'Will Helen really marry Dimitris?!'
   b. Η Μαρία θα παντρευτεί **ποιον;**!
   (exclamatory intonation with emphasis on ποιον)
   c. **Ποιον** θα παντρευτεί η Μαρία;!
   (exclamatory intonation with emphasis on ποιον)
   'Who will Helen marry?!'
   d. Η Μαρία θα κάνει **τι;**!
   (exclamatory intonation with emphasis on τι)
   e. **Τι** θα κάνει η Μαρία;!
   (exclamatory intonation with emphasis on τι)
   'What will Mary do?!'

There are also exclamations introduced by the interrogative word πού followed by a να-clause which expresses some sort of amazement. Such expressions are generally equivalent to 'You won't believe this, but . . .'

(3)a. (Και) Πού να σ' τα λέω; Η Μιμή δεν του μιλάει πια
   'You won't believe this, but Mimi is not speaking to him any
   more'

5.1.6.3   Wishes and curses

Wishes and curses are included here because, despite the fact that their intonation is not exactly the same as that used in more typical exclamations, they too have a marked intonation expressing emotion, and they are often structurally marked by using special particles or by being elliptical. Some examples are given below.

Wishes and curses may be introduced by μακάρι να or που να, or simply the subjunctive particles να or ας.

(1)a. Μακάρι να γίνει καλά!
   'May s/he get well!'
   b. Που να μη σε είχα ποτέ συναντήσει!
   'Would that I had never met you' or 'I wish I had never met you!'

c. Βρε που να χαθεί το παλιόπαιδο!
   'I wish that bloody kid would get lost!'
d. Να/ας τον δω κι ας πεθάνω!
   'May I see him and then I don't mind if I die!'
e. Ας/να τέλειωνε πια αυτός ο χειμώνας!
   'If only this winter would come to an end!'

There are other idiomatic expressions for a variety of wishes.

(2)a. Καλώς τον/την! (etc.) 'Welcome!'
   b. Μπράβο σου! 'Good for you (bravo to you)!'
   c. Συγχαρητήρια! 'Congratulations!'
   d. Να σου ζήσει το παιδί! 'Long life to your child!' [said, for example, after a baptism]
   e. Αλίμονό σου! 'Woe betide you!'
   f. Ζήτω η Ελλάδα! 'Long live Greece!'
   g. Κάτω οι φασίστες! 'Down with the fascists!'
   h. Α να χαθείς, βρε βλάκα! 'Get lost, you idiot!'

5.2 THE ORDER OF MAIN CONSTITUENTS IN A CLAUSE

In Greek the position of the main constituents of the clause, namely subject, verb and object, is very flexible and allows for all possible arrangements to produce well-formed sentences.

(1)a. Η μητέρα μου μάλωσε τον πατέρα μου
   b. Μάλωσε η μητέρα μου τον πατέρα μου
   c. Μάλωσε τον πατέρα μου η μητέρα μου
   d. Τον πατέρα μου μάλωσε η μητέρα μου
   e. Η μητέρα μου τον πατέρα μου μάλωσε
   f. Τον πατέρα μου η μητέρα μου μάλωσε

All of the examples in (1) can be translated into English as:

'My mother told my father off'

The reason for this flexibility is the fact that noun phrases and pronouns have inflectional endings which mark the **case** (nominative, accusative, genitive), and this case marking indicates the function of the noun phrase in the sentence: nominative = subject, accusative = direct object, genitive = indirect object. Therefore it is unnecessary for the noun phrase to be placed in a fixed position within the sentence in order to indicate its function.

The six orders of (1) are variations of the same statement, but each one of the alternatives is more appropriate in certain discourse contexts than in others. More specifically, the order of the constituents in a sentence is influenced by the following factors: (i) whether the whole sentence is presented as completely *new* information or whether it is partly new and partly *given*, i.e. information which has already appeared in the previous discourse, and (ii) which of the constituents is presented as the **topic** (see Section 5.2.2) of the sentence, i.e. the item that the sentence is about, and which element, if any, is given emphasis or constitutes the **focus** (see Section 5.2.4) of the sentence. In most cases the *topic* of the sentence is part of the *given* information, while the *focus* is the main element within the *new* information (*comment*) section of the sentence. These factors influence the choice of the alternative arrangements as shown in Sections 5.2.1–5.2.4.

5.2.1   SENTENCES PRESENTED AS NEW INFORMATION WITH NEUTRAL INTONATION

Such sentences often occur at the beginning of the discourse or are, explicitly or implicitly, preceded by something equivalent to τα ᾽μαθες τα νέα; 'have you heard the news?' (1a) or in other contexts where the information expressed in the sentence is completely unpredictable (1e), as in the following examples:

(1)a. Τα ᾽μαθες τα νέα;
     'Have you heard the news?'
   b. Συνάντησε ο Γιάννης τη Μαρία
     'John met Mary'
   c. Ο Γιάννης συνάντησε τη Μαρία
     'John met Mary'
   d. Τα παιδιά άκουγαν σιωπηλά τη δασκάλα
     'The children were listening quietly to the teacher'
   e. Αλλά ξαφνικά ανοίγει η πόρτα και μπαίνει μέσα ένας
      αστυφύλακας
     'But suddenly the door opens and in comes a policeman'

In such contexts the most likely choices are two: either verb-subject-object or subject-verb-object, as in (1b) and (1c) respectively. Both of these sentences are normally accompanied by neutral intonation, i.e. none of the constituents is pronounced with emphasis.

5.2.1.1   The order verb-subject-(object)

Sentences in which the verb appears before the subject and object are found more frequently with intransitive verbs, i.e. where the object noun phrase is absent (examples 2–6). But such sentences may also be found with transitive verbs which have a full noun phrase object (1). The various factors which contribute to the choice of sentences where the verb is placed before subject and object are as follows:

(a) The sentence presents new unpredictable information:

> (1) Ξαφνικά αρπάζει ο Γιάννης το παλτό του και φεύγει
>   'Suddenly John grabs his coat and leaves'

(b) The subject is indefinite and non-specific:

> (2) Κυκλοφορούν διάφορες φήμες τώρα τελευταία ότι ...
>   'Various rumours have been circulating recently that ...'

(c) The subject is the indefinite non-specific κανείς (or κάποιος) in a non-interrogative and non-negative sentence:

> (3) Ίσως να 'ρθει κανείς/κάποιος να με ζητήσει
>   'Someone may come asking for me'

(d) The verb is one of appearing, entering, being, coming, beginning, etc.:

> (4) Δε μου παρουσιάζονται συχνά τέτοιες ευκαιρίες
>   'Such opportunities do not present themselves to me often'
> (5) Άρχισαν χθες τα γυρίσματα της νέας ταινίας του Τζέιμς
>   Μποντ
>   'The filming of the new James Bond picture started yesterday'

(e) There is another element, perhaps some adverb, occupying the first position in the sentence:

> (6) Πίσω από τα παρασκήνια ακούστηκε το κλάμα της
>   'Behind the scene one could hear her crying [lit. 'was heard her crying']'

With the exception of (3), with the subject κανείς, the sentences above can also appear with the subject before the verb, but then there is a slight change in the communicative value of the utterance. For example, if the subject τα γυρίσματα της νέας ταινίας του Τζέιμς Μποντ was placed before the verb:

> (7) Τα γυρίσματα της νέας ταινίας ... άρχισαν χθες

it would imply that there was some previous discussion about this film and that the beginning of the filming was an issue of some interest or a cause for some concern. Thus sentence (7) is about the starting of the filming, whereas the alternative with the verb in initial position (5) is simply announcing a totally new event which could not be predicted from the previous discourse.

5.2.1.2 The order subject-verb-object

Although the order subject-verb-object may convey new, unpredictable information and is thus appropriate in contexts such as τα 'μαθες τα νέα;

and the like, it is rather different from the order verb-subject-object which we discussed above. The subject tends to be placed in initial position when it constitutes part of the background knowledge of the speakers; for example, if it is a name referring to someone the interlocutors already know or if it is a definite, specific noun phrase. Thus, although the sentences in (1) communicate new information and the intonation associated with them is neutral, they contain the subjects ο Γιάννης and ο Υπουργός Παιδείας, which by referring to persons already known to the interlocutors may be treated as topics.

The order subject-verb-object with neutral intonation is more likely to occur when the following conditions are satisfied:

(a) The sentence is transitive with an object noun phrase and the subject is an animate, definite noun phrase referring to someone known to the interlocutors, while the object may be definite or indefinite:

(1) a. Ο Γιάννης αγόρασε καινούριο αυτοκίνητο
   'John bought a new car'
   b. Ο Υπουργός Παιδείας κάλεσε αντιπροσώπους των
   φοιτητών σε μια συνάντηση
   'The minister of education invited student representatives to a meeting'

(b) The subject is indefinite but specific and known to the interlocutors:

(2) Κάποιοι υπουργοί αποκρύπτουν την αλήθεια για την
   οικονομική κατάσταση
   'Certain ministers are hiding the truth about the economic situation'

5.2.1.3 The order verb-object-subject

The order verb-object-subject may also be used to convey entirely new information in contexts such as τα 'μαθες τα νέα; with neutral intonation, but it is more appropriate when both the verb and the object constitute part of the known background information. It is more likely to occur under the following circumstances:

(a) The object is a word more or less predictable from the meaning of the verb:

(1) Φόρεσε το σακάκι του ο Τάσος και έφυγε
   'Tasos put on his coat and left'

(b) The verb and its object form some sort of idiomatic expression:

(2) Έτσι κάνει την πλάκα του ο Δημήτρης
   'This is how Dimitris amuses himself'

(c) The subject is either introduced into the discourse for the first time or is reintroduced:

(3)a. Ύστερα μας είπε τα δικά του κι ο Γιάννης
'Later it was John who told us his stories'
  b. Εκεί που τρώγαμε **ανοίγει την πόρτα ένας παπάς** και ...
'As we were eating, a priest opens the door and ...'
  c. Τώρα **μαθαίνει πιάνο η Ελένη**, του χρόνου **θα αρχίσει και η Μαίρη**
'Now it is Helen who is learning the piano, next year Mary will start too'

5.2.2   TOPICALIZATION

The sentences which we presented above are all associated with neutral intonation and they are all appropriate for presenting completely new information. Such sentences do not have a clear division into what is referred to as the *topic* of the sentence and the remainder of the sentence, which is known as the *comment* on that topic. However, in other sentences such a division into topic and comment is clearly indicated by intonation and by grammatical elements such as the weak personal pronouns, and by changes in the order. The topic is usually some entity which has already been introduced into the discourse and is thus something or somebody known, while the *comment* is saying something new about the topic. A sentence may also have a constituent which is more emphatically presented. This constituent is referred to as the *focus* of the sentence; it carries more prominent stress and is part of the comment (the new part of the information). (See also Section 5.2.4.) In what follows we will present the variety of constructions associated with choice of topic and focus.

5.2.2.1   The subject as topic

The constituent of the sentence which most naturally serves as the topic, about which the rest of the sentence is predicated, is the subject, especially if it is definite and specific, for instance some proper name referring to somebody known to the interlocutors, etc. The characteristics of a topic are: (a) it does not carry the main stress of the sentence, (b) it is placed at the beginning of the sentence, and (c) to demarcate the topic more clearly there is a fall in intonation immediately after it. This intonation break is not always present when the subject as topic is in sentence-initial position because subjects are the most natural constituents to form topics and thus the least in need of special intonational marking. The natural coincidence of subject with topic and the preference for topics being placed at the beginning of the sentence leads to the prevalence of the subject-verb-object order.

       topic   *comment*
(1) Η μητέρα μου ↓ μάλωσε τον πατέρα μου
    'My mother scolded my father'

In (1) the topic of the sentence is the subject noun phrase η μητέρα μου and the comment is μάλωσε τον πατέρα μου. This sentence presupposes that the entity η μητέρα μου has been introduced before in the discourse and that the discussion is about her. It is thus more appropriate as an answer to a question, explicit or implicit, such as τι έκανε η μητέρα σου; 'what did your mother do?' or ποιον μάλωσε η μητέρα σου; 'who did your mother scold?' Accordingly the most prominent piece of the new information, under normal intonation, is the last constituent of the sentence, i.e. τον πατέρα μου, which constitutes the focus. Example (2a) is appropriate as an answer to τι κάνει ο Νίκος; 'what is Nick doing?' or ποια είναι τα νέα του Νίκου; 'what is Nick's news?', while (2b) presupposes a conversation where the appropriate behaviour of adults and children is discussed and it states that 'as far as the children are concerned, they should not . . .'

       topic   *comment*
(2)a. Ο Νίκος ↓ κέρδισε το λότο
    'Nick won the lottery'

       topic   *comment*
b. Τα παιδιά ↓ δεν πρέπει να βλέπουν τόσες ώρες τηλεόραση
   'The children should not watch television for so many hours'

The subject is the most natural constituent to be the topic of a sentence. However, the situation may also arise where the object noun phrase (or indeed other constituents) needs to be presented as the topic of a sentence. Furthermore, while in most cases the subject as topic is given (known) information, there are some occasions when the subject is introduced as a new topic, as in (3):

       topic   *comment*
(3) Ένας γιατρός στην Αμερική ↓ ανακάλυψε το φάρμακο κατά
    της φαλάκρας
    'A doctor in America has discovered the cure for baldness'

The above sentence is all new information, but the subject noun phrase may be considered as a newly introduced topic. The function of the noun phrase ένας γιατρός στην Αμερική as topic in (3) will be shown by the use of falling intonation after it.

5.2.2.2   Direct objects as topics

In the two most frequent orders, verb-subject-object and subject-verb-object, and in the absence of any prepositional phrases or adverbials, the object is the last main constituent. It has been mentioned above (Section 5.2.1.1) that the order verb-subject-object is most appropriate when there is no topic in the sentence, while the order subject-verb-object presents the subject as known information and indeed in most cases as the topic. Therefore, in both of these arrangements the object is part of the comment; i.e. the new information of the utterance. Furthermore, since the object is the last major constituent, it receives the main stress of the sentence, which indicates that it expresses the most important new piece of information.

To use the object as the topic of the sentence it is necessary that the corresponding weak object pronoun (τον, την, το, τους, με, σε, μας, etc.) be added to the verb; in addition, the object noun phrase may be placed at the beginning of the sentence, since this is the most typical topic position. The following examples present the object as the topic:

> *topic   comment*
> (1)a. Το Γιάννη τον διόρισαν στην τράπεζα
>   'John was appointed at the bank'

> *topic   comment*
>   b. Το συνέδριο αυτό το διοργανώνει το Πανεπιστήμιο Κρήτης
>   'This conference is organized by the University of Crete'

Sentence (1a) is appropriate in a context where John is known to the interlocutors and where there has been previous discussion about him and his affairs.

The presence of the appropriate weak pronoun is necessary in object topic constructions because it indicates that the object is not new information. The function of the weak pronoun, as the device that removes the object from the comment (new part) of the sentence and renders it part of the background (known) information, is further revealed by the fact that when the weak pronoun is present the object cannot receive the main stress of the sentence. Thus in (1a) the main stress must fall either on the prepositional phrase στην τράπεζα or on the verb διόρισαν, while in (1b) it will fall on the subject το Πανεπιστήμιο Κρήτης, or on the verb διοργανώνει. These stressed constituents will now constitute the most salient piece of new information, i.e. the focus. Remember that focus is located within the comment part of the utterance as the most stressed and thus most important piece of new information.

The explicit mention of the object noun phrase at the beginning of the sentence in conjunction with its weak pronoun marks the object as the topic. Thus sentence (1a) is about John, while example (1b) is about the conference. Example (1a) is an appropriate answer to the question, implicit or explicit, 'what about John?' or 'what became of John?' and (1b) to the question 'what about this conference?' or the request 'give me more information about this conference'.

It is worth noting that constructions with the object as topic, as in (1) above, are more naturally translated as passive sentences in English. This is because in English, in order to bring the object to the beginning of the sentence and render it as the topic, we must change the verb into the passive. Greek, on the other hand, can achieve the same effect through the use of clitics with verbs in the active voice.

For an object to become the topic of the sentence it must generally be a definite noun phrase, as the examples above show. On rare occasions we may find objects with indefinite noun phrases accompanied by their weak pronouns and also placed in initial topic position. In such cases, the indefinite noun phrase is interpreted as something specific and as something which is mentioned or implied in the previous discourse.

(2)a. Θα το 'πινα ευχαρίστως ένα ουζάκι τώρα
       'I would drink gladly a little ouzo now'
   b. Έναν τέτοιο άνθρωπο δεν τον βρίσκεις εύκολα πια
       'Such a man you will not find easily any more'

In these sentences the indefinite noun phrase ένα ουζάκι accompanied by its weak pronoun το implies that if an ouzo were to be offered to the speaker he would not say no to it; in (2b) it is obvious that the speaker has a certain man in mind known to the interlocutors.

5.2.2.3   Personal pronouns as topics

To present personal pronouns as topics the emphatic form of the corresponding pronouns must be used: εγώ, εμένα, εσένα, εμείς, εσάς, αυτός, etc. If these pronouns are objects of the sentence the appropriate weak pronouns will also accompany the verb:

(1)a. Εμένα, δε με θέλει καθόλου
       'As for me, she can't stand me' [lit. 'Me, she doesn't want me at all']
   b. Εσάς, θα σας δω την άλλη Κυριακή
       'As for you, I will see you next Sunday'

The characteristic way of topicalizing the object is to place it before the weak pronoun + verb (1a–b). However, both the weak pronoun and the lexical object may be present in sentences in which the lexical object does not appear at the beginning:

(2)a. Πρέπει να τον απαλλάξουμε αυτόν από αυτή την ευθύνη
'We must relieve him of this responsibility'

   b. Νομίζω ότι σας θυμούνται εσάς περισσότερο
'I think that they remember you more'

5.2.2.4 Indirect objects as topics

Indirect objects are expressed either by a noun phrase in the genitive case
or, more often, by a prepositional phrase. The indirect object usually
follows the verb directly, as in (1a); otherwise it comes later in the sentence
(1b). The topic is indicated in bold, the focus in bold italics:

     topic   *focus*
(1)a. **Η Μαρία** χάρισε του Νίκου ***ένα ωραίο πορτοφόλι***
'Mary gave Nick a beautiful wallet'

     topic   *focus*
   b. **Ο Νίκος** δεν είπε το μυστικό ***κανενός***
'Nick did not tell the secret to anyone'

In both sentences the genitive noun phrases του Νίκου and κανενός belong
to the comment (the new part of the information) and are appropriate to
a context where the discussion is about Mary and her actions (1a) or about
Nick and his actions (1b), i.e. in a context where Mary and Nick are the
topics of the corresponding sentences. In (1a), however, the indefinite
direct object ένα ωραίο πορτοφόλι, occurring at the end of the sentence,
is more likely to receive the main stress of the sentence and thus to be
the focus. In (1b), on the other hand, the genitive κανενός is placed at
the end of the sentence and is most likely to receive the main stress of
the sentence, thus expressing the most important piece of new information, i.e. the focus. Thus (1a) is more appropriate in a context such as Η
Μαρία τι δώρο χάρισε στο Νίκο; 'What present did Mary give to Nick?',
while (1b) is appropriate in the context Είπε ο Νίκος το μυστικό (σε
κανένα); 'Did Nick tell the secret [to anyone]?'

The indirect object, if it is expressed by a noun phrase in the genitive
case, may also be topicalized in ways parallel to a direct object. To indicate
that the indirect object does not convey new information and to show
that it is already known and part of the background information, we must
again add the corresponding genitive weak pronoun to the verb.

     topic   *focus*
(2)a. **Η Μαρία** του χάρισε του Νίκου ***ένα ωραίο πορτοφόλι***
'Mary gave Nick a beautiful wallet'

       topic   *focus*
  b. **Ο Νίκος** δεν της έδωσε ***τίποτα*** της Ειρήνης
    'Nick did not give anything to Irene'

(2a) is appropriate after a question such as 'what did Mary give to Nick?' while (2b) is appropriate after a question such as 'what did Nick give to Irene?'. The new piece of information in (2a) is 'a wallet' while in (2b) it is 'nothing'. Notice that in (2b) the most salient piece of new information is the pronoun τίποτα, which also receives the main stress of the sentence. This is so in spite of the fact that the noun phrase της Ειρήνης occurs at the end of the sentence. The noun phrase της Ειρήνης in (2b) cannot receive main stress and thus cannot be the new piece of information, because it is accompanied by its weak clitic pronoun, which indicates that it is part of the already known information.

In order to present the indirect object as the topic of the sentence we may place it at the beginning of the sentence:

      topic   *focus*
(3)a. **Του Νίκου** του χάρισε η Μαρία ***ένα ωραίο πορτοφόλι***

      topic   *focus*
  b. **Της Ειρήνης** δεν της έδωσε ***τίποτα*** ο Νίκος

(3a) is equivalent to 'as for Nick, Mary gave him a beautiful wallet', while (3b) is equivalent to 'as for Irene, Nick gave her nothing'.

5.2.2.5 Sentences with more than one topic

Examples (3a) and (3b) in the previous section show that when the indirect object is placed at the beginning of the sentence and is accompanied by a clitic pronoun it constitutes the topic of the sentence. Therefore, in (3) above, each sentence has only one noun phrase as its topic: του Νίκου in (3a) and της Ειρήνης in (3b). It is, however, possible to have sentences with two topics. The most frequent combinations are subject and direct object (1a–b) or subject and indirect object (2a–b) while the combination of direct object and indirect object as topics is not very common (2c):

(1)a. **Η Μαρία, το Νίκο** τον αγαπάει πολύ
  b. **Το Νίκο, η Μαρία** τον αγαπάει πολύ
    'Mary loves Nick very much'
(2)a. **Η Μαρία, του Νίκου** του χάρισε ένα ωραίο πορτοφόλι
  b. **Του Νίκου, η Μαρία** του χάρισε ένα ωραίο πορτοφόλι
    'Mary gave Nick a beautiful wallet as a present'
  c. **Του Νίκου, το πορτοφόλι** τού το χάρισε η Μαρία
    'Mary gave Nick the wallet'

(1) in either order (a or b) is appropriate after a question about Mary's feelings about Nick and is equivalent to 'If you ask me about Mary and how she feels about Nick, she loves him very much'. (2a or b) is appropriate after a question asking about Mary's action towards Nick. (2c) is appropriate after a question equivalent to 'If you want to know about the wallet in connection with Nick, Mary gave it to him'. Thus in (2c) the most salient piece of new information is the verb phrase του το χάρισε or the subject η Μαρία. Notice, however, that (2c) is more acceptable and more natural if we interpret the genitive του Νίκου as a possessive 'Nick's wallet was given to him by Mary' and not as the indirect object.

In spite of the fact that both objects can be found at the beginning of the sentence accompanied by weak personal pronouns and constituting thus two topics, as shown above, it is also possible to have only one of them in this position:

(3) **Του Νίκου** του το χάρισε η Μαρία **το πορτοφόλι**

(3) is equivalent to 'If you want to know about Nick and the wallet, Mary gave it to him'. Here again the most salient piece of new information, and therefore the focus, is either the subject η Μαρία or the verb phrase του το χάρισε according to which one of these the main stress of the sentence will fall on.

5.2.2.6   Other constituents as topics

Adverbs and prepositional phrases may also be used as topics by being placed at the beginning of a sentence and given the appropriate intonation (medium pitch with slight fall after the topic constituent). For example:

(1) a. **Σήμερα** θα πάμε στη δουλειά αλλά **αύριο** έχουμε αργία
   'Today we will go to work but tomorrow we have a holiday'
   b. **Στην Ελλάδα** πήγαμε πέρσι και μάλλον δε θα πάμε και φέτος
   'We went to Greece last year and it is likely that we will not go this year'
   c. **Με τον αδελφό της** μαλώνει συχνά και χωρίς λόγο
   'With her brother she quarrels often and with no reason'

5.2.3   DISLOCATION

Dislocation is a more extreme form of topicalization, although in many cases it is difficult to distinguish a topic from a *dislocated constituent*. A dislocated constituent is in a more peripheral position in the sentence, either at the very beginning or at the very end, and there is a comma after the dislocated topic, or a marked fall in intonation between it and the rest of the sentence. The dislocated constituent is more naturally translated as 'As far as X is concerned' (1a). Since a dislocated constituent is a peripheral element, the sentence may also contain its own local topic (1b). It is also possible for the dislocated constituent to be only semantically and not syntactically connected with the sentence (1c). The syntactic distance between a dislocated topic and the clause it accompanies is also shown by the fact that it may appear in the nominative case while the weak personal pronoun that corresponds to it may be in another case, thus creating a so-called 'anacoluthon' (1c–d).

(1)a. **Το Γιάννη**, δεν τον είδαμε ποτέ να χαμογελάει
    'As far as John is concerned, we have never seen him smile'
  b. **Στην Ελλάδα**, εγώ και τα παιδιά θα πηγαίνουμε κάθε χρόνο
    'As far as Greece is concerned, the children and I will be going every year'
  c. Α! **Η Αθήνα** (nom.), δε θα ξεχάσω ποτέ τα ταβερνάκια **της** (gen.)
    'As for Athens, I will never forget its little tavernas'
  d. **Εκείνος ο πατέρας** (nom.) **του Γιάννη**, δεν **τον** (acc.) βλέπεις ποτέ θυμωμένο
    'As for John's father, you never see him angry'

Notice that the difference between topicalization and dislocation for examples like those in (1a–b) is only a matter of the length of the pause between the topicalized or dislocated constituent and the rest of the sentence. The longer the pause and the deeper the intonation fall, the closer we get to dislocation.

A dislocated constituent may also appear at the very end of the sentence, sometimes even separated from its own clause by some intervening clause; it always follows a fall in the intonation (comma intonation). That is, the constituent dislocated to the end of the sentence is pronounced with weak stress and a fall in the pitch, while the main stress of the sentence falls on one of the other constituents of the sentence. A constituent dislocated to the end of the sentence always sounds like an afterthought aiming at clarification.

(2)a. Δεν τον βλέπεις ποτέ να χαμογελάει, το Γιάννη
    'You never see him smile, John'
  b. Θα του το πάρουνε, είμαι σίγουρη, το μαγαζί
    'They will take it away from him, I am sure, the shop'
  c. Ο καημένος φαίνεται πολύ άρρωστος, ο Γιάννης
    'The poor man seems very ill, John'

5.2.4   FOCUSING

In sections 5.2.2–5.2.3 we discussed sentences which consist of two parts: the topic and the comment. We also pointed out that the topic is generally part of the given, background information, while the comment is the new information expressed by the sentence. The topic is usually a definite noun phrase within the known section of the sentence. Within the new information section, the comment, there is an element which carries the main stress of the sentence, and this element is the focus. The topic is usually found at the beginning of the sentence, while the focus, which is the most salient piece of new information, is found at the end of the sentence unless the last constituent is an object noun phrase accompanied by its weak clitic pronoun or is a dislocated constituent. Intonationally a neutral sentence (with no dislocation and no emphasis at the beginning) will progress from unstressed constituents to more stressed ones. The focus of the sentence may also be an element which in addition carries extra emphasis to indicate contrast, surprise, amazement, etc.

With neutral intonation on an utterance the main stress falls naturally on the last constituent, interpreted as the focus. However, there is an alternative strategy for rendering a constituent focal, and this is by placing emphatic stress on it irrespective of its position within the sentence. Thus, a constituent may be focused by being pronounced with extra stress and at a higher pitch level without changing the structure of the sentence at all. All constituents are possible candidates for focus except syntactically weak elements such as weak personal pronouns and particles and object noun phrases accompanied by their weak pronouns. Some particles, such as δεν and μην, may exceptionally be focused. The bold italics in the sentences in (1b–f) indicate focus.

(1)a. Ο Μιχάλης θέλει να γράψει στον πατέρα του *αύριο*
      'Michael wants to write to his father tomorrow'
   b. *Ο Μιχάλης* θέλει να γράψει στον πατέρα του αύριο
      'Michael [not somebody else] . . .'
   c. Ο Μιχάλης *θελει* να . . .
      'Michael sure wants to . . .'
   d. Ο Μιχάλης θέλει να *γράψει* . . .
      'Michael wants to write [not to telephone] . . .'
   e. Ο Μιχάλης θέλει να γράψει *στον πατέρα του* . . .
      'Michael wants to write to his father [not to his mother] . . .'
   f. Ο Μιχάλης θέλει να γράψει στον πατέρα του *αύριο* . . .
      'Michael wants to write to his father tomorrow [not today . . .]'

A constituent in focus may also be moved to the beginning of the sentence while keeping its emphatic stress. It is impossible for a weak pronoun to accompany an object noun phrase in focus (cf. Section 1.1.1.7). Weak pronouns and focus are mutually exclusive features of objects.

(2)a. *Η κόρη του* έκανε όλες αυτές τις ανοησίες
      'His daughter [not his son] did all these stupid things'
   b. *Το Γιάννη* θέλω να μου φέρεις αύριο
      'I want you to bring John [not Nick] to me tomorrow'
   c. *Στον πατέρα του* θέλει να γράψει ο Μιχάλης
      'Michael wants to write to his father [not his mother]'

If a sentence contains both a topic and a focus at the beginning of the sentence, the topic is placed before the focus (3a–b). The preferred arrangement in such cases is to start with the topic and place the focus immediately before the verb. The topic in such constructions is more likely to represent a dislocated topic and to be accompanied by intonation fall:

(3)a. Η Ελένη, *το συμφέρον της* κοιτάζει
      'As for Helen, she is looking after her own interest'
   b. Και τα μαλλιά του, *η κόρη του* του τα κόβει
      'Even his hair, it is his daughter who cuts it'

Only one focused constituent is possible for each sentence.

5.3   EMBEDDED (SUBORDINATE) CLAUSES

Embedded or subordinate clauses are clauses which form part of another clause. They serve a variety of functions. According to their function they are divided into relative clauses (Section 5.3.1), indirect questions (5.3.2), indirect commands (5.3.3), complement clauses (5.3.4), and adverbial clauses, which are subdivided into conditional (5.3.5), concessive (5.3.6), etc. In general, though not always, embedded clauses are introduced by special particles. For example, some types of complement clauses are introduced by complementizers such as ότι, πως or που; relative clauses are introduced either by the suitable form of o οποίος or by the uninflected που, while adverbial clauses are introduced by the appropriate conjunction.

   Unlike English, Greek does not have infinitives and for this reason all embedded clauses are finite, i.e. they contain verbs which are fully inflected for person and number in agreement with their subject. The only non-finite verb form which forms the nucleus of an adverbial embedded clause is the gerund (see Section 1.7). Another characteristic of some embedded clauses, such as purpose clauses introduced by για+να and nominal clauses introduced by το+να, is that they require that the verb be the first constituent of the clause. This is also true for indirect questions and for relative clauses unless the relativized or questioned element is the subject itself.

5.3.1   RELATIVE CLAUSES

Relative clauses which modify nouns are also referred to as adjectival clauses. They are introduced either by the pronominal phrase ο οποίος or by the relative complementizer που. These elements are, in many cases, interchangeable but there are pragmatic factors, as well as structural ones, which make one preferable to the other. For example, ο οποίος, which is of learned origin, is more frequently used in formal discourse. It is also used instead of που, even in less formal discourse, when the relativized constituent is in the genitive or within a prepositional phrase.

5.3.1.1   Restrictive and non-restrictive relative clauses

Relative clauses are divided into *restrictive* and *non-restrictive*. The function of a restrictive relative clause is to further specify a noun in such a way so as to enable the hearer to identify its referent. A non-restrictive relative clause is used simply to add some additional piece of information about the noun. This information is not crucial for the identification of the referent but is added as an afterthought, and this is made clear by the fact that non-restrictive relative clauses are set off by pauses. This difference is exemplified below:

(1)a. Ο καθηγητής **που** μας έκανε ιστορία ήταν πολύ καλός
   'The teacher who taught us history was very good'
   b. Ο καινούριος μας καθηγητής, **που** σπούδασε στο Reading, είναι πολύ καλός
   'Our new teacher, who studied at Reading, is very good'

In (1a) the relative clause helps to identify the teacher in question, while in (1b) the noun phrase ο καινούριος καθηγητής is sufficient to identify the person we are talking about; therefore the relative clause in (1b) simply adds some relevant piece of information.

In general the relative clause immediately follows the head noun, also known as the **antecedent**, as in (1), but it is also possible for the relative clause, both restrictive (2a) and non-restrictive (2b), to be separated from its antecedent by a verb. In such cases the restrictive relative clause is more likely to be introduced by που than ο οποίος, while the non-restrictive is much more likely to be introduced by ο οποίος than που.

(2)a. Η κοπέλα έφυγε **που/η οποία** ήθελε να σου μιλήσει
   'The girl who wanted to talk to you has left'
   b. Ήρθε κι ο Γιάννης να τη δει, **ο οποίος/που** δεν είναι πολύ φίλος της
   'John came to see her too, who is not a close friend of hers'

This separation of the relative clause from its antecedent is more likely to occur when the relative clause is a long one.

Especially when the relative clause is separated from its antecedent, but in other cases too, it is possible to use the expression ο οποίος not as a pronominal but as a determiner followed by a repetition of the head noun, as in (3). Such constructions are possible only with non-restrictive relative clauses:

(3) Σκορπάει τα λεφτά του εδώ κι εκεί, **τα οποία λεφτά** τα βγάζει
    με μεγάλο κόπο
    'He throws his money around, money which he earns with a lot
    of toil'

5.3.1.2   Relative clauses introduced by *ο οποίος*

The expression ο οποίος introducing a relative clause must agree in gender and number with the noun phrase it modifies but it must be in the case appropriate to its function within the relative clause itself.

(1)a. Η συζήτηση **την οποία** κάναμε πρέπει να μείνει μεταξύ μας
     'The conversation which we had must remain between us'
   b. Καταλαβαίνω πάντα τους ανθρώπους **οι οποίοι** λένε ψέματα
     'I can always tell people who lie'
   c. Αυτός είναι ο άνθρωπος **του οποίου/στον οποίο** έχω μιλήσει
     επανειλημμένως
     'This is the man to whom I have spoken repeatedly'
   d. Κάθε παιδί **του οποίου ο πατέρας** είναι πολύτεκνος δεν
     πληρώνει δίδακτρα
     'Every child whose father has many children does not pay fees'

In (1a) the noun modified by the relative clause is feminine nominative singular; the relative pronominal την οποία agrees in gender and number with the head noun but it is in the accusative case, as required by the fact that it is the direct object of the verb within the relative clause. In (1b) οι οποίοι is masculine plural, agreeing with the head noun, but in the nominative case because it is the subject of the relative clause. In (1c) the relative is either in the genitive or in a prepositional phrase introduced by σε because its function is that of indirect object while in (1d) it is in the genitive because the relative pronominal has the function of the possessor within the relative clause.

If the noun phrase modified by the relative clause contains animate nouns conjoined, either in the singular or in the plural, and the combination is either feminine+masculine, neuter+masculine, or feminine+neuter, the relative pronominal appears in the masculine plural. This rule of gender agreement is as in Section 1.9.1. (See also Appendix 4.)

(2)a. Απέλυσαν τους καθηγητές και τις καθηγήτριες **οι οποίοι**
   έκαναν απεργία
   'They fired the male and female teachers who went on strike'

  b. Οι γυναίκες και τα παιδιά **τους οποίους** πλησιάσαμε ήταν
   χάλια
   'The women and the children who we approached were in an
   awful state'

  c. Ο άνδρας και η γυναίκα **οι οποίοι** περπατούσαν μπροστά . . .
   'The man and the woman who were walking in front . . .'

In the examples in (1) and (2) the relative pronominal is the subject, the direct object, the indirect object or the possessive within the relative clause and it appears accordingly in the nominative, the accusative or the genitive. It is possible, however, for the relative pronominal to be the noun phrase complement of a prepositional phrase within the relative clause. In such cases the expression ο οποίος introducing the relative clause is always preceded by its preposition, as below:

(3)a. Ο άνθρωπος **από τον οποίο** πήρα τα λεφτά
   'The man from whom I took the money'

  b. Η γυναίκα **με την οποία** τον είδαμε χθες
   'The woman with whom we saw him yesterday'

  c. Ο σκοπός **για τον οποίο** πολεμήσαμε
   'The aim for which we fought'

  d. Ο μαθητής **στον οποίο** έδωσες το βιβλίο
   'The student to whom you gave the book'

The relative pronoun may also be within an adverbial phrase; in this case too the relative clause is introduced by the adverbial phrase followed by the relative pronominal.

(4)a. Η κοπέλα **κοντά στην οποία** καθόσουνα είναι η
   αρραβωνιαστικιά του
   'The girl you were sitting near is his fiancée'

  b. Τον κ. Φωκά, **δίπλα στον οποίο** καθόμουνα δυο χρόνια, τον
   ξέρω καλά
   'Mr Fokas, next to whom I lived for two years, I know very
   well'

If the relative pronoun in the genitive functions as part of another noun phrase as a possessive, subjective or objective genitive, partitive genitive, etc., we find either the genitive relative pronoun followed by the noun phrase it modifies or the noun phrase followed by the relative pronoun.

(5)a. Ο άνδρας **του οποίου το παιδί** είναι μαθητής μου
   Ο άνδρας **το παιδί του οποίου** είναι μαθητής μου
   'The man whose child is a student of mine'

b. Η πόλη **της οποίας η καταστροφή** ήταν πλήρης
   Η πόλη **η καταστροφή της οποίας** ήταν πλήρης
   'The city whose destruction was complete'

c. Ο Γιάννης, **του οποίου η πρόταση** με συγκίνησε
   Ο Γιάννης, **η πρόταση του οποίου** με συγκίνησε
   'John, whose proposal touched me'

d. Αυτός είναι ο αγρός **του οποίου το μεγαλύτερο μέρος** ανήκει
   στη Χριστίνα
   Αυτός είναι ο αγρός **το μεγαλύτερο μέρος του οποίου** ...
   'This is the field the largest part of which belongs to Christina'

In most cases the relativized noun phrase appears at the beginning of the relative clause itself. However, there are situations when it is possible to find the relativized noun phrase separated from the relative clause itself by one, two or possibly more clauses:

(6)a. Ο φοιτητής **ο οποίος** μας είπε η Ελένη ότι **δε διαβάζει**
      'The student who Helen told us does not study'

b. Ο νεαρός **τον οποίο** μας είπαν ότι **δεν (τον) ξέρουν**
   'The youth whom they told us they do not know'

c. Εκείνος ο φίλος της **στον οποίο** μας έλεγαν ότι **δεν έχουν**
   εμπιστοσύνη
   'That friend of hers whom they said they did not trust'

In sentences such as (6b), where the relative pronominal is the object of the relative clause and is separated from its clause by another intervening clause, it is much more usual for a clitic pronoun corresponding to the relative pronoun to accompany the verb.

5.3.1.3 Relative clauses introduced by *που*

The relative clauses introduced by the invariable relative complementizer που may contain no word referring to the antecedent if it is the subject, direct object or indirect object:

(1)a. Ο άνθρωπος **που** ήρθε και σε γύρευε
      'The man who came looking for you'

b. Ο νεαρός **που** είδαμε στην ταβέρνα
   'The young man whom we saw at the taverna'

c. Το παιδί **που** δώσαμε το βιβλίο
   'The child to whom we gave the book'

With direct and indirect object it is also possible to use the corresponding clitic pronoun in the relative clause. Indeed, with the indirect object this is preferable.

(2)a. Ο νεαρός **που τον** είδαμε χθες στην ταβέρνα
'The young man whom we saw in the taverna yesterday'
  b. Το παιδί **που του** δώσαμε το βιβλίο
'The child to whom we gave the book'

A relative clause introduced by που may also represent or stand for a prepositional phrase, as in (3). The precise relationship between such a που and the rest of the clause is inferred from the semantic and/or pragmatic context.

(3)a. Το κουτί **που** (locative) έβαλε το δώρο
'The box **in which** she put the present'
  b. Το μαχαίρι **που** (instrumental) έκοψε το τυρί
'The knife he cut the cheese with'

With a relativized adverbial phrase in a relative clause introduced by που we find the adverb optionally followed by a clitic pronoun corresponding to the relativized noun phrase.

(4)a. Το πρώτο μου σπίτι **που κοντά (του)** ήταν ένα πάρκο
'My first house near to which there was a park'
  b. Το καφενείο **που απέναντί (του)** ήταν το ξενοδοχείο μας
'The café opposite which was our hotel'

When the relativized constituent is the subject there is no corresponding clitic in the που-clause because such an item is not freely available. We may however find the emphatic form of the personal pronoun.

(5) Κάλεσαν τον φίλο τους, **που** νομίζω ότι **μόνο αυτός** θα
μπορέσει να τους βοηθήσει
'They called their friend, who I think is the only one who could help'

Cases like (5) are usually non-restrictive relative clauses.

As a general rule the greater the distance separating the element introducing the που-clause from the relativized constituent in that clause, the more likely it is to find its clitic pronoun present. This strategy is also used occasionally with relative clauses introduced by ο οποίος.

All the examples presented above contain relative clauses whose verb is in the indicative. It is possible however, though not as common, to find relative clauses that do not make positive assertions, such as negatives, interrogatives, imperatives, suggestions, requests, etc., introduced by either ο οποίος or που followed by the subjunctive mood, as in the following sentences:

(6)a. Πρέπει να βρούμε ξεναγό **ο οποίος/που να** μιλάει σουηδικά
'We must find a tour guide who speaks Swedish'
  b. Πρέπει να βρούμε ξεναγό **να** μιλάει . . .
'We must find a tour guide speaking . . .'

(7)a Ξέρεις άνθρωπο **ο οποίος/που** να μη λέει ποτέ του ψέματα;
     'Do you know anybody who never lies [such that he wouldn't
     lie]?'
  b. Ξέρεις άνθρωπο **να** μη λέει ποτέ του ψέματα;
     'Do you know a man telling no lies?'

In (6a) and (7a) the nouns ξεναγός and άνθρωπος are modified by a relative clause in the subjunctive; in (6b) and (7b), on the other hand, there
is no relative clause. Instead the noun is modified by a subjunctive clause
directly. This subjunctive clause modifying a noun is equivalent to the
English active participle, i.e. 'speaking' and 'saying' in the above sentences.

5.3.1.4 Free or headless relative clauses

Free relative clauses are characterized by the fact that there is no explicitly
stated antecedent for the relative clause. Such clauses may be either
nominal or adverbial. Nominal free relatives are introduced by the appropriate correlative pronouns, όποιος, όσος, ό,τι, οποιοσδήποτε, οτιδήποτε,
etc. (See also Section 2.8.3.9.) The indefinite correlative pronouns may
also be used as determiners: όποιος άνθρωπος, 'whichever person', ό,τι
φόρεμα 'whatever dress'.
Adverbial free relatives are introduced by an indefinite correlative
adverb: όπως 'as', όπου, οπουδήποτε, 'wherever', όποτε, οποτεδήποτε,
'whenever', όσο, οσοδήποτε 'however much'.

(1)a. **Φάγαμε ό,τι** βρήκαμε
      'We ate whatever we found'
  b. Θα φάμε **ό,τι φαγώσιμο** βρούμε
      'We will eat whatever edible thing we find'
  c. Πήραμε μαζί μας **όποιον(δήποτε)** ήθελε να 'ρθει
      'We took along whoever wanted to come'
  d. Μετά από ένα μήνα θα μιλάς **όπως** μιλάω εγώ
      'After a month you will speak as I do'
  e. Θα πάει **όπου(δήποτε)** τον στείλεις
      'He will go wherever you send him'

Notice that the compound οπωσδήποτε is not used to introduce relative
clauses. It is used only as an adverb meaning 'by all means, certainly', as
in (2a). The other compounds with -δήποτε may be used either to introduce relative clauses (1c and e) or as pronominals or as adverbials
respectively, as in (2b–c).

(2)a. Πρέπει να πάμε **οπωσδήποτε** να του μιλήσουμε
      'We must certainly go and talk to him'
  b. Αυτό μπορεί να το κάνει **οποιοσδήποτε**
      'Anybody can do this'

   c. Τώρα βρίσκεις φτηνά και καλά ρολόγια **οπουδήποτε**
      'You can now find cheap and good watches anywhere'

A distinct characteristic of free relatives introduced by a pronominal is that the case of this pronominal is not determined by its function within the relative clause but by the function of the whole relative clause within the main clause. Thus in (3a) όποιον is the subject of the relative clause and yet its case is not nominative but accusative. This is because the whole relative clause functions as the direct object of the main verb and receives its accusative from it. In some sentences (3b) a clitic pronoun corresponding to the correlative pronoun may accompany the main verb:

   (3)a. Θα πάρουμε μαζί μας **όποιον** θέλει να 'ρθει
        'We will take along whoever wants to come'
    b. Θα **τον** σκοτώσει **όποιον** της κάνει κακό
       'He will kill whoever does her harm'

If a free relative clause functioning as an object is placed before the main clause the presence of the corresponding clitic pronoun within the main clause becomes obligatory:

   (4) **Όποιον** πει την αλήθεια θα **τον** συγχωρήσω αμέσως
     'I will forgive immediately whoever tells the truth'

In constructions such as (4) where the free relative clause, which is the direct object of the main clause, is placed at the beginning, the clitic pronoun must be present within the main clause. In such constructions the correlative pronoun may also appear in the nominative, as in (5) below. This nominative satisfies the requirement of its subject role within the relative clause, while the clitic in the accusative, which refers to the relative clause as a whole, shows that the relative clause is the object of the main clause.

   (5) **Όποιος** πει την αλήθεια θα **τον** συγχωρήσω αμέσως

With the indefinite correlative όσος we have constructions similar to those we find with όποιος, as in (6), but also constructions with a main clause containing the corresponding τόσος, as in (7):

   (6)a. Πάντα φιλοξενεί **όσους** έρχονται στο σπίτι του
     b. Πάντα **τους** φιλοξενεί **όσους** έρχονται στο σπίτι του
     c. **Όσους/όσοι** έρχονται στο σπίτι του **τους** φιλοξενεί πάντα
       'He always offers hospitality to all who come to his house'
     d. **Όσοι ήρθαν** πήραν δώρο
       'All that came got a present'
     e. **Όσοι κι αν ήρθαν** πήραν δώρο
       'However many came, they all got a present'

Notice the difference between (6d), where the verb immediately follows the correlative όσοι, and (6e), where after όσοι we have the hypothetical κι αν. The second implies that there were so many presents available that it did not matter how many guests came, they were all able to get a present. Thus whereas (6a) is a statement of fact, (6e) constitutes a praise of the generosity of the hosts.

(7)a. **Όσα λεφτά** του δώσεις **τόσα** θα ξοδέψει
  'He will spend just the amount of money you give him'
  b. **Όσα ψάρια** μου φέρεις **τόσα** θα σου πληρώσω
  'I will pay for just as many fish as you bring me'

Free relatives are also found in prepositional phrases and may introduce adverbial clauses:

(8)a. **Σε όποιο καφενείο** πας θα ακούσεις την ίδια συζήτηση
  'Whatever café you go to you will hear the same conversation'
  b. **Από όπου** περάσεις σου χαμογελούν
  'Wherever you go they smile at you'
  c. Θα σε πάρω μαζί μου **οπουδήποτε** πάω
  'I will take you with me wherever I go'
  d. **Όπως** στρώσεις (έτσι) θα κοιμηθείς
  'As you make your bed, so you will sleep on it'

All indefinite correlative words, whether pronominal or adverbial, whether used as pronouns or as determiners, may be accompanied by the expression κι αν or και να, which has the effect of strengthening their indefiniteness.

(9)a. **Όση αγάπη κι αν/και να** του δώσεις δεν είναι ευχαριστημένος
  'No matter how much love you give him, he is not satisfied'
  b. **Όποιος κι αν** με ζητήσει πες του ότι δεν είμαι εδώ
  'Whoever may ask for me tell him that I am not here'
  c. **Όπου κι αν πας** θα θυμάσαι τον ουρανό της Ελλάδας
  'Wherever you may go you will remember Greece's sky'

Any correlative pronoun, determiner or adverb may be followed by the coordinating conjunction και + the hypothetical particle αν or the particle να (όποιος κι αν, όσος κι αν, ό,τι κι αν, όπου κι αν, όποτε κι αν) without change in the meaning except to stress that, no matter how remote the possibility might seem, something will happen.

It is also possible to find a correlative pronoun or adverb followed directly by the subjunctive, as in the following examples:

(10)a. **Όποιος να** 'ρχότανε τον φιλοξενούσαν
  'They entertained anyone who came'
  b. **Ό,τι να δει** θέλει να το αγοράσει
  'She wants to buy anything she sees'

5.3.2   INDIRECT QUESTIONS

Indirect questions follow main verbs of asking, questioning and equivalent expressions such as δεν ξέρω, δεν έμαθα etc.

5.3.2.1   Questioning the whole sentence

An indirect question may question the truth or falsity of the whole embedded sentence. Such sentences constitute the indirect form of yes/no direct questions. They are introduced by the conjunction αν 'if, whether' or μήπως 'if by any chance' followed by the embedded clause with a verb in the indicative:

(1)a. Ο Γιάννης με ρώτησε **αν/μήπως** ήθελα να πάω μαζί τους
       'John asked me if I wanted to go with them'
   b. Δεν μπορούσα να καταλάβω **αν** μου έλεγε αλήθεια ή ψέματα
       'I could not understand if s/he was telling me the truth or lies'

Indirect questions may also have a verb in the subjunctive with the particle να and no other introductory conjunction or particle.

(2) Η Μαρία με ρώτησε **να φύγει ή όχι**
       'Mary asked me whether to leave or not'

The indirect question in (2) is very similar to the corresponding direct one:

(3) Να φύγω ή όχι;   'Should I leave or not?'

but (2) is considered an indirect question because its verb is in the third person to agree with the third person of the subject of the main clause which is reported as asking the question. On the other hand, in (3) the verb in the first person is in agreement with the person doing the asking. Furthermore, the intonation contour of (2) is that of a statement, whereas in (3) it is that of a question.

5.3.2.2   Questioning one of the constituents

If the questioned constituent is a noun phrase, the indirect question is introduced by the appropriate question word (see Section 5.1.4.4), which may be used either as a pronoun, completely replacing the noun phrase (1a and c), or as a determiner followed by the noun itself (1b and d).

(1)a. Με ρώτησε **ποιος** του τηλεφώνησε
       'He asked me who phoned him'
   b. Δεν ξέρουν ακόμη **ποιον υποψήφιο** θα ψηφίσουν
       'They do not know yet which candidate they will vote for'
   c. Αναρωτιέμαι **ποιανού** θα δώσουν την υποτροφία
       'I am wondering who they will give the scholarship to'

d. Ήθελα να μάθω **ποιανού φοιτητή** θα δώσουν υποτροφία
   'I would like to know which student they will give a scholarship
   to'

If the questioned noun phrase is a genitive which is part of another noun phrase (possessive, subjective, objective etc.), the indirect question may be introduced either by the question word (1c) or by the whole noun phrase containing the questioned genitive (2a–b):

(2)a. Ρώτησαν **ποιανού η κόρη** διορίστηκε στην τράπεζα
   b. Ρώτησαν **η κόρη ποιανού** διορίστηκε στην τράπεζα
      'They asked whose daughter was appointed at the bank'

The genitive ποιανού in all cases (1c–d) and (2) may be replaced by τίνος. Indirect questions may also be used to question a prepositional phrase or an adverbial, as the following examples show:

(3)a. Με ρώτησε **από ποιον** πήρα τα λεφτά
      'He asked me who I got the money from'
   b. Μάθε **με ποιον** ήταν η Ελένη στην ταβέρνα
      'Find out who Helen was at the taverna with'
   c. Πες μου **από πού/από ποιο μέρος** κατάγεται ο Ανδρέας
      'Tell me where/which place Andreas comes from'
   d. Θέλει να μάθει **δίπλα σε ποιον/σε ποιον δίπλα** καθόμουνα
      'She wants to find out who I was sitting next to'
   e. Δεν έχουμε αποφασίσει **πώς/με ποιο τρόπο/με τι τρόπο** θα
      πάμε
      'We have not decided how/by what means we will go'
   f. Πες μου **γιατί/για ποιο λόγο** δε μου μιλάς
      'Tell me why/for what reason you are not talking to me'

An indirect question concerning the nominal or adjectival predicate is introduced by the question word τι 'what':

(4) Τον ρώτησα **τι** είναι ο Γιάννης
    'I asked him what John was'

Like direct questions, indirect questions may have their verb either in the indicative, as in all the examples presented above, or in the subjunctive, as in the sentences below:

(5)a. Με ρώτησε **ποιον να** φέρει μαζί του
      'He asked me who to bring with him'
   b. Δεν ξέρει **με ποιον (άνθρωπο) να** μιλήσει
      'She doesn't know who (which person) to speak to'

The element which introduces the clause is immediately followed by the verb, although it is marginally possible to find the subject following adverbial question words such as γιατί 'why', πότε 'when'. Thus the order subject-verb-object is excluded in indirect questions, as in direct ones, unless the questioned phrase is the subject itself.

5.3.3   INDIRECT COMMANDS

When imperative sentences are presented as indirect commands, i.e. as embedded clauses after verbs of requesting, ordering, commanding etc., they are expressed in the subjunctive with the particle να. There is no other introductory particle.

(1)a. *Direct command*:
Φέρε μου το βιβλίο
'Bring me the book'
   b. *Indirect command*:
Μου είπε **να του** φέρω το βιβλίο
'He told me to bring him the book'

In (1) we see that the imperative mood of a positive direct order of (1a) is changed to the subjunctive with the particle να and with the clitic pronoun before the verb rather than after it. When the direct command is in the negative form, as in (2a), the mood of the verb is already the subjunctive, so the changes from the direct to the indirect command (2b) concern only the personal ending of the verbs and the person of the relevant pronouns.

(2)a. *Direct command*:
(Σε παρακαλώ) **(να) μη** μου μιλάς όταν γράφω
'Please do not talk to me when I am writing'
   b. *Indirect command*:
Με παρακάλεσε **να μην** του μιλάω όταν γράφει
'He asked me not to talk to him while he is writing'

5.3.4   COMPLEMENT CLAUSES

Complement clauses are embedded clauses governed by a verb (1a–c), an adjective (1d) or a noun (1e).

(1)a. Πιστεύει **ότι/πως** δε θα γίνει πόλεμος
'He believes that war will not take place'
   b. Ο Γιάννης παρακαλούσε **να μην** τον στείλουνε στο μέτωπο
'John was pleading not to be sent to the front'
   c. Μετάνιωσα **που** τον άφησα να φύγει
'I regret that I let him go'
   d. Είναι βέβαιος **ότι/πως** η κατάσταση θα βελτιωθεί
'He is sure that the situation will improve'
   e. Η απόφασή της **να** τον ακολουθήσει είναι αξιοθαύμαστη
'Her decision to follow him is admirable'

5.3.4.1   Object complement clauses governed by a transitive verb

There are two types of complement clause: those expressed by the indicative mood (see Section 1.3.1) and those expressed by the subjunctive (see Section 1.3.2). Indicative complement clauses are further subdivided into those introduced by the complementizer ότι/πως (see (1a) in Section 5.3.4 above, and (1a) below), those introduced by μήπως as in (5–6) below, and those introduced by the complementizer που (see (1c) in Section 5.3.4 above, and (1b) below). Subjunctive complement clauses have no complementizer element introducing them but begin directly with the subjunctive marker να (see (1b) in Section 5.3.4 above). According to the kind of complement clause they take, main verbs are divided into four types: (i) verbs of saying, thinking, believing, and similar ones, which take an indicative complement clause introduced by ότι/πως; (ii) factive verbs, i.e. verbs which presuppose that their complement clauses express a fact and are followed by an indicative complement clause introduced by που; (iii) future referring verbs of wishing, planning, desiring, requesting, ordering etc., which take a subjunctive complement clause; and (iv) verbs of fearing, which may take either an indicative introduced by ότι, a subjunctive introduced by να, or even an indicative introduced by μη or μήπως.

The examples in (1) show the difference between a non-factive (1a) and a factive (1b) complement clause:

(1)a. Νομίζω **ότι/πως** μου λες πάλι ψέμματα
    'I think that you are telling me lies again'
  b. Λυπάμαι **που** έχασε ο Νίκος τη δουλειά του
    'I am sorry that Nick lost his job'

In (1a) the ότι/πως-clause expresses something which may or may not be true, while the που-clause in (1b) presupposes that Nick has lost his job and the speaker expresses his sadness at this fact. Although in most cases the verbs that take ότι/πως-clauses are different from those that take a που-clause, there are verbs which can combine with either type. In such cases the meaning of the main verb in the different constructions is slightly changed in order to combine appropriately with factivity:

(2)a. **Φοβήθηκε ότι** θα τον μεταθέσουνε σε καμιά επαρχία
    'He is afraid that they will transfer him somewhere to the
    provinces'
  b. **Φοβάται που** δεν του έχει ακόμη τηλεφωνήσει η Μαρία
    'He is fearful that/because Mary has not phoned yet'
(3)a. **Βλέπεις ότι** η Ελένη είναι πολύ κουρασμένη
    'You see that Helen is very tired'
  b. **Βλέπεις που** δεν τον σέβεται καθόλου;
    'Do you see/realize the fact that she does not respect him at
    all?'

In (2a) the speaker fears the *possibility* that they will transfer him, while in (2b) the speaker is worried by the *fact* that Mary has not called. In (3a) the meaning of the complement clause allows for the *possibility* that Helen may only appear tired, while in (3b), where the complement clause is introduced by που, the meaning of the complement clause is presented as a *fact*.

Που may also be used as an alternative to ότι in some idiomatic expressions, again in order to stress that the embedded clause is presented as a fact.

(4) Δε λες **ότι/που** της έχτισε ολόκληρη βίλα!
     'Why don't you also consider (the fact) that he built her a whole villa!'

Verbs of fearing, such as φοβάμαι 'I fear', ανησυχώ 'I worry', στενοχωριέμαι 'I worry', αγωνιώ 'I am anxious' and others with similar meaning, may also take a complement clause introduced by μη or μήπως 'in case' followed by a verb in the indicative mood, as shown by the choice of δεν as the negative particle. The particle μη, which introduces these complement clauses, is not a negative marker as such, since the clause it introduces has its own negative. Μη in this context combines the meaning of the complementizer ότι with a wish that what the clause conveys will be averted and thus will not happen. These cases are exemplified below:

(5)a. **Φοβάται μην** τον δούνε
   b. **Φοβάται μήπως** τον δούνε
       'He is afraid they might see him'
   c. **Φοβάται μήπως δεν** τη συναντήσει
       'He is afraid he might not meet her'
(6) **Ανησυχούσε μήπως δεν** πετύχαινε στις εξετάσεις του
     'He was worried he might not pass his exams'

Subjunctive clauses follow verbs of wishing, planning, desiring, etc., as mentioned above, and such verbs are different from those which combine with the indicative. However, there are also verbs which may combine with either an ότι/πως-clause or a να-clause. Again the choice of one type of complement clause over another after the same verb has some semantic consequences. Verbs of this type are ελπίζω, πιστεύω, and νομίζω in its negative form.

(7)a. **Ελπίζω ότι** θα τον προλάβω στο γραφείο του
       'I hope that I will catch him at his office'
   b. **Ελπίζω να** τον προλάβω στο γραφείο του
       'I hope to catch him at his office'
   c. **Ελπίζω ότι/να** τον πρόλαβες στο γραφείο του
       'I hope that you caught him at his office'

(8)a. **Νομίζω ότι** δε θα μας καλέσει
    'I think that he will not invite us'
  b. **Δε νομίζω ότι** θα μας καλέσει
    'I don't think that he will invite us'
  c. **Δε νομίζω να** μας καλέσει
    'I don't think (and I am sorry about it) that he will invite us'

In (7a) the speaker simply hopes that he will find a certain person at his office, while in (7b), where the complement clause is in the subjunctive, the speaker both hopes and wishes to find this person at his office. The subjunctive complement adds to the main verb some emotional involvement and colours the hoping with wishing.

The verbs ξέρω, μαθαίνω, διδάσκω, and similar ones, may also occur with either an ότι-clause, in which case they are related to other verbs of cognition, or a να-clause, in which case they have the meaning of knowing, teaching and learning a skill (i.e. knowing how to do something):

(9) a. Η Μαρία **ξέρει ότι** ο Γιάννης δεν έχει λεφτά
    'Mary knows that John does not have money'
  b. Η Μαρία **ξέρει να** κρατάει μυστικά
    'Mary knows how to keep a secret'
(10)a. Έμαθα **ότι** πήρες το πτυχίο σου
    'I heard [was informed] that you got your degree'
  b. Έμαθα πια **να** μην περιμένω πολλά
    'I finally learned not to expect too much'

The majority of verbs which take an object complement clause may also take the third person neuter clitic pronoun το 'it'. Το πιστεύω 'I believe it', το θέλω 'I want it', το μετανιώνω 'I regret it', το ξέρω 'I know it', etc. In addition, they can also combine the clitic with the complement clause, in which case the complement clause acts as an apposition, an explanation of the pronoun.

(11)a. Δεν **το** πιστεύει **ότι** όλα τέλειωσαν μεταξύ τους
    'He cannot believe [it] that everything is over between them'
  b. Δε θα **το** ήθελα ποτέ **να** σε στενοχωρήσω
    'I would never have wished [it] to upset you'
  c. **Το** μετάνιωσα **που** του μίλησα άσχημα
    'I regretted [it] that I spoke to him badly'
  d. Δεν **το** ήξερα **ότι** ο Πέτρος ήταν φίλος σου
    'I did not know [it] that Peter was your friend'

Verbs such as ξέρω, with the 'know how' meaning, followed by a να-clause, do not combine with the neuter pronoun το 'it', nor do verbs of strong emotion such as λυπάμαι 'I feel sorry', πονώ 'I feel pain', etc., which are followed by a που-clause. In the latter cases the που-clause is not strictly nominal but rather a causative adverbial, where που can be interpreted as 'because', as in (1b) and (11c) above.

In the previous examples the complement clause functions as the direct object of the transitive verb. There are also situations where the main verb has both a noun phrase as direct object and also a να-clause, as in the following examples:

(12)a. Έπεισα **το Γιάννη να** μας φέρει την κόρη του
'I persuaded John to bring his daughter to us'

b. Ανάγκασαν **τους εργάτες να** κάνουν απεργία
'They forced the workers to strike'

c. Έβαλα **του Γιάννη να** φάει
'I served John his food [lit. I put (food) for John to eat]'

Verbs of perception such as βλέπω 'I see', ακούω 'I hear', αισθάνομαι 'I feel', αντιλαμβάνομαι 'I perceive', also take a noun phrase direct object and a να-clause, as in the following examples:

(13)a. **Άκουσα τη Μαρία να** κλαίει
'I heard Mary crying'

b. **Βλέπω το Γιάννη να** σου χαμογελά
'I see John smiling at you'

c. Η Ελένη **αισθάνθηκε τα χέρια της να** παγώνουν
'Helen felt her hands freezing'

The same verbs may be used for 'realize' or 'acquire the knowledge', 'I am informed', etc. In this case they are followed by an ότι-clause:

(14)a. **Άκουσα ότι** η Μαρία κλαίει συχνά
'I heard [was informed] that Mary cries often'

b. **Είδα τελικά ότι** είχα άδικο
'I realized finally that I was wrong'

The να-clause after these verbs has no explicit subject because it is understood to be identical with either the main clause direct object (12a–b) or with the main clause indirect object (12c). There are also verbs which take only a να-clause, whose subject is not expressed and is understood to be identical with the main subject:

(15)a **Προσπάθησα να τον αποφύγω** αλλά δεν τα κατάφερα
'I tried to avoid him but I did not succeed'

b. Ο Γιάννης **ξέρει να κολυμπά**
'John knows how to swim'

The verbs in (12), (13) and (15) whose complement clause has obligatorily the same subject as either main clause subject or main clause object are referred to as *verbs of control*. The phenomenon of control is discussed further in Section 5.4.3.

5.3.4.2 Complement clauses with intransitive and impersonal verbs

Intransitive verbs in the third person singular, such as με πειράζει 'it bothers me', με ενοχλεί 'it annoys me', μου φαίνεται 'it seems to me', and impersonal expressions formed by the verb είναι and a neuter adjective such as καλό 'good', κακό 'bad', πιθανό(ν) 'likely', απίθανο(ν) 'unlikely', δυνατό(ν) 'possible', αδύνατο(ν) 'impossible', ευχάριστο, 'pleasant' δύσκολο 'difficult', εύκολο 'easy', take as their subject either an indicative clause introduced by ότι/πως or, more frequently, a που- or a να-clause. With some of these verbs or expressions all three types of complement clause are possible (1a–b) with very small semantic differences.

(1)a. Με **πειράζει ότι/που** δεν μου μιλάει
      'It bothers me that he does not talk to me'
   b. Με **πειράζει** πολύ **να** μην ξέρω τι κάνει
      'It upsets me a lot not to know what she is doing'
   c. Μου **φαίνεται ότι** δε με ξέρεις καλά
      'It seems to me that you don't know me well'
   d. Είναι **ξεκάθαρο ότι** η κυβέρνηση έχει χάσει την εμπιστοσύνη
      του λαού
      'It is clear that the government has lost the confidence of the
      people'
   e. Δεν είναι **σωστό να** παραπονιέσαι συνέχεια
      'It isn't right to complain continuously'
   f. Είναι **λυπηρό που** έχασε τη δουλειά του σ' αυτήν την ηλικία
      'It is sad that he lost his job at his age'

It is also possible to place the complement clause before the main verb and introduce it optionally with the neuter definite article το. In such constructions the complement clause is used as the topic of the complex sentence, while the main clause constitutes the focus.

(2)a. **(Το) ότι** δε μου μιλάει με πειράζει πάρα πολύ
      'That he does not talk to me bothers me a great deal'
   b. **Το ότι** με ξέρεις τόσο λίγο μου φαίνεται περίεργο
      'That you know me so little seems strange to me'
   c. **Το να** παραπονιέσαι συνέχεια δεν είναι καθόλου σωστό
      'To complain all the time is not at all proper'
   d. **Το ότι** έχασε τη δουλειά του είναι πολύ λυπηρό
      'That he lost his job is very sad'

The definite article το cannot precede a που-subject clause. Therefore, in order to prepose the complement clause in constructions like (1f) the complementizer ότι or πως is used instead, as in (2d) above.

5.3.4.3   Complement clauses governed by adjectives and nouns

The same three types of complement clause which combine with verbs can also be found as complements of adjectives and nouns and with the same semantic features.

(1)a. Είναι **βέβαιος ότι** τα πράγματα θα βελτιωθούν
   'He is sure that the situation will improve'
   b. Είναι **ευχαριστημένη που** μπόρεσε να πάει στην Ελλάδα το καλοκαίρι
   'She is pleased that she was able to go to Greece in the summer'
   c. Είναι **ανυπόμονη να** τον συναντήσει
   'She is impatient to meet him'
(2)a. Έχει την **απαίτηση να** τον θαυμάζουν όλοι
   'He demands that everybody admires him'
   b. Ζει με την **ελπίδα ότι** θα ξανάρθει σύντομα
   'He lives with the hope that he will return soon'
   c. Θα τρελαθεί από τη **χαρά της που** θα τον δει
   'She will be mad with joy that she will see him'

5.3.4.4   Nominalized clauses

In examples (2) of Section 5.3.4.2 above we found clauses which were introduced by the neuter definite article το. These are clauses which have become nominals and which function as a neuter noun phrase within the sentence. The definite article precedes the complementizer ότι or που and the subjunctive particle να, as shown below:

(1)a. Τον ενοχλεί **το ότι** παντρεύτηκε τόσο γρήγορα η Μαρία
   'It annoys him that Mary got married so soon'
   b. **Το ότι** χώρισαν τόσο γρήγορα δε μου έκανε καθόλου εντύπωση
   'That they divorced so soon did not surprise me at all'
   c. Είναι απαράδεκτο **(το) να** δουλεύεις και να μην αμείβεσαι
   'It is unacceptable to work without getting paid'
   d. **Με το που** έφυγε η Μαρία μπήκε μέσα ο Νίκος
   'Just as Mary left, in came Nick'
   e. Δεν κερδίζεις φίλους **με το να** γκρινιάζεις συνέχεια
   'You will not win friends by complaining all the time'
   f. Στενοχωριέται **εξαιτίας του ότι** δεν μπορεί να βρει δουλειά
   'S/he is worried because s/he cannot find a job'
   g. Είναι πολύ καλός **στο να** φυλάει μυστικά
   'He is very good at keeping secrets'

A nominalized clause with the article typically serves as the subject of an impersonal verb (1a–b) or as the subject of a linking verb (1c). This is possible only with an ότι- or να-clause but not with a που-clause. A nominalized clause may also serve as the complement of a preposition (1d–f). After a preposition we may find all three types of complement clauses introduced by ότι (1f), να (1e) and που (1d). Such clauses following a preposition are also found as complements to adjectives (1g).

It is less common to find nominalized clauses preceded by the definite article occupying the object position of a verb, although it is possible to find optionally the neuter singular form of the weak (clitic) pronoun το accompanying the main verb and referring to the object clause (2a–c). This clitic pronoun indicates that the object complement clause is also nominalized. The function of the clitic pronoun here is to present the embedded clause as background information and thus allow for the focus to be placed on the main clause. (On focus see Section 5.2.4.)

(2)a. **Το** ξέρει **ότι** δεν τον αγαπάει η Μαρία
  'He knows that Mary does not love him'
 b. Δεν **το** θέλει κι αυτός **να** κάνει τόσα λάθη
  'He does not want to make so many mistakes either'
 c. **Το** μετάνοιωσε **που** δεν του έγραψε
  'S/he regretted that s/he did not write to him'

5.3.5   CONDITIONAL CLAUSES

Conditional clauses are subordinate clauses introduced typically by the conditional conjunctions αν, εάν. There are also some more marginal conjunctions introducing conditionals such as άμα, which is both temporal and conditional ('if and when'), έτσι και, which often implies some sort of threat, and the more analytic expression σε περίπτωση που 'in the event that'. There are also conditional clauses consisting of two parts which are introduced by είτε ... είτε or ή ... ή 'whether ... or'. The negative particle in these clauses is δεν. The conditional clause, referred to as the **protasis**, may either precede or follow the main clause, which is referred to as the **apodosis**.

(1)a. Δεν πρόκειται να φύγω **αν** δεν του μιλήσω
  'I will not leave unless I speak to him' [lit. 'if I don't speak to him']
 b. **Αν** δεν του μιλήσω δεν πρόκειται να φύγω
  'Unless I speak to him I am not leaving'
 c. Δεν μπορείτε να εργαστείτε εδώ **εάν** δεν έχετε διδακτορικό
  'You cannot work here if you do not have a doctorate'
 d. Άμα θέλεις έλα να τα πούμε
  'If you want, come and have a chat with me'

e. Έτσι και τολμήσει να σε κατηγορήσει θα τον βρίσω
   'If he dares accuse you I will give him a piece of my mind'

f. Σε περίπτωση που η τράπεζα είναι κλειστή θα σας δώσω εγώ λεφτά
   'If the bank is closed, I will give you money'

g. Είτε το θέλεις είτε όχι η Μαρία θα παντρευτεί το Σπύρο
   'Whether you want it or not, Mary will marry Spyros'

h. Είτε/ή το θέλεις είτε/ή δεν το θέλεις, το ίδιο μου κάνει
   'Whether you want it or not it's all the same to me'

There are also conditional clauses introduced by other means, such as εκτός αν, εκτός και αν 'unless', ακόμη και αν or έστω και αν 'even if':

(2)a. Πάρε ακόμη λίγο μουσακά, **εκτός και αν** δε σου αρέσει
     'Take some more mousaka, unless you don't like it'

 b. Είναι σίγουρο ότι θα σε εντυπωσιάσει **έστω κι αν** δεν τον εγκρίνεις
     'It is certain that he will impress you even if you don't approve of him'

The above types of conditional clause are all expressed in the indicative. However, there is also a conditional use of να-clauses:

(3) **Να** τον δεις τώρα μετά την εγχείρισή του δε θα τον γνωρίσεις
   'If you were to see him now after his operation you wouldn't recognize him'

Although conditional clauses are usually combined with a main clause, the apodosis, there are situations where the conditional clause is used alone to express an exclamation or a question.

(4)a. **Αν έβλεπες** την Ελένη με το φόρεμα του χορού!
     'If only you could have seen Helen in her ball dress!'

 b. **Κι αν** ξαφνικά **μας δούνε**;
     'What if they see us suddenly?'

According to the verb form and their semantic force, conditional clauses may be divided into *factual* and *counterfactual* clauses.

5.3.5.1   Factual conditional clauses

Factual or suppositional conditional clauses are those where if what is described in the if-clause (the protasis) is fulfilled or can be fulfilled, then what is expressed in the main clause (the apodosis) is or will be or should be fulfilled too. The verb in the protasis may be in any tense or aspect; the verb in the apodosis may be either in the same tense as that of the protasis or it may be a modal or an imperative. Thus in (1a) the if-clause

contains a present tense, 'if you [consistently] work hard', and the main
clause also contains a present tense, 'you succeed'; if and when the condition of working hard is satisfied, then the consequence will be success,
which will automatically follow. In the protasis of (1b) the verb is in the
perfective non-past (dependent) and the apodosis is in the simple future.
The sentence says that if the sending of the letter is fulfilled today it
follows that the letter will be received tomorrow. In (1c) the if-clause also
contains a perfective non-past but the conjunction άμα introducing the
protasis indicates 'whenever'. The whole sentence means that on each
occasion that he meets a friend he immediately invites him. In (1d) the
protasis contains a simple past tense and the apodosis another simple past.
This sentence indicates that if it turns out to be true that he read the
letter then it is also true that he has found out what there is to know. In
(1e) both the protasis and the apodosis contain a perfect tense and the
meaning is that if it turns out to be true that he has telephoned Manolis
then it will follow that it is also true that Manolis has spilled the beans.
In (1f) the protasis in the present tense is followed by an apodosis with
a modal in the present and in (1g) by an imperative:

(1)a. **Αν δουλεύεις** σκληρά πάντα **πετυχαίνεις**
       'If you work hard you always succeed'
   b. **Αν (θα) στείλεις** το γράμμα σήμερα **θα το πάρει** αύριο
       'If you send the letter today, he will receive it tomorrow'
   c. **Άμα συναντήσει** φίλο του **τον καλεί** αμέσως στο σπίτι
       'If ever he meets a friend he immediately invites him to his
       house'
   d. **Έτσι και διάβασε** το γράμμα **τα έμαθε** όλα
       'If he read the letter he has found out everything'
   e. **Αν έχει τηλεφωνήσει** του Μανόλη **του τα έχει πει** όλα
       'If he has telephoned Manolis he has told him everything'
   f. **Αν θέλεις** να πετύχεις **πρέπει να** δουλεύεις σκληρά
       'If you want to succeed you must work hard'
   g. **Αν σε ενδιαφέρει** να τον γνωρίσεις **έλα** μαζί μου αύριο
       'If you are interested in meeting him, come with me tomorrow'

5.3.5.2 Counterfactual conditional clauses

Counterfactual constructions express situations where the content of the
protasis has not been fulfilled in the past or most likely will not be fulfilled
in the future; as a consequence, the content of the apodosis is also unre-
alized or unrealizable. In the protasis we find either the imperfect or the
pluperfect, occasionally preceded by θα, while in the apodosis we find θα
followed by the imperfect (conditional) or the pluperfect (perfect conditional). If both the protasis and the apodosis contain the imperfect

(conditional) and there is no negation, the construction may be interpreted as suppositional, as in (1f).

(1)a. **Αν τον ήξερες** δε **θα μιλούσες** έτσι
'If you knew him you wouldn't speak like that'

b. **Αν δεν τον ήξερα** καλύτερα **θα τον παρεξηγούσα**
'If I didn't know him better, I would have misunderstood him'

c. **Ακόμη κι αν σου είχα πει** την αλήθεια, **δε θα με πίστευες/
δε θα με είχες πιστέψει**
'Even if I had told you the truth you wouldn't have believed me'

d. **Αν είχες πάρει** λαχείο, **μπορεί να είχες κερδίσει**
'If you had bought a lottery ticket you might have won'

e. **Να τον έβλεπες** τώρα **δε θα τον γνώριζες**
'Were you to see him now you wouldn't recognize him'

f. **Αν μου το έλεγες θα το πίστευα**
'If you told me I would believe it' ['It is possible that you will tell me']

In (1a) the protasis is in the imperfect and the apodosis contains θα followed by the imperfect. It means that if it were the case that you knew him (which it isn't because you do not know him), then you would not be speaking the way you are speaking. The fact is that you do not know him and this is why you are speaking the way you do. In (1c) the protasis contains a pluperfect and the apodosis may contain either an imperfect or another pluperfect. The meaning is that even if it had been the case that I had told the truth (which is not the case because I didn't) it would still have been true that you would not have believed me. Thus, the counterfactual conditionals combine a protasis in the imperfect or pluperfect with an apodosis containing θα and either the imperfect or pluperfect; all four combinations are possible. The protasis expresses situations which were not fulfilled, and the apodosis also expresses situations which were not fulfilled in consequence. In (1e) the conditional particle αν is replaced by the subjunctive marker να. In (1f) both the protasis and the apodosis are in the imperfect and there is no negation present in the apodosis. Here the two imperfects may refer either to past or present or even future time, and the conditional is more suppositional than counterfactual. It means either (a) you may or may not have told him yesterday but if you did then he believed you, or (b) you may tell him now or in the future and if you do he will believe you.

5.3.6 CONCESSIVE CLAUSES

Concessive clauses are subordinate indicative clauses typically introduced by αν και, 'although, even though' or less frequently by παρά το ότι, παρ' ότι, παρ' όλο που, παρ' όλον ότι, μολονότι, 'in spite of', παρά το γεγονός ότι 'in spite of the fact that'. In more formal discourse the learned origin particle καίτοι 'though' may be found. Although it is more frequent to find the concessive clause before the main one, as in (1a), the reverse order is also possible. When the main clause follows the concessive it is possible to introduce the main clause with the word εντούτοις 'nevertheless', as in (1d).

(1)a. **Αν και** δεν τον ξέρω πολύ καλά τον συμπαθώ
    'Even though I do not know him very well I like him'
  b. Θα το αγοράσω **αν και** δεν το χρειάζομαι
    'I will buy it though I do not need it'
  c. **Μολονότι** δεν έχει λεφτά κάνει πολλά έξοδα
    'Although he does not have much money he spends a lot'
  d. **Παρόλον ότι** είναι απρόσεκτος εντούτοις τα καταφέρνει
    'Even though he is rather careless, nevertheless he manages all right'

Another type of concessive clause is one introduced by κι ας 'even though', which is negated by the particle μη(ν).

(2)a. Εγώ θα πάω στο πάρτι **κι ας μην** έρθει ο Τάσος
    'I will go to the party even if Tasos does not come [lit. 'and let Tasos not come']'
  b. Συνέχιζε να στενοχωριέται **κι ας** της είχα μιλήσει
    'She continued to worry even though I had spoken to her'

There is an overlap in the meaning of concessive κι ας and the conditionals introduced by κι αν ακόμη κι αν, έστω κι αν, 'even though' and όσο κι αν/όσο και να 'no matter how much'.

(3)a. Στενοχωριέται πάρα πολύ **κι ας** μην το δείχνει
    'She is very worried even though she is not showing it'
  b. Στενοχωριέται πολύ **ακόμη κι αν** δεν το δείχνει
    'She is very worried even though she is not showing it'
  c. Πρέπει να ζητήσεις συγνώμη **όσο και να μην** το θέλεις
    'You must apologize no matter how much you do not want to'
  d. Πρέπει να 'ρθεις κι εσύ **έστω κι αν** δε θέλεις
    'You must/should come too even if you do not want to'
  e. **Κι αν** δεν έρθεις εσύ εγώ θα πάω
    'Even if you do not come I will go'

5.3.7 TEMPORAL CLAUSES

Temporal clauses are adverbial clauses which describe an event which either took place before or after or at the same time as the event described in the main clause. The most neutral temporal conjunction and the most frequently used one is όταν 'when'. Other conjunctions introducing the temporal clause are πριν or προτού 'before', τώρα που 'now that', τότε που 'at the time that', μετά που 'after', αφού 'after, since', αφότου, από τότε που 'since', ώσπου 'until', ενώ, ενόσω, την ώρα που 'while', καθώς 'as', όποτε, οπόταν 'whenever', οπότε 'at which point', σαν 'when, as', μόλις (που), με το που 'as soon as', εφόσον 'as long as', μέχρι που/να, ώσπου να 'until', πάνω που 'just as'.

Πριν and προτού 'before' are always followed by the *dependent* verb form, which may or may not be preceded by να (see Section 1.5.2). A clause introduced by πριν (προτού) may not be negated.

   (1)a. **Πριν (να)** πάτε στη διάλεξη περάστε από το σπίτι μου
         'Before you go to the lecture drop in at my house'
      b. Πρέπει να συζητήσεις το θέμα με τη Μαρία **πριν (να)** της μιλήσεις
         'You must discuss the issue with Mary before you speak to her'

Μέχρι and ώσπου (also *katharevousa* έως ότου) 'until' express both time (2a) and result (2b). When they refer to the future, they are followed by να and the dependent verb form. They can combine with the negative.

   (2)a. Ανησυχούσε πολύ **μέχρι να** τον δει
         'She was very worried until she saw him'
      b. Θα δουλεύω **μέχρι να μην** αντέχω πια
         'I will carry on working until I cannot stand it any more'

Μέχρι που 'until', expressing result, when it refers to the past, is combined with an indicative past tense verb form.

   (3)a. Τον βασάνισαν **μέχρι που τα ομολόγησε** όλα
         'They tortured him until he confessed everything'
      b. **Μέχρι που δεν έκλαιγε** ήταν καλά
         'While she was not crying it was fine'

All the other temporal conjunctions are followed by the indicative and combine fairly freely with any verb form appropriate to the rest of the context. The temporal clause usually precedes the main clause, though the reverse order is also possible.

   (4)a. **Όταν** τον βλέπω θυμάμαι τον πατέρα μου
         'When I see him I remember my father'
      b. **Όταν** του φώναξα ήρθε αμέσως
         'When I called him he came immediately'
      c. **Μόλις** τον έβλεπε να κουράζεται του έλεγε να σταματήσει τη δουλειά
         'As soon as she would see him getting tired she would tell him to stop working'

d. **Αφού** δεν ξέρει αγγλικά πώς θα σπουδάσει στην Αγγλία;
'Since she does not know English, how will she study in England?'

e. **Καθώς** κατέβαινα τη Σόλωνος είδα τη Δήμητρα με τον Παναγιώτη
'As I was coming down Solonos street I saw Dimitra with Panayotis'

f. Δώσε του αυτό το γράμμα **όταν τον δεις**
'Give him this letter when you see him'

g. **Μόλις τον φωνάξω** έρχεται
'He comes the moment I call him'

h. Κάθισε και **αφού πιεις** ένα καφέ μας λες την ιστορία σου
'Sit down and after you drink a coffee you can tell us your story'

i. **Όποτε της μιλήσει** ο Γιάννης κοκκινίζει
'Whenever John speaks to her she blushes'

j. **Πάνω που** ήμουν έτοιμος να φύγω εμφανίστηκε η Σούλα
'Just as I was ready to leave Soula appeared'

As shown in (4f–i), the temporal conjunctions όταν, μόλις, αφού and όποτε may be followed by the dependent verb form when they refer to an indefinite future time. The conjunctions αφότου and ενώ may not be followed by the dependent form. In (4f) and (4g) the dependent is a covert future since the negative particle possible here is δεν.

5.3.8 ADVERBIAL CLAUSES OF MANNER

Adverbial clauses of manner are introduced by the conjunctions όπως, σαν, καθώς 'as' or with the relative clause expressions έτσι που, με τον τρόπο που 'in the way/manner that', με τον ίδιο τρόπο που 'in the same way that'. Όπως κι αν (or και να) is used with the meaning 'however, no matter how'. The verb in these clauses is in the indicative after όπως, με τον τρόπο που, έτσι που, and in the subjunctive after σαν; the tense and aspect are those which are appropriate to the context:

(1)a. **Όπως** έστρωσες θα κοιμηθείς
'As you made your bed so you will sleep'

b. Πρέπει να γράφεις **όπως** γράφει κι ο Πέτρος
'You must write the way that Peter writes'

c. Ήθελε να πάει στο Πανεπιστήμιο **όπως** έκανε η Μαρία
'She wanted to go to the University as Mary did'

d. **Έτσι/με τον τρόπο που** μιλάς δε σε καταλαβαίνει κανείς
'The way you speak, no one understands you'

e. Ο Νίκος γελούσε **σαν να** ήταν πάλι παιδί
'Nick was laughing as if he were a child again'

 f. Μιλούσαν **σαν** ο Νίκος **να** ήταν παιδί
  'They spoke as if Nick were a child'

The conjunction σαν is normally directly followed by να, and no major constituent, including a subject, intervenes between them (1e). On rare occasions it is however possible to place the subject between σαν and the verb, as in (1f).

 A clause introduced by όπως may also be used parenthetically:

 (2)a. **Όπως** σου είχα πει, η Μαρία δεν τη δέχτηκε αυτή την
   πρόταση
   'As I had told you, Mary did not accept that proposal'
  b. Η κατάσταση χειροτέρεψε, **όπως** το είχαν προβλέψει
   'The situation got worse, as they had predicted'
  c. Εγώ πάντως θα πάω στην Ελλάδα, **όπως κι αν** έχουν τα
   πράγματα
   'I will go to Greece whatever the situation is like'
  d. **Όπως κι αν** της το εξηγήσεις αυτή δε θα σε καταλάβει
   'No matter how you explain it to her, she will not understand
   you'

5.3.9 ADVERBIAL CLAUSES OF PURPOSE (FINAL CLAUSES)

Purpose clauses are typically introduced by για να 'in order that'. Occasionally a purpose clause may also appear without για, i.e. introduced directly by να, especially after verbs of motion.

 (1)a. Η Λουίζα έφυγε νωρίς **για να** τον προλάβει
   'Louisa left early in order to catch him'
  b. Έφερα τα παιδιά **(για) να** τους κόψεις τα μαλλιά
   'I brought the children so that you can give them a hair-cut'

The subject of a purpose clause, if it is explicitly stated, must always follow the verb. Furthermore, no constituent may be placed between για and the particle να; the two elements για να must always be adjacent to each other.

 There are also some idiomatic uses of για να-clauses where a combination of the semantics of purpose, cause and result seems to be present. In (2a–b) the για να-clause expresses result or consequence.

 (2)a. Της πήρε τα λεφτά, **για να μην** της τα επιστρέψει ποτέ
   'He took the money from her, never to return it'
  b. **Για να** μιλάει έτσι κάτι πρέπει να έχει μάθει
   'For him to speak like this he must have found out something'

5.3.10   ADVERBIAL CLAUSES OF RESULT

Adverbial clauses of result are introduced by the conjunctions που or ώστε 'so that'. The verb in a result clause after the conjunction ώστε, if it refers to the future, is usually in the subjunctive (1a). Notice also that the subject of the adverbial clause introduced by ώστε may occur after ώστε and before να (1b):

(1)a. Δε θα αγοράσω τη μπλούζα αυτή εγώ **που να** την αγοράσεις εσύ
      'I will not buy this blouse so that you can buy it'
   b. Έκανε **έτσι ώστε** η Μαρία **να** μπορεί να αποφασίσει μόνη της
      'He acted in such a way that Mary will be able to decide on her own'
   c. Μίλησέ του αγγλικά **ώστε/που να** σε καταλάβει
      'Speak to him in English so that he will understand you'
   d. Του μίλησε με τόση αγένεια **που** αυτός θύμωσε πολύ
      'She spoke to him so rudely that he got very angry'

Another use of ώστε is to introduce a main clause presented as a conclusion drawn by the speaker.

(2)a. **Ώστε** αυτά του κάνεις και τον τρελαίνεις
      'So that is what you are doing to him that's driving him crazy'
   b. **Ώστε** δεν έδωσες το δώρο στη Χρυσούλα;
      'So you did not give the present to Chrysoula?'

A certain kind of result clause may also be introduced by για να, as in the following examples:

(3)a. Θα είναι πολύ χαζός **για να μη** δεχτεί μια τέτοια δουλειά
      'He must be very stupid not to accept such a job'
   b. Είναι πολυ μικρός **για να** καπνίζει
      'He is far too young to smoke'

5.3.11   ADVERBIAL CLAUSES OF CAUSE

Adverbial clauses of cause are introduced by a number of conjunctions: γιατί or more formal διότι 'because', καθώς 'as', επειδή, αφού, εφόσον, colloquial μια και 'since, as long as'. The verb is in the indicative and in the tense and aspect appropriate to the situation described.

(1)a. Κάθισε **γιατί** ήταν κουρασμένη
      'She sat down because she was tired'
   b. Θύμωσα **διότι με απείλησε**
      'I got angry because he threatened me'

c. Δεν πρόκειται να πάω στο θέατρο **επειδή/καθώς** δεν έχω λεφτά
'I will not go to the theatre as I have no money'

d. Θα σου κάνει τη χάρη αυτή **αφού** του το ζήτησα εγώ
'He will do you this favour since/because I am the one who
asked him'

e. Μην αγοράσεις καινούριο αυτοκίνητο τώρα **μια και** δεν έχεις
λεφτά
'Do not buy a new car now since you have no money'

f. **Εφόσον** δε θέλεις να καταλάβεις θα πάψω να σου μιλώ
'Since you are refusing to understand I will stop talking to you'

When the adverbial clause is introduced by the conjunctions γιατί and
διότι it must follow the main clause; with the other conjunctions either
order is possible.

5.4 OTHER SYNTACTIC PHENOMENA

In this section we will examine some important syntactic phenomena which
have not been dealt with so far: *coordination*, *comparison*, and *anaphora*.

5.4.1 COORDINATION

There are two types of coordination: clause coordination and constituent
coordination, as described below.

5.4.1.1 Clause coordination

Clause coordination is marked by the use of a coordinating conjunction.
The most typical conjunctive coordinating conjunction is και 'and' (sometimes κι before a word with an initial vowel), while the most typical
adversative coordinating conjunction is αλλά 'but', or less commonly
and more colloquially μα 'but', all of which occur between the two coordinated clauses.

(1)a. Η Χριστίνα είναι φοιτήτρια **και** σπουδάζει γλωσσολογία
'Christina is a university student and she is studying linguistics'

b. Σήμερα θα μελετήσω το κείμενό σου **κι** αύριο θα σου πω τη
γνώμη μου
'Today I will study your paper and tomorrow I will tell you my
opinion'

c. Ο Δημήτρης χρειάζεται χρήματα **αλλά** κανείς δεν έχει να του
δώσει
'Dimitris needs money but no one has any to give him'

d. Του το έχω εξηγήσει πολλές φορές **μα** δε με πιστεύει
'I have explained it to him many times but he doesn't believe me'

If the verb of the two coordinated clauses is understood to be the same, it may be omitted from the second.

(2)a. Ο Γιάννης έφαγε τη σούπα **κι** ο Νίκος το κρέας
'John ate the soup and Nick the meat'

b. Ο Γιάννης θέλει να μετακομίσουν **αλλά** η γυναίκα του όχι
'John wants them to move house but his wife does not'

Another adversative coordinating conjunction is όμως 'but, however'. This occurs either between the two clauses or at the very end of the second clause, or after one of the constituents of the second clause.

(3)a. Η Μαρία συμπαθεί την Ελένη, **όμως** ο Γιάννης δεν τη θέλει

b. Η Μαρία συμπαθεί την Ελένη, ο Γιάννης **όμως** δεν τη θέλει

c. Η Μαρία συμπαθεί την Ελένη, ο Γιάννης δεν τη θέλει **όμως**
'Mary likes Helen but John does not want her'

Another type of coordination involves the use of the disjunctive ή 'or' or one of the two expressions ή ... ή ... 'either ... or ...' and είτε ... είτε ... 'whether ... or ...' (see Section 5.3.5):

(4)a. Δεν ξέρει τι να κάνει, **να πάει** στο στρατό **ή να συνεχίσει** τις σπουδές του
'He does not know what to do, go to the army or continue his studies'

b. **Ή** θα αλλάξεις συμπεριφορά **ή** εγώ θα φύγω από το σπίτι
'Either you change your behaviour or I will leave home'

c. **Είτε** τον μαλώνεις **είτε** δεν τον μαλώνεις το ίδιο κάνει
'Whether you tell him off or not, it makes no difference'

To express the English equivalent 'whether or not' it is also possible to omit είτε ... είτε ... and leave the two clauses next to each other without any connecting element except for the negative particle δεν at the beginning of the second (5). These expressions are also equivalent to κι αν ... κι αν δεν ... 'whether or not'. Their common characteristic is that the verb of the first clause is repeated in the second but is accompanied by the negative δεν.

(5)a. **Τον μαλώνεις δεν τον μαλώνεις** το ίδιο κάνει
'Whether you tell him off or not it is all the same'

b. Πρέπει να τον δεις **φοβάσαι δεν φοβάσαι**
'You must see him, whether you are afraid or not'

Analogous to the repetition of the disjunctive ή ... ή ... and είτε ... είτε ... is the use of και ... και ... 'both ... and ...' as in (6a) or the adversative ούτε ... ούτε ... 'neither ... nor ...', as in (6b):

(6)a. **Και** τη δουλειά μου θα τελειώσω **και** στο πάρτι θα πάω
'I will both do my work and also go to the party'

b. **Ούτε** να σπουδάσει θέλει **ούτε** να βρει δουλειά
'She neither wants to study nor to find a job'

There are cases where the conjunction και is not a 'pure' coordinator but has a meaning equivalent to a number of different subordinating conjunctions as in the following examples:

Και with a temporal meaning 'and then':

(7) Έφαγε **και** πήγε να κοιμηθεί
'He ate and (then) went to bed'

Και after verbs of perception replaces either a να-clause or a που-clause, as in (8):

(8)a. Την άκουσα **κι** έκλαιγε instead of
Την άκουσα **να** κλαίει or
Την άκουσα **που** έκλαιγε
'I heard her cry'

b. Την είδα **και** χόρευε με το Γιάννη
'I saw her dancing with John'

Και may also replace a να-clause after verbs of beginning and verbs with similar meaning, as in (9), always followed by the imperfective:

(9) Ξαφνικά άρχισε **και** μου κατηγορούσε την Όλγα
'Suddenly she started to criticize [and criticized] Olga'

Και may express result, as in (10):

(10)a. Ήθελε **και** το έκανε
'He wanted (to do it) and (so) he did it'

b. Του μίλησες πάλι άσχημα **κι** έφυγε
'You spoke badly to him again and (so) he left'

c. Τι συμβαίνει **και** δεν έφτασαν ακόμα;
'How come they have not arrived yet?'

Και may replace a relative clause, as in (11):

(11) Ήρθε μια γυναίκα **και** κρατούσε ένα μεγάλο καλάθι
'A woman came who [and] was carrying a big basket'

Και may be used to express reason:

(12) Φώναξε το Νίκο **και** θέλω να του πω κάτι
'Call Nick because [and] I want to tell him something'

Και may be used to express the consequence of a condition:

(13) Μη μου κάνεις το χατήρι αυτό **και** θα σου δείξω εγώ
'If you do not do me this favour I will show you'

The option of using και in conditionals like (13) is not available if the protasis contains αν, εάν etc.

5.4.1.2 Constituent coordination

The coordination of two constituents is marked either by the conjunctive particle και (κι) or by the disjunctive ή 'or' or ούτε 'neither'. The particles και and ή may occur once between the two conjuncts, or else they may accompany each conjunct and thus be repeated as many times as there are conjuncts, as in (1) and (2) below. Ούτε occurs in negative sentences and must be repeated before each conjunct. The other coordinating conjunctions, αλλά, μα, όμως 'but' are used less frequently in constituent coordination.

(1)a. Ήρθε η Μαρία **και** ο Πέτρος
  'Mary and Peter came'
 b. Ήρθε **και** η Μαρία **και** ο Πέτρος **και** ο Βασίλης
  'All three came, Mary, Peter and Basil'
(2)a. Λέω να αγοράσω το φόρεμα **ή** το ταγέρ
  'I am thinking of buying the dress or the suit'
 b. Λέω να αγοράσω **ή** το φόρεμα **ή** το ταγέρ
  'I am thinking of buying either the dress or the suit'
(3) Δε μου αρέσει **ούτε** ο τραγουδιστής **ούτε** η τραγουδίστρια
  'I do not like either the male or the female singer'
(4) Μιλάει αργά **αλλά/όμως** προσεκτικά
  'She speaks slowly but carefully'
(5) Δεν είναι **ούτε** έξυπνος **ούτε** βλάκας
  'He is neither clever nor stupid'

When there are two or more coordinated noun phrases functioning as subjects of the verb, the verb is either in the singular, as in examples (1) and (3), or in the plural, as in (6a). We may also have the singular verb if the subject follows:

(6)a. Ο Πέτρος και η Μαρία **ήρθαν** να σε δουν
  'Peter and Mary came to see you'
 b. Ήρθε η Μαρία και ο Πέτρος
  'Mary and Peter came'
 c. Δε μου **αρέσουν/αρέσει** ούτε ο τραγουδιστής ούτε η
   τραγουδίστρια
  'I do not like either the man or the woman singer'

When one of the two coordinates of the subject is the first person pronoun (either singular or plural) the verb is usually in the first person plural, as in (7):

(7)a. Εγώ κι ο Γιάννης **φύγαμε** νωρίς
'John and I left early'

   b. Θα σου **τηλεφωνήσουμε** ή εγώ ή ο Γιάννης
'Either John or I will telephone you'

   c. Ούτε ο Γιάννης ούτε εγώ **ακούσαμε** τίποτα
'Neither John nor I heard anything'

All types of phrase as well as single words may be coordinated: noun phrases (1–3), adjective phrases (5 and 8), adverbial phrases (4 and 9), prepositional phrases (10), verb phrases (11) or single words (12–13):

(8)   Ο Πάνος είναι **πολύ θυμωμένος και πολύ απογοητευμένος**
'Panos is very angry and very disappointed'

(9)   Το σπίτι της δεν είναι **ούτε κοντά ούτε μακριά**
'Her house is neither near nor far'

(10)   Πρέπει να είναι **ή στο σπίτι ή στο γραφείο**
'She must be either at home or in her office'

(11)   Δεν μπορεί να κάνει τίποτα, μόνο **να τρώει και να κοιμάται**
'He cannot do anything, only eat and sleep'

(12)   Μπορείς να έρθεις **με ή χωρίς** το Γιάννη
'You may come with or without John'

(13)   **Πάρε και δώσε** τα λεφτά στο Νίκο
'Take the money and give it to Nick [lit. take and give the money to Nick]'

Although it is more common to coordinate phrases or words of the same category, as in the previous examples, it is also possible to find coordination of dissimilar categories such as an adjective phrase with a prepositional phrase (14), an adverbial phrase with a prepositional phrase (15), a noun phrase with a nominalized clause (introduced by the neuter definite article) (16), etc.

(14)   Του αρέσει το κρέας **καλοψημένο και με μπόλικο αλάτι**
'He likes his meat well done and with lots of salt'

(15)   Μιλάει πάντα **προσεκτικά και με ακρίβεια**
'He always speaks carefully and with precision'

(16)   **Η αναίδειά του και το ότι** ποτέ δε σου κάνει μια χάρη τον κάνουν πολύ αντιπαθητικό
'His insolence and the fact that he never does you a favour make him very unlikeable'

5.4.2 COMPARISON

There are a number of ways used to compare two constituents. These are described below.

5.4.2.1 Normal comparison

A comparison normally consists of two parts. The first part, referred to as the first term of comparison, contains the comparative element, while the second term of the comparison is introduced by the preposition από (1 and 3), or the genitive (2) or παρά (4).

(1) Ο Γιάννης είναι **εξυπνότερος από την Ελένη**
    'John is cleverer than Helen'
(2) Ο Νίκος είναι **μικρότερός μου**
    'Nick is younger than me'
(3) Αυτή η υπόθεση είναι **χειρότερη από την προηγούμενη**
    'This case is worse than the previous one'
(4) Είναι **καλύτερα να** τον πάρουμε μαζί μας **παρά να** τον
    αφήσουμε εδώ
    'It is better to take him with us than to leave him here'

However, the second term of the comparison may occasionally be omitted, where it is easily understood:

(5) Αυτό το επιχείρημα είναι **περισσότερο πιστευτό**
    'This argument is more convincing'

For all adjectives, including those that also have a morphologically marked comparative (1–4), adverbs, and other types of phrases which may appear in a comparison, there is a syntactic means of marking the first member by the particle πιο 'more', or less frequently περισσότερο 'more' (5). The second member of the comparison, in this case, is again introduced by either the preposition από or by παρά. The genitive of a clitic pronoun cannot combine with this type of comparison.

(6)a. Ο Γιάννης είναι **πιο ενθουσιώδης από το Γιώργο**
      'John is more enthusiastic than George'
   b. Ο Μιχάλης είναι **πιο φιλάρεσκος από την αδερφή του**
      'Michael is more vain than his sister'

In example (6) the first member of the comparison is presented as in some way exceeding the second. To express the opposite, i.e. that the first member possesses some quality to a lesser extent than the second member of the comparison, we use the comparative degree of the adverb λίγο 'little', i.e. λιγότερο 'less', followed by the same elements, από or παρά.

(7) Το βιβλίο αυτό είναι **λιγότερο ενδιαφέρον από/παρά το**
    προηγούμενο
    'This book is less interesting than the previous one'

If the second member of the comparison is a noun phrase after a morphologically formed comparative, it is most commonly accompanied by the
preposition από 'than', followed by the second member of the comparison in the accusative case. If the second member of the comparison is a
clitic pronoun it appears in the genitive without από.

(8)a. Αυτό το κουστούμι ειναι **φτηνότερο από το άλλο** που είδαμε
      στην Ερμού
      'This suit is cheaper than the other one we saw in Ermou
      Street'
   b. Δεν πιστεύει ότι υπάρχει κανείς που να είναι **καλύτερός του**
      'He does not believe that there is anybody better than him'
   c. Το φαγητό του Βασίλη είναι **πιο νόστιμο από (το φαγητό) της
      Αγνής**
      'The food prepared by Basil is tastier than that of Agnes'

Since in (8c) the noun phrase το φαγητό in the second part of the comparison is identical to the noun phrase in the first part, it may be omitted.
In this case it may appear that the preposition από is followed not by the
expected accusative but by the genitive case. However, the object of από
is actually the understood noun phrase το φαγητό, which, if it were present,
would have been in the accusative.

Instead of the preposition από the second term of the comparison may
be introduced by παρά 'than' which can function as a preposition and
thus be followed by an accusative noun phrase, exactly as in the case of
από, or as a conjunction when it may be followed by a noun phrase in
any case, and indeed by any type of phrase. Clitic pronouns may not
follow παρά.

(9)a. Ο πατέρας τους αγαπά **περισσότερο** τη Μαρία **παρά την
      Ελένη**
      'Their father loves Mary more than Helen'
   b. Ο Γιάννης αγαπά τη Μαρία **περισσότερο παρά ο Νίκος**
      'John loves Mary more than Nick does'
   c. Η μητέρα τους δίνει **περισσότερα λεφτά του Νίκου παρά της
      Ειρήνης**
      'Their mother gives more money to Nick than to Irene'
   d. Ο καφές μού φαίνεται νοστιμότερος **στην κουζίνα παρά στην
      τραπεζαρία**
      'Coffee tastes better to me in the kitchen than in the dining-
      room'

If the comparison is not between noun phrases but between other types
of phrase the second member of the comparison can only be introduced
by παρά, not από, as in (9d) and (10–12). Παρά is also obligatory when
comparing indirect object noun phrases, as in (9c) above.

(10) Είναι πάντα **καλύτερα στο σπίτι σου παρά** σε ξένο σπίτι
'It is always better in your house than in somebody else's'

(11) Είναι **πιο σωστό να λες την αλήθεια παρά να** λες ψέματα
'It is better to tell the truth than to tell lies'

(12) Είναι **προτιμότερο να έχεις λεφτά παρά να είσαι φτωχός**
'It is preferable to have money than to be poor'

The second member of the comparison may be introduced by από, in cases like (11–12) above, but only if the second clause has been nominalized by the addition of the neuter definite article:

(13) Είναι **προτιμότερο να λες την αλήθεια από το να** λες ψέματα
'It is preferable to tell the truth than to tell lies'

Comparison between two indicative clauses may also be expressed by means of a relative clause structure. In this case the second term of the comparison is expressed by either από or παρά followed either by the correlative neuter pronoun ό,τι or the quantitative correlative όσος.

(14) Η Όλγα είναι **πιο πεισματάρα από/παρά ό,τι** είναι η Ελένη
από/παρά ό,τι η Ελένη
από/παρά όσο είναι η Ελένη
από/παρά όσο η Ελένη
'Olga is more persistent than Helen is'

(15) Ο Κώστας λέει **πιο πολλά** ψέματα **από/παρά όσα** λέει ο
Μιχάλης (*or* **από/παρά όσα ο Μιχάλης**)
'Kostas tells more lies than Michael does'

5.4.2.2 Correlative comparison

A correlative comparison also contains two parts which are judged to be equal with respect to some property or characteristic. The first part of such a construction is marked by the quantitative correlative όσος 'as much' while the second part of the comparison is introduced by the quantitative demonstrative τόσος 'this much/many, so much/many'.

(1)a. **Όσο** επιμένεις **τόσο** θα απογοητεύεσαι
'The more you insist the more you will be disappointed'

b. **Όσο** πιο πολύ/περισσότερο τρως **τόσο** πιο πολύ/περισσότερο
βλάφτεις τον οργανισμό σου
'The more you eat the more you damage your health'

c. **Όσο** πιο καλά γράψεις στις εξετάσεις σου **τόσο** μεγαλύτερους
βαθμούς θα πάρεις
'The better you perform in your exams the higher marks you
will get'

d. Όσες ψευτιές μου είπε η Μαρία άλλες τόσες μου είπε και η
   Αντιγόνη
   'Antigoni told me as many lies as Maria did'

In (1a) the correlative comparison is between two clauses. The expression
όσο ... τόσο is sufficient in this case. It is however possible to use the
comparative degree of the adverb πολύ (i.e. πιο πολύ or περισσότερο)
following both elements τόσο ... όσο, as in (1b), where the comparison
is again between two clauses. In example (1d) the quantitative demonstrative of the second term of the comparison is accompanied by άλλες
to express 'as many again'.

5.4.2.3 Equation

In equation the comparison concerns two phrases: noun phrases, adjective
phrases, prepositional phrases, etc. These elements are compared and
found identical in respect of the degree to which they possess a certain
property. Equation is expressed by σαν, ως, όπως or όσο.

The noun phrase or the pronoun which may follow σαν may be in the
accusative case if it is definite, as in (1) and (2a). If the noun or even
adjective phrase following σαν is indefinite, then it agrees with the case
of the first term of the comparison. In (2b), where the case of the first
member is nominative, the case of the indefinite noun phrase following
σαν will also be nominative. It is possible to suggest that in (2b) the verb
να είναι '[as if] he were' is understood after σαν.

(1)a. Είσαι **σαν την Ελένη**
      'You are like Helen'
   b. Ο Νίκος είναι **σαν εσένα** ψηλός
      'Nick is as tall as you'
(2)a. Ο Αλέκος είναι προστατευτικός **σαν τον αδελφό μου**
      'Alec is protective like my brother'
   b. Ο Αλέκος είναι προστατευτικός **σαν αδελφός**
      'Alec is protective like a brother'
   c. Μιλάει **σαν δικηγόρος**
      'He speaks like a lawyer'

As the examples in (2) show, σαν is used in the sense of 'like'. Thus in
(2a–b) Alec is said to behave as if he were the brother or a brother with
the implication that he is not necessarily a brother. In (2c) someone is
said to show the ability to speak as if he were a lawyer, although he may
not be a lawyer.

Σαν is therefore used differently from the conjunction ως, which also
introduces a noun phrase:

(3)a. **Ως Υπουργός** των Εξωτερικών πρέπει να πάει στο Παρίσι
'As the minister of foreign affairs he must go to Paris'

b. Εργάζεται **ως γραμματέας** του προέδρου
'S/he works as the secretary of the Prime Minister'

c. Σου μιλάω **ως φίλος** και όχι **ως γιατρός**
'I am speaking to you as a friend and not as a doctor'

d. Ανέθεσαν την υπόθεση στο Νίκο **ως τον πιο κατάλληλο άνθρωπο**
'They assigned the case to Nick as the most appropriate person'

(3a) says that somebody has to go to Paris in his capacity as minister, i.e. he is the minister of foreign affairs and in this capacity he has to go to Paris. Similarly in (3b) the subject has been appointed to the office of secretary, i.e. s/he is the secretary. In (3c) the speaker explains that he is speaking in the way he speaks in his capacity as the friend of the addressee and not in his professional capacity as a doctor. In (3d) it is stated that a certain case was entrusted to Nick because it is believed that Nick is the most appropriate person. Thus ως introduces a noun phrase expressing a characteristic or an attribute which is possessed by the noun to which the ως-phrase applies. Notice that the case of the noun phrase following ως is the same as the case of the noun phrase to which it applies; in (3a–c) it is in the nominative, agreeing with the subject to which it applies, while in (3d) it is in the accusative, agreeing with the noun phrase within the prepositional phrase στο Νίκο.

Όπως may be used as a conjunction followed by a noun phrase or a pronoun in the same case as the first term of the comparison:

(4)a. Η Ελένη είναι όμορφη **όπως εσύ**

b. Η Ελένη είναι **όπως εσύ** όμορφη
'Helen is beautiful like you'

Another way of expressing equation is by the use of τόσο . . . όσο (και). Τόσο may either immediately precede the first of the compared phrases, as in (5a), or it may follow it and be placed immediately before the τόσο, as in (5b):

(5)a. Ο Νίκος ενδιαφέρεται **τόσο** για την Ελένη **όσο** και για την Όλγα
'Nick is interested as much in Helen as he is in Olga'

b. Ο Νίκος ενδιαφέρεται για την Ελένη **τόσο όσο** και για την Όλγα
'Nick is interested in Helen as much as he is interested in Olga'

c. Οι φοιτητές είναι **τόσο** κουρασμένοι **όσο** και βαριεστισμένοι
'The students are as much tired as they are bored'

d. Τελικά είναι **τόσο** όμορφη η Σούλα **όσο** μας έλεγαν;
'Finally, is Soula as pretty as they used to tell us?'

It is possible to omit the first element of the equation τόσο:

(6)a. Ο καινούργιος μας καθηγητής είναι καλός **όσο** και ο
προηγούμενος
'Our new teacher is as good as the previous one'
b. Δεν είναι καλή **όσο** (είσαι) εσύ *or*
Δεν είναι **όσο** εσύ καλή
'She is not as good as you are'

5.4.3 ANAPHORA

Anaphora is the term used for the part of grammar that describes the
rules and conditions which regulate the ways in which elements traditionally classified as ***pronominals*** establish their point of reference.

5.4.3.1 Absence of overt subjects

In Greek the subject of a finite verb is regularly omitted, as in sentence
(1a). In this example the personal ending of the verb (3rd person plural)
indicates that the missing subject is equivalent to a 3rd-person plural
pronoun. An actual pronoun is only used as the subject of a verb if it is
emphatic or contrastive, as in example (1b).

(1)a. Έφυγαν ξαφνικά
'They left suddenly'
b. **Εκείνοι** έφυγαν ξαφνικά ενώ **εμείς** μείναμε
'They left while we stayed'

The missing subject of a clause which we may refer to as 'zero subject'
may find its antecedent (the noun phrase with which it is coreferential)
either in the larger linguistic or non-linguistic context, as in (1a), or in a
higher clause, as in (2), where the zero subject of the embedded clause
may refer to the main clause subject ο καθηγητής.

(2) Ο καθηγητής είπε στους φοιτητές ότι θα τους βοηθήσει
'The teacher told the students that he will help them'

The matching of person and number is an essential condition in choosing
an antecedent for the zero subject. In (2) the personal ending of the verb
βοηθήσει indicates that the missing subject is a 3rd-person singular noun
phrase and this is matched by the 3rd-person singular noun phrase ο
καθηγητής.

Another necessary condition for co-indexing (establishing co-reference
between) the zero subject with a noun phrase is that the zero subject must
occur in a more dependent position than the antecedent. Compare (3a)
with (3b):

(3)a. Λένε ότι **οι φίλοι μου** δε θα επιμείνουν
'They say that my friends will not insist'
   b. **Οι φίλοι μου** λένε ότι δε θα επιμείνουν
'My friends say that they will not insist'

In (3a) there is a zero subject in the main clause, while the noun phrase οι φίλοι μου is the subject of the embedded clause. As a consequence the more embedded οι φίλοι μου cannot provide the antecedent for the less embedded zero subject and therefore the zero main subject must refer to an entity outside the construction, to some other group of people. In (3b) the noun phrase οι φίλοι μου is the subject of the main clause and therefore it is in a less embedded position than the zero subject of the embedded verb επιμείνουν. Thus it is possible to interpret οι φίλοι μου as the antecedent of the missing embedded subject. It is also possible however that the missing subject of the embedded clause in (3b) refers to some other people. (3b) may, for example, mean that my friends say that the Americans or the Russians etc. will not insist.

Thus, a zero embedded subject pronoun may either have an independent reference outside of the construction or, if there is a noun phrase with matching person and number features in a higher clause, this noun phrase may be interpreted as the antecedent. This freedom of a zero subject in an embedded clause to establish independent reference holds not only for indicative ότι/πως- or που-clauses but also for most subjunctive να-clauses too.

(4)a. **Ο Γιάννης** επιμένει να φύγει
   (i) 'John insists on (his own) leaving'
   (ii) 'John insists on somebody else's leaving'
   b. **Ο Γιάννης** φρόντισε να πάρει προαγωγή
   (i) 'John acted so that he [John] will get a promotion'
   (ii) 'John acted so that he [somebody else] will get a promotion'

It is true that out of context the most likely interpretation of the zero subject of a να-clause is the one in which the zero subject has an antecedent in the main clause (the main subject in the above examples). But that the second possibility is available is evident from the fact that we can extend the sentence in ways which show clearly that the zero subject is different from the main one. This is shown in (5a–b), where the gender of μόνη της and προαγωγή της shows that the subject of the embedded verb is feminine, not masculine like the subject of the main clause:

(5)a. **Ο Γιάννης** επιμένει να φύγει **μόνη της**
'John insists on her leaving by herself'
   b. **Ο Γιάννης** φρόντισε να πάρει την **προαγωγή της**
'John acted so that she would get her promotion'

However, there are a number of verbs, called *control verbs*, which must be followed by a zero subject that is obligatorily coreferential with either the main subject (*subject-control verbs*) or the main object (*object-control verbs*). Examples of control constructions are as follows:

Subject control:
(6)a. Όλοι οι Κρήτες ξέρουν να χορεύουν
      'All Cretans know how to dance'
   b. Πού έμαθε η Γιαννούλα να παίζει κιθάρα;
      'Where did Giannoula learn to play the guitar?'
(7)   Ο Στέφανος υποσχέθηκε να 'ρθει νωρίτερα
      'Stephen promised to come earlier'

Object control:
(8)a. Ανάγκασαν **το Γιάννη** να παραιτηθεί
      'They forced John to resign'
   b. Έβαλαν **το παιδί** να κοιμηθεί
      'They put the child to bed'

5.4.3.2 Absence of overt objects

Whereas a missing or zero subject is very common and always refers to a definite noun phrase, a missing or zero object is uncommon and it is possible only if it refers to an indefinite noun phrase:

(1) Ήθελα να πάρω **ένα σπίτι** κοντά στη θάλασσα αλλά δε βρήκα
    'I wanted to buy a house by the sea but I did not find [one]'

The zero object here involves a non-referring expression ένα σπίτι.

5.4.3.3 Clitic pronouns

Clitic pronouns serving as direct or indirect object behave exactly like the missing or zero subject in the way in which they establish reference. They may refer (i) to an entity outside the construction in which they occur or (ii) to a noun phrase in a higher clause. A third possibility is to accompany a noun phrase within their own clause in what is referred to as a *clitic doubling construction*. This is possible only if both the noun phrase and the clitic have the same function in the clause and thus have the same case, either both accusative or both genitive. These possibilities are exemplified in (1, 2 and 3) respectively.

(1)a. Πρέπει να ξέρεις το Νάσο
      'You must know Nasos'
      Όχι, δεν **τον** ξέρω
      'No, I don't know him'

b. Μίλησες του Νάσου;
'Did you speak to Nasos?'
Όχι, δεν **του** μίλησα
'No, I did not speak to him'
c. Ο Γιάννης δεν **τον** ξέρει
'John does not know him'

In the above examples the clitic pronouns refer to an entity which was mentioned in the previous discourse. In (1a) the clitic τον, in the response sentence, refers to το Νάσο and in (1b) the clitic του refers to the genitive noun phrase mentioned in the previous sentence, του Νάσου. In (1c) the object clitic cannot refer to the subject of the same clause, ο Γιάννης, but must refer to some other individual.

(2)a. **Ο Γιάννης** είπε ότι θα τηλεφωνήσει αλλά δεν **τον** πιστεύω
'John said that he would call but I do not believe him'
b. Φώναξέ μου **το Γιάννη** γιατί θέλω να **του** μιλήσω
'Call John for me because I want to talk to him'

In (2) the clitics refer to the noun phrases ο Γιάννης and το Γιάννη in the main clause.

(3)a. **Τον** έχεις γνωρίσει **το Γιάννη**;
'Have you met John?' [lit. 'have you met him John']
b. **Το Γιάννη τον** έχεις γνωρίσει;
'Have you met John?'
(4)a. **Του** έδωσες **του Γιάννη** λεφτά;
'Did you give John money?'
b. **Του Γιάννη του** έδωσες λεφτά;
'Did you give money to John?'

In (3) and (4) the clitic pronouns combine with the noun phrases το Γιάννη and του Γιάννη respectively, which occur within the same clause, but unlike (1c) these clitics have the same function as the noun phrases to which they refer. (See Section 5.2.2 on topicalization.)

5.4.3.4 Emphatic pronouns

Instead of the zero subject or object and the clitic object pronouns it is possible to use the emphatic form of personal pronouns, εγώ, εσύ, αυτός, etc., but only if they are emphasized, as in (1) (see also Section 2.8.1.1.2).

(1)a. **Εσύ** μην ανησυχείς. Θα πάω **εγώ**
'Don't you worry; I will go'
b. Γνωρίζετε τον υπουργό; Και βέβαια **αυτός** μας κάλεσε εδώ
'Do you know the minister? Of course it was he who invited us'

Emphatic pronouns, like any other noun phrases, may be topicalized within their own clause; in this case they combine with their clitic pronoun, as in (2):

(2)a. **Αυτόν τον** ξέρουμε από τα φοιτητικά μας χρόνια
'We have known *him* since our student days'

b. **Εσένα** πότε θα **σε** δούμε;
'When are we going to see *you*?'

5.4.3.5   Reflexive expressions

Greek has three different ways of expressing reflexivity: by mediopassive verb morphology (Section 5.4.3.5.1), by the reflexive verbal prefix αυτο- (5.4.3.5.2; see also Section 1.4.2.1), and by the reflexive pronoun phrase ο εαυτός μου 'myself' (5.4.3.5.3).

5.4.3.5.1   Passive reflexives

The passive forms of some verbs, mainly those expressing grooming or bodily care, often express reflexivity, especially when their subjects are humans who have the ability and the interest to carry out the action described by the verb, as in the following examples:

(1)a. Η Μαρία **ντύνεται** πάντα πολύ κομψά
'Mary always dresses very elegantly'

b. Ο Γιάννης φαίνεται πως **ξυρίζεται** μόνο μέρα παρά μέρα
'John seems to shave only every other day'

c. Δεν του αρέσει η Ελένη γιατί **βάφεται** πάρα πολύ
'He does not like Helen because she uses too much make-up'
[lit. 'paints herself too much']

5.4.3.5.2   Reflexives with verbal prefix αυτο- 'self'

The prefix αυτο- is attached to a passive verb form to express reflexivity, indicating that the subject, which in the case of a passive verb is the patient, is also the initiator of that action. Grooming verbs cannot use this means to express reflexivity.

(1)a. Με αυτά που κάνει **αυτοκαταστρέφεται**
'With the things he does he is destroying himself'

b. Πάψε να **αυτοκολακεύεσαι**
'Stop flattering yourself'

The prefix αυτο- may also be found attached to some nouns, αυτοκριτική 'self-criticism', αυτόγραφο 'autograph', and adjectives such as αυτόματος 'automatic', αυτάρκης 'self-sufficient', αυτάρεσκος 'vain', etc.

5.4.3.5.3   Reflexive pronoun phrase

The most common way to indicate reflexivity is by the use of the reflexive pronoun phrase. This is a definite noun phrase consisting of the masculine definite article, singular or plural, followed by the masculine singular noun εαυτός 'self' or plural εαυτούς 'selves' and the possessive pronoun μου, σου, του, της for the singular and μας, σας, τους for the plural in agreement with their antecedent. The case of the definite article and the head noun εαυτός is determined by the syntactic function of this phrase within the clause. The case is most commonly accusative since the reflexive expression is most frequently used as the direct object, but it may also be the genitive and even the nominative. Notice that, as in any typical noun phrase, these expressions may contain an adjective modifying the head noun εαυτός, as in ο καλός του εαυτός 'his good self'.

Reflexive expressions are generally used as referentially dependent elements which must establish co-reference with an appropriate *ante-cedent*. Furthermore, the antecedent for the reflexive must be found within the same clause as the reflexive itself. In the majority of cases where the reflexive is either the direct or indirect object of the sentence the antecedent is the subject of that clause, as in the following examples:

(1)a. Πρέπει **κανείς** να σέβεται **τον εαυτό του**
'One must respect oneself'

   b. **Ο Γιάννης** συνέχεια καμαρώνει **τον εαυτό του** στον καθρέφτη
'John constantly admires himself in the mirror'

   c. **Αυτή** αγαπά **τον εαυτό της** μόνο και κανέναν άλλο
'She loves herself only and nobody else'

   d. Να φροντίζεις **τον εαυτό σου**
'You must take care of yourself'

   e. Ξέρουν **τους εαυτούς τους** πολύ καλά
'They know themselves very well'

In (1a) the antecedent of the reflexive is the subject of the να-clause, κανείς, which is masculine singular; thus the possessive pronoun inside the reflexive expression is also masculine singular. In (1b) the antecedent is the masculine singular subject of the clause, namely ο Γιάννης. In (1c) the antecedent is the subject of the clause, αυτή, which is feminine singular, as is the possessive pronoun της inside the reflexive expression. In (1d) the antecedent of the reflexive, which contains the second person singular possessive pronoun σου, is the zero subject. Finally in (1e) the antecedent is the zero subject third person plural. Accordingly, the possessive in the reflexive expression is third person plural.

The reflexive pronoun phrase may also constitute the indirect object, in which case it may appear in the genitive but more often in a prepositional phrase; again its antecedent will be the subject of its clause:

(2)a. Έδωσα **του εαυτού μου/στον εαυτό μου** κουράγιο και
προχώρησα
'I gave myself courage and I proceeded'
b. Έκανε (κι **αυτή**) ενα δώρο **στον εαυτό της**
'She [too] made a present to herself'

The reflexive pronoun phrase may also occur after the prepositions με
'with', για 'for', από 'from'. Again the antecedent is the subject of the clause:

(3)a. Τσακώνεται **με τον εαυτό του**
'He is quarrelling with himself'
b. Δε δουλεύεις μόνο **για τον εαυτό σου** αλλά και για την
οικογένειά σου
'You do not work only for yourself but also for your family'
c. Βγάλε τώρα **εσύ** συμπέρασμα **από τον εαυτό σου**
'Draw your conclusion from yourself'
d. Κλείστηκε **μέσα στον εαυτό του**
'He shut himself up within himself'

The reflexive pronoun phrase does not combine with adverbs of place,
which may be followed instead by a genitive weak pronoun:

(4) Έβαλε τη Μαρία **κοντά του/δίπλα του/απέναντί του/μακριά του**
'He placed Mary near him/next to him/opposite him/away from
him'

In (4) the weak pronoun within the adverbial phrases may refer to the
subject of its own clause, or to somebody else mentioned or implied in
the discourse. In Greek, unlike English, there is no possibility of using
the reflexive expression here.

It is possible, though very rare, for the reflexive expression to refer not
to the subject of the clause but to another noun phrase inside the clause.
In (5) the reflexive expression refers to the indirect object:

(5)a. Η Μαρία τόλμησε να αποκαλύψει **στο Γιάννη τον εαυτό του**
'Mary dared to reveal to John his true self [lit. himself]'
b. **Της** μιλήσαμε **για τον εαυτό της**
'We spoke to her about herself'

It is also possible to have a reflexive pronoun phrase within an embedded
clause, after verbs of saying, requesting, instructing, etc., referring not to
the subject of its own clause but to the main clause subject doing the
saying, requesting and instructing.

(6) Η Μαρία είπε στα παιδιά να πάρουν ένα κουτί σοκολάτες για
τη μητέρα τους κι ένα **για τον εαυτό της**
'Mary told the children to buy a box of chocolates for their
mother and one for her'

However, the more appropriate element in (6) would be the expression για την ίδια (lit. 'for the same').

The phrase ο εαυτός μου may also be used as the subject of the clause, in which case it is not expressing reflexivity but means 'one's own self':

(7)a. **Ο εαυτός της** φταίει και κανένας άλλος
    'Her own self is to blame and nobody else'
  b. **Ο εαυτός σου σε** βασανίζει **εσένα**
    'Your own self tortures you'

Reflexive expressions may also occur as complements of deverbal nouns; in such cases, either their antecedent is not expressed, or it occurs within the noun phrase.

(8)a. Τον ενοχλεί η υπερβολική ενασχόληση **της Μαρίας με τον
    εαυτό της**
    'He is annoyed by Maria's excessive preoccupation with herself'
  b. Τα παράπονά **του για τον εαυτό του** δε με συγκινούν
    'His complaints about himself do not move me'

5.4.3.6 Reciprocal expressions

Reciprocity is expressed by the passive verb inflections (Section 5.4.3.6.1), the verbal prefix αλληλο- 'each other' (5.4.3.6.2), or the reciprocal periphrasis ο ένας τον άλλο 'each other' (5.4.3.6.3).

5.4.3.6.1 Reciprocity expressed by passive verb morphology
Reciprocity may be expressed by the passive forms of verbs expressing love, affection and their opposites, as well as actions motivated by these feelings, such as kissing, quarrelling, etc. The subject must be plural and animate (usually human):

(1)a. Πρέπει να **αγαπιούνται** πολύ, **φιλιούνται** και **χαϊδεύονται**
    συνέχεια
    'They must love each other very much, they kiss and caress
    each other all the time'
  b. **Αρπάχτηκαν** και **σκοτώθηκαν** στο ξύλο
    'They grabbed each other and beat each other to death [lit.
    'killed each other to the wood']'
  c. **Χτυπηθήκανε** σώμα με σώμα
    'They came to blows'

5.4.3.6.2 Reciprocity expressed by the prefix αλληλο-
The prefix αλληλο- is attached to the passive verb forms with plural animate (usually human) subjects to express reciprocity:

(1)a. Ο Γιάννης και η Μαρία **αλληλοσπαράζονται** καθημερινά
'John and Mary tear each other apart daily'

b. Αυτοί οι δυο **αλληλοθαυμάζονται** και **αλληλοϋποστηρίζονται**
'These two admire each other and support each other'

The prefix αλληλο- can also combine with nouns: αλληλοβοήθεια 'mutual help' and with adjectives: αλληλοβοηθητικός 'reciprocally helpful'.

5.4.3.6.3   Reciprocity expressed by reciprocal periphrases

The reciprocal periphrasis consists of two parts: (i) ένας, μια, ένα preceded by the appropriate definite article, and (ii) the pronominal άλλος, άλλη, άλλο, also preceded by the appropriate definite article. This expression too accompanies a verb expressing love, hate and similar feelings as well as verbs expressing actions motivated by such feelings, but the verb, in this case, is either in the active voice, or is a deponent verb (see Section 1.4.3) such as σέβομαι 'I respect'. The reciprocal expression refers to a plural animate (usually human) subject. Both constituents of the reciprocal expression are always in the singular, and their gender is determined by the gender of the noun phrase, explicit (1a–b) or implicit (1c–e), to which they refer. The case of the first constituent is nominative because it refers to the subject of the sentence, while the case of the second constituent or the choice of the preposition to govern it depends on the meaning of the verb in each case and its associated complement structure (direct or indirect object, prepositional phrase, etc.).

(1)a. **Οι αδελφές του** αντιπαθούν έντονα **η μια την άλλη**
'His sisters dislike each other intensely'

b. **Τα καλά παιδιά** πρέπει να βοηθούν **το ένα το άλλο**
'Good children should help each other'

c. Κάνουν πολλά παράπονα **ο ένας στον άλλο**
'They complain a lot to each other'

d. Θυσιάζονται **ο ένας για τον άλλο**
'They sacrifice themselves for each other'

e. Δεν μπορούν να ζήσουν **ο ένας χωρίς τον άλλο**
'They cannot live without each other'

In all of the above examples the first constituent of the reciprocal expression is in the nominative. In (1a–b), the second constituent of the reciprocal expression is in the accusative because the complement, to which this part of the expression refers, is the direct object of the verbs and as such it must be in the accusative. In (1c) the second constituent is in the prepositional phrase introduced by σε, and so on. In spite of the different cases of its two constituents the reciprocal expression behaves as a single unit in some important ways: (i) the two constituents can never be separated, and (ii) their order ο ένας τον άλλο cannot be changed.

If the first phrase of the reciprocal expression, namely ο ένας, is used independently and separately from the second phrase, namely τον άλλο, ο ένας with the meaning 'the one' constitutes the subject of the verb, which must now be in the singular, while τον άλλο constitutes the complement, meaning 'the other'.

(2)a. **Ο ένας** κοίταζε **τον άλλο** χωρίς να μιλούν
'The one was looking at the other without speaking'
b. Σε δύσκολες στιγμές **ο ένας** συμβούλευε **τον άλλο**
'In difficult times the one would advise the other'
c. Σε δύσκολες στιγμές συμβούλευε **ο ένας τον άλλο**
'In difficult times one would advise the other'

As is clear from (2), the two phrases ο ένας and τον άλλο may either be separated in this sense, as in (2a–b), or they may be adjacent to each other (2c). What is crucial for this usage is that the verb is in the singular, so that the first noun phrase ο ένας is its subject while the second τον άλλο is its complement. Again the order of the two elements, whether separate or adjacent, requires that ο ένας precedes τον άλλο.

5.4.3.7   The use of the phrase *ο ίδιος* 'the same'

Ίδιος 'same' is an adjective, as in (1):

(1) Είναι **ίδιος** ο πατέρας του
'He is just like his father'

Accompanied by the definite article, ο ίδιος, η ίδια, το ίδιο, etc., modifies a noun phrase in order to emphasize that it is this person or thing and no one or nothing else, as in (2):

(2)a. Ήρθε **ο Νίκος ο ίδιος** και τη ζητούσε *or*
Ήρθε **ο ίδιος ο Νίκος**
'Nick himself came looking for her'
b. Να δώσεις τα λεφτά **στο Βασίλη τον ίδιο** *or* **στον ίδιο το Βασίλη**
'You should give the money to Basil himself'

In (2) the expression ο ίδιος is adjacent to the noun phrase that it modifies and it may either precede or follow it.

It is also possible to find the two of them separated, as in (3), with the expression ο ίδιος towards the end of the sentence. This places even more emphasis on it.

(3)a. **Ο Γιάννης** ήρθε **ο ίδιος**
'John came himself'
b. **Στη Μαρία** να δώσεις τα λεφτά **την ίδια**
'You should give the money to Mary herself'

In all cases where ο ίδιος combines with a noun phrase it is equivalent to the emphatic use of the English reflexive pronoun, as the translations of the Greek sentences indicate.

The phrase ο ίδιος may also occur either in combination with αυτός or on its own within a subordinate clause in order to refer to a noun phrase within the main clause, as in (4):

(4)a. Ο Βασίλης είπε στην Πέπη να δώσει την αίτηση **σ' αυτόν τον ίδιο**
  b. Ο Βασίλης είπε στην Πέπη να δώσει την αίτηση **στον ίδιο**
     'Basil told Pepi to deliver the application to him in person'
(5)a. Ο Μανόλης είπε στον Κώστα ότι πρέπει να πάει **αυτός ο ίδιος**
  b. Ο Μανόλης είπε στον Κώστα ότι πρέπει να πάει **ο ίδιος**
     'Manolis told Kostas that he should go himself'

In (4a–b) the expression αυτόν τον ίδιο, or simply τον ίδιο, can only refer to the noun phrase ο Βασίλης in the main clause and not to some other entity within the previous discourse. In (5), where the main clause contains two noun phrases in the same number and gender, the expression αυτός ο ίδιος or simply ο ίδιος in the subordinate clause may refer to either of them. Thus ο ίδιος in (5) may refer either to Manolis or Kostas.

APPENDICES

APPENDIX 1: CORRESPONDENCE TABLE OF PRONOUNS, DETERMINERS, AND ADVERBS

The Table opposite shows the correspondence among certain pronouns, determiners, and adverbs.

¹ Gender here refers to the gender of these words when they are used as pronouns; when they are used as determiners they take the gender of the noun which they accompany.

² Also (of reason) γιατί 'why'.

³ To these could be added the uninflected distributive determiner κάθε 'each, every'.

	Pronouns and determiners		Adverbs			
	Masc./fem./neuter[1]	Neuter only[1]	Place	Time	Manner	Quantity
Indefinite (specific)	κάποιος 'some[one]' / ένας [some]one' / μερικοί 'some (pl.)'	κάτι, κατιτί 'something'	κάπου 'somewhere'	κάποτε 'at some time; once'	κάπως 'in some way; somehow'	κάπως 'somewhat'
Indefinite (non-specific)	κανένας 'any[one]'; no [one]	τίποτα 'no[thing]; any[thing]'	πουθενά 'anywhere; nowhere'	ποτέ '[n]ever'	καθόλου '[not] at all'	καθόλου '[not] at all'
Interrogative and exclamatory[2]	ποιος 'who; which' / πόσος 'how much/many'	τι 'what' / πόσο 'how much'	πού 'where'	πότε 'when'	πώς 'how'	πόσο 'how much'
Demonstrative	αυτός 'he; this/that' / τούτος 'he; this' / εκείνος 'he; that'	αυτό 'this/that' / τούτο 'this' / εκείνο 'that'	εδώ 'here' / αυτού 'there' / εκεί 'there'	τώρα 'now' / τότε 'then'	έτσι 'in this/that way'	τόσο 'so much'
Qualitative demonstrative	τέτοιος 'such a [one]'				έτσι 'in such a way'	
Relative	ο οποίος, που 'who, which, that'	ό,τι 'that which, what[ever]'	όπου 'where'	όταν 'when'	όπως, καθώς 'as'	
Correlative	όποιος 'he who; whoever; whichever' / όσος 'as much as'	ό,τι 'that which, what[ever]'	όπου 'wherever'	όποτε 'whenever' / οπότε 'at which time, whereupon'	όπως 'however'	όσο 'as much as'
Universal[3]	καθένας 'each one' / όλοι 'everyone; all'	καθετί 'each thing' / όλα, το παν, τα πάντα 'everything'	παντού 'everywhere'	πάντα 'always'	πάντως 'in any case'	
Universal correlative	οποιοσδήποτε 'anyone [whatever]'	οτιδήποτε '[anything] whatever'	οπουδήποτε 'anywhere'	οποτεδήποτε 'whenever'	οπωσδήποτε 'in any case'	οσοδήποτε 'however much'
Contrastive	άλλος 'someone else; other'	άλλο 'something else; other'	αλλού 'elsewhere'	άλλοτε 'at another time'	αλλιώς 'otherwise'	άλλο 'more, further'

APPENDIX 2: PREPOSITIONS AND ADVERBS USED IN THE EXPRESSION OF SPATIAL AND TEMPORAL RELATIONS

2.1 SPATIAL RELATIONS

at, to, in (location at/in or
  motion [in]to)
  σε

from (location away from or
  motion from/out of)
  από

for (destination)
  για

above (either directly over or
  generally above [at a higher
  level than])
  πάνω

below (either directly under or
  generally below [at a lower
  level than])
  κάτω

inside
  μέσα

outside
  έξω

in front of
  μπροστά

behind
  πίσω

near
  κοντά

next to
  δίπλα

beside
  πλάι

distant
  μακριά

beyond
  πέρα

between, among
  ανάμεσα

opposite
  απέναντι

around
  γύρω

through, past, along, across
  [περνώ] **από**
  'through' also διά μέσου
  + gen.
  'along' also κατά μήκος
  + gen.
  'across' also από τη μιαν
  άκρη στην άλλη + gen.

2.2 TEMPORAL RELATIONS

time when: at, on, in
σε (or bare accusative)

duration: for
για

during
κατά [τη διάρκεια], επί

before
πριν

after
μετά

from, since
από

until, by
μέχρι, ως, ίσαμε

within
μέσα σε

APPENDIX 3: EXPRESSIONS OF MEASUREMENT: SPACE, TIME AND QUANTITY

3.1 SPACE

The measurement of space is usually expressed by means of constructions using the accusative case (see also Part III, Section 2.4.2.1(v)):

(1) Έτρεξα **δυο χιλιόμετρα**
    'I ran **two kilometres**'

(2)a. ένα ξύλο **δέκα πόντους** μακρύ
    'a stick **ten centimetres** long' *or*

   b. ένα ξύλο **δέκα πόντους μήκος**
    'a stick **ten centimetres [in] length**'

(3)a. Αυτό το σπίτι είναι **δέκα μέτρα** ψηλό
    'This house is ten metres high'

   b. Αυτό το σπίτι έχει ύψος **δέκα μέτρα**
    'This house has [a] height [of] **ten metres**'

(4)a. ένα σπίτι **δέκα μέτρα** ψηλό
    'a house **ten metres** high'

   b. ένα σπίτι **δέκα μέτρα ύψος**
    'a house **ten metres [in] height**'

(5) ένα σίδερο **πέντε μέτρα μήκος με δέκα εκατοστά φάρδος**
    'a piece of iron **five metres long by ten centimetres thick**'

(6) ένα κελί **τρία επί τέσσερα**
    'a cell **three by four** [metres]'

(7) Το σπίτι μου είναι **δυο χιλιόμετρα** μακριά
    'My house is **two kilometres** away'

In the above examples, (2a) and (2b) are equivalent in meaning, as are (3a) and (3b), and (4a) and (4b).

In more formal contexts, however, the genitive of measurement may be used (see also Part III, Section 2.4.3.2(viii)):

(8) μια τηλεόραση **είκοσι τεσσάρων ιντσών**
    'a **24-inch** television'

(9) σε απόσταση **εκατό μέτρων**
    'at a distance **of 100 metres**'

(10) Έπεσα σ' ένα λάκκο **βάθους σαράντα εκατοστών**
    'I drove [lit. 'fell'] into a forty-centimetre-deep pothole [lit. 'a pothole **of-depth of-forty centimetres**']'

3.2   TIME

The names of the days of the week are as follows:

Κυριακή	'Sunday'
Δευτέρα	'Monday'
Τρίτη	'Tuesday'
Τετάρτη	'Wednesday'
Πέμπτη	'Thursday'
Παρασκευή	'Friday'
Σάββατο	'Saturday'

They are all feminine singular, except Σάββατο, which is neuter singular.

Most of the *months* have two alternative names; the first given here is the standard version, while the second is a colloquial alternative:

Ιανουάριος	Γενάρης	'January'
Φεβρουάριος	Φλεβάρης	'February'
Μάρτιος	Μάρτης	'March'
Απρίλιος	Απρίλης	'April'
Μάιος	Μάης	'May'
Ιούνιος	Ιούνης	'June'
Ιούλιος	Ιούλης	'July'
Αύγουστος		'August'
Σεπτέμβριος	Σεπτέμβρης	'September'
Οκτώβριος	Οχτώ[μ]βρης	'October'
Νοέμβριος	Νοέμβρης	'November'
Δεκέμβριος	Δεκέμβρης	'December'

All the names of the months are masculine singular.

Like space, the measurement of time is normally expressed by means of constructions using the accusative case (see also Part III, Section 3.4.2.1(i–iii)):

(i)   Duration

(1) Δούλεψα **όλο το χρόνο**
    'I worked **all year**'
(2) Κράτησε **ένα μήνα**
    'It lasted **a month**'
(3) πολλή ώρα *or* πολύν καιρό
    'for a long time'

Note that πολλή ώρα is used for shorter times (less than a day), while πολύν καιρό is used for longer periods; both expressions are in the accusative.

In many cases the preposition για may optionally be added:

(4) Έμεινε κλεισμένη στο σπίτι [για] πέντε ώρες
'She remained shut indoors for five hours'

(ii)   Point in time

(5)   τη νύχτα
'during the night'
(6)   το μεσημέρι
'at midday; in the middle of the day'
(7)   τα μεσάνυχτα
'at midnight'
(8)   την Τρίτη το πρωί
'on Tuesday morning'
(9)   τον Απρίλιο
'in April'
(10)   το Πάσχα
'at Easter'
(11)   το χειμώνα
'in the winter'
(12)   το 1997 [also στα 1997]
'in 1997'
(13)   τον εικοστό αιώνα
'in the twentieth century'

Dates are expressed with the feminine accusative singular of the ordinal numeral for the 'first' of the month only, and thereafter by στις and the feminine plural of the cardinal numeral:

(14)   την πρώτη Οκτωβρίου
'on the first of October'
(15)   στις είκοσι μία Απριλίου *or* στις είκοσι μία του Απρίλη
'on the twenty-first of April'

Note that the article is normally used with the colloquial names of the months.

Times of day are also expressed with στις 'at', while 'o'clock' is expressed by the nominative expression η ώρα:

(16)   στις δώδεκα η ώρα
'at twelve o'clock'

Minutes are expressed by the neuter forms of the cardinal numerals, while parts of the *hour* are expressed by the neuter noun τέταρτο 'quarter' and the substantivized feminine adjective μισή 'half'; alternatively, the morpheme -μιση/-μισι 'and a half' may be added to the numeral (see Part III, Section 2.7). Minutes and parts of the hour are linked to the hour by either και 'past' or παρά 'to':

(17) στις τρεις και είκοσι
      'at twenty past three'
(18) Είναι τέσσερις και τέταρτο
      'It's a quarter past four'
(19) Είναι δώδεκα και μισή or Είναι δωδεκάμιση
      'It's half past twelve'
(20) στις πέντε παρά τέταρτο
      'at a quarter to five'
(21) στις οχτώ παρά πέντε
      'at five to eight'

There are two ways of expressing the starting- and end-points of a durative action: with the prepositions από and μέχρι (22: with και the meaning is 'up to and including' ['through' in US]), or with the preposition με (23):

(22) Οι εκδηλώσεις του φεστιβάλ θα κρατήσουν από την Τρίτη
          μέχρι και την Κυριακή
      'The festival events will last from Tuesday until Sunday'
(23) Έχουμε μάθημα δέκα με έντεκα
      'We have a class from ten till eleven'

The space of time within which something takes place (24) and the lapse of time before something takes place (25) are both expressed with the preposition σε:

(24) Τελειώσαμε τη δουλειά σε μισή ώρα
      'We finished the job in half an hour'
(25) Θα φτάσουμε σε μισή ώρα
      'We'll arrive in half an hour'

The point in time *by* which an action is complete is expressed by μέχρι (or ως):

(26) Θα έχουμε τελειώσει τη δουλειά μέχρι την Κυριακή
      'We'll have finished the job **by** Sunday'

Ages are normally expressed with the genitive:

(27) Είμαι **είκοσι τριών χρονών**
      'I am **twenty-three years old**'
(28) –**Πόσω[ν] χρονών** είσαι; –Τριάντα δύο
      '"**How old** [lit. 'of how many years'] are you?" "Thirty-two"'
(29) ένα μωρό **δέκα μηνών**
      'a ten-month-old baby'

Nevertheless, in colloquial usage, the declinable numerals ένας, τρεις, τέσσερις may appear in the nom./acc., especially when they are not accompanied by the genitive form χρονών (ένα is in fact quite commonly found even with χρονών):

(30) Είμαι είκοσι **ένα** χρονών
'I'm twenty-one years old'

(31) – **Πόσω[ν] χρονών** είσαι; – Τριάντα **τρία**
(more formally, τριών)
'"**How old** are you?" "Thirty-three"'

(32) – **Πόσω[ν] χρονών** είσαι; – Τριάντα **τέσσερα**
(more formally, τεσσάρων)
'"**How old** are you?" "Thirty-four"'

In more formal styles the measurement of time in general, like the measurement of space, may be expressed by means of the genitive (see also Part III, Section 3.4.3.2(viii)):

(33) μια αναβολή **δύο χρόνων**
'a **two-year** delay'

(34) κατά τη μακρά περίοδο **τριάντα ετών**
'during the long period **of thirty years**'

'How often' is expressed by κάθε πόσο, 'how long' by various expressions according to the meaning:

(35) Κάθε πόσο έχει τραίνο για Πειραιά;
'How often is there a train to Piraeus?'

(36) Από πότε δουλεύετε εδώ;
'How long have you been working here?' (i.e. since when?)

(37) Μέχρι πότε θα κρατήσει η απεργία;
'How long will the strike last?' (i.e. till when?)

(38) Πόση ώρα κάνει το ταξίδι από την Κηφισιά στον Πειραιά;
'How long does the journey take from Kifisia to Piraeus?' (i.e. how many hours/minutes?)

(39) Πόσες μέρες θα μείνετε;
'How long will you be staying?' (i.e. how many days?)

Expressions such as πόση ώρα and πόσες μέρες are in the accusative.

3.3   QUANTITY

The measurement of quantity may be expressed by a number of appositional constructions (consisting of two noun phrases in the same case), introduced by a cardinal numeral or quantifier (see also Part III, Section 2.12). For the sake of convenience, all of the following examples show the noun phrases in the nominative:

(1) δυο κιλά πατάτες
'two kilos of potatoes'

(2) μια ώρα δρόμος
'an hour's journey' [lit. 'one hour road']

(3) δέκα τόνοι τσιμέντο
    'ten tons of cement'
(4) τρεις χιλιάδες άνθρωποι
    'three thousand people'

Less specific expressions of quantity (i.e. those not specifying precise numbers) also use appositional constructions:

(5) μια παρέα γυναίκες
    'a group of women'

In more formal usage, and when the expression is more complex, such non-specific expressions use the genitive (see also Part III, Section 3.4.3.2(ix)):

(6) μια μεγάλη παρέα **καλοντυμένων γυναικών**
    'a large group of well-dressed women'

Rate can be expressed by two noun phrases in the accusative:

(7) Αυτό το αυτοκίνητο πάει **διακόσια χιλιόμετρα την ώρα**
    'This car goes **two hundred kilometres an hour**'
(8) Η ντομάτα έχει **τριακόσιες δραχμές το κιλό**
    'Tomatoes [lit. 'the tomato'] cost **three hundred drachmas a kilo**'

Με may be used to express 'at' a certain rate:

(9) Οδηγούσα **με διακόσια**
    'I was driving **at two hundred** [kilometres an hour]'

For *arithmetical operations* see Part III, Section 2.7.

APPENDIX 4: AGREEMENT

The rules of gender, case, and number agreement are summarized below.

4.1 AGREEMENT WITHIN THE NOUN PHRASE

All words in the same noun phrase and modifying the noun agree with each other in gender, number and case. Thus all declinable modifiers (articles, adjectives, numerals, and determiners), except possessive pronouns, indicate in their inflection their gender, number, and case agreement with the noun they modify:

(1)a. ο άλλος μικρός μαρκαδόρος (masc. nom. sg.)
   b. τον άλλο μικρό μαρκαδόρο (masc. acc. sg.)
   c. του άλλου μικρού μαρκαδόρου (masc. gen. sg.)
     'the other small marker'

(2)a. οι άλλοι μικροί μαρκαδόροι (masc. nom. pl.)
   b. τους άλλους μικρούς μαρκαδόρους (masc. acc. pl.)
   c. των άλλων μικρών μαρκαδόρων (masc. gen. pl.)
     'the other small markers'

(3)a. η άλλη μικρή θάλασσα (fem. nom. sg.)
   b. την άλλη μικρή θάλασσα (fem. acc. sg.)
   c. της άλλης μικρής θάλασσας (fem. gen. sg.)
     'the other small sea'

(4)a. οι άλλες μικρές θάλασσες (fem. nom. pl.)
   b. τις άλλες μικρές θάλασσες (fem. acc. pl.)
   c. των άλλων μικρών θαλασσών (fem. gen. pl.)
     'the other small seas'

(5)a. το άλλο μικρό γραφείο (neut. nom. and acc. sg.)
   b. του άλλου μικρού γραφείου (neut. gen. sg.)
     'the other small desk/office'

(6)a. τα άλλα μικρά γραφεία (neut. nom. and acc. pl.)
   b. των άλλων μικρών γραφείων (neut. gen. pl.)
     'the other small desks/offices'

When a single modifier modifies attributively *two or more nouns* denoting inanimates, it usually appears in the gender and number of the noun nearest to it:

(7) ελληνική (fem. sg.) μουσική (fem. sg.) και τραγούδια (neut. pl.)
    'Greek music and songs'

Greek-speakers normally avoid using a single modifier for two or more nouns in different genders denoting humans.

Two or more modifiers may modify a singular noun attributively even when the noun denotes two or more entities. When such a noun acts as the subject of a verb, the verb normally appears in the plural:

(8) Ο Έλληνας (sg.) και ο Τούρκος (sg.) **αντιπρόσωπος** (sg.)
    πρότειναν (pl.) ένα κοινό σχέδιο
    'The Greek and Turkish **representatives** proposed a joint plan'

Compare (9), where the noun denotes a single entity and therefore has a singular verb:

(9) Ο έξυπνος και μορφωμένος **δάσκαλος** (sg.) **πρότεινε** (sg.) τη
    λύση
    'The clever and [highly] educated **teacher** proposed the solution'

4.2 AGREEMENT BETWEEN NOUN PHRASES IN APPOSITION

Noun phrases in apposition to each other (see Part III, Section 2.12) appear in the same case. Compare (1), where the two noun phrases are in the nominative, with (2), where the noun phrases are both in the accusative:

(1) Ήρθε **η φίλη** (nom.) μου **η Καίτη** (nom.)
    '**My friend Katy** came'
(2) Είδα **τη φίλη** (acc.) μου **την Καίτη** (acc.)
    'I saw **my friend Katy**'

A phrase in apposition that does not include a noun agrees with the head noun not only in case but in gender and number too:

(3) Είδα **τη φίλη** (acc.) μου, **τη μικρή** (acc.)
    'I saw my friend, the little one'

4.3 AGREEMENT BETWEEN A PREDICATE AND THE SUBJECT OR OBJECT

A subject predicate consisting of an adjective, numeral, etc. displays gender, case and number agreement with the subject (1–3); similarly, an object predicate agrees with the object (4):

(1) Ο Γιάννης είναι **καλός** (masc. nom. sg.)
    'John is **nice**'

(2) Η Μαρία είναι **καλή** (fem. nom. sg.)
'Mary is **nice**'
(3) Ο Γιώργος τον ξέρει τον Γιάννη από **μικρός** (masc. nom. sg.)
'George has known John since he [George] was a child'
(4) Ο Γιώργος τον ξέρει τον Γιάννη από **μικρόν** (masc. acc. sg.)
'George has known John since he [John] was a child'

If the predicate noun phrase includes a *noun*, it agrees with the subject or object in case, but it does not necessarily agree in number and gender:

(5) Ο Γιώργος είναι **φίλος** μου (masc. nom. sg.)
'George is [a] friend of mine'
(6) Οι Άγγλοι είναι **περίεργος λαός** (masc. nom. sg.)
'The English are [a] strange people'
(7) Η Μαρία είναι **καλός άνθρωπος** (masc. nom. sg.)
'Mary is a nice person'

The predicative noun φίλος in (5) happens to agree with the subject in number and gender as well as in case. In (6), however, the predicative noun λαός is singular, since it denotes a single people, even though here it is a predicate of the plural noun Άγγλοι. The noun άνθρωπος is always masculine, even when it denotes a female, as it does in (7). In both (6) and (7) the modifiers of the predicative nouns (περίεργος and καλός) agree in number and gender with these nouns, not with the subject.

When there is no noun present in the clause for a predicative modifier to agree with, it appears in the gender and number appropriate to the subject, while its case depends on whether it is a subject predicate (8–11) or an object predicate (12):

(8) Πήγα μικρός (masc. nom. sg.) (*or* μικρή (fem. nom. sg.)) στο
Παρίσι
'I went young to Paris'
(9) Πήγε μικρός (masc. nom. sg.) στο Παρίσι
'He went young to Paris'
(10) Πήγε μικρή (fem. nom. sg.) στο Παρίσι
'She went young to Paris'
(11) Πήγαμε μικροί (masc. nom. pl.) [*or* μικρές (fem. nom. pl.)] στο
Παρίσι
'We went young to Paris'
(12) Σ᾽ ακούω βραχνό (masc. acc. sg.) (*or* βραχνή (fem. acc. sg.))
σήμερα
'You sound hoarse today' [lit., 'I hear you hoarse today']

In the above examples the predicative adjective is masculine or feminine according to the gender of the subject or object of the clause, and it is singular or plural according to the number of the subject or object.

The only exception to this rule is where the polite plural forms of the personal pronoun and the verb are being used to address a single person, in which case the words that denote the person addressed appear in the singular:

(13) Εσείς (pl.) να είστε (pl.) πολύ προσεκτικός (masc. sg.)
     'You should be very careful'
(14) Εσείς (pl.), η αδελφή (fem. nom. sg.) του, είστε (pl.) και η
     καθηγήτριά (fem. nom. sg.) του;
     'Are you, his sister, also his teacher?'

Similarly, a predicate after ως 'as' appears in the same case as the word it modifies:

(15) η ιδιότητά μου ως πολίτη
     'my status as a citizen'

Here the predicative πολίτη is in the genitive to agree with the possessive pronoun μου, which is also genitive.

When *two or more* nouns denoting *humans* of different genders have a single predicate not containing a noun, the predicate normally appears in the masculine plural:

(16) Ο Πέτρος (masc. nom. sg.) και η Μαρία (fem. nom. sg.) είναι
     πολύ συμπαθητικοί (masc. nom. pl.)
     'Peter and Mary are very nice'
(17) Οι γυναίκες (fem. nom. pl.) και τα παιδιά (neut. nom. pl.) να
     είναι έτοιμοι (masc. nom. pl.)
     'The women and children should be ready'

When it modifies two or more singular nouns of different genders that do not denote humans, the predicate normally appears in the neuter plural (18):

(18) Ο κομμουνισμός (masc. sg.) και η ελεύθερη αγορά (fem. sg.)
     είναι ασυμβίβαστα (neuter pl.)
     'Communism and the free market are incompatible'

When a predicate modifies two or more plural nouns of different genders that do not denote humans, it may appear either in the neuter plural or in the gender of the noun nearest to it:

(19) Οι δρόμοι (masc. nom. pl.) και οι πλατείες (fem. nom. pl.)
     ήταν γεμάτες (fem. nom. pl.) *or* γεμάτα (neut. nom. pl.)
     κόσμο
     'The streets and squares were full of people'

The same principles apply to the gender of doubling clitics (see also Part III, Section 5.4.3.3):

(20) Τον Πέτρο (masc. sg.) και τη Μαρία (fem. sg.) τους (masc. pl.)
θεωρώ φίλους μου
'I consider Peter and Mary to be friends of mine'

(21) Τις γυναίκες (fem. pl.) και τα παιδιά (neut. pl.) τους (masc. pl.) είδα το πρωί
'I saw the women and the children in the morning'

(22) Τον έρωτα (masc. sg.) και την επιθυμία (fem. sg.) τα (neut. pl.)
θεωρεί κορύφωμα της φιλίας
'He considers love and desire to be the culmination of friendship'

(23) Τους δρόμους (masc. pl.) και τις πλατείες (fem. pl.) δεν τις
(fem. pl.)/τα (neuter pl.) είδα
'I didn't see the streets and squares'

Nevertheless, where the object includes a feminine noun and a neuter noun denoting humans (as in 21), it is possible for the clitic pronoun to appear in the neuter to agree with the nearest noun (here, τα).

4.4　NUMBER AGREEMENT BETWEEN SUBJECT AND VERB

A verb normally agrees in number with its grammatical subject:

(1) Ήρθε (sg.) ο Πέτρος (sg.)
'Peter has come'

(2) Ήρθαν (pl.) τα παιδιά (pl.) του Πέτρου
'Peter's children have come'

When the subject consists of more than one noun phrase, the verb is normally plural:

(3) Ήρθαν (pl.) η Μαρία (sg.) και ο Πέτρος (sg.)
'Mary and Peter have come'

Nevertheless, in colloquial use, if a subject consisting of more than one phrase follows the verb and the first subject is singular, the verb may be in the singular:

(4) Ήρθε (sg.) η Μαρία (sg.) και ο Πέτρος (sg.) (=3)

In such cases, the noun phrase or phrases after the first one seem to be uttered as an afterthought.

Conversely, again in colloquial use, a verb may be in the plural even though the subject is grammatically singular, when two or more noun phrases are considered as forming the subject:

(5) Ήρθαν (pl.) ο Πέτρος (sg.) με τη Μαρία
'Peter has come with Mary'

In example (5), the subject ο Πέτρος is once again grammatically singular, but it is clear that Mary has come as well as Peter.

When the subject consists of two or more singular noun phrases co-ordinated by ή 'or', είτε ... είτε ... 'whether ... or ...', or ούτε ... ούτε ... 'neither ... nor ...', the verb usually appears in the plural:

(6) Ούτε ο Πέτρος (sg.) ούτε η Μαρία (sg.) [δεν] είναι ικανοί (pl.)
        να σε καταλάβουν (pl.)
     'Neither Peter nor Mary is capable of understanding you'
(7) Ο Πέτρος (sg.) ή η Μαρία (sg.) θα σε ειδοποιήσουν (pl.)
     'Peter or Mary will let you know'

Example (6) shows that a predicative adjective modifying the subject is also plural in such circumstances.

For further discussion of number agreement between subject and verb see Part III, Section 5.4.1.2.

GLOSSARY OF GRAMMATICAL TERMS

This glossary should be used in conjunction with the Index of grammatical categories and concepts, which refers to the specific sections of the Grammar where these terms are discussed. Words in italics are terms that are defined in the glossary.

abstract noun	a *noun* denoting an unobservable notion (e.g. μουσική 'music', δυσκολία 'difficulty')
accent	the symbol written over a vowel to show that it receives *stress* (άνθρωπος 'person')
accusative	see *case*
active voice	when a *verb* is in the active voice its *subject* is typically the person or thing doing the action (cf. *passive*)
adjective	a word that specifies an attribute of a noun (ένα **κόκκινο** πουλί 'a **red** bird')
adjective phrase	a *phrase* whose *head* is an *adjective*
adverb	a word indicating the manner, time or place of the action of a verb (έλα **γρήγορα** 'come quickly', έλα **αύριο** 'come tomorrow', έλα **δω** 'come **here**')
adverb phrase	a phrase with an *adverb* as its *head*
adverbial	an *adverb* or any phrase or clause that functions as an adverb
adverbial clause	a *clause* that functions as an *adverbial*, modifying the *verb* of another *clause*
affix	a single *morpheme* attached to a *stem*, either to produce a separate word (πρόσωπ-**ο** 'person', προσωπ-**ικός** 'personal') or to produce a different inflectional form of the same word (πρόσωπ-**α** 'persons')
agent	the entity (typically a person) carrying out the action of the *verb* (the term is usually applied to the *noun phrase* after από with passive verbs: Σκοτώθηκε **από τους στρατιώτες** 'S/he was killed **by the soldiers**')
agreement	the way of showing that two words have a

	certain feature in common (i.e., *number*, *gender*, or *case*)
allophone	any of the different phonetic realizations of a single *phoneme*
anaphora	the structural conditions under which an anaphoric element (*pronoun*, reflexive, reciprocal) finds its *antecedent*
antecedent	a linguistic unit (usually a *noun phrase*) to which an anaphoric element refers (see *anaphora*)
apodosis	the *clause* in a *conditional sentence* that expresses the action that would take place if the condition expressed in the *protasis* were fulfilled (Αν πήγαινες στην Αθήνα **θα έβλεπες την Ακρόπολη** 'If you went to Athens **you would see the Acropolis**')
apposition	the relationship between two usually consecutive *noun phrases* in the same *case* and denoting the same entity (ο φίλος μου ο Νίκος 'my friend Nick')
article	modifier placed before a *noun* to limit, individualize or give definiteness to the *noun phrase*. There are two kinds of article: definite (ο, η, το 'the') and indefinite (ένας, μια, ένα 'a[n]')
aspect	grammatical property of *verbs* that indicates whether the action is presented as completed (*perfective*) or as progressive or repeated (*imperfective*)
assimilation	a phonological process by which one phonological segment changes its features in order to become like an adjacent sound (/ton patéra/ → [to**mb**atéra], where the dental nasal at the end of the definite article becomes a labial like the following consonant, while the voiceless consonant /p/ becomes voiced under the influence of the preceding voiced nasal) (cf. *dissimilation*)
attributive	refers to the role of an *adjective* phrase or *noun phrase* used to modify the *head* of a *noun phrase* (το **μεγάλο** σπίτι 'the **big** house') (cf. *predicative*)
augment	the *prefix* added to certain *verb stems* to

make certain forms of the past tenses (έγραψα 'I wrote')

bitransitive
a *verb* with two *objects*, one *direct* and the other *indirect*

case
one of the forms of a noun (or other member of the *nominal system*) indicating the syntactic function of the noun in the clause; the nominative indicates the *subject*, the accusative the *direct object*, and the *genitive* normally the *indirect object*, the *complement* of a noun, or the possessor; the *vocative* is used for addressing someone or something

clause
a *syntactic* unit consisting of at least a *finite verb* (i.e. verb that is not a *gerund*, *participle* or *non-finite*); a clause may be a *main* (*independent*) clause or a *subordinate* (*embedded*) clause

clitic pronoun
a monosyllabic *personal pronoun* that cannot stand on its own but is structurally and accentually dependent on another word (also called weak personal pronoun)

collective noun
a noun whose singular denotes a group of items

comment
see *topic*

common gender
a *noun* of common gender may be either masculine or feminine without changing its form; all words that modify it are accordingly in the masculine or feminine form

comparative
see *degree*

complement
(a) a major constituent (phrase or subordinate clause) in the *clause* which (i) obligatorily completes the action of the verb (*direct* and *indirect objects*: Έδωσα **τα λεφτά στο Νίκο** 'I gave **the money to Nick**'), or (ii) restricts the meaning of a *noun* (η δημοσίευση **του βιβλίου** 'the publication **of the book**'), an *adjective* (Είναι αγαπητός **στους φίλους του** 'He's loved **by his friends**'), an *adverb* (κοντά **στο σχολείο** 'near the school'), or a *preposition* (από **το σχολείο** 'from **the school**') (b) see *subject complement, object complement*

complementizer
a conjunction introducing a *complement* clause (i.e. ότι, που, and πως)

complex word	a word composed of one of more *affixes* and a *stem* (α-φύσικος 'un-natural')
compound word	a word made up of two *stems* (τραπεζο-μάντηλο 'table-cloth')
concessive clause	a *clause* expressing concession (**Αν και δε μου αρέσει** θα το κάνω '**Even though I don't like it**, I'll do it')
conditional	*tenses* of the *verb* formed by θα+imperfect or pluperfect to express actions that would take place if certain conditions were fulfilled (θα έγραφα 'I would write', θα είχα γράψει 'I would have written'); also *sentences* that express conditions (Αν πήγαινες στην Αθήνα θα έβλεπες την Ακρόπολη 'If you went to Athens you would see the Acropolis')
conjugation	(a) the way a *verb* inflects to indicate *person*, *number*, *voice*, *tense* and *aspect*; (b) a group of verbs that inflect in the same way
conjunction	a word that links phrases or clauses (και 'and', αν 'if', όταν 'when')
co-ordination	the process of combining two or more linguistic units of the same or equivalent status (ο Γιάννης και η Μαρία 'John and Mary', Θα πάω και θα του πω 'I'll go and tell him')
copular verb	*linking verb*
dative	*case* (inherited from Ancient Greek and very rarely found in the modern language) typically governed by certain *prepositions*
declension	the way a *noun* (or other member of the *nominal system*) inflects to indicate *number*, *gender* and *case*; (b) a group of nouns (or other members of the *nominal system*) that inflect in the same way
defective verb	*verb* that has only *imperfective aspect* (ανήκω 'I belong')
defining relative clause	a *relative clause* that is necessary in order to restrict the reference of the *head noun* so as to identify it more easily (ο νεαρός **που έφερε το δέμα** 'the young man **who brought the parcel**')
definite	a specified entity, typically a *noun phrase* containing the *definite article*

degree

Greek distinguishes four degrees of comparison in *adjectives* and *adverbs*: positive (ωραίος 'lovely'), comparative (ωραιότερος or πιο ωραίος 'lovelier', relative superlative (ο ωραιότερος or ο πιο ωραίος 'the loveliest') and absolute superlative (ωραιότατος 'very lovely')

demonstratives

the *pronouns* and *determiners* αυτός, τούτος, εκείνος 'this; that'

demotic

the traditional spoken form of Greek, which evolved naturally from Ancient Greek, as opposed to the artificial learned form of the language known as *katharevousa*

dependent

the perfective non-past form of the verb (sometimes called aorist subjunctive) (γράψω)

deponent

a verb without active forms (at least in the imperfective) (κάθομαι, 'I sit', κοιμάμαι 'I sleep')

derivative

a word derived from another word

determiner

a word that is not an adjective or numeral but accompanies a *noun* (e.g. κάθε 'each', κάποιος 'some', κανένας 'any; no')

diacritic

a sign written over a letter (e.g. an *accent*)

diphthong

a combination of two different vowels in a single *syllable*

direct object

a *weak pronoun* or *noun phrase* in the accusative indicating the person or thing that the action of the verb is done to

direct question

a question expressed in a *main clause* (Θα έρθεις; 'Will you come?') (cf. *indirect question*)

dissimilation

a phonological process by which a phonological segment changes its features in order to become dissimilar to an adjacent segment (/páv-so/ → [pápso], where one of the two fricatives becomes a plosive) (cf. *assimilation*)

embedded clause

a *clause* that is dependent on one of the elements of another clause

emphatic pronoun

a *personal pronoun* that is structurally independent (contrast *clitic pronoun*)

finite

a verb form that displays person and number; in Greek all verb forms are finite except the *gerund*, the *participles*, and the *non-finite*

focus	refers to the part of the sentence that carries the main stress and constitutes the most important emphasis or contrast
fricative	a consonant sound made by the movement of air between two vocal organs placed very close together (e.g. English 'f, v, th') (cf. *plosive*)
gender	one of three classes to which every noun belongs (masculine, feminine, neuter); all words modifying the noun must agree with it in gender
genitive	see *case*
gerund	an uninflected non-finite verb form that has an *adverbial* function (γράφοντας 'writing')
head	refers to the central element of a phrase (the *noun* is the head of a *noun phrase*, the *verb* is the head of a *verb phrase*, etc.); the head determines the properties of the whole phrase
imparisyllabic	a *noun* whose *plural* forms have one more *syllable* than the corresponding *singular* ones (γιαγιά 'grandmother', γιαγιάδες 'grandmothers')
imperative	*verb* or *verb phrase* used to express a command (γράψε! 'write!', μη γράψεις! 'don't write!')
imperfect	the *imperfective past* form of the *verb* (έγραφα 'I was writing; I used to write')
imperfective	the *aspect* of the *verb* that refers to an action that is presented as progressive or repeated
impersonal verb	a *verb* in the third person singular which has no *subject*
indeclinable	a word (noun or adjective) that does not inflect for number and case
indefinite	an *article, determiner* or *noun phrase* is indefinite if it has no definite reference point; an indefinite *noun phrase* is typically one without the *definite article*
independent clause	*main clause*
indicative	refers to the *mood* of a *verb* that typically makes a statement that can be judged as either true or false; it also asks a question whether or not it is the case that . . .; the indicative takes the negative δεν and does

	not combine with the *particles* να and ας
indirect object	a *weak pronoun* or *noun phrase* or *prepositional phrase* denoting the entity to or for which the action denoted by the verb takes place (**Της** το έδωσα 'I gave it **to her**', Το έδωσα **στη Μαρία** 'I gave it **to Mary**')
indirect question	a question reported by a third person and presented in an *embedded clause* (Με ρώτησε **αν θα έρθω** 'S/he asked me **if I was coming**') (cf. *direct question*)
inflect	to change the form of a word to indicate (in verbs) *tense, aspect, person* and *number*, or (in the *nominal system*) *number, gender* and *case*
interrogative	a word, sentence, etc., used to ask a question
intransitive	a verb that does not normally have an object (βήχω 'I cough', κάθομαι 'I sit')
katharevousa	a form of Greek, using a mixture of words and forms from Ancient and Modern Greek, formerly used as the official language of Greece
lexical object	an *object* in the form of a *noun phrase* (as distinct from a *weak personal pronoun*)
linking verb	a verb that links the *subject* with the *subject complement* (typically the verb είμαι 'I am'); also called *copula*
main clause	a *clause* that can stand independently as a sentence
modal verb	*verb*, usually *impersonal*, expressing *modality* (e.g. μπορεί 'it may be', πρέπει 'it is necessary')
modality	a number of *semantic* functions (possibility, probability, necessity, counterfactuality) expressed by a variety of means, including *impersonal modal verbs*, combinations of *particles* with *verbs*, etc.
modify	make the meaning of some word more specific by means of a phrase; e.g. an *adjective* may modify a *noun* (**μεγάλα** σπίτια 'big houses'), or an *adverb* may modify a *verb* (Ήρθες **γρήγορα** 'You came quickly')
monolectic	a verb form consisting of a single word
monotransitive	a *verb* that takes only one *object*

mood	refers to a set of morphological/syntactic contrasts correlating with semantic differences indicating the way in which the speaker wishes to present the information of the sentence, as a statement of fact (*indicative*), a wish (*subjunctive*), or an order (*imperative*)
morpheme	the smallest functioning unit in the composition of words; includes *stems* and *affixes*
morphology	the study of the way in which words inflect and form derivatives
nominal	a word or phrase functioning as a *noun*
nominal clause	a *clause* that functions as a *noun phrase*
nominal system	*nouns* and *adjectives*, plus those *pronouns* and *determiners* that inflect in a similar way to nouns
nominalized clause	a να- or που-clause that becomes a nominal clause by being introduced by the neuter singular form of the definite article
nominative	see *case*
non-defining relative clause	a *relative clause* that is not used in order to restrict the reference of the *head noun* but simply adds another piece of information about the head noun (Ο Νίκος, **που είναι ο καλύτερος φίλος μου,** με συμβούλεψε ... 'Nick, **who is my best friend**, advised me ...')
non-finite	a verb form that does not display number and person; in particular, the form used with έχω to form the perfect and pluperfect tenses (έχω **γράψει** 'I have written') (cf. *finite*)
non-past	a *verb* form referring to an action that takes place in the present or future
noun	a word that denotes a thing, a person, a place, a process, a concept, etc. (τραπέζι 'table', Μάρκος 'Mark', κίνηση 'motion', ελπίδα 'hope')
noun phrase	a *phrase* with a *noun* (or a word acting as a noun) as its *head* (το μικρό κορίτσι 'the little girl'); the head of a noun phrase may be an *emphatic pronoun*
number	the distinction between *singular* and *plural* in a *noun* (or other member of the *nominal system*) or a *verb*

numeral	a word expressing number; cardinal numerals are the basic forms (ένας 'one', δύο 'two'), while ordinal numerals express order or sequence (πρώτος 'first', δεύτερος 'second')
object	a *noun phrase* or *weak personal pronoun* that indicates an entity that is acted upon by the *subject* (see *direct object* and *indirect object*)
object complement	an *object predicate*, i.e. an *adjective phrase* or *noun phrase* used as a *predicate* to an *object* (Τον θεωρούν **χαζό** 'They consider him **stupid**')
oxytone	a word with *stress* on its final *syllable*
paradigm	the complete set of forms for an *inflected* word
parisyllabic	(*noun*) whose *plural* forms have the same number of *syllables* as the corresponding *singular* ones
paroxytone	a word with *stress* on the second to last *syllable*
participle	a *non-finite* form of the verb used as an *adjective* (κουρασμένος 'tired')
particle	an auxiliary word preceding the *verb* in order to indicate either the *subjunctive mood* (να and ας) or the *future* and *conditional tenses* (θα)
passive voice	when a *verb* is in the passive voice its subject is not the person or thing doing the action but typically the person or thing acted upon (cf. *active*)
past	a *verb* form referring to an action that took place in the past
perfect	a *tense* of the *verb* consisting of the *present* forms of έχω followed by the *non-finite*; refers to an action that took place in the past but whose consequences are felt in the present (έχω γράψει 'I have written')
perfective	the *aspect* of the *verb* that refers to an action presented as being complete (cf. *imperfective*)
periphrastic	a verb consisting of more than one word
person	one of three categories indicated by the verb and the *personal pronouns*; the first person indicates the speaker, the second person the

	addressee, and the third person indicates what is being talked about
personal pronoun	a *pronoun* that indicates *person*
phoneme	the minimal unit of the sound system of a language; a sound is recognized as a separate phoneme if by using it instead of another sound a different word is obtained (the pair [kóri] 'daughter', [xóri] 'areas' indicates that /k/ is a separate phoneme from /x/ in Greek; each phoneme may be realized by one or more phonetic variants called *allophones*)
phonology	the study of the sound system of a language
plosive	a consonant sound produced when a complete closure in the vocal tract is suddenly released (as in Eng. 'p, b, t') (cf. *fricative*)
pluperfect	a *tense* of the *verb* formed with the past forms of έχω followed by the *non-finite*; it is used to express the completion of an action before a specified past time (είχα γράψει 'I had written')
plural	form of a *noun* (or other member of the *nominal system*) indicating more than one entity; form of a *verb* indicating that the *subject* consists of more than one entity
predicate	an *adjective phrase* or *noun phrase* assigned to the *subject* or *object* by a *copular verb* (see also *subject complement, object complement*)
predicative	refers to an adjective or other word that forms the *predicate* of a *clause* (i.e. unlike an *attributive* adjective, it does not form part of the same *noun phrase* as the noun it modifies)
prefix	an *affix* added to the front of a *stem*
preposition	a word introducing a *prepositional phrase* that typically indicates time, place or manner
prepositional phrase	a phrase introduced by a *preposition* ('Ηρθα από την Αθήνα 'I came from Athens')
pronominal	any word acting as a *pronoun*
pronominal phrase	a *phrase* functioning as a *pronoun* (ο οποίος 'who, which, that' [relative])
pronoun	a word that has the function of a *noun*

	phrase; it may be an emphatic personal pronoun (εμένα 'me'), a weak (clitic) personal pronoun (με 'me'), or some other kind of pronoun (ποιος; 'who?', κάποιος 'someone', κανένας 'no one; anyone'); most Greek pronouns other than personal pronouns may also act as *determiners*
proparoxytone	a word with *stress* on the third to last *syllable*
protasis	the *clause* in a *conditional sentence* that expresses the condition that must be fulfilled if the action of the verb in the main clause (the *apodosis*) is to take place (**Αν πήγαινες στην Αθήνα** θα έβλεπες την Ακρόπολη '**If you went to Athens** you would see the Acropolis')
quantifier	a word that expresses quantity (e.g. όλος 'all', πολύς 'much')
reciprocal expression	the expression of an action that the multiple subjects of a verb do to each other (Μισούν **ο ένας τον άλλο** 'They hate **each other**')
reduplication	a *prefix* added to some verbs in the *passive perfect participle* (**πε**πεισμένος 'convinced')
reflexive expression	the expression of an action that the subject does to him/herself (Δε φροντίζει **τον εαυτό του** 'He doesn't look after **himself**')
register	a variety of language according to its use in social situations (e.g. formal, colloquial)
relative clause	an *embedded clause* modifying a *noun phrase* (το κορίτσι **που ήρθε** 'the girl **who came**')
semantic	regarding the meaning of words, phrases, etc.
sentence	a *syntactic* unit that contains a complete meaning and consists of one or more *clauses*
simple past	the *perfective past* form of the *verb* (έγραψα 'I wrote')
singular	form of a *noun* (or other member of the *nominal system*) indicating a single entity; form of a *verb* indicating that the *subject* is a single entity
stem	the part of an inflected word (noun, verb, adjective, etc.) to which *affixes* are added
stress	prominence of a *syllable* (in terms of loudness and clarity) (cf. *accent*)

subject	the *noun phrase* denoting the person or thing doing the action of an *active verb* (**Ο Πέτρος** ήρθε 'Peter came') or undergoing the action of a *passive verb* (**Ο Πέτρος** σκοτώθηκε 'Peter was killed')
subject complement	a *subject predicate*, i.e. an *adjective phrase* or *noun phrase* assigned to a *subject noun phrase* by a *copular verb* (Ο Νίκος είναι **πολύ έξυπνος** 'Nick's **very clever**', Ο Νίκος είναι **δάσκαλος** 'Nick's **a teacher**')
subjunctive	the *mood* of the *verb* that typically presents the contents of a clause as wished for, planned, etc.; the subjunctive is marked by the particles να and ας, and it takes the negative μη
subordinate clause	*embedded clause*
substantivization	the process whereby a word that is not a noun is used as a noun (το πιστεύω 'the creed')
suffix	an *affix* added to the end of a *stem*
superlative	see *degree*
syllable	consists of a vowel, optionally accompanied by one or more consonants (άν-θρω-πος 'person')
syntactic	regarding the way that words, phrases, etc., are joined to make phrases, clauses and sentences
temporal clause	an *embedded clause* indicating the time at which an action took place ('**Οταν έφτασα,** ο Κώστας είχε φύγει '**When I arrived,** Kostas had left')
tense	grammatical property of a *verb* that primarily refers to the time of the action; in this book we make two different types of distinction between tenses: (a) the general categories of *past* and *non-past*; and (b) the specific verb-forms present, *imperfect*, *simple past*, future, *perfect*, etc.
termination	the ending of an inflected word, attached to its stem; two-termination adjectives are *adjectives* which have only two sets of forms, one for masculine and feminine, and one for neuter, instead of the normal three sets, one for each gender

topic	the person or thing about which something is said, whereas the statement made about the topic is called the *comment*
transitive	a verb that may have an object (βλέπω [κάτι] 'I see [something]')
verb	a word that denotes an action or a state (τρέχω 'I run', υπάρχω 'I exist')
verb phrase	consists of a *finite verb* form, optionally accompanied by an *object*, a *complement*, and/or an *adverbial*
vocative	see *case*
voice	see *active* and *passive voice*
voiced	indicates a consonant produced with vibration of the vocal cords (e.g. 'd, m, v, z'); all vowels are voiced
voiceless	indicates a consonant produced without vibrating the vocal cords (e.g. 't, f, s')
weak personal pronoun	*clitic pronoun*

INDEX

Note: This index of grammatical categories and concepts is intended to be used in conjunction with the table of contents; there the reader will gain a clear view of how the material is arranged, particularly in the case of topics covered extensively. Many of the terms below are also defined in the glossary. At the end of the index we list a number of important Greek words which are mentioned frequently in the Grammar.

ADDENDA TO PART II: MORPHOLOGY

Page 55, after 2.1.5 add:

2.1.6   IRREGULAR NOUNS

The masculine noun μυς 'muscle' does not conform to any of the foregoing patterns. It is declined as follows:

		Sg.		*Pl.*
Nom.	ο	μυς	οι	μυς/μύες
Acc.	τον	μυ	τους	μυς/μύες
Gen.	του	μυός	των	μυών

The first of the two alternative forms for the nom. and acc. pl. is the one more frequently used, though some speakers regard the second as more 'correct'.

Two other masculine nouns present patterns which differ from any of those given above; note particularly the plural forms:

ο πρύτανης   'vice-chancellor, rector (of university)'

		Sg.		*Pl.*
Nom.	ο	πρύτανης	οι	πρυτάνεις
Acc.	τον	πρύτανη	τους	πρυτάνεις
Gen.	του	πρύτανη	των	πρυτάνεων
Voc.		πρύτανη		πρυτάνεις

The noun πρέσβης 'ambassador' follows the same pattern, with the stress remaining on the same syllable throughout.

Page 68, at end of Section 2.4.8 add:

There are two neuter nouns ending in -υ which have forms like those of the neuter of the adjectives in Section 3.5:

το οξύ 'acid'

		Sg.		*Pl.*
Nom.	το	οξύ	τα	οξέα
Acc.	το	οξύ	τα	οξέα
Gen.	του	οξέος	των	οξέων

το ήμισυ 'half' (no plural forms)

		Sg.
Nom.	το	ήμισυ
Acc.	το	ήμισυ
Gen.	του	ημίσεος

For other neuter nouns ending in -υ see Section 2.4.3.

Page 166, after line 2 add:

Another type of second-conjugation (oxytone) verb, which does not exist in Modern Greek as a complete paradigm, has the following forms in the passive present (the bracketed forms are very formal):

δικαιούμαι   'I am entitled (to)'

Sg.	1	δικαιούμαι	*Pl.*	1	δικαιούμαστε (δικαιούμεθα)
	2	δικαιούσαι		2	δικαιούστε (διακαιούσθε)
	3	δικαιούται		3	δικαιούνται

The imperfect, which is rare, follows the pattern of the passive imperfect of θεωρώ (see Section 7.4.2.2), but is often avoided by the use of a periphrasis, e.g. είχα το δικαίωμα 'I had the right'. This verb has no perfective forms. (Note, however, the related verb δικαιώνω 'I vindicate, prove right', which does have perfective forms, e.g. active simple past δικαίωσα, passive simple past δικαιώθηκα and passive perfect participle δικαιωμένος.)

    Similarly, υποχρεούμαι 'I am obliged (to)' (a more formal alternative to υποχρεώνομαι). (The imperfect of υποχρεούμαι is very rare; instead, the periphrasis ήμουν υποχρεωμένος 'I was obliged' is used.)